YOUTH AT RISK
and YOUTH JUSTICE

YOUTH AT RISK
and YOUTH JUSTICE

A CANADIAN OVERVIEW

Edited by
JOHN WINTERDYK
RUSSELL SMANDYCH

OXFORD
UNIVERSITY PRESS

Oxford University Press is a department of the University of Oxford.
It furthers the University's objective of excellence in research, scholarship, and education
by publishing worldwide. Oxford is a registered trade mark of Oxford University Press
in the UK and in certain other countries.

Published in Canada by
Oxford University Press
8 Sampson Mews, Suite 204,
Don Mills, Ontario M3C 0H5 Canada

www.oupcanada.com

Library and Archives Canada Cataloguing in Publication

Youth at risk and youth justice : a Canadian overview / edited by John A. Winterdyk & Russell Smandych.

Includes bibliographical references and index.
ISBN 978-0-19-544130-7

1. Juvenile delinquency—Canada—Textbooks. 2. Juvenile justice, Administration of—Canada—Textbooks.
I. Winterdyk, John II. Smandych, Russell Charles

HV9108.Y67 2012   364.360971   C2012-900068-X

Cover image: homydesign/veer

Page 3: © iStockphoto.com/Frances Twitty; page 26: © iStockphoto.com/Cyril Hou; page 54: AP Photo/Remy de la Mauviniere;
page 80: © iStockphoto.com/Mehmet Salih Guler; page 108: © iStockphoto.com/webphotographeer; page 130: © iStockphoto.com/
Brandon Laufenberg; page 156: © iStockphoto.com/Philipp Baer; page 181: © iStockphoto.com/RMAX; page 204: © iStockphoto.com/
diego cervo; page 228: AP Photo/The Santa Fe New Mexican, Natalie Guillén; page 253: © iStockphoto.com/Lorie Slater;
page 279: Toronto Star/John Mahler; page 307: © imagebroker/Alamy; page 335: © iStockphoto.com/GH01;
page 358: Winnipeg Free Press/Joe Bryksa; page 379: © iStockphoto.com/Viorika Prikhodko.

Oxford University Press is committed to our environment.
This book is printed on Forest Stewardship Council® certified paper and comes from responsible sources.

Printed and bound in Canada

1 2 3 4 — 15 14 13 12

Contents

Part II   Understanding Contemporary Youth Crime and Justice: Theories and Perspectives   105

Part IV   Keeping Kids Out of the System: Restorative Justice and Other Progressive Approaches to Youth Crime and Justice   333

Contributor Bios

Sibylle Artz is a full professor in child and youth care at the University of Victoria. Her research focuses on youth aggression with an emphasis on girls' use of violence. She has undertaken numerous community-based collaborative research projects, including community-based violence prevention; a community-based approach for dealing with violent youth who are under the age of 12; collaborative work undertaken with service providers on developing girls' custody units; and a project that involved three Vancouver Island communities focused on developing a gender-sensitive community needs assessment tool for supporting at-risk girls and young women. Dr Artz has also published more than 50 refereed articles, written two books—*Feeling as a Way of Knowing* (1994) and *Sex, Power and the Violent School Girl* (1997)—and co-edited a third book, *Working Relationally with Girls* (2004), with Dr Marie Hoskins. In addition to her many other honours and awards, she was chosen, in 1998, as Academic of the Year by the Confederation of University Faculty Associations of British Columbia and, in 2004, received the Award of Distinction for Research from the McCreary Youth Foundation of Vancouver. Dr Artz is also currently participating as the Canadian partner in an international research project on girls and aggression that involves six European countries.

Nicholas Bala has law degrees from Queen's and Harvard. His research focuses on children, youth, families, and the justice system, including such issues as juvenile justice and youth offending; child welfare law, child abuse, and child witnesses in the criminal justice system; family violence; parental rights and responsibilities after divorce; and the legal definition of the family. Much of his research work is interdisciplinary, and he has collaborated with psychologists, criminologists, social workers, and doctors. He recently co-authored, with Sanjeev Anand, *Youth Criminal Justice Law*, second edition (2009). The first edition of that book (2003) was extensively cited by the courts, including the Supreme Court of Canada, in interpreting the Youth Criminal Justice Act (YCJA).

Stephen W. Baron is a professor of sociology in the department of sociology at Queen's University. His research focuses primarily on homeless street youth and crime and substance abuse. He is concerned with how various criminological theories can be used to help and understand these forms of behaviour among the homeless street youth population. His work on these types of issues has appeared in a variety of academic journals, including *Criminology*, *Journal of Research in Crime and Delinquency*, *Justice Quarterly*, *Journal of Criminal Justice*, and *Deviant Behavior*.

Peter J. Carrington is professor of sociology and legal studies at the University of Waterloo and editor of *Canadian Journal of Criminology and Criminal Justice*. His current research project, the Canadian Criminal Careers and Criminal Networks Study, combines his long-standing interests in social network analysis and the development of crime and delinquency. His other research interests include police discretion and the impact of the Canadian Youth Criminal Justice Act. His recent articles appeared in *Criminology*, *Canadian Journal of Criminology and Criminal Justice*, and *Criminal Justice Policy Review*. He is co-editor of *The SAGE Handbook of Social Network Analysis* (2011) and *Models and Methods in Social Network Analysis* (2005).

Louis-Georges Cournoyer is currently associate professor at the School of Criminology of Montreal University. He has a Ph.D. in psychology and has been a psychologist for 22 years and has worked with various clientele, especially with high-risk young people and families at Centre jeunesse de Montréal—Institut universitaire (CJM-IU), with which he is now affiliated as a researcher. His research interests centre on the rehabilitation processes and effectiveness of treatments for youth offenders and drug addicts. He has conducted a major study with Jacques Dionne on the impact of the Montreal Youth Centre's intensive probation with treatment, which has since been acknowledged in Québec as representing an important approach for rehabilitating youth offenders.

Jacques Dionne has for the past 20 years been an educator, psychoeducator, chief of unit, program director, research and professional staff training director of Boscoville, Montreal (Institution for youth offenders). He is also a full professor at the Université du Québec en Outaouais and researcher at l'Institut de recherche pour l'adaptation des jeunes du CJM-IU. Dr Dionne specializes in staff training, program development, and evaluation for youth offenders and adolescents in difficulty. Over the past 10 years he has also been the leader of many international collaboration projects on rehabilitation, especially in Chile and Brazil.

Sarah Gilliss is an instructor in the criminal justice and police techniques program in the Health and Human Services Department of the New Brunswick Community College in Miramichi, New Brunswick. She is currently completing her thesis for a master's degree in sociology at the University of New Brunswick with a focus on youth justice policy. She has had experience on the front line as a youth worker and correctional officer working with youth in the youth criminal justice system.

Michèle Goyette, Director of Specialized Services for Young Offenders at Centre jeunesse de Montréal—Institut universitaire, has worked for 30 years mainly as a criminologist or manager for young offenders' services. She participated in the development of different programs for young offenders and also collaborated with Québec's major research partners working on the provincial organization and orientation of services. A member of the board of directors of Québec's Society for Criminology and of the Child Welfare League of Canada, Ms Goyette uses every possible platform in Québec or Canada to promote the rehabilitation and social reintegration of young offenders.

Ross Green is a judge of the Provincial Court of Saskatchewan, sitting in Yorkton. Before his appointment to the bench in 2004, he practised criminal and family law with legal aid for many years. He was appointed as Queen's Counsel by the Saskatchewan Minister of Justice in 2001. He holds bachelor degrees in Commerce and Law from the University of Saskatchewan, and an LL.M. degree from the University of Manitoba. He is also the author of *Justice in Aboriginal Communities: Sentencing Alternatives* (1998) and the co-author, with Kearney Healy, of *Tough on Kids: Rethinking Approaches to Youth Justice* (2003). His first book was nominated for a Saskatchewan Book Award in the First Book category, and his second received the Saskatchewan Book Award for Scholarly Writing.

Hirsch Greenberg was born in Montreal and has spent the past 48 years in Saskatchewan working for community-based organizations in Regina and File Hills (First Nations communities) as line staff, administrator, and volunteer. He is currently the practicum coordinator in the Department of Justice Studies at the University of Regina, is actively doing research on housing and homelessness,

and is chairperson of the newly constituted Saskatchewan Justice Institute at the University of Regina. He is an active board member of the Regina Alternative Measures Program. Hirsch received the Regina YMCA Peace Medal in 2009 and was recognized by Correctional Service of Canada in 2010 for his work in restorative justice. Hirsch has a BA in sociology and a master's in social work from the University of Regina.

Jana Grekul is assistant professor of sociology and Director of criminology at the University of Alberta. Her research interests include the eugenics movement and sterilization program (1928—1972) in Alberta, gender and pedagogy in the university classroom, the study of punishment within the criminal justice system, street and prison gangs, and in particular Aboriginal gangs. She teaches a variety of sociology and criminology courses and is co-author of *Sociology Matters*, *Sociology*, and *Criminology*.

Attorney **Pierre Hamel** is a trained lawyer and has worked for many years in the litigation department at the Centre Jeunesse de Montréal-Institut Universitaire. Being a specialist in juvenile delinquency policy, he was responsible for the Reference Manual guiding the application of the Youth Criminal Justice Act for youth centres throughout Québec. Mr. Hamel is also the author of a 2009 book on the application of the YCJA in Québec. Hamel is now Director of the legal department l'Association québecoise des centres jeunesse, where he plays a key role preserving the philosophy of the Québec model of juvenile delinquency intervention.

Bryan Hogeveen is associate professor of sociology at the University of Alberta. He is co-author (along with Joanne Minaker) of *Youth, Crime and Society: Issues of Power and Justice* (2009). He has published on a variety of his academic interests, which include socio-legal theory, violence, martial arts in society, young offenders and the law, and justice. His Social Sciences and Humanities Research Council (SSHRC)-funded research examines neo-liberalism's impact on the marginalized inner-city residents of Edmonton and Winnipeg. Dr Hogeveen has been invited to share his ideas with both national and international audiences. He recently returned from giving the keynote address at the Federal University of Rio de Janeiro.

Bruce MacLaurin is an assistant professor at the faculty of social work, University of Calgary. He is currently the co-investigator on the third cycle of the Canadian Incidence

Study of Reported Child Abuse and Neglect (CIS 2008), as well as the principal investigator for provincial maltreatment studies in BC, Alberta, and Saskatchewan. In collaboration with Worthington and community agencies, he was a co-investigator on the Calgary Youth, Health, and the Street Study funded by CIHR. His research and publishing has focused on street-involved youth and homelessness, child welfare service delivery, foster care outcomes, and child maltreatment. He has more than 15 years experience in non-profit children's services.

Chris McCormick is professor in the criminology department at St Thomas University in Fredericton, New Brunswick. He teaches courses on wrongful conviction, crime, and media, and visual criminology. His most recent book is *Constructing Danger: The Mis/Representation of Crime in the News (2010)*.

Susan McIntyre has over 25 years experience working with families and children in the treatment of juvenile justice arenas, which has allowed Dr McIntyre to develop expertise in program management and development. She has a strong track record in identifying and meeting the needs of the organization and was responsible for the start-up of 30 operations in the private and public sectors, guiding them from the concept stage through to full implementation and evaluation. Susan is recognized for her expertise on child sexual abuse and child sexual exploitation, and she is an international research and policy advisor. Susan is also the president of a retrospective research firm called The Hindsight Group, a leading-edge research and project management firm (see www.hindsightgroup.com).

Joanne C. Minaker is assistant professor in the sociology department at Grant MacEwan University in Edmonton, Alberta. Her work raises questions regarding identity, power, choice, social exclusion, and social justice. Dr Minaker's main areas of expertise are criminalized girls/women and the sociology of motherhood. Among her recent publications are a book, co-authored with Bryan Hogeveen, on *Youth, Crime, and Society: Issues of Power and Justice* (2009), and various articles on mothering. She can often be found with her infant daughter and partner watching her sons play hockey in Edmonton rinks.

Brenda Morrison is co-chair of the Safe Schools and Communities Special Interest Group of the American Education Research Association and a member of the Scientific Committee of the International Observatory of Violence in Schools. She has presented papers at UNESCO, in Paris, and to the House of Lords in London, and chaired many panels on restorative justice and schools for the World Congress of Criminology as well as a number of other associations. She is a research partner with PREVNet (Promoting Relationships and Eliminating Violence Network) within Canada's Networks of Centres of Excellence. In British Columbia, she is a member of the working group for Social Responsibility and Collaborative Learning in Education. In her home community, she is an active board member for the North Shore Restorative Justice Society.

Rhonda Nelson, B.Ed, BA, M.Ed, is currently completing her doctorate with the Faculty of Graduate Studies and Research, University of Regina. As a long-time resident of Saskatchewan, she has worked as a classroom teacher, a special education teacher, and a central office administrator within school divisions in the province. With the Saskatchewan Ministry of Education she served in the capacities of provincial consultant, regional superintendent, and regional director. Currently, she teaches as a sessional lecturer for the University of Regina, acts as director of education for the Paul Dojack Youth Centre, which is a closed custody facility, and does private consulting.

Colleen Pawlychka is a doctoral student at Simon Fraser University, School of Criminology. She currently participates in the Alternatives to Violence Program, and her research interests include youth justice, trauma, violent offenders, and presentation and evaluation of restorative justice. Her rich and varied background in restorative justice includes lived experiences, academic and research development, as well as work and volunteer experience. She graduated from the University of Winnipeg with an interdisciplinary BA, Honours, degree focusing on restorative justice, and from the University of Manitoba with an MA degree in sociology. She is the recipient of the SSHRC and Manitoba graduate scholarships as well as numerous scholarships in peace and conflict studies, humanities, criminal justice, and sociology, including the SFU Law Foundation Graduate Scholarship in Restorative Justice. Colleen has spent several years as a Winnipeg Youth Justice Committee co-chair and as a member of the Winnipeg Council of Justice Committees.

Darryl Plecas is the RCMP Research Chair and Director of the Centre for Public Safety and Criminal Justice Research at the University of the Fraser Valley. He is the author or co-author of more than 150 articles and research reports addressing a wide range of criminal justice issues, including numerous recent works dealing with drug production, trafficking, and use. He has an active interest in drug prevention and treatment, and has been a member of the board of directors for the Canadian Centre on Substance Abuse since 2006. He received his BA and MA from Simon Fraser University, and his Ed.D. from the University of British Columbia.

Susan Reid is a professor of criminology and criminal justice at St Thomas University in Fredericton, New Brunswick. She is also the Director of the Centre for Research on Youth at Risk, which is the eastern hub of the Students Commission of Canada/Centre of Excellence for Youth Engagement at St Thomas. Her research interests include youth justice, youth at risk, youth voice, and youth engagement. She has been actively involved in promoting adult–youth research partnerships and being an adult ally to youth through the New Brunswick Network *Youth Matters.*

Marge Reitsma-Street is a professor in studies in policy and practice at the University of Victoria, and is cross-appointed to the School of Social Work. Educated as a social worker with a doctorate in social policy from the University of Toronto, her current research interests and activist work centre on poverty, welfare, women's provisioning work, and community organizations. She has written extensively on female delinquency, juvenile justice, and correctional policies. A particular methodological interest is in developing the processes and possibilities of action research in community. Her scholarship is embedded in years of experience as co-facilitator or academic advisor on poverty, housing, and neighbourhood projects while living in Victoria, Sudbury, and North Bay. In 2009 Dr Reitsma-Street received the Dick Weiler Award in honour of her exceptional contributions to community and social development in Canada.

Julian V. Roberts is a professor of criminology in the faculty of law, University of Oxford, and a member of the Sentencing Council of England and Wales. He is editor-in-chief of the *European Journal of Criminology* and associate editor of the *Canadian Journal of Criminology and Criminal Justice.* Recent books he has written, edited, or co-edited include the following: *The Role of Previous Convictions at Sentencing* (2010); *Hearing the Victim* (2009); *Principled Sentencing* (2008); *Punishing Persistent Offenders* (2008); *Understanding Public Attitudes to Justice* (2005); and *The Virtual Prison* (2004).

Lorinda Stoneman is a doctoral student in the School of Child and Youth Care at the University of Victoria, and is engaged in research and writing on youth justice policy. Having received her master's degree in criminology from Simon Fraser University in 2008, the intersections between the disciplines of criminology and child and youth care form a key area of interest. Since 2009 she has managed the Victoria site for a project called The Study on Incarcerated Serious and Violent Young Offenders. She has also worked in the non-profit sector since 2006 for the Safe OnLine Outreach Society, a grassroots organization dedicated to education and policy change in light of new technologies. Other interests range from qualitative and community-based research methods to criminological and post-structural theory.

Mark Totten collaborates with groups across Canada and internationally on evidence-based practices and program evaluation in the areas of gangs, sexual exploitation, crime prevention, mental health, family violence, and corrections. He is president of Totten and Associates and is past director of research at the Youth Services Bureau (1987–2007) and has worked with high-risk young people and families for 30 years. He has a MSW and a Ph.D. in sociology. An expert witness on gangs and a certified social worker, he has authored over 60 books, articles, and reports, including *Guys, Gangs and Girlfriend Abuse* (2000), *When Children Kill: A Social-Psychological Study on Youth Homicide* (2002), *Promising Practices for Addressing Youth Involvement in Gangs* (2008), and *From Children to Outcasts: The Tragic Lives of Canadian Gang Members* (2011). He is a frequent media commentator and keynote speaker at Canadian and international conferences.

Catherine Worthington is an associate professor at the School of Public Health and Social Policy, University of Victoria. Her research focuses on quality of and access to health and social services for vulnerable populations. In research studies funded by the Canadian Institutes for Health Research (CIHR) and the Social Sciences and Humanities Research Council (SSHRC), she has worked with people living with HIV, street-involved youth, African immigrant communities, and Aboriginal youth to develop services that meet the needs of client groups. While an associate professor and CIHR new investigator at the University of Calgary, she worked with MacLaurin and community agencies as a principal investigator on the Calgary Youth, Health, and the Street Study.

Preface

We are extremely pleased about having been able to edit this book and we hope that you will not only enjoy reading it but also learn and be inspired to inquire further. As co-editors of this book, we have both taught courses on young offenders and youth justice as well as published nationally and internationally on the general subject of youth crime. In addition to lending our own knowledge and experience to this book, we have assembled a list of contributors, who are all well-established experts in their chapter themes. This brings a richness and an elevated level of comprehensiveness to the book that we could not have matched otherwise. As a result, the readers are the beneficiaries of the collaborative effort that has allowed us to prepare this textbook.

The study of youth crime and youth justice is one of the most intriguing and invigorating areas within criminology and criminal justice. Yet as much as researchers and scholars have studied youth crime and youth justice over the past 160 years, it is still very much an enigma. For example, whether locally, provincially, or nationally (and even internationally), criminologists and social scientists in general have been intrigued by the challenges of youth crime and its prevention and control. At a more fundamental level, everyone reading this book has at one time or another likely wondered why young people commit delinquent or criminal acts and what we can or should do about it. While this book does not profess to provide answers to all the questions, the book does explore a wide range of topics and issues that will provide the reader with a thorough understanding of the richness and complexity of youth crime and youth justice.

In an effort to provide an appropriate overview of youth crime and youth justice we have intentionally attempted to avoid endorsing any particular ideological agenda. However, we have asked the chapter authors to be reflective and, where appropriate, critical about the topics or subjects they have covered. The editors feel that by exposing students to not only the history of youth justice but also to a variety of theoretical perspectives and a range of topical issues (e.g., gangs, substance abuse, etc.) that are framed within an informative but also reflective manner, students will learn to think critically about the various chapter topics and form their own observations and conclusions about the different issues and topics being covered.

As such, we solicited chapters for this book with several key goals in mind. First, we wanted to ensure that the book was comprehensive in its coverage, in-depth in content, and yet reader friendly so as to encourage students to not only read but be challenged by the questions offered and intrigued by the additional sources identified. Although the book is divided into four main parts, each with its own introduction, the sections and chapters do not need to be followed in sequence, nor do they necessarily all need to be covered. Yet, collectively, they serve to provide a solid foundation for almost any undergraduate-level Canadian course on youth at risk, young offenders, and the workings of the youth justice system.

Second, we were keen to include pedagogical materials and features that are intended to not only enliven student understanding of the topic but also to stimulate further questioning, further reading, and possibly a desire to take more advanced or specialized courses on one or more of the chapter themes. The questions for review and critical thinking, suggested readings and helpful web links, as well as key terms (and glossary) combine to make the book student friendly and to serve as a primary text at the undergraduate level. Where appropriate, chapters also include information textboxes, tables, and figures that are intended to enrich the chapter content without detracting from the main message.

A third goal we had in mind was to ensure topical coverage. Each chapter devotes attention to a specific topic that is seen as fundamental to understanding the complexity of youth crime and youth justice. In addition, we wanted to include important topics that were timely but not commonly addressed in as much detail in other undergraduate textbooks. For example, the chapters on street-involved youth (Chapter Twelve), adolescent male prostitution (Chapter Thirteen), the Québec approach to youth justice (Chapter Fourteen), and the coverage of restorative justice (Chapter Fifteen) have received little to no attention in textbooks with a similar focus. Yet we also wanted to ensure that the core themes typically introduced in youth crime and justice courses were covered as well—as is the case with all the other chapters, which range from a historical overview of youth justice in Canada to an examination of current youth justice legislation, to young female offenders, youth gangs and substance abuse, and Aboriginal youth in conflict with the law.

Organization of the Book

As indicated above, the textbook is organized into four parts. 'Part One: History, Trends, and Legislation' presents four chapters that collectively serve to provide a foundation for better understanding the development of legislative and policy approaches taken in Canada over the last century to define, measure, and deal with at-risk, delinquent, and criminal youth. Part One includes chapters aimed at accounting for historical and contemporary trends in delinquency and youth justice legislation (Chapter One), understanding how we measure and use different data sources to describe and explain contemporary youth crime (Chapter Two), describing the current Youth Criminal Justice Act (YCJA) (Chapter Three), and assessing the effects of the YCJA to date on youth crime and the treatment of young persons in the criminal justice system (Chapter Four). The chapters follow a similar format so as to facilitate reading, critical reflection, and understanding of these important topics.

'Part Two: Understanding Contemporary Youth Crime and Justice: Theories and Perspectives' shifts attention to examining the different ways a student can try to develop a knowledge of youth crime and justice in today's society. Chapter Five begins by critically examining the role of the media in creating public knowledge and awareness of youth crime and youth justice, while the subsequent chapters focus more on the various theoretical approaches that have been developed to explain juvenile delinquency and youth crime. Because the behaviour of females is often influenced by different factors than is the behaviour of young males, Chapter Six focuses on young female offending behaviour while the remaining two chapters in Part Two focus on new theoretical perspectives on youth crime (Chapter Seven) and the need for a critical criminological perspective on youth and crime that pays attention to issues of power and justice (Chapter Eight).

Inevitably when we think of young offenders we tend to categorize their behaviour as either offenders or victims. And within each category we then attempt to refine our labelling based on the behaviour(s) they are engaged in. In 'Part Three: At-Risk and Criminalized Youth Crime in Canada: Selected Types and Problems', we focus on five areas that in addition to being topical also serve to reflect the complexity of young persons' behaviour. For example, in Chapter Nine we cover the age-old problem of drug use/abuse among young persons to see what, if anything, has changed and how well it is working. Chapter Ten focuses on a dark period in the history of Canada that persists even today—the overrepresentation of Aboriginal youth in the youth criminal justice system. Also included in this section is a chapter on the topical issue of youth gangs (Chapter Eleven). Chapter Twelve covers the unfortunate plight of homeless youth, who, while commonly seen as victims of social and personal circumstances, often turn to crime to survive. In an era where awareness and resources have never been so plentiful the question of whether or not we really care takes centre stage. Part Three concludes with a chapter on adolescent male prostitutes (Chapter Thirteen).

After reading all, or parts, of this section of the book students will have a deeper appreciation for the diversity of what constitutes youth crime as well as for the complexity of trying to address the problem. For example, it is clear that while young people may engage in anti-social and illegal activity, such behaviour is not always a matter of choice. To this end we might reflect on the chapters in Parts One and Two and ask, again, if we are 'doing the right thing'.

What lies ahead for the administration of youth justice in Canada remains unclear. Notwithstanding, in 'Keeping Kids out of the System: Restorative Justice and Other Progressive Approaches to Youth Crime and Justice' we will see that a number of different initiatives are being utilized with varying degrees of success and controversy. Collectively, they speak to public policy and legislative issues that show promise in the possible refinement (or overhauling) of the youth justice system. For example, in Chapter Fourteen the authors provide an overview of the multidisciplinary assessment and intervention approach as used in Québec, while in Chapter Fifteen the authors explore the history and feasibility of restorative justice. Meanwhile, Chapter Sixteen offers an evocative discussion as to why we need to maintain a separate youth justice system in which young persons' unique needs are recognized and supported. The authors also place the examination of Canada's youth justice system within an international context by referring to the United Nations (UN) Convention on the Rights of the Child.

Finally, to paraphrase the esteemed 1970s psychiatrist Karl Menninger, who once said that society gets the youth crime it deserves, it may be argued that if we fail to understand youth crime and respond with poorly informed evidence then we cannot blame anyone but ourselves for the current state of affairs. As is reflected throughout this textbook, over the past century we have seen a considerable transformation of youth justice policy and practices, from the introduction of the Juvenile Delinquents Act in 1908 and the Young Offenders Act (YOA) in 1984, to the implementation of the Youth Criminal Justice Act in 2003. During this history we have shifted from a welfare model, which emphasized a social-work approach that focused on diagnosing the problem and providing treatment under the premise of *parens patriae*—the state knows best—toward a justice model with the YOA, in which due process and accountability were emphasized but in measured ways (see Chapter Three). Arguably the YCJA, with its revised objectives, is reflective of what Reid and Reitsma-Street (1984) referred to as a 'community change model' or 'modified justice model' that attempts to strike a balance between crime control and providing rehabilitative and restorative options for young offenders.

We realize that in spite of our effort to prepare a textbook that would span the spectrum of course curriculums that focus on youth crime and youth justice, we may have come up short in some areas. We debated long and hard about including more content but in the end, due in part to practical constraints, we had to make informed decisions about what to include and what not to. These decisions were in part guided by the helpful feedback from the various anonymous reviewers whom we would like to acknowledge and thank, but in the end we are responsible for the final product. Along the way, should you have any constructive feedback, we would welcome hearing from you because we are always receptive to trying to improve on the approach we have taken to understanding youth risk and youth justice in Canada.

Acknowledgements

Although I did not know it at the time, my nearly 30-year involvement with writing and editing books on young offenders and juvenile justice dates back to when I agreed to run a wilderness adventure program in Ontario for an eager and creative probation officer by the name of Rick Mazur (we are still dear friends to this day). My experience over those two years eventually drew me back to school, intent on learning more about young offenders and youth at risk. And while much has transpired since the days of ACTION (Accepting Challenge Through Interaction with Others and Nature), my interest in young offenders and youth justice remains steadfast.

In the preparation of this textbook, little has changed. Co-editing this collection of original articles requires considerable teamwork and dedication by all involved. Although the process never seems to get any easier, it has also been a joyous experience to witness how well so many different ideas, agendas, and personalities can come together with dedication to a common cause. Therefore, for my part, I would like to express my deepest appreciation to all the contributors who were kind enough to prepare their chapters and who graciously worked with us as we finalized their submission for the book. Without their contribution, the book would never have been published.

I am particularly appreciative of having Russell Smandych join me as co-editor. Our friendship dates back to our days as students at Simon Fraser University, and it has been a genuine pleasure and honour to work on this project (our first together) after so many years.

I would also be remise if I did not thank my students, who diplomatically endured being subjected to portions of the new material and who regularly offered constructive feedback. It is for you that this book has been written and edited with the hope that it will inspire you to want to make a difference for our youth, especially those youth who are at risk in society today.

Finally, but most definitely not least of all, is my partner in life and happiness, Rosemary Buck. While she continues to likely question the sanity of my academic commitments, I am truly blessed to have a partner who has stood by and been my confidant and best friend over the past few decades. And to our two sons, who, now as teenagers, must wonder at times why I do not take my own advice when it comes to understanding them! Thanks, guys, for being who you are.

— John Winterdyk

I am also appreciative of finally having an opportunity to work with John Winterdyk, my long-ago fellow graduate student friend from Simon Fraser University. Unlike John, however, my interest in youth crime and justice has been more recent, starting, rather ironically, in the middle of the 1990s, during the peak of the moral panic over youth crime that soon led to the introduction of the YCJA, which appeared at the time to symbolize a further shift toward the 'adulteration' of young offenders, that is, the move toward treating young people more like adults in the criminal justice system. I began to ask questions like 'What is happening to youth in the criminal justice system?' and 'How did we get to where we are today?' The lack of adequate answers to these questions led me to try to answer these questions myself and share what I learned with my students. Along the way, I have incurred many professional and personal debts: first, to the many other youth justice researchers who inspired and provided a foundation for my own work; and second, to my friends and family who supported me along the way. The most important of these are my partner, Kathryn, and our children, Timothy, Amelia, and Alissa, who survived my years of learning how to be a parent and are now, quite amazingly, all carving out their own interesting educational paths and adult careers. Among my many friends and colleagues who have also been a huge help, I would especially like to thank my cross-country ski partner, Rod Kueneman, my always encouraging head of department, Elizabeth Comack, and my reliable home-province (Saskatchewan) contact, Ross Green, who usefully helps to keep me humble by reminding me where I came from. Thanks to all of you!

— Russell Smandych

To the staff at Oxford—words cannot express our gratitude. A special thanks goes to David Stover, president of Oxford University Press Canada, who embraced this project and encouraged us to follow through with it after incurring a number of stumbling blocks; to Patti Sayle, our developmental editor, who adeptly helped to get this project on track and keep us all within a reasonable timeframe; and to Mark Thompson, acquisitions editor, who skilfully helped to guide the project along and to keep us within the time constraints. A special thanks to Colleen Ste. Marie, who provided invaluable copy editing.

Finally, the caveat that so often appears at the end of acknowledgement sections and remains true in this edition: any shortcomings within this text still remain ours alone. Just as we must learn to have compassion for each other rather than sympathy, we hope you will see the intent in this edition and provide feedback so that the book can continue to evolve to serve its readers even better.

John Winterdyk
Director, Centre for Criminology and Justice Research, Department of Justice Studies
Mount Royal University
Calgary, Alberta

Russell Smandych
Department of Sociology
University of Manitoba
Winnipeg, Manitoba

About the Editors

John Winterdyk is the current director of the Centre of Criminology and Justice Research at Mount Royal University. He is also an adjunct professor at St Thomas University in Fredericton, NB, at the University of Regina, as well as at the Polytechnic of Namibia in Windhoek, Namibia. John has held two visiting positions at the Max Planck Institute in Freiburg, Germany. He has published extensively in the areas of youth justice, human trafficking, international criminal justice, and criminological theory. To date he has authored/edited some 20 textbooks and is currently co-editing a textbook on human trafficking (Taylor & Francis Group) and one on fear of crime and punitivity (Bochum University Press), among other initiatives.

Russell Smandych is a professor of sociology and criminology in the department of sociology at the University of Manitoba, and an adjunct professor of criminology in the department of justice studies at Mount Royal University. His current research and teaching interests include global criminology and criminal justice, comparative legal history, and comparative youth justice. He is the editor and co-editor of seven books and has published widely in leading Canadian and international journals in the fields of legal history and criminology. He has held honorary appointments as a distinguished visiting professor and scholar at universities in Canada, Ireland, Australia, New Zealand, and England, and in 2010 he was awarded the University of Manitoba Faculty of Arts Award in Internationalization for his work at promoting student awareness of international culture, perspectives, and issues through his teaching and research.

Contributors

Russell Smandych—University of Manitoba
John A. Winterdyk—Mount Royal University
Ross Green—Provincial Court of Saskatchewan
Nicholas Bala—Queen's University
Peter J. Carrington—University of Waterloo
Julian V. Roberts—University of Oxford
Chris McCormick—St Thomas University
Sibylle Artz—University of Victoria
Lorinda Stoneman—University of Victoria
Marge Reitsma-Street—University of Victoria
Stephen W. Baron—Queen's University
Bryan Hogeveen—University of Alberta

Joanne C. Minaker—Grant MacEwan University

Hirsch Greenberg—University of Regina

Jana Grekul—University of Alberta

Rhonda Nelson—University of Regina

Jordan Diplock—University of the Fraser Valley

Darryl Plecas—University of the Fraser Valley

Mark Totten—Totten and Associates

Bruce MacLaurin—University of Calgary

Catherine Worthington—University of Victoria

Susan McIntyre—The Hindsight Group

Louis-Georges Cournoyer—Université de Montréal

Jacques Dionne—Université du Québec

Michèle Goyette—Centre jeunesse de Montréal—Institut universitaire

Pierre Hamel—Centre jeunesse de Montréal—Institut universitaire

Brenda Morrison—Simon Fraser University

Colleen Pawlychka—Simon Fraser University

Susan A. Reid—St Thomas University

Sarah Gilliss—New Brunswick Community College

Part I
History, Trends, and Legislation

In order to understand current problems and issues surrounding youth at risk and the operation of the Canadian youth justice system, there are several steps we must first take: (1) develop a knowledge of youth justice history; (2) learn how we go about acquiring information about youth crime and youth justice; and (3) determine the objectives and purposes of youth justice legislation. Specific historical and comparative questions we need to address include the following:

- Why do we have a youth justice system in Canada?
- How did that system develop?
- How well is it working across the country and in comparison to youth justice systems in other countries?

We also need to attempt to answer questions about how, over time, criminologists and governments have attempted to assess trends in 'juvenile delinquency' and 'youth crime' and respond to them in various ways.

One of the most common ways Western countries have responded to juvenile delinquency and youth crime since the late nineteenth century has been to enact and implement legislation to treat and punish at-risk youth and young offenders. Since the beginning of the twentieth century, the Canadian federal government has followed this pattern by putting into place three succeeding legislative regimes: the Juvenile Delinquents Act (JDA) (1908); the Young Offenders Act (YOA) (1984); and the Youth Criminal Justice Act (YCJA) (2002). Collectively, the chapters included in Part One help us to better appreciate how the approach taken in Canada to define, measure, and deal with at-risk and criminalized youth has developed over the past century and evolved into its current form.

In Chapter One, Russell Smandych adopts a critical historical and comparative approach to explain the development of Canada's youth justice system. He argues that in order to answer the question of why we have a youth justice system, one has to start by developing a knowledge of the factors that contributed to the creation of the early juvenile justice systems in Canada and the United States beginning in the late nineteenth century. Similarly, in order to understand current developments occurring in the Canadian youth justice system—including the apparent trend toward a more punitive approach to dealing with youth crime—one needs to take into account comparable cross-national developments that also may be influencing these changes. In addition to emphasizing the need for a broader comparative perspective, Smandych closely examines historical literature on the development of early juvenile courts in the United States and Canada. In doing so, he points to a variety of different accounts of youth-justice-system reform, including, most notably, Thomas Bernard's perspective on the cyclical nature of changes in juvenile justice. Smandych argues that although Bernard's cyclical theory of juvenile justice reform does not provide a specific explanation of the reasons underlying historical changes in Canada's youth justice legislation, the theory nonetheless provides a relevant perspective on youth-justice-system reform that can be applied to Canada. In particular, Smandych notes that Bernard's theory provides a useful starting point for explaining the ostensibly cyclical nature of the legislative shift from the JDA to the YOA and the YCJA.

In addition to understanding the social, political, and legislative context of youth justice, one must also have a clear understanding of how 'youth crime' is defined and measured in Canada. The study of youth crime and/or delinquency poses many of the same challenges as the study of crime in general. For example, just as more general concepts and definitions of crime have changed over time, the concept of 'youth crime' has only in recent years come to be used by governments, criminologists, and the media in most of the Commonwealth countries, including Canada, England and Wales, New Zealand, and Australia. On the other hand, the earlier popular concepts of 'juvenile delinquency' and 'juvenile crime' continue to be more commonly used in other countries, like the United States. While at first glance this might appear to be an unimportant difference, these various concepts also imply different views about the level of culpability and responsibility that the legal system should attribute to young people who break the law, with juvenile 'delinquency' implying less culpability than youth 'crime'. In Chapter Two, John Winterdyk provides an overview of the concepts and data-collection methods that criminologists have developed to study what we now commonly refer to in Canada as youth crime. Importantly, this discussion illustrates that one of the main purposes of governments' measuring and recording 'juvenile delinquency' and 'youth crime' has been to provide justification for the state to control 'the problem'. Consequently, as Winterdyk carefully outlines, one must develop a thorough understanding of the strengths and weaknesses of the major data-collection methods used to study and develop and/or inform government policy on the perceived contemporary problem of 'youth crime'.

In Chapter Three, Judge Ross Green offers a systematic overview of key provisions of the YCJA. In doing so, he outlines similarities and differences between the YCJA and the earlier YOA, and highlights how the new legislation is now being interpreted by the courts and how it is being formally implemented. Judge Green examines the policy objectives underlying the YCJA and how these objectives are reflected in the act's provisions, the youth court process through which the act is enforced, the rights and obligations of young people and parents under the act, and issues surrounding the use of discretion in determining the most appropriate measures for dealing with young persons who may be charged with criminal offences. Judge Green's chapter is important for the perspective it provides on how judges who work on a day-to-day basis in the Canadian youth justice system are interpreting the YCJA and attempting to apply it—both in the best interests of young people and in the better protection of society from crime. The chapter is also valuable for the information it provides on some of the challenges judges face in applying the legislation, including issues surrounding the sentencing of Aboriginal young people and the problem of finding adequate ways of dealing with young people who suffer from developmental challenges (such as fetal alcohol spectrum disorder) and mental health issues.

Chapter Four offers a complementary examination of how the YCJA has been implemented across Canada and the effects it appears to be having on the way the justice system responds to young persons in conflict with the law. The chapter, which is written by Nicholas Bala, Peter J. Carrington, and Julian V. Roberts, examines Canadian data on the processing of young persons in the justice system both before and after the enactment of the YCJA in 2002. Bala et al.'s data analysis in essence shows that while under the YCJA the use of courts and custody in dealing with young offenders has decreased, there has been no corresponding apparent increase in youth crime. According to the authors, this finding runs contrary to what many 'tough on youth crime' opponents of the YCJA initially forewarned, and demonstrates that overall the manner in which the YCJA has been implemented has reduced incarceration rates for young offenders and increased the use of potentially more effective extrajudicial measures and community-based sentences. Despite the major change brought about in the youth justice system in Canada through the pre-court diversion and sentencing provisions of the YCJA, Bala et al., along with the authors of other chapters in Part One, are also concerned with the possibility that these evident improvements in the administration of youth justice in Canada may be undone in the future if federal politicians elected to Parliament endorse a 'crime control' approach that leads to further efforts aimed at toughening the YCJA.

1 From 'Misguided Children' to 'Criminal Youth': Exploring Historical and Contemporary Trends in Canadian Youth Justice

Russell Smandych

Overview

This chapter offers a historical and comparative perspective on the development of juvenile justice legislation in Canada and other Western countries from the late nineteenth to the early twenty-first centuries. Particular attention is given to accounting for the development of early juvenile justice systems in the United States and Canada in the late nineteenth century and the more recent contemporary shift—referred to by some as the punitive turn in youth justice—that now appears to be occurring in a number of Western countries. The primary purpose of this chapter is to develop an understanding of the importance of historical and comparative research in helping to explain contemporary trends in youth justice in Canada.

Key Objectives

After reading this chapter, you should be able to:

- Explain how 'deviant' and 'dependent' children were typically dealt with in Western countries prior to the invention of juvenile courts.
- Understand the factors that led to the creation of early delinquency legislation and juvenile courts in the nineteenth and early twentieth centuries.
- Identify factors linked to changes in early juvenile delinquency and to more recent youth criminal justice legislation in Canada.
- Understand the role of historical and comparative research in helping to explain contemporary trends in youth justice in Canada.

Introduction

juvenile delinquency

The legal term, which came into popular use in the nineteenth century to describe violations of the law by persons who had not reached the legal age of adulthood.

juvenile courts

Specialized courts first created in the late nineteenth century to apply juvenile justice laws in the care of dependent and delinquent children.

youth criminal justice system

A term often used today as a substitute for *juvenile courts*. Critical criminologists argue that it signifies a shift toward treating young offenders more like adults offenders.

reformable young offender

A term coined by Bryan Hogeveen (2005) to describe the discursive construction of some young offenders as 'troubled' and therefore needing intervention in the hope they can be rehabilitated.

In the past century Canada has seen the introduction of three different legislative regimes for administering juvenile justice: the Juvenile Delinquents Act (JDA) of 1908, the Young Offenders Act (YOA) of 1984, and the Youth Criminal Justice Act (YCJA) of 2002 (Smandych 2001). In the course of this legislative history, Canada has followed a pattern of legislative change that appears similar to that of many other Western countries, including Britain, Australia, and the United States. In each of these jurisdictions, recent decades have witnessed an earlier, predominately child-welfare model of juvenile justice eroded and replaced with more legalistic, and arguably more punitive, justice and crime-control models of juvenile justice procedure (Corrado, Gronsdahl, MacAlister, and Cohen 2010; Corrado and Markwart 1992; Hogeveen 2005).

These changes in legislation and models of juvenile justice have also been accompanied in some countries by changes in the terminology used to refer to young people who are caught up in the criminal justice system. Most notable among these is the shift in language that has occurred from considering such young people as 'misguided children' or 'juvenile delinquents', who have committed acts of **juvenile delinquency** that are best dealt with in **juvenile courts**, to viewing them as 'criminal youth' whose alleged anti-social and criminal acts are best dealt with through more formal **youth criminal justice systems**. Stated somewhat differently, Bryan Hogeveen and Joanne Minaker (Hogeveen 2005; Minaker and Hogeveen 2009, pp. 12–18) have argued that in Western countries like Canada discussions of how society should deal with troubled and/or troubling youth have oscillated over time between the two competing discourses; first, the discourse of the **reformable young offender**, which prevailed for much of the nineteenth and twentieth centuries and proposed that troubled youth 'required intervention and could be rehabilitated', and second, that of the **punishable young offender**, which has been prominent in debates since the 1990s and proposes that 'troubling' youth require 'punishment first and foremost, leaving reform and rehabilitative interventions as secondary measures'. Indeed, criminologists such as Minaker and Hogeveen argue that recent decades have witnessed a 'punitive turn' in youth justice in Canada that parallels similar trends in both the adult (Garland 2001; Pratt, Brown, Brown, Hallsworth, and Morrison 2005) and juvenile (or youth) justice systems of a number of other Western countries (Muncie 2005; Muncie and Goldson 2006). On the other hand, other prominent Canadian criminologists disagree with this **punitive turn thesis** and contend that there is very little evidence to support the claim that Canada's more recent approach to dealing with young people in conflict with the law (under the Youth Criminal Justice Act) is any more punitive in practice than it was in earlier decades (when the Juvenile Delinquents Act and Young Offenders Act were in effect) (Bala, Carrington, and Roberts 2009; Doob and Sprott 2006).

One of the aims of the current chapter is to evaluate the merit of competing views on historical and contemporary developments in Canadian youth justice, including, in particular, the origins of Canada's early juvenile delinquency legislation, and the alleged punitive turn in youth criminal justice since the 1990s. As we will see, this task is complicated because attempting to account for changes in Canadian youth justice must also take into consideration the way in which Canadian developments have often been tied to and influenced by similar changes in other countries. Indeed, a key argument made in this chapter is that the nature and direction of historical and contemporary trends in Canadian youth justice cannot be adequately understood without taking into account the connected experiences of other countries. The essential questions addressed in this chapter are as follows:

- Where did our modern (Western) juvenile or youth justice systems come from, and why did they come about when they did?
- What are the key changes that have occurred in juvenile justice administration over the course of the twentieth and early twenty-first centuries, and to what extent have Canadian developments been influenced by developments in other countries?

The essential point we will learn is that while there are many commonalities that link the historical development and current state of juvenile systems across various Western countries, there are also important historical, cultural, and political differences that make Canada's current approach to youth justice unique. In turn, as we attempt to show in this chapter, understanding these commonalities and differences can help us to better appreciate how Canadians, in general, and Canadian youth justice law and policy makers, in particular, can more fruitfully undertake the complicated task of improving the way we deal with the recurrently perceived problems of juvenile delinquency and youth crime.

The Development of Modern Juvenile Justice Systems

From 'Little Adults' to 'Misguided Children': The Changing Role and Status of Children in Western Society

In order to understand why young people are viewed the way they are by the criminal justice system today, we must begin by exploring the meaning of childhood and how this meaning has changed over time (Empey 1982). In recent decades, social historians have devoted a great deal of attention to examining the changing role and status of children in Western European and North American countries (see, for example, Gottlieb 1993). These studies have covered a broad array of topics, including, for example, the changing nature of parental attitudes toward children; the evolution of adult child-rearing practices; changes in the use of child labour and the eventual exclusion of children from much of the world of so-called adult work; and changing adult sensibilities about child abuse, discipline, and delinquency (see Stearns 1994). Significantly, criminologists have drawn on the work of historians of childhood and the family for evidence of how changing adult sensibilities about the meaning of childhood and the changing social and economic status of children in Western society were connected to the development of early child-welfare-model juvenile justice systems in the late nineteenth and early twentieth centuries. As such, a first step we need to undertake in order to explain where our first modern Western juvenile or youth justice systems came from is to learn how criminologists have made use of the evidence and arguments advanced by historians on the nature of influential changes in the role and status of children in Western society.

Of all of the historians who have written on the topic, criminologists have, arguably, been most influenced by the work of Philippe Ariès. In his influential book *Centuries of Childhood: A Social*

punishable young offender

A term coined by Bryan Hogeveen (2005) to describe the discursive construction of some young offenders as 'troublesome' and therefore requiring punishment in order to make them accountable for their criminal acts.

punitive turn thesis

The argument that in recent decades the criminal justice systems of many Western countries have become more punishment oriented, with longer prison sentences and higher rates of incarceration.

History of Family Life, Ariès (1962) undertook a detailed historical study of the treatment of children in Western Europe from the Middle Ages to the nineteenth century, and in doing so was the first social historian to propose an argument explaining how children were viewed and treated by adults in earlier times, and about how these views and practices changed over the centuries.

Ariès boldly argued that the modern concept of childhood was 'discovered' in Western Europe in the seventeenth century. According to Ariès, prior to this time few distinctions were made between individuals on the basis of age, and young people were fully integrated into the mainstream of social life. For example, this integration was evident in children's wearing essentially the same clothes as adults from a very early age. Ariès also pointed out that prior to the seventeenth century most of the education received by young people took the form of apprenticeships that involved learning a trade or profession through working daily for many years in the company of adults. For Ariès, evidence like this showed that the concept of childhood as we know it today did not exist in Western Europe in the Middle Ages.

Another important part of Ariès's thesis is the claim that the very high infant mortality rate that existed until the seventeenth century discouraged parents from wanting to invest emotionally in their children. In other words, he claimed that because the death rate for young children was so high, parents consciously avoided developing strong bonds and emotional ties to their children. This emotional detachment was reflected in the practice of wet-nursing, whereby mothers hired other women to breastfeed their babies, and in the practice of sending children away from home at an early age, either to go to boarding school or to work as a servant or apprentice in someone else's home. According to Ariès, this attitude of indifference toward children protected parents from the otherwise tragic loss they would feel when a number of their children died.

That many more children died prematurely in the Middle Ages than in later periods is a well-known demographic fact (Shahar 1990). However, Ariès offered the rather provocative argument that despite the high mortality rate and the lack of emotional investment they received from parents, children living prior to the seventeenth century were probably happier than they were in later periods. According to Ariès, because pre-seventeenth century Western European society was not preoccupied with raising the young and severely restricting their lives, conditions for children were relatively good. Indeed, he claimed that much of the status ambiguity and inter-generational conflict that now exists because of the way children are treated in modern Western society did not exist before the 'discovery' of childhood in the seventeenth century. Indeed, he argues that 'Rather than repressing, judging, or attempting to protect children with a special set of moral rules, adults shared all aspects of existence with them. The years of littlehood, as a consequence, were sociable and happy' (Empey 1982, p. 33).

Over the years a number of criminologists have drawn uncritically on Ariès's research to try to explain the reasons for the 'invention' of juvenile delinquency and the juvenile court. Most notable among these is Lamar Empey, who, in his influential textbook *American Delinquency: Its Meaning and Construction* (1982), relies mostly on Ariès (1962) to provide support for the argument that 'It was not until Europe began to awaken from the intellectual hibernation and social stagnation of the Middle Ages that a handful of moral philosophers began to question the customary treatment of children' and that '[o]ver a period of the next two or three centuries, age-old tendencies either to ignore or to exploit them were replaced with an ardent concern for their moral welfare'. Simultaneously, over this period 'parental care for children became a sacred duty; the school gradually replaced the apprenticeship system as the second most important child-raising institution; and childhood became a transitional period in which protection from, rather than indulgence in, adult activities became the rule'. According to Empey,

> Out of this process grew the modern concept of childhood stressing the idea that children
> have value in their own right and that because of their sweetness and simplicity they

require a careful preparation for the harshness and sinfulness of an adult world [and] [f]urthermore, it was only after childhood became a special status in the life cycle that the concept of a special court for juveniles began to develop. (Empey 1982, p. 8)

Ariès's thesis has also been drawn on to explain early twentieth century developments in Canada, particularly by the criminologist Tulio Caputo (1993), who argued that '[t]he establishment of a separate system of justice for young people in Canada followed similar developments in a number of western countries.' This development was based, in part, on the 'discovery' of childhood, outlined above, which Ariès (1962) describes as taking place in Western Europe between the sixteenth and nineteenth centuries.

In earlier work, I have criticized juvenile justice historians who have drawn on Ariès's thesis for creating an oversimplified account of the invention of juvenile delinquency and the juvenile court (Smandych 2001). In particular, I have pointed out how these authors have ignored the work of later historians of childhood and the family, including Linda Pollock (1983), Shulamith Shahar (1990), and Beatrice Gottlieb (1993), among others (Spagnoli 1981; Wilson 1984), whose studies raise serious concerns about the validity of Ariès's thesis on a number of grounds. The most damaging of these concerns is the apparent manner in which Ariès allowed his personal religious and ideological beliefs about the role of parents in child rearing and the need to maintain traditional conservative family values to bias his historical analysis (Spagnoli 1981).

In addition, historians like Beatrice Gottlieb (1993) show that it is misleading to talk about the 'discovery of childhood' as having occurred at a specific point in time since both historically and in more recent times adults have displayed a great deal of ambiguity in their thinking about the definition and treatment of children and youth. The currency of this continuing dilemma of parenting is captured well in Box 1.1 in the discussion and quote from Gottlieb's (1993) study. Moreover, Gottlieb's findings are consistent with evidence provided in more recent North American historical and sociological studies of parenting and the challenges of youth transition to adulthood (Comacchio 2006; Côté and Allahar 2006; Gleason, Myers, Paris, and Strong-Boag 2010).

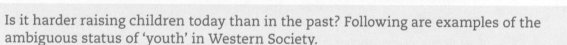

Box 1.1 Youth Justice in Action

Is it harder raising children today than in the past? Following are examples of the ambiguous status of 'youth' in Western Society.

In her study *The Family in the Western World from the Black Death to the Industrial Age*, Beatrice Gottlieb provides many examples that illustrate how ambiguous the category of 'youth' was in Western countries prior to the nineteenth century. Gottlieb (1993, pp. 156–57) notes that prior to the nineteenth century '(y)oung people were subject to full parental authority as long as they were under the parental roof, and the father's legal authority usually continued after they left home'. In addition, regardless of how old they were, '(i)t was next to impossible for single people to be considered adults'. With the exception of young men in Catholic countries who entered the celibate clergy, adulthood did not begin for males until they were married. Not entirely unlike today, Gottlieb (1993, p. 157) further notes that '(t)he adulthood of women was an even more ambiguous matter' since '(t)he only grown women who could function as full legal adults were widows in certain localities and under certain circumstances'. In her discussion of the ambiguity of youth in pre-industrial Western society, Gottlieb (1993) makes another statement that probably sounds quite familiar to many parents of today's Canadian youth, who are usually under the age of 30 but are sometimes even older:

Since most people did not marry until their middle or late twenties, it is plain that a sizeable chunk of the population drifted in a no-man's land between childhood and adulthood, the ill-defined territory called 'youth'. It was generally assumed that by fourteen, or at the latest sixteen, nobody could any longer be considered a little child. On the other hand, before being established in the religious life or as the head of a household, a male over sixteen was necessarily a dependent of some sort . . . Youth of both sexes constituted a large mobile population that formed only temporary attachments to households. Some journeymen and maidservants spent years moving about before they finally settled into marriage, the only conceivable end to youth. (pp. 157–58)

Source: Smandych (2001, p. 9).

The lesson that stands out from reading this historical and sociological literature is that parents have always found raising children to be a complicated and difficult task. The literature also points to the persuasiveness of the argument that while changing adult sensibilities about childhood in seventeenth century Europe may have had some influence on thinking about the need for a different way of dealing with juvenile delinquency, there were many other local, national, and more broadly international influences that need to be taken into account. In the following section, we describe and offer a critical analysis of the various explanations juvenile justice historians have developed to account for the creation of late nineteenth and early twentieth century delinquency legislation and juvenile courts in the United States, in selected European countries, in Britain, and in Anglo white-settler colonies, including Canada. However, before turning to this comparative historical discussion it is relevant to note some important common facts about the how juvenile delinquents were dealt with in the legal systems of Western countries before the creation of specialized delinquency legislation and juvenile courts. As well, we describe some common features of how juvenile delinquents were dealt with after early child-welfare-model delinquency legislation came into force.

Precursors to the Creation of Delinquency Legislation and Juvenile Courts

The term *juvenile delinquency* was first used in the eighteenth century, primarily as a legal term to describe 'violations of the law by persons below the community's legal age of adulthood' (Graebner 1994, p. 379). By the late nineteenth century, however, the term was in widespread use, and new juvenile justice systems had begun to be put into place in order to deal with the special needs of perceived delinquent and dependent children. Although, as we will see in this chapter, it is clear that a transformation in the way that young people were dealt with by the criminal justice system did occur in the nineteenth century, one must be careful not to over-exaggerate the extent of this transformation. In particular, it is not true that prior to the development of juvenile courts young offenders were dealt with in exactly the same way as adult offenders. Historians who have examined the operation of English-based criminal courts in common-law countries prior to the mid-nineteenth century have shown that the severity of the criminal law was often mitigated by sympathetic juries and paternalist judges who showed mercy toward those accused of serious crimes (see Beattie 1986; Hay 1975; Langbein 1992; Smandych 1991). Evidence also shows that young people who were accused of crimes that made them liable to the same punishment as adults were usually shown an even greater degree of mercy than adults who came before the courts (Carrigan 1998; Sutton 1988). It is also significant that under English common law, persons below the age of seven years could not be convicted of committing an offence, while 'youths between the ages of seven and fourteen were subject to the doctrine of **doli incapax**, which involved a presumption of incapacity that could be contested by the Crown' (Griffiths and Verdun-Jones 1994, p. 597).

Common Features of Early Child-Welfare-Model Delinquency Legislation

Before examining the development of delinquency legislation and juvenile courts in specific countries, it is also important to highlight a number of common features shared by juvenile justice systems. Although the timing of their establishment varied from jurisdiction to jurisdiction, there were three common features that came to characterize the operation of all newly invented juvenile courts and the laws that provided for their establishment.

First, the laws commonly recognized that there were three distinct age-graded levels of criminal accountability: no criminal accountability for youth under a certain legislatively determined age (for example, under 10 years old); limited criminal accountability for youth who were subject to the jurisdiction of the legislation because they fell within a certain legislatively determined age range (for example, 10 to 15 years old); and full criminal accountability for youth above a certain age (for example, 16 years old). In other words, all late nineteenth- and early-twentieth-century juvenile delinquency legislation came to be formally premised on the concept of **diminished criminal responsibility** for so-called juvenile delinquents.

A second general feature, related to both legislation and the operation of early juvenile courts, was that they were based on the principle of **parens patriae**—the idea that the state had a duty to intervene in the lives of children and assume the role of a substitute parent for those who were found to be either 'delinquent' or 'dependent'.

A third feature of the delinquency legislation enacted in many jurisdictions—including the United States, France, Belgium, England and Wales, Australia, and Canada—was the extent to which it reflected the common belief that juvenile delinquents should be viewed as 'misguided children' and treated with 'friendly helpfulness' (Hogeveen 2001). Most commonly, this was made operational in juvenile courts by giving judges wide discretionary power to deal with juvenile delinquents as they saw fit, and by appointing probation officers to give individual attention to the cases of young people who were brought before the court. Indeed, throughout Western countries where new juvenile justice systems were created in the late nineteenth and early twentieth centuries, probation officers came to assume a key role in the development and operation of those systems. While these were important common features of how early delinquency legislation and juvenile courts were in theory supposed to operate (as we will see in the following discussion), across all of the jurisdictions where they came into being the development of juvenile courts was also uneven, and in some cases took many decades to evolve from inception to more uniform practical implementation.

The Invention of the Juvenile Court in the United States

A great deal has been written in the past and continues to be written today about 'the invention of the juvenile court' in the United States (see Bernard 1992; Colomy and Kretzmann 1995; Getis 2000; Harris, Welsh, and Butler 2000; Krisberg 2005; Platt 1969; Redding, Goldstein, and Heilburn 2005; Rosenheim, Zimring, Tanenhaus, and Dohrn 2002; Rothman 1980; Springer et al. 2011; Tanenhaus 2004; Zimring 2005). One reason for this is that the United States, and more specifically the state of Illinois, was arguably the first jurisdiction where a juvenile justice system was created based explicitly on a child-welfare model. It may be that another reason for the attention US criminologists and juvenile justice historians have given to the topic is that in recent decades the juvenile justice system in the US has been under constant attack from critics, many of whom have argued

---

doli incapax

A legal doctrine that literally translated means 'incapable of doing harm' and refers to the English common-law presumption that children between 7 and 14 years of age could not be prosecuted for committing criminal offences, unless this presumption was contested by the Crown.

diminished criminal responsibility

The general view that individuals who are not adults should not be held fully responsible for their criminal behaviour.

parens patriae

The legal doctrine that the state has a duty to assume the role of a substitute parent in the case of delinquent or dependent children who do not have parents who are able to adequately control or care for them.

for major reforms including the more frequent waiver of juvenile cases to adult court and the use of tougher 'more adult-like' sentences for juvenile offenders (see Dolgin 1999; Feld 1999; Simon 1995; Thorson 1999). Several of the more recent histories of the original juvenile court movement in the US have clearly been written with knowledge and concern about these contemporary trends in mind. It is obviously not possible in this chapter to extensively review the wealth of literature on the early development of the juvenile court systems in the US. However, it is important to develop an understanding of the evidence and arguments advanced by specific key authors, both for what they have to tell us about the invention of the juvenile court in the US and for what their studies reveal about the shortcomings of existing historical writing on the topic—the primary one being the manner in which US historians have remained largely oblivious to the cross-national connections that linked the US and other late-nineteenth-century juvenile justice reform movements.

The focal point of much of the US historiography on the juvenile court are histories of the circumstances and events that surrounded the creation of the first state-wide juvenile court system in Illinois in 1899, and its evolution, which began with the establishment of the Cook County Juvenile Court in Chicago. The first criminologist to undertake a detailed study of the origin and operation of the famous Chicago Juvenile Court was Anthony Platt, in his (also soon to be famous) book on *The Child Savers: The Invention of Delinquency* (1969). Platt argued that the Illinois juvenile justice system and the Chicago juvenile court came about as a result of the child-saving movement that emerged in Chicago and many other US cities in the late nineteenth century. This movement was led mainly by conservative middle-class social reformers. More specifically, Platt portrayed the child-saving movement in the United States as a middle-class, Anglo-Saxon, Protestant movement dedicated mainly to attempting to control the moral behaviour of lower-class families and immigrants, who were perceived to pose a threat to moral values as well as to economic interests of the more 'respectable' middle class. In his study, Platt shows that rather than being the product of an outpouring of genuine humanitarian concern for 'saving children' from lives of poverty and parental neglect that often contributed to dependency and delinquency (as earlier historical accounts claimed), the child-saving movement was an ideologically conservative movement that was influenced in particular by ideas associated with 'social Darwinism and European [criminological] positivism' (Platt 1969, p. 13). According to Platt:

> The child-saving movement, like all moral crusades, reaffirmed ideal values and stressed the positive capacities of traditional institutions. The child savers' ideology was an amalgam of convictions and aspirations. From the medical profession, they borrowed the imagery of pathology, infection, immunization, and treatment; from the tenets of social Darwinism, they derived their pessimistic views about the intractability of human nature and the innate moral defects of the lower classes; [and] finally, their ideas about the biological and environmental origins of crime can be attributed to the positivist tradition in European criminology and anti-urban sentiments associated with the Protestant, rural ethic. (1969, p. 19)

In essence, according to Platt's analysis, racism and class discrimination were the most important factors that led to the enactment of juvenile delinquency statutes and the establishment of juvenile courts throughout the United States. He notes that in the years following the enactment of the Juvenile Court Act of Illinois, the act came to be used 'as a model statute by other states and countries', such that '[b]y 1917 juvenile court legislation had been passed in all but three states and by 1932 there were over 600 independent juvenile courts throughout the United States' (Platt 1969, p. 10). While Platt does not extend his critical analysis in any way to take into account simultaneous developments that were occurring in Canada, it is notable that his interpretation, which he advanced even more explicitly in later writing (Platt 1974), was later criticized by the Canadian juvenile justice historians John Hagan and Jeffery Leon (1977, 1980) for its inability to explain the factors surrounding the emergence of the child-saving movement and the juvenile court in Canada. As we will also see a little later, in their early and rather unique comparative historical research Hagan and Leon (1977, p. 240) did draw attention to the 'cross-fertilization of ideas that occurred between Canada and the United States in the juvenile justice context'.

A second and quite different account of the invention of the juvenile court in the United States is given by David Rothman (1980) in his book on *Conscience and Convenience: The Asylum and Its Alternatives in Progressive America*. Whereas Platt (1969, 1974) stresses the importance of examining changes in the social structure and economy of American society to explain changes in juvenile justice, Rothman examines the power of the ideas and rhetoric of social reformers involved in the late-nineteenth-century child-saving movement. In particular, Rothman links the efforts of child-saving reformers and 'the invention of the juvenile court' to a much broader range of social reform movements that emerged in the United States toward the end of the nineteenth century. Specifically, he shows that reform innovations in the areas of child welfare and juvenile justice were linked to more sweeping changes that were also occurring in the adult criminal justice system and in the mental health system in the US. According to Rothman (1980, p. 43), the 'Progressive era' in American history (which continued through the first two decades of the twentieth century) 'marked a major divide in attitudes and practices toward the deviant, creating new ideas and procedures to combat crime, delinquency, and mental illness'. The emergence of these new sensibilities regarding the methods to be employed in treating deviant individuals was reflected in the Progressive era in the dramatic rise of alternatives to, and innovations in, institutional confinement. In the same period that 'Americans enacted probation, parole, and indeterminate sentences for adult offenders', measures were taken to establish 'juvenile courts for delinquents' and 'outpatient clinics for the mentally ill'. In each of the areas of criminal justice, mental health, and child welfare, Rothman points to the growing occupational and professional status of reformers, and to the increasing extent to which they relied on social-scientific knowledge about the causes and treatment of deviant behaviour to justify the introduction of new methods of treatment and control.

According to Rothman (1980, pp. 207–211), the person who perhaps best epitomized the social-scientific approach that came to underpin the Progressive-era juvenile court movement was the psychologist G. Stanley Hall, 'who made the first systematic studies of childhood in the United States'. Hall introduced the term **adolescence** to describe the critical period of human development when people move through a distinct stage in which they progress, both biologically and emotionally, from being a child to being an adult. Hall's extensive two-volume book *Adolescence*, published in 1904, sold over 25 000 copies, which did much to cement his reputation as the leading American child psychologist of the period (Comacchio 2010; Hall 1904). Rothman notes the profound influence that Hall's ideas on adolescence and delinquency had on educated Americans, from women who belonged to the 'National Congress of Mothers (the forerunner of the Parent Teacher Association)', to criminologists, social workers, and advocates of the juvenile court. Significantly, Hall identified several causes of delinquency, which, although mostly environmental, included everything from 'heredity, bad antenatal conditions, bad homes, unhealthful infancy and childhood', to 'extremes of wealth and poverty' and 'overcrowded slums with their promiscuity and squalor' (Hall 1904; cited in Rothman 1908, p. 210). Hall also 'strongly advocated a juvenile court system' in which 'juveniles had to be treated completely apart from adults'.

According to Rothman, two of the juvenile court advocates who perhaps did more than any others to promote Hall's ideas on the causes and prevention of delinquency were Richard Tuthill, the first judge appointed to the Chicago Juvenile Court, who 'was persuaded that the delinquent's faults were "due not to hereditary taint, but to bad environment"', and Ben Lindsey, who presided

adolescence

A term popularized by the child-development expert G. Stanley Hall to refer to the stage of life during which a person progresses, both biologically and emotionally, from being a child to being an adult.

as judge in the first juvenile court in Denver, Colorado, and became a proverbial 'one-man traveling road show' in the cause of promoting the juvenile court movement throughout the United States (Rothman 1980, pp. 211, 215). Significantly, the original age of jurisdiction for both the Chicago Juvenile Court and the Denver Juvenile Court was under sixteen years of age for any child but that within five years Illinois extended the age of jurisdiction upward 'to include boys under the age of seventeen and any female child under the age of eighteen' (Dohrn 2002, p. 271.) While offering important insights into the broader reform process that influenced the establishment of delinquency legislation and juvenile courts in the United States—particularly regarding the undeniable power of the social-scientifically informed ideas and rhetoric of child-saving reformers—Rothman can also be criticized for ignoring the cross-fertilization of ideas on juvenile justice that occurred between the United States and other countries, as we will see later in this chapter when we turn to looking at the overlapping and interconnected experiences of other countries, including Canada.

More recently, David Tanenhaus (2004) has published a richly detailed study of the origin and early development of the Chicago Juvenile Court that moves beyond the work of Rothman and other American juvenile justice historians by focusing more attention on 'the actual working of juvenile courts in the early twentieth century'. In doing so, Tanenhaus (2004, pp. 164–165) shows that rather than being born in an 'institutionally intact' or fully complete form, it took several decades of 'trial and error' innovations for the Chicago Juvenile Court to evolve into the model child-welfare court that it was, rather inaccurately, reputed to represent from its beginning in 1899. Like Rothman and other earlier US juvenile justice historians, however, Tanenhaus (2004, pp. xxiv–xxv) only gives passing attention to noting that the Chicago Juvenile Court soon became 'a model . . . for policy makers in European, South American, and Asian nations' and that many of the 'child savers' from other countries 'looked to this American creation to learn how to divert children from the criminal justice system and to handle their cases in a less punitive fashion'.

Another significant observation made by Tanenhaus (2004, p. 165), which has an important parallel to the work of Thomas Bernard (1992), a leading US criminologist who has studied juvenile justice reform, is his view that 'child savers in the early twentieth century struggled with many of the same issues that twenty-first-century policy-makers must address'. This observation is consistent with Bernard's (1992) argument about the cyclical nature of juvenile justice reform, which he proposed in his attempt to explain the late-nineteenth-century juvenile court movement in the United States. Unlike other juvenile justice historians, Bernard develops theoretically based arguments about the recurrent nature of cycles of juvenile justice reform in order to explain the invention of the juvenile court in the late nineteenth century. Specifically, he accounts for the establishment of the Chicago Juvenile Court in 1899 by arguing that it represented another example of how adults have recurrently tended to respond to growing perceptions that juvenile crime is on the increase. According to Bernard's (1992, p. 3) cyclical theory of juvenile justice reform, a movement toward reform

> . . . begins at a time when justice officials and the general public are convinced that juvenile crime is at an exceptionally high level, and there are many harsh punishments but few lenient treatments for juvenile offenders. In this situation, justice officials often are forced to choose between harshly punishing juvenile offenders and doing nothing at all. As a consequence, many minor offenders are let off scot-free because lenient treatments are not available and because justice officials believe that the harsh punishments will make the minor offenders worse.

Bernard documents this cyclical pattern of juvenile reform by comparing the circumstances that surrounded the creation of the Chicago Juvenile Court in 1899 with earlier reform movements that also led to the introduction of a more lenient approach to dealing with juvenile delinquents.

Specifically, he shows how the introduction of a more lenient justice system for juveniles in Chicago in 1899 was preceded 75 years earlier by a similar attempt, in New York, to create 'Houses of Refuge' for the care and confinement of dependent and delinquent children. In a manner analogous to the Chicago Juvenile Court, the establishment of the New York House of Refuge by the Society for the Reformation of Juvenile Delinquents in 1825 was aimed at introducing a less punitive alternative for juvenile offenders who otherwise might be sentenced to an adult penitentiary. However, Bernard argues that prior to the establishment of the New York House of Refuge, what occurred more often was that juries who were disturbed over the harshness of current punishment practices simply acquitted youth who were accused of crimes that could have led to them being jailed in an adult penitentiary. Given the choice of continuing to do nothing at all, or working to introduce a more middle-of-the-road approach, supporters of the New York House of Refuge chose the latter approach. According to Bernard (1992, p. 99) this cycle was repeated in the late nineteenth century, at which time similar perceptions of 'high juvenile crime rates were accompanied by a firm belief that these could be lowered by the proper policy response'—namely, the 'middle-of-the-road' approach promised by the juvenile court. According to Bernard,

> The juvenile court, as a reform, was designed to provide leniency for those who would have been harshly punished by being sent to Chicago's jails and poorhouses, and to do something for juveniles for whom nothing would have been done by the adult criminal justice system. That is, it was designed to provide a middle ground between punishing harshly and doing nothing at all. In terms of 'criminal justice thermodynamics', the juvenile court reduced the severity of the penalty to increase the frequency of its application.

As we will see in the following sections of this chapter, Bernard's cyclical theory of juvenile justice reform, along with Tanenhaus's observation that many of the issues faced by early-twentieth-century juvenile justice reformers are the same as those that policy-makers struggle with today, are useful insights to keep in mind when examining historical and contemporary trends in juvenile or youth justice.

Paths of Juvenile Justice Reform in other Western Countries

The cross-fertilization of ideas on juvenile justice reform pointed to in some of the works of US and Canadian researchers is an important but, for the most part, largely overlooked aspect of juvenile justice history. Among US researchers it invariably takes the form of noting how the US juvenile court model 'influenced' developments in other countries, rather than being 'interconnected' with and, perhaps, reciprocally influenced by ideas on juvenile delinquency and juvenile justice reform in other countries. Part of our interest in this chapter is with learning about the broad range of factors associated with the creation of early delinquency legislation and juvenile courts in the nineteenth and early twentieth centuries. As such, we will explore what researchers have documented about the origin and outcome of juvenile justice reform movements that emerged in other Western countries during the same period, and about how these different paths of juvenile justice reform may have been interconnected.

In an article written in the year of 'the centennial of the Chicago Juvenile Court', Jean Trépanier (1999), the leading French-Canadian criminologist and juvenile justice historian, reflected on the operation of juvenile courts in North America and other mainly European countries over the century. While Trépanier recognizes that the Chicago Juvenile Court undeniably served as the model that was later followed in a number of other countries, he also points out that 'the diversity that characterises the history and evolution of juvenile courts in Western societies' makes it important to examine the coinciding but also sometimes noticeably different paths of development that were followed elsewhere (Trépanier 1999, p. 303).

One of the commonalities Trépanier points to is the gradual separation of juveniles and adults in court proceedings and institutions of confinement. For example, in France, Penal Codes enacted in 1791 and 1810 instituted a different court process for children under 16, while in the United States similar laws separating minors' trials from adults' were passed in 1874 in Massachusetts and 1892 in New York State. Also, in the same year the New York State passed its legislation, a new Criminal Code of Canada was enacted which 'provided for the possibility of private trials for children' (Trépanier 1999, p. 310). Along the same lines, in Canada back as early as 1857 two statutes were passed in the Province of Canada: one that provided for 'more expeditious trials' for young persons [An Act for the More Speedy Trial and Punishment of Young Persons] and another that created separate 'reformatory prisons' for young offenders [An Act for Establishing Prisons for Young Persons]. Similarly, in the United States, the House of Refuge movement started in the 1820s and marked the beginning of the gradual removal of children from adult prisons. This movement coincided closely with a parallel reform movement in Britain that between 1840 and 1900 led to the wide-scale transfer of young offenders from adult prisons to variously titled youth 'reform prisons', 'reform schools', and 'industrial schools' (Trépanier 1999, p. 310; Minaker and Hogeveen 2009). This pattern of gradual separation of juveniles from adults in court proceedings and institutions of confinement also occurred in many other Western countries during the nineteenth century, as shown in a summary form in Table 1.1. What this comparative historical data clearly shows is that there was an international dynamic to nineteenth century juvenile justice reform that most likely involved an extensive cross-fertilization of reform ideas between various countries (see also Shore 2003; Vanstone 2008; Weijers 1999). However, while this pattern occurred across many jurisdictions, the specific ages of young people who came under the jurisdiction of new juvenile justice systems varied between different Western countries and sometimes even between different provinces and states within a country. For example, similar to the case of states like Illinois and Colorado in the United States, with the enactment of the **Juvenile Delinquents Act (JDA)** in Canada in 1908, individual provinces were allowed to set their own maximum age of jurisdiction of the JDA at anywhere between 15 and 17 years old, while different age categories could also be selected for males and females. This was the case in Alberta, where the maximum age of jurisdiction was 15 for boys and 17 for girls (Hacker 1978).

Although all Western countries eventually established separate criminal court processes and institutions for dealing with juvenile offenders, the specific nature and timing of these developments varied considerably and, in some jurisdictions, occurred only quite gradually over the course of the first half of the twentieth century (Shore 2003). One example of this is England and Wales, where the early juvenile courts provided for under the Children Act of 1908 were simply 'special sittings of magistrates' courts . . . [that] were empowered to act in criminal cases and in cases of begging and vagrancy, though they remained, in essence, criminal courts' (Newburn 2002, p. 549). Or, as Henri Giller (1999, p. 395) explains in more detail, in England and Wales the original juvenile court 'was primarily a court with modified procedural arrangements which, in part, recognised the immaturity of youth', and it was not until 25 years later, with the passing of the Children and Young Person Acts of 1932 and 1933, that the court was formally allowed to make 'the welfare of the child a particular (although [still] not overriding) consideration when determining what was an appropriate disposition for an offence'. Similarly, Cunneen and White (2007, p. 15) have noted that although created as separate courts, early juvenile courts in Australia were 'not as different from the adult courts' as they were in the US.

On the other hand, France was a country that patterned its juvenile justice system explicitly on the Chicago Juvenile Court model. This was apparently in large part through the influence of Edouard Julhiet, the son of a French Appeal Court judge, who lived in the United States from

Juvenile Delinquents Act (JDA)

Canada's first juvenile delinquency legislation enacted in 1908 and in force until 1984.

Table 1.1 Juvenile Justice Reforms in Selected Western Countries

Country or State	Date of Earliest Delinquency Legislation and/or Functioning Juvenile Court	Date of Earliest Separate Juvenile Houses of Refuge, Prisons, Reformatories, and Industrial Schools
Australia (by state)[1]	1895 to 1918	Most states, from 1863 to 1874
Belgium[2]	1912	1847
Canada[3]	1908	1858 (Québec); 1859 (Ontario)
England and Wales[4]	1908	1838
France[5]	1912	1830
Germany[6]	1923	1833
Netherlands[7]	1922	1857
New Zealand[8]	1906	1867
Sweden[9]	1902	1838
United States[10]	1899	1825

Data Sources:

1. Cunneen and White (2007, pp. 5, 8–9, 14); O'Connor and Cameron (2002, p. 211); Trépanier (1999, p. 310).
2. Shore (2003, p 117); Trépanier (1999, pp. 304, 312); Trépanier and Tulkens, (1993).
3. Minaker and Hogeveen (2009, p. 48); Trépanier (1999, pp. 307, 310).
4. Corrado and Turnbul (1992, p. 78); Cunneen and White (2007, pp. 8–9); Graham (2002, p. 81); Newburn (2002, p. 549); Shore (2003, pp. 113, 117); Trépanier (1999, pp. 304, 313–314).
5. Blatier (1999, p. 241); Shore (2003, p. 112); Trépanier (1999, pp. 304, 310, 316).
6. Albrecht (2004, p. 443); Crofts (2002, p. 107); Trépanier (1999, pp. 304, 316).
7. Shore (2003, p. 117); Trépanier (1999, pp. 304, 316).
8. Morris (2004, pp. 247–248).
9. Janson (2004, p. 394); Shore (2003, p. 113).
10. Trépanier (1999, pp. 306, 310).

1902 to 1906, where he learned about the Illinois system and returned to France to advocate for the establishment of a similar system (Vanstone 2003, p. 742). This was also the case for Germany, where 'the youth court movement' that led to the enactment of the country's first Youth Court Law in 1923 'relied heavily on the thinking of the North American child-saving movement and on North American experiences with juvenile courts' (Albrecht 2004, p. 444).

From these comparative examples, we can more adequately appreciate the diversity that characterized the history and evolution of juvenile courts and also how the development of the juvenile court in Canada was influenced by ideas and practices that already existed in other countries.

Paths to Reform in Canada and the Origins of the Juvenile Delinquents Act of 1908

While the history of the origin of the juvenile court model has not been seriously contested, a few claims have been made that the Chicago Juvenile Court was not the first. Some have claimed that South Australia 'introduced the first juvenile court in the world' through state legislation enacted in 1895 (O'Connor and Cameron 2002, p. 212; Cunneen and White 2007). It has also been claimed that the state of Colorado established a juvenile court by way of enacting an education law that came into effect earlier in 1899 than the Juvenile Court Act of Illinois (Hagan and Leon 1977, p. 239). In addition, in the Canadian context, it was also claimed early on by none other than J.J. Kelso, one of the key lobbyists for the enactment of the Canadian Juvenile Delinquents Act of 1908, that it was he who actually did more than anyone else to create the modern juvenile court. Although Kelso's claim was eventually effectively repudiated by his critics, the fact that he could make this claim and create the debate he did with his contemporaries shows a great deal about how Canada's Juvenile Delinquents Act of 1908 came into being.

J.J. Kelso was a 'young, passionate and crusading Toronto newspaper reporter' who became a key leader in the child-saving movement in Ontario in the 1880s (Davis-Barron 2009, p. 31). Kelso recalled later that as a young reporter in Toronto, he witnessed first-hand the miserable conditions experienced by poor and neglected street children and pledged 'to devote his life to "plead for these little ones" who perished by the wayside "in a land abounding in Christian activities"' (cited in Sutherland 1976, p. 112). Kelso figured prominently among the 'new breed of child-savers' that emerged in Ontario and elsewhere in the 1880s, and along with them, he argued for an expansion of 'the definition of needy children to include those who suffered from parental neglect or cruelty' while also promoting 'the idea of foster homes as the most efficient, humane, and economical approach to child-welfare' (Bullen 1991, p. 136). In 1887, at the age of 22, Kelso 'founded the Toronto Humane society, a voluntary organization dedicated to the protection of women, children, and animals', and by the following year he successfully lobbied for the enactment of new Ontario legislation entitled An Act for the Protection and Reformation of Neglected Children, which, among other significant changes, empowered local municipalities to appoint commissioners 'to conduct trials of juvenile offenders apparently under the age of sixteen' while also providing that all defendants under the age of twenty-one 'be tried apart from other offenders, "as far as practicable"'. In the same year, 'he founded a charitable society known as the Fresh Air Fund for the purpose of providing poor city children with summer excursions' and in 1891, he founded and became the first voluntary president of the Toronto Children's Aid Society. In 1893, Kelso was recognized for his child-welfare and juvenile justice reform efforts by being appointed Ontario's first superintendent of Neglected and Dependent Children, a position created under a new child-welfare act (entitled An Act for the Prevention of Cruelty to, and Better Protection of Children, commonly called 'The Children's Act'), which Kelso himself had lobbied the provincial government to enact. This position, which Kelso occupied for the next 41 years, gave him the power to directly oversee the implementation of The Children's Act of 1893 as well as to lobby for additional child-centred social reforms (Bullen 1991, pp. 138–145).

Kelso was also in a good position to lobby the federal government to enact legislation that would enshrine Ontario's approach to dealing with dependent and delinquent children, and he began to do this with the help of Ottawa lawyer and president of the Ottawa Children's Aid Society, W.L. Scott. Kelso and Scott worked together to campaign for the enactment of federal delinquency legislation. In the course of this effort, they both took every opportunity to strengthen support for their campaign from constituencies like the police, judges, and federal politicians in Ottawa. Toward this end, Kelso and Scott both corresponded with and travelled to the US to meet with juvenile justice reform experts, and through their efforts prominent American juvenile court proponents were invited to Ottawa 'to address Senators and Members of the House of Commons regarding the benefits of a juvenile justice system for Canada' (Davis-Barron 2009, p. 36). Among their many cross-border connections, one of the most notable is Kelso's long-time acquaintance and correspondence with both Judge Harvey B. Hurd, who drafted the Illinois legislation, and Judge Ben Lindsey of Denver, whom he met while travelling to conferences in the US. Significantly, however, the historian Neil Sutherland claims that 'Canadians . . . turned neither to Chicago or Denver but to Philadelphia for the model for their first systematic effort to put the notion [of a juvenile court] into practice'. This stemmed from an event in May 1906. W.L. Scott, as president of the Ottawa Children's Aid Society (CAS), and his paid secretary, John Keane, attended an annual meeting of the National Conference of Charities and Correction in Philadelphia, where they learned about the system of juvenile probation used in the city and subsequently returned to Ottawa to persuade the executive committee of the Ottawa CAS to adopt the same system. Later that year, W.L. Scott and his influential father, Senator R.W. Scott, invited Mrs Hannah Kent Schoff, chairman of the Philadelphia Court Committee, to come to Ottawa to 'address a special meeting of senators and members of Parliament' on the benefits of creating a juvenile court system like the one in Philadelphia (Sutherland 1976, pp. 119–121). Scott also shortly afterward hosted Judge Ben Lindsey in Ottawa to address Members of Parliament on the benefits of enacting legislation for creating a specialized juvenile court (Hogeveen 2001; Trépanier 1991).

It is true that historians commonly recognize that it was W.L. Scott who drafted the Juvenile Delinquents Act of 1908 and, with his father's help, lobbied most vigorously for the passage of the legislation first through the Canadian Senate and then the House of Commons. However, in later years J.J. Kelso claimed that the juvenile court movement started neither in Chicago nor in Philadelphia but actually in Ontario, beginning with the effort he undertook in 1888 to lobby for the enactment of An Act for the Protection and Reformation of Neglected Children, which provided for separate trials for juveniles. Moreover, Kelso claimed that he actually influenced the creation of the Chicago Juvenile Court by corresponding with 'officials in Chicago' and attending three conferences there in 1893, where he advocated his 'Children's Court ideas as one of the chief solutions of juvenile crime' (cited in Hagan and Leon 1980, p. 240). In response to lingering stories about the role Kelso claimed for himself in the creation of the Juvenile Delinquents Act, in 1933 W.L. Scott wrote a letter in which he disputed Kelso's story with his own claim that he himself drafted the original legislation, taking into account mainly the juvenile court acts of Illinois and Colorado (Hagan and Leon 1980). In the end, however, it would be misleading to give credit for the origin of Canada's modern juvenile justice system solely to the humanitarian conscience and power of the ideas and rhetoric of social reformers like J.J. Kelso and W.L. Scott, as Rothman (1980) analogously did in the US context. In addition, we must take into account a number of other factors, including earlier precursors to the juvenile court, the changing social and economic climate of the last half of the nineteenth century, the gradual rise of the social welfare state in many countries, and other international influences including the cross-fertilization of ideas about juvenile justice reform (for a more detailed discussion of these factors, see Hogeveen 2001; Minaker and Hogeveen 2009).

The Juvenile Delinquents Act nonetheless represented a fundamental shift in the way juvenile justice was administered in Canada. In addition to making the supervision of juvenile offenders in the community by way of probation a central feature, the act did this by casting a wide net in defining the types of delinquent and dependent children who would henceforth come under the jurisdiction of the legislation. Specifically, the JDA originally defined a juvenile delinquent as 'any child who violates any provision of *The Criminal Code* . . . , or of any Dominion or provincial statute, or of any by-law or ordinance of any municipality, for which violation punishment of a fine or imprisonment may be awarded; or, who is liable by reason of any other act to be committed to an industrial school or juvenile reformatory under the provisions of any Dominion or provincial statute'. A 1924 revision to the act further broadened the definition of *juvenile delinquent* to include any child 'who is guilty of sexual immorality or any similar form of vice' (cited in Davis-Brown 2009, p. 41). This broadened definition of delinquent youth led to the creation of what later came to be referred to as **status offences**, or offences that a youth could be found guilty of simply because he or she was underage. These included 'offences' like 'the consumption of alcohol, truancy, running away from home, refusal to obey parents, having delinquent friends, and the use of profanity' (Tanner 2010, p. 31). In many provinces children were committed to industrial or training schools for such offences or for being found guilty of either 'unmanageability' or 'incorrigibility' (Bala 1997; Hatch and Griffiths 1991). The doctrine of *parens patriae* embodied in the JDA also gave juvenile court judges and corrections officials the discretion to sentence children to **indeterminate sentences** of incarceration, which meant that they would not be released until 'they were no longer a threat to

status offences
Behaviours that are considered delinquent or criminal only because the person who engages in the behaviour is not yet an adult. Examples include truancy (skipping school), underage drinking, and promiscuous sexual behaviour.

indeterminate sentences
Sentences of incarceration that have no fixed expiration date, which means that a person can be held in custody until he or she is deemed by correctional officials either to be rehabilitated or to no longer pose a threat to society.

the public . . . or until they reached the age of 21' (Minaker and Hogeveen 2009, p. 59). As a general rule, the JDA exerted jurisdiction over children ranging from 7 to 15 years of age. However, the act also allowed for considerable variation between provinces; each province was allowed to decide the cut-off age, above 15, at which point a case involving a young person would be held in adult court. In most provinces the age was set at 16 years, while in Manitoba and Québec it was set at 18 years, and, as noted previously, in Alberta these age cut-offs were also made gender specific (Hacker 1978). As in the case of the juvenile courts established in other countries, the child-welfare orientation of the JDA was also reflected in the informal nature of proceedings in juvenile courts, where judges, many of whom had no legal training themselves, acted to give hopefully wise advice to 'misguided children', and where lawyers were discouraged from appearing in order to 'to ensure that "unnecessary technicalities" would not interfere with or delay the treatment considered to be in the child's best interests' (Bala 1997, p. 44).

When the JDA came into effect in 1908, juvenile courts and probation services, as in other countries, developed unevenly across Canada, and it was well into the twentieth century before many rural and remote areas had a functioning juvenile justice system. This, along with the differences in the cut-off age for juvenile offenders, not surprisingly contributed to a great deal of inter-provincial and regional variation in applying the legislation (Carrigan 1998; Hatch and Griffiths 1991; Hogeveen 2001; Myers 1999; Sangster 2002; Sutherland 1976; Woloschuk 2009).

Yet even before the JDA became more evenly implemented across the country, its operation began to be criticized on a number of grounds. By the 1960s and 1970s, the move toward juvenile justice reform in Canada, again noticeably influenced by parallel developments in the United States, was well under way (Corrado and Markwart 1992; Minaker and Hogeveen 2009). When the **Young Offenders Act (YOA)** was finally introduced in 1984 to replace the JDA, many criminologists and youth justice policy-makers viewed it as a long-overdue reform that finally brought in needed 'due process' rights and safeguards for young offenders, which included most importantly a guaranteed right to obtain and instruct legal counsel (Bala 1997; Corrado and Markwart 1992; Leschied, Jaffe, and Willis 1991). At the same time, however, critics of the new legislation viewed it as representing an unfortunate shift away from the child-welfare-based child-saving approach of the JDA toward a more justice- and crime-control based child-blaming approach, in which priority would be given to holding young offenders accountable for their criminal behaviour (Havemann 1986, 1992).

The relatively short 15-year life of the YOA was marked with controversy from the outset, and the act underwent a number of significant amendments before it was finally replaced with the **Youth Criminal Justice Act (YCJA)** in 2003 (see generally, Bala 1997; Doob and Sprott 2004: Hogeveen and Smandych 2001). In the remaining part of this chapter, we give more attention to more recent contemporary trends in youth justice and, in particular, to the question of whether in recent years Canadians have taken a more punitive approach to dealing with young criminals.

Contemporary Trends in Youth Justice Law and Practice in Canada

With the enactment of the Youth Criminal Justice Act (YCJA) in 2002, and its formal implementation on 1 April, 2003, Canada entered into a new era in the administration of juvenile or youth justice. As in the years following the enactment of the JDA (in 1908) and the YOA (in 1982), youth justice professionals from across Canada—including police, lawyers and judges, and youth corrections personnel—have now taken up the task of attempting to interpret and apply the legal principles underlying the YCJA. Criminologists and government policy analysts, meanwhile, are now beginning to assess how in fact the YCJA has been implemented in practice, and what the outcomes

Young Offenders Act (YOA)
The federal legislation that replaced the Juvenile Delinquents Act from 1984 to 2003.

Youth Criminal Justice Act (YCJA)
The federal legislation enacted in 2002 to replace the Young Offenders Act, and which came into effect on 1 April, 2003.

of its application have been to date. A number of the authors of later chapters of this book make contributions of this type to our knowledge of the YCJA (see Green, Chapter 3; Bala et al., Chapter 4, in this textbook), and thus should be read along with the current chapter, which is concerned more with highlighting the role of historical and comparative research in helping to explain contemporary trends in youth justice in Canada.

The Origins of the YCJA and the Punitive Turn Debate

Like its predecessors, the JDA and the YOA, the enactment of the YCJA was clearly part of a broad international shift away from a child-welfare model of juvenile justice toward more legalistic and ostensibly punitive justice and crime-control models. However, in many countries this shift was not solely in the direction of moving from what were perceived as lenient juvenile crime prevention and response strategies to more harsh ways of punishing wayward youth (Bernard 1992; Muncie 2008). This appears to be particularly the case in Canada, since, when it was enacted in 2002, the YCJA contained sections that provided for the harsher, adult-like punishment of violent young offenders, while also restricting the use of custody sentences for youth convicted of non-violent crimes. The act also introduced a wide range of formal and informal extra-judicial measures for diverting first-time and less serious young offenders out of the youth justice system. Such measures included police warnings, cautions, and community-based conferences (for details, see Chapter 3). In effect, these measures made Canada's new youth criminal justice system, at least formally on paper, a **bifurcated youth justice system**—'wherein petty and non-serious offenders would he handled through community-based and diversionary programs while serious and violent offenders would be subject to more carceral and punitive interventions' (Minaker and Hogeveen 2009, pp. 78–79).

One of the issues currently being debated by Canadian criminologists is the degree to which the implementation of the YCJA has resulted in a shift in the direction of making more use of 'carceral and punitive interventions' in the youth justice system in comparison to the use of 'community-based and diversionary programs', which are generally perceived to be more 'lenient'. It is not my purpose in this chapter to try to resolve this debate but, rather, to show that a better understanding of both the factors that led to the creation of the YCJA and the 'punitive turn' debate itself can be obtained by placing both of these in their respective historical and comparative contexts.

In a study published just prior to the enactment of the YCJA in 2002, Hogeveen and Smandych (2001) located the immediate origins of the YCJA in the political discourse surrounding the perceived crises in youth crime in Canada in the 1990s. To carry out this research, they drew on the approach of other criminologists and historians mentioned in this chapter who had earlier attempted to explain the origins of the JDA and the YOA by analyzing parliamentary debates and media reports (e.g., Havemann 1986; Trépanier 1991). From their examination of parliamentary debates and media reports of the period, Hogeveen and Smandych found that in the speeches of most federal politicians at the time and in reports on the need for youth justice reform found in newspapers, the dominant discourse was one that viewed the YOA as ineffective and in need of replacement; the act was considered too lenient on youth offenders and unable to effectively address what was perceived to be a growing crisis of youth crime. While Hogeveen and Smandych began here to contribute to what would later come to be referred to by others as the punitive turn debate, they did not at the time attempt to predict how young offenders would be dealt with under the YCJA in the future, noting only that the legislation marked a significant discursive shift from referring to deviant youth 'officially as either "juvenile delinquents" or "young offenders," signifying their reduced responsibility' toward viewing them as 'young criminals' and making them 'appear much closer to adult criminals' (2001, p. 166). Significantly, Hogeveen and Smandych's study drew on the theoretical and methodological insights of earlier historical studies of juvenile justice reform to

bifurcated youth justice system
Literally, a two-pronged justice system, meaning that it provides avenues for the diversion of first-time and less serious young offenders out of the system, while at the same time making possible more punitive forms of punishment for more serious offenders.

offer an account of the origins of the YCJA at the same time that it indirectly addressed the contemporary issue of the alleged punitive turn in youth justice.

More recently, in two separately authored studies, Hogeveen (2005) and Smandych (2006) offer skeptical views of the YCJA's ability to facilitate promoting community-based extra-judicial ways of dealing with young offenders. They also point to the continuing potential for the YCJA, and its possible perceived failures, to be used to justify more punitive responses to various types of broadly defined 'youth violent crime' and 'serious violent offenders' (Tanner 2010). Both authors also point out how the growing demand in Canada in the 1990s for tougher legislation to deal with criminal youth paralleled contemporary trends in other countries, such as the United States and Britain, toward 'the further dismantling of traditional "child-welfare" juvenile court procedures' (Smandych 2006, p. 23) and the introduction of new legislation aimed at getting tough on juvenile crime (Hogeveen 2005, p. 77).

While it is comparatively too short a time since the introduction of the YCJA to offer 'any definitive statements about its impact on the administration of juvenile justice in Canada' (Tanner 2010, p. 250), other criminologists have argued that available youth court processing and sentencing data show that there has been no real increase in the punitiveness of the Canadian youth criminal justice system in recent years (Bala, Carrington, and Roberts 2009; Doob and Sprott 2006). Anthony Doob and Jane Sprott (2006, p. 224), in a critique of Hogeveen's (2005) study, also make the historically based claim that the intention of the government of Canada when it introduced the YCJA was not to actually create more tough legislation but simply to make it appear that it was doing so, in order to deflect criticism from political opposition parties that it was too soft on youth crime. According to Doob and Sprott, by formally creating a bifurcated youth justice system, federal government legislative drafters quite astutely 'crafted a law' that offered more opportunities than existed before to 'reduce the level of punitiveness' of the youth criminal justice system (Doob and Sprott 2006, p. 224; Tanner 2010). Despite whether or not this was actually the case, it is difficult to predict the direction that the administration of juvenile justice in Canada will move in the future (Mann 2011). One reason for this, as we have begun to learn in this chapter, is that we must consider contemporary trends in Canadian youth justice within the context of comparable juvenile justice developments in other countries (see Merlo and Benekos 2010; Muncie 2008).

In addition, in order to arrive at more definitive conclusions about whether the Canadian youth justice system is taking a punitive turn, we need to also take into account whether trends in the punishment of youth are moving in a similar or different direction than punishment trends in the adult criminal justice system (Garland 2001; Meyer and O'Malley 2005; Moore and Hannah-Moffat 2005; Pratt et al. 2005). As of now, perhaps the most accurate observation that can be made is the one offered by Julian Tanner (2010, p. 250), who states that 'It remains to be seen how the Youth Criminal Justice Act will be judged by members of the voting public, especially victims' rights organizations, who are inclined to view all juvenile justice legislation as being too lenient. It seems unlikely that the popular appeal of "get tough" approaches to young offenders will ever completely go away.'

Summary

This chapter has stressed the value of historical and comparative research in understanding contemporary trends in Canadian youth justice. It has shown that Canada's current approach to dealing with young people who come in conflict with the law evolved over many centuries and involved many significant turning points along the way. One of these was the gradual shift that occurred in adult sensibilities about childhood—or what Ariès argued amounted to 'the discovery of childhood'—which over time led young people from being viewed as little adults from a very early stage in life, to them later being viewed and treated by adults as innocent and vulnerable children who needed to be nurtured and protected for a more extended period of time. By the late nineteenth century this extended period of 'growing up, or the transitional years from childhood to adulthood, came to be referred to as adolescence. Social-scientific knowledge about this newly defined stage in life in turn had a noticeable influence on the thinking of social reformers about the causes of juvenile delinquency and the value of having a separate juvenile court for dealing with troubled youth, who now were perceived mainly as either dependent, neglected, or misguided and therefore mostly in need of friendly helpfulness.

However, historical research shows that there were also many other factors in operation that help to account for the enactment of the Juvenile Delinquents Act in 1908, including earlier precursors to the juvenile court, the changing social and economic climate of the last half of the nineteenth century, the gradual rise of the social welfare state in many countries, and the international cross-fertilization of ideas about juvenile justice reform. Through describing the essential findings of research on the origins of the Youth Criminal Justice Act and the debate over the alleged recent punitive turn in Canadian youth justice, this chapter also highlights the value of historical and comparative research for understanding more recent, and possibly future, trends in the Canadian youth criminal justice system.

Key Terms

adolescence
bifurcated youth justice system
diminished criminal responsibility
doli incapax
indeterminate sentences
juvenile courts
juvenile delinquency
Juvenile Delinquents Act (JDA)

parens patriae
punishable young offender
punitive turn thesis
reformable young offender
status offences
Young Offenders Act (YOA)
Youth Criminal Justice Act (YCJA)
youth criminal justice systems

Review Questions

1. What can we learn from studying the history of childhood that is relevant to understanding the development and operation of modern juvenile justice systems?

2. What were the major factors that contributed to the development of specialized youth justice systems in Western countries, including Canada in the late nineteenth and early twentieth centuries?

3. How important was humanitarian conscience and the rhetoric of social reformers in the development of early juvenile delinquency legislation and juvenile courts in the US and Canada?

4. What is Bernard's cyclical theory of juvenile justice reform, and how might it be used to explain reforms in Canadian youth justice legislation, such as the introduction of the JDA (in 1908) and the YCJA (in 2002)?

Critical Thinking Questions

1. Is it harder to raise children today than in the past? Why?

2. Do we really need a specialized youth justice system in Canada? Why or why not?

3. Has there been a punitive turn in youth justice in Canada? What types of data could you use to try to answer this question?

4. If you were given the power to make changes in the Canadian youth criminal justice system, would you want the system to be more lenient or more punitive? Why?

Suggested Readings

Bernard, Thomas J. (1992). *The cycle of juvenile justice*. New York: Oxford University Press.

Gleason, M., Myers, T., Paris, L., and Strong-Boag, V. (Eds.). (2010). *Lost kids: Vulnerable children and youth in twentieth-century Canada and the United States*. Vancouver: University of British Columbia Press.

Muncie, J., and Goldson, B. (Eds.). (2006). *Comparative youth justice: Critical issues*. London: Sage.

Tanenhaus, D.S. (2004). *Juvenile justice in the making*. New York: Oxford University Press.

Suggested Weblinks

The Canadian Encyclopedia
www.thecanadianencyclopedia.com/index.cfm?PgNm=TCE&Params=A1ARTA0001579
• A history of childhood.

Mapleleafweb: Youth Justice in Canada
www.mapleleafweb.com/features/youth-justice-canada-history-debates
• A discussion of the history of youth justice in Canada.

Canadian Children's Rights Council
www.canadiancrc.com/default.aspx
• A non-profit advocacy organization.

References

Albrecht, H.-J. (2004). Youth justice in Germany. In M. Tonry and A. Doob (Eds.), *Youth crime and youth justice: Comparative and cross-national perspectives* (pp. 443–93). Chicago: Chicago University Press.

Ariès, P. (1962). *Centuries of childhood: A social history of family life*. New York: Vintage Books.

Bala, N. (1997). *Young offenders law*. Toronto: Irwin.

Bala, N., Carrington, P., and Roberts, J. (2009). Evaluating the Youth Criminal Justice Act after five years: A qualified success. *Canadian Journal of Criminology and Criminal Justice, 51*(2): 131–67.

Beattie, J. (1986). *Crime and the courts in England 1600–1800*. Princeton: Princeton University Press.

Bernard, T. J. (1992). *The cycle of juvenile justice*. New York: Oxford University Press.

Blatier, C. (1999). Juvenile justice in France. *British Journal of Criminology, 39*(2): 240–52.

Bullen, J. (1991). J.J. Kelso and the 'new' child-savers: The genesis of the children's aid movement in Ontario. In R. Smandych, G. Dodds, and A. Esau (Eds.), *Dimensions of childhood: Essays in the history of children and youth in Canada* (pp. 135–58). Winnipeg: University of Manitoba, Legal Research Institute.

Caputo, T. (1993). The Young Offenders Act: Children's rights, children's wrongs. In T. O'Reilly-Fleming, T. and Clark, B. (Ed.). (1993). *Youth injustice: Canadian perspectives* (pp. 1–30). Toronto: Canadian Scholars' Press.

Carrigan, D.O. (1998). *Juvenile delinquency in Canada: A history*. Toronto: Irwin.

Colomy, P. and Kretzmann, M. (1995). Projects and institution building: Judge Ben B. Lindsey and the juvenile court movement. *Social Problems, 42*(2): 191–215.

Comacchio, C. (2006). *The dominion of youth: Adolescence and the making of modern Canada, 1920 to 1950*. Waterloo, ON: Wilfrid Laurier University Press.

Comacchio, C. (2010). Lost in modernity: 'Maladjustment' and the 'modern youth problem', English Canada, 1920–50. In M. Gleason, T. Myers, L. Paris and V. Strong-Boag (Eds.), *Lost kids: Vulnerable children and youth in twentieth-century Canada and the United States* (pp. 53–71). Vancouver: University of British Columbia Press.

Corrado, R., Gronsdahl, K., MacAlister, D., and Cohen, I. (2010). Youth justice in Canada: Theoretical perspectives of youth probation officers. *Canadian Journal of Criminology and Criminal Justice, 52*(4): 397–426.

Corrado, R. and Markwart, A. (1992). The evolution and implementation of a new era of juvenile justice in Canada. In N.B.R. Corrado, R. Linden, and M. Le Blanc (Eds.), *Juvenile justice in Canada: A theoretical and analytical assessment* (pp. 137–227). Toronto: Butterworths.

Corrado, R. and Turnbull, S. (1992). A comparative examination of the modified justice model in the United Kingdom and the United States. In N.B.R. Corrado, R. Linden, and M. Le Blanc (Eds.), *Juvenile justice in Canada: A theoretical and analytical assessment* (pp. 75–136). Toronto: Butterworths.

Côté, J.E. and Allahar, A.L. (2006). *Critical youth studies: A Canadian focus.* Toronto: Pearson.

Crofts, T. (2002). *The criminal responsibility of children and young persons: A comparison of English and German law.* Aldershot: Ashgate.

Cunneen, C., and White, R. (2007). *Juvenile justice: Youth and crime in Australia* (3rd ed.). Melbourne: Oxford University Press.

Davis-Barron, S. (2009). *Canadian youth and the criminal law.* Markham, ON: LexisNexis Canada.

Dohrn, B. (2002). The school, the child, and the court. In M.K. Rosenheim, F.E. Zimring, D.S. Tanenhaus, and B. Dohrn (Eds.), *A century of juvenile justice* (pp. 267–309). Chicago: University of Chicago Press.

Dolgin, J.L. (1999). The age of autonomy: Legal reconceptualizations of childhood. *QLR, 18*(3): 421–50.

Doob, A.N. and Sprott, J. (2006). Punishing youth crime in Canada: The blind men and the elephant. *Punishment and Society, 8*(2): 223–33.

Empey, L. (1982). *American delinquency: Its meaning and construction.* Chicago: Dorsey Press.

Feld, B.C. (1999). A funny thing happened on the way to the centenary: Social structure, race and the transformation of the juvenile court. *Punishment and Society, 1*(2): 187–214.

Garland, D. (2001). *The culture of control.* Chicago: University of Chicago Press.

Getis, V. (2000). *The Juvenile court and the progressives.* Urbana: University of Illinois Press.

Giller, H. (1999). From center stage to spear carrier: The repositioning of the English juvenile court. *European Journal on Criminal Policy and Research, 7*(3): 395–403.

Gleason, M., Myers, T., Paris, L., and Strong-Boag, V. (Eds.). (2010). *Lost kids: Vulnerable children and youth in twentieth-century Canada and the United States.* Vancouver: University of British Columbia Press.

Gottlieb, B. (1993). *The family in the Western world from the Black Death to the Industrial Age.* New York: Oxford University Press.

Graebner, W. (1994). Juvenile delinquency. In P. Stearns (Ed.), *Encyclopedia of social history* (pp. 379–81). New York: Garland Publishing.

Griffiths, C. and Verdun-Jones, S. (1994). *Canadian criminal justice.* Toronto: Harcourt Brace.

Hackler, J. (1978). *The prevention of youthful crime: The great stumble forward.* Toronto: Methuen.

Hagan, J. and Leon, J. (1977). Rediscovering delinquency: Social history, political ideology, and the sociology of law. *American Sociological Review, 42*(August): 587–98.

Hagan, J. and Leon, J. (1980). The rehabilitation of law: A social-historical comparison of probation in Canada and the United States. *Canadian Journal of Sociology/Cahiers canadiens de sociologie, 5*(3): 235–51.

Hall, G.S. (1904). *Adolescence: Its relation to physiology, anthropology, sociology, sex, crime, religion, and education.* New York: D. Appleton.

Harris, P.W., Welsh, W.N., and Butler, F. (2000). *A century of juvenile justice criminal justice 2000, vol. 1: The nature of crime, continuity and change* (pp. 363–425). Washington, D.C.: United States, Department of Justice, Office of Justice Programs.

Hatch, A.J. and Griffiths, C.T. (1991). Child saving postponed: The impact of the Juvenile Delinquents Act on the processing of young offenders in Vancouver. In R. Smandych, G. Dodds, and A. Esau (Eds.), *Dimensions of childhood: Essays in the history of children and youth in Canada* (pp. 233–66). Winnipeg: University of Manitoba, Legal Research Institute.

Havemann, P. (1986). From child saving to child blaming: The political economy of the Young Offenders Act 1908–1984. In Brickery, S. and Comack, E. (Ed.), *The social basis of law* (p. 225) Comack. Toronto: Garamond.

Havemann, P. (1992). Crisis justice for youth: Making the Young Offenders Act and the discourse of penality. In Currie, D. and MacLean, B. (Eds.), *Rethinking the administration of justice* (pp. 86–112). Halifax: Fernwood.

Hay, D. (1975). Property, authority, and the criminal law. In D. Hay, P. Linebaugh, J. Rule, E.P. Thompson, and C. Winslow (Eds.), *Albion's fatal tree: Crime and society in eighteenth century England* (pp. 17–63). London: Pantheon Books.

Hogeveen, B. (2001). 'Winning deviant youth over by friendly helpfulness': Transformations in the legal governance of deviant children, 1857–1908. In R. Smandych (Ed.), *Youth justice: History, legislation, and reform* (pp. 43–63). Toronto: Harcourt.

Hogeveen, B. (2005). 'If we are tough on crime, if we punish crime, then people get the message': Constructing and governing the punishable young offender in Canada during the late 1990s. *Punishment and Society, 7*(1): 73–89.

Janson, C.-G. (2004). Youth justice in Sweden. In M. Tonry and A. Doob (Eds.), *Youth crime and youth justice: Comparative and cross-national perspectives* (pp. 391-441). Chicago: Chicago University Press.

Krisberg, B. (2005). *Juvenile justice: Redeeming our children.* Thousand Oaks, CA: Sage.

Langbein, J. (1992). *The London hanged: Crime and civil society in the eighteenth century.* Cambridge: Cambridge University Press.

Leschied, A., Jaffe, P., and Willis, W. (Eds.). (1991). *The Young Offenders Act: A revolution in Canadian juvenile justice.* Toronto: University of Toronto Press.

Mann, R. (2011). A specialized criminal justice system for Canadian youth: Critical overview of historical and contemporary developments in law and procedures governing youth offending. In K. Kramer (Ed.), *Criminology: Critical Canadian perspectives* (pp. 57–77). Toronto: Pearson.

Merlo, A.V. and Benekos, P.J. (2010). Is punitive juvenile justice policy declining in the United States? A critique of emergent initiatives. *Youth Justice, 10*(1), 3–24.

Meyer, J. and O'Malley, P. (2005). Missing the punitive turn? Canadian criminal justice, 'balance', and penal modernism. In J. Pratt, D. Brown, M. Brown, S. Hallsworth, and W. Morrison (Eds.), *The new punitiveness: Trends, theories, perspectives* (pp. 201–17). Cullompton, Devon: Willan Publishing.

Minaker, J. and Hogeveen, B. (2009). *Youth, crime, and society: Issues of power and justice.* Toronto: Pearson.

Moore, D. and Hannah-Moffat, K. (2005). The liberal veil: Revisiting Canadian penality. In J. Pratt, D. Brown, M. Brown, S. Hallsworth, and W. Morrison (Eds.), *The new punitiveness: Trends, theories, perspectives* (pp. 85–100). Cullompton, Devon: Willan Publishing.

Muncie, J. (2005). The globalisation of crime control—The case of youth and juvenile justice: Neo-liberalism, policy convergence and international conventions. *Theoretical Criminology, 9*(1), 35–64.

Muncie, J. (2008). The 'punitive turn' in juvenile justice: Cultures of control and rights compliance in Western Europe and the USA. *Youth Justice, 8*(2), 107–21.

Muncie, J. and Goldson, B. (Eds.). (2006). *Comparative youth justice: Critical issues.* London: Sage.

Myers, T. (1999). The voluntary delinquent: Parents, daughters, and the Montreal juvenile delinquents' court in 1918. *Canadian Historical Review, 80*(2), 242–68.

O'Connor, I. and Cameron, M. (2002). Juvenile justice in Australia. In A. Graycar and P. Grabosky (Ed.), *Cambridge handbook of Australian criminology* (pp. 211–34). Sydney: Cambridge University Press.

Platt, A.M. (1969). *The child savers: The invention of delinquency.* Chicago: University of Chicago Press.

Platt, A.M. (1974). The triumph of benevolence: The origins of the juvenile justice system in the United States. In R. Quinney (Ed.), *Criminal justice in America* (pp. 356–89). Boston: Little, Brown.

Pollock, L. (1983). *Forgotten children, parent–child relations from 1500 to 1900.* Cambridge: Cambridge University Press.

Pratt, J., Brown, D., Brown, M., Hallsworth, S., and Morrison, W. (Eds.). (2005). *The new punitiveness: Trends, theories, perspectives.* Cullompton, Devon: Willan Publishing.

Redding, R., Goldstein, N.S., and Heilbrun, K. (2005). Juvenile delinquency: Past and present. In K. Heilbrun, N.S. Goldstein, and R. Redding (Eds.), *Juvenile delinquency: Prevention, assessment, and intervention* (pp. 3–18). New York: Oxford University Press.

Rosenheim, M.K., Zimring, F.E., Tanenhaus, D.S., and Dohrn, B. (Eds.). (2002). *A century of juvenile justice.* Chicago: University of Chicago Press.

Rothman, D.J. (1980). *Conscience and convenience: The asylum and its alternatives in progressive America.* Boston: Little Brown.

Sangster, J. (2002). 'She is hostile to our ways': First Nations girls sentenced to the Ontario Training School for Girls, 1933–1960. *Law and History Review, 20*(1), 59–96.

Shahar, S. (1990). *Childhood in the Middle Ages.* London: Routledge.

Shore, H. (2003). 'Inventing' the juvenile delinquent in nineteenth century Europe. In C. Emsley and G. Dunstall (Eds.), *Comparative crime histories* (pp. 110–23). Cullompton: Willan.

Simon, J. (1995). Power without parents: Juvenile justice in a postmodern society. *Cardozo Law Review, 16,* 1363–426.

Smandych, R. (1991). Tory paternalism and the politics of penal reform in Upper Canada, 1830–1834: A 'neo-revisionist' account of the Kingston Penitentiary. *Criminal Justice History: An International Annual, 12,* 57–83.

Smandych, R. (2001). Accounting for changes in Canadian youth justice: From the invention to the disappearance of childhood. In R. Smandych (Ed.), *Youth justice: History, legislation, and reform* (pp. 1–23). Toronto: Harcourt.

Smandych, R. (2006). Canada: Repenalisation and young offenders' rights. In J. Muncie and B. Goldson (Eds.), *Comparative Youth Justice: Critical Issues* (pp. 19–33). London: Sage.

Spagnoli, P.G. (1981). Philippe Aries. Historian of the family. *Journal of Family History*, 6, 434–41.

Springer, D., Roberts, A., Brownell, P., Torrente, M., Lippman, A.D.P., and Deitch, M. (2011). A brief historical overview of juvenile justice and juvenile delinquency. In D. Springer and A. Roberts (Eds.), *Juvenile justice and delinquency* (pp. 3–22). Boston: Jones and Bartlett Publishers.

Stearns, P.N. (Ed.). (1994). *Encyclopedia of social history.* New York: Garland Publishing.

Sutherland, N. (1976). *Children in English-Canadian society: Framing the twentieth-century consensus.* Toronto: University of Toronto Press.

Sutton, J. (1988). *Stubborn children: Controlling delinquency in the United States 1640–1981.* Berkeley: University of California Press.

Tanenhaus, D. S. (2004). *Juvenile justice in the making.* New York: Oxford University Press.

Tanner, J. (2010). *Teenage troubles: Youth and deviance in Canada.* Toronto: Oxford University Press.

Thorson, A.M. (1999). From parens patriae to crime control: A comparison of the history and effectiveness of the juvenile justice systems in the United States and Canada. *Arizona Journal of International and Comparative Law, 16*(3), 845–71.

Trépanier, J. (1991). The origins of the Juvenile Delinquents Act of 1908: Controlling delinquency through seeking its causes and through youth protection. In R. Smandych, G. Dodds, and A. Esau (Ed.), *Dimensions of childhood: Essays in the history of children and youth in Canada* (pp. 205–32). Winnipeg: University of Manitoba, Legal Research Institute.

Trépanier, J. (1999). Juvenile courts after 100 years: Past and present orientations. *European Journal on Criminal Policy and Research, 7*(3), 303–27.

Trépanier, J. and Tulkens, F. (1993). Juvenile justice in Belgium and Canada at the beginning of the century: Two models or one? *International Journal of Children's Rights, 1*, 189–211.

Vanstone, M. (2008). The international origins and initial development of probation. *British Journal of Criminology*, 48, 735–55.

Weijers, I. (1999). The double paradox of juvenile justice. *European Journal on Criminal Policy and Research, 7*(3), 329–51.

Wilson, S. (1984). The myth of motherhood a myth: The historical view of European child-rearing. *Social History*, 9, 181–98.

Woloschuk, C. (2009). Protecting and policing children: The origins and nature of juvenile justice in Winnipeg. In E.W. Jones and G. Friesen (Eds.), *Prairie metropolis: New essays on Winnipeg social history* (pp. 63–81). Winnipeg: University of Manitoba Press.

Zimring, F.E. (2005). *American juvenile justice.* New York: Oxford.

2 'Nothing but the Facts': Measuring Youth Crime in Canada

John A. Winterdyk

Overview

This chapter provides an overview of the official and unofficial facts about youth crime in Canada. To provide a contextual framework, a brief historical description of the social and historical influences on youth crime will serve to help understand how and why we measure youth crime today. The chapter then reviews the types of data and information that can be gleaned from official data sources as well as from unofficial data sources (i.e., self-report surveys and victimization surveys). A review of various youth crime characteristics and trends will be presented along with an examination of some provincial variations. The findings are discussed within the context of describing some of the key trends and patterns of youth crime.

Key Objectives

After reading this chapter, you should be able to:

- Understand the importance of social and historical influences on the evolution of youth justice and the measuring of youth crime in Canada.
- Understand how we define youth crime.
- Recognize that measuring and recording youth crime is influenced by formal social control mechanisms.
- Describe some of the facts and trends of youth crime over the past several decades.
- Understand the strengths and weaknesses of official statistics in relation to self-report and victimization data.
- Critically reflect on what the three measurement methods tell us about youth crime as well as what they do not tell us.

Introduction

As a social scientist who has been studying youth crime since the early 1970s, I am regularly asked by the media and my students to explain the apparent nature and extent of delinquency and/or youth crime. How serious and how common is it? Is it getting worse? Is the legislation too lenient? Who is committing these criminal and/or deviant acts and why do they do it? Unfortunately, researchers are seldom able to provide succinct answers to these questions and unless the media seeks out informed opinions, the presentation of youth crime in the media and through political debate is not always based on empirical reality but on what Schissel (1997, p. 72) describes as 'constructed versions that serve political and moral purposes'. Nevertheless, Brantingham and Brantingham (1984, p. 41) have pointed out the ongoing motivation for investigating youth crime: 'counting crime seems to satisfy some fundamental urge to know the dimensions of our misery, as if knowing by itself makes things better'.

In order to better understand, explain, and eventually predict any social phenomenon such as youth crime, we need to draw from a variety of sources of measurement, each of which has strengths and weaknesses. In this chapter, we begin by examining the major factors that have contributed to the historical emergence of youth crime and youth justice. Next, we draw on two separate sources of measurement that help describe the nature and extent of delinquency and youth crime: (1) official accounts of social control (e.g., police, courts, and corrections); and (2) unofficial sources, such as self-report studies and victimization surveys. Self-report and victimization surveys allow researchers to determine the nature and extent of unrecorded delinquency, the so-called **dark figure of crime**, and compare the results with official accounts of delinquency. Before we review the evidence from these different methods, however, we must first appreciate the complexity of the terms *youth crime* and **youth at risk**.

Although delinquency and youth crime can be, and have been, defined in a number of different ways by sociologists (see Kratcoski and Kratcoski 1990) and psychologists (see Bartol and Bartol 2008), we will briefly review the legal definition as it is largely used in the measurement of youth crime.

Defining Youth Crime

Delinquency or *juvenile delinquency* were terms used in the 1908 Juvenile Delinquents Act (JDA) to describe 'any child who violates any provision of the Criminal Code or any federal or provincial statute. . . ' (sec. 2.1). With the passing of the Young Offenders Act (YOA) in 1984, the terms were

dark figure of crime
Refers to incidents of crime or delinquency that go undetected or unreported by the police.

youth at risk
Refers to young people who are 'at risk' of offending or being victimized because of various social, family, and/or personal factors.

then replaced with the less pejorative phrase *young person* (sec. 2.1), which continues to be used (also sec. 2.1) under the Youth Criminal Justice Act (YCJA) (2003). A young person who commits an offence is referred to as a 'young offender' and when formally acknowledged and counted, the offence becomes a 'youth crime' even though it violates the same laws as those that apply to an adult. The shift in terminology, while perhaps appearing subtle, has also had an impact on how we measure youth crime. For example, Bartol and Bartol (2009, p. 29) note that *juvenile delinquency* was 'an imprecise, nebulous, social, clinical and legal label for a wide variety of law- and norm-violating behaviour'. The term *young offender*, by contrast, refers only to behaviours against the Criminal Code. Hence, it is important to understand how youth crime is defined and how its meaning has changed over time.

Legal Definition

Historically, Canadian criminologists have tended to focus on the legal rather than on the psychological or sociological definitions of youth crime. The YCJA defines a young person as 'a person who is or, in the absence of evidence to the contrary, appears to be twelve years old, or older, but less than eighteen years old and, if the context requires, includes a person who is charged under the Act with having committed an offence while he or she was a young person or who is found guilty of an offence under this Act'. Should the young person meet these conditions, his or her act then constitutes a 'youth crime'.

Although the JDA definition of *juvenile delinquency* (sec. 291) was intended to support the concept of family and to build an informal system of social control (Hak 1996), the YCJA places a greater emphasis on a legalistic approach under which young offenders are held legally responsible for their actions (Fetherston 2005; also see Chapters 1 and 3).

Limitations in Assuming a Purely Legal Definition

Although clearly restrictive from a social science perspective, notwithstanding the technical offence of administrative-type transgressions (e.g., breach of conditions), the legal definition of youth crime focuses primarily on predatory (e.g., break-and-enter, robbery, etc.) and aggressive (e.g., assault, homicide, etc.) behaviour that is deemed punishable by law (Winterdyk 2006). As the legal definition only enables us to describe the problem, there are a number of limitations to its use:

- *Theoretical insight.* The legal definition does not take into account victimless crimes, and due to the vague meaning of youth crime, the definition limits the scope of theoretical insight.
- *Demographic.* Changes in the age distribution, particularly for high-risk (15- to 24-year-old) offender groups, can influence crime rates.
- *Case filtration and dismissal.* Depending on the nature of the deviance, cases of youth crime are often eliminated because they are perceived as lacking sufficient gravity, or are deemed unlikely to result in a conviction due to insufficient evidence. Local police policies and procedures may also affect recording rates.
- *Policy and administration variation.* How the YCJA is interpreted varies among, and even within, provinces and territories (see Prevost 2011; Chapter 4 in this volume). Similarly, the policies of police departments that report these crimes are likely to vary with the level of public pressure, police administration, and available personnel.
- *Method of gathering statistics.* The data used to track youth crime trends, cleared crime, and patterns of youth crime are derived from different administrative sources: police records, judicial records, and correctional records. Although these findings are published annually

by Statistics Canada, the resulting statistics can be misleading because the enumeration of youth crime gives us a measure of political success (or failure) of our crime-control policies and Statistics Canada does not enumerate all crimes. For example, historically Statistics Canada enumerates only those offences made known to the police, court, and/or corrections. In other words, whoever gathers the statistics can have an (unintended) agenda that goes beyond the published data (see Huff 1954).

- *Reporting rates.* The extent to which youth crime is reported often depends on the public's willingness to report youth crime as well as varying social and economic factors (see Charron 2009). Reporting rates are intimately related to society's attitudes toward law enforcement, the perceived gravity of the offence, and society's level of punitiveness. Reporting rates are therefore connected to what Wheeler, Bonacich, Cramer, and Zola (1968) refer to as the 'cultural climate'.

- *Public perception.* At any given time, society's perception of youth crime can profoundly affect the legal implementation of the youth justice legislation. Referring to various national polls (e.g., Environics and the National Gallup Poll) a Department of Justice report notes that while Canadians in general support the YCJA, they feel the legislation is not punitive enough (Public perception of crime… 2010). As discussed in Chapter 5, numerous researchers point to the influence of the media and the lack of public education about the act as the impetus for this change in attitude. Given the observations of crime data noted above, obtaining a realistic picture of the extent of youth crime can be difficult.

- *Technologies.* Changes in technology create new opportunities for complex crimes to emerge and go undetected (e.g., cyber- and internet-based crimes). Until the crime is recognized and defined, it is not legally a crime.

As we will discuss later in this chapter, the answer to whether youth crime has increased and public fear is justified is subject to continuous debate. This chapter attempts to shed light on what is happening by examining both official and unofficial sources of data on youthful offending behaviour.

Measuring Delinquency: A Historical Overview

Juvenile delinquency is a social construction and a normative term that has evolved over time and has created certain dilemmas for the youth justice system. Until recently, however, most interpretations of youth crime have lacked a sense of history. Yet to understand the nature and extent of youth crime today, we need to become familiar with how law-violating children and youth have become a concern and focus of attention. As the philosopher George Santayana (1905) has said, 'those who cannot remember the past are condemned to repeat it'.

For illustrative purposes, the history of youth-crime trends in Canada can be divided into three periods: pre-Confederation, state intervention, and the twentieth century. The overview will serve to show how and why we created the term *delinquency* and how and why we started to count delinquent acts.

Delinquency Trends: Pre-Confederation to the Nineteenth Century

Given the frontier spirit of the Canadian pioneers during the early seventeenth century, children were likely allowed considerable freedom, resulting in crime and hooliganism. Carrigan (1998) notes that children were, indeed, involved in petty theft, brawling, and vandalism, and young girls, in prostitution, as they were swept up in the violence that permeated the fur trade. J.G. Moylan, Inspector of Penitentiaries in New France at this time, claimed that 'immigrant children greatly added to the criminal ranks and that their immigration should be stopped' (cited in Carrigan 1998, pp. 82–83).

Youth crime during the seventeenth century was also most likely caused by the uncontrolled growth of New France. Many young families were enticed to the New World with promises of land, prosperity, and opportunity. However, many of these families soon broke up due to extreme economic and physical hardships (Carrigan 1991). This disintegration of families ultimately resulted in numerous young people being abandoned, neglected, or abused. It was this lack of supervision that led to crime and subsequently official attention by social service–type agencies (Carrigan 1998).

Until 1876, when the Dominion Bureau of Statistics (now Statistics Canada) began to record official statistics in Canada, accounts of juvenile delinquency were obtainable only through limited newspaper sources that were often based on first-hand observational reports. As a result, the delinquency problem in pre-Confederation Canada cannot be accurately quantified. However, some information is available. Based on the First Annual Report of the Board of Inspectors of Asylums and Prisons in 1860, Carrigan (1998) notes that of 11 268 incarcerations, 6 per cent were young offenders under the age of 16 of which only 23.2 per cent were female. Between 1869 and 1889, the rate of juvenile incarceration fluctuated between 23.2 and 31.6 per cent of all offences. And as we will see shortly, the delinquency problem at the end of the nineteenth century, in many ways, resembles the trends we are experiencing at the beginning of the twenty-first century. Now, as then, boys continue to be disproportionately represented in the youth justice system, most crimes are property related, most delinquencies occur in urban centres (see below), and familial problems are often associated with youth crime. Being the product of parental neglect and/or maltreatment is still seen as one of the more common characteristics, or risk factors, among young offenders (see Carrigan 1998; Hoge and Andrews 2010).

Table 2.1 provides an overview of juvenile convictions for indictable (i.e., serious) offences between 1885 and 1889 in the existing provinces and territory. As noted above, during this time period significantly more young males than young females were convicted. Males accounted for over 90 per cent of all convictions. However, what is not clear is to what extent the official data reflect, as noted above, reporting and/or recording bias (also, see Chapter 5).

Table 2.1 Youth Crime Convictions for Indictable Offences by Province, 1885–1889

Provinces	Under 16 years		16–20 years	
	Male	Female	Male	Female
Ontario	5687	242	6550	580
Québec	2516	200	3095	256
Nova Scotia	367	14	446	42
New Brunswick	181	4	218	16
Manitoba	209	7	311	22
British Columbia	174	1	192	19
Prince Edward Island	81	1	57	9
Northwest Territories	21	0	94	4
Totals	9236	469	10963	948

Source: 'Youth Crime Convictions for Indictable Offences by Provinces, 1885–1889,' from Carrigan 1998, p. 93.

State Intervention:
The First Step to Defining and Officially Counting Delinquency

The American sociologist Anthony Platt (1977), in the postscript to his acclaimed book *The Child Savers*, suggests that the dramatic increase in youth crime throughout the 1870s can be attributed, in large part, to the deterioration in economic conditions in North America. He noted that, at that time, more than a half-million young men and women were neither in school nor employed. By the late nineteenth century the social-support networks that had typically characterized rural or agrarian communities were in the process of deteriorating. Urbanization and industrialization were changing the ways in which people lived. Children were less and less supervised, and, as a result, they became more criminally active, particularly in the growing cities.

As the nature and extent of delinquency grew, it was believed, especially among the dominant middle and upper social classes, that the problem could be solved by state intervention. Universal public education was the first step the state took to help alleviate growing delinquency. In 1871, Ontario made school attendance compulsory for 7- to 12-year-olds for four months a year. Several industrial schools (also referred to as residential schools)[1] for boys and girls were also established across the country (Carrigan 1991). The impetus for this came primarily from the middle-class 'child savers' who believed that the root causes of delinquent behaviour rested in a child's environment, especially the family. By keeping count of children's delinquent behaviour it was then possible to measure the impact of the state's efforts.

The state intervention philosophy marked a new era in youth crime, and the need to record and measure delinquent activity was also reflected in early twentieth century law. The JDA was intended to support the young offender within the context of the family as a social unit. The JDA also sought to build an informal system of social control as opposed to a formal system. As discussed in Chapter 1, J.J. Kelso (1864–1935) was instrumental (along with W.L. Scott) in establishing the first Ontario juvenile court system.

Youth Crime Trends: The Twentieth Century

The early twentieth century marked a new era in youth crime as we experienced 'the introduction of juvenile courts and a generally more efficient system of responding to juvenile crime' (Carrigan 1991, p. 228). For example, between 1911 and the early 1940s, the rate of conviction for youth between the ages of 10 and 15 rose from 172 to 423 per 100 000. This represents over a 200 per cent increase as compared to just over a 30 per cent growth in the population of youth aged 10 to 15 years (Carrigan 1998).

Although the increase is dramatic, most of the offences committed during the early twentieth century were petty property-related offences and the increase was a reflection of the shift in formal attention to young offenders. The fluctuation in property crime (a high of 36 per 100 000 in 1930 to a low of 24 per 100 000 in 1945), it has been suggested, coincided with the changing social and demographic climate and to some extent with the increasing desire for the state to exercise social control. DeMause (1988, p. 52) refers to this period (circa nineteenth century to mid-twentieth century) as the 'socialization mode', during which youth were given extra attention by their parents and society. Fathers, in particular, began to invest more time and effort in training/raising their children as well as relieving their wives of child-care chores.

From 1940 onward, the youth crime rate slowly dropped until 1955 when the youth crime rate was just under 300 per 100 000. DeMause (1988, p. 54) refers to this stage as the 'helping mode', during which there was an explosion of faddish techniques for child rearing and discipline. Children were brought up to feel 'unconditionally loved'.

This phase appears to have been short-lived, however, as delinquency rates began to climb precipitously again. The increase has been attributed, in part, to improved social and economic conditions as the country emerged from the hardships of World War II. By 1966, the delinquency rate had climbed to 459 per 100 000, as North American society experienced a social and cultural revolution. Families in which both parents worked had become more common, the influence of the mass media was everywhere, and there was a general erosion of values. According to Carrigan (1998), these social changes, among others, prompted calls for the revision of the JDA. A special committee report in 1965, entitled 'Juvenile Delinquency in Canada', stated that the increase in juvenile crime had become 'alarming' and that it could be expected to continue to increase (Carrigan 1998, p. 159).

Comparing these numbers to those of the 1980s and 1990s is revealing. By 1989, the youth crime rate was 5.5 times that of the 1960s (i.e., 2568 per 100 000)! During the same year, young offenders between the ages of 12 and 17 represented 22 per cent of all persons charged with Criminal Code offences (CCJS 1992a). Then, in 1991, the overall youth crime rate began to decline for the second time in the twentieth century. However, as we discuss below, this decline does not pertain to all offences and it was short-lived.

Further State Intervention: Solutions for a Changing Society

As described within a different context in Chapters 3 and 4 in this volume, by the early 1980s there was a growing sentiment that new laws were needed to address the growing problem of youth crime even though there was no unanimous agreement that the increase was even due to the JDA (see Tanner 2010). Nevertheless, this socio-political-motivated need resulted in the introduction of the YOA of 1984. During its 20-year tenure, the YOA underwent numerous reforms and received considerable criticism for not being able to fulfill its objectives of reducing youth crime and/or providing the appropriate response to the needs of young offenders (see Bala 1994). The YOA was eventually replaced with the YCJA in 2003. Since the purpose of this chapter is not to examine the relative impact of the YCJA on youth crime (see instead Chapter 4),[2] this chapter will focus on presenting some of the facts about youth crime in Canada as obtained through **official** and **unofficial data** sources.

Characteristics of Today's Young Offenders— The Official Picture

As was suggested at the outset of this chapter, the public tends to have a pejorative image, fuelled mostly by the mass media (see Chapter 5), of the extent, nature, and gravity of youth crime (see Schissel 2006; Brooks and Schissel 2008). There is little question that youth crime is damaging not only to our youth but also to our communities. Therefore, it is important to know the facts before recommending, or exploring, responses to youth crime.

The term *official data* refers to the records of youth whose illegal activities have come to the attention (i.e., reported to or discovered by) of the various social-control agencies (i.e., law enforcement, youth courts, and youth corrections). Agencies in each of the provinces and territories are expected to provide Statistics Canada with their data, which is then compiled and aggregated, and is made available through standardized publications and/or posted on the Statistics Canada website (see 'Suggested Weblinks' at the end of this chapter). Not all data received is presented or published; however, if specific data has been collected it can be purchased from Statistics Canada. Therefore, only youth with a public record are official young offenders as opposed to those who commit an infraction but do not become part of the official record because they remain unknown to officials. As mentioned, the latter are referred to as the dark figures of crime.

official data
The Canadian Centre for Justice Statistics, a branch of Statistics Canada, collects offender and offence data from the police, courts, and corrections for administrative purposes. The Centre produces regular reports that are readily available to the public.

unofficial data
Refers to data that is collected and usually published by private or independent researchers or research facilities. The primary data collection techniques are self-report surveys and victimization surveys. Unofficial data is often used to enrich official data.

While the accuracy of official statistics has been the subject of much debate (Brantingham and Brantingham 1984), these statistics remain the most consistent source of measurement for youth offending and are readily available through the Canadian Centre for Justice Statistics (CCJS) at Statistics Canada in Ottawa. In terms of youth crime, CCJS expresses crime data in three ways: (1) the number of youth charged; (2) the rate of youth charged per 100 000 youth aged 12 to 17; and (3) the percentage of change in total youth rate between the reporting year and previous year. Within this context, the offences reported are limited to '132 Criminal Code offence categories and several drug and trafficking offences' (Creechan 1995, p. 99). We will provide an overview of some of the information that can be gleaned from various official sources.

Demographic Facts of Young Offenders

Gender

As already mentioned, ever since Canada started collecting official data on young offenders, such statistics have shown that young males tend to commit more reported crimes than females do (see Box 2.1 below). According to a 2008/09 Statistics Canada report, almost 72 per cent of youth court cases involved accused males while 21 per cent involved a female accused[3] (Milligan 2010). This pattern shows a slight shift in the gender balance since 2003 when the percentage of young males involved in youth crime was around 80 per cent and for young females was around 20 per cent. Also, since the introduction of the YCJA in 2003, the youth court data reveal that those cases completed tend to be older young persons, and that male involvement in crime increases with age, while female involvement peaks at around 15 years of age (Milligan 2010; also, see Chesney-Lind and Sheldon 1992). Males are more likely to be accused of sexual assault (92 per cent), drug possession (85 per cent), attempted murder (82 per cent), and weapons offences (82 per cent) while the highest representation of females involved prostitution (44 per cent), common assault (36 per cent), and fraud (35 per cent) (Milligan 2010).

However, it is still unclear whether the increase in violent crimes (e.g., assault, attempted murder, etc.) among young persons and the difference in rates and frequency between young males and females can be attributed to changes in reporting patterns, media sensationalism, the 'crime funnel' effect, the alleged growth of 'girl gangs', the use of extra-judicial measures to formal processing, and/or young females becoming more like their male counterparts. For example, some researchers have been paying more attention to crimes committed both by young males and young females, and they are relying on different sources of data (i.e., police vs. court administrative records) to clarify the apparent trends. But the fact remains that males have always committed, and continue to commit, most of the youth crimes (also see Chapter 6). Official measurement of youth crime is also unable to tell us what role the various risk and protective factors in society play in helping to explain the gender differences in offending patterns.

Age

Next to gender, age is one of the most important determinants that researchers focus on to explain youth crime trends and patterns (see, generally, Blumstein 1995). As illustrated in Figure 2.1, the rate of persons accused of crimes steadily increases from age 12 to 17, the peak age, and then begins to decline for all offence types. Is this due to social, psychological, and/or biological factors or a possible interaction of the consequences of formal legislation? Official data is unable to provide any direct answers.

According to various official reports by the CCJS, the age-related pattern of being accused of an offence has remained fairly consistent over the past two decades. What is perhaps more revealing

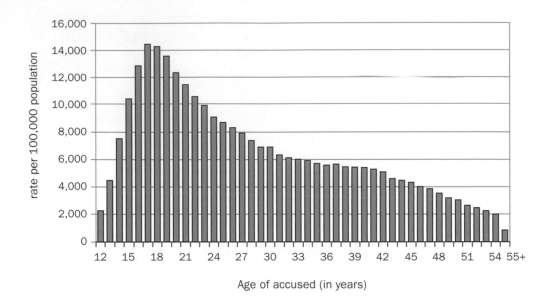

Figure 2.1 Persons Accused of Crime, by Age, Canada, 2009

Source: Dauvergne, M. and Turner, J. (2010). Uniform Crime Reporting (UCR2) Survey. Statistics Canada: Canadian Centre for Justice Statistics, 30(2) (adapted from Chart 14, p. 22).

administrative offences

Under sec. 4 of the YCJA there are provisions under the extrajudicial measures that allow for charges to be laid if the young person fails to comply with his or her disposition or fails to appear before the court. The charge can be initiated by either the police or the Crown.

disposition

For young offenders, this is the equivalent of sentencing for adults. Under the YCJA, a disposition should in theory be more rehabilitative and/ or restorative than retributive.

is the type of offences different age groups engage in. For example, as shown in Table 2.2, below, those who are younger are more likely to engage in property-related crimes (approximately 45 per cent of all of their offences vs. about 37 per cent among 17-year-olds). Older youth, on the other hand, are proportionately more likely to commit **administrative offences** (e.g., charges not generally considered to be criminal, such as failure to appear in court and failure to comply with **disposition**—the two most common guilty findings [Sanders 2000]) than are 12- or 13-year-olds (e.g., 12 per cent vs. 4 per cent, respectively).[4] What is perhaps noteworthy from the official data on the cases completed in youth court by age is that 12- and 13-year-olds are proportionately being more frequently charged with 'crimes against the person' than are 16- and 17-year-olds (i.e., 41 per cent and 36 per cent vs. 24 per cent and 23 per cent, respectively). Again, although the official data do not offer any explanation, Doob and Cesaroini (2004) have suggested that young persons, proportionately, engage in more anti-social behaviour because they are less organized and more spontaneous that their older peers. If so, what effect, if any, is the YCJA having on the different age groups?

As pointed out, one of the advantages of using official data is the ability to examine trends and patterns over a period of time. According to CCJS data, since the 1990s young people appear to have been getting involved in delinquent activities at an earlier age than ever before. For example, 2001/02 data reveal that in spite of the introduction of the alternative measures program, the proportion of youth-court caseloads dealing with 12- and 13-year-olds still increased from 10 per cent in 1992/93 to 11 per cent for 2001/02, while for 16- and 17-year-olds, the proportion increased from 52 per cent to 54 per cent during the same years (Thomas 2003). While perhaps the increase was an artefact of the way data were collected as well as police charging practices, there did appear to be a slight increase during the two time periods. For the recording period of 2008/09 the percentage of youth court cases for youths aged 12 to 13 dropped to 3.2 per cent, while for 16- and 17-year-olds the proportion of cases continued to increase up to 63.4 per cent (Milligan 2010). The trend may also, in part, be explained by one of the objectives of the YCJA—to use police diversion and extrajudicial

Table 2.2 Cases Completed in Youth Courts by Offence Category and Age of Accused, Canada, 2008/2009

Offence Category	Total Cases Number	Age of Accused													
		12 years old		13 years old		14 years old		15 years old		16 years old		17 years old		Other[1]	
		Number	% of total	Number	% of total	Number	% of total	Number	% of total	Number	% of total	Number	% of total	Number	% of total
Total offences	58 379	1 307	2.2	3 583	6.1	7 120	12.2	11 780	20.2	15 387	26.4	18 019	30.9	1 183	2.0
Total Criminal Code offences	47 890	1 263	2.6	3 309	6.9	6 266	13.1	9 855	20.6	12 349	25.8	13 974	29.2	874	1.8
Crimes against the person	15 457	543	3.5	1 287	8.3	2 143	13.9	3 224	20.9	3 841	24.8	4 166	27.0	253	1.6
Crimes against property	22 001	593	2.7	1 578	7.2	3 141	14.3	4 726	21.5	5 766	26.2	5 910	26.9	287	1.3
Administration of justice offences	6 284	57	0.9	268	4.3	624	9.9	1 215	19.3	1 698	27.0	2 179	34.7	243	3.9
Other Criminal Code offences	3 021	67	2.2	168	5.6	327	10.8	580	19.2	808	26.7	989	32.7	82	2.7
Criminal Code traffic offences	1 127	3	0.3	8	0.7	31	2.8	110	9.8	236	20.9	730	64.8	9	0.8
Other federal statute offences	10 489	44	0.4	274	2.6	854	8.1	1925	18.4	3 038	29.0	4 045	38.6	309	2.9
Drug offences	4 356	22	0.5	94	2.2	302	6.9	706	16.2	1 276	29.3	1 909	43.8	47	1.1
Youth Criminal Justice Act	5 880	19	0.3	171	2.9	531	9.0	1 179	20.1	1 690	28.7	2 039	34.7	251	4.3
Other federal statutes	253	3	1.2	9	3.6	21	8.3	40	15.8	72	28.5	97	38.3	11	4.3

1. Other age group includes cases where the accused was older than 17 at the time of the offence (i.e., YCJA sections 136 to 139) or the age was unknown.

Notes: Due to rounding, percentages may not add to 100. Age of accused is at the time of offence.

Source: S. Milligan (Summer 2010). Juristat. Ottawa: Statistics Canada. (From Table 4).

measures (see Chapter 4 for further discussion) as well as the host of new programs and/or resources being made available under the YCJA.

Box 2.1   Youth Justice and Gender Factor?

Question to Ponder

Until fairly recently, gender in regard to delinquency has been largely ignored (Heidensohn 1995). However, as reflected in this chapter's section on gender (also see Milligan 2010), the differences in offending rates between the genders has remained relatively constant, with males responsible for committing most types of youth crimes. From a theoretical perspective, how might we best explain the gender difference in offending patterns? How might we be able to use the evidence presented to better inform public misconceptions about the gender disparity? Consider engaging in a class discussion to explore possible risk and protective factors that might help explain the difference between gender offending patterns as well as to explore how any differences between the genders can be explained within a socio-cultural context (e.g., gender inequality, abuse, self-defence, etc.).

Measuring Youth Violent and Nonviolent Crime

Violent Crime

In the mid-1990s there were two opposing interpretations of whether youth violent crime had been increasing in Canada. Corrado and Markwart (1994) claimed that violent crime among young persons had increased while Carrington (1995) argued that the violent incident rate among young persons had not increased. In the late 1990s, Gabor (1999) suggested that while youth crime may not have increased dramatically, the level of seriousness had. A few years later, in 2004, Sally Spencer, executive director for the group Youth Assisting Youth in Toronto, reinforced Gabor's observation when she stated that 'the severity of what is happening is definitely on the rise' (Violent Crime in Canada 2008). However, if we take into consideration the youth **Crime Severity Index** (CSI), which was introduced in 2009, we get a slightly different official picture. Instead of simply relying on measures of police-reported crime, the CSI measures the seriousness of crime reported to the police. The CSI scores for all crimes have declined steadily between 1999 and 2009. In 2009, the CSI was 22 per cent lower than in 1999. The same trend holds for youth crime between 1999 and 2009, when the index scores dropped from 100.6 to 93.7 in 2009. Specifically, the youth violent CSI has remained relatively stable in recent years (around 95)[5] while the nonviolent crime index score has dropped from 110.8 in 1999 to 92.4 in 2009; however, the CSI was still 10 per cent higher than it was in 1999 (Dauvergne and Turner 2010, p. 23). But the facts may not be that simple.

> **Crime Severity Index (CSI)**
>
> Developed and introduced by Statistics Canada, the CSI uses a weighting system to measure (youth) offences according to their seriousness. Although introduced in 2009, CSI data are available back to 1998.

    While the overall violent crime rate has stabilized in recent years and the CSI has dropped in recent years, if we look at certain types of violent crimes, we see that the 'quality' of violent crime tells a different story. For example, Beattie and Cotter (2010) observed that youth homicide rates were the highest they had been in 30 years with the greatest increase and number of incidents occurring in Manitoba. Conversely, between 1999 and 2009 robbery declined 6 per cent and serious assaults dropped 5 per cent, but homicide rose from 56 to 79—a 74 per cent increase. However, since the absolute numbers are comparatively low, they don't have a comparable impact on the violent crime rate or the CSI (see Figure 2.2).

    Official sources also reveal that regionally, in 2009, Québec had the lowest rate of violent youth crimes (i.e., 64.4) while (outside of the Yukon, Nunavut, and the NWT) Saskatchewan had the

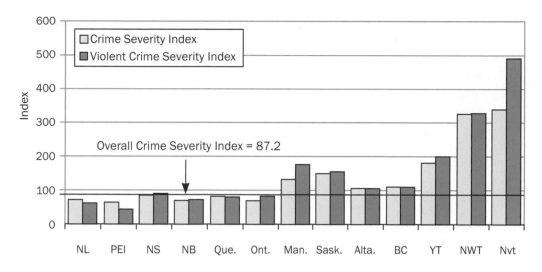

Figure 2.2 Police-Reported Crime Severity Indexes, 2009

Source: M. Dauvergne and J. Turner. Police-reported crime statistics in Canada, 2009. (2010: 10). *Juristat*, 30(2). Ottawa: Statistics Canada.

highest CSI (i.e., 239). In the majority of violent offence cases, the principal charge is assault, with a rate of 264 per 100 000. Robbery is a distant second, at 162, while the rate for attempted murder and murder cases in 2008/09 was 79 per 100 000—accounting for less than 1 per cent of cases heard in court (see Figure 2.3). The regional variations speak to a host of different economic, demographic makeup, cultural, social, availability of supporting resources, and political factors across the country, as well as potential variations in public fear about youth crime that prompted more reporting (see Carrington 1995). And while it has been suggested that such variations are reflective of the

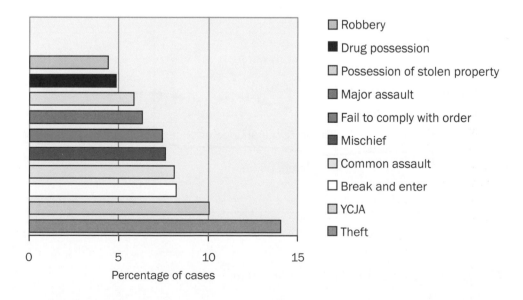

Figure 2.3 Type of Youth Crime Offence 2008/2009

Source: Adapted from S. Milligan (Summer 2010: 4). *Juristat*. Ottawa: Statistics Canada.

punitive nature of official legislation, the trends cannot be explained solely by the introduction of the YOA or YCJA. As Prevost (2011) recently observed, there is considerable variability between the provincial and territorial jurisdictions in how the YCJA is applied.

Manitoba, for example, had the highest number of youth homicide charges at 24, followed by Ontario at 16, while a number of provinces had none (Dauvergne and Turner 2010). In terms of sexual assault (levels 2 and 3) Manitoba had the highest rate (655) while PEI had the lowest (183); the national average was 274 per 100 000.

While official violent crime data are interesting, they do not provide insight into the richer social-science interests and issues. For example, to what extent are the rates of different crimes, as well as the crime seriousness, perhaps related to the growth of youth gangs (see Chapter 11), an escalation in the use/accessibility of weapons, and an apparent increase in female violence (see Chapter 6)?

Nonviolent Crime

Property crimes have been declining since the late 1980s: from 72 per cent in 1968 to 31.8 per cent in 2008. Yet these crimes still account for the greatest proportion of all youth crime, followed by crimes against the person (28 per cent), then offences against the administration of justice (11 per cent), other Criminal Code offences (5 per cent), etc. (Milligan 2010) (see Figure 2.4). As noted in *The Daily Report* (May 16, 2008) the drop in property crime can be explained 'by a 47% decline in

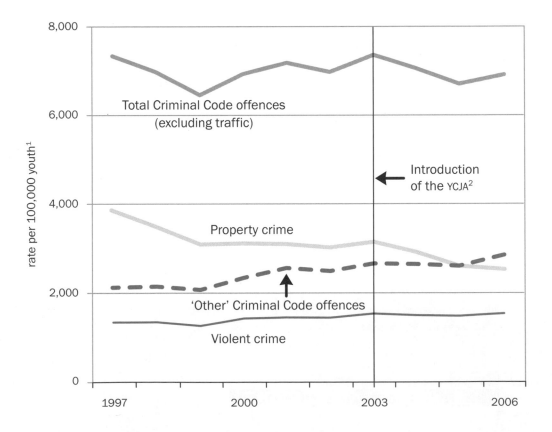

Figure 2.4 Youth Crime Rates, 1996–2006

1. Youth aged 12 to 17.

2. Youth Criminal Justice Act (YCJA).

Source: A. Taylor-Butts and A. Bressan. (2008). *Juristat* 28(3). Ottawa: Statistics Canada. (Chart 1).

the rate for break-ins, as well as a 33% drop in minor theft rates (i.e., theft under $5000), the criminal offences for which youth were most commonly apprehended'. As noted above, proportionately, those charged with property crimes tend to fall within the 12- to 13-year-old age spectrum and are mostly young males. In spite of the declining rates in youth crime, the Conservative government (at the time of preparing this chapter) appeared determined to want to revamp the YCJA and shift away from rehabilitation toward retribution (*The Gazette* 2010; see also Chapter 4).

Again, as is evidenced with any of the characteristics regarding the nature and extent of youth crime, there is considerable variation across the country as well as among the different crime categories. For example, while property crimes have been going down, certain types of illicit drug offences have been going up. Between 1996 and 2006, cocaine charges went up 135 per cent while 'other' drug offences went up 156 per cent over the same period. Only heroin-related offences dropped (i.e., 56 per cent) between 1996 and 2006 but increased 156 per cent from 2005 to 2006 (Youth crimes reported to police for selected Criminal Code offences 2009) (see Chapter 9).

In summary, while it is encouraging that the overall youth crime rates have been dropping in recent years, it is perhaps more disconcerting that violent crime has not followed the same trend. Future research should endeavour to better understand and predict such behaviour so as to better identify relevant risk and protective factors. In addition, we need to be careful when examining crime trends over any period of time because, for various reasons, some provinces do not report in certain years. In addition, depending on the official source, the numbers are only a valid representation of the youth criminal activity known to the police, the courts, or youth corrections. Hence such data is a more realistic measure or indicator of youth justice involvement than of youth crime. And yet we typically rely on such information to construct our 'reality' of youth crime!

Youth Court–Related Facts

Court Dispositions

Contrary to public opinion (see Chapter 5), data from the CCJS reports throughout the 1990s suggest that until the introduction of the YCJA there was a shift toward finding more young offenders guilty and moving toward harsher sentencing practices for young offenders. However, after 2004, the trend appears to change to being less punitive. When examined in more detail (see below), the patterns and trends, however, have not been consistent and are subject to interpretation (see, for example, Chapter 4). For example, between 1992/93 and 1996/97 the percentage of those youth who were found guilty of a crime and were placed on probation increased from 48 to 66 per cent and then peaked at 70 per cent by 2002/03 before steadily declining to 60.3 per cent by 2008/09. Yet, again, there remained considerable geographic variation in the use of probation. For example, in 2008/09 PEI had the highest percentage of youth being placed on probation (over 78 per cent) and Saskatchewan had among the lowest (43 per cent) (Milligan 2010). Keep in mind, however, that official statistics provide no insight into why the variation exists or how the length of probation is determined (see Table 2.3).

As regularly reflected in the media, Canadians tend to believe we are too lenient when it comes to holding young offenders accountable for their crimes (see Box 2.2). Officially, there would appear to be mixed evidence to support such a statement. In 1986/87, just over 6 per cent of young offenders were placed in secure custody, while in 1997/98, this portion had jumped to 16 per cent and peaked at 26.9 per cent in 2002/03 (Thomas 2004). However, consistent with the objectives of the YCJA, since 2003/04 fewer youth are being placed in secure custody (see Chapter 4 for further discussion).

Additional evidence would also appear to be reflected in the decline in the number of youth court cases: between 1991/92 and 2002/03 the number of youth court cases declined by 19.8 per cent (CCJS 1992a; Thomas 2005, p. 14). Perhaps what is more telling is that since the introduction of the YOA,

Table 2.3 Percentage of Guilty Youth Cases Sentenced to Custody in Canada: 2002/2003 to 2008/2009

Province/Territory	2002/ 2003	2003/ 2004	2004/ 2005	2005/ 2006	2006/ 2007	2007/ 2008	2008/ 2009
	Percentage						
Canada	26.9	21.9	21.1	18.4	16.6	15.9	15.4
Newfoundland and Labrador	38.5	21.3	23.5	20.3	18.0	12.0	15.6
Prince Edward Island	39.5	19.7	16.0	17.3	18.7	15.8	19.4
Nova Scotia	32.8	14.7	13.3	11.5	13.7	12.1	11.0
New Brunswick	25.8	23.2	20.9	16.1	16.5	13.5	12.2
Québec	21.2	15.9	15.3	12.5	11.2	11.3	12.0
Ontario	28.1	27.5	26.3	23.8	20.9	21.7	20.3
Manitoba	26.0	15.9	15.7	8.6	7.9	6.7	6.2
Saskatchewan	30.9	26.1	21.2	18.0	16.7	14.8	16.3
Alberta	19.3	12.9	13.3	12.4	12.5	11.1	10.5
British Columbia	31.6	22.1	21.5	21.6	18.6	16.7	15.6
Yukon	46.9	27.3	25.0	44.1	31.8	34.1	41.2
Northwest Territories[1]	39.2	19.1	15.6	20.1	20.3	17.3	17.3
Nunavut	24.7	21.3	23.2	22.2	18.8	9.7	14.6

1. From 2004/2005 to 2008/2009, for the Northwest Territories, the number of custody orders has been under-reported and the number of probation orders has been overreported by unknown amounts due to clerical procedures. The majority of custody orders were captured as probation.

Source: S. Milligan (Summer 2010). *Juristat*. Ottawa: Statistics Canada. (From Table 8).

and then the YCJA, the incarceration rate has steadily dropped from a rate of 18.7 per 100 000 young persons in 1995/96 to 8.1 in 2004/05 (Thomas 2007). This dramatic decline is largely attributed to the increased use of diversion and other extra-judicial measures as well as the fact that, under the YOA, youth custody sentences were often followed by a period of probation to ensure some form of supervision on reintegration into the community. Furthermore, since the introduction of the YCJA, the youth court caseload has stabilized and (as reflected in Figure 4.2 in Chapter 4) is dramatically lower than it was prior to the introduction of the YCJA.

Since the early 1990s there has been an apparent shift to greater accountability of young offenders engaged in serious offences. For example, the percentage of youth who received secure custody and supervision orders or sentences of less than one month increased steadily, from 6 per cent in 1986/87 to 30 per cent in 1995/96, and then to 49 per cent in 2003/04 (Thomas 2005). However, in 2008/09, custody and supervision dropped dramatically to 15.4 per cent but again showed considerable variation across the country. The percentage of those placed in custody ranged from a low of 6.2 per cent in Manitoba to a high of 20.3 per cent in Ontario (Milligan 2010).

For the fiscal year 2008/09, the number of youth placed in any type of custody was the lowest it had been in 15 years: 5307. In addition to fewer youth being placed in custody, they are also serving shorter sentences than a decade ago. Although some 14 per cent of those case convictions received secure custody versus 12 per cent in 1992/93, the average length of sentences in secure custody declined from 94 days in 1992/93 to 68 days in 2002/03—just prior to the enactment of the YCJA

Box 2.2 Youth Justice in Action

Question to Ponder: Class or Individual Exercise

In the previous sections we have reviewed some of the official and unofficial characteristics of youth crime. As an individual, class, or group exercise, consider collecting at least a dozen different, yet recent, media stories on youth crime in your area and/or province. What impressions are you left with about the young offenders' age, gender, and crime seriousness? The types of crimes being committed by young persons? The type of sentence/disposition that they receive? Do the media reflect the facts that have been presented throughout this chapter? Do the stories appear to support the assertion that we are too lenient on young offenders when it comes to holding them accountable? What, if any, lessons have you learned by doing this exercise?

(Milligan 2010). So, even though proportionately more convicted offenders are being placed in secure custody, they were serving noticeably less time until the introduction of the YCJA. By 2008/09 the average length of secure custody had climbed to 119 days with a median of 65 days.

One of the stated objectives of the YCJA was to ensure that justice would be administered more quickly; however, increasingly we hear about delays in our youth justice system. The concern would appear to be somewhat justified. As reflected in Figure 2.5, since the early 1990s the court case completion time remained fairly steady until the introduction of the YCJA when there was a dramatic spike in the length of time it takes to complete a court case.

Again, as with other trends and patterns across the country, there is considerable variation. For example, the longest average case processing time occurred in Manitoba (153 days) and the shortest time occurred in New Brunswick (46 days) (Thomas 2004, p. 4). And although the provinces and territories are responsible for administrating the YCJA, such variations raise concerns about the fairness, efficiency, and effectiveness of youth justice.

After the introduction of the YCJA, the median number of days to complete youth court cases has steadily risen to the point that for 2008/09 the median elapsed time to process a case in youth court was 119 days—over a month longer than in the year prior to the enactment of the YCJA (see Figure 2.6). As with most other facts presented in this chapter, there continues to be considerable variation in the processing time between the provinces. For example, in 2006/07, Saskatchewan averaged the most days to process a case at 182 days followed by Manitoba at 177 days, with PEI being the most expedient at 51 days (Thomas 2008).

The increase in case processing time with the introduction of the YCJA may, in part, be due to the fact that the courts are hearing lengthier cases as a result of less serious cases being diverted from the court process (e.g., extra-judicial measures) (Milligan 2010). This is consistent with the principles and objectives of the YCJA (see Chapter 4).

Yet official statistics provide less insight into the complex set of factors that can contribute to case processing delays (e.g., resources and workload, jurisdiction size, case characteristics such as offence type and severity, various procedural factors, and the informal norms and values of a court) (see Box 2.3).

Transfers to Adult Court—Adult Sentencing

Under the JDA and during the first few years of the YOA, their respective juvenile justice models have been described as a 'tug of war' between one of *welfare* (i.e., informality, indeterminate sentencing, and a focus on individuals needs and rehabilitation) and *modified justice* (i.e., due process informality, determinate sentences, and sanctioning of behaviour and provision of treatment) (Winterdyk 2002). As a result, transfers to adult court were relatively infrequent until the early 1990s when amendments to Section 16 of the YOA were introduced to facilitate transfers due to Parliament's concern about the

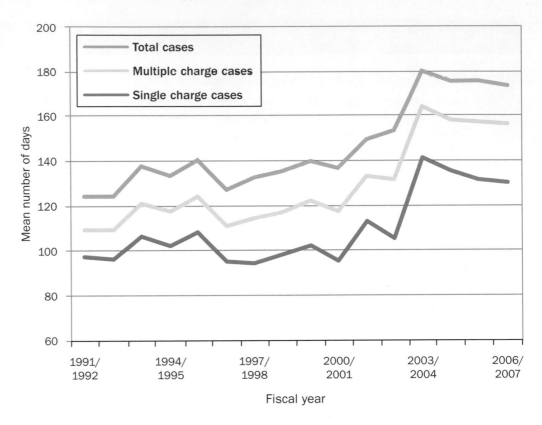

Figure 2.5 Youth Court Cases Are Taking Longer to Process

Source: Thomas, J. (2008). Youth court statistics, 2006/2007. *Juristat*, 28(4).

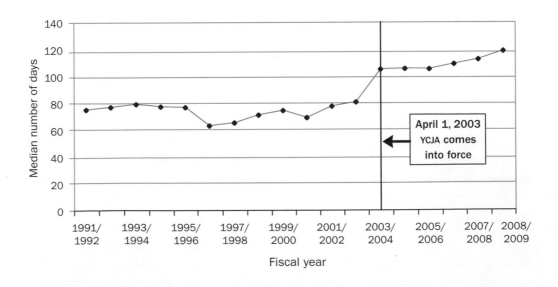

Figure 2.6 Median Number of Days to Complete Youth Court

Source: Milligan, S. (Summer 2010: 5). *Juristat*. Ottawa: Statistics Canada. (Chart 3).

Box 2.3 Youth Justice in Action

Question to Ponder: How Do We Reduce Variations between Provinces?

Although some have argued that the YCJA is an improvement over the JDA and YOA (see Chapters 3 and 4 in this volume; also, generally, see www.justice.gc.ca/eng/pi/yj-jj/information/diff.html), we have seen in this chapter that there are, in some cases, notable differences between the provinces. How might we be able to reduce the variations and discrepancies between the provinces? Is it even necessary? Explain.

public perception that the YOA was too lenient. The amendments were limited to the most serious offence cases involving youth between the ages of 16 and 17 (unless otherwise ruled by the court).

Between 1986/87 and 1989/90, the number of transfers to adult court dropped from around 80 to approximately 25; however, after the amendments were introduced, the number of transfers increased to a high of 85 cases in 1994. At that point, critics argued that youth incarceration was being overused. In fact, Canada, at one point, had the highest youth incarceration rate in the world—even higher than that in the United States. Various scholars began to point out that the transfer process was unfair, too complex, and contributed to lengthy delays. For example, while transfers were being used, there was considerable variation between the provinces with Québec and Manitoba tending to have the most transfers and the Maritime provinces having very few transfers (Thomas 2003).

The current legislation no longer provides for the transfer of youth to adult court as the focus of the YOA has shifted toward *rehabilitation* and re-entry into society. Rather, in accordance with strict criteria as outlined in Section 61, a convicted young person may receive an adult sentence only if 'found guilty of an offence for which an adult could be sentenced to imprisonment for more than two years'. Since the amendments were introduced, the number of adult sentences has dropped precipitously. In 2004 there were only four cases for which a young offender received an adult sentence. More recently, there have been a number of high-profile cases reflecting the extreme circumstances under which the option can and has been exercised. For example, in 2006, a Montreal youth was given an adult sentence for the vicious murder of another young person at a house party (Young offenders gets. . . 2006), and in September 2010, a 17-year-old male youth was given an adult sentence in Ontario after having violently murdered his mother (Nasmith 2010). In both cases, it took in excess of two years for the sentence to be delivered. Hence, we could argue that the intent of Section 61, and the YCJA in general, is fulfilling its objective—to limit adult sentences to only the most grievous of crimes committed by young persons. But the system's ability to process such cases efficiently still appears to pose a challenge if justice is to be swift and certain (i.e., fair).

Recidivism

It has been suggested that the success, or failure, of punishment can be measured by **recidivism**, or the rate at which convicted individuals reoffend. However, as reflected in a report by Correctional Service Canada, the concept is not that straightforward. For example, what is called 'recidivism' may also actually refer to return to custody on technical violations, and/or new offences (FORUM on Correctional Research 2009). Therefore, for the purpose of this section, we will rely on the general definition of an individual's reoffending.

Recidivism data on young offenders in Canada are not regularly recorded. Given the limitations of official information in such cases (many crimes go unreported or unrecorded by official agencies), official recidivism should perhaps be viewed as 'a measure of political success . . . how well (or poorly) our crime control policies are working' (Brantingham and Brantingham 1984, p. 41).

recidivism

Repetition of criminal and/or delinquent behaviour. Recidivism can be measured through official sources or through self-report surveys.

Notwithstanding this cautionary comment, official data tell us that in the early 1990s about 18.6 per cent of young offenders who appeared in court had five or more prior convictions (Moyer 1992). The same report notes that approximately 46 per cent of those charged in youth court had one or more prior convictions since 1984. By the late 1990s, official youth court statistics for 1998/99 showed that nearly 42 per cent of cases with convictions involved repeat offenders (Carrierre 2000). Furthermore, the older a youth gets, the more likely it becomes that he or she has had prior charges. And as with other youth crime facts presented in this chapter, for recidivism data there are also regional variations. For example, using data obtained from the Manitoba corrections branch, the reoffending rate for those young offenders who had been incarcerated was a staggering 100 per cent (Morris 2010).

Finally, one of the most comprehensive studies whose data should provide considerable insight to the criminal careers of young persons is the work being undertaken by Carrington, Matarazzo, and Souza (2005). They are involved in the first quasi-national Canadian study of the criminal careers of a birth cohort. It uses linked data from the Youth Court Study and Adult Criminal Court Survey for youths born in 1979/80. Their preliminary data from six provinces tends to parallel the recidivism results presented above; however, in the future the richness of their data set should provide a deeper understanding of criminal career trends and provide evidence-based insight into how to better address youth crime.

Before we examine the unofficial measures of youth crime, we should reiterate that a number of real and artificial pitfalls affect the accuracy of official data. Furthermore, official data reflect the action (or inaction) of social-control agencies (e.g., police) rather than the real numbers and features of delinquent behaviour. Nevertheless, if we view the data longitudinally, for the most part, the facts remain relatively consistent. As long as we remain sensitive to some of the pitfalls surrounding the use of official data, these data can provide insight into how official agencies have responded to youth crime over the years.

Measures of Youth Crime—The Unofficial Picture

As we noted earlier, we will now highlight some of the facts about youth crime based on self-report studies and victimization surveys. These are referred to as *'unofficial' sources of data* because criminal justice agencies are not required by law to collect this information. Instead, academics and research centres usually compile such data.

Self-report Surveys

self-report survey
A social-science questionnaire survey designed to ask respondents to report on their involvement in criminal or delinquent activities.

West (1984, p. 86) suggests that **self-report (SR) surveys** and related scales were developed during the 1940s and 1950s because 'police and court statistics were too hopelessly biased'. Although self-report studies have become more popular and are proving to be useful in helping to uncover the 'dark figure' (i.e., unreported or unrecorded crimes) for certain offences, they are not without their limitations. Some of the more common limitations to conducting self-report studies with youth include young people's literacy level and ability to comprehend questions, their short-term versus long-term memory, the extent to which they are willing to give information voluntarily, and the fact that respondents may exaggerate their answers in order to conform—or may even telescope their answers by admitting to something that took place before the actual reference period.

Research methodology texts today are quick to point out that, despite the preceding problems with self-report surveys, a great deal of progress has been made in improving the validity and reliability of this method, to the point that SR surveys have gained acceptance as a valid measure of young offenders. Over the years, various studies have repeatedly shown that most youth engage in acts that would have qualified as an offence had these youths been caught. In fact, offending among young persons is far more prevalent than official data or the media report (Le Blanc and Tremblay 1988). Over 80 per cent of youths surveyed admitted to at least one delinquent act while less than 3 per cent of these acts had been detected by the police. However, one of the first SR studies to be conducted on young offenders in the 1960s revealed that while offending was common among young people, the nature of offending among middle-class youth was less serious in nature than among lower-class youth (Vaz 1966). Nevertheless, as West (1984) observed in Canada: (1) there is little SR evidence to suggest that youth crime has increased over the years, and (2) the difference between the amount of delinquent activity that males and females engage in is not as dramatic as official data would lead us to believe. For example, West (1984, p. 88) reported the male to female offending ratio to be about 5:1 and 3:1, whereas official statistics indicate that the ratio is between 5:1 and 10:1. In a slightly more recent study, Simourd and Andrews (1996) found the ratio to be 3:1, male to female.

Based on the results from the National Longitudinal Survey of Children and Youth (NLSCY), which has collected data every two years since 1994, the most recent results show that about 38 per cent of young persons engaged in a repeated offence in the previous year, of which almost 70 per cent involved 'minor' offences (Correlates . . . 2010). However, the NLSCY only includes youth between the ages of 11 and 13 and asks only very general questions about the nature and extent of victimization (see Sprott, Doob, and Jenkins 2001).

In addition to examining issues around unreported delinquent behaviour, researchers could also begin to probe specific offence variations, compare demographic relationships, do comparative studies with other countries, and conduct follow-up surveys. Some of these concerns are already being addressed internationally in several ongoing studies involving researchers at the University of Southern California and the Dutch Research and Documentation Centre (see Junger-Tas, Terlouw, and Klein 1994; Junger-Tas et al. 2003; and Junger-Tas 2010). The research involves the largest self-report study of young people in the world: the International Self Reported Delinquency Survey (ISRD). During the second round of this survey, some 30 countries were included. In 2006 Canada participated for the first time with its International Youth Survey, which was limited to the city of Toronto. Among its other findings, the study reported that second-generation immigrant youth remained at higher risk of reporting delinquent acts than their native-born counterparts (Self report delinquency. . . 2010; also see Sprott and Doob 2010).

In summary, while the use of self-report surveys has increased, the methodologies and designs used have not been consistent, hence limiting interpretation, comparison, and extrapolation. However, such surveys do serve to provide qualified insight that is not always captured by official statistics.

Victimization and Victimization Surveys

Although society and the media tend to focus on the offences committed by young people, we must remember that young people are also the victims of a great deal of violence, not only from members of their own age group but also from adults. **Victimization survey** data indicate that young people are more likely to be victims of crimes than are adults. In fact, several years ago an international report observed that even though 190 countries—including Canada—have signed the United Nations Convention on the Rights of the Child, victimization of children is on the rise (Chin 1998). The report also observed that young people were at greater risk of being victims of assault, sexual assault, and robbery than those over the age of 24 (AuCoin 2002).

In the early 1990s, based on information from 13 major police departments across the country, nearly one-quarter of all violent crime victims were teenagers (CCJS 1992b). More recent data reveal that most of these victims were males and that children under 12 years of age were most often the victims of common assault (43 per cent) or sexual assault (34 per cent) (CCJS 1999).

victimization survey
A social-science questionnaire survey designed to measure the experiences of respondents as victims of crime(s).

A review of other Canadian research suggests that victimization rates have continued to increase since 2000. This is appears to be evident in such areas as bullying, street youth (see Chapter 12), and in particular among Aboriginal youth (see Chapter 9). For example, Brzozowski, Taylor-Butts, and Johnson (2006) note that Aboriginal youth are three times more likely to be victimized than non-Aboriginal youth. However, the rates were lower for new immigrants and for visible minorities than for non-immigrants and non-visible minorities. The initial results from the 2009 General Social Survey (GSS) indicated that young people (i.e., those aged 15 to 24) were almost 15 times more likely to have been a victim of a violent crime than seniors 65 and older (Perreault and Brennan 2010). Unfortunately, the GSS only collects victimization of persons 15 years of age or older.

One of the most ambitious Canadian victimization studies, the Canadian Urban Victimization Survey (CUVS), which began in 1983 and was repeated every few years, involved seven major cities (Vancouver, Edmonton, Winnipeg, Toronto, Montreal, Halifax–Dartmouth, and St. John's) and included more than 61 000 interviews. The 2004/05 cycle of the survey included 25 000 participants. However, because only youths 15 years of age and older were interviewed for this survey, the results were somewhat limited in terms of adolescents. Using data from the CUVS, Sacco and Johnson (1990) found the following:

- Young persons (comprising a 15–24 age group) were the most victimized age group (37 per cent versus 24 per cent for all age groups).
- The age group of 15–24 had the highest incidence of repeat victimization (16 per cent had been victimized two or more times) compared with all other age groups.
- Contrary to popular opinion, the difference between males and females in the percentage of victimization was not all that large (18 per cent for males, and 14 per cent for females, aged 15–24).
- The group aged 15–24 consistently had higher rates of victimization for personal theft, violent incidents, robbery, sexual assault, and common assault.

In 1999, Paetsch and Bertrand conducted a victimization survey of young persons in Calgary and their results were generally similar to those reported by Sacco and Johnson (1990) but they focused more specifically on the relative influence of school. Several of their key findings included the following:

- Overall, males were more likely than females to report they were victimized but the difference was in type: victimization was greater among those young persons who attended school than those who did not.
- The strongest predictors of victimization were type of peer group, weak family relations, and socializing more with youth of similar age than with adults.
- Difficulties in school (e.g., suspension, dropping out, negative attitude toward school) correlated with higher likelihood of being victimized.
- Students with psychological challenges (e.g., conduct disorder, hyperactivity, etc.) were more likely to be victims than those not expressing psychological problems.

Over the years, there have been at least three major *Juristat* reports that have examined children and youth as victims of violent crime. Given the dates of publication, they allow for a general comparison. When 1996 data (Fitzgerald 1997) is compared to that of 2003 (AuCoin 2005), young females are more often the victims of assault crimes than young males are. More specifically, young females are more likely to be the victims of sexual assault than are young males, and their victimization is more likely at the hands of friends and/or acquaintances rather than strangers.

Conversely, in terms of physical assault young males are more likely to be victims than are their female counterparts. However, similar to sexual assault offences, the perpetrators tend to be friends and acquaintances. A more recent *Juristat* report prepared by Ogrodnik (2010), and drawing upon victimization data from the General Social Survey, points out that about 80 per cent of 'youth aged 15–17 who had been victimized did not report the incident to police' (p. 1). The report indicated that violence against children and youth was highest in Saskatchewan (2136 per 100 000) and lowest in Prince Edward Island (894 per 100 000).

In one of the largest victimization studies of its kind, Tanner and Wortley (2002) found that more than half of 3400 high school students in Toronto and 400 local street youth surveyed failed to report to an adult that they had been victimized. With the recent concerns surrounding bullying, hazing, and media-profiled cases, the implications of this 'code of silence' is alarming; the dark figure for young victims is not only quite large but there are also no clear provisions in the Criminal Code to address the problem. As Tanner and Wortley note, there is no easy solution to the problem of victimization, but it requires school- and family-oriented intervention. We must send the message to youth that it is okay to report such incidents.

Notwithstanding the previous observation, the overall trends of victimization among young persons sharply contrast with what one might be led to believe from most media reports. For example, Mathews (1996) cites research that found that the first time many victimized teens receive attention is when they come in contact with the legal system because of an offence they have committed. This finding suggests that prior victimization may be a key risk factor to criminal activity and that we need to look more carefully at the causes underlying youth crime and determine whether accountability and punishment are more important than treatment, counselling, or other forms of support. The underlying assumption is that it is more cost effective and cost efficient to invest and prevent crime from happening than waiting to respond to it (see, for example, Safe Communities . . . 2011).

As we will see in Part Three, a notable number of these victimized youths end up turning to a life of drugs, joining gangs, becoming involved in prostitution, and/or following a general path of self-destruction—including suicide (see Coloroso 2004). Consequently, one can ask, do these facts lend support to the need not only to understand the risk factors that lead to victimization but also to learn more about the protective factors that might help to build resiliency among such youth?

Before concluding this section, we should briefly address the relationship between young offenders and young victims of crime. Some academics have argued that these may be artificial categories (see Fagan, Piper, and Cheng 1989), based on the general observation that victims of crime and abused youth are the most likely to become offenders (abusers) themselves. These assertions, however, tend to rely on single disciplinary and theoretical perspectives. For example, why don't all victims become offenders? Why do some non-victims become offenders? Supporters of victim–offender causality typically subscribe to the influence of the nurture assumption, which asserts that anything that goes wrong in our lives can be attributed to our upbringing (see Harris 1998, 2006). Thanks, in large part, to improved research strategies, we can explore the relationship between biological traits and a host of social and psychological factors, and how they might more accurately explain the similarities as well as differences between young offenders and young victims. As Ezzat Fattah (1991), a Canadian pioneer of victimology, has noted, this will require a new theoretical orientation (see Goodey 2005; Giannini and Rossi 2009).

Finally, although the quality of victimization and self-report studies has improved over the years, they are by no means perfect. The true nature and facts about youth crime will always remain somewhat elusive. After all, youth crime, as something separate from adult crime, has existed ever since the term *delinquency* was coined; and, as reflected above, the trend and patterns have not changed significantly over the years. However, as we continue to examine the strengths and weaknesses of data collection, we will better be able to confirm or reject existing theoretical formulations and to develop new ones that have a more practical application in controlling and preventing youth crime. In an effort to more accurately uncover the 'dark figure' of crime or 'hidden crime' researchers can and often do rely on a process that is referred to as **triangulation**. The term refers to the process of using different sources of data to help provide a richer factual accounting of facts being examined.

triangulation
A research methods technique that involves using more than one source of criminological data to assess the validity of what is being observed. For example, this technique can include combining official crime data with self-report data to obtain a clearer picture of crime or delinquency facts.

Summary

In this chapter, we provided a broad overview of three major sources of information on youth crime in Canada from the pre-Confederation era to the present day. We can make a number of observations about these trends. Although there have been periods of increases, since 1991 (and based largely on official statistics) there appears to have been a marked decline in official youth crime. However, the picture is not absolutely clear because of the nature and quality (i.e., reliability and validity) of our data sources, changes in legislation, shifts in demographics, etc. The one exception to the declining crime rates among young persons has been violent crimes. This has been particularly evident since the beginning of the new millennium. Furthermore, although somewhat controversial, what is perhaps more alarming is the apparent fact that young persons are not only engaging in more serious youth crime but they are also becoming active criminals at an earlier age. As well, recidivism rates have steadily risen over the years, the courts have become backlogged, and the public has become increasingly dissatisfied with the judicial system's ability to control the problem. These challenges, in part, explain why we saw a number of major changes to the former YOA, which was eventually replaced by the YCJA, as well as a move toward alternative solutions, such as restorative justice initiatives, alternative measures programs, and a range of outreach programs (see Chapters 3 and 4 for further discussion).

Finally, considering that we continue to allocate considerable resources to trying to control youth crime with marginal returns, it is even timelier that we refine our crime measurement techniques before we make assumptions about how to best to respond to youth crime. As much as it has become fashionable to focus on identifying and responding to risk factors, and on supporting the protective factors and/or helping to build resiliency in our youth (see, for example, Howell 2009), we need to have our facts straight first. While it is relatively easy to identify risk and protective factors associated with youth offending, it is a different matter when it comes to applying and implementing protective factors in intervention. In the meantime, while each measurement method provides useful information, no one technique is better than the other, and until we are able to improve the quality of how we measure youth crime the dark figure of crime will remain somewhat elusive for most crimes. Therefore, we are limited to speaking in generalities and, as stated at the beginning of this chapter, there is no clear answer to the question, 'How serious is youth crime?' Hence, as informative and interesting as the data from measuring youth crime might be, the quality of the data still remains relatively imprecise and relying on it to predict future youth crime trends and patterns remains speculative.

Key Terms

administrative offences
Crime Severity Index
dark figure of crime
disposition
official data
recidivism

self-report (SR) survey
triangulation
unofficial data
victimization survey
youth at risk

Review Questions

1. Identify some of the major factors that appear to have led to increased state intervention in the lives of young persons.

2. Identify several advantages and disadvantages of relying on official statistics to provide a picture of youth crime issues.

3. How can self-report studies and victimization surveys be used to better understand youth crime?

4. Review and discuss how violent crime has changed over the years. What explanations can you offer? Try to substantiate your explanations with evidence.

5. What types of youth crime activities appear to be most problematic for Canadians today? Explain your answer and offer a possible creative and constructive solution.

Critical Thinking Questions

1. Review and discuss how violent crime has changed since the early 1990s. What explanations can you offer? Try to substantiate your explanations with evidence.

2. Why is it considered useful to practise triangulation when describing youth crime trends?

3. Throughout this chapter, we have looked at youth crime trends. Based on the information presented, what do you predict for the future? What, if anything, should we as a society focus on in regard to youth crime? Are there particular problem-related areas that might require extra attention?

4. There have been a number of notable changes in the trends and patterns of youth crime and youth court cases since the enactment of the YCJA. In light of the changes in the trends and patterns since the YCJA came into force, does the act appear to be fulfilling its objective in addressing youth crime? What, if any, might be some of the long-term benefits or challenges?

5. We have presented a number of cautionary comments about the reliability and validity of youth crime data. Do you agree? If so, how might we begin to improve the collection of such information?

Suggested Readings

Carrigan, D.O. (1998). *Juvenile delinquency in Canadian history*. Toronto: Irwin Pub.

Carrington, P. (1995). Has violent youth crime increased? Comments on Corrado and Markwart. *Canadian J. of Criminology*, 37: 61–74.

Corrado, R. and Markwart, A. (1994). The need to reform the YOA in response to violent young offenders. Confusion, reality or myth? *Canadian J. of Criminology*, 36: 347–78.

Schissel, B. (1997). *Blaming children: Youth crime, moral panic and the politics of hate.* Halifax: Fernwood.

Taylor-Butts, A. and Bressan, A. (2007). Youth crime in Canada, 2006. *Juristat*, 28(3).

Suggested Weblinks

Canadian Journal of Criminology and Criminal Justice

www.utpjournals.com/cjccj/cjccj.html

- The official journal for Canadian criminology and criminal justice. It regularly has youth justice–related articles, which may include studies involving the use of official and unofficial statistics.

Statistics Canada

www.statcan.gc.ca

- The website for Statistics Canada, where students can find a wealth of official data on youth crime from the police, youth courts, etc. Links can also be found to *The Daily* and *Juristat* reports.

Department of Justice Canada

www.justice.gc.ca

- This government site is rich with youth justice information as well as a range of official data sources.

Statistics Canada: National Longitudinal Survey of Children and Youth

www.statcan.gc.ca/dli-ild/data-donnees/ftp/nlscy-elnej-eng.htm

- At this federal site students can find access to the numerous cycles of the National Longitudinal Survey of Children and Youth. Although not completely deviance- or youth-crime-related, it is the most extensive and standardized self-report survey of its kind in Canada.

The 2004/05 International Crime Victims Survey

http://rechten.uvt.nl/icvs

- Although not specific to Canada, this international crime victimization survey does include Canada in several cycles and provides an overview of youth victimization internationally.

Endnotes

1.   For an overview of industrial schools in Canada see Milloy (1999).
2.   Given that the YCJA has only been in use fewer than 10 years at the time of this book being published, the time period is considered too short for any definitive statement about the impact of the act on the administration of youth justice in Canada.
3.   For the other 7 per cent gender was not recorded.
4.   Note that the police index crime category of 'other' offences only includes Criminal Code charges while in court statistics the 'other' category also includes administrative charges. These charges only came into effect after the introduction of the YOA.
5.   The overall youth violent crime rate was, however, 11 per cent higher in 2009 than in 1999.

References

AuCoin, K. (2005). Children and youth as victims of violent crime. *Juristat (25)*1. Ottawa: Statistics Canada Catalogue no. 85-002-XIE.

Bala, N. (1994). What's wrong with YOA bashing? What's wrong with the YOA? Recognising the limits of the law. *Canadian Journal of Criminology*, 36, 247–70.

Bartol, C.R. and Bartol, A. (2009). *Criminal behavior: A psychological approach* (9th ed.). Englewood Cliffs, NJ: Prentice-Hall.

Beattie, S. Cotter, A. (Fall 2010). Homicide in Canada, 2009. *Juristat.* Ottawa: Canadian Centre for Criminal Justice Statistics.

Blumstein, A. (1995). Youth violence, guns and the illicit drug industry. *Journal of Criminal Law and Criminology, 86*(1): 10.

Brantingham, P.J. and Brantingham, P.L. (1984). *Patterns in crime.* New York: Macmillan.

Brooks, C. and Schissel, B. (Eds.). (2008). *Marginality and condemnation* (2nd ed). Halifax: Brunswick Books (formerly Fernwood Books).

Brzozowski, J-A, Taylor-Butts, A., and Johnson, S. (2006). Victimization and offending among the Aboriginal population in Canada, *Juristat, 26*(3). Ottawa: Canadian Centre for Justice Statistics.

Carrier, D. (2001). Youth court statistics, 1989/90 highlights. *Juristat, 21*(2). Ottawa: Canadian Centre for Criminal Justice Statistics.

Carrigan, D.O. (1991). *Crime and punishment in Canada: A history.* Toronto: McClelland and Stewart.

Carrigan, D.O. (1998). *Juvenile delinquency in Canada: A history.* Toronto: McClelland and Stewart.

Carrington, P. (1995). Has violent crime increased? Commenting on Corrado and Markwart. *Canadian J. of Criminology, 37*: 61–73.

Carrington, P.J., Matarazzo, A., and deSouza, P. (2005). *Court careers of a Canadian birth cohort.* Ottawa: Statistics Canada.

Cases completed in youth courts by offence category and age of accused, Canada, 2008/2009 (2010). Retrieved 6 Oct., 2010, from http://www.statcan.gc.ca/pub/85-002-x/2010002/article/11294/tbl/tbl04-eng.htm

CCJS (Canadian Centre for Justice Statistics). (1992a). Sentencing in youth court, 1986–87 to 1990–91. *Juristat Service Bulletin, 12*(16).

CCJS (Canadian Centre for Justice Statistics). (1992b). Teenage victims of violent crime. *Juristat Service Bulletin. 12*(6).

Charron, M. (2009). Neighbourhood characteristics and the distribution of police-reported crime in the city of Toronto. *Crime and Justice Research Series.* Ottawa: Statistics Canada Cat. No. 85-561-MEI-No. 18. Retrieved 16 April, 2010, from http://www.statcan.gc.ca/pub/85-561-m/85-561-m2009018-eng.htm

Chesney-Lind, M. and Shelden, R. (1992). *Girls, delinquency and juvenile justice.* Belmont, CA: West/ Wadsworth.

Coloroso, B. (2004). *The bully, the bullied, and the bystander: From preschool to high school—how parents and teachers can help break the cycle of violence.* NY: Harper Collins.

Corrado, R. and Markwart, A. (1994). The need to reform the YOA in response to violent young offenders: Confusion, reality or myth? *Canadian Journal of Criminology, 36*: 343–78.

Correlates of delinquency: A look at gender differences. (2009). Retrieved 2 Oct., 2010, from http://www.csc-scc.gc.ca/text/pblct/forum/e061/e061g-eng.shtml

Creechan, J. (1995). How much delinquency is there? In J. Creechan and R. Silverman (Eds.), *Canadian delinquency.* Scarborough, ON: Prentice Hall Canada.

Dauvergne, M. and Turner, J. (2009). Police reported crime in Canada, 2009. *Juristat.,* Ottawa: Canadian Centre for Justice Statistics.

DeMause, L. (Ed.). (1988). *The history of childhood.* New York: Peter Bedrick.

Doob, A. and Cesaroni, C. (2004). *Responding to youth crime in Canada.* Toronto: University of Toronto Press.

Doob, A. and Sprott, J.B. (2006). Punishing youth in Canada. *Punishment and Society, 8*(2): 223–33.

Fagan, J., Piper, E., and Cheng, Y-T. (1989). Contributions of victimization to delinquency in inner cities. *Journal of Criminal Law and Criminology, 78,* 586–613.

Fattah, E. (1991). *Understanding criminal victimization.* Scarborough: Prentice Hall.

Fetherston, D. (2005). The law and young offenders. In J. Winterdyk (Ed.), *Issues and perspectives on young offenders in Canada* (3rd ed.). Toronto: Nelson.

Fitzgerald, R. (1997). Assault against children and youth in the family, 1996. *Juristat (17)*11. Ottawa: Statistics Canada Catalogue no. 85-002-XIE.

FORUM on correctional research. (2009). Retrieved 6 Oct., 2010, from http://www.csc-scc.gc.ca/text/pblct/forum/e053/e053h-eng.shtml

Gabor, T. (1999). Trends in youth crime: Some evidence pointing to increases in the severity and volume on the part of young people. *Canadian Journal of Criminology, 41*(3): 385–92.

Gannon, M. and Mihorean, K. (2005). Criminal victimization in Canada–2004. *Juristat, 25*(7). Ottawa: Canadian Centre for Justice Statistics.

Giannini, A.M. and Rossi, C. (Eds.). (2009). *Victim's care: A handbook.* Milano, Italy: Echo Communications.

Goodey, J. (2005). *Victims and victimology: Research, policy and practice.* Essex, England: Pearson Education.

Hak, J. (1996). The Young Offenders Act. In J. Winterdyk (Ed.), *Issues and perspectives on young offenders in Canada.* Toronto: Nelson.

Harris, J.R. (1998). *The nurture assumption: Why children turn out the way they do.* New York: Free Press.

Harris, J.R. (2006). *No two alike.* New York: W.W. Norton and Co.

Heidensohn, F. (1995). *Women and crime.* Basingstoke: MacMillan.

Hoge, R.D. and Andrews, D.A. (2010). *Evaluation for risk of violence in juveniles.* NY: Oxford University Press.

Howell, J.C. (2009). *Preventing and reducing juvenile delinquency: A comprehensive framework* (2nd ed.). Thousand Oaks CA: Sage.

Huff, D. (1954). *How to lie with statistics.* NY: W.W. Norton and Co.

Junger-Tas, J. (2010). The significance of the International Self-report Delinquency Study (ISRD). *European Journal on Criminal Policy and Research, 16*(2), 71–87.

Junger-Tas, J., Marshall, I., and Ribeaud, D. (2003). *Delinquency in an international perspective: The International Self-Report Delinquency Study (ISRD).* New York: Kugler.

Junger-Tas, J., Marshall, I.H., and Ribeaud, D. (2010). The significance of the International Self-report Delinquency Study. *European J. of Criminal Policy and Research, 16*(2): 71–87.

Junger-Tas, J., Terlouw, G-J., and Klein, M.W. (Eds.). (1994). *Delinquent behavior among young people in the Western world: First results of the International Self-Report Delinquent Study.* New York: Kugler.

Kowalski, M. and Caputo, T. (1999). Recidivism in youth court: An examination of the impact of age, gender, and prior record. *Canadian Journal of Criminology, 41*(1), 57–84.

Kratcoski, P.C. and Kratcoski, L.D. (1990). *Juvenile delinquency* (3rd ed.). Englewood Cliffs, NJ: Prentice-Hall.

Le Blanc, M. and Tremblay, R.E. (1988). Homeostasis: Social change plus modifications in the basic personality of adolescents equal stability of hidden delinquency. *International J. of Adolescence and Youth, 1*(3): 269–91.

Le Blanc, M., Vallières, E., and McDuff, P. (1993). The prediction of males' adolescent and adult offending from school experience. *Canadian Journal of Criminology, 35*(4), 459–78.

Mathews, F. (1996, March). *The invisible boy.* Ottawa: National Clearing House of Family Violence, Health Canada.

Milligan, S. (Summer 2010). Youth court statistics, 2008/2009. *Juristat.* Ottawa: Canadian Centre for Justice Statistics.

Milloy, J.S. (1999). *A national crime: The Canadian government and the residential school system, 1879 to 1986.* Winnipeg: University of Manitoba Press.

Morris, J. (March 4, 2010). Criminal recidivism rates in Canada. Retrieved 6 Oct., 2010, from http://www.employeescreen.com/iqblog/criminal-recidivism-rates-in-canada/

Nunn, D.M. (2006). Spiraling out of control: Lessons learned from a boy in trouble: Report of the Nunn Commission Inquiry. Province of Nova Scotia. Retrieved 19 April, 2011, from http://www.nunncommission.ca/media_uploads/pdf/109.pdf

Ogrodnik, L. (2010). Child and youth victims of police-reported violent crime, 2008. *Juristat,* 23. Ottawa: Statistics Canada Catalogue no. 85F0033M.

Paetsch, J.J. and Bertrand, L.D. (Summer 1999). Victimization and delinquency among Canadian youth. *Adolescence, 34*(134): 351–67.

Perreault, S. and Brennan, S. (2010). Criminal victimization in Canada, 2009. Retrieved from: http://www.statcan.gc.ca/pub/85-002-x/85-002-x2010002-eng.htm (accessed Nov. 30, 2011).

Platt, A.M. (1977). *The child savers* (2nd ed.). Chicago: University of Chicago Press.

Police-reported youth crime for selected offences, by province and territory, 2009 (2010). Retrieved 10 Oct., 2010, from http://www.statcan.gc.ca/pub/85-002-x/2010002/article/11292/tbl/tbl9-eng.htm

Prevost, A. (2011). Empirical exploration of the importation, deprivation and integrated models concerning types of aggression in youth custody. Unpublished PhD thesis. Burnaby, BC: Simon Fraser University, School of Criminology.

Public perception of crime and justice in Canada: A review of opinion pools. Retrieved 2 Oct., 2010, from http://www.justice.gc.ca/eng/pi/rs/rep-rap/2001/rr01_1/p6.html

Sacco, V.F. and Johnson, H. (1990, March). Patterns of criminal victimization in Canada. Cat. no. 11-612E, No. 2. Ottawa: Statistics Canada (Housing, Family and Social Statistics Division), Ministry of Supply and Services Canada.

Sanders, T. (2000). Sentencing of young offenders in Canada, 1998/99. *Juristat, 20*(7).Ottawa: Canadian Centre for Justice Statistics.

Santayana, G. (1905). *The life of reason.* London: Constable.

Schissel, B. (1997). *Blaming children.* Halifax, Fernwood.

Schissel, B. (2006). *Blaming children* (2nd ed.). Halifax, Fernwood.

Self-report delinquency of immigrant youth: Toronto 2006. Retrieved 2 Oct., 2010, from http://www.statcan.gc.ca/pub/81-004-x/2008005/article/10799-eng.htm

Simourd, L. and Andrews, D. (1996). Correlates of delinquency: A look at gender. In R. Silverman, J. Teevan, and V. Sacco (Eds.), *Crime in Canadian society*. Toronto: Harcourt Brace and Co.

Solicitor General Canada. (1983). Canadian urban victimization survey. Ottawa: Solicitor General.

Sprott, J.B. and Doob, A.N. (2008). Youth crime rates and the youth justice system. *Canadian Journal of Criminology and Criminal Justice, 50*(5), 621–39.

Sprott, J.B. and Doob, A.N. (2010). Gender treatment: Girls and treatment order in Bail Court. *Canadian Journal of Criminology and Criminal Justice, 52*(4), 427–41.

Sproot, J.B., Doob, A.N.M., and Jenkins, J.M. (2001). Problem behaviour and delinquency in children and youth. *Juristat*. Ottawa: Canadian Centre for Justice Statistics.

Statistics Canada. (1992). *Canada Year Book 1992*. Ottawa: Ministry of Industry, Science and Technology.

Statistics Canada. (2000, August 1). Sentencing of young offenders. *The Daily*. Retrieved August 2000 from http://www.statcan.ca/Daily/English/000801/d000801b.htm

Statistics Canada. (2010). General social survey: Victimization 2009. Retrieved 4 Oct., 2010, from http://www.statcan.gc.ca/cgi-bin/imdb/p2SV.pl?Function=getSurveyandSDDS=4504andlang=enanddb=imdbandadm=8anddis=2

Taylor-Butts, A. and Bressan, A. (2008). Youth crime in Canada, 2006. *Juristat 28*(3). Ottawa: Statistics Canada.

Tanner, J. and Wortley, S. (2002). *Toronto youth crime and victimization survey: Overview report*. Toronto: University of Toronto, Centre of Criminology.

Tanner, J. (2010). *Teenage troubles: Youth and deviance in Canada* (3rd ed.). Toronto: Oxford University Press.

The correlates of self-reported delinquency: An analysis of the national longitudinal survey of children and youth. (2010). Retrieved 1 Oct., 2010, from http://www.justice.gc.ca/eng/pi/rs/rep-rap/2003/rr03_yj2-rr03_jj2/p3.html#sec3_1

The Daily. (2008, May 16). Youth crime. Retrieved 18 Nov., 2010, from http://www.statcan.gc.ca/daily-quotidien/080516/dq080516a-eng.htm

The Gazette. (2010, March 22). Making things worse for young offenders. Retrieved 14 July, 2010, from http://www.montrealgazette.com/news/Making+things+worse+young+offenders/2710007/story.html

Thomas, J. (2003). Youth court statistics, 2001/02. *Juristat, 23*(3). Ottawa: Canadian Centre for Justice Statistics.

Thomas, J. (2005). Youth court statistics, 2003/04. *Juristat, 25*(4). Ottawa: Canadian Centre for Justice Statistics.

Thomas, J. (2008). Youth court statistics, 2006/07. *Juristat, 28*(4). Ottawa: Canadian Centre for Justice Statistics.

Vaz, E. (1966). Middle-class adolescents: Self-reported delinquency and youth culture activities. *Canadian Review of Sociology and Anthropology, 2*, 52–70.

Violent crime in Canada (2008). Retrieved 18 April, 2011, from http://www.thefreeradical.ca/Violent_crime_in_Canada_fact_sheet.pdf

Wasserman, D., Cheng, Q., and Jiang, G-X. (2005). Global suicide rates among young people aged 15–19. *World Psychiatry, 4*(2): 114–20.

West, G. (1984). *Young offenders and the state: A Canadian perspective on youth crime*. Toronto: Butterworths.

Wheeler, S., Bonacich, E., Cramer, R., and Zola, J.K. (1968). Agents of delinquency control. In S. Wheeler (Ed.), *Controlling delinquents*. New York: John Wiley and Sons.

Winterdyk, J. (Ed.). (2002). *Juvenile justice systems: International perspectives* (2nd ed.). Toronto: Canadian Scholars' Press.

Winterdyk, J. (Ed.). (2005). *Issues and perspectives on young offenders in Canada* (3rd ed.). Toronto: Thomson.

Winterdyk, J. (2006). *Canadian criminology* (2nd ed.). Toronto: Pearson.

Young offender gets adult sentence for murder. (Sept. 7, 2006). Retrieved 20 April, 2011, from http://www.cbc.ca/news/canada/montreal/story/2006/09/07/youthsentencedasadult.html

Youth court survey, number of cases, by sex of accused, annual, CANSIM (database), Using E-STAT (distributor). (2010). Retrieved 28 Sept., 2010, from http://www.statcan.gc.ca/pub/85-002-x/2009002/article/10846-eng.htm

Youth Court Statistics, 2008–2009. (2010). Retrieved 6 Oct., 2010, from http://www.statcan.gc.ca/pub/85-002-x/2010002/article/11294-eng.htm#a12

Youth crimes reported to police for selected Criminal Code offences. (2009). Retrieved 10 Oct., 2010, from http://www.statcan.gc.ca/daily-quotidien/080516/t080516a-eng.htm

Youth Criminal Justice Act: Changing the law on young criminal. (June 23, 2006). Retrieved 20 Dec., 2010, from http://www.cbc.ca/news/background/crime/ycja.html

Youth Violence: A report of the (US) Surgeon General, 2001. Retrieved 27 Sept., 2010, from http://www.surgeongeneral.gov/library/youthviolence/chapter4/appendix4b/html

3 Explaining the Youth Criminal Justice Act

Ross Green

Overview

This chapter offers an overview of key aspects of the Youth Criminal Justice Act (YCJA) that was enacted by the Parliament of Canada in 2002 and implemented in 2003. It focuses in particular on explaining policy objectives underlying the YCJA and how these objectives are reflected in the act's provisions, the youth court process through which the act is enforced, the rights and obligations of young people and parents under the act, and issues surrounding the use of discretion in determining the most appropriate measures for dealing with young persons who may be charged with criminal offences and made subject to provisions of the act.

Key Objectives

After reading this chapter, you should be able to:

- Explain the policy objectives underlying the YCJA and how these objectives are reflected in the act's provisions.
- Explain the youth justice and youth court process through which the act is enforced.
- Explain the sentencing provisions in the YCJA.
- Summarize the rights and obligations of young people and parents under the act.
- Discuss the interrelation or distinction between criminal procedures and other social measures made in the act.
- Discuss why the mental health of young people, and in particular the presence of fetal alcohol spectrum disorder (FASD), is an important consideration in youth court.

Introduction

The Youth Criminal Justice Act (YCJA) came into force in 2003, replacing the Young Offenders Act (YOA). The YCJA is a complex statute that is significantly longer than the YOA, spanning 165 substantive sections in comparison to 70 sections in the YOA. As a result, the following discussion of the YCJA is not intended to be a comprehensive analysis of all aspects of this act but, rather, an outline of its important features.[1]

Policy Objectives Underlying the Youth Criminal Justice Act (YCJA)

The content and structure of the YCJA reflects key policy objectives held by the federal government of the day. Minister of Justice Anne McLellan, in introducing the YCJA for second reading in the House of Commons, said that this act was intended to reduce the unacceptably high level of incarceration under the YOA, and that the YCJA was drafted so as to ensure that the most serious interventions in the youth justice system should be reserved for the most serious crimes, thereby reducing the over-reliance on custody. Ms McLellan further said that, in contrast to the YOA, the YCJA reserves custody primarily for violent offenders and serious repeat offenders.[2] At the same time, the government's view was that the youth justice system was being overburdened by minor offences that could be better dealt with outside of court. Ms McLellan said experience in Canada and elsewhere had shown that out-of-court measures could provide effective responses to youth crime (Davis-Barron 2009, p. 65).

This suggested a tradeoff: the youth justice system would be able to better deal with more serious offences and offenders if fewer resources—especially court resources—were spent on less serious offences and offenders. As McLellan said, 'The proposed youth criminal justice act is intended to enable the courts to focus on serious youth crimes by increasing the use of effective and timely non-court responses to less serious offences'.[3]

Richard Barnhorst, a lawyer with the federal Department of Justice and a drafter of the act, summarized the main components of the philosophy underlying the act as including the following:

- *Restraint,* encompassing both sentencing and the decision of whether to use the formal court process in the first place

- *Accountability*, with a focus on holding youth accountable for their actions by imposing meaningful consequences that will promote the rehabilitation and reintegration of the youth into society
- *Proportionality*, meaning that consequences imposed on young people be proportionate to the seriousness of the offence and the youth's degree of responsibility
- *Protection of the public*, which the system can contribute to through holding youths accountable in a fair and proportionate manner, while acknowledging that 'there are many factors outside the youth justice system that can have as much effect, or greater effect, on public protection than the activities of the youth justice system'
- *Rehabilitation and addressing needs*, ensuring that the 'seriousness of the offence sets the degree of intervention, and efforts to address the rehabilitative needs of youths fit within the proportionate response'
- *Structured discretion*, reflecting Parliament's view that officials in the youth justice system be given more legislative direction on how to exercise their discretion in a way that is consistent with the act's objectives (Barnhorst 2004, pp. 233–5).

The YCJA is divided into a preamble (containing definitions and a declaration of principle) and nine parts, the most significant of which deal with extrajudicial measures (handling offending behaviour outside of court), the organization of the youth criminal justice system, judicial measures (procedures and processes to be following in **youth court**), the sentencing of young people, procedures governing youth custody sentences and supervision following release, and rules governing the publication of names.

The preamble of this act states that members of society share a responsibility to address the developmental challenges and the needs of young people and to guide them into adulthood. At its core, the YCJA establishes a separate legal and sentencing regime for young people. The Supreme Court of Canada, in *R. v. D.B.*, said this was because 'young people are entitled to a presumption of diminished moral blameworthiness or culpability flowing from the fact that, because of their age, they have heightened vulnerability, less maturity and a reduced capacity for moral judgment'.[4]

A frequently heard criticism of the statement of principles in the YOA was that it contained 'a number of potentially conflicting, inconsistent, and un-prioritised principles' (Anand 1999, p. 251). Although the declaration of principle in s. 3 of the YCJA contains more guidance than did its counterpart in the YOA, these general principles still retain the often-conflicting goals of accountability, on the one hand, and rehabilitation, on the other. To some extent, these ambiguities are addressed in three other areas of the YCJA, which now sets the principles and objectives of extrajudicial measures (in sections 4 and 5), the purpose and principles of sentencing (in s. 38), and the purpose and principles of custody and supervision (in s. 85).

The YCJA establishes procedures for young people that, in most respects, are simpler than the procedures for adults under the Criminal Code. A **young person**, defined as being between 12 and 17 years of age, must appear before and be tried in a youth court. For the vast majority of youth charged under the act, that will mean appearing before a youth court judge who also acts as a provincial court judge for adults. For a small number of serious offences, a young person can elect to be tried in a Superior Court of Justice. These include offences for which the Crown has given notice that an adult sentence is being sought for a youth who has reached 14 years of age or for the offences of first- or second-degree murder for a youth who has not yet reached 14 years (s. 67(1)).

In what the government described as a 'bifurcated' approach, the YCJA, at a number of junctures, makes a distinction between the treatment of youth who commit violent offences and those who commit less serious, and nonviolent, offences (Minaker and Hogeveen 2009, p. 78). Regarding sentencing, the prerequisites to custody are set out in s. 39, making it clear that committing an

youth court
The court in which young people charged with an offence under the Criminal Code or the Controlled Drugs and Substances Act appear, in order to enter a plea and then to have their trial or to be sentenced.

young person
A youth aged 12 to 17 years charged under the YCJA with having committed an offence.

offence of violence automatically makes custody a possible sentence for a youth. Further, the sentence of a deferred **custody and supervision order**, which is served in the community and not in a custodial facility, is not available to a youth who has committed a serious violent offence.[5] Finally, when applying for bail, a rebuttable presumption exists, in s. 29(2), that a youth who cannot be sentenced to custody under the act should not be detained on the so-called secondary ground (which questions whether there is a substantial likelihood that the youth will commit another offence or interfere with the administration of justice if released). This means that no rebuttable presumption of release on bail exists when a youth is charged with an offence of violence.[6]

Extrajudicial Measures: Dealing with Less Serious Offences and Less Experienced Young Offenders Outside of Court

A key issue in the youth justice system is whether young offenders without any significant involvement can be diverted from youth court and instead dealt with by so-called **extrajudicial measures**, which were called 'alternative measures' under the YOA. The YOA contained only a general statement of principle (in s. 3) that, where not inconsistent with protection of the public, police or prosecutors should consider either taking no measures (e.g., doing nothing) or taking measures other than judicial proceedings (e.g., informal police warnings). In the YCJA, the declaration of principles respecting extrajudicial measures is much broader. Section 4 of the YCJA states that extrajudicial measures are

- often the most appropriate and effective way to address youth crime;
- able to allow for effective and timely interventions focussed on correcting offending behaviour;
- presumed to be adequate to hold a young person accountable for his or her offending behaviour if the young person has committed a non-violent offence and has not previously been convicted of an offence; and
- [to be] used if they are adequate to hold a young person accountable for his or her offending behaviour and, if the use of extrajudicial measures is consistent with the principles set out in this section, nothing in this Act precludes their use in respect of a young person who: (i) has previously been dealt with by the use of extrajudicial measures, or (ii) has previously been found guilty of an offence.

In addition, s. 5 states that extrajudicial measures should be designed to:

- provide an effective and timely response to offending behaviour outside the bounds of judicial measures;
- encourage young persons to acknowledge and repair the harm caused to the victim and the community;
- encourage families of young persons—including extended families where appropriate—and the community to become involved in the design and implementation of those measures;
- provide an opportunity for victims to participate in decisions related to the measures selected and to receive reparation; and
- respect the rights and freedoms of young persons and be proportionate to the seriousness of the offence.

While alternative-measure programs were the only alternative to court proceedings defined in the YOA, the YCJA formally sets out a number of alternatives, other than laying charges. The range and prominence of front-end options in the YCJA parallel similar developments in New Zealand

custody and supervision order
A period of youth imprisonment followed by a period of community supervision.

extrajudicial measures
A process by which young people who admit responsibility for an offence can be dealt with outside of the court system.

and England (Green and Healy 2003). More specifically, similar to legislation in these countries, s. 6(1) of the YCJA compels a police officer, faced with a young person alleged to have committed an offence and before 'starting judicial proceedings or taking any other measures' under the act, to consider the following: (1) taking no further action; (2) warning the young person; or (3) with the consent of the young person, referring the young person to a program or agency in the community that may assist the young person in ways that help him or her not to commit further offences. Although these options were previously within the discretion of police officers under the YOA, the formalization of these alternatives in the YCJA lends priority to considering approaches other than proceeding to youth court. Another front-end option contained in the YCJA is *the caution*. Specifically, s. 7 of the act provides that the Attorney General of each province may establish a program authorizing the police or prosecutors 'to administer cautions to young persons instead of starting judicial proceedings'.

Greater consideration of front-end options in the Canadian youth justice system came as a result of the reality that, in 2000, less serious offences made up over 40 per cent of youth court cases. Such offences included theft under $5000, possession of stolen property, and failure to appear and failure to comply with a disposition (i.e., breach of probation) (Hogeveen and Minaker 2009, p. 103). Keeping less serious and first-time offenders out of the court system leaves more of the system's scarce resources available to deal with more serious offences.[7]

Rights and Obligations of Young People and Parents under the YCJA

Procedural Protection for Young People

Section 3(1)(b)(iii) of the YCJA provides that the criminal justice system for young people must emphasize 'enhanced procedural protections to ensure that young persons are treated fairly and that their rights, including their rights to privacy, are protected'. In *R. v. R.W.C*,[8] Justice Fish of the Supreme Court of Canada stated that 'in keeping with its international obligations, Parliament has sought as well to extend to young offenders enhanced procedural protections, and to interfere with their personal freedom and privacy as little as possible'.[9] In recognition of the range of procedural protections afforded to Canadian young people, the preamble of the YCJA states that

> WHEREAS Canada is a party to the United Nations Convention on the Rights of the Child and recognizes that young persons have rights and freedoms, including those stated in the *Canadian Charter of Rights and Freedoms* and the *Canadian Bill of Rights*, and have special guarantees of their rights and freedoms; . . .

For the purposes of this discussion, the key sources of procedural protections for young people come from the Canadian Constitution, specifically the Canadian Charter of Rights and Freedoms, and from additional protections set out in the YCJA. A discussion of the procedural protections for young people found under the Charter is an enormous endeavour that goes far beyond the scope of this chapter (see Davis-Barron 2009, ch. 6). The most important protections for youth under the Charter can be summarized as follows:

- *Section 7* provides that 'Everyone has the right to life, liberty and security of the person and the right not to be deprived thereof except in accordance with the principles of fundamental justice'. These rights have been held to encompass the right of a young person to remain silent during the police investigation and the trial, the right to full disclosure from the Crown of the case against the young person, and the right to make full answer and defence in response to a charge.

- *Section 8* provides the right to be secure against unreasonable search and seizure.
- *Section 9* provides the right not to be arbitrarily detained or imprisoned.
- *Section 10* provides the right, on arrest or detention, to be informed promptly of the reasons for being taken into police custody and the right to retain and instruct a lawyer and to be told of this right.
- *Section 11(b)* provides the right to be tried within a reasonable time.
- *Section 11(d)* provides the right to be presumed innocent.
- *Section 12* provides the right not to be subjected to any cruel and unusual treatment or punishment.

In addition to, and at times as an adjunct to, the rights provided for young people under the Charter, the YCJA sets out a series of rights that protect the interests of young people charged under the act. These include the following:

- The presumption that extrajudicial measures will be adequate to hold a young person accountable for his or her offending behaviour if the young person has committed a non-violent offence and has not previously been found guilty of an offence (in s. 4(c)).
- The right, upon arrest, detention, or otherwise being ordered to appear on a charge in youth court, to have a parent or guardian notified about the young person's status before the court (s. 26) and, further, the qualified right to have his or her parent or guardian attend court (as a judge under s. 27 can order such attendance if deemed to be in the best interests of the young person).
- The right to be represented by a lawyer, and the right to be advised of this by the judge at various stages during the proceeding (s. 25(3)). If the young person is not able to obtain a lawyer, the judge can appoint one (s. 25(6)), who, where the interests of parent and child differ, can be a separate lawyer from the parent's counsel (s. 25(8)).
- The right, on first appearance in court, to have the charge read aloud and to receive an explanation of the right of the young person to be represented by a lawyer (s. 32(1)). If the youth does not understand the charge, the judge is obligated to enter a not-guilty plea (s. 32(4)). If the youth is unrepresented and does not understand the charge, the right to plead guilty or not guilty, or the possibility of an adult sentence (if applicable), the judge shall appoint a lawyer to assist the young person (s. 32(3)).
- If denied bail by a justice of the peace (as opposed to a youth court judge) to have that decision reviewed—in effect to have another bail hearing—before a youth court judge (s. 33). This provision is utilized most often in Ontario, where many initial bail hearings for young people are done before a justice of the peace.
- The qualified right to be held in custody separate from adults, including while on remand (s. 84 and s. 30(3)).

Another key protection for young people charged under the act is a restriction on the admissibility of statements given by the young person to a person in authority, such as a police officer. The YOA contained a series of requirements to be met before a young person's statement could be admitted as evidence in a court proceeding.[10] These requirements have been repeated in s. 146 of the YCJA, and prevent admission of such statements unless the statement is voluntary and the person to whom the statement is made has explained, in language appropriate to the age and understanding of that young person, a number of factors. These include the young person's right to silence; that any statement may be used against him or her; his or her right to consult a lawyer, parent, or other adult; and the right to have the person consulted present during the statement. Any waiver of these rights by a young person must be formerly recorded, either on tape or on paper, and signed by the young person.

In *R. v. J.(J.T.)*,[11] the Supreme Court of Canada ruled that a statement that did not comply with the strict requirements of s. 56 of the YOA was inadmissible, regardless of how street-wise the youth was. Apparently in response to this interpretation, the YCJA now allows a youth court, under s. 146(6), to admit a statement into evidence despite a technical irregularity if satisfied that 'the admission of the statement would not bring into disrepute the principle that young persons are entitled to enhanced procedural protection to ensure that they are treated fairly and their rights are protected'. Further, under s. 146(5), a court can accept as valid a waiver of rights not made in strict compliance with the act as long as the court is satisfied that the young person was informed of his or her rights and voluntarily waived those rights.

Parents under the YCJA

parent
Includes any person who is under a legal duty to provide for a young person or any person who has the custody or control of a young person.

The preamble to the YCJA specifically mentions **parents** as a participant in attempts to (1) reduce crime by addressing its underlying causes; (2) respond to the needs of young persons; and (3) provide guidance and support to those at risk of committing crimes. Under specific provisions of the act, parents are given both rights and responsibilities. The rights include the following:

- The right to receive notice from the police when their child is arrested or detained or otherwise summoned to court (s. 26)
- The right to be advised of the sanction when their child is dealt with by way of an extrajudicial sanction (s. 11)
- The right to receive a copy of any document their child is entitled to receive if that youth is the subject of a mental-health proceeding under Part XX.1 of the Criminal Code, such as a psychiatric remand (s. 141(2))
- The right to request that their child, if subject to a custody sentence, be brought before the youth court to review the youth's sentence, subject to minimum time limitations and to grounds for the review set out in the act (ss. 94(3) and (6))

And following are the responsibilities:

- To attend court with their child if so ordered by the youth court judge (s. 27(1)) and, if they fail without reasonable excuse to do so, to be subject to a warrant compelling their attendance or to being punished for contempt of court (s. 27(4) and (5))
- The legal responsibility of complying with any condition placed on that parent by a judge when a youth is released to that parent as a responsible person (s. 31(3)) and potentially to being charged under s. 139(1) for a breach of that condition

Outside of the power to set reasonable conditions on a parent to whom a child is released or the power to order a parent to attend court, a judge has no power under the YCJA to order a parent to follow any course of conduct or programming. That stands in contrast to the situation in England and some states in the United States, where a youth court can order a parent to take part in counselling to help understand adolescent development and to improve parenting skills (Bala and Anand 2009, pp. 155–156). It also stands in contrast to Canadian child-protection proceedings, where, under provincial child-protection legislation, a court could, in appropriate circumstances and when deemed to be in the best interests of the child, order a parent to take specific programming. Nor is there any provision in the YCJA to make parents financially liable to victims for crimes committed by their children. However, some provincial governments—in particular Manitoba, Ontario, and British Columbia—have passed legislation that 'imposes limited civil liability to victims by parents of young offenders' (Bala and Anand 2009, p. 157).

Sentencing under the YCJA

A substantial part of the YCJA deals with sentencing young people. As a result, this section discusses the following:

- Sentencing principles set out in the act
- Variety of sentences available
- Limitations on custody
- Provisions regarding the sentencing of Aboriginal young people
- Circumstances under which a youth can be sentenced as an adult
- Provisions for the community supervision and reintegration of young people

Sentencing Principles

In *R. v. P.(B.W.)*,[12] the Supreme Court noted that the sentencing principles in the YCJA 'have been characterized as "the most systematic attempt in Canadian history to structure judicial discretion regarding the sentencing of juveniles"'.[13] Whereas the YOA contained no separate statement of purpose guiding the sentencing of young offenders, the YCJA states, in s. 38(1), that the purpose of sentencing is to 'hold a young person accountable for an offence through the imposition of just sanctions that have meaningful consequences for the young person and that promote his or her rehabilitation and reintegration into society, thereby contributing to the long-term protection of the public'.

Major changes were made to the Criminal Code sentencing provisions (for adults) in 1996. These amendments included a set of broad-ranging, competing, and at times contradictory, sentencing principles. The YCJA has now adopted this approach, with a detailed set of sentencing principles contained in s. 38(2). These require that

- the sentence must not result in a punishment that is greater than the punishment that would be appropriate for an adult who has been convicted of the same offence committed in similar circumstances;
- the sentence must be similar to the sentences imposed in the region on similar young persons found guilty of the same offence committed in similar circumstances;
- the sentence must be proportionate to the seriousness of the offence and the degree of responsibility of the young person for that offence;
- all available sanctions other than custody that are reasonable in the circumstances should be considered for all young persons, with particular attention to the circumstances of Aboriginal young persons; and

[subject to the principle of proportionality, the sentence must:]

i)   be the least restrictive sentence that is capable of achieving the overall purpose of sentencing in s. 38(1),

ii)   be the one that is most likely to rehabilitate the young person and reintegrate him or her into society, and

iii)   promote a sense of responsibility in the young person, and an acknowledgment of the harm done to victims and the community.

Under s. 38(3) of the YCJA, the youth court, in determining a sentence shall consider:

- the degree of participation by the young person in the commission of the offence;
- the harm done to victims and whether it was intentional or reasonably foreseeable;
- any reparation made by the young person to the victim or the community;
- the time spent in detention by the young person as a result of the offence;
- the previous findings of guilt of the young person; and
- any other aggravating and mitigating circumstances related to the young person or the offence that are relevant to the purpose and principles set out in this section.

Two principles of sentencing *not* contained in the YCJA are deterrence (deterring the youth in question and others from this form of conduct) and denunciation (society's denunciation of the behaviour). Section 50 of the YCJA sets out the adult sentencing principles made applicable to youth under this act. The only sentencing principle listed in s. 50 is from s. 718.2(e) of the Criminal Code, the provision requiring a judge to consider all reasonable alternatives to imprisonment, with particular attention to the circumstances of Aboriginal offenders. In *R. v. B.W.P.; R. v. B.V.N.*, Justice Charon of the Supreme Court of Canada concluded that Parliament's omission of the word *deterrence* was deliberate, and as a result this principle was not incorporated into the YCJA's sentencing regime.[14] Despite the inapplicability of deterrence as a distinct sentencing principle under the act, Justice Charon nevertheless noted that the focus in the act on young people being held accountable in court, together with other specified sentencing principles, may in turn have the effect of deterring a young person or others from committing a crime.[15]

In September 2011, the new Conservative majority government led by Stephen Harper introduced an omnibus crime bill (Bill C-10, The Safe Streets and Communities Act), which included several changes to 'toughen' the YCJA. Included among these was an amendment that would allow judges to include deterrence and denunciation as sentencing principles for youth receiving youth sentences. Whether the inclusion of these sentencing principles in the YCJA will significantly change the sentencing decisions of judges in cases that come before them if this amendment is fully implemented remains to be seen. One reason for this uncertainty is the opposition that the Canadian Bar Association (CBA) voiced when the amendment was first included in changes to the YCJA (Bill C-4) proposed in 2010 by the then Conservative minority government. In expressing its concern about adding deterrence and denunciation to sentencing principles included in the YCJA, the CBA pointed out the following:

> This proposed amendment appears to respond to a previous SCC decision in *R. v. P. (B.W.); R. v. N. (B.V.)* to make youth court sentences more onerous. However, this represents a radical departure from the stated goals of the YCJA as discussed in the Court's decision in *D.B.*, for example. In the *P. (B.W.)* case, the SCC states that omitting 'deterrence' is not a mere oversight but rather an intentional recognition of the fact that it is a controversial theory. There is little evidence that general deterrence is an effective sentencing principle when applied to adult offenders; indeed, it has been criticized in both judicial and academic spheres. It is highly unlikely that it is in any way effective for young persons, considering their diminished capacities. The wording of the current YCJA recognizes this.

Studies show that the principle of 'deterrence' primarily affects one group—judges. Including deterrence in the sentencing principles would suggest to judges that they should impose longer, harsher sentences. But for immature offenders unable to anticipate or appreciate consequences in the same way that adults do, it is particularly troubling that this principle would be grafted onto an otherwise progressive sentencing regime. This amendment would offer judges considering the imposition of a jail sentence a 'peg to hang their coat on', but would go against other sections of the *Act* that clarify that jail should be avoided, and used only as a 'last resort'. Those sections are based on sound social science that shows imposing jail time is generally *not an effective deterrent* as against a young person, which has been proven conclusively over the last seven years. (CBA 2010, p. 7; footnotes omitted)

Regardless of how judges decide to interpret the new amendments to the YCJA introduced in Bill C-10, it is likely that their decisions will result in more legal debate and public controversy among the public, given the varied viewpoints Canadians appear to hold on how youth should be dealt with in the courts. Box 3.1 provides an example of the broader public controversy and debate that existed in Canada leading up to the introduction of bills C-4 and C-10, and the types of divided opinion highlighted in Box 3.1 will no doubt continue to exist in the future.

Box 3.1 Youth Justice in Action

Tory 'Tough-On-Crime' Bill Has Youth Advocates Worried: Legislation Would Alter the Youth Criminal Justice Act's Aim to Incarcerate Only the Most Violent Teens

Globe and Mail, July 18, 2011
By Anna Mehler Paperny

The idea behind Canada's current strategy to fight youth crime was deceptively simple: Put teens in jail if you have to, but only if you have to.

It was supposed to strike a balance between two competing anxieties: that young people were committing heinous crimes and not being punished appropriately; and that locking up impressionable teens created criminals who would spend the rest of their lives bouncing in and out of the penal system.

'There was considerable concern around whether the balance was quite right in terms of protection of the public and rehabilitation,' says Anne McLellan, the Liberal justice minister who brought in the Youth Criminal Justice Act in the late 1990s.

The act was both stricter and more lenient than the preceding Young Offenders Act: It sought to ensure that violent, repeat young offenders were locked up—but that they were the only teens who were. Other offenders would be handed alternative sentences or diverted from the system altogether.

In some ways, the law has succeeded. Since it came into effect in 2003, the proportion of the prison population under the age of 18 has fallen from 10 to 4.6 per cent. But Canada's youth incarceration rates are still considered high—thanks, some argue, to inconsistent application between jurisdictions and a lack of consistent funding for alternative programs.

When it comes to youth justice, argues Simon Fraser University criminologist Ray Corrado, the devil is in the details of the way each province deals with young offenders. British Columbia and Quebec, for example, have historically lower rates of youth incarceration; the rates in the Prairie provinces, and to a lesser extent Ontario, are higher.

'You have to go by province. . . . That sort of distorts the national picture,' Mr. Corrado says. 'Some provinces have done a great job. And the provinces that have high custody rates, they often have a distinctive profile of kids who have huge needs.'

Manitoba's among them. It has a significant aboriginal population and has been struggling with youth gangs. That's what makes child advocate Darlene MacDonald so leery of the federal government's move to change the Youth Criminal Justice Act. Bill C-4, part of the Conservatives' omnibus crime bill to be passed in this government's first 100 days, would expand the crimes for which youth can be incarcerated and the amount of time they might spend in custody.

'The No. 1 way to create more gang members is to keep kids locked up together,' she says. 'That's probably the No. 1 recruitment.'

Part of the problem simply boils down to a lack of cash.

In some places, community-based programs to help reintegrate youth into the community are working well, providing police and prosecutors with alternatives to incarceration. In other places, their records are poor.

'The resources didn't come with the [Youth Criminal Justice Act],' says Ontario youth advocate Lee Tustin. 'In some communities there might be something available. In others, there's not.'

Daren Dougall's job is to make those options available.

Frontenac Youth Diversion, the program he has run out of Kingston, Ont., for almost 40 years, provides alternative programs for youth who've committed crimes—anything from minor property offences to serious assaults.

Officers can send teens Mr. Dougall's way instead of charging them. Or they can serve their sentence in the community, through the program, after they're convicted. The consequences are determined through consultation with police and the victim, among others, and can include compensation or restitution. But the idea is to go a step further.

'In the case of kid-on-kid acts of aggression, they're usually going to be in the same social circle,' Mr. Dougall says. 'We really want to make sure those relationships are repaired.'

When Canada's youth justice system is in the spotlight, it's usually because of extreme, individual cases of kids in serious trouble. When the federal Conservatives introduced Bill C-4 last fall, they named it after Sebastien Lacasse, the 19-year-old whose beating death earned his teenaged killer an adult sentence five years ago.

'It does go to people's underlying values,' Ms. McLellan says. The very concept of young people committing heinous crimes provokes anxieties 'that something more broadly in society has gone wrong.'

It was one of these horror stories that precipitated one of the Youth Criminal Justice Act's most scathing indictments—Justice Merlin Nunn's 2006 report on a Nova Scotia woman killed by a repeat young offender who had just been released from custody despite facing numerous other charges. But damning as Justice Nunn's 378-page report is, it does not find fault with the act itself as much as how it's administered: Too many corners cut, too many under-resourced aspects of the system.

That's what has some critics worried about this latest piece of legislation. Youth advocacy offices for nine provinces and Yukon lobbied Parliament in March to stop discussion on the bill, provide evidence it would actually lower youth crime and improve public safety and, in the meantime, provide adequate funding to non-custody alternatives the Youth Criminal Justice Act was supposed to include. 'Adopting the proposed amendments will not provide the desired public safety outcomes,' the joint submission reads. 'As recent literature points out, increasing incarceration rates does not work.'

(PEI does not have a member on the council that made the submission.)

Ms. Tustin worries the push for laws like this stokes a politicized 'fear of youth.'

'The whole purpose of the [existing] legislation is to reserve custody for those serious and violent and repeat offenders . . . [This act] would enable a court to justify sending any young person to custody.'

Variety of Sentences

Section 42 of the YCJA sets out the potential sentences for young persons. Like the YOA, the YCJA allows a youth court judge to grant a conditional or absolute discharge; to fine the young person; to order the young person to pay restitution to victims of his or her crime; to order the young person to do either personal service for a victim or community service hours; to make an order of prohibition, forfeiture, or seizure against the young person as authorized under any act of Parliament; or to place the young person on probation for up to two years. Section 51 of the YCJA further allows the judge to make a firearms prohibition against the young person for up to two years.

The YCJA, however, provides additional sanctions. A youth court judge can reprimand a young person, which is an oral statement condemning the youth's behaviour. Subject to agreement by the provincial director, a youth may now be ordered into an intensive support and supervision program or may be ordered—assuming the young person is a suitable candidate and that such programming would not interfere with their work or education—to attend a nonresidential program approved by the provincial director over a period not exceeding six months. For a young person convicted of an offence that is not a serious violent offence, the court can make a deferred custody and supervision order that is for a specified period not exceeding six months. This order is similar to a conditional sentence order for an adult under the Criminal Code.

The intensive rehabilitation custody and supervision order (as per ss. 42(2)(r) and 42(7)) provides an option to other available youth sentences, or to an adult sentence, for a youth convicted either of first- or second-degree murder, attempted murder, manslaughter, or aggravated sexual assault or for a youth convicted of a serious violent offence for which an adult is liable to imprisonment for more than two years when that youth has been previously convicted twice of serious violent offences. Such an order may be made, for the same duration as a normal custody and supervision order, if

- this youth is suffering from a mental illness or disorder, a psychological disorder or an emotional disturbance;
- a plan of treatment and intensive supervision has been developed for the young person, and there are reasonable grounds to believe that the plan might reduce the risk of the young person repeating the offence or committing a serious violent offence; and
- the provincial director has determined that an intensive rehabilitative custody and supervision program is available and that the young person's participation in the program is appropriate.

The YOA provided two levels of custody for young persons: open and secure. The appropriate level was to be determined at sentencing by the judge. The YCJA, in s. 85, also requires each province to establish two levels of custody, 'distinguished by the degree of restraint'. According to that section, the decision as to level of custody is to be made by the provincial director, not by the judge. However, s. 88 allows each province, rather than adopting this new process of determining custody levels, to retain the YOA's process of letting the judge determine whether open or secure custody is to be imposed on a young person. While it appears to have been Parliament's intent to allow the provincial director the discretion to make this decision—as that person presumably had the most accurate and up-to-date information on the progress and needs of a young person—the reality is that all provinces and territories chose to retain the previous system (Tustin and Lutes 2005, p. 132).

As a result, youth court judges continue to make this decision, based on section 24.1 of the YOA. In deciding between open custody and secure custody, the judge must consider the following factors:

(a) that a young person should be placed in a level of custody involving the least degree of containment and restraint, having regard to
    (i) the seriousness of the offence in respect of which the young person was committed to custody and the circumstances in which that offence was committed,
    (ii) the needs and circumstances of the young person, including proximity to family, school, employment and support services,
    (iii) the safety of other young persons in custody, and
    (iv) the interests of society;
(b) that the level of custody should allow for the best possible match of programs to the young person's needs and behaviour, having regard to the findings of any assessment in respect of the young person;

(c) the likelihood of escape if the young person is placed in open custody; and

(d) the recommendations, if any, of the youth court or the provincial director, as the case may be.

The total length of a custody and supervision order under the YCJA shall not exceed two years or, if the young person is found guilty of an offence for which the punishment provided by the Criminal Code or any other act of Parliament is imprisonment for life, it shall not exceed three years from the date the order comes into force. These maximums are the same as those that were contained in the YOA. Likewise, the maximum sentences for first- and second-degree murder remain unchanged under the YCJA: ten years for first-degree murder and seven years for second-degree murder (with each sentence including a period of conditional supervision).

Limitations on Custody

Despite calls for a more punitive response toward young offenders in the debate leading up to passage of the YCJA, the act contains language that suggests limiting the scope of custody for young offenders. As noted earlier in this chapter, this change in policy came about because of concern with the overuse of custody. Writing in 1999 in *R. v. J.K.E.*,[16] Chief Judge Lilles of the Yukon Territorial Court recounted the high rates of youth incarceration in Canada, in comparison to other countries:

> Adults are incarcerated at a rate of 130 inmates per 100,000 population in Canada, less than the rate in the United States. Yet Canada incarcerates young people under the age of 18 at a much higher rate than adults, 447 per 100,000. Moreover, this is considerably higher than the corresponding youth incarceration rate of 311 per 100,000 for the United States, 86 per 100,000 for Scotland and 69 per 100,000 for England and Wales . . . Further, more than one-half are incarcerated for property and process offences rather than for offences involving personal injury . . .[17]

As an apparent response to these alarming rates, s. 39(1) states that a youth court shall not sentence an offender to custody unless that young person:

(a) has committed a violent offence;

(b) has failed to comply with noncustodial sentences;

(c) [has committed an indictable offence for which an adult could be jailed for over two years while possessing a history indicating a pattern of criminality; or]

(d) in exceptional cases, has committed an indictable offence, the aggravating circumstances of which are such that the imposition of a noncustodial sentence would be inconsistent with the purpose and principles set out in s. 38.

Not surprisingly, the issue of when a young person can receive a sentence of custody has resulted in much debate. While litigation over s. 39(1) is certain to continue and evolve, to date the following has been determined:

- *Under s. 39(1)(a)*, a 'violent offence' excludes pure property offences and means an offence in the commission of which a young person causes, attempts to cause, or threatens to cause bodily harm (*R. v. D (C.); R. v. K. (C.D.)*, [2005] 3 S.C.R. 668 (S.C.C.)).[18]
- *Under s. 39(1)(b)*, the young person must have failed to comply with two separate noncustodial sentences (Davis-Barron 2009, p. 369).

- *Under s. 39(1)(c)*, the only findings of guilt that the judge can consider in deciding whether a pattern of criminality exists are the convictions entered as of the date of the offence for which the young person is being sentenced. Further, the Crown must generally present evidence of at least three prior findings of guilt, although findings need not relate to similar or to indictable offences (*R. v. S.A.C.* [2008] S.C.J. No. 48 (S.C.C.)).[19]
- *Under s. 39(1)(d)*, 'exceptional circumstances' refer to cases where the circumstances of the offence are so extreme that only a sentence of custody would reflect societal values; hence, the application of this provision is limited to the clearest of cases where a custodial disposition is the only one that can be justified (*R. v. R.E.W.* (2006), 79 O.R. (3d) 1 (Ont. C.A.)).[20]

The wording of s. 39(1) makes clear Parliament's attempt to restrict significantly the number of young people who can be incarcerated for property or other nonviolent offences. Yet even if the restrictions in s. 39(1)(a) to (c) (above) apply, s. 39(2) of the act further restricts the applicability of a custody sentence by requiring the youth court judge, before imposing custody, to consider 'all alternatives to custody raised at the sentencing hearing that are reasonable in the circumstances' and to determine that there is no alternative to custody that is consistent with principles of sentencing set out in the act.

Provisions Regarding the Sentencing of Aboriginal Young People

One of the final amendments to the YCJA before final passage in the House of Commons was made to the principles of sentencing as they relate to Aboriginal young people. Section 38(2)(d) provides that 'all available sanctions other than custody that are reasonable in the circumstances should be considered for all young persons, with particular attention to the circumstances of aboriginal young persons'.

In *R. v. Gladue*,[21] the Supreme Court of Canada interpreted s. 718.2(e) of the Criminal Code, which requires sentencing judges to consider a similar provision for adult Aboriginal offenders. In *Gladue*, Justices Cory and Iacobucci interpreted this subsection as a 'direction to sentencing judges to undertake the process of sentencing aboriginal offenders differently, in order to endeavour to achieve a truly fit and proper sentence in the particular case'.[22] The court considered the 'circumstances of aboriginal offenders' within the context of what was described as the 'tragic history of the treatment of aboriginal peoples within the Canadian criminal justice system'.[23]

Trial courts were directed to pay particular attention to so-called systemic and background factors that may have played a part in bringing an Aboriginal offender before the court. These factors were said to include the effects of poverty, substance abuse, a lack of or the irrelevance of education, and community breakdown.[24] In addition to these factors, however, the Supreme Court outlined the following:

> . . . it must be recognized that the circumstances of aboriginal offenders differ from those of the majority because many aboriginal people are victims of systemic and direct discrimination, many suffer the legacy of dislocation, and many are substantially affected by poor social and economic conditions. Moreover, as has been emphasized repeatedly in studies and commission reports, aboriginal offenders are, as a result of these unique systemic and background factors, more adversely affected by incarceration and less likely to be 'rehabilitated' thereby, because the internment milieu is often culturally inappropriate and regrettably discrimination towards them is so often rampant in penal institutions.[25]

As a result, the court urged judges to seek alternatives to jailing Aboriginal offenders in appropriate circumstances, given their overrepresentation in the prisons of Canada. The search for alternative sentences was to utilize, wherever possible, restorative principles of justice, including healing and rehabilitation and restoration of the relationship between the offender, victim, and community.[26]

The *Gladue* decision was held to apply to young persons under the YOA, despite there being no mention of the circumstances of Aboriginal young people in that act.[27] The specific reference to paying 'particular attention to the circumstances of aboriginal young people' in s. 38(2)(d) makes the *Gladue* decision directly applicable to the sentencing of Aboriginal young people under the YCJA.[28]

The complexity of the issue of overrepresentation of Aboriginal young people in the youth justice system cannot be overstated. The Manitoba Aboriginal Justice Implementation Commission stated that the roots of such overrepresentation are not 'found only in the justice system, but in the broader social setting, and will require concerted action from all three levels of government in Canada'. The Commission also said this:

> Aboriginal people who are at risk of becoming involved in crime often face multiple problems: racism, domestic violence, community violence, poor access to health care and education, inadequate housing and limited employment options. These problems generate hostility, stress and demoralization, and can lead to criminal behaviour. (Chartrand and Whitecloud 2001, p. 135)

The Commission suggested a coordinated crime-prevention approach, addressing all these issues in a co-ordinated fashion.[29]

Despite the goal of reducing the number of Aboriginal young people in custody, recent statistics suggest that the number of Aboriginal youth in custody has actually increased, rather than decreased, since the implementation of the YCJA. The proportion of Aboriginal youth admissions on remand, during 2007/2008, was about four times their representation in the youth population and had increased from 23 per cent in 2004/05 to 25 per cent in 2007/08. Furthermore, the proportion of Aboriginal youth in sentenced custody was more than five times their representation in the population, and, since the implementation of the YCJA, the proportion of Aboriginal youth in sentenced custody had increased from 28 per cent in 2002/03 to 33 per cent in 2007/2008. And yet Aboriginal youth represented only 6 per cent of the youth population in 2007/2008.[30]

Circumstances under Which a Youth Is To Be Sentenced as an Adult

The YOA provided for the transfer of a youth charged under the act to adult court, and hence permitted a youth to be tried as an adult. The YCJA provides that a youth can only be tried in youth court, regardless of the charge, but that in some circumstance a youth can be sentenced as an adult.

A major feature of the YCJA, when put into force, was the definition of so-called presumptive offences—those for which there was a presumption, unless rebutted by the youth, that a youth convicted of such an offence would be sentenced as an adult. These offences, which apply only to a youth who has reached 14 years of age, were defined in s. 2 to include murder, attempted murder, manslaughter, and aggravated sexual assault or, in the alternative, a serious violent offence where the youth has twice before committed such an offence. This presumption, however, was determined to be unconstitutional, as a violation of s. 7 of the Charter, by the Supreme Court of Canada in *R. v. D.B.*[31] As a result, while it is still possible for a youth to receive an adult sentence—for an offence for which an adult would be liable to imprisonment of more than two years and alleged to have been committed after the youth attains the age of 14 years—the onus is on the Crown to show why an adult sentence would be appropriate for the youth.[32]

Provisions for Community Supervision and Reintegration

Section 83 of the YCJA states the purpose of the youth custody and supervision system to be two-fold: (1) to carry out sentences imposed by courts through the safe, fair, and humane custody and supervision of young persons; and (2) to assist young persons to be rehabilitated and reintegrated into the community as law-abiding citizens by providing effective programs to young persons in custody and while under supervision in the community. The principles to be used in achieving that purpose, in addition to the general principles in s. 3 of the act, are said to include the following:

- That the least restrictive measures consistent with the protection of the public and of personnel working with young persons and of young persons be used
- That young persons sentenced to custody retain the rights of other young persons, except the rights that are necessarily removed or restricted as a consequence of a sentence under the YCJA or another act of Parliament
- That the youth custody and supervision system facilitate the involvement of the families of young persons and members of the public
- That custody and supervision decisions be made in a forthright, fair, and timely manner, and that young persons have access to an effective review procedure

While a youth court previously had discretion as to whether or not to place a young person on probation in addition to or as an alternative to custody, the YCJA now provides that any custody sentence be followed by a supervision order, which, in most cases, is one-half as long as the period of custody and contains conditions defined in s. 97. The supervision order—similar to conditional supervision, which formed the latter part of a sentence for murder under the YOA—brings the process of youth custody and release closer to that set out in the Criminal Code and to the associated correctional legislation for adults. An adult offender receives remission or 'good time' usually equal to one-half of the time actually served in jail. After two-thirds of the total sentence, such offenders are to be released on mandatory supervision unless the authorities apply, in limited cases, to have them held in prison until their warrant-of-expiry date, the so-called gating or detention-hearing process. In the case of a young person sentenced to custody for a serious crime of violence—including murder, manslaughter, or aggravated sexual assault—the Attorney General can apply under s. 104 of the YCJA (and similar to the gating provision for adults) to revoke the community supervision part of the sentence. Such an application can be granted where there are reasonable grounds to believe that the young person is likely to commit an offence causing death or serious bodily harm before the end of his or her sentence.

Multidisciplinary Approaches to Youth Justice and Crime Prevention

There is often an interrelation between the supports available to a young person from their family and community, or the lack of these, and the presence of that young person in youth court. In many cases, that interrelation can best be described as a breakdown. Many police officers, lawyers, youth workers, and judges encounter, daily, youth who they believe would be more appropriately dealt with by child-protection or mental-health workers, rather than being processed through the criminal justice system. This has led some commentators to suggest that the criminal justice system has become our society's default system, taking in all those youth that fall between the cracks of other systems and resources (Green and Healy 2003, pp. 70–83).

The Young Offenders Act, in s. 24(1.1)(a), provided that custody should 'not be used as a sub-stitute for appropriate child protection, health or other social measures'. Similarly, the YCJA now provides in s. 29(1) that a young person shall not be detained in custody prior to sentence 'as a sub-stitute for appropriate child protection, mental health or other social measures' and in s. 39(5) that custody shall not be used 'as a substitute for appropriate child protection, mental health or other social measures'. The YCJA, in s. 35, further provides that 'a youth justice court may, at any stage of proceedings against a young person, refer the young person to a child welfare agency for assessment to determine whether the young person is in need of child welfare services'.

While the YCJA clearly evidences an intent that criminal sanctions are not to be used where other social measures would be appropriate, at the same time the drafters of this legislation also foresaw the need for multidisciplinary and wide-ranging approaches to youth justice. The YCJA contains, in its preamble, a statement that 'communities, families, parents and others concerned with the development of young persons should, through multi-disciplinary approaches, take rea-sonable steps to prevent youth crime by addressing its underlying causes, to respond to the needs of young persons, and to provide guidance and support to those at risk of committing crimes'.[33] These multidisciplinary approaches necessitate co-operation among a broad spectrum of people and organizations, including employees working in various services and agencies and other groups and individuals within each community. This approach suggests putting an emphasis on a co-operative view of justice. In a society where public-sector cutbacks have at times become a reality, there is an obvious need to pool resources in attempting to address the causes and effects of crime and, as a result, to provide for safer communities.

The goal of multidisciplinary co-operation within the justice system has, however, proven to be a challenge at times. The extent to which the justice system has remained aloof from the rest of society, in contrast to many other institutions, was questioned by Chief Judge Stuart of the Yukon Territorial Court in R. v. M.N.J.:[34]

> How can a system remain so robust when no one can make the case it is succeeding and everyone can agree it should be doing much better on almost every front? When the evidence for changing to a holistic, coordinated, value-based approach is so overwhelm-ing, how can the justice system remain a jungle of complex, disjointed interactions that preserve numerous self-serving fiefdoms, all with different values, different objectives? When the public has not merely challenged, but penetrated and participated directly in the shaping of other public processes (Education, Health, Environment, Labour Relations, etc.), how has the justice system managed to keep the public at its outer gates, misinformed and ineffective in changing our arcane processes? We have achieved, often despite our best intentions to be otherwise, a level of excellence in maintaining the status quo, despite constant external pressures to change.[35]

As a signal that those employed within the justice system must now be open to new partnerships with other agencies and community members, the general principles of the YCJA state that measures taken against young persons who commit offences should, 'where appropriate, involve the parents, the extended family, the community and social or other agencies in the young person's rehabilita-tion and reintegration'.[36] This provision represents a recognition of the complexity of today's soci-ety, and hence of the need to pool and focus the efforts of people and organizations in providing both services and supports to young people and an increased sense of safety at the local level.

Although there is much to be said about how inter-agency and multidisciplinary approaches to justice can help youths already caught up in the justice system, another significant aspect of this form of co-operation lies in the area of crime prevention—that is, helping young people stay out of court in the first place. In recognition of the importance of this goal and of the interrelationship between the causes of crime and crime prevention, the YCJA provides, as a key principle of interpretation, that the youth criminal justice system is meant to 'prevent crime by addressing the circumstances underlying a young person's offending behaviour.'[37]

And education is a key part of crime prevention. As an example of this, the Manitoba Aboriginal Justice Implementation Commission recognized the interconnectedness of young people, their families, and their communities, and stated that 'there is clear evidence that money spent on early years' education decreases the likelihood of a young person's coming into conflict with the law' (Chartrand and Whitecloud 2001, p. 137).

Conferencing under the YCJA

The YCJA promotes the involvement of a broad cross-section of people and organizations in assisting young people within the youth justice system in general and within youth court in particular. Under the community **conferencing** provisions of this act (in s. 19), a 'youth justice court judge, the provincial director, a police officer, a justice of the peace, a prosecutor or a youth worker may convene or cause to be convened a conference for the purpose of making a decision required to be made under this Act'.[38] These conferences can involve the participation of a variety of people who previously would not have had their voices heard in youth court or elsewhere in the youth justice system.

conferencing
A collaborative and nonconventional approach to decision making in youth court.

The most frequent use of conferencing has been in considering whether a youth is to be released pending completion of a charge (i.e., during the bail stage) or in considering a fit sentence for a young person. Although these conferences may focus on a variety of purposes and results, some of which are not necessarily restorative in nature, this section does provide considerable latitude for the use of restorative practices at different stages of the youth justice process. In a Canadian context, this provision represents a formalization of the conferencing processes a number of courts have already employed through the use of sentencing circles in Aboriginal communities (see Green 1998, Ch. 5).

There are many potential benefits of conferencing. One is allowing voices other than judges, lawyers, and police to enter the youth justice dialogue. In the context of court organization and circle sentencing, Judge Barry Stuart of the Yukon Territorial Court—a pioneer in bringing restorative processes to Canadian courts—explained the need to look outside of status quo court procedures and processes in seeking new approaches to justice, and new alternatives for the participation of offenders, victims, and community members:

> For centuries, the basic organization of the court has not changed. Nothing has been done to encourage meaningful participation by the accused, the victim or by the community. . . . If the objective of the sentencing process is now to enhance sentencing options, to afford greater concern to the impact on victims, to shift focus from punishment to rehabilitation, and to meaningfully engage communities in sharing responsibility for sentencing decisions, it may be advantageous for the justice system to consider how court procedures and the physical arrangements within court-rooms militate against these new objectives.[39]

Under s. 18 of the YCJA, youth justice committees can also act as a conference. These committees—which can be appointed by the federal government or the relevant provincial government—are organizations that can play a part in promoting community-wide consultation and co-operation on youth justice matters. The YCJA provides that the functions of youth justice committees include 'ensuring that community support is available to the young person by arranging for the use of services from within the community, and enlisting members of the community to provide short-term mentoring and supervision' and 'when the young person is also being dealt with by a child protection agency or a community group, helping to coordinate the interaction of the agency or group with the youth criminal justice system'.[40]

Mental Health Issues as a Consideration in Youth Court

The first preamble to the YCJA provides that 'members of society share a responsibility to address the developmental challenges and the needs of young persons and to guide them into adulthood'. Key to addressing these developmental challenges and needs are an understanding of the mental health issues faced by young people who come before the court. Section 34 of the YCJA provides that a judge may, at any stage of proceedings against a young person, require that the young person be assessed by a qualified person who is required to report the results in writing to the court. These assessments may be completed in conjunction with a presentence report (PSR) prepared by a youth worker. Such an assessment can be ordered if the judge believes a medical, psychological, or psychiatric report regarding the young person is necessary for a purpose such as considering a bail application or passing sentence, and if one of the following applies:

> (i) The court has reasonable grounds to believe that the young person may be suffering from a physical or mental illness or disorder, a psychological disorder, an emotional disturbance, a learning disability, or a mental disability.
> (ii) The young person's history indicates a pattern of repeated findings of guilt under this Act or the Young Offenders Act, Chapter Y-1 of the Revised Statutes of Canada, 1985.
> (iii) The young person is alleged to have committed a serious violent offence.

Fetal Alcohol Spectrum Disorder (FASD)

Among the many mental-health issues that appear in youth court, neurological damage and cognitive impairment resulting from prenatal exposure to alcohol has become a significant focus of youth court judges, lawyers, youth court workers, and others employed within the youth justice system. In addition to prenatal exposure to alcohol, a diagnosis of fetal alcohol syndrome (FAS) requires evidence of a delay in growth, a distinctive pattern of facial features, and a central nervous system (or brain) dysfunction (Conry and Fast 2000, p. 1). Fetal alcohol effect (FAE) refers to those young people who have suffered prenatal exposure to alcohol and who meet some but not all of the formal criteria for FAS (Boland et al. 1998, p. 14). Experts in this field stress that FAE 'is not a "milder" form of FAS, and people with FAE have the same risk of developmental and behavioural disabilities as those with FAS' (Conry and Fast 2000, p. 1). The range of cognitive disabilities stemming from prenatal consumption of alcohol has come to be known as **fetal alcohol spectrum disorder** (FASD).

fetal alcohol spectrum disorder (FASD) The range of cognitive disabilities that are caused by prenatal consumption of alcohol by a youth's mother.

The neurological damage resulting from prenatal alcohol consumption is permanent and irreversible, and the effects of FASD are wide-ranging and profound. Judge Mary Ellen Turpel-Lafond of the Provincial Court of Saskatchewan, in *R. v. W. D.*, stated this:

> The prenatal brain damage which causes FAS leaves its victims with neuro-developmental abnormalities such as diminished IQ, fine and gross motor delays, learning disabilities relating to language dysfunction, verbal learning and memory deficits, and behaviour effects such as impulsivity and a failure to learn from mistakes.[41]

The inability of young people suffering from FASD to connect unacceptable behaviour with consequences is of paramount concern. As Judge Henning of the Provincial Court of Saskatchewan stated in *R. v. R.C.P.*, in sentencing an offender diagnosed with a form of FASD (who had spent much of his youthful years either in foster care or in custody), 'socially unacceptable and criminal behaviours may result without any true appreciation of why such behaviour is not acceptable'.[42]

Information gained through assessments ordered under s. 34 or otherwise provided by a youth worker within a presentence or bail report is important to the court as the dangers of incarcerating individuals suffering from FASD cannot be overstated. These include the following:

- A significant risk of being victimized while in custody
- A difficulty in comprehending and following institutional rules, often leading to an inaccurate labelling of such youth as resistant and defiant
- A significant risk of negative influence through association with criminal peer models (Conry and Fast 2000, pp. 69–73)

To show how concerns over the treatment of youth with FASD continue at the forefront of the youth criminal justice system, the Canadian Bar Association recently passed a resolution urging all levels of government to allocate additional resources for alternatives to the current practice of criminalizing individuals with FASD; to develop policies designed to assist and enhance the lives of those with FASD; and to prevent persistent overrepresentation of FASD-affected individuals in the criminal justice system. The resolution also urged the federal government to amend criminal sentencing laws to accommodate the disability of those with FASD.[43] Box 3.2 provides a recent media example of the increased concern over the treatment of young persons suffering from mental health and cognitive disabilities, including FASD, who are caught up in the youth criminal justice system. In particular, this newspaper article highlights the continuing frustration experienced by criminal justice professionals, including lawyers and judges, who are tasked with trying to find services that effectively address the complex treatment needs of young offenders with cognitive and mental-health challenges.

The Public's Right to Know vs. Young People's Right to Privacy

Youth courts in Canada, in many respects, function like adult courts. Members of the public are free to attend the court proceeding, at all stages, subject to a few exceptions. The power of a youth court to exclude any person from the court is set out in s. 132: in effect when the judge considers the presence of the person in question to be unnecessary to the proceeding, and is further of the opinion that: (1) information to be heard in court would seriously injure or prejudice the young person, a youthful witness, or a youthful victim; or (2) excluding any or all members of the public from the courtroom would be in the interest of public morals, the maintenance of order, or the proper administration of justice. This is broader than, but still similar to, the power of an adult court judge to exclude the public (under s. 486(1) of the Criminal Code).

There is, however, a key difference between youth and adult court respecting public access to the proceeding—and that involves the publication of the names of young persons who appear in youth court. This difference has led to much public debate. At the root of that debate stands a conflict between the right to privacy of young people charged or convicted under the act, on the one hand, and 'the public's historic right to know who stands accused in the criminal court rooms of the nation', on the other hand (Davis-Barron 2009, p. 433, and, in general, ch. 9).

Box 3.2 Youth Justice in Action

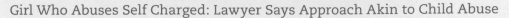

Girl Who Abuses Self Charged: Lawyer Says Approach Akin to Child Abuse

Winnipeg Free Press, January 6, 2011
By Gabrielle Giroday

A 17-year-old girl who was shackled when she tried to harm herself inside a youth prison has since been charged with a weapons breach after cutting herself with a kitchen knife last month.

Corey La Berge, a Legal Aid lawyer for the girl, said he considers the charge against his client a form of child abuse because it harms a vulnerable child.

The girl pleaded guilty to another breach in December after taking over-the-counter sleeping medication in order to hurt herself days before the knife incident, La Berge said.

'We seem to be endorsing criminalization of a young person, a young, vulnerable person for having a disability and mental-health problems,' La Berge said.

'I think what we're doing is we're taking public health problems and turning them into criminal ones. . . . We're using the criminal legal system to address barriers within other systems like mental health [and] Child and Family Services.'

The girl, who cannot be named under the Youth Criminal Justice Act, has suffered abuse and trauma, and is from outside Winnipeg. She also grapples with a cognitive disability and self-harm behaviour such as cutting.

Her breaches of court conditions relate to a conviction for being unlawfully in a dwelling house in March 2009, as well as failing to comply with previous court conditions.

She's banned from having alcohol, drugs or weapons. She is also under a curfew.

La Berge said prosecuting the teen is hurting her. 'It's not serving the public interest in terms of protecting the public, and it's not in her rehabilitative interests.'

A spokeswoman for Manitoba Justice said the Crown cannot comment on a case before the court. 'In every case, they assess whether there's a reasonable likelihood of conviction and whether it's in the public interest to proceed,' said an email.

The issue of mental health among youth in trouble with the law has come to attention in recent months after the suicides of two teenage girls incarcerated at the Manitoba Youth Centre. In the province's throne speech in November, a new mental-health court was promised, based on a family court model.

On Wednesday, Justice Minister Andrew Swan said it hasn't been determined yet whether that court will handle young people facing charges.

'We hope to get the mental-health court up and running and we haven't finalized what [its] parameters are going to be,' he said.

'Obviously, we know there's a substantial number of people involved in the system—both in the youth system and the adult system—that [deal] with mental-health issues.

We're always looking at what other jurisdictions are doing, to see if there are best practices in dealing with people with mental-health issues.'

In July, a 15-year-old girl who had a history of suicidal behaviour died after she hanged herself in one of the Manitoba Youth Centre's cottages.

Last month, a 17-year-old charged with second-degree murder hanged herself at the youth prison. She died at hospital.

Those were the first suicides at the youth jail since 1975.

La Berge's client has been in and out of jail since spring 2010.

Her self-harm behaviours include trying to bite through her lip while she was in jail last summer so she could go to the hospital, her lawyer said.

Under the province's Fatality Inquiries Act, an inquest will be called to look at the circumstances surrounding the two suicides at the youth jail.

In a prepared statement, Louis Goulet, Manitoba Justice's executive director for youth correctional services, said the youth centre is adopting a new program to help teen girls in custody.

'Plans to introduce that are proceeding, and in fact it will be in place as early as the first week of February,' he said.

Source: Gabrielle Giroday, *Winnipeg Free Press*, January 6, 2011.

Subject to a few exceptions, the YCJA (in s. 110(1)) prohibits publication of the name of a young person or any other information that would identify the young person as being dealt with under the act. Further, regarding youth victims or youth witnesses in youth court, s. 111(1) prohibits the publication of any information that would identify the youth as a victim or witness.

One of the exceptions to non-publication of names in the YCJA allows for the publication of the name of a young person sentenced as an adult.[44] This provision follows a similar one in the YOA that allowed for the publication of the names of young persons transferred to adult court. In addition, the YCJA provides in s. 75(3) that a youth court judge has the discretion to allow the publication of the names of youths who receive a youth sentence for 'presumptive offences'. That exception must now be considered in the context of the Supreme Court of Canada decision in *R. v. D.B.*,[45] which found that this section violated s. 7 of the Charter of Rights and Freedoms to the extent that it placed the onus on the young person to show why the publication ban should be maintained. At the least, the onus of dispensing with the ban for these offences now appears to be on the prosecution.

The Preamble of the YCJA states that information about youth justice, youth crime, and the effectiveness of measures taken to address youth crime should be publicly available. However, it appears that both the substantive provisions of the YCJA and judicial interpretation of this issue favour protecting the right to privacy of young people over the public's right to know the name of young people charged or convicted under the act. As an example of the latter, Justice Binnie of the Supreme Court of Canada, in *R. v. F.N.*,[46] stated that '[s]tigmatization or premature "labelling" of a young offender still in his or her formative years is well understood as a problem in the juvenile justice system' and that a 'young person once stigmatized as a lawbreaker may, unless given help and redirection, render the stigma a self-fulfilling prophecy'. Further, Justice Abella of the Supreme Court in *R. v. D.B.*[47] stated that international youth protocols and prevailing judicial comment in Canada recognized 'that lifting a ban on publication makes the young person vulnerable to greater psychological and social stress' and, as a result, that the sentence for such a youth is rendered 'significantly more severe'.[48]

Summary

The YCJA was intended to reduce the overreliance on custody and to reserve custody for the most serious crimes and young offenders. It was also intended to enable youth courts to focus on more serious youth crimes by increasing the use of effective and timely non-court responses—called extrajudicial measures—for less serious (and often nonviolent) offences and for less experienced offenders. Other policy objectives addressed in the act are holding young people accountable for their transgressions, ensuring a proportionate response to the wrongdoing, protecting the public, rehabilitating young people, and allowing for a structured discretion in decision making under the act.

The YCJA contains a distinct legal and sentencing regime for young people, separate and apart from that for adults under the Criminal Code. The YCJA provides enhanced procedural protections for young people charged under the act and, at the same time, establishes both procedural rights and responsibilities for their parents. The act also restricts the publication of the names of young people charged under the act, with a few exceptions that include public access to the name of a youth who is sentenced as an adult.

Unlike the YOA before it, the YCJA now has a separate statement of the purpose and principles of sentencing. This includes a provision that all available sanctions other than custody that are reasonable in the circumstances be considered for all young people, with particular attention to the circumstances of Aboriginal young people (the so-called *Gladue* clause for Aboriginal young people). The possible sentences under the act include a discharge, a reprimand, a restitution order, a fine, a deferred custody and supervision order, open or closed custody, an intensive support and supervision program order, and an intensive custody and supervision order.

Because of the goal of reducing the use of custody, a custodial sentence can only be a possibility if the youth has (1) committed a violent offence; (2) failed to comply with noncustodial sentences; (3) committed an indictable offence for which an adult could be jailed for over two years while possessing a history indicating a pattern of criminality; or (4) in exceptional cases, committed an indictable offence, the aggravating circumstances of which are such that the imposition of a non-custodial sentence would be inconsistent with the purpose and principles of sentencing in the act.

The YCJA draws a distinction between criminal procedures or sanctions, on the one hand, and other interventions—such as child protection, mental health, or other social measures—on the other. Custody is not to be used as a substitute for these later social interventions either pending sentence or as a sentence in itself. The YCJA further allows a judge, at any stage of the proceedings, to refer a young person to a child-welfare agency for assessment to determine whether the young person is in need of child-welfare services. While the act, in effect, draws a distinction between criminal and non-criminal interventions, the YCJA nevertheless encourages multidisciplinary approaches to youth justice, seeking to encourage the coordination of resources to support a young person and the co-operation of various players within the justice and youth court system

Conferencing is a nonconventional approach to decision making recognized in the YCJA. In particular, conferencing can be used when a youth court judge is considering whether to release a young person on bail or considering a fit sentence for a youth. Conferences may be restorative in nature and involve a cross-section of participants that would not normally be heard from in youth court.

The mental health of young people is a key consideration for judges in youth court. The YCJA provides a means to obtain a professional assessment of a range of mental-health challenges a young person may have. Of particular concern is fetal alcohol spectrum disorder. A young person with FASD suffers from a multiple of deficits, including difficulties in cognition and an inability to learn from his or her mistakes and is generally at a greater risk than other youth of being victimized.

Key Terms

conferencing

custody and supervision order

extrajudicial measures

fetal alcohol spectrum disorder (FASD)

parent

young person

youth court

Review Questions

1. What were the policy issues and concerns that the federal government sought to address through passage of the YCJA?

2. What are the procedural protections for young people under the YCJA?

3. What are the issues that arise in the sentencing of a young person under this act?

4. What are the factors a youth court should consider in dealing with a young person diagnosed with fetal alcohol spectrum disorder?

Critical Thinking Questions

1. Are the YCJA's overriding sentencing goals of accountability, on the one hand, and rehabilitation, on the other, conflicting?

2. Should there be a separate justice system for young people? If so, why?

3. Can you give some examples of how custody could be used as a substitute for appropriate child-protection measures, health measures, or other social measures?

4. What are the benefits of a youth court using a conference as opposed to the conventional court proceeding?

Suggested Readings

Bala, N. and Anand, S. (2009). *Youth criminal justice law*. Toronto: Irwin.

Bala, N., Carrington, P., and Roberts, J. (2009). Evaluating the Youth Criminal Justice Act after five years: A qualified success. *Canadian Journal of Criminology and Criminal Justice, 51*(2), 131–67.

Davis-Barron, S. (2009). *Canadian youth and the criminal law*. Markham, ON: LexisNexis Canada.

Minaker, J. and Hogeveen, B. (2009). *Youth, crime, and society: Issues of power and justice*. Toronto: Pearson.

Jones, B. (2009). Meaningful consequences? Sentencing and the Youth Criminal Justice Act. 62 *Criminal Reports (6th)*, 233–46.

Tustin, L. and Lutes, R. (2005). *A guide to the Youth Criminal Justice Act*. Toronto: Lexis-Nexus Butterworths.

Suggested Weblinks

Department of Justice: The Youth Criminal Justice Act: Summary and Background

www.justice.gc.ca/eng/pi/yj-jj/YCJA-lsjpa/back-hist.html

- A summary and background of the YCJA.

Department of Justice: Research and Analysis

www.justice.gc.ca/eng/pi/yj-jj/res-rech/res-rech.html

- Research and reports on various youth justice topics.

Canadian Legal Information Institute: Youth Criminal Justice Act

www.canlii.org/en/ca/laws/stat/sc-2002-c-1/latest/sc-2002-c-1.html

- Various versions of the act from its passage in 2002.

The John Howard Society: The Youth Criminal Justice Act Handbook

www.johnhoward.ab.ca/pub/youthcrim/youth.pdf

- A description of the YCJA.

John Howard Society of Ontario: Fact Sheet

www.johnhoward.on.ca/pdfs/FactSheet_26_FASD_and_the_Criminal_Justice_System.pdf

- FASD and the criminal justice system.

Department of Justice: Youth Criminal Justice Act

http://laws.justice.gc.ca/en/Y-1.5

- The text of the YCJA.

Endnotes

1. Portions of this chapter are taken or adapted from *Tough on Kids: Rethinking Approaches to Youth Justice* (Purich Publishing, 2003), with the consent of Purich Publishing and my co-author, Kearney Healy.

2. House of Commons Debates, 14 February, 2001, p. 704. The full quotation, with an analysis, can be found in Jones 2009.

3. House of Commons Debates (14 February, 2001): 1530, in Davis-Barron, 2009, p. 66.

4. [2008] 2 S.C.R. 3, par. 41.

5. Section 2 of the act defines a 'serious violent offence' as 'an offence in the commission of which a young

person causes or attempts to cause serious bodily harm'. Bill C-10, introduced in Parliament in September 2011, amends the definition of 'serious violent offence' to mean the offences of first- or second-degree murder, attempted murder, manslaughter, or aggravated sexual assault.

6. Bill C-10 eliminates the rebuttable presumption of release and, as a result and in effect, broadens the offences for which a youth may well be detained in custody while maintaining the onus on the Crown to show why the youth should be detained.

7. Bill C-10 also contains an amendment that police officers shall keep a record of any extra-judicial measures they use to deal with a young person. This amendment, in turn and based on another amendment in the bill, may be used in considering whether the youth may be sentenced to custody on a subsequent charge because changes to s. 39(1)(c) in this bill now allow custody to be considered where the youth has a pattern of convictions or extrajudicial sanctions.

8. (2005), 201 C.C.C. (3d) 321 (S.C.C.).

9. At par. 41.

10. In s. 56.

11. [1990] 2 S.C.R. 755, 79 C.R. (3d) 219, 59 C.C.C (3d) 1.

12. (2006), 38 C.R. (6th) 1 (S.C.C.).

13. Ibid, par. 19.

14. [2006] 1 S.C.R. 941, par. 23.

15. Ibid, par. 4. For a full discussion of the purpose and principles of sentencing under the YCJA, see Bala, Carrington, and Roberts 2009.

16. [1999] Y.J. No. 119 (Yukon Ter. Ct.).

17. Ibid, par. 60.

18. Bill C-10 includes a definition of violent offence, which is an offence committed by a young person that includes an element of the causing of bodily harm, or an attempt or threat to commit such an offence, or an offence in the commission of which a young person endangers the life or safety of another person by creating a substantial likelihood of causing bodily harm.

19. Ibid, p. 375. However, Bill C-10 redefines the pattern as being comprised of either extrajudicial sanctions or findings of guilt under the YCJA.

20. Ibid, p. 377. See Davis-Barron, generally, at pp. 357–383, regarding the interpretation of s. 39(1).

21. [1999] 1 S.C.R. 688.

22. Par. 33.

23. Par. 34.

24. Par. 67.

25. Par. 68.

26. Par 74 and 93.

27. See *R. v. J.K.E.*, [1999] Y.J. No. 119 (Yukon Youth Ct.).

28. See *R. v. T.D.P.*, [2004] 3 C.N.L.R. 318 (Sask. Youth Ct.).

29. Ibid.

30. Taken from a PowerPoint presentation entitled Youth Justice under the YCJA: 2003–2010, by Richard Barnhorst (Department of Justice, Canada) on April 15, 2010, at an educational conference of the British Columbia Provincial Court Judges Association in Victoria.

31. [2008] S.C.J. No. 25.

32. However, Bill C-10 includes a provision requiring the Crown to consider whether a youth should be sentenced as an adult for a serious violent offence committed after the youth reached the age of 14 years.

33. This is contained within the second Whereas in the Preamble.

34. [2002] Y.J. No. 49 (Yukon Territorial Court).

35. At par. 129.

36. Section 3(1)(c)(iii).

37. In s. 3(1)(a)(i).

38. In s. 19(1).

39. *R. v. Moses* (1992), 71 C.C.C. (3d) 347 (Yuk. Ter. Ct.), 355-356.

40. In subsections 18(2)(iii) & (iv).

41. [2001] S.J. No. 70 (QL) (Sask. Yth. Ct.) at par. 25.

42. [2000] S.J. No. 373 (QL) (Sask. Youth Ct.).

43. Resolution passed by the Council of the Canadian Bar Association at the Annual Meeting held in Niagara Falls, Ontario, August 14–15, 2010.

44. In s. 110(2)(a). However, Bill C-4, introduced in Parliament in April 2010, includes a provision requiring the youth court to consider allowing the publication of the name of a young person convicted of a violent offence and receiving a youth sentence.
45. Supra note 4, par. 95.
46. 146 C.C.C. (3d) 1.
47. Supra note 4.
48. Par. 85–87.

References

Anand, S.S. (1999). The good, the bad, and the unaltered: An analysis of Bill C-68, the Youth Criminal Justice Act. *Canadian Criminal Law Review, 4,* 249–70.

Bala, N. and Anand, S. (2009). *Youth criminal justice law.* Toronto: Irwin.

Bala, N., Carrington, P., and Roberts, J. (2009). Evaluating the Youth Criminal Justice Act after five years: A qualified success. *Canadian Journal of Criminology and Criminal Justice, 51*(2), 131–67.

Barnhorst, R. (2004). The Youth Criminal Justice Act: New directions and implementation issues. *Canadian Journal of Criminology and Criminal Justice, 46*(3), 231–50.

Boland, F., Burrill, R., Duwyn, M., and Karp, J. (1998). Fetal alcohol syndrome: Implications for correctional service [unpublished: July, 1998].

Canadian Bar Association. (2010). Submission on Bill C-4 *Youth Criminal Justice Act* amendments. Ottawa: Canadian Bar Association, National Criminal Justice Section.

Chartrand, P. and Whitecloud, W. (2001). *Aboriginal Implementation Commission: Final report and recommendations.* Winnipeg: Statutory Publications Office.

Conry, J. and Fast, D. (2000). *Fetal alcohol syndrome and the justice system.* Vancouver: Law Foundation of British Columbia.

Davis-Barron, S. (2009). *Canadian youth and the criminal law.* Markham, ON: LexisNexis Canada.

Green, R. (1998). *Justice in Aboriginal communities: Sentencing alternatives.* Saskatoon: Purich Publishing.

Green, R. and Healey, K. (2003). *Tough on kids: Rethinking approaches to youth justice.* Saskatoon: Purich Publishing.

Jones, B. (2009). Meaningful consequences? Sentencing and the Youth Criminal Justice Act. 62 *Criminal Reports* (6th), 233–46.

Minaker, J. and Hogeveen, B. (2009). *Youth, crime, and society: Issues of power and justice.* Toronto: Pearson.

Tustin, L. and Lutes, R. (2005). *A guide to the Youth Criminal Justice Act.* Toronto: Lexis-Nexus Butterworths.

4 Implementing Youth Justice Reform: Effects of the Youth Criminal Justice Act

Nicholas Bala, Peter J. Carrington, and Julian V. Roberts*

Overview

This chapter explores the impact of the YCJA on youth crime and on the justice system in Canada. After providing some contextual material, we describe the most important elements of the legislation. We then present and interpret data that reveal how the YCJA has changed the way that the justice system responds to young persons in conflict with the law. The result has been a decrease in the use of courts and custody, with no apparent increase in youth crime. The chapter concludes with a summary of recent amendments to the YCJA (Bill C-10).

Key Objectives

After reading this chapter, you should be able to:

- Understand the context for Canadian youth justice reform.
- Be familiar with Supreme Court of Canada decisions interpreting the YCJA.
- Understand the effect of the YCJA on youth crime in Canada.
- Understand the effect of the YCJA on diversion from youth court.
- Understand the effect of the YCJA on youth custody.
- Understand the effect of the YCJA on pre-trial detention.
- Be familiar with the Conservative government's concerns about the YCJA and be aware of the recent amendments to the act.

Introduction

In this chapter, we review the first seven years of implementation (2003–2009) of the Youth Criminal Justice Act (YCJA), with a particular focus on issues related to police decision-making, **diversion** from court, sentencing, and the use of custody. We examine the salient provisions of the act, especially those relating to diversion and sentencing, and discuss Supreme Court of Canada (SCC) decisions interpreting the YCJA. We also present statistical data from the first six years under the YCJA, including data on youth justice caseloads at several stages in the system, culminating in rates of young persons in custody. The chapter concludes with a brief discussion of continuing controversy about the YCJA, and some of the recent amendments to the act.

diversion

A justice-system practice, procedure, or program that substitutes an informal response to offending for a formal response, thus diverting people out of the formal justice system.

The Context for Canadian Youth Justice Reform

Although enacted with the unanimous support of Parliament, the Young Offenders Act (YOA) became a highly controversial statute soon after it came into force in 1984. While conservative politicians criticized the law for being 'soft on youth crime', there were also concerns about the increase in the use of courts and custody under the YOA. The result was that by the early years of the millennium Canada had one of the lowest rates of youth diversion and one of the highest rates of youth custody in the world (Canada 2002; Doob and Sprott 2004). Successive federal governments responded to these criticisms by enacting amendments to the YOA in 1986, 1992, and 1995 and, finally, by having a parliamentary committee review the act in 1998.

In 2002 the then Liberal government enacted a completely new statute to replace the YOA, the Youth Criminal Justice Act (YCJA), which came into force in 2003. The most prominent objectives of the YCJA were to address the two major concerns about the YOA: to reduce the use of courts and custody for the majority of adolescent offenders, and to improve the effectiveness of the responses to the relatively small number of young offenders convicted of serious crimes of violence (Canada 2002). Although the provisions set out in the YCJA to achieve these intended purposes have already been reviewed in detail in Chapter 3, we will discuss those purposes further in this chapter. We will show how implementing specific provisions of the YCJA has affected young offenders and the operation of the Canadian youth criminal justice system since 2003.

In many ways the YCJA represented an astute political compromise. The legislation attempted to address continuing public anxiety about a relatively small number of highly publicized cases involving the most violent youth offenders (as exemplified in Box 4.1), while also responding to the growing concerns of juvenile justice professionals, advocates for youth, and academic critics about the large numbers of youth being processed through the courts and placed in custody. At the time that the YCJA was introduced, a prominently publicized aspect of the act was the provisions intended 'to respond more firmly and effectively to the small number of the most serious, violent young offenders' in order to respond to the 'disturbing decline in public confidence in the youth justice system' in Canada (Canada 1999). The provisions of the YCJA that facilitate imposing adult sentences for the most serious offenders addressed these concerns. However, the preamble to the YCJA itself made it clear that the act was intended to address Canada's 'over-reliance on incarceration' for young offenders.

Box 4.1 Youth Justice in Action

Public Reaction to Serious Violent Crime by Juveniles

One source of pressure on the government to 'get tough' with young offenders is public opinion. Members of the public tend to call for harsher youth court sentencing every time a high-profile crime of violence is reported in the news media. A number of such high-profile cases have generated public concern in recent years. For example, the killing of a vulnerable victim (Reena Virk) by a group of teenagers in British Columbia led to calls for harsher sentencing. News media coverage of this and other cases has generated public criticism of the youth justice system. However, systematic research into public views of youth court sentencing generally shows that when people are asked to sentence young offenders and are given an adequate amount of information about the case, they become far less punitive. So while public opinion polls suggest that the Canadian public simply want harsher sentencing for young offenders, more sophisticated public opinion research shows considerable public support for community-based sentences (see Roberts 1997; Roberts and Hough 2005).

Reducing the Use of Courts and Custody

Relative to other Western nations, the use of juvenile custody in Canada was high under the YOA (e.g., Bala and Anand 2009; Doob and Sprott 2004; Doob and Cesaroni 2004). Most scholars agreed that the YOA provided little real guidance either for the exercise of police discretion in laying charges or diverting youth from the formal court process (see Carrington 1999; Carrington and Schulenberg 2003), or for judges sentencing youth to custody (e.g., Anand 1999b; Doob and Sprott 2004). This lack of guidance may have contributed to the relatively low diversion rates and high rates of youth custody, as well as to the substantial variation across jurisdictions in Canada with respect to the use of courts and custody.

The over-use of courts and custody is generally acknowledged to be more problematic at the juvenile level than the adult level as involvement in the formal justice system and imprisonment can have more profound and deleterious effects on adolescents. Community-based responses represent a cost-effective way to deal with juvenile offenders, especially those who have committed less serious offences and who do not have an extensive history of offending. Juveniles' experiences of imprisonment are often more damaging, especially for first offenders, than adults' experiences because they are less able to cope with penal sequestration, and they may be more susceptible to the negative effects of the inmate subculture (Cesaroni and Peterson-Badali 2005). Further, even though there is generally a greater emphasis on **rehabilitation** in youth custody facilities, imprisonment deprives adolescents of the social milieu on which they depend for their moral and psychological development and this may increase the likelihood of school failure, a well-established contributor to delinquency (Howell 1997).

While there is a need to imprison some adolescent offenders, the inappropriate use of custody is expensive, ineffective, and inhumane, and may contribute to a cycle of reoffending. For example,

rehabilitation

A penological theory that an offender can be returned by appropriate programs to a state of non-offending; also, practices and programs based on that theory.

research has suggested that the deeper a young person penetrates into the youth justice system, the less likely he or she is to desist from further offending (see McAra and McVie 2007; Laub and Sampson 2003). Thus, one of the goals of any youth justice system—encouraging desistance and reducing reoffending—can be impeded by the use of more intensive forms of intervention, such as custody.

Accordingly, early in the new millennium the federal government set as a primary goal of its reform a reduction in the number of juveniles being sentenced to custody (Canada 2002). The clarity of the government's position at that time with respect to the goal of the legislation played an important role in significantly reducing the number of admissions to youth custodial facilities. This level of clarity for sentencing legislation has rarely been achieved before in Canada. A Royal Commission on Sentencing (Canada 1987) and a number of academics (e.g., Anand 1999a; Manson 2001) recommended that Canada adopt formal sentencing guidelines for adult offenders. Despite the use of guidelines in many other common-law jurisdictions, Canadian governments have rejected this approach although the recent introduction of additional minimum sentences for adult offenders (Bill C-10) has reduced judicial discretion in adult sentencing.

The YCJA and Supreme Court Judgments

The discussion that follows summarizes the major provisions of the YCJA that deal with sentencing and diversion and reviews Supreme Court of Canada (SCC) jurisprudence interpreting the act. The SCC has affirmed that the YCJA requires that custody is to be used as a 'last resort' for adolescent offenders, and has thereby contributed to the reduction in the use of custody. The SCC has also emphasized that youth are to be treated differently from adults, and has ruled unconstitutional provisions of the YCJA that created a **presumption** that youths found guilty of the most serious offences would receive adult sentences, thus limiting the effect of provisions of the act directed at serious violent offenders.

The preamble to the YCJA makes clear the intent of Parliament that Canada should 'have a youth criminal justice system that reserves its most serious interventions for the most serious cases and reduces the over-reliance on incarceration for non-violent young persons'. In its 2005 decision in *R. v. C.D.*,[1] the SCC cited the preamble as a justification for adopting a 'narrow' interpretation of the term 'violent offence', restricting the possibilities for utilizing s.39(1)(a) to impose a **custodial sentence**. Similarly, in *R. v. B.W.P.*,[2] the SCC cited the preamble as a justification for ruling that general **deterrence** is not a legitimate consideration in the sentencing of adolescents under the YCJA. According to the principles spelled out in Section 3 of the act, rehabilitation is as important as preventing crime and imposing meaningful consequences upon the offender. Further, the long-term protection of the public is seen as the consequence of rehabilitation and accountability, rather than as an independent objective of the youth justice system. Importantly, the YCJA directs judges to impose sentences that facilitate the rehabilitation of young offenders rather than those that will merely incapacitate them.

The Declaration of Principle of the YCJA also articulates a set of principles for responding to young offenders that places the greatest emphasis on the proportionality of the response, with s.3(1)(c) emphasizing that 'fair and proportionate' accountability is the central principle for responding to youth offending. The principles recognize, however, that it is to be a limited accountability in comparison to adults, 'consistent with the greater dependency of young persons and their reduced level of maturity'. Judicial concerns about heightened vulnerability and limited accountability of adolescents are illustrated by *R. v. R.W.C.*,[3] the first SCC decision interpreting the YCJA, where the court ruled that 'young offender' status is a mitigating factor when deciding how to apply the provisions of s. 487.051 Criminal Code that governs taking a DNA sample from a person found guilty of a primary designated offence. These concerns are also reflected in the 2008 SCC decision in *R. v. D.B.*,[4] which held unconstitutional those provisions of the YCJA that create a presumption of adult

presumption

A rule of law that permits a court to assume something is true until such time as there is evidence that disproves (rebuts) the presumption.

custodial sentence

A sentence that is served in a custodial facility; under the YCJA this may be an open or a closed facility.

deterrence

A penological theory that criminal sanctions will discourage people from committing crime; a penological practice based on that theory.

sentencing for the most serious offences (for more detailed discussion of these Supreme Court decisions, see Chapter 3).

The YCJA encourages the diversion of cases from youth court, providing for both **extrajudicial measures** and **extrajudicial sanctions**. In a growing number of Canadian communities, extrajudicial sanctions programs have been established to deal with minor violent youth offences through, for example, victim–offender reconciliation or family group conferencing. Such programs may result in an apology to the victim, restitution, community service, or counselling for the offender (Bala 2003; see also Box 4.2). While the YCJA encourages police and prosecutors to make greater use of diversionary programs, it also makes it clear that the decision of police and prosecutors to lay charges and send a matter to youth court rather than divert a case is not subject to judicial review (ss.3(1)(d)(i) and 6(2)). Although a judge may informally signal that a case should be diverted or may impose the mild sentence of a reprimand for a case that should have been diverted, the success of the diversionary provisions of the YCJA is dependent on the attitudes and policies of police and prosecutors, and on the availability of community-based alternatives to youth court. There is substantial variation across the provincial policies and in local attitudes and community programs, but the introduction of the YCJA was accompanied by transitional federal government funding to encourage the establishment of more community-based programs for responding to youth offending. In addition, at the time of implementation of the YCJA the federal government funded a number of professional educational initiatives directed at police and prosecutors, which were intended to encourage the use of community-based responses to youth offending.

Trends in Youth Justice and the Impact of the YCJA

The next part of this chapter presents statistical data bearing on trends in youth justice both before and after the enactment of the YCJA. It is our argument that these data provide quite clear evidence of the impact the YCJA has had to date on the treatment of youth in the Canadian youth criminal justice system.

1. Youth Crime Statistics

Canadians have long been concerned with the problem of youth crime (Carrigan 1998, p. ix et passim), and one popular fear has been that the introduction of the YCJA, by reducing the use of custody and by increasing the use of alternatives to a criminal charge, would encourage more offending. It is important, therefore, in the contemporary context, to assess whether the YCJA had this possible unintended effect.

The top line in Figure 4.1 shows that the **rate per 100 000** of youth identified by police as **chargeable**—generally known as the **recorded youth crime rate**—has decreased slightly since the YCJA came into effect. Although the rate fluctuated during the 1990s, it was almost constant from 2000 to 2007 at about 8000 per 100 000—the same level as in the late 1980s—and then decreased to about 7600 per 100 000 by 2009. The slight decline in recorded youth crime since 2003 has two major implications. First, it demonstrates that the YCJA has not resulted in an increase in recorded youth crime. Second, since the per capita rate of youth **apprehended** by police did not increase, and in fact decreased slightly, any 'downstream' decreases in numbers of court cases or custodial populations following the introduction of the YCJA must be due to changes in the functioning of the youth justice system.

Box 4.2 Youth Justice in Action

Youth Criminal Justice Act: s. 6, Police Options Checklist for Police Officer

1. Do you have *reasonable grounds to believe* that the youth has committed an offence?

    - If you do not, then you should not continue with this checklist.
    - If yes, then you may continue with this checklist.

    Note: you should ensure that you have advised the youth of his or her right to counsel and afforded him or her access to counsel wherever that is required during any exercise of police procedures or powers with respect to this incident.

    Before Starting Judicial Proceedings or Considering an Extrajudicial Sanction, a police officer must consider whether it would be sufficient to administer one of the measures listed in section 6: take no further action, warn, caution, or refer the young person.

    Note: you should be aware that you may use a conference where you think it might assist you in decision-making in this part of the process.

2. An extrajudicial measure is often the most appropriate, effective and timely response to criminal conduct by youth.

    In this instance, you should consider using one of the measures listed in section 6 (take no further action, warn, caution, or referral), unless there are *clear indications* that this would not be adequate to hold the youth accountable for his or her conduct.

3. If this is a non-violent, first offence by this youth, an extrajudicial measure is presumed to be adequate to hold the youth accountable for his or her conduct.

    Do you believe that the youth has committed a non-violent offence and has not previously been found guilty of an offence? If so, you must consider using one of the measures listed in section 6 unless there are *exceptional circumstances* that indicate it would not be adequate to hold the youth accountable for his or her conduct.

4. You may choose between one of four measures in order to hold the youth accountable for his or her offence. You may choose

    - to take no further action against the youth,
    - to give the youth a warning,
    - to issue a caution to the youth, or
    - to refer the young person, with his or her consent, to a program or agency in the community that may assist him or her not to commit offences.

The measure that you use should be applied fairly and be proportionate to the offence. You should use the least restrictive measure that will hold the youth accountable, ensuring the minimum intervention warranted to respond to the conduct. The measure should always be less than one a court would impose for this conduct should the youth have been tried and found guilty of the offence.

Within the limits of fair and proportionate accountability, the measure should be designed and applied with the following principles and objectives in mind

- emphasize timeliness (ensuring the measure is applied with as close a link to the conduct as possible, to help the youth understand the relationship between action and consequences)
- be an effective intervention
- promote the rehabilitation of the youth
- offer meaningful consequences to the youth
- encourage the youth to acknowledge harm he or she may have caused
- encourage the youth to repair harm he or she may have caused
- involve the family of the youth
- respect the youth's rights, and especially any special protections or guarantees of rights applying to youth

Source: Department of Justice Canada, *Youth Criminal Justice Act: Resource Manual for Police*. Ottawa: Department of Justice Canada, 2003.

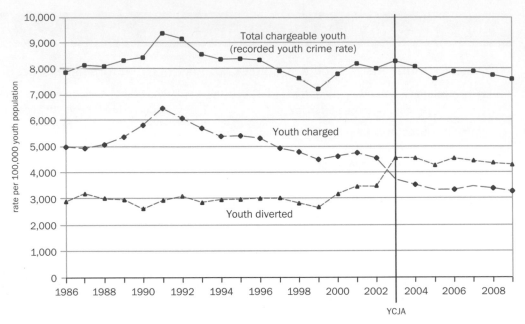

Figure 4.1 Rates of Police-Reported Youth Crime, Youth Charged, and Youth Cleared Otherwise, Canada, 1986–2009

Source: Statistics Canada, Canadian Centre for Justice Statistics, Uniform Crime Reporting Survey.

2. Rates of Charging and Rates of Diversion

You will recall that one of the explicit goals of the YCJA was to increase the use of diversion and reduce the rate at which youth in conflict with the law were charged. Did the legislation achieve this objective?

The YCJA has clearly resulted in a significant drop in the number of youth charged by police, as well as an increase in the use of various methods of police diversion. Figure 4.1 shows the changes from 1986 to 2009 in the rates per 100 000 of youth who were charged and diverted by police. In 2003, the year that the YCJA came into effect, the rate of youth charged by police dropped by 18 per cent from the previous year—from 4557 per 100 000 to 3740—and the rate of youth dealt with by alternatives to charging (diverted) increased by a similar amount. For the first time since youth justice statistics began to be collected, more youth apprehended by police were dealt with by alternatives to charging than by criminal charges. Since 2003, the rates of youth charged and diverted have both decreased slightly, consistent with the small decrease in the number of chargeable youth, and show no signs of returning to their pre-YCJA levels.

charge ratio
The proportion of chargeable persons who were charged.

In Figure 4.2, the relative levels of the rates of youth charged and diverted are summarized in one statistic. The **charge ratio** indicates the relative degree to which police are clearing cases by charge rather than by alternatives to charging. This indicator declined gently from 1991 to 2002. Since 2003 the charge ratio dropped by one-fifth from 57 per cent to 45 per cent charged, and has fluctuated between 42 per cent and 44 per cent since then. This reflects a substantial and ongoing increase in the diversion by police of apprehended young people from the formal court process, using other 'extrajudicial' responses to their alleged criminal behaviour.

Regional Variation in Charging Practices

Table 4.1 shows the percentage of chargeable youth who were charged in the five regions of Canada for three years. Under the YOA, the charge ratio increased substantially in Ontario and decreased

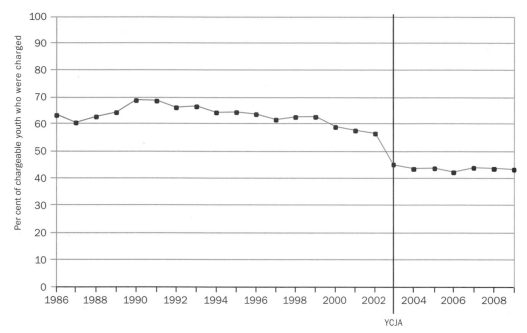

Figure 4.2 The Proportion of Chargeable Youth Who Were Charged, Canada, 1986–2009

Data source: Statistics Canada, Canadian Centre for Justice Statistics, Uniform Crime Reporting Survey.

in the other regions so that Ontario went from having the lowest charge ratio in 1986 to the highest in 2002. In 2002, regional charge ratios ranged from 38 per cent in British Columbia to 70 per cent in Ontario: a spread of 32 per cent. By 2009, charge ratios had dropped in all regions but most markedly in Ontario, reducing the regional spread to 15 per cent. Thus the YCJA appears not only to have caused a substantial increase in the use of alternatives to charging but also to have caused a considerable reduction in regional differences in the use of alternatives to charging.

Changes over time in the per capita rate of cases in youth court reflect changes in the numbers of youth charged (see Figure 4.1). As a whole, there was a gentle decline from fiscal 1991/92 to 2002/03, followed by a sharp drop when the YCJA came into effect in 2003/04, a further drop in 2004/05, and then relative stability. Roughly similar patterns are evident in Ontario and the Atlantic region. In Québec, the per capita rate of youth court cases over the entire period was much lower, reflecting that province's unique system of pre-court screening. In Québec, the rate of youth court cases hardly changed from 1991/92 to 2002/03, but decreased somewhat in 2003/04 and then levelled off. Per capita rates of youth court cases in the Prairies and British Columbia declined substantially during the decade before 2003 and continued to decline at about the same rate until 2004/05, bringing the rate in British Columbia down to the level in Québec. Thereafter, the rate of youth court cases was stable in British Columbia but increased somewhat in the Prairie region. Thus the main impact of the YCJA on the use of youth court appears to have been in the Atlantic region and Ontario, with a much smaller impact in Québec, and little to no impact in the Prairies and British Columbia, where forces other than the YCJA appear to have been at work since at least the early 1990s.

3. Restrictions on Use of Pre-Trial Detention

As noted earlier, the YCJA contains provisions intended to reduce use of **remand custody**. Here the legislation appears to have been less successful than it was in reducing use of court and custody.

remand custody

The practice of holding a person in a custodial facility before or during his or her court appearance(s); also known as *pre-trial detention*.

Table 4.1 Charge Ratios by Region, 1986, 2002, and 2009

Region	1986	2002	2009
Canada	63.3	56.8	43.4
Atlantic	63.1	54.9	38.9
Québec	**79.9**	46.5	38.3
Ontario	**56.9**	**69.9**	**47.9**
Prairies	66.3	58.8	47.1
British Columbia	59.1	**37.8**	**32.6**
Spread	23.0	32.1	15.3
Standard deviation	9.1	12.2	6.5

Notes: Cell entries are the per centage of chargeable youth who were charged.
The highest and lowest values for each year are in bold font.
'Spread' refers to the difference between the highest and lowest values.
Data source: Statistics Canada, Canadian Centre for Justice Statistics, Uniform Crime Reporting Survey.

pre-trial detention

The practice of holding a person in a custodial facility before or during his or her court appearance(s); also known as *remand custody*.

rebuttable presumption

A presumption that can be disproved by evidence to the contrary.

Section 29(1) of the YCJA specifies that **pre-trial detention** shall not be used as a 'substitute for appropriate child protection, mental health or other social measures'. Section 28 of the YCJA makes it clear that a youth should only be detained before sentencing in circumstances in which an adult could be detained, generally on the primary grounds of ensuring attendance in court, or on secondary grounds if detention is 'necessary for the protection or safety of the public', or because there is a 'substantial likelihood' of offending or of witness intimidation (s.515(10) Criminal Code). Further, s. 29(2) creates a **rebuttable presumption** that detention on the secondary grounds—that is, for the protection or safety of the public—should occur only if the youth could receive a custodial sentence under the YCJA s. 39(1)(a) to (c).

It is difficult to assess the impact of the YCJA on national rates of youth in remand custody because data are not available for Ontario prior to 2003/04—and Ontario accounts for almost half the national total number of young persons in remand custody in Canada. Omitting Ontario, there was a decrease in the number of youth in remand custody in Canada in 2003/04, but it was preceded by decreases of similar magnitude in 2002/03 and in 1998/99 and 1999/2000; and was followed by increases in 2006/07, 2007/08, and 2008/09. By 2008/09, the rate of youth in remand custody had returned to its level in 1998/99. The rate of remand custody in Québec—already relatively low—dropped by about one-quarter in 2003/04 and has remained at the new lower level since then.

There is no evidence of decreases in the use of pre-trial detention under the YCJA for youth in the other regions; in fact, there are recent substantial upward trends in the Atlantic and Prairie regions. Regional variations, then, persist, and in some cases are increasing. In 2008/09, on a per capita basis, more than five times as many youth were in remand custody in the Prairie region as in Québec.

4. Impact on Sentencing

reintegration

The re-entry of an offender into society.

As discussed in Chapter 3, the YCJA articulates the purpose of sentencing in youth court, and then sets out specific principles of youth sentencing. Section 38(1) states that 'The purpose of [youth court] sentencing . . . is to hold a young person accountable for an offence through the imposition of just sanctions that have meaningful consequences for the young person and that promote his or her rehabilitation and **reintegration**'.

The omission of reference to deterrence in the YCJA statement of sentencing purpose, as originally enacted, may have contributed to lowering the number of custodial sentences imposed in youth court (Cesaroni and Bala 2008). Its absence in the act, in contrast to the Criminal Code, suggests that general and specific deterrence are not to be objectives of sentencing in youth court. A number of early judgments under the YCJA emphasized the absence of explicit mention of deterrence as a reason for imposing a **noncustodial sentence** (Roberts and Bala 2003). In 2006, in one of the first cases under the new act, the Supreme Court of Canada rendered a unanimous decision in *R. v. B.W.P.*[5] to uphold a trial decision that emphasized the importance of rehabilitation. In this case, the SCC discussed the role of deterrence in sentencing, observing that for adults 'general deterrence is factored in the determination of the sentence, the offender is punished more severely, not because he or she deserves it, but because the court decides to send a message to others who may be inclined to engage in similar criminal activity'. The SCC recognized that under the previous statute, the YOA, general deterrence had been an objective of sentencing youths, albeit to a lesser extent than for adults. The court accepted, however, that the YCJA established 'a new sentencing regime' for young offenders in Canada. The Supreme Court also recognized that while general deterrence should not be an objective in sentencing youth offenders, the fact that a youth is to be held accountable in youth court undoubtedly has 'the effect of deterring the young person and others from committing crimes'.

> **noncustodial sentence**
> A sentence that is served in the community (and therefore, not in a custodial facility); also known as a *community-based sentence.*

The Effect of Section 39 of the YCJA

Under the former legislation, the YOA, a judge could not commit a young offender to custody unless the court considered 'a committal to custody to be necessary for the protection of society having regard to the seriousness of the offence and the circumstances in which it was committed, and having regards to the needs and circumstances of the young person' (s.24(1)). This vague provision offered little real guidance as to when youths should be imprisoned even though it was accompanied by a direction to exercise restraint in imposing custodial sentences. This lack of clear sentencing guidelines tailored to young offenders may account for the fact that adolescent custody rates were among the highest in the world (Canada 2002). At the adult level there are no specific offence-based criteria that must be met before an adult offender is imprisoned, and this was similarly the case under the YOA. In contrast, the YCJA provisions relating to the imposition of a custodial sentence in youth court are far more restrictive, with s. 39(1) establishing four 'gateways'[6] to custody:

1. The level of violence entailed in the offence
2. The young person's failure to comply with noncustodial sentences
3. A prior history of committing offences for which an adult could receive a sentence of more than two years
4. Exceptional cases where a young person has committed a serious indictable offence (see Chapter 3).

Thus there are only four circumstances in which a young offender may be committed to custody. Significantly, in its first sentencing decision under the YCJA, *R. v. C.D.*, the Supreme Court held that s. 39(1) should be 'narrowly construed', emphasizing that this provision should be interpreted in a manner that is consistent with the intent of the act, as set out in the preamble, in a way that restricts the use of custody.[7] The SCC held that the offence of dangerous driving, involving a high-speed police chase of a youth in a stolen vehicle, was not a 'violent offence' as it did not involve actual bodily harm or the intent to cause harm; accordingly, a youth found guilty of this offence could not receive a custodial sentence.

Section 39 is likely a cause of the reduction in the use of custody since under the YOA there were significant numbers of young offenders who were imprisoned but who fell outside any of the four conditions now identified by the YCJA as justifying imprisonment. It is noteworthy that a youth can receive a custodial sentence for **breach of probation** or some other **community-based sentence** only if the youth has breached a previous community-based sentence. Under the YOA, a significant portion of custodial sentences were imposed for breach of probation; although this still occurs under the YCJA, it is less common. Further, apart from exceptional circumstances or where a youth has previously failed to comply with noncustodial sentences, a nonviolent offence can result in a custodial sentence only if the offence is reasonably serious (i.e., an offence for which the maximum adult sentence is greater than two years) and there is a 'history that indicates a pattern of findings of guilt' (s. 39(1)(c)).

In 2008, the SCC again emphasized the need to narrowly construe the sentencing provisions of the YCJA, ruling that the provision regarding a prior history of committing offences generally requires a minimum of three prior judicial findings of guilt.[8] If the case before a youth court satisfies one of the four conditions in s. 39(1), a number of other custody-related principles must still be considered before a court can imprison the young offender. The first restriction is a clear reminder to judges in s. 39(2) of the principle of restraint with respect to the use of custody, even if one of the conditions of s. 39(1) is satisfied:

> if [one of the criteria for custody] apply, a youth justice court *shall not impose a custodial sentence* . . . unless the court has considered all alternatives to custody raised at the sentencing hearing that are reasonable in the circumstances, and determined that there is not a reasonable alternative, or combination of alternatives, that is in accordance with the purpose and principles [of sentencing at the youth court level]. (emphasis added)

A second principle to be observed before a custodial sentence is imposed is designed to discourage judges from escalating the severity of the sentence in response to subsequent offending. Section 39(4) attempts to constrain this judicial practice, providing that 'The previous imposition of a particular non-custodial sentence on a young person does not preclude a youth justice court from imposing the same or any other non-custodial sentence for another offence'. While this provision does not prohibit judges from following the 'step principle' logic at sentencing, the provision does mean that the same alternative sanction may be imposed on consecutive occasions.

A third principle that restricts the use of custody is more clearly binding on youth court judges, with s. 39(5) explicitly stating that a youth court 'shall not' use custody as a substitute for a child protection, mental health, or other social measure. Under the YOA, a common justification for imposing a custodial sentence was that the judge could see no other way of providing the necessary social intervention for an adolescent at risk. Under the YCJA, this justification for the imposition of custody is prohibited.

Finally, a youth court is obliged, prior to imposing custody, to consider a pre-sentence report prepared by a probation officer as well as any sentencing proposal made by the young offender or his or her counsel. The YCJA also permits a judge to convene a conference or refer a case to a community-based conference before imposing a sentence. This step might facilitate receiving advice from family or community members, or could allow for a victim–offender meeting before sentencing (s. 41).

Section 39(9) requires youth court judges who impose a term of custody to provide reasons why 'it has determined that a non-custodial sentence is not adequate' to achieve the purpose of sentencing ascribed to the youth court system. This is yet another provision of the YCJA that creates a condition to be satisfied before the imposition of a custodial term in youth court.

New Community-based Sentences

In order to encourage judges to sentence fewer youths to custody, the YCJA created a number of new community-based sanctions at the youth court level. Some of these new sentences, such as nonresidential orders and intensive supervision and support, are intended to provide youth with more supervision and support in the community. These new sentences may only be imposed where the provincial government decides to provide services. Although significant efforts have been made to establish these services in all provinces, there has been little recorded use of the sentence of intensive supervision and support outside of British Columbia. Of the 470 recorded sentences of intensive supervision and support in Canada in 2008/09, 385 were in British Columbia (Milligan 2010, Table 11, p. 36).

The most significant community-based sentence introduced by the YCJA was the **deferred custody and supervision order (DCSO)**, which the court can impose even without special programming being introduced by a provincial government. This sentence allows the court to permit the youth to remain in the community for the duration of the order, subject to supervision by probation officers. In the event of an apprehended breach of the terms of release, the youth may be immediately placed in custody for the balance of the sentence without the prior necessity of another court hearing before apprehension, although there may be a review after the youth has been returned to custody. This sentence can be imposed for a period of up to six months, provided that the youth has not committed a serious violent offence. The DCSO is only to be imposed if the court concludes that a custodial sentence is warranted. This new sanction represents the last opportunity for the court to spare the offender committal to custody.

Youth court sentencing statistics show that the DCSO has been imposed in about 4 per cent of sentenced cases each year, with wide provincial variations (Milligan 2010: Chart 5, pp. 13–14). Although it is not possible to be certain, it would appear that this sentence is generally being used as intended: that is, in cases where a custodial sentence would otherwise have been ordered rather than in cases where probation would otherwise have been ordered (Carrington and Roberts 2011). Thus the DCSO appears to have had a 'decarcerating' effect, not a 'net-widening' effect.

Custody and Community Supervision

As under the YOA, the maximum custodial sentence that may be imposed under the YCJA is three years, except for murder which is ten years. Under the YOA, juveniles sentenced to custody generally remained in an institution until the end of the sentence unless a judicial review modified the sentence. (Under the YOA, no conditional release mechanism like parole existed for juvenile prisoners.) In practice, however, judicial review under the YOA was cumbersome to arrange and did not regularly occur; further, when review hearings were held, some judges were reluctant to modify a previously imposed sanction (Bala and Anand 2009).

Under the YCJA, all custodial sentences are composed of custodial and community phases; for all but the most serious offences, the first two-thirds of the sentence is served in custody and the last third under supervision in the community. For the most serious offences, there is judicial discretion about how to divide the sentence between custody and community supervision, and for all custodial sentences there is the possibility of judicial review to allow early release or continued detention after the presumptive release date. Further, for all but the longest sentences a period of supervision under probation may follow the completion of the sentence of custody and supervision.

The YCJA also introduced the sentence known as intensive rehabilitative custody and supervision order (IRCS). The IRCS order allows a court to confine a youth to a mental health facility or to approve an individual plan that includes confinement and treatment; however, it does not allow for involuntary medical treatment. This sentence may only be imposed on a juvenile offender who has committed one of a small number of very serious offences and who is suffering from a psychological disorder. As a result of the statutory restrictions on their use, very few of these orders are made—so few, in fact, that they are not reported by Statistics Canada.

Figure 4.3 shows changes over time in the use of custodial sentences in youth court, as indicated by two statistics. The rates per 100 000 show the number of custodial sentences, standardized by

deferred custody and supervision order (DCSO)

In the YCJA, a community-based alternative to a custodial sentence, under which the young person will serve his or her sentence in the community under a set of strict conditions. If these conditions are not followed, the young person may be sent to custody to serve the balance of that sentence.

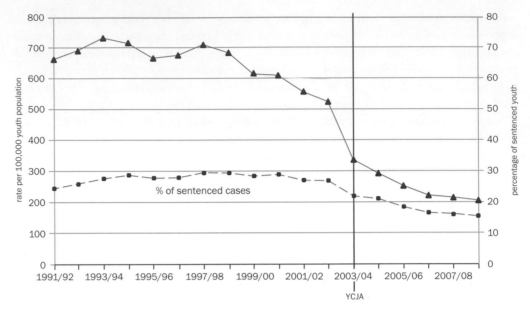

Figure 4.3 Rates and Proportions of Custodial Sentences in Youth Court, Canada, 1991/92–2008/09

Data source: Statistics Canada, Canadian Centre for Justice Statistics, Youth Court Survey.

population, and reflect any changes in the number of cases coming to court, in the proportion of cases with a finding of guilt, and in sentencing patterns. The proportions of sentenced cases show the use of custodial sentences, standardized by the total number of sentences handed down, and reflect only changes in custodial sentencing itself. Both indicators show a decline after the YCJA came into force.

The per capita rate of custodial sentences dropped by 36 per cent in 2003/04, and by a further 25 per cent over the following five years. These dramatic declines reflect both the decrease in the proportion of custodial sentences handed down and the decrease, as noted earlier, in the volume of cases coming to youth court. As a result, the rate of custodial sentences handed down in youth court in 2008/09 was less than half of the rate in 2002/03 (206 vs. 524 per 100 000).

The proportion of sentenced cases receiving a custodial disposition also dropped: from 27 per cent in 2002/03 to only 15.4 per cent in 2008/09. Due to police diversion of less serious cases (see above), the cases reaching court under the YCJA were, on average, more serious; thus, the observed reduction in the proportion of custodial sentences is strong evidence for the effectiveness of the provisions of the YCJA that restrict the use of custodial sentences.

Regional Variation

Table 4.2 shows regional variations in the proportions of sentenced cases receiving a custodial sentence in three years: fiscal 1991/92, which was early in the YOA sentencing regime; 2002/03, the last year of the YOA; and 2008/09. While the use of custodial sentences has decreased substantially in all regions under the YCJA, the difference between Ontario and the other regions remains substantial.

As a result of the decrease in the volume of cases coming to youth court and in the proportion of cases with a finding of guilt that received custodial sentences, the per capita rate of youth admitted in **sentenced custody** in Canada also decreased dramatically after the YCJA came into force in 2003: by 60 per cent from 2001/02 to 2003/04 and a further 13 per cent to 2008/09. On a per capita basis, only about one-quarter as many youth were admitted in sentenced custody in 2008/09 as in 2001/02. In

sentenced custody
Being held in a custodial facility as a result of a court sentence (as opposed to *remand custody*).

Table 4.2 Custodial Sentencing Ratios by Region, 1991/92, 2002/03, and 2008/09

Region	1991/92	2002/03	2008/09
Canada	24.3	26.9	15.4
Atlantic	25.8	**32.2**	12.7
Québec	26.4	21.2	12.0
Ontario	**29.7**	28.1	**20.3**
Prairies	19.6	**23.9**	**11.3**
British Columbia	**18.4**	31.6	15.6
Spread	11.3	8.3	9.0
Standard deviation	4.8	4.3	3.7

Notes: Cell entries are the per centage of cases sentenced in youth court that received a custodial sentence.

The highest and lowest values for each year are in bold font.

'Spread' refers to the difference between the highest and lowest values.

Source: Statistics Canada, Canadian Centre for Justice Statistics, Youth Court Survey.

2008/09, more than four times as many youth were admitted in remand custody (14 198) as in sentenced custody (3334). It may be that some youth who actually received a custodial sentence under the YCJA had been remanded in custody on a pre-trial basis, and the sentence eventually imposed was 'time served', which for reporting purposes is not included as a custodial sentence.

With decreasing numbers of youth sentenced to custody, the average daily rate of youth in actual custody also decreased dramatically after the YCJA came into force (see Figure 4.4): by 43 per cent in 2003/04 and a further 24 per cent over the following five years. On a per capita basis, only one-third as many youth were in custodial institutions on an average day in 2008/09 as in 2002/03 (35 vs. 106 per 100 000). In contrast, the average daily rate of youth in remand custody does not appear to have been affected by the YCJA. Pre-YCJA data are not available for Ontario (see above), but in the rest of the country the level of remand custody was just as high in 2008/09 as it was a decade earlier. As a result of the continuing decrease in the number of youth in sentenced custody, the proportion of youth in custodial facilities who were on remand increased from less than one-quarter (23 per cent) in 2002/03 to more than one-half (52 per cent) in 2008/09. The number of youth in **pre-adjudication** remand custody on an average day in 2008/09 in Canada was 981—somewhat more than the 899 youth in sentenced custody.

pre-adjudication
Occurring before adjudication.

The large decrease in youth in sentenced custody in 2003/04 and subsequent smaller decreases are reflected in all five regions: with drops in 2003/04 of 45 per cent in the Atlantic region, 27 per cent in Québec, 53 per cent in Ontario, 31 per cent in the Prairie region, and 41 per cent in British Columbia. There is no evidence of regional convergence in numbers of youth in sentenced custody: in fact, there has been a small divergence. Over the past 12 years, British Columbia and Québec have had similar low rates, while the Atlantic and Prairie regions have had similar high rates. On a per capita basis, in 1997/98 about 2.5 times as many youth were in sentenced custody in the Prairies and Atlantic regions as in Québec; by 2008/09 the sentenced **incarceration rate** in the Prairies was 3 times as high as in British Columbia. In Ontario, rates of youth in sentenced custody were similar to those of the Atlantic and Prairie regions before the YCJA came into effect, and have fallen much closer to those in British Columbia and Québec since then. Thus, there are still large regional variations under the YCJA in the extent of the sentenced incarceration of youth.

incarceration rate
The rate (usually per 100 000) of persons in custodial facilities on an 'average' day of the year; it is the sum of the sentenced custody and the remand custody rates.

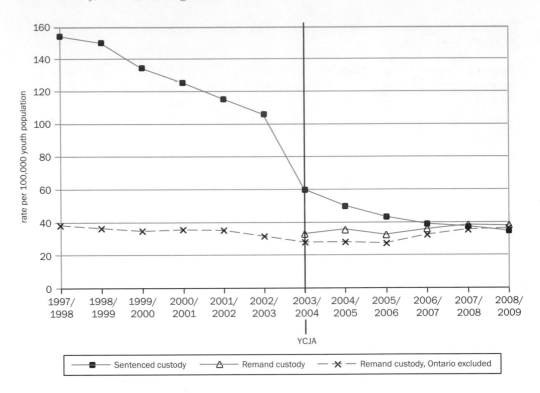

Figure 4.4 Average Daily Rates of Youth in Sentenced and Remand Custody, Canada, 1997/98–2008/09

Note: Due to missing data, the Northwest Territories and Nunavut are omitted from all series.

Data source: Statistics Canada, Canadian Centre for Justice Statistics, Corrections Key Indicators Report. Table 251-0008.

The sum of youth in sentenced custody and in remand custody is the total youth incarceration rate: the per capita rate of incarcerated youth on an 'average' day of the year. Regional and national trends in youth incarceration are shown in Figure 4.5. Since the rate of remand custody in Ontario prior to 2003/04 is not known, both the Ontario and Canada series begin in 2003/04. The reductions in 2003/04 in the incarceration rate in the four regions are similar to, but less pronounced, than those in the sentenced custody rate. They are more modest because of the minimal changes in 2003/04 in the remand custodial rates. However, the drops in 2003/04 in total youth incarceration are still substantial: 41 per cent in the Atlantic region, 26 per cent in Québec, 24 per cent in the Prairie region, and 30 per cent in British Columbia.

Regional variations in the incarceration of youth actually increased after the YCJA came into effect. In 1997/98, the rate in the Prairies was 2.7 times as high as in Québec. This ratio changed little until 2004/05, after which it began to increase steadily as youth incarceration decreased in Québec and increased in the Prairies. By 2008/09, on a per capita basis, 3.9 times as many youth were incarcerated in the Prairie region as in Québec (and 3.4 times as many as in British Columbia). This widening in regional variations is not necessarily due, or entirely due, to the YCJA as it did not begin until 2004/05, but it is clear that the YCJA did not result in a decrease in regional variations in the incarceration of youth.

Sentencing Young Offenders as Adults

While much of the YCJA was intended to reduce the use of courts and custody for less serious young offenders, the YCJA also included provisions to facilitate sentencing of the most serious young

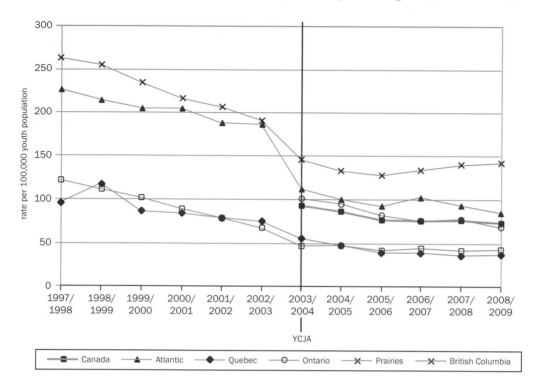

Figure 4.5 Youth Incarceration Rates, Canada and by Region, 1997/98–2008/09

Note: The Canada series omits the Northwest Territories and Nunavut, due to missing data. The Ontario and Canada series are not shown prior to 2003/04, due to missing data for Ontario.

Data source: Statistics Canada, Canadian Centre for Justice Statistics, Youth Key Indicators Report. Table 251-0008.

offenders as adults (Bala 2006). The YCJA changed the process from that under the YOA by abolishing the pre-**adjudication** transfer hearing that could result in a trial in adult court and adult sentencing. The YCJA provides that the decision about whether to impose an adult sentence is to be made at a **post-adjudication** hearing, just prior to sentencing, with the court having full awareness of the circumstances of the offence and offender. This allows for a more expeditious and fairer process for deciding whether to impose an adult sentence.

In 1995 the YOA was amended to create a presumption of transfer in certain cases, placing an onus on 16- and 17-year-old youths charged with the most serious offences (murder, attempted murder, manslaughter, or aggravated sexual assault) to satisfy a judge why they should not have an adult court trial and sentencing. The YCJA expanded the concept of the **presumptive offence**, placing onus on a youth found guilty of the same four presumptive offences to satisfy the court why an adult sentence should not be imposed, and added to the list of named 'presumptive offences' cases in which a youth is found guilty of a third 'serious violent offence' (a variation on the 'three strikes' sentencing laws for adult offenders in some American states). The YCJA also lowered to 14 years the age at which the onus was on a youth found guilty of a presumptive offence to justify not being subject to an adult sentence.[9]

There were a number of conflicting court of appeal decisions on the constitutionality of s.72(2) of the YCJA, which placed an 'onus' on a youth found guilty of a 'presumptive offence' to satisfy the court why an adult sentence should not be imposed.[10] In May 2008 the Supreme Court of Canada resolved the controversy, ruling in *R. v. D.B.* that it is a violation of the 'principles of fundamental justice' and s. 7 of the Canadian Charter of Rights and Freedoms to have presumptive offences.

adjudication

The making of the decision by a court as to the guilt of the accused person. A person may also be adjudicated not guilty or not criminally responsible due to a mental disorder.

post-adjudication

Occurring after adjudication.

presumptive offence

Under the YCJA, an offence for which, if a young person is found guilty, there is a presumption of an adult sentence.

The SCC accepted that it is a principle of fundamental justice that young people are entitled to a presumption of 'diminished moral blameworthiness' or culpability flowing from the fact that, because of their age, they have heightened vulnerability, less maturity, and a reduced capacity for moral judgment. (See Box 4.3 for an example of a case in which the age of the accused was taken into consideration in sentencing.) The presumption of an adult sentence in s. 72(2) is inconsistent with the principle of fundamental justice that young people are entitled to a presumption of diminished moral culpability. The SCC made clear that the Charter does not preclude imposing an adult sentence on a young person as the seriousness of the offence and the threat to society posed by the youth may require an adult sentence.[11] However, the Charter requires that the Crown must always justify imposing an adult sentence on a youth.

If an adult sentence is imposed, s. 76 of the YCJA creates a presumption that a young person who is under 18 years of age at the time of receiving the adult sentence will be placed in a youth custody facility, with provisions for transfer to an adult facility upon reaching the age of 18. However, the sentencing court may order that a youth who is under the age of 18 and who is subject to an adult

Box 4.3 Youth Justice in Action

An Adult Sentence? The Bathtub Girls Murder

One of the first reported decisions dealing with the question of whether to impose an adult sentence was the highly publicized 'bathtub girls murder' case. It involved two sisters, aged 15 and 16 years of age at the time of their crime (Mitchell 2008). The girls lived with their mother, who was divorced and an alcoholic. The girls were embarrassed and very angry about their situation, and decided to kill their mother. There was some financial motivation for the crime as the girls expected to collect on their mother's life insurance policy, but the primary motivation was the girls' anger and resentment at their mother's alcohol-influenced attitude toward them and her behaviour around them and their friends.

With the assistance of some friends, the girls searched the internet to find out how to kill a person, leaving as little evidence as possible. One evening the girls drugged their mother's drink and invited her to take a warm bath, and then held her head under water to drown her. They then went out with some friends for dinner, and when they came back home made a 911 call, hysterically asking for an ambulance. The police and EMS workers rushed to the scene, where the girls were crying about the 'accidental' drowning of their mother. After the funeral, the girls went to live with their father's family.

There was no police investigation at that time, but the girls told a few friends at school what they had done. Word spread quickly among the student body at their high school, and literally hundreds of youth

had some knowledge of the crime, but it took almost a year for any of them to report it to the police. The girls were eventually taped discussing the crime with a friend, who had agreed to help the police, and the mother's body was then exhumed and a forensic investigation conducted.

Although the girls pled not guilty, there was a great deal of evidence to support their conviction for first-degree murder, including extensive email discussions with friends before, after, and even during the commission of the crime. The Crown sought an adult-length sentence, but Justice Duncan decided to impose a youth sentence. He explained that s. 72 of the YCJA requires a judge to impose a youth sentence unless the Crown can satisfy the court that this sentence would be insufficient to hold the youth 'accountable'. He explained:

The issue then becomes whether the blend of considerations—the aggravating and mitigating circumstances of the offence, age, background . . . and those considerations and principles in section 38—are such as to render this case exceptional and to take it outside of the range where the youth sentence can hold the offender to account—again, importantly, keeping in mind that we are talking about 'fair and proportionate accountability' that is consistent with the greater dependency of young persons and their reduced level of maturity. ([2006] O.J. 2982) sentence be placed in an adult facility if this is in the 'best interests' of the young person or necessary to ensure 'the safety of others'. If a person was a youth at the time of the offence and receives a life sentence for murder, there will be eligibility for parole at an earlier date than for an adult, reflecting the limited accountability of even those youth convicted of the most serious offences.

There are no reliable data on adult sentencing of youth under the YCJA although, based on the reported case law, it is clear that adult sentences are rarely imposed and only for the cases involving the most serious offences, and for youth who have a history of violence and who seem unlikely to be rehabilitated by a youth sentence (Bala 2007).

Recent Reforms: Bill C-25 and Bill C-10

Despite the YCJA's success in achieving its principal objective of reducing youth sentenced custody rates, youth justice issues remain controversial in Canada. Concerns about the continued high rate of use of pre-trial remand custody remain, and it has been suggested that there could be further legislative reforms to reduce the use of remands (Canada 2007). On the other hand, the Conservative government has a 'get tough on crime agenda', which clearly includes changes to the sentencing provisions of the youth court process (Campion-Smith 2008). In 2007 the government introduced Bill C-25, which included provisions to amend the YCJA by adding 'denunciation' and 'deterrence' as principles of youth sentencing (Cesaroni and Bala 2008). This bill was not enacted prior to the 2008 election, but in the period before the election, Conservative prime minister Stephen Harper denounced Canada's approach to handling young offenders as 'an unmitigated failure', in that it did not 'hold young lawbreakers responsible for their behaviour and . . . make them accountable to their victims and society'.[12] The Conservative Party's 2008 election platform policy on youth crime went beyond the limited amendments in Bill C-25. That platform included adding deterrence and denunciation as sentencing principles, but also went on to propose 'automatic, stiffer sentences for persons 14 and older convicted of serious and violent crimes' as well as provisions that would allow increased publication of the names of serious young offenders. While there is some public support for 'toughening' the law, the other political parties rejected the Conservative approach during the 2008 election campaign on the basis that such an approach would not reduce youth crime. Particularly strong opposition came from the Québec-based Bloc Québécois (Galloway 2008; Kari 2008; Canadian Broadcasting Corporation 2008). However, in the months leading to the Canadian federal election in May 2011, and since then under a Conservative majority government in Ottawa, several changes to 'toughen' the YCJA have been introduced that will have a significant effect on the operation of the youth criminal justice system.

In March 2010, the Conservative government re-introduced amendments to the YCJA in Bill C-4,[13] and in September 2011, it incorporated these amendments into its post-election-victory omnibus crime bill (Bill C-10, The Safe Streets and Communities Act). Some of the most important changes to the YCJA included in Bill C-10 are highlighted in Box 4.4.

Significantly, Bill C-10 proposes to add denunciation and specific deterrence as principles of youth sentencing. The bill, when enacted, will also expand the definition of *violent offence*, reversing the effect of the Supreme Court decision in *R. v. C.D.*,[14] to allow for the imposition of a custodial sentence if the youth has endangered others even if the conduct itself is not intended to cause bodily harm and does not result in bodily harm (as also discussed in Chapter 3).

Interestingly, however, Bill C-10 may also have the effect of limiting some situations in which pre-trial detention has in the past been used with youth accused of less serious offences, like breach of probation. Under Bill C-10, youth can only be detained pre-trial if charged with a 'serious offence', defined as 'an indictable offence for which the maximum punishment for an adult is imprisonment for five years or more, or if they have' a history that indicates a pattern of either outstanding

Box 4.4   Youth Justice in Action

Bill C-10

- Amends the Declaration of Principle (Section 3(1)) to state:

(a) the youth criminal justice system is intended to protect the public by

(i) holding young persons accountable through measures that are proportionate to the seriousness of the offence and the degree of responsibility of the young person,

(ii) promoting the rehabilitation and reintegration of young persons who have committed offences, and

(iii) supporting the prevention of crime by referring young persons to programs or agencies in the community to address the circumstances underlying their offending behaviour;

- Changes to the law regarding pre-trial detention of youth (Section 29), to provide that:

(2) A youth justice court judge . . . may order that a young person be detained in custody only if

(a) the young person has been charged with

(i) a serious offence, or

(ii) an offence other than a serious offence, if they have a history that indicates a pattern of either outstanding charges or findings of guilt [and]

(b) the judge . . . is satisfied, on a balance of probabilities,

(i) that there is a substantial likelihood that, before being dealt with according to law, the young person will not appear in court when required by the law to do so,

(ii) that detention is necessary for the protection or safety of the public, including any victim of or witness to the offence, having regard to all the circumstances, including a substantial likelihood that the young person will, if released from custody, commit a serious offence, or

(iii) in the case where the young person has been charged with a serious offence and detention is not justified under subparagraph (i) or (ii), that there are exceptional circumstances that warrant detention and that detention is necessary to maintain confidence in the administration of justice, having regard to the principles set out in section 3 and to all the circumstances, including

(A) the apparent strength of the prosecution's case,

(B) the gravity of the offence,

(C) the circumstances surrounding the commission of the offence, including whether a firearm was used, and

(D) the fact that the young person is liable, on being found guilty, for a potentially lengthy custodial sentence; and

(c) the judge . . . is satisfied, on a balance of probabilities, that no condition or combination of conditions of release would, depending on the justification on which the judge or justice relies under paragraph (b),

(i) reduce, to a level below substantial, the likelihood that the young person would not appear in court when required by law to do so,

(ii) offer adequate protection to the public from the risk that the young person might otherwise present, or

(iii) maintain confidence in the administration of justice.

(3) The onus of satisfying the youth justice court judge . . . as to the matters referred to in subsection (2) is on the Attorney General [Crown prosecutor].

charges or findings of guilt. While there is no longer a rebuttable presumption of pre-trial release, there continues to be an onus on the Crown to justify detention. Further, the bill prohibits placing a young person in an adult jail prior to reaching the age of 18 years, even if an adult sentence is imposed. Although Bill C-10 is clearly intended to appeal to 'law and order' voters, and, if fully implemented, some of its provisions will result in increases in the use of custody for certain types of cases, other provisions of the bill might actually result in other youth being *less* likely to be incarcerated, especially on a pre-trial basis. Despite the rhetorical support of the Conservative government for 'toughening' the YCJA, the government may recognize that incarcerating significantly more youth would increase the cost of youth justice services without increasing public safety. Unlike some of the changes to laws governing adults, all of the changes to the YCJA continue to give judges discretion about how to apply the law, and their ultimate effect will depend on how youth court judges, probation officers, prosecutors, and police decide to interpret the law.

Summary

Although there has been some variation in how different justice-system professionals have interpreted and applied some of the provisions of the YCJA, in general, the police, prosecutors, and judges in Canada have responded to the declaration in the preamble that the act is intended to 'reduce the over-reliance on the incarceration of . . . young persons'. Youth courts have generally recognized the limited accountability of youth in comparison to adults and have focused on the need to impose community-based sentences that 'promote . . . rehabilitation and reintegration into society'. However, in cases involving more serious offences or involving youths with lengthy records who have not responded to community-based options, youth courts have continued to impose custodial sentences. Further, while the presumption of adult sentencing for the most serious youth offenders has been ruled unconstitutional, adult sentences are still imposed in a small number of cases involving very violent youth where the Crown satisfies the youth court that this is an appropriate sentence.

The pre-court diversion and sentencing provisions of the YCJA have brought about a major change in the youth justice system in Canada. The implementation of the new law was accompanied by professional education and program changes, as well as transitional federal funding that undoubtedly reinforced the effects of the YCJA; however, it is apparent that enacting a clear, new legislative regime had a significant effect. The data from the first seven years under the new legislation demonstrate that the act has had a significant impact on both recourse to youth court and the use of custody as a sanction. Without increasing the volume of recorded youth crime, the YCJA has resulted in a very significant reduction in the use of courts and custody for adolescent offenders in Canada and, hence, allowed for a significant reduction in spending on youth courts and custody facilities. This was generally accompanied by shifting resources to community-based programs. On the other hand, the regional variations in the use of youth courts and custody have remained substantial.

Key Terms

adjudication
apprehended person
breach of probation
charge ratio
chargeable person
community-based sentence
custodial sentence
deferred custody and supervision order
  (DCSO)
deterrence
diversion
extrajudicial measures
extrajudicial sanctions
incarceration rate

noncustodial sentence
post-adjudication
pre-adjudication
presumption
presumptive offence
pre-trial detention
rate per 100 000
rebuttable presumption
recorded youth crime rate
rehabilitation
reintegration
remand custody
sentenced custody

Review Questions

1. How has the YCJA succeeded in reducing the use of court for young persons accused of offending?

2. How has the YCJA succeeded in reducing the use of custody for young persons found guilty of offences?

3. Describe the trends over the past two decades in the volume of recorded youth crime and in the use of police discretion whether to charge apprehended youth.

4. Under the YCJA, what alternatives to charging are available to police who have reasonable grounds to believe a young person has committed an offence?

5. How has the YCJA made it difficult for judges to sentence young persons to custody?

6. What, if any, has been the impact of the YCJA on the use of pre-trial detention for accused young persons?

Critical Thinking Questions

1. One of the YCJA's stated objectives (and the main theme of this chapter) is reducing the number of accused young persons who are sent to court or who are sentenced to custody. Do you agree with this objective? Why or why not?

2. The chapter suggests that the YCJA has had a limited effect in reducing differences in the way that different parts of the country respond to young offenders. Some people may feel that in a country like Canada, regional variation is a strength rather than a weakness. What do you think?

3. What are the principal justifications for creating a youth justice system that treats young offenders differently from adult offenders?

4. There has recently been much talk about restorative justice. This is an alternative to the traditional 'retributive' model of criminal justice. Restorative justice attempts to reconcile victims and offenders by bringing the two parties together. The victim benefits from receiving an apology and an explanation from the offender while the offender might benefit from receiving a more lenient sentence in return for apologizing and

trying to make amends for his or her crime. Do you think this restorative approach to crime should be used more often in the area of youth crime? Why or why not?

5. The current age of criminal responsibility in Canada is 12 years. Some people think it should be lower—say, 10 years—while others argue that it should be higher and that a juvenile should not be prosecuted in court unless he or she is 14 years or older. What is your opinion?

6. The YCJA makes it harder for courts to impose custody as a sanction in youth court. Some youth justice workers argue that it should be impossible for a judge to send a young offender to a youth custody facility unless the juvenile has been convicted of a more serious offence or has a history of repeat offending. Do you agree that even fewer young offenders should be incarcerated?

7. The YCJA, as interpreted by the Supreme Court, does not allow judges to take account of deterrence when sentencing a youth. Why did the SCC interpret the act this way? Do you agree with this judicial approach?

Suggested Readings

Bala, N. and Anand, S. (2009). *Youth criminal justice law.* Toronto: Irwin.

Doob, A.N. and Cesaroni, C. (2004). *Responding to youth crime in Canada.* Toronto: University of Toronto Press.

Roberts, J.V. (2004). Public opinion and the evolution of juvenile justice policy in Western nations. In M. Tonry and A.N. Doob (Eds.), *Youth crime and youth justice: Comparative and cross-national perspectives (Volume 31 in Crime and Justice).* Chicago: University of Chicago Press.

Smith, D. (Ed.). (2010). *A new approach to youth justice.* Cullompton: Willan Publishing.

Tonry, M. and A.N. Doob (Eds.). (2004). *Youth crime and youth justice: Comparative and cross-national perspectives (Volume 31 in Crime and Justice).* Chicago: University of Chicago Press.

Suggested Weblinks

Department of Justice Canada, Youth Justice
www.justice.gc.ca/eng/pi/yj-jj/index.html
* An explanation of the youth justice process from the Department of Justice.

Endnotes

1. 2005 SCC 78, at para. 36
2. 2005 SCC 61.
3. The term *gateway* is commonly used among justice system professionals, and was adopted by the Supreme Court of Canada in *R. v. C.D.*, 2005 SCC 78.
4. *R. v. C.D.*, 2005 SCC 78.
5. Section 61 allowed a province to set a higher age for the presumptive offence provisions; Québec and Newfoundland set 16 years of age.
6. See e.g., *R. v. A.O.*, [2007] O.J. 800 (C.A.).
7. Bill C-4, 40th Parliament, 3rd Session, 1st reading March 16, 2010.
8. *R. v. S.A.C.*, 2008 SCC 47.
9. Section 61 allowed a province to set a higher age for the presumptive offence provisions; Québec and Newfoundland set 16 years of age.
10. This provision was held unconstitutional in Reference Re Bill C-7 (2003), 10 C.R. (6th) 281 (Que. C.A.) and *R v. D.B*, [2006] O.J. 1112 (C.A.), but it was upheld in *R v K.D.T.*, [2006] B.C.J. 253 (C.A.)
11. See e.g., *R. v. A.O.*, [2007] O.J. 800 (C.A.).

12. Canwest News Service, reporting on a speech given by the prime minister to the Canadian Crime Victims Foundation in Vaughan, Ontario (Canwest 2008).

13. Bill C-4, 40th Parliament, 3rd Session, 1st reading, March 16, 2010.

14. *R. v. C.D.*, 2005 SCC 78.

References

Anand, S. (1999a). The good, the bad, and the unaltered: An analysis of Bill C-68, the Youth Criminal Justice Act. *Canadian Criminal Law Review, 4*, 249–70.

Anand, S. (1999b). Sentencing, judicial discretion and juvenile justice, part II. *Criminal Law Quarterly, 41*(4), 485–500.

Bala, N. (2003). Diversion, conferencing, and extrajudicial measure for adolescent offenders. *Alberta Law Review, 40*(4), 991–1027.

Bala, N. (2006). Charter challenges to presumptive adult sentences for serious youth offenders. *Criminal Reports (6th series) 37*, 287–300.

Bala, N. (2007). Responding to adolescent offenders: The YCJA & Sentencing Youth as Adults *The Verdict, 113*, 54–59.

Bala, N. and Anand, S. (2009). *Youth criminal justice law.* Toronto: Irwin.

Bala, N., Carrington, P., and Roberts, J. (2009). Evaluating the Youth Criminal Justice Act after five years: A qualified success. *Canadian Journal of Criminology and Criminal Justice, 51*(2), 131–67.

Campion-Smith, B. (2008, July 30). Tories push crime agenda. *Toronto Star.*

Canada. (1987). *Sentencing reform: A Canadian approach. Report of the Canadian Sentencing Commission.* Ottawa: Department of Justice Canada.

Canada. (1999, May 12). Press release. Ottawa: Department of Justice Canada.

Canada. (2002). YCJA explained. Ottawa: Department of Justice Canada. Retrieved 6 Feb., 2009, from http://canada.justice.gc.ca/eng/pi/yj-jj/repos-depot/index.html

Canada. (2007). Pre-trial detention under the Youth Criminal Justice Act: A consultation paper. Ottawa: Department of Justice Canada.

Canwest. (2008, June 6). Harper vows changes to 'failed' youth justice Act.

Carrigan, D.O. (1998). *Juvenile delinquency in Canada: A history.* Toronto: Irwin.

Carrington, P.J. (1999). Trends in youth crime in Canada, 1977–1996. *Canadian Journal of Criminology, 41*(1), 1–32.

Carrington, P.J. and Roberts, J.V. (2011). The last chance sanction in youth court: The deferred custody and supervision order. In S. Anand (Ed.), *Paradoxes of children's rights: Essays in honor of Professor Nicholas Bala.* Toronto: Irwin Law.

Carrington, P.J. and Schulenberg, J.L. (2003). Police discretion with young offenders. Ottawa: Department of Justice Canada.

Carrington, P.J. and Schulenberg, J.L. (2005). The impact of the Youth Criminal Justice Act on police charging practices with young persons: A preliminary statistical assessment. Ottawa: Department of Justice Canada.

Carrington, P.J. and Schulenberg, J.L. (2008). Structuring police discretion: The effect on referrals to youth court. *Criminal Justice Policy Review, 19*, 349–67.

CBC. (2008, Sept. 22). Conservatives vow to toughen youth justice act. Retrieved from http://www.cbc.ca

Cesaroni, C. and Bala, N. (2008). Deterrence as a principle of youth sentencing: No effect on youth, but a significant effect on judges. *Queen's Law Journal, 39*, 447–81.

Doob, A.N. and Cesaroni, C. (2004). *Responding to youth crime in Canada.* Toronto: University of Toronto Press.

Doob, A.N. and Sprott, J.B. (2004). Changing models of youth justice in Canada. In M. Tonry and A. Doob (Eds.), *Youth crime and youth justice: Comparative and cross-national perspectives. 31 Crime and Justice* (pp. 185–242). Chicago: University of Chicago Press.

Galloway, G. (2008, Sept. 26). Poll shows support for Tories' justice plan for youths. *Globe and Mail*, p. A13.

Howell, J.C. (1997). *Juvenile justice and youth violence.* Thousand Oaks, CA: Sage.

Kari, S. (2008, Oct. 6). Candidates still believe crime pays: Play on public's concerns to win votes. *National Post.*

Laub, J.H. and Sampson, R.J. (2003). *Shared beginnings, divergent lives: Delinquent boys to age 70.* Cambridge: Harvard University Press.

McAra, L. and McVie, S. (2007). Youth justice? The impact of system contact on patterns of desistance from offending. *European Journal of Criminology, 4*, 315–45.

Manson, A. (2001). *The law of sentencing.* Toronto: Irwin Law.

Milligan, S. (2010). Youth court statistics, 2008/09 *Juristat, 30*(2).

Mitchell, B. (2008). *The class project: How to kill a mother—The true story of Canada's infamous bathtub girls.* Toronto: Key Porter.

Mitchell, B. (2009, June 22). Bathtub girl granted release to attend school. *Toronto Star.*

Roberts, J.V. and Bala, N. (2003). Understanding sentencing under the Youth Criminal Justice Act. *Alberta Law Review, 41*, 395–423.

Roberts, J.V. and Hough, M. (2005). Sentencing young offenders: Public opinion in England and Wales. *Criminal Justice, 5*, 211–32.

Statues Cited

All federal legislation in Canada can be accessed at http://laws.justice.gc.ca/en/index.html.

Criminal Code, R.S.C. 1985, chap. C-46, as amended.

Young Offenders Act, R.S.C. 1985, c. Y.-1, in force 1 April, 1984, to 31 March, 2003.

Youth Criminal Justice Act, S.C. 2002, c. 1, in force 1 April, 2003.

Part II
Understanding Contemporary Youth Crime and Justice:
Theories and Perspectives

There are many different ways one can approach attempting to develop an understanding of youth crime and justice in today's society. What most people believe about youth crime and youth justice is likely based on a variety of sources (e.g., mass media, authority, tradition, personal experience, and common sense) that are not necessarily scientifically based yet serve to inform us about social issues. While these methods might serve us well personally, they risk the problems of overgeneralization and selective observation and, therefore, have been viewed with skepticism by most criminologists, who, depending on their training, prefer instead to rely on a wide range of disciplinary and theoretical perspectives. In this part, we present four chapters that collectively highlight and contrast the different approaches that have been taken in society and among criminologists to try to understand youth crime and justice today.

As it is probably the most familiar of the approaches, we begin with an examination of the role of the media and in constructing knowledge. Most people, who have no training in criminology or direct experience with the youth justice system, learn what they know about these topics from the media, including both traditional print and electronic media, such as newspapers and television, and more recent media like the internet. In Chapter Five, Chris McCormick provides a thoughtful analysis of the role of the media in producing knowledge about youth crime and justice. He contrasts this with other ways of learning about reported and unreported youth crime, including official statistics and self-report studies. McCormick critically argues that while most people, including criminologists, tend to privilege 'one way of knowing youth crime over the other', it is more useful and valuable to look at a variety of information sources, including the media, statistics, and self-report studies, as complementary but different ways of making sense of youth crime. McCormick's chapter is particularly unique in that it critiques the work of criminologists and media sociologists who tend to either ignore or discount the important role played by the media in contributing to public debate over crime and justice issues generally, and public debate concerning youth crime and justice more specifically. In essence, McCormick points out that the media provide a crucial public arena in which youth crime and the justice system are debated and that as such the media contribute to a different way of understanding youth crime and justice than that offered through the more narrow study of official crime statistics or self-report studies.

Other ways that criminologists have attempted to learn more about youth crime and justice are, first, through carrying out research with the aim of developing formal, testable theories of juvenile delinquency and youth crime, and, second, through developing critical theoretical insights on the operation of youth justice agencies and practices. In Chapter Six, Sibylle Artz, Lorinda Stoneman, and Marge Reitsma-Street combine these approaches by providing an overview of traditional and contemporary theories of female crime, along with a critical analysis of the failure of the Canadian youth justice system to adequately address the needs of girls who come into conflict with the law. Artz et al. cover the wide variety of theories that have been used to try to explain female crime and delinquency, ranging from individual-focused early biological and more recent biopyschosocial theories, to more sociologically based strain, control, and gender role theories. The authors also discuss promising directions that are now being taken to more adequately theorize the causes of female crime and delinquency and to more effectively intervene in the lives of girls who are at risk of becoming involved in crime. Particular attention is given to developing an 'intersectional' approach for guiding interventions that addresses the unique 'strains faced by girls and their complex and varied pathways to social and delinquent behaviours'. According to Artz et al., one of the reasons for the continuing failure of social agencies and the youth justice system to adequately address the needs of at-risk and 'delinquent' girls has been the lack of sensitivity to the manner in which variables like age, gender, race, class, ethnicity, and sexuality intersect in shaping the life circumstances and behaviour of individuals. In addition, the authors suggest that the failure of even well-intended social agencies and youth justice workers to develop an awareness of these types of complex 'demographic intersections' leads to piecemeal and typically overly punitive approaches to dealing with female youth crime. As critical counter-examples of this, the authors note that attending to demographic intersections

> means not placing Aboriginal girls in centres thousands of miles from home and culture. It means radically changing correctional practices to reflect Aboriginal respect for spirit and land . . . It [also] means not charging one in three Canadian girls for administrative offences . . .

In Chapter Seven, Stephen Baron examines a number of more recent theoretical perspectives that have been offered to help explain and understand youth crime. Particular attention is given to recent sociologically based control, strain, and coercion theories that have attempted to improve on the earlier theories discussed by Artz et al. in Chapter Six. While some of these new perspectives, like Gottfredson and Hirschi's general theory of crime, build on specific earlier theories, others, like Sampson and Laub's age-graded theory and Tittle's control balance theory, attempt to bring together or integrate a number of the previously examined perspectives to create new explanations of criminal behaviour. Baron provides a systematic examination of the main causal factors identified by each theory, the key research studies that have been carried out to test the amount of empirical support for each theory, and the extent to which these theories complement or conflict with one other. Baron's review of these recent theoretical perspectives on youth crime shows the variety of ways in which positivist-oriented criminologists, who believe in the need for scientifically rigorous theory formulation and testing, have approached the topic. Baron concludes that in order to successfully understand youth crime, we must identify and include ideas from a range of complementary theoretical perspectives that help to better explain the causal process of youth crime, thus allowing for a more complex and nuanced understanding of how youth crime emerges and evolves.

In Chapter Eight, Bryan Hogeveen and Joanne Minaker contribute to the discussion by offering a series of insights on youth crime and the operation of the youth justice system from the perspective of critical criminology. Hogeveen and Minaker argue that while mainstream positivist criminology has tended to focus attention on the 'causes, consequences, and control of youth crime', critical criminology attempts to unmask the structural inequalities that marginalize young people and thereby contribute to their behaviours being criminalized and dealt with through various agencies of governmental control, including the youth justice system. For example, critical criminologists have begun to show how social inequalities linked to age, class, race, and gender work to 'structure the life chances of the marginalized other—Aboriginal youth, the poor, and racial minorities—and translate into overrepresentation in the contemporary youth justice system'. Consequently, rather than thinking of youth crime as 'freely chosen' behaviour on the part of youth that can therefore be simply deterred through the threat of punishment, critical criminologists like Hogeveen and Minaker link the criminalization of youth to 'systemic conditions of marginalization, exclusion, and social inequality' and advocate forms of 'social justice praxis' that are 'dedicated to making meaningful changes to improve the life chances of young people'. In their chapter, Hogeveen and Minaker offer an engaging introduction to key concepts, theories, and practical experiences that are informing the efforts now being undertaken by critical criminologists in promoting justice for Canadian youth.

5 Youth Deviance and the Media: Mapping Knowledge and the Limits to Certainty

Chris McCormick

Overview

The media—including traditional print and electronic media, such as newspapers and television, and more recent media like the internet—are one of society's key indices and sources of knowledge about crime. Despite the media's popularity and influence, however, over the years criminologists and media sociologists have been skeptical of the accuracy and usefulness of media representations of crime and justice and have instead given more weight to officially produced data (like crime statistics) and data acquired through other data-collection techniques (like self-report and victimization studies). This chapter provides a somewhat different discussion of the media, acknowledging that although the media are often guilty of distorting and sensationalizing crime news stories, they nonetheless may be seen to provide a crucial public arena in which youth crime and the youth criminal justice system are debated and understood.

Introduction

In October 2004, 16-year-old Archie Billard ran a red light and crashed into Theresa McEvoy, a teacher's aide and mother of three, killing her instantly. He was speeding, driving a stolen car and being chased by police. He was so high he had no memory of the incident but pled guilty to negligence causing death in 2006. The public was outraged because he had a string of convictions and was awaiting trial on other offences (CTV 2006). The circumstances surrounding the case led to a provincial inquiry (the Nunn Inquiry) that recommended changes to the federal Youth Criminal Justice Act. After pleading guilty to criminal negligence in McEvoy's death, Billard was sentenced to four years in prison, was released in 2009, and was then readmitted twice for statutory violations in that and the following year (CBC 2010). Typical comments at the time were that he was unremorseful, that he was irresponsible, and that he was playing the system.

This chapter is a reflection on (what we know about) youth crime and juvenile deviance. Before we can do anything about a social problem, we must lay out the methods for knowing that problem and the limitations of those methods. In this chapter the premise is that what we know about youth crime and juvenile deviance is based on the particular methods we use to map that knowledge. Although there are other methods, this chapter focuses specifically on an analysis of the role of media in the production of knowledge about youth crime and justice, contrasting it with other data-collection techniques, including official statistics and self-report and victimization studies.

It is important to compare official statistics, unofficial data, and the media as indices or sources of knowledge. While these three sources of knowledge are complementary, they differ both in kind and degree. Official statistics record in detail what is known and reported to the police, while self-report and victimization studies are used to fill out those incidents not reported to the police. The media, however, are the main sources of crime news information for the public (Surette 1998), and significant ones because they highlight emotional and violent extremes of crime (Fishman 1981; Graber 1980). Furthermore, the media create a feedback loop, where discussions of youth crime influence public perception and to some extent public policy with calls for more punitive measures (Garofalo 1981).

Numerous studies by criminologists and media sociologists have empirically supported the argument that the media play a significant role in shaping public attitudes toward youth crime (Best 1999; Cohen 1972; Faith and Jiwani 2002; Muncie 2004; Schissel 1997, 2006). One of the earliest and most famous of these is Stanley Cohen's influential book, *Folk Devils and Moral Panics: The Creation of the Mods and Rockers* (1972). Cohen's study, which involved field-research interviews and analysis of media reports, showed how rather haphazardly organized groups of youth (or 'youth gangs') known as Mods and Rockers came to be famous in England in the 1960s mainly through the sensationalist stories that were written about them in newspapers of the day. Cohen coined the 'term **moral panic** to describe exaggerated fears about youth deviance that were generated

moral panic
Exaggerated fears about social problems, including youth deviance, partly generated by the media.

folk devils

Any group that is unjustifiably perceived to pose a threat to the traditional values and institutions of society.

by the media, while he used the term **folk devils** to capture the idea that—much like witches in seventeenth-century New England—English youth of the 1960s came to be viewed by adults as a group that posed a potentially serious threat to the traditional values and institutions of English society' (Smandych 2001, p. 66).

While the findings of researchers like Cohen (1972) have been influential in evoking skepticism about the accuracy and usefulness of information on youth crime and justice derived from the media, this does not mean that criminologists should entirely discount examining the ways in which the media may contribute to a different, if not better, knowledge of these topics. Overall, in this chapter we will come to see that the study of youth crime and deviance is more than just counting because the conditions for creating and knowing meaning are more complex. Knowing crime and deviance is both actuarial yet interpretive, and is socially constructed in the media as a way of looking at the world. The topic of youth crime will be used here as a mirror to reflect on our methods for knowing about crime and understanding its occurrence. By grounding the analysis of youth crime against the context of other ways of knowing, we may create a more adequate method of analyzing how knowledge of youth crime and justice are generated in today's contemporary society.

The Official Version: Statistics on Youth Crime

First, we will look at the official statistics on (youth) crime and consider what they do and do not tell us. Overall, these statistics attempt to portray crime as a pattern through uniform descriptions. However, in doing so, artificial categories are often created that mask important details about events and processes connected with crime. Consequently, to know about youth crime from official crime statistics is like trying to dine out using restaurant reviews—entertaining but ultimately unfulfilling.

The Creation of an Official Statistic

The Canadian Centre for Justice Statistics (CCJS) has collected information on crime every year since 1962, which is called the Uniform Crime Report (UCR) survey. It is an aggregate count because it lumps crime into categories based on reports from over 1000 separate police detachments from over 200 different police forces across Canada. The UCR is the official source that represents crimes substantiated through police investigation.

UCR data is an invaluable resource to study crime in society, and a revised version has even more detailed information on accused and victim characteristics (e.g., age, gender, alcohol and drug consumption, victim–offender relationship, and level of injury) and incident characteristics (e.g., location, time, secondary violations, and weapons). The revised version, the UCR2, gives the police and the public a more specific sense of what offences occur.

Each month, police agencies report to the CCJS the number of crimes known to them, taken from all complaints of crime received from victims, from members of the public, or from officers who discovered the infractions. The initial reports of crime are investigated and if they are unfounded they are eliminated from the total. This crime total represents only what the police know about crime because of course some crimes are never detected and many are not reported to the police at all. Called the 'dark figure' of crime, such crimes are discovered in a different way, usually through victimization surveys or self-reports (see the earlier, more detailed discussion of this in Chapter 2).

The UCR thus does not reflect the total amount of crime in society, although it might be understood that way. Rather, it was created as a way to measure police work, although it is now used to compare crime across jurisdictions and to justify the use of police resources. And, of course, in order to be a meaningful statistic, police have to count crime the same way, consistently and systematically.

The UCR uses several terms to express crime data. For homicide, the 'actual number' is expressed as a raw figure (for example, 611 homicides occurred in 2008). Second, the 'percentage change' in the amount of crime between years is computed. For example, this 2008 number increased from 594 homicides in 2007, or 2 per cent. In 2007, the property crime rate decreased 8 per cent, and the violent crime rate decreased 2.5 per cent, with all categories of violent crime declining. The percentage change is important because, read literally, it is an indicator of whether society is becoming more dangerous. The percentage change can also be made to reflect on the effectiveness of the police, courts, and corrections, and the direction of public policy. If the crime rate increases, then it can be used to comment on, for example, whether the police are doing a good job or whether politicians need to get tough on crime. The third way of expressing crime data is the crime 'rate' per 100 000 people. The crime rate involves dividing the total crimes by the population (33 million), which creates a relative rate of changes in crime. For example, the homicide rate was 1.8 in 2009, which means that fewer than 2 people in every 100 000 were killed between January 1 and December 31 of that year. Thus, the likelihood of being murdered is very low in Canada, especially when compared to the United States (5.4), Russia (14.9), South Africa (37), or Jamaica (58) (Wikipedia 2010).

Within Canada, homicide rates vary as well. For example, in 2009 Ontario had 178 homicides while Newfoundland and Labrador had only 1. However, it is obvious that Ontario also had a far greater population base than did Newfoundland and Labrador, skewing the relative number of crimes. When the relative population is factored in, Newfoundland and Labrador's homicide rate is 0.2, and Ontario's is 1.4. Saskatchewan had only 36 homicides in 2009, but its homicide rate per 100 000 people is 3.5. The only jurisdiction with a higher homicide rate was the territory of Nunavut (18.6) (Beattie and Cotter 2010).

In 2007, the national crime rate for adult offenders was at its lowest in 30 years, and continued to decline. This can be taken to mean that at the aggregate level Canadians were at an unprecedented safety level, especially when seen with the new Crime Severity Index. This measure of serious crime showed a decrease of 22 per cent since 1999 (Dauvergne and Turner 2010). Moreover, violent crime is usually low compared with the amount of property crime. In 2009, the property crime rate was 4081 compared to 1314 for violent crime. Other offences, such as prostitution and gaming, had a rate of 1011, while drugs were 289 per 100 000. Historically, crime rates have increased from east to west across Canada (Dauvergne and Turner 2010). However, little attempt has been made to measure or explain this phenomenon.

In addition to incidence and crime rate, police agencies report the total number of 'crimes cleared', which means that at least one person is arrested and charged unless something prevents the physical arrest, such as when a suspect dies or leaves the country. A case can also be 'cleared otherwise' even if no charge is laid, as in the case of a young offender diverted to an extrajudicial measures program.

In general, the clearance rate for violent offences is around 70 per cent but is only about 20 per cent for property crimes. The national weighted clearance rate was 38 per cent in 2009, its highest point since data were first available in 1998 (Juristat 2010). The highest clearance rate is usually for homicide, while the lowest is often motor vehicle theft. If 70 per cent of violent offences and 20 per cent of property violations were cleared, that means conversely that 30 per cent of violent crimes and 80 per cent of property violations go uncleared (and apparently unsolved). Violent crimes are more likely to be solved than property crimes, because police devote more resources to these more serious acts (Cloninger and Sartorius 1979). Also, witnesses and the victim are available to identify offenders because usually the victim and offender are previously acquainted.

The Youth Crime Statistic

Statistics Canada reports in its annual publication on crime that there were about 176 000 youth (aged

12 to 17 years) accused of a criminal offence in 2007. The youth crime rate decreased by 2 per cent in 2007, but had increased 3 per cent in 2006. To put it in a larger time frame, the youth crime rate peaked in 1991, decreased substantially over the next decade, and has remained relatively stable over the past decade. However, in contrast to the declining pattern of the youth crime rate, overall, the rate of *violent* youth crime has been steadily increasing since the mid-1980s. Significantly, this rate is double what it was 20 years ago and is largely made up of increases in common assault, which accounts for about 6 in 10 violent incidents committed by youth. This increase is accounted for in part by an actual increase in crime, but also might be due to increased reporting and charging practices.

A more stable statistic, the youth homicide rate was at a record high in 2006 and decreased in 2007 from 85 to 74 (Juristat 2008; see also, Chapter 2). The decrease of 13 per cent is due to only 11 cases, and shows that youth homicide rates can vary considerably from one year to the next because of the relatively small number of offences. This can lead to misunderstanding, especially if such a change is reported in the media without the underlying absolute change. However, despite this decrease, the 2007 youth homicide rate was the second highest since 1961.

Youth drug crimes were mostly cannabis-related offences (84 per cent) in 2006, and were nearly double those of 1997 (Juristat 2007). The rate of drug crime was 693 youth per 100 000, or less than one per cent. While the majority of drug offences are for marijuana, other drug offences have grown as well, such as cocaine, ecstasy, and crystal methamphetamines. Part of this increase is artificial, in that the Controlled Drugs and Substances Act (CDSA), which was introduced in 1997 and which replaced the Narcotic Control Act, strengthened law enforcement. The CDSA also broadened the range of illegal substances to include amphetamines, LSD, and anabolic steroids (CanLII 1996).

Before moving on to discuss the limits of official statistics, what also deserves mention in terms of the official statistics on youth crime is that in 2006, about 6 in 10 youth who could have been charged with an offence (who came to the attention of the police) were handled outside the formal justice system. The decline in charges against youth accused of a crime followed the introduction of the Youth Criminal Justice Act (YCJA) in 2003. Since the YCJA was introduced, the proportion of accused youth who were cleared by means other than a charge increased for most offences. As discussed in Chapter 3, a primary objective of the YCJA was to divert youth involved in minor, nonviolent crimes from the formal justice system, creating procedures for the police use of discretion. Obviously, charges are still the norm for serious offences, such as homicide, while less serious offences such as minor theft are more likely to be diverted from the criminal justice system (Barnhorst 2004).

For reasons associated with these legal changes, the youth crime rate can increase while the charge rate itself drops. Obviously, this means that accused youth are dealt with through means other than the formal system. Since about 2000, the proportion of youth apprehended but not charged has been on the rise, but this trend increased sharply after the introduction of the YCJA (as discussed in Chapter 4). When it comes to cases like Archie Billard, mentioned at the beginning, such changes can lead to charges that the system is now too lenient when it comes to young offenders.

Limits of the Official Version of Youth Crime

Official crime statistics are produced through work: people reporting crime to police, who investigate, record, and lay charges, and which are then prosecuted in court. The machinery of (law and) order, so to speak, creates the product of crime because until a crime is accepted, defined, and convicted, it is not a tangible thing. Crime is, as noted at the outset of this chapter, a social construct. However, the quality of the raw material going into the crime machine is affected by five factors because (1) crime is report-sensitive, which means the willingness of the victim to report the crime determines whether the police know about it; (2) crime is policing-sensitive, which means the level of police enforcement determines whether the crime gets counted; (3) crime is definition-sensitive, which means that a change in the law affects whether something is called a crime; (4) crime is media-sensitive, which means that if crimes are publicized, a 'feedback loop' can change the public's perceptions and their willingness to report; and (5) real trends in the number of crimes in society change over time (McCormick 2008). Let's deal with three of these issues briefly because they are relevant to the topic of youth deviance: law enforcement, legal definitions, and media practices.

Law Enforcement Practices

The ways in which police departments enforce and record criminal activity also affect the UCR statistics. This ranges from low clearance rates to police discretion (Black 1970). Ironically, increasing police efficiency can also increase crime rates as departments adopt more sophisticated computer technology, hire better-trained employees, and improve record-keeping ability. In addition, discretion affects the way in which police enforce the laws on prostitution, drug crimes, traffic offences, and internet crimes. For example, cannabis possession went from 2300 cases in 1968 to 44 000 cases in 2006 due to increased use but also to increased police enforcement. Drug enforcement is higher in jurisdictions where forfeiture laws allow police to retain seized assets, raising drug arrest rates by about 18 per cent (Mast, Benson, and Rasmussen 2000). This enforcement disproportionately affects the young.

Legal Definitions

Changes to the law affect the crime rate. For example, broadening the Criminal Code's definition of arson 20 years ago to include mischief or suspicious fires resulted in an increase of 17 per cent in the arson rate (McCormick 2008). An even more dramatic example is sexual assault, where in 1983, 1988, and 1991 changes were made to remove barriers affecting a victim's willingness to report and thus increasing the rate. Another legislative change that could be studied is the Youth Criminal Justice Act (YCJA), which diverts youths who have committed nonviolent crimes from the formal criminal justice system. Early on, the charge rate dropped from 56 per cent to 42 per cent, resulting in an apparent decrease in youth crime while in fact the number of youths who came into contact with police actually increased.

Media Practices

The media also have a role in the distortion of crime knowledge, as measured by what is known by the police. For example, news of crimes committed in public by strangers against innocent victims encourages the perception that crime is random, sensitizing the public to fear crime, which then is transformed into police enforcement or legislative changes (Kappeler 1996). News about crime and deviance can also desensitize the public in the opposite direction. For example, in the 1990s when sex-trade workers started disappearing on the Lower Mainland in Vancouver, media accounts ran stories about 'hookers' who had simply moved away, according to police. This became a predominant version to account for the disappearances even though there were those insisting that a serial killer was to blame. Years before the name *Robert Pickton* became common knowledge, the message the public got was one that encouraged apathy and disinterest (McCormick 2010).

When we extrapolate this theme to youth crime, if there is a disproportionate number of articles on the topic or a disproportionate stress on violent crimes, for example, this is the version the public has knowledge of. Whether it is an accurate version is irrelevant because it becomes the template for reporting and policing youth crime. In the media analysis discussed later in this chapter, the national news almost consistently reports only on homicides committed by youths; thus the reader gets the predominant impression of violent youths.

Interestingly, the CCJS Juristat series is an important source of data for the media, presenting complex information in a way that makes it appealing for the media to report the facts. The creation of UCR statistics originally was as much about providing journalists with information about crime as it was about measuring police workload. Today, the media influence the timing and wording of press releases, the type of statistics used, and the types of information presented. Furthermore, 'information officers' provide the media with crime stories as it is often beyond the scope of a reporter's ability to gather such information otherwise.

In conclusion, the official version of crime is the normative version, being the officially produced and thus authoritarian representation of crime. Its character as mathematically produced and textually presented contributes to its authenticity. However, its limit is that it represents what the state knows and decides is worthy to count as crime. The official version is a pallid facsimile and aggregated conglomerate of youth crime and gives little voice to the practices that produced youth crime or to the violence that is often at its core. Understanding the limits of official statistics, however, does not mean they are easily rectified, although other attempts to discover the more accurate reality of crime have been tried.

The Unofficial Version: Alternative Methods of Measuring Youth Crime

The various limits of official statistics have led criminologists to seek alternative sources of information to measure crime not reported to police and also to measure victimless crimes, such as substance abuse. The assumption is that techniques can be devised to catch the dark figure of crime missed in official statistics and thus supplement and expand official data. As discussed in Chapter 2, one way in which unreported crime is measured is through victimization surveys, and a way in which deviant behaviour is measured is through self-report surveys. However, it is relevant to comment further on these data-collection methods here in connection with a discussion of the comparable role of the media in generating knowledge about youth crime.

Self-Report and Victimization Surveys

Self-report surveys ask participants to reveal information about deviance that may have been committed by or against them. Through interviews, telephone surveys, or anonymous questionnaires, self-reports are viewed as a way to get at delinquency in particular, which is missed by official statistics.

Using self-report studies to collect information on young offenders in school is convenient and practical because many young people can be questioned at the same time. And because school attendance is mandatory up to the age of 16, a school-based self-report survey provides a fairly reliable snapshot of a cross-section of the population. Self-reports have also been used to examine the offence histories of prison inmates, drug users, and other groups (for example, see Cantor and Lynch 2000). Self-reports are not used very often, however, perhaps because of the reliance on official statistics. However, self-reports provide a broader picture of the distribution of criminality than do official data, and they also provide a check on that data. For example, racial bias may be present if surveys indicate that white and non-white people report unequal levels of police attention, but official data indicate similar rates of whites and non-whites being arrested or stopped by police. It is in the self-reports that disclosure about treatment is made available. Such surveys are also a way to see the distribution of criminal behaviour across racial, class, age, and gender lines (for example, see Smart and Adlaf 1991).

An example of a self-report study is a 1999 survey of 2001 students aged 12 to 18 conducted in over 67 Alberta junior and senior high schools. The study assessed students' perceptions of violence and personal safety, their own victimization and delinquent behaviour, and their weapons possession. The survey revealed more information than would generally be known through other means (Gomes et al. 2003).

Another example is a 2002 study by Tanner and Wortley that surveyed 3400 high-school students and 400 street youth in Toronto about experiences of victimization, perceptions of youth crime, and participation in gangs. What was revealing about this study was the contribution of youths' opinions about what their options were, and how criminality was often chosen as a means of survival (Tanner and Wortley 2002).

In 2004, the Centre for Addiction and Mental Health also conducted a national random survey of alcohol and drug use (the Canadian Campus Survey) of over 6000 undergraduate students from Canadian universities, which showed heavy drinking (16 per cent), cannabis use (32 per cent), and other illicit drug use (9 per cent). There is no victim in the traditional sense in such deviance and so self-report studies are almost the only way to collect such information. Various other drug use surveys include those done by the Addiction Research Foundation and the Canadian Centre on Substance Abuse, the Canadian Community Health Survey, and the Canadian Addiction Survey (see Canadian Centre on Substance Abuse 2011).

Victimization data have also been collected alongside self-report data in international youth surveys. A 2007 International Youth Survey study of more than 3200 youth in middle school revealed that 37 per cent of Toronto students had committed acts of violence, property crime, or drug dealing (Savoie 2007). The survey is part of the International Youth Survey (IYS) conducted in over 30 countries in 2006. Over 40 per cent of surveyed students in Toronto said they had been victimized at least once in the previous year. Many, however, did not report the incidents to the authorities, which means that often crimes are known about only by the offender and the victim. The findings of this survey would be surprising to anyone whose knowledge of youth crime is confined to official statistics. For example, in the previous year 20 per cent of youths also reported committing at least one delinquent act. Of the 11 800 youth surveyed who reported about 115 000 separate delinquent acts, the vast majority (91 per cent) of the acts were committed by about half of the youths. This shows that those youth are responsible for a high number of repeated acts of deviance. Overall, about 13 per cent of Toronto youth reported violent behaviour, and about the same amount reported property-related crime. Carrying a weapon and participating in fights accounted for 88 per cent of violent acts, and vandalism and shoplifting were common property offences. Delinquency was highest in public places, where there was less supervision.

Other research has shown that the early onset of delinquency is a significant factor in repeat offences, with youths who began their 'court career' at age 12 having an average of about 8 incidents. In comparison, those whose first incident was at age 21 had an average of about 1 incident. Most of the time these youth were with other people when they participated in delinquent acts, such as arson (92 per cent), vandalism (81 per cent), breaking and entering (80 per cent), threatening someone (70 per cent), and assault (60 per cent). In 58 per cent of the cases the delinquency was undiscovered, but when it was, it was punished (67 per cent). Youths reported being victimized by theft (28 per cent) or bullying (21 per cent), but reported the incidents in only 14 per cent of the cases. The reasons given for not reporting to the police were 'not important enough' (36 per cent) or that it was dealt with another way (20 per cent). Delinquency itself appeared to contribute significantly to victimization, with 56 per cent of delinquent youth reporting being victimized compared to those who were not (36 per cent) (Carrington et al. 2005).

The risk factors for delinquency have also been studied using data from self-report and victimization surveys (Savoie 2007). In the study conducted by Savoie, risk factors included being in step- or single-parent families (35 per cent and 25 per cent, respectively), rather than in double-parent families. Not surprisingly, over one-third of youth who reported that they did not get along with their parents had engaged in delinquency compared to 20 per cent of youth who reported that they did get along well with at least one of their parents. Even less surprisingly, delinquency was relatively rare among youth who said their parents always knew who they were with when they went out (12 per cent), compared to youth

(56 per cent) who said their parents never knew who they were with when they went out. Delinquency was highest among those who used drugs (60 per cent) and alcohol (35 per cent), compared to those who didn't use drugs (16 per cent) or those who didn't drink (9 per cent). Overall, what is significant about Savoie's findings are the high rate of both offending and victimization, much higher than the rate reported in official crime statistics. At 6885 per 100 000 (7 per cent), the official rate is far lower than that admitted in the self-report survey population (37 per cent). The rate of both offending and victimization is also much higher than that found in either the UCR or the GSS surveys. Also, what we see is that youths commit both violent and property offences relatively equally, quite often undetected, in the company of others with predictable underlying risk factors. And, finally, we also see that most offences are committed by a disproportionally smaller portion of the population (Savoie 2007).

Overall, official statistics and unofficial data are complementary sources of information. Official statistics reflect those crimes that come to the attention of the police, while self-report and victimization studies reflect a wide range of incidents that might not. In addition, forms of unofficial data get at a broader range of behaviour since the deviance they study is quite often soft, for example drug use or truancy. Moreover, these types of studies show the importance of asking people directly about crime, deviance, and victimization.

Youth Crime in the Media

We have looked at youth crime in two ways, discussing both official statistics and unofficial data. Official statistics show a steady decline in youth crime, except for a gradual increase in violent crime. Much youth crime is property-related, gender-biased, and reflects an interest in diversion since the introduction of the YCJA. On the other hand, unofficial data show that youths commit property and violent crime almost equally, and show a much higher rate of offending than is disclosed in official statistics. The data is complementary in that it fills out the details of crime not reported to the police, and also begins to reveal some of the context in which youth crime occurs. However, the difficulty with both sources of information is they are not the way in which most people know about youth crime. For most people, media coverage is the main way of knowing about youth crime. For example, a recent government report published on the primary source of information used by Canadians to learn about the youth justice system shows that the vast majority derive their information from newspapers, TV, or radio news, and other media (see Figure 5.1). Consequently, it is important to see if youth crime in the media is portrayed in a way that is similar to or different than the other two ways of knowing discussed here.

Social scientists have frequently looked at media coverage of crime and deviance (see, generally, Chiricos et al. 1997; Fishman 1981; Hindelang 1974). They have not looked at the media as a source of information as much as a source of misinformation, as in exaggerating the impact of street crime (Fishman 1978) or misconstructing the nature of corporate crime. This is a main approach to crime and media analysis. For example, one way to explain the discrepancy between the reality of dropping rates of youth crime and the perception that youth crime is out of control is that media coverage is distorted (Schissel 1997). Whether in the reporting of freeway crashes, shark attacks, serial killers, or youth super-predators, the media can be blamed for getting it wrong and misinforming the public (Best 1999).

This leads to the second approach to crime and media analysis: that is, that the misrepresentation of crime in the media causes fear or anxiety. For example, by distorting the frequency or severity of youth crime, the media create the impression that youth crime is more of a problem than it really is. Among the elderly, for example, it is believed that the media create unnecessary fears of victimization. However, this is a curious argument because it assumes that we know what crime is and that the media should do as good a job in showing that truth as we do in knowing it.

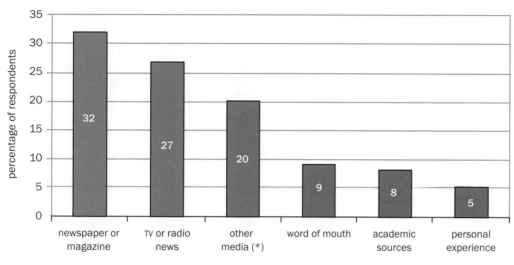

(*) includes movies, TV shows, and the internet

Figure 5.1 Primary Source of Information about the Canadian Youth Criminal Justice System

Respondents were also asked to identify their primary source of information about the youth criminal justice system in Canada. More than half (59 per cent) relied primarily on newspapers, magazines, or news stories from television or radio. Very few (8 per cent) relied on more academic sources, such as university courses, government reports, or books, and even fewer relied on first-hand experience (5 per cent).

Source: Canada, Department of Justice, *The 2008 National Justice Survey: The Youth Justice System in Canada and the Youth Criminal Justice Act*. Retrieved from www.justice.gc.ca/eng/pi/rs/rep-rap/2008/rr08_yj1-rr08_jj1/p3.html

The Construction of the Research

There is not much research on media coverage of youth crime. Most crime and media research focuses on more hot-button social-panic issues, such as child abuse and abduction, diseases, and homicide (Best 1993; Jenkins 1994)—crimes where it is easy to see that the media distort the danger of strangers, risks to children, and the amount of serial homicide in society. However, Jane Sprott's article (1996) gives a good example of how we can begin an analysis using a **context analysis**. Based on the premise that the reality constructed by the news media might not reflect other images of reality (which might suggest a parity), she compared newspaper articles on youth crime in three Toronto papers over a two-month period to the so-called Bala and Lilles Young Offenders Reporting Service over a two-year period.

context analysis
Analyzing media content for themes such as sensationalism or distortion.

What Sprott found is that the youth court cases were broken down as follows: charges involving violence (22 per cent), property crime (50 per cent), other Criminal Code offences (18 per cent), YOA offences (7 per cent), and other federal offences (3 per cent). In comparison, the media (*The Globe and Mail*, *The Toronto Star*, and *Toronto Sun*) focused almost exclusively on violent crime (94 per cent). Homicide, for example, constituted 0.02 per cent of youth court cases, was summarized in the Bala and Lilles Report slightly more often (7.8 per cent), and comprised a weighty 70.4 per cent of Toronto newspaper coverage. On the other hand, property crime was reported in the news far less often than it appeared in court (5.3 per cent compared to 50 per cent) or than was summarized in the reports (19.7 per cent). We might surmise, then, that property crime is not as interesting to cover.

This type of research methodology is quite simple. Take a sample of media coverage and compare the incidence of its stories to another source of information. In this case youth court statistics were used, but the source could have been police reports or even self-report survey results. The objective will always be to point out that media coverage is distorted in comparison to the more objective information, yielding the conclusion that the media exaggerate crimes of violence. The objective will never be to show that court statistics are not entertaining or interesting to read.

As well as a context difference, Sprott also noticed a content difference between the newspaper articles and the reports: the former focused more on the impact of the crime, while the sentencing reports focused more on the reasons for judicial disposition. Privileging the latter, she criticized the media for not giving enough information for the public to understand the reasons for sentencing. If the media did a better job, then the public would have a better understanding of the courts. However, that logic also cuts the other way: it also means that the newspaper focuses on the affective dimension by foregrounding the victim while the sentencing report does not. Which is doing the better job?

Sprott then goes on to argue that because the news media distort the proportion of youth violent crime, it is useful to measure the public perception of youth crime as it probably effects policy changes. She found that those who thought sentences were too lenient were usually thinking specifically of repeat offenders, and were slightly more likely to want harsher sentences. Those who believed that sentences were too lenient were also more likely to overestimate the amount of violent youth crime and to think that it has increased. Again, as we will see in the media analysis, this is an easy conclusion to come to when the majority of youth crime stories are about violence. Conclusively, Sprott ends with the sentiment that the public cannot be blamed for having little knowledge of how youth court works because the media do such a poor job in reporting cases.

Sprott's research dovetails nicely with Baron and Hartnagel's (1996), who found that respondents were quite punitive toward juvenile justice issues. This attitude was not based in experience of victimization but coincided with more conservative social values, which they hypothesized occurred as a result of how the media constructed youth crime. Fully 78 per cent of their respondents felt that youth courts were too lenient, but the level of victimization was only 22 per cent. Baron and Hartnagel speculate that high-profile coverage surrounding the YOA combined with simplistic coverage of sensational cases bring to awareness 'latent public fears', the first step in the spiral of events that can lead to a full public crusade. This is called the 'amplification of deviance'. While their study was not intended to be a systematic analysis of media coverage, it fits within the 'distorted coverage produces public fear' equation.

A more recent study of juvenile homicide in Chicago newspapers (see Boulahanis and Heltsey 2004) between 1992 and 2000 found that juvenile homicide rates declined but that the number of cases receiving media coverage increased. There is no good reason for one to reflect the other, but it does mean that the media can overrepresent the amount of violent crime and thus distort public perception. Furthermore, this study found that news articles do a good job of covering youth crime but also tend to focus on atypical cases. Most homicides are committed by males (90 per cent), but females make up 30 per cent of media coverage. Additionally, homicides committed against females were covered more than twice as often as cases involving male victims. In Chicago, black youth commit the most murders, but a case gets more coverage if it is committed by a white youth. Specifically, more than 59 per cent of cases involving Caucasian offenders received media coverage, compared to those involving African-Americans (21 per cent) and Latinos (17 per cent). The study also found that every one-year increase in offender age corresponded to a 28 per cent reduction in the odds of getting newspaper coverage, and homicides involving victims younger than 14 were 480 per cent more likely to receive coverage than homicides involving victims aged 20 to 29.

cultivation hypothesis
The hypothesis that the media inundates the public with ideas about crime.

After establishing these patterns and using a model called the **cultivation hypothesis** (Gerbner et al. 1980; Hawkins and Pingree 1980), the researchers felt that distorted media coverage made people more fearful. It was not that atypical cases were getting covered and typical cases were not but, rather, that there was a mix of coverage with atypical cases getting disproportionately more coverage than the typical cases. They conclude that this mixture makes it difficult to see patterns of victimization, just as Sprott (1996) concluded that media coverage makes it difficult for the public to understand sentencing patterns. Boulahanis and Heltsey (2004, p. 155) say this 'uncertainty produces a fear that anyone can be a victim and anyone can be a perpetrator', but go on to say that the resulting distortions include the perception that homicides committed by young persons represent a growing problem, which may or may not be the case.

For example, as indicated in Chapter 2, in 2007 the youth crime rate actually decreased by 2 per cent, following a 3 per cent increase in 2006, the first increase since 2003 (Juristat 2007). As with most crime, the highest rates were in Saskatchewan and Manitoba. Since the introduction of the YCJA in 2003, the proportion of apprehended youths formally charged with crimes has dropped; the YCJA diverts youths from the court system. So while in 2006 the rate of youths charged by the police dropped 1 per cent, there was a 6 per cent increase in the rate of youths cleared because of the new provisions of the YCJA. However, as this is perhaps not general knowledge, this does not reassure the public when they hear news reports of youth violence.

The Social Constructionist Analysis

There is now a large literature on **social constructionism**, developing over the past 40 or so years (see, for example, Altheide 2006; Best 1995; Goode 2009). This approach is more complicated than the context analysis approach in that we are not comparing indices, so to speak, or asking how well the media report reality. Rather, we are looking more closely at the discursive constructions used in media texts. In the analysis of prostitution in the Vancouver news mentioned earlier, for example, it is argued that the word *hooker* desensitizes viewers and actually destroys any empathy the public might have for the victims of a serial killer (McCormick 2010). This discursive construction contributed to what John Lowman (2000) called the 'discourse of disposal'—that is, how media descriptions of the attempt of politicians, police, and residents' groups to get rid of street prostitution from residential areas actually contributed to a sharp increase in murders of street prostitutes in British Columbia after 1980. His analysis trades on how there was a geographic and political marginalization of street prostitution that was aided by the symbolic marginalization created in the media that ultimately allowed for violence against street prostitutes.

Social constructionist analysis usually has several main themes. First, there is the suggestion that the media presents violence as a growing social problem, much like an epidemic or plague (for example, see Best and Horiuchi 1985). In addition, there are usually innocent victims and guilty predators who prey on those victims (for example, see D'Arcy 2007). Third, there is also usually a link or **convergence** between a new problem and an existing one—for example, stalking and domestic violence, or internet luring and pedophilia (for example, see Doyle 2000). And fourth, there are claims-makers, such as police, politicians, or advocates, who advance the idea that the described social problem is growing, is out of control, or needs attention (for example, see Dowler 2003). These are all basic elements of a constructionist approach that are easily applied to an analysis of youth crime in the media.

In the first example of constructionist research considered here, Spencer (2005) looks at select high-profile coverage of youth violence in 1994. In contrast to accounts that focus simplistically on media distortions and that create a sense of (un)certainty in the audience, Spencer adopts the view that the media trades on the ambiguous culpability of youth in that they are both victimizer and victimized. He chose 1994 because it was prior to the Columbine school shooting, youth violence had peaked, and there were several sensational cases (in the US and abroad) that were the focus of media attention. He chose commentary sections of the news, in venues such as *The New York Times*, *Time* magazine, *Newsweek*, and *US News & World Report*.

social constructionism
An approach that sees social problems as constructed in the media; see *moral panic*.

convergence
When a current issue is framed in terms of its relation to a previous one.

Among his findings are that youth violence was promoted as at a crisis level, that numerical estimates of its magnitude portrayed it as growing, that it was spreading geographically and could strike anyone and anywhere, and that atrocity tales were used to highlight the sensationalism of the issue. The crisis of youth violence was also linked to existing social problems, such as unemployment, single-parent families (single-mom or missing-dad), crack cocaine, child abuse, and the growing use of guns. These are standard elements of a constructionist analysis, and show how the public can get a distorted perception of youth crime (from the perspective of official statistics, for example).

Moreover, contextualizing the issue in this way raised issues of how culpable these youths were, and how the audience was to relate to them emotionally. This raised the issue of whether they were victims or victimizers, or both. These are two contradictory images: are they to be feared or sympathized; are they responsible or lost? Spencer (2005) calls this an **ideological flexibility**, and he suggests that the ambiguity in portrayal might be extended to analysis of other topics, such as mothers who kill their children, female partners who kill their abusive partners, or people who (knowingly) transmit the AIDS virus. This is a stronger version of 'uncertainty' in media portrayal than was suggested earlier, and presents a more complicated reality for the public to digest. This ideological flexibility also creates a confusion when we cannot easily distinguish the victims from the villains.

In general, constructionist analysis states that violent youth crime is overrepresented in the media, while youth property crime is under-represented. The public gets the message that violent youth crime is a significant problem, and connects these patterns through an inordinate focus on victims. This message distorts perception, which in turn affects the reported rates of youth crime and the public's willingness to press charges, eventually resulting in pressure on politicians to change the law.

ideological flexibility
Where the portrayal of persons is ambiguous—e.g., a young offender is portrayed as both villain and victim.

The Implication of the Patterns in Media Coverage of Youth Crime

As we have seen, there are certain patterns in media coverage of youth crime. Violent youth crime is overrepresented in the media while youth property crime is under-represented; atypical cases get disproportionately more coverage than typical cases, and the resulting product is a public misperception about youth crimes. However, simply comparing media coverage to police statistics or court cases and criticizing the former presumes that the media has an obligation to report faithfully what is known by those other venues. That is, critics often argue that if the media's coverage of crime is distorted and sensationalized in comparison to other sources, then it is inaccurate and responsible for more punitive attitudes on the part of the public, and inevitably politicians seeking to cash in on those fears.

This way of characterizing the relationship between media knowledge and crime knowledge makes the mistake of privileging the latter while ignoring the problems inherent in generating official and unofficial crime data. As we saw earlier, there are problems with both police information and with self-report studies, but they are complementary in giving us different images of what is putatively the same universe of behaviours: youth deviance. But they are images only, each with its own benefits and limits. Media knowledge is similarly a window on the world (see McCormick 2010), but there seems to be no ready reason for why the media should mirror what is known by the police any more than police statistics should mirror juvenile self-reports. Instead of being antagonistic bodies of knowledge, I suggest that they are imbricated scales, ways of measuring behaviour that are slightly overlapping (as shown in Figure 5.2).

To think of media knowledge in this way gives it a legitimacy that media knowledge often lacks in shallow versions of social constructionism, such as context analysis. Instead of seeing how well the media conform to a different way of measuring youth crime, we can use an alternative model such as **frame analysis** to see how the media frame or portray youth crime, and how the media allow us

frame analysis
Analyzing media content to see how crime and criminals are depicted.

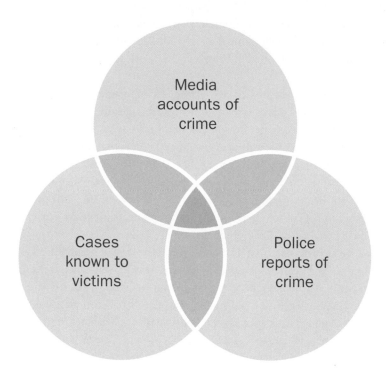

Figure 5.2 Different Ways of Knowing Youth Crime

to get at deeper cultural understandings of youth, especially when we combine frame analysis with a **critical discourse analysis** (Fairclough 2003; Wodak 2000) to see the link between those portrayals and the larger political structure of society.

Using such an approach also opens the door to analyzing in more detail the role of the media in the public sphere. And for there to be a role for the media in the public sphere, the media have to be construed as more than a simple conduit for political opinion or police knowledge. Rather, the media have to be seen as a forum for debate. Debates that are divided and difficult do not rely on the idea that hegemony does not somehow simply exist, but show us that it is accomplished through discourse. Making claims about putative conditions and the persons who are suggested to be responsible for those conditions, especially if we are not quite clear about their responsibility, are a good case study in the building of consensus.

A study that has looked at this issue of public debate in more detail is Hogeveen (2005). Through an analysis of House of Commons debates and some media reports, he explores the construction of the category of 'the punishable young offender'. His analysis is that media reports of debates in the House of Commons in the late 1990s created a new discursive category that emphasized protecting the public from risks associated with youth crime. The public concern about young offenders in Parliament and in the media centred on replacing the YOA with a tougher law based on accountability—the YCJA.

The selection of media articles that Hogeveen uses does not appear systematic, but is especially apropos in the discussion of the valorization of victims. For example, several years ago, former Alliance MP Jay Hill from British Columbia was able to name victims (who would have been in the news) as if everyone knew who they were, as in the following:

> In my home province of British Columbia, the names of Reena Virk, Dawn Shaw, and Trygve Magnusson represent just a few victims who died at the hands of violent youth.

critical discourse analysis

An approach in socio-linguistics that links discourse with political structure.

> Their senseless deaths demand laws from the government that punish and deter those who commit violent acts and provide mandatory rehabilitation programs during incarceration. (*Hansard*, October 21, 1999 , cited in Hogeveen 2005, 84)

As well, the late British Columbia MP Chuck Cadman, an important critic of the YOA, championed victims' rights after his son was victim of an unprovoked attack in Surrey. Joe Wambach became another important claims-maker after his son was victimized in Toronto. These claims-makers are important for their role in the valorization of victims, and for laying the groundwork for establishing that juveniles are 'getting away with crime'.

Hogeveen argues that the construction of the 'punishable young offender' in political and media discourse is based on the perceived inadequacy of current law, on the centrality of victims, on a get-tough discourse, and of course, on emotionality, as in former MP Mark Crawford's comments: 'Where does it end? Local parents and other citizens are calling for vigilante justice. They do not trust our current system of justice, that it lets off criminals with a slap upon the wrist while the victims are left in limbo for the rest of their lives' (*Hansard*, May 2, 1994 , cited in Hogeveen 2005, 79). This comment from 1994 does not reflect current discourse, perhaps, but it is uttered in the leadup to changing juvenile justice legislation. This symbiotic relation between violent offenders, valorized victims, and calls for tougher legislation is accomplished through debate. And we argue here that it is through the public arena of the media that this building of consensus happens. It is not as simple as privileging one form of knowledge over another, say official statistics over media stories. That is too easy a criticism. The media is a site for sensationalism and exaggeration, and at the same time it is also a place of debate and correction. For example, in a letter to the editor written in June 1998, Anthony Doob, a leading University of Toronto criminologist, made the following point:

> It is not surprising to see a Globe and Mail editorial (March 16) suggesting, once again, that the Young Offenders Act be toughened up. . . . What is surprising, however, is that the Globe and Mail editorial board used patently false information . . . to support its editorial position. . . . The manner in which we as a society deal with young offenders is important. We have to decide, for example, whether we are interested in focusing more on ways to make Canada a safer place to live or on making symbolic gestures that make older people feel that they are being tough. These are legitimate choices that should be debated. The debate is not served, however, by dishonest (or incompetent) reporting of what the current law is.

In the next section, we introduce research findings from an ongoing critical discourse analysis media study of newspaper reporting on young offenders in Canada. This sample of findings from ongoing research supplements the data reported by Hogeveen (2005) and helps us to further appreciate the key role that the media plays in producing knowledge about youth crime.

An Example of the Media Analysis of Newspaper Articles on Youth Crimes

The following media analysis research findings described here are derived from a study carried out by the author that involved searching the *National Post* newspaper from 1995 to 2003 for the term *young offender*. The search yielded 121 relevant articles. The results were separated by year and by subject matter, and were analyzed for discursive trends using critical discourse analysis, a qualitative approach that looks for themes in media discourse related to structural issues. The intent was to see what themes, if any, could be found in this national newspaper that would support a tougher approach to juvenile offenders. Five themes were identified: editorializing, moral outrage, atrocity tales, problems defining events, and the valorization of victims.

Although the *National Post*, being a national newspaper, was found to not have as many local stories about young offenders, it did contain articles that reflected the national debate over youth crime and the lack of effectiveness of the youth justice system and the disproportionate attention given to youth violent crimes. Between 1995 and 1998 there were no stories in the *National Post* directly related to young offenders. However, from 1999 onward stories about young offenders began to appear more frequently, and they dealt typically with more national trends and issues and youth violent crimes.

Description of Findings

There were ten stories about young offenders in 2000; three, in 2001; four, in 2002; and six, in 2003. Stories with little length were put into 'briefs'; articles that were really about something else, like the accidental shooting of an officer by another during pursuit of young offenders, were put into 'tangents'; and articles really making comments on some aspect of the system were put into 'overviews'. Some briefs, such as 'Ontario: Teen Convicted of Animal Cruelty after Barbecuing Dog' (*National Post*, Nov 29, 2001, p. A7), are horrifying because of their briefness, but in general there was little to comment on. So-called tangential articles were about prison reform, young offender facilities, and politicians inadvertently releasing the names of young offenders, which is against the law.

It was in the category of 'overviews' that general comments were often the most measured and the most interesting, such as comments on the law being too soft on young offenders, or Anthony Doob's dispute with Ontario's Justice Minister over the effectiveness of boot camps in reducing recidivism (2004). The government had taken the recidivism statistics from a boot camp facility and then compared them to those in regular jails and found a significant difference. However, the government had taken out those who had dropped out of the program before comparing the two groups statistically. And in 2001, Vic Toews, the new Canadian Alliance justice critic, voiced his wide-ranging objections to the youth justice reform that was to be tabled by Anne McLellan, the Justice Minister. On February 5, 2001, it was reported in the *National Post* that

> He opposes the new law's emphasis on cautions and out-of-court sanctions and its end to the practice of sending the worst offenders to adult court. 'If we don't bring accountability into our youth justice system, we are breeding criminals in youth courts,' he said. 'Violent, repeat offenders need to be held accountable in adult court.' He also wanted broader publication of names of young offenders. 'I think it's wrong that people in a community can't be warned about a young offender living among them.'

Similarly, David Young, the Attorney General of Ontario was quoted as saying on June 15, 2001, that 'None of these concerns [about the YCJA] were addressed in the bill. [The] Act is weak-kneed. It fails to protect the public.' These 'overview' articles with their comments on the system at large contextualize individual stories that might be published or aired about young offenders committing crimes. The year 2001 confirms the suspicion that unusual cases are highlighted. There are two stories about a Québec teenager with racist tendencies and psychotic delusions who lured a Cuban-born girl to a gravel pit to kill her, and the one about the girl who barbecued the family dog.

Between 2000 and 2003, the *National Post* contained 23 stories on young offenders. Because of this small sample it is difficult to generalize about the nature of the coverage. However, using an inductive method we can see if there are any patterns. The year 2000 saw an article about the murder by a cross-dressing teenager; two articles on the extradition hearing of an Israeli soldier wanted for murder in a park; one on a carjacking in Forest Hill; one on a first-degree murder case in Newfoundland; two articles on the trial for the accused in the case of the Chatham, Ontario, boy found hanging from a hook in a school bathroom; two on the swarming death trial for Reena Virk's assailants; and one on the trial of the youth who killed a shop owner by stabbing him 50 times. These cases, mostly murder, are also fairly unusual and highly violent. Given the number of youth crimes in Canada that year, and the number that went to court, the 'national reader' is left reading a highly select group of articles. The *Juristat* publication on crimes in Canada in 2000 reports that there were 22 635 youths charged with violent crime, of which 16 404 were assaults. Of those charged with homicide, eight per cent were youths, a total of 41 cases.

One year, however, stands out in comparison to the rest in the 1995 to 2003 period. In 1999, there were a total of 50 articles, about half of which were primarily articles about crimes. This is a remarkable spike in coverage, in sheer numbers alone. They include an article about a man who threatened police, who then arrived at his home to arrest him and a scuffle ensued and people were shot; another article about the shooting of an 11-year-old by a 13-year-old neighbour after a dis-agreement; two articles on a 16-year-old driving a van who struck and killed a police officer who was trying to lay down a nail belt to stop a high-speed chase outside Sudbury; another about an 11-year-old set ablaze with kerosene and a lighter; an article about a 14-year-old boy who murdered a taxi driver with a baseball bat on a Hobbema reserve while his friends stole the alcohol he was delivering; two on the so-called Reena Virk case; two on a young woman who killed her parents on a ranch in Alberta; and one on a young man who severed the hand of another with a machete outside a bar in North York. Again, these articles were almost all about murders, unusual enough events in themselves, and all were told in a sensationalist style.

In 1999 several more general pieces on victims, including greater compensation for crime vic-tims; one on a new section of the YCJA that would punish parents if their children continued to com-mit crimes while at home (March 6), introduced in 1997 by Chuck Cadman; a comment by Priscilla de Villiers (March 9) on the need to get tough on the causes of crime; and several on recidivism in youth care facilities. Chuck Cadman also spoke out on the need to lift publication bans in the cases of young offenders (March 12), and was criticized by then Justice Minister, Anne McLellan, for not understanding the youth crime legislation. There were also many other general articles on provi-sions of the Youth Criminal Justice Act and its implementation, and there were two on the rise in female offenders, and trends in juvenile offenders.

What sense can we make of this? Looking at the sheer frequency of articles, 1999 is an important turning point. Examined critically, newspaper reporting shows a connection between individual crime stories and the larger political structure. Several features of the 1999 coverage bear this out. There are a lot of overview pieces—more than half of the coverage for 1999—with commentary by experts, claims-makers who wished to advocate certain points of view about youth crime and its treatment, and politicians. These create a discursive context within which to see youth crime. These are enhanced by primary news articles that also serve as platforms for the valorization of victims and the vilification of young offenders. In one article, 'Dead Girl's Dad Says Youth's Sen-tence a "Joke": Dangerous Driving: Teenager Gets One Year for Accident that Killed Two' (May 11), for example, a youth is given a sentence of open custody for dangerous driving causing death. The victim's father, who is by extension also a victim, uses the occasion of a specific crime to criticize the larger workings of the criminal law. Similarly, the use of headlines to accomplish a quick reading of the cases is easily demonstrated, as in 'Daughter Charged in Brutal Slaying of Parents: First-degree Murder: Two Teens Also Face Charges in Killing of Alberta Couple' (May 26); '15-year Sentence Given in Home-Invasion Attack: Judge Calls Assault on Elderly Couple Horrific' (July 1); and 'Beat-ing Victim Still Comatose: "Gang-Style Attack"' (July 10), which involved the beating of Jonathan Wamback. There was also the Forest Hill carjacking, 'Teen in Forest Hill Carjacking Gets 3 Years:

Lawyer and Wife Kidnapped, Beaten and Robbed' (September 3); and 'Women Asked to Identify Their Underwear: Teen Charged after Bedroom Search Turns up Booty' (November 5).

The headlines draw in the national reader, who reads about salacious and horrific crimes in the context of a general commentary, which is pro-victim and critical of the way youths are treated by the court and under the law. The year 1999 was a year for headlines on articles about highly violent and senseless crimes, but also an opportunity for those who wished to make young offenders a social and political issue. In this way specific crime discourse is tied to a larger political discourse, a discourse that reflects and promotes a view of the world and of young offenders. The media then becomes a forum of debate, a punitive forum that is symbolic and communicative, regardless of youths' actual crimes or their ultimate dispensation. For most, the public forum of the media is the forum of the spectacle, and it is very real.

The key themes identified in this study, and examples of specific newspaper articles in which they appeared, are highlighted in Box 5.1. These themes arguably frame the claim that the law on young offenders needed to be changed to make it less lenient on youths. The findings show that overall the *National Post* often served as a venue for giving voice to the claim that youth crime was out of control. However, it is not simply that the media gets it wrong. The fact is that both sensationalism and correction, outlandish exaggeration and sober caution are part of the public sphere that is the media. This debate, carried on in the public arena, creates a different way of knowing than is available through official crime statistics and/or self-report and victimization studies. It is important to see how the media constructs the reality that is youth crime and at the same time it is important to realize that for most people that *is* their reality.

Summary

It is easy to privilege one way of knowing youth crime over another, for example, using official statistics to criticize the way in which the media portray youth crime. Similarly, we could use self-report surveys to criticize police statistics, as if the former is better than the latter. Such approaches as context analysis are useful in using one measure to understand the limits of another. However, such approaches suggest that one way of 'knowing' youth crime is inherently better than another.

Instead of privileging one way of knowing youth crime over the other, we suggest here that they are, at best, complementary forms of knowledge, and, even better, different ways of knowing the world of youth crime. Yes, the media exaggerates and distorts youth crime (from the perspective of official statistics), but perhaps the media is contributing to the public debate in a way that is unaccountable to official statistics and self-report surveys.

Some analysts (for example McCormick 2010) have begun to get at some of the reasons for why this happens by suggesting that the media is part of a public debate at the beginning of the twenty-first century that is not accountable to official ways of knowing. For some reason we have moved to a harsher way of categorizing and conceptualizing youth crime, and the media is an important forum for that public debate.

Box 5.1 Youth Justice in Action

Media Sample

1. Editorializing

'A Young Killer Gets Kid-Glove Treatment: Special Hearing May Set Murderer Free after Just 29 Months'

'He may be the luckiest young killer in Canada, and if his luck continues to hold, he could end up serving only 29 months for the vicious murder of an elderly Holocaust survivor he stabbed nine times in the throat in broad daylight. . . .' (1106 words)

Byline: Christie Blatchford, *National Post,* Page: A1, Feb. 26, 1999

2. Moral Outrage

'Dead Girl's Dad Says Youth's Sentence a 'Joke': Dangerous Driving: Teenager Gets One Year for Accident that Killed Two'

'. . . he was driving struck and killed two other teens. Court heard that the accused, who can not be named as he is a young offender, drank six beers in two hours before getting behind the wheel. He was originally charged with impaired driving causing. . .' (326 words)

Byline: Kelly Egan *(Ottawa Citizen)*, Page: A10, *National Post,* May 11, 1999.

3. Atrocity Tales

'Teen Convicted of Animal Cruelty after Barbecuing Dog'

'A 17-year-old girl was convicted this week of animal cruelty after she beat and then barbecued her family's Pomeranian. The 12-year-old dog, named Peppy, had been a family pet for the past seven years. The young offender could face up to six months in jail, but the horrific case has renewed calls for stiffer penalties.' (57 words)

Source: Brief, *National Post,* Page: A7, Thurs. Nov. 29, 2001.

4. Problem Defining Event

'"Killer Kelly" Was Toughest Girl in the Gang, Friends Said: Results of Psychiatric Examinations Contradictory'

'. . . At the time of the fatal attack, Ellard was 15 and could have been tried as a young offender. In deciding whether to try her as an adult, the court turned to the evidence of a battery of experts, including. . .' (563 words)

Byline: Mark Hume, *National Post,* Page: A8, Apr. 1, 2000.

5. Valorization of Victims

'Bill to Give Victims of Crime More Rights: Offenders Would Pay into Fund to Help Injured Party'

'. . . Reform MP who has campaigned for increased victims' rights since his 16-year-old son, Jesse, was murdered by a young offender almost seven years ago, welcomed the new legislation. Mr. Cadman noted MPs from all parties supported victims . . .' (461 words)

Byline: Tim Naumetz (Southam News), Page: A7, *National Post,* Apr. 16, 1999.

We emphasize once again that this kind of media-based editorializing has been shown in many research studies to have measurable impacts on public perceptions and legislation affecting at-risk youth, young offenders, and the youth justice system.

Key Terms

content analysis

context analysis

convergence

critical discourse analysis

cultivation hypothesis

folk devils

frame analysis

ideological flexibility

moral panic

social constructionism

Review Questions

1. This chapter describes three ways of knowing youth crime. What are these ways of knowing and how do they overlap?

2. What are the major problems with official statistics on youth crime as outlined in this chapter?

3. This chapter emphasizes the media as an important way for the public to know about youth crime.

4. How do 'atrocity tales' and other media patterns create a distorted reality of youth crime for the public?

Critical Thinking Questions

1. The valorization of victims in the media anchors the claim that politicians should get tougher on youth crime. Does this benefit the cause of victims in our society?

2. What would be a way to revise media coverage of youth crime to make it more accurate, less sensationalistic, and more educational for the public?

3. Imagine that you were a journalist who was asked to explain and defend why youth crime is reported in the media in the way that it is. How would you do this? What kinds of arguments would you put forth?

Suggested Readings

Herman, E.S. and Chomsky, N. (1988). *Manufacturing consent: The political economy of the mass media.* New York: Pantheon Books.

Fawcett, B. (1986). *Cambodia: A book for people who find television too slow.* Vancouver: Talonbooks.

McLuhan, M. and Fiore, Q. (1967). *The medium is the message: An inventory of effects.* New York: Bantam.

Suggested Weblinks

Manufacturing Consent: Video
http://video.google.ca/videoplay?docid=-5631882395226827730#
• The documentary *Manufacturing Consent*, which takes a look at the propaganda model of the media.

Project Censored: Media Democracy in Action
www.projectcensored.org
• Covers the media's most underreported (but important) stories.

The Marshall McLuhan Center on Global Communications
www.mcluhanmedia.com/m_mcl_page_index.html
• About Marshall McLuhan and the Center, which was formed by his daughter.

References

Altheide, D. (2006). Terrorism and the politics of fear. *Cultural Studies, 6*(4): 415–39.

Barnhorst, R. (2004). The Youth Criminal Justice Act: New directions and implementation issues, *Canadian Journal of Criminology and Criminal Justice, 46*(3): 231–50.

Baron, S. and Hartnagel, T. (1996). 'Lock 'em up': Attitudes toward punishing juvenile offenders. *Canadian Journal of Criminology, 28*(2): 191–212.

Beattie, S. and Cotter, A. (2010). Homicide in Canada, 2009. *Juristat.*

Best, J. (1993). Threatened children: Rhetoric and concern about child victims. Chicago: University of Chicago Press.

Best, J. (Ed.). (1995). *Images of issues: Typifying contemporary social problems.* New York: Aldine de Gruyter.

Best, J. (1999). *Random violence: How we talk about new crimes and new victims.* Berkeley: University of California Press.

Best, J. and Horiuchi, G. (1985). The razor blade in the apple: The social construction of urban legends. *Social Problems 32*(5): 488–99.

Black, D. (1970). Production of crime rates. *American Sociological Review, 35*(4): 733–48.

Blatchford, C. (1999, Feb. 26). A young killer gets kid-glove treatment: Special hearing may set murderer free after just 29 months. *National Post*, A1.

Booth, A., Johnson, D., and Choldin, H. (1977). Correlates of city crime rates: Victimization surveys versus official statistics. *Social Problems, 25*(2): 187–97.

Boulahanis, J. and Heltsey, M. (2004). Perceived fears: The reporting patterns of juvenile homicide in Chicago newspapers. *Criminal Justice Policy Review 15*(2): 132–60.

Canadian Centre on Substance Abuse (2011). Canadian Addiction Survey (CAS). Retrieved from: http://www.ccsa.ca/eng/priorities/research/canadianaddiction/pages/default.aspx.

CanLII. (1996). Controlled Drugs and Substances Act, 1996. Retrieved 23 Dec., 2010, from http://www.canlii.org

Cantor, D. and Lynch, J. (2000). Self-report surveys as measures of crime and criminal victimization, *Criminal Justice*, 4.

Carrington, P.J., Matarazzo, A. and deSouza, P. (2005). Court careers of a Canadian birth cohort. Crime and Justice Research Paper Series. Statistics Canada Catalogue no. 85-561-MIE, no. 006. Ottawa.

CBC 2010. Archie Billard back in prison. Retrieved from: http://www.cbc.ca/news/canada/nova-scotia/story/2010/10/25/ns-archie-billard-release-revoked.html. Chiricos, T., Eschholz, S. and Gertz, M. (1997). Crime, news and fear of crime: Toward an identification of audience effects. *Social Problems 44*(3): 342 M. 57.

Cloninger, D. and Sartorius, L. (1979). Crime rates, clearance rates and enforcement effort: The case of Houston, Texas. *American Journal of Economics and Sociology, 38*(4): 389–402.

Cohen, S. (1972). *Folk devils and moral panics: The creation of the mods and rockers.* London: MacGibbon and Rae.

CTV. (2006, Jan. 11). N.S. teen gets adult sentence for woman's death.

D'Arcy, S. (2007). The 'Jamaican criminal' in Toronto, 1994: A critical ontology. *Canadian Journal of Communication*, 32: 2.

Dauvergne, M. and Turner, J. (2010). Police reported crime statistics in Canada, 2009. *Juristat*. Ottawa.

Doob, A. (1998, June 1). Young Offenders Act, *Globe and Mail,* Letter to the editor.

Doob, A. and Cesaroni, C. (2004). Responding to youth crime in Canada. Toronto: University of Toronto Press.

Dowler, K. (2003). Media consumption and public attitudes toward crime and justice: The relationship between fear of crime, punitive attitudes, and perceived police effectiveness. *Journal of Criminal Justice and Popular Culture, 10*(2): 109–26.

Doyle, V. (2000). Lead us not into temptation: The London, Ontario, 'kiddie-porn ring' and the construction of a moral panic. *International Journal of Canadian Studies*, 21.

Egan, K. (1999, May 11). Dead girl's dad says youth's sentence a 'joke': Dangerous driving: Teenager gets one year for accident that killed two. *National Post, (Ottawa Citizen)*, A10.

Faith, K. and Y. Jiwani. (2002). The social construction of 'dangerous' girls and women. In B Schissel and C. Brooks (Eds.), *Marginality and condemnation: An introduction to critical criminology* (pp. 83–107). Halifax: Fernwood Press.

Fairclough, N. (2003). *Analyzing Discourse: Textual Analysis for Social Research*. London: Routledge.

Fishman, M. (1978). Crime waves as ideology. *Social Problems, 25*(5): 531–43.

Fishman, M. (1981). Police news: Constructing an image of crime. *Urban Life 9*(4): 371–94.

Garofalo, J. (1981). Crime and the mass media: A selective review of research. *Journal of Research in Crime and Delinquency 18*, 319–50.

Gerbner, G., Gross, L., Morgan, M., and Signorielli, N. (1980). The mainstreaming of America: Violence profile no. 11. *Journal of Communications 30*, 10–29.

Gomes, J., Bertrand, L., Paetsch, J., and Hornick, J. (2003). Self-reported delinquency among Alberta's youth: Findings from a survey of 2,001 Junior and senior high school students. *Adolescence*, 38.

Goode, E. (2009). *Moral panics: The social construction of deviance*. Blackwell.

Graber, D. (1980). *Crime news and the public*. New York: Praeger.

Hawkins, R. and Pingree, S. (1980). Some progress in the cultivation effect. *Communication Research 7*, 193–226.

Hindelang, M.J. (1974). Public opinion regarding crime, criminal justice, and related topics. *Journal of Research in Crime and Delinquency* 11: 101–16.

Hogeveen, B. (2005). 'If we are tough on crime, if we punish crime, then people get the message': Constructing and governing the punishable young offender in Canada during the late 1990s. Punishment and Society, 7(1): 73–89.

Hume, M. (2000, April 1). 'Killer Kelly' was toughest girl in the gang, friends said: Results of psychiatric examinations contradictory. *National Post*, A8.

Jenkins, P. (1994). *Using murder: The social construction of serial homicide.* New York: Aldine de Gruyter.

Juristat (2007). Police-reported crime statistics in Canada, 2009. Retrieved from: http://www.statcan.gc.ca/pub/85-002-x/2010002/article/11292-eng.htm.

Juristat. (2008, May 16). Youth crime. *The Daily.*

Juristat. (2010, Oct.). Police personnel and expenditures. Statistics Canada.

Kappeler, V. (1996). *The mythology of crime and criminal justice.* Prospect Heights: Waveland Press.

Lowman, J. (2000). Violence and the Outlaw Status of (Street) Prostitution in Canada. *Violence Against Women*, 6(9): 987 -1011.

Mast, B., Benson, B., and Rasmussen, D. (2000). Entrepreneurial police and drug enforcement policy. *Public Choice, 104*(3-4), 285–308.

McCormick, C. (2008). *Criminology in Canada: Theories, patterns and typologies.* Toronto: Nelson.

McCormick, C. (2010). *Constructing danger: The mis/representation of crime in the news.* Halifax: Fernwood.

Muncie, J. (2004). *Youth and crime* (2nd ed.). London: Sage.

Naumetz, T. (1999, April 16). Bill to give victims of crime more rights: Offenders would pay into fund to help injured party. *National Post* (Southam News), A7.

Savoie, J. (2007). Youth self-reported delinquency, Toronto, 2006. Statistics Canada–Catalogue no. 85-002-XPE, Vol. 27, no. 6.

Schissel, B. (1997). *Blaming children: Youth crime, moral panic and the politics of hate.* Halifax: Fernwood.

Schissel, B. (2006). *Still blaming children: Youth conduct and the politics of child hating.* Halifax: Fernwood.

Smandych, R. (2001). *Youth justice: history, legislation, and reform.* Toronto: Harcourt.

Smart, R. and Adlaf, E. (1991). Substance use and problems among Toronto street youth. *British Journal of Addiction, 86*(8): 999–1010.

Spencer, J. (2005). It's not as simple as it seems: Ambiguous culpability and ambivalent affect in news representations of violent youth. *Symbolic Interaction 28*(1), 47–65.

Sprott, J. (1996). Understanding public views of youth crime and the youth justice system. *Canadian Journal of Criminology, 38*(3): 271–90.

Surette, R. (1998). *Media, crime, and criminal justice: Images and realities.* New York: Wadsworth Publishing.

Tanner, J. and Wortley, S. (2002). The Toronto youth crime & victimization survey: Overview report. Toronto: Centre of Criminology, University of Toronto.

Wikipedia. (2010). List of countries by intentional homicide rate. Retrieved 23 December, 2010.

Wodak, R. and Meyer, M. (2000). *Methods of critical discourse analysis.* Thousand Oaks, CA: Sage.

6 Canadian Girls and Crime in the Twenty-First Century

Sibylle Artz, Lorinda Stoneman, and Marge Reitsma-Street

Overview

This chapter offers a broad overview of the way in which girls who encounter the criminal justice system are dealt with in Canada. Readers are presented with material that will assist them in understanding and critiquing Canadian judicial responses to female youth crime and in identifying new promising directions for dealing with female youth offenders. Readers will also learn that in Canada, despite the shift in legislation initiated by the Youth Criminal Justice Act (YCJA) in 2003, far too many girls, notably Aboriginal girls, are being locked up and that Aboriginal girls are vastly overrepresented in Canada's youth justice system. This overrepresentation is a perpetual problem in Canada, a problem that the YCJA seems to have exacerbated because the funding necessary to administer extrajudicial measures has not been distributed in ways that make community-based intervention possible, especially in less affluent and remote communities. As a result, Canadian custody centres are filled with marginalized, under-resourced girls who are often victims of childhood abuse and neglect and who suffer from mental-health and addiction challenges. Recommendations are provided for instituting policies and practices to reverse systemic and personal discrimination based on gender and racial inequity and for keeping neo-liberal and neo-conservative crime-control policies in check.

Key Objectives

After reading this chapter, you should be able to:

- Identify and discuss Canadian female youth offending patterns.
- Understand and critique Canadian judicial responses to female youth crime.
- Outline traditional and contemporary explanations of female crime.
- Identify promising new directions in responding to female youth crime.

Introduction

In order to understand and respond to girls and crime, it is necessary to examine patterns of crime and trends in juvenile justice. We begin this chapter by looking at such patterns using official statistics and self-report surveys. Next, we present a brief review of theories that seek to explain female crime and delinquency along with a critique of the ways in which female youth crime is conceptualized. The chapter ends with a discussion about the challenges of working effectively with delinquent girls in a system that, since 2006, has been under considerable political pressure from the Harper Conservative federal government with its 'tough on crime' agenda, an agenda that has been heavily criticized by experts for being wasteful, counterproductive, and ultimately ineffective in dealing with youth crime (Cesaroni and Bala 2008).

Most delinquent girls commit minor crimes. Any apprehension or conviction, however, can have costly implications for girls, for their families, for their friends, and for society. Looking at the various ways that female crime is understood and responded to in law and practice can help reveal how social order is established and held in place, sometimes despite the fact that solid research suggests that the opposite of what is being done should be done. Examining crime and punishment critically shows that crime is not a static phenomenon but one that changes as our ideologies and knowledge about crime and punishment change.

Patterns of Crime and Trends in Juvenile Justice

Girls, like boys, break the law but not often. Although girls do engage in illegal behaviours, they rarely develop crime specialties (Chesney-Lind and Pasko 2004). Self-report data on delinquency in the US show that incidence rates have not substantially changed in more than a decade. Indeed, rather than showing increases in serious behaviours like engaging in fights, girls are reporting lower, not higher, rates of the use of aggression and violence in recent years (Chesney-Lind 2010). In Canada, Barron and Lacombe (2005) argue that recent public concern suggesting girl violence is increasing is largely a social construction and a 'product of a moral panic' (p. 52). They also note that data that supports this notion of a rising violent crime rate among girls fail to take into account policy changes and changes to the ways we count crime. Still, despite relatively low rates of offending, the study of girls' offending remains an important social science task because, if not considered separately, girls easily become lost in comparison to the male population (Kong and AuCoin 2008). Although girls join with other girls and with boys to commit crime, they may do so for reasons that are different than the reasons that boys have for engaging in these actions (see Miller 2001). However, as we will discuss later in the chapter, we should exercise caution when framing girls as different than boys because 'gender differences are often pathologized' (Irwin and Chesney-Lind 2008, p. 842), locating differences in girls as weaknesses in their biological and psychological chemistry.

Canadian Judicial Responses to Female Youth Crime

Official Charges

An accurate summary of the crime rates of youth or of adults of either gender is illusive. Official police and court statistics, however, can provide key indicators of how the Canadian judicial system responds to some of the illegal behaviours of some girls (see Figure 6.1). To ensure a reliable estimate of Canadian girls' involvement in crime, it is necessary to use more than one indicator and more than one source and to interpret indicators in a comparative context—over time and as a ratio of the general population.

As Figure 6.1 suggests, only 3 per cent of all Canadians charged and brought to court in 2006 were girls (Statistics Canada 2006a; 2006b). It is not youth, but adults, especially adult men, who are likely to enter the court system for crimes against persons, property, or the public order. Additionally, although there are nearly equal numbers of girls and boys under the age of 18 in the Canadian population, most of the charges laid in youth court continue to be against boys. In the early 1980s, one in ten cases in youth courts were against girls. Twenty years later, the gender ratio narrowed to one in five, and data from 2006/07 show that the ratio is nearing about 1:3.5 for all cases (Statistics Canada 2006b). While youth crime for both genders appears to have increased somewhat until the mid-1990s, a significant drop in crime rates for both girls and boys (20 per cent and 14 per cent, respectively) in 2003/2004 and a further 12 per cent drop for girls and a 10 per cent drop for boys in 2005/06 have led to an overall decrease despite recent slight increases of 1.5 per cent for girls and 0.5 per cent for boys in 2006/2007 (Kong and AuCoin 2008). Although the causes of the increase in the 1990s remain unclear, it is widely agreed that the statistics do not illustrate an explosion of female crime. One reason for the apparent increase is that the upper age limits for minors in the youth justice system changed from 16 to 18 years of age in 1984. The total population of youth also

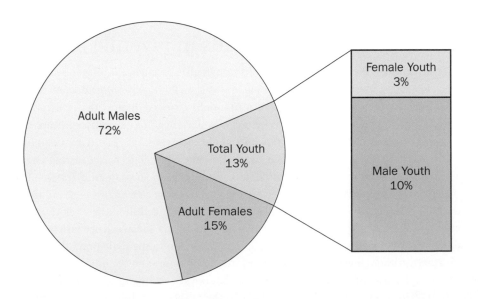

Figure 6.1 2006 Total Canadian Court Cases

Source: Statistics Canada, CANSIM Table 2520048, Youth Court Survey, Number of Cases, by Sex of Accused, Annually; Table 2520044, Adult Criminal Court Survey, Number of Cases by Sex of Accused, 2006.

increased until the mid-1990s, at the same time that changes in charging patterns by school officials, police, and prosecutors pushed crime rates up (Doob and Sprott 1998; Estrada 2001).

In 2005, Steffensmeier, Schwartz, Zhong, and Ackerman found that the upward trend of girls' offending behaviour could not be replicated using unofficial longitudinal sources. They hypothesized that changes in enforcement, in youth justice policy, and in culture are better explanations of the changing charge rates. Because policy has changed in a more expressive and punitive direction (Steffensmeier et al. 2005), actions that previously would not have come to the attention of police are reclassified as criminal matters. These exacerbating policies include zero tolerance policies in schools, a lower threshold for what constitutes criminality in domestic arguments, and the inclusion of parent–child and sibling altercations as chargeable domestic offences (Woolford 2009), along with the net-widening effect of using criminal charges for minor offences to preventing anticipated future criminal risk (Steffensmeier et al. 2005). These policy changes might help to explain why there appears to be an upward trend in female major assault charges from 1991 to 2001—an increase from 644 to 1041 charges for major assault, (Statistics Canada 2002c) that is continuing through to 2006/2007 (Statistics Canada 2006b). Also, more girls were charged with minor assault, such as shoving, punching, and verbal threats, in schoolyards in 2001 than in 1991, although the numbers fluctuated considerably over the years.

Further, despite the data showing that girls are 'catching up' to boys in their commission of criminal offences, Sprott and Doob (2009) affirm that this is not so. In fact, because fewer boys are becoming involved in the justice system as compared to the early 1990s, it is only the ratio of girls to boys that is narrowing. Sprott and Doob suggest that what is really a difference in offending patterns for boys is being interpreted as a reason to become alarmed about girls. Instead, they show quite convincingly that delinquent adjudication for girls has remained quite stable, and even dipped slightly, while that for boys has noticeably declined. For these reasons, we need to be cautious when assessing female offending (Sharpe and Gelsthorpe 2009).

The rates of females charged by police started to decline late in the 1990s, and the comparable rate for boys has dropped even more. The number of females charged by police was 2230 per 100 000 Canadian female youth in 1996; 1891 in 1999; 2046 in 2001 (Statistics Canada 2002b) and; 1366 in 2006 (Taylor-Butts and Bressan 2007). According to Statistics Canada data, this represents a 34 per cent decrease in charges for female youth and a 38 per cent drop in charges for boys between 1997 and 2006. Looking solely at the years since the inception of the YCJA, the decrease in charges is more pronounced for girls than for boys: the period from 2002 to 2006 saw a 31 per cent decrease in charges for girls and a 25 per cent decrease in charges for boys (Taylor-Butts and Bressan 2007). As we will discuss later, this difference can be explained with attention to the differences in frequency and types of offence commissions typical for girls as compared to boys. For example, female youth were charged with minor theft at nearly twice the rate of young males. Such minor, nonviolent offences are most 'likely to be targeted for diversion under the YCJA' (Taylor-Butts, and Bressen 2007, p. 6). Accordingly, girls' delinquency is more likely to be dealt with outside of the formal justice system through police warnings and cautions.

Another reason that caution is required as we examine girls' delinquency as represented by percentage-based quantitative statistics is that the base number of girls involved in crime is so small. For example, in 2005 four girls were charged with homicide. The following year, six girls faced homicide charges (Statistics Canada 2006b), accounting for a 50 per cent jump in these violent offences but representing only two more girls being involved.

Table 6.1, which shows the most recent data available, presents the types of crimes for which girls and boys made court appearances in 2006 by principal charge, listed in descending order of seriousness. The most frequent charge resulting in a court appearance for girls is minor assault followed closely by theft and **administrative offences**; these three offences amount to nearly 60 per cent of

administrative offences

Offences against the administration of justice, that is, violations of court-ordered behavioural requirements, such as complying with a curfew, attending mandated programs, and following through on all manner of bail conditions and probation orders.

Table 6.1 Specific Youth Court Cases, 2006, By Gender

Specific Youth Court Cases—Principal Charge for 2006	Female %	Male %
Murder & Attempt	0.07	0.13
Robbery	2.2	4.5
Against Person Major*	6.2	6.0
Against Person Minor**	**21.2**	**13.1**
Sexual Offences	0.3	2.6
Theft	**19.9**	**12.0**
Break & Enter	4.9	10.0
Fraud	2.6	1.2
Possess Stolen Goods	6.4	6.3
Trafficking/Possession	4.4	7.4
Mischief	5.3	7.5
Administrative/Against YCJA***	**18.3**	**16.1**
Other Property Crimes	0.3	0.7
Criminal Code Traffic	1.2	2.1
Other Criminal Code	4.2	8.5
Residual Federal Statutes	2.5	1.8
Total by Sex	**100%**	**100%**

*Major assault; assault with a weapon (Assault Level II, section 267), aggravated assault (Assault Level III, section 268), and other assaults (assaulting a police officer and unlawfully causing bodily harm). Excludes murder, attempt, and robbery.

** Common assault, harassment, and other crimes against the person.

***Includes failure to comply with disposition; failure to comply with undertaking; assist/interfere/other; contempt against youth court; breach of recognizance; failure to appear; failure to comply with probation order; escape custody; unlawfully at large and charges against the YCJA.

Source: Statistics Canada 2006b, CANSIM table 2520048.

charges for girls in court. For boys, the most frequent charge resulting in a court appearance is for administrative offences (and has been for several years). Next in frequency for both genders are charges for theft under $5000 and possession of stolen goods. Infrequent are major serious violent crimes against people.

For over 30 years, Canadian girls have been charged with fewer than 20 murders or attempted murders per year and usually fewer than 10 (see also Reitsma-Street 1999)—a rate that holds in the most recently available data (Statistics Canada 2006b). The number of females accused of homicides varied from 8 in 2007 to 4 in 2008 (Beattie 2009, p. 26). Additionally, fluctuations are noted when rates of total violent charges are calculated in relation to the total population of female youth. For example, there were 452 charges laid against girls for major and minor violence per 100 000 female youth in 1996, compared to 444 in 1999, and 502 in 2001 (Sprott and Doob 2003). In 2006, female youth were responsible for 26 per cent of violent youth crime, 25 per cent of property crime involving youth, and 17 per cent of mischief involving youth (Statistics Canada 2006b). However, as we noted earlier, these percentages are difficult to interpret because of the decline in male charges and the stability in female charges. We cannot, therefore, use simple arithmetic to make sense of our computations.

Whether we believe there is an increase or a decrease in the crime rate of girls depends in part on an accurate understanding of the information presented and how calculations are made and interpreted (compare Sprott and Doob 2009; Estrada 2001). An important issue with the data is that the category of 'violent' crime suggests acts of terror and serious harm. But media reports on numbers of violent crime can be misleading as they usually include both the more frequent minor assault charges and infrequent major aggravated assaults with deadly weapons and murder. Sensational media portrayals of female involvement in crime have fuelled the popular perspective of females acting more like males, a perspective that has been refuted by research over the past two decades (Chesney-Lind and Pasko 2004; Males 2010). Chesney-Lind and Irwin (2008) argue that the media propels a 'misogynistic framing of girlhood' (p. 3), continuing the oppression and subservience of girls and young women by warning them of the repercussions for non-normative female behaviour. In essence, the media performs a strong social-control role. Further, when public perception is informed solely by media accounts of violence, the very important contexts for violence are usually missing, leading to the scapegoating of youth for family and societal problems that are beyond their control (Green and Healy 2003), and the development of moral panics that exaggerate girls' involvement in violent and serious crimes (Dean 2005; Males 2010).

Administrative Offences

What is perhaps most surprising is how often Canadian girls have been charged with administrative offences in the past two and more decades. Violations of administrative orders include failure to appear in court, failure to comply with a condition of bail or a probation order, the infrequent escape from custody, and the more frequent committing an offence 'against the Youth Criminal Justice Act'—a new offence added as an amendment in 1985 to the YOA (and now the YCJA) that makes not complying with a probation order, for example coming home later than one's court-ordered curfew or consuming alcohol, a criminal offence. In 1985–86, about one charge in twenty (5.1 per cent) against girls was for failure to comply with administrative orders. Since that time, there has been a sharp increase in the rates: 27.3 per cent in 1995–96; 31 per cent in 1997–98; and 33.8 per cent by the year 2000. Rates for administrative charges against boys also increased rapidly during those years, from 3.9 per cent in 1985 to 22.5 per cent in 2000, but not as much as for girls. Just before the introduction of the YCJA, one charge in three of all charges laid in youth court for girls was for noncompliance.

The striking increase in administrative charges throughout the 1990s illustrates how difficult it can be to obtain an accurate picture of girls and crime. We need to appreciate that changes in laws and regulations and problematic practices have implications for crime rates and our perceptions of reality. Sprott and Doob (2009) suggest that the trend of the 1990s is continuing and that in North America administrative offences are still being used disproportionately with girls. Such charges can push girls further into the youth justice system, turning them into recidivists and leaving them with sizable criminal records.

The increase in charging girls (and boys) with technical administrative violations under the YOA was a trend much recognized and examined in research (Doob and Sprott 1998; Reitsma-Street 2005). A central question in this research was this: What is the reason for this trend—especially among girls? The answer to this question is that judges were adding more conditions to probation orders than before, including attending drug courses, keeping sometimes unreasonable curfews, not associating with certain peers, and going to school. Failure to comply with these probation conditions, then, became the new offences. Sometimes judges feel pressured to add treatment and other conditions to probation, to custody, or to conditional sentences as insurance companies and governments cut back on funds for mental health, addictions, and other services (Chesney-Lind and Pasko 2004). In 2000, Corrado, Odgers, and Cohen reported that 44 per cent of the charges laid against girls in a study of two Canadian custody centres were for breaches of court orders; therefore, girls were spending more time in custody for administrative than for serious substantive offences. To explain these findings, Corrado and his colleagues (2000) suggest that professionals were frustrated in their attempts to deal with the difficulties girls in their study faced: half were Aboriginal and there were few services on the street or in the girls' home communities. Thus, administrative charges and custodial sentences appear to be used by youth justice personnel to prevent girls from returning to unsafe streets or possibly to sex trade work.

The Youth Criminal Justice Act

One of the reasons for the development of the Youth Criminal Justice Act (YCJA) in 2003 was to respond to the growing youth incarceration rate that we have discussed above. It was widely known that, throughout the 1990s, Canada's incarceration rate for youth was one of the highest in the Western world, higher than even that of the US. The Department of Justice approached the new youth justice legislation 'with a more inclusive framework, focusing on public awareness, crime prevention, education, child welfare, health, family and the community' (Calverley 2007, p. 2). An important part of the YCJA is a clearer delineation of serious and minor offences such that the most serious intervention (such as custody) can be given to the most serious offenders while minor offenders have the opportunity to be diverted from the formal system and take part in a community-based program or receive a warning.

While an initial key feature of the YCJA was the intent to decrease custody for minor and administrative offences, as the act was moving through the legislative process on its way to becoming law, many expressed concern that the YCJA's post-custody supervision regulations might increase the number of administrative charges as new charges might be laid and a return to custody be possible if supervision conditions are not complied with (see Box 6.1).

Box 6.1 Youth Justice in Action

Administrative Offences Under the YCJA

Sprott and Doob (2009) discuss the 2007 case of M.B. as an example of why we should carefully consider how the spirit of policy might be lost in practice. M.B. was a 16-year-old girl, who, under the YCJA, was given a maximum custodial sentence of six months after being charged with damage to property (she damaged her room in her parents' home). Her offence triggered a charge for the failure to comply with her previous disposition (that she keep the peace and exhibit good behaviour). Although the YCJA has made it tougher to sentence youth to custody—with guidelines stating that custody should only be used for youths charged for a violent offence, those who have multiple past sentences, or those who have failed to comply with noncustodial sentences—incarcerating nonviolent youth like M.B. is still permitted. In fact, M.B.'s custodial sentence due to her failure to comply was lengthier than 93 per cent of custodial sentences.

Sprott and Doob (2009) speculate that such occurrences signal the existence of cases where, despite the YCJA's clarity that youth cannot be held in custody for welfare purposes, detention—especially for girls—is still being used for this reason instead of solely for the protection of the public.

Perhaps of greater concern, Sprott and Doob (2010) indicate that although girls usually commit nonviolent offences and have shorter histories of criminal involvement compared to their male peers, girls are typically given more conditions upon their release from remand and custody. Those girls who commit nonviolent offences are also just as likely as those who commit violent offences to receive counselling or treatment orders.

What are the implications of these patterns for the treatment of girls under the YCJA?

As we mentioned earlier, since the introduction of the YCJA in 2003, decreases in charge rates have been greater for female youth when compared to their male counterparts, likely because more girls are being diverted. Sharpe and Gelsthorpe (2009) discuss community-based alternatives to custody (diversion) but also highlight the concerns that girls who fail community programs will then be 'fast-tracked into custody' (p. 202). Likewise, in Canada a key concern is that community programs will continue to experience a lack of government funding, thereby deterring judges from utilizing these options at the sentencing stage and undermining the effectiveness of useful programs.

In 2006, measures other than formal charges (police cautions, formal warnings, extrajudicial measures) were used to handle 64 per cent of accused female youth compared to 55 per cent of male youth (Taylor-Butts and Bressen 2007). Interestingly, for youth involved in property and violent crime, a greater proportion of females (72 per cent and 59 per cent, respectively) were dealt with by means other than a formal charge than males were (62 per cent and 51 per cent, respectively). One suggestion is that when females commit these offences, they are less likely than males to use a weapon and that in some cases their offence histories may be shorter (Taylor-Butts and Bressen 2007).

Current Responses Have Led to an Overrepresentation of Aboriginal Girls

One glaring issue that has a long history in Canada is the overrepresentation of Aboriginal female youth in custody. In 2008–09, Aboriginal female youth represented 44 per cent of all female youth sentenced to custody (Calverley et al. 2010, p. 14). This is up from 29 per cent to 35 per cent in 2004–05. Additionally, Aboriginal girls make up 34 per cent of females on remand, and 31 per cent of those admitted to probation. These are all higher percentages than those for Aboriginal boys' correctional services involvement (Calverley et al. 2010). While the number of females admitted to remand has increased and the number of females admitted to sentenced custody has decreased overall, the decline was much smaller for Aboriginal females. At present, 58 per cent of girls in BC custody centres are Aboriginal while only 8 per cent of the BC youth population is Aboriginal (Sharpe and Gelsthorpe 2009). Canada's current youth justice practices seem to be especially problematic for Aboriginal girls, who experience very high rates of administrative charges. Custody admissions for administrative offences in one youth custody centre in BC in 1999–2000 illustrate the disparity between gender and Aboriginal status. While 16.5 per cent of all young offenders were admitted to custody for an administrative offence, the rate was 47.8 per cent for Aboriginal females (Ministry for Children and Families 2000).

Court Decisions and Dispositions for Convicted Girls

Not all girls charged in youth court are convicted and sentenced. Every year a substantial proportion of girls—38 per cent in 1999–2000—have their cases withdrawn, dismissed, or stayed (held in abeyance). As with the rest of the justice system, where female youth are found in far fewer numbers than male youth, female youth are admitted to correctional services at a much smaller rate than male youth. Research concludes that the trend of admissions to correctional services has been declining for nearly a decade and was hastened by the YCJA. Consistent with trends from 2004–05, in 2008–09, female youth made up 24 per cent of all youth admitted to supervised probation, 21 per cent of those admitted to remand, and 17 per cent of those admitted to sentenced custody (Calverley et al. 2010). While the incarceration rate for female youth is 2 per 10 000, the rate for male youth is 7 times that, at 15 per 10 000 (Calverley et al. 2010). Although the total incarceration rates for both boys and girls have been relatively consistent since 2005–06, a closer look yields an increase in youth on remand who are awaiting trial or sentence, which is up 17 per cent for both girls and boys alongside a decline in sentenced custody (-14 per cent for girls and -22 per cent for boys).

The most common sentence or disposition for girls, like boys, is probation. Community service can also be added as a condition to a probation order, with the unintended consequence of increasing the chance for girls to not comply and being charged with noncompliance and as a consequence returned to court as recidivists, as mentioned earlier in this chapter. Since the YCJA, several new community corrections sanctions are available with the aim of correcting the upward trend in youth incarceration rates. In order to allow for reintegration following a custodial sentence, youth are sentenced to community supervision to commence once released from custody (akin to statutory release after serving a third of the sentence in the adult system). Taylor-Butts and Bressen (2007) noted the likelihood that conjoined sentencing would decrease the use of probation under the YCJA since the community portion of the custodial sentence is now automatic. Along with the YCJA, in 2003 deferred custody and supervision orders (similar to adult conditional sentences) were introduced as the newest available sanctions in cases where the judge wishes to impose conditions on the youth where the penalty for noncompliance is custody (Kong 2009). Since the YCJA, there has been a marked decrease in not only charge rates for all youth but also court rates (Taylor-Butts and Bressen 2007).

Under the old laws, justice officials had to request permission of a youth court to transfer a girl to adult court for serious crimes. In 1995 presumptive offences were added to the YOA, placing the onus on girls (and boys) aged 16 and 17 to prove to a judge that they should not be sentenced as an adult for serious violent offences (Bala, Carrington, and Roberts 2009). There have been very few Canadian girls transferred per year over the past two-and-a-half decades. In 2003 presumptive offences were expanded with the YCJA, stating that prosecutors and judges must consider adult sentences in youth court for youth 14 and older convicted of presumptive offences, including murder, attempted murder, other serious violent offences and the 'three-strikes' offender who is convicted of three serious violent offences that caused or created a substantial risk of causing serious harm (YCJA, Sec. 42(9); 70(1)(2); see also Chapter 3). These adult sentences for presumptive offences (where the onus was on the youth to argue against the use of adult sentences) were expected to significantly increase the numbers of Canadian girls sentenced to custody and to lengthen their stay in custody. Although the YCJA also introduced new legal safeguards regarding the use of adult sentences (e.g., judges were called upon to determine the seriousness of the violence and girls were to be provided with legal counsel in order to apply for a youth sentence), the presumptive nature of these offences was deemed unconstitutional by the Supreme Court of Canada in 2008. Now, the onus is on the Crown to prove that an adult sentence is appropriate for youth aged 14 and over who have committed a serious violent offence (Bala et al. 2009). Due to a lack of recent, reliable data on youth serving adult sentences (Bala et al. 2009), we have yet to see how this will play out where girls are concerned.

Theories of Female Crime and Delinquency

gender gap
Acknowledges the difference in the rates at which males and females do things. In the field of criminology, there exists a persistent and well-documented difference in the arrest rates for males and females, with males consistently committing significantly more crime than females.

Before the 1970s, few mainstream sociological and criminological theories concerned themselves with female crime and delinquency. Those that did grounded most of their thinking in male experience and in the notion that if females were delinquent, it was most likely because they were sexually deviant and pathological. When females *were* considered, the focus was generally on the **gender gap** (i.e., the proportionally lower crime participation of females in comparison to males), rather than on either the conditions or the motivations that move females toward crime and delinquency (Artz 1998; Tanner 1996).

Three categories of theory emerged from the early literature: (1) those that explain the gender gap in crime and delinquency as given in the biological differences between the sexes; (2) those that explain the gender gap as derived from differences in gender role socialization; and (3) those that focus on increased female deviance relative to males, and explain this rise in terms of a 'masculinization' of women brought on by women's liberation and the feminist movement (see Adler 1975; Simon 1975). All three categories of theory explain female crime and delinquency as a move away from the feminine toward the masculine and support the notion that delinquency and crime is in effect a masculine pursuit (Cohen 1955). Claims that feminism has perpetrated a rise in delinquency in children as mothers leave their homes and the domestic realm to pursue careers have been carefully examined and shown to be erroneous (Chesney-Lind and Shelden 1998; Miller 1986). Still, it was not until the mid-1980s and afterward that theorists called for a shift away from theories of delinquency that are uncritically grounded in male behaviour (Campbell 1991; Chesney-Lind and Shelden 1998; Reitsma-Street 1998; Chesney-Lind and Pasko 2004; Zahn 2009; Chesney-Lind and Jones 2010). While the question of the gender gap still remains, the focus among researchers has shifted quite considerably toward understanding female delinquency as it pertains to females rather than merely as compared to males.

Biological Theories

Early theories of crime, whether focused on males or females, were largely informed by the notion that biology was destiny. Cesare Lombroso (1835–1909), for example, suggested that if females did become criminals, it was largely because they were degenerate, unwomanly aberrations without maternal instinct. Lombroso's explanations regarding biology and criminal behaviour have long fallen into disrepute although even well into the twentieth century criminologists continued to explain girls' and women's lower involvement in delinquency and crime in terms of females' supposed biological inferiority—some even proposed premenstrual syndrome (PMS) as a cause for female criminality (for example, see Binder, Geis, and Bruce 1988; Cowie, Cowie, and Slater 1968; Pollack 1950; Wilson and Herrnstein 1985).

Gisela Konopka (1966, 1983) was one of the first to turn directly to adolescent girls to examine with them their involvement in delinquency. While she emphasized the effects on female behaviour of the sexual double standard, psycho-social problems, and women's changing cultural position, she still assumed that girls and women were largely controlled by biology and sexuality.

Current work on biology and crime continues, but in a different vein. For example in research on aggression and violence, Tremblay (2003) argues that 'all humans are at risk for using physical aggression given the appropriate circumstances' (p. 195), and makes the case that aggression is innate rather than learned as was widely claimed in the 1980s and 1990s (see Reiss and Roth 1993). Tremblay states that aggression is 'a natural behavior that one learns to control' (p. 183), that is, aggression and violence must be unlearned. He further suggests that variability in early aggression is due, in part at least, to some genetic effects (Dionne, Tremblay, Boivin, LaPlante, and Perusse 2003) and cites the example of fetal exposure to testosterone as playing a role in how easily a child learns to control physical aggression (Rubinow and Schmidt 1996). Additionally, Tremblay suggests that there is good evidence that low levels of serotonin are implicated in impulsive and aggressive behaviour (see Moffit, Brammer, Caspi, Fawcett, Raleigh, Yuwiler, and Silva 1998; Raine 2002). Interestingly, while Tremblay emphasizes the need to understand the physiological underpinnings of behaviour that influence the ability to unlearn the use of aggression and violence—the behaviours of greatest concern when we consider youth crime—his theory ultimately turns on the use of socialization to shift what is biologically given. In further work, Tremblay, Nagin, Séguin, Zoccolillo, Zelazo, Boivin, Pérusse, and Japel (2005) underline the importance of learning to regulate physical aggression in early childhood and emphasize the contribution of parental conflict and antisocial behaviour, low income, early child bearing, and maternal smoking to later problematic outcomes for children.

We have certainly learned to reconsider notions of biological determinism when it comes to understanding human behaviour and have learned to appreciate the importance of understanding

biopsychosocial model
An approach used to study the involvement of girls in the criminal justice system that addresses biological, psychological, and social risk factors related to female criminality.

the ways in which biologically based sensitivities and potentials intersect and interact with psychological and social factors in the lives of delinquent youth. So, for example, Kenneth Dodge and Gregory Pettit (2003) offer us a **biopsychosocial model** to explain chronic antisocial and delinquent behaviour in adolescents and show us that we need to pay attention to the reciprocal influences of biological and socio-cultural contexts on behaviour. These researchers show that for both girls and boys, biological dispositions influenced by prenatal factors—such as exposure to toxic substances—along with autonomic nervous system hyperactivity, intelligence potential, and temperament can be mediated positively or negatively in a child's life by socio-cultural context variables. Such variables may include family income, occupation and education, age of the mother, the absence or presence of parental conflict, divorce, and family violence; and, as the child matures, variables may include the mediating effects of positive or negative peer, school, and neighbourhood influences. As well, Dodge and Pettit note that these dispositions and socio-cultural interactions are not merely linear but reciprocal, so that a child's sensitivities and temperament can influence parenting behaviour and the behaviour of other significant children and adults in the child's life. As well, the child's early experiences serve to set in place a child's cognitive models and beliefs, that is, the child's social knowledge structures about how the world works. These internalized structures influence how the child makes sense of what is expected and what is acceptable and exerts a strong influence on behaviour and personal choice where delinquency is concerned, thus adding to the interactive nature of the development of delinquency.

Fishbein, Miller, Winn, and Dakof (2009), in their extensive examination of biopsychological factors, gender, and delinquency found that, for girls, the most salient biological disposition and vulnerability for delinquency appears to be early pubertal maturation. But as Fishbein et al. point out, early pubertal maturation is not simply a matter of fixed individual biological timing; it also involves heredity, body weight, and weight-to-height ratio, the hormonal and other biopsychological effects of stressful life events, and the quality of a girl's family relations, including the absence or presence of an adult male in the girl's household. Nor is early maturation by itself a causal factor for delinquency. Whether an early maturing girl becomes involved in delinquency depends on the quality of her home life, her school, and neighbourhood; the effects of context and relationships and interpersonal trauma, such as sexual and other forms of abuse, deprivation on her mental health and wellness, and the presence and influence of older males who may seduce her and include her in their criminal activities. The interplay of multiple influences and their effect on mental health play an enormous role in how an early maturing girl, or for that matter any girl, becomes involved in delinquency and crime. As Fishbein and colleagues also note, the incidence of mental illness and of co-morbidity—that is, two or more psychiatric disorders—is extremely high in delinquent girls. These disorders are not merely intrinsic to some girls and not others; they have their origins in a complex interplay of personal, relational, social, and cultural factors and can by no means be explained by biological disposition alone.

Sociological and Gender Role Theories

gender role theories
Those explanations of delinquent and criminal behaviour that focus on the role that gender plays in the lives and behaviours of both females and males.

Socialization theories of delinquency and crime emerged in the 1950s (Grosser 1951) and have grown in strength and number to the present day (Chesney-Lind and Shelden 1998; Chesney-Lind and Jones 2010; Hagan, Gillis, and Simpson 1985; Zahn 2009). **Gender role theories** explain the difference in male and female participation in delinquent behaviour as the outcome of differential gender socialization that imposes higher moral expectations and greater social controls on girls and women. Three mainstream sociological approaches to crime and delinquency that fit with a gender role analysis are (1) differential association or social learning theories, (2) social control theories, and (3) strain theories.

Social Learning and Differential Association Theories

The primary source of social learning is, of course, the family, however multiply constructed and variously defined families are in the twenty-first century. In an extensive review of the research on family and youth delinquency and crime, Kruttschnitt and Giodarno (2009) found that girls and boys both suffer the negative consequences of family conflict, harsh and coercive parenting, and other problematic emotional family dynamics, including exposure to crime by family members, abuse within the family, divorce, and living in stressed lone-parent households. These researchers found few consistent gender differences with regard to the effects of these factors on the socialization of children except in the area of sexual abuse, where girls consistently suffer far higher rates of such abuse, and with that, the long-term negative effects of this kind of trauma especially when combined with family criminality. Kruttschnitt and Giordano's 'state of the art' analysis of the research on family and delinquency in girls calls into question the commonly held belief that girls have stronger connections with their families and are thus more positively socialized and therefore less inclined to become involved in crime and delinquency. They point instead to a better, more nuanced under-standing of the acquisition of gender roles and the consequent learned gender performance for dealing with emotional and interpersonal processes as a more promising area for further research. Whatever their social location, girls learn early that being 'nice' and being 'good' have enormous social value and may therefore have internalized greater constraints on delinquent behaviour.

Kruttschnitt and Giordano's (2009) analysis echoes that of Dodge and Pettit (2003), who also found few gender effects for delinquency and crime. They too point to problematic family contexts, inconsistent and harsh discipline, abuse, a lack of warmth, and an absence of positive social teaching on the part of parents as being strongly linked with delinquency in later life for both girls and boys. As well, they note that by the time conduct problems and delinquency emerge, usually in adoles-cence, multiple factors beyond family also come into play, particularly relationships with peers.

Peer influence has for some time been known to be significant for delinquency. Based on the observations that delinquents appear to gather in groups and gangs and have more interaction with others who engage in crime than with those who do not, Sutherland (1939) and others (Sutherland and Cressey 1978) argued that the techniques, motives, and values that facilitate criminal behaviour are transmitted through social and antisocial learning opportunities that arise from close associa-tion with others who engage in delinquency and crime. Although Sutherland and his associates studied only males, differential association (or learning theory) holds some promise with regard to explaining female delinquency and is supported by research that indicates that females who have frequent contact with other deviant youth appear to engage in deviant behaviour to a greater degree than those who do not (Giordano, Cernkovich, and Pugh 1986).

Giordano (2009), in her extensive examination of peer influences and crime, shows that some socialization practices seem to be involved in protecting girls from greater involvement with delin-quent peers: girls generally spend more time in structured social activities than boys and less time simply 'hanging out'. As well, while the norms of the friendship group they most identify with help to shape the behaviour of both girls and boys, more girls than boys report affiliating with and knowing a greater range of peers than boys and therefore experience a wider range of possible social norms and models than boys do. Giordano's assessment of the current literature on delinquency and peers suggests that the girls who are more vulnerable to negative peer influences are those who gravitate toward delinquent friends, especially mixed-gender groups of delinquent friends, and who become involved with delinquent romantic partners. Still, Giordano cautions us to refrain from over-emphasizing the corrupting influence of males as an explanation for female delinquency.

So, is delinquency learned—that is, the outcome of exposure to delinquent models—or is the capacity for delinquency present in all humans, thereby placing the onus not on learning devi-ant behaviour but on learning self-restraint, deferred gratification, empathy, self-regulation, and positive social skills? As we saw earlier, Tremblay (2003) and Tremblay et al. (2005) point out the importance of self-regulation of the negative behaviour for which all humans have the capacity; in so doing, they align with social control theories.

Social Control Theories

Social control theories of crime and delinquency focus on the capacity of all human beings to engage in deviance and crimes. For social control theorists, personal control or inner containment of deviant urges grounded in a positive and socially conventional self-concept are central to the containment of delinquency and crime (Reckless 1961; Reiss 1951), as are effective family functioning and the existence of a positive social structure (Nye 1958; Toby 1957), and the presence of a social bond (Hirschi 1969). Positive bonds with family, friends, peers, school, and neighbourhood are of central importance to social control theorists, as they are to learning theorists.

Hirschi (1969) describes the social bond that keeps deviance in check as made up of four components: (1) attachment, (2) commitment, (3) involvement, and (4) belief. In applying Hirschi's notions to research with girls, Jensen and Eve (1976) and Cernkovich and Giordano (1987) found that attachment to conventional others and a belief in the legitimacy of rules have predictive power for both male and female delinquency. Cernkovich and Giordano also found that lower rates of female delinquency could be partly explained by higher levels of parental supervision and more intimate communication between parents and daughters.

Hagan, Gillis, and Simpson (1985), Hagan, Simpson, and Gillis (1987), and Hagan (1988, 1990) who developed **power-control theory**, a variant of social control theory, suggest that social control, power, and constraint vary across gender. Specifically, power-control theory suggests that patriarchal families are structured such that they support, and thus provide greater access for, males' risk-taking behaviour. In contrast, much tighter restrictions are placed on the behaviours of female children, thus lending some explanatory power to the impacts of familial gender socialization and lower rates of girls' involvement in crime. Conversely, in an egalitarian family, one that sets an equal threshold of risky behaviour for both boys and girls, one might expect more similar involvement in delinquency between the sexes. In the various articles by Hagan and his colleagues listed above, they point out that females generally experience more social control and constraint and less power, especially in more traditional, patriarchal families. Sons on the other hand, experience fewer controls, are expected to take risks, and are therefore more likely to be involved in risky, deviant, and delinquent behaviour and victimization than girls are. Further, this theory suggests that as families move away from traditional models toward systems where adult women take up more equal power with males or find themselves in the position of being single heads of households, girls will become more like boys and, as a consequence, also take more risks, including deviant risks, and may experience more victimization.

Such theorizing seems to suggest that women's labour force entry and female equality contribute to higher delinquency and higher victimization rates for girls. In fact, based on self-report and official statistics, female delinquency typically declines or remains stable in spite of the rise in number of female-headed households (Chesney-Lind and Shelden 1998). Further, power control theory also falls short in trying to explain victimization. Despite the consistent finding that boys are more likely than girls to be victims and offenders, patriarchal households do not necessarily protect girls from victimization (Blackwell, Sellers, and Schlaupitz 2002). Girls are often victimized in their homes by those closest to them and may be more vulnerable than boys to abuse at home. Ethnographic work by Artz (1998) suggests that patriarchal households where fathers exert dominance through intimidation and fear may in fact contribute to delinquency and aggression in girls. Additionally, there appears to be a consistent and strong relationship between females' sexual and emotional victimization in the context of misogynist (i.e., one who hates all women) and stereotypical gender relations based on hierarchies of power dominated by males, and female

power-control theory
Refers to John Hagan and colleagues' 1989 integrated (conflict and social control theories), feminist-informed explanation of the role of gender socialization on crime distributions.

participation in delinquency and crime (Acoca and Dedel 1998; Chesney-Lind and Okamoto 2001; Katz 2000; Means 2002).

In a recent study on girls' use of aggression, Artz, Nicholson, and Magnuson (2008) noted that both males and females use aggression to hold in place males' expectations of female sexual behaviour in that females actively participate in the privileging of males' sexual expectations of their own sex and in containing their own resistance to male domination. Where dominance and aggression is concerned, both males and females carry what Holland, Ramazanoglu, Sharpe, and Thompson (1998) call 'the male in the head' and enact the involuntary and asymmetric institutionalization and regulatory power of males and patriarchy in heterosexual relations (p.171).

Recent work (see Hagan, McCarthy, and Foster 2002) carries forward the examination of the effects of gender-stratified family practices, gendered control of power and resources, and patriarchy on the life course. Such research also explores the link between gender differences in types of delinquency and different forms of distress and despair in adulthood by taking a closer look at fathers' impacts on children. Foster and Hagan's (2007) examination of the difficult transitions to adulthood of the children of incarcerated fathers shows that the daughters of such fathers are at greater risk for abuse and neglect by nonbiological father figures and for homelessness during the transition to adulthood. In following this line of thinking, power-control theory converges with developmental criminology and the life course perspective work of, for example, Laub, Nagin, and Sampson (1998), Piquero and Mazarolle (2000), and Thornberry (1997), who examine the developmental aspects of delinquency and crime. Power control theory also converges with strain theory.

Strain Theory

Arising out of Durkheim's (1933) anomie concept, strain theory builds on the notion that delinquency can be explained as a response to being denied access to socially and conventionally approved opportunities for power and material success. In other words, where legitimate and conventional means of success are unavailable, strain and stress ensue and deviance becomes a means to an end. And indeed, an examination of male subcultures involved in delinquency and crime show that for lower-class males, delinquency could be construed as both a response to being thwarted in the achievement of middle- and upper-class success and a defence of masculinity (Cloward and Ohlin 1960; Cohen 1955; Miller 1958).

Strain theory has, however, been critiqued as not readily applicable to girls and women because females continue to suffer from unequal opportunities and more limited means for achieving success than males while at the same time committing significantly fewer crimes than males (see Agnew 1995; Artz 1998). But the theory has also been favourably reconsidered by those who argue for an expanded version, one that takes into account the different strains experienced by males and females and their different adaptations and responses to strain (Agnew 1992; Berger 1989; Naffine 1987; see also, Chapter 7). Broidy and Agnew (1997) suggest that Agnew's (1992) general strain theory (GST) offers potential for explaining both higher rates of male crime and the causes of female crime because it extends the focus of classic strain theory on the failure to achieve positively valued material goals. GST incorporates not only blocked access to monetary success and middle-class status but also the loss of family, friends, and romantic partners and experiences with all forms of abuse and deprivation as part of strain.

In their own application of general strain theory, Broidy and Agnew (1997) argue along lines similar to those proposed by social control theorists regarding constraint: that the overall differences in female and male rates of crime can be explained by the differences in types of strain to which females and males are subjected. Because of gender role stereotypes, males are more often subject to material- and status-related strains, and females are more subject to oppression in the forms of family violence, sexual abuse, and high levels of social controls and restrictions, including restriction related to criminal opportunity.

Additionally, Broidy and Agnew (1997) suggest that the female and male differences in crime rates can be further explained by gender differences in the processing of the negative emotions associated with strain. Males 'act out' with other-directed overt anger, aggression, and violence. Females, in contrast, 'act in' with depression, guilt, and shame and inner or relationally directed, more covert aggression. Females also disperse their negative emotions by gaining support from others in their more developed social networks and have been socialized to espouse values and use coping styles that discourage the commission of crimes. Males, on the other hand, are typically rewarded for their displays of aggression and encouraged to use coping styles that support the commission of crime. It seems that, on occasion, the distinction between constraint and strain appear to blur, but strain focuses more on what is withheld rather than on how one is controlled.

No single factor is known to predict delinquent behaviour and no single path to delinquency is known to exist either for girls (or for boys) although the strains that contribute to both have by now been well documented. As well, no homogeneous set of strains or conditions apply to all girls or all boys and within-group differences in strain also need to be considered (see, for example Katz 2000, 2004). Lanctôt, Émond, and Le Blanc (2004) note that previous approaches in research and intervention that treat delinquent females as a homogeneous group have done little to further our knowledge about delinquent females.

General strain theory helps us to understand the differential nature of strain and has implications for improved analysis of gender, class, and ethnicity by acknowledging the role of conditions and contexts within which the social bonds of attachment, commitment, involvement, shared beliefs, and power are structured, shaped, and distributed (see Agnew 2009, Chapter 7). GST also helps to avoid one of the pitfalls associated with gender role theory: backlash, such that gender role theories are used as the basis for the notion that a change in women's roles and the emancipation of women will ultimately lead to greater participation of women in criminal activity and create ground for other negative effects.

Promising Directions: Toward an Intersectional Approach

Although we may have made considerable advancements from the rehabilitative, treatment-focused paternalism of the early twentieth century as it concerns boys involved in the justice system, progress for girls has lagged somewhat (Sprott and Doob 2010). We propose that promising directions regarding girls' delinquency must be both intersectional and contextual in nature to arrive at interventions that address the strains faced by girls and their complex and varied pathways to social and delinquent behaviours.

intersectionality

Refers to a movement away from thinking categorically and toward thinking about the connections and crossroads between social facets. Intersectional thinking and theorizing recognizes the multiple, changing, and often overlapping dimensions, demographics, roles, and identities of criminals, victims, other individuals, and collectives.

Intersectionality refers to a movement away from thinking categorically and toward thinking about the connections and crossroads between social facets (e.g., race, sexuality, and gender) (Daly 2008). Intersectional thinking and theorizing recognizes the multiple, changing, and often overlapping dimensions, demographics, roles, and identities of criminals, victims, other individuals and collectives (Berger and Guidroz 2009). This approach moves beyond 'essential,' uniform identities and appreciates that the lives of girls who partake in delinquency are much more complex than the label 'delinquent/bad girl' implies. For example, those engaged in crime may also suffer from social marginalization and/or victimization.

Intersectionality as a theoretical concept emerged in the 1980s and is now widely popular in feminist criminology (Daly 2010). This approach bares the assumption that gender, race, class, ethnicity, sexuality, age, and nation and their intersections are crucial to understanding one's position in society (Berger and Guidroz 2009) and, especially, the positions of criminalized girls (Chesney-Lind and Jones 2010). By rejecting the 'universal' girl in favour of the 'inessential' girl (an approach from Elizabeth Spelman's 1988 book *Inessential Woman*), we highlight the need to refrain from focusing only on discrete aspects of girls, such as gender, and move toward a more nuanced understanding. This approach necessitates (1) theoretical and practical attention to demographic intersections experienced by girls, (2) an expansion of practices based on intersectionality, and (3) the mobilization of political change.

Attending to Demographic Intersections

There are several directions to pursue as part of attending to these intersections:

- Discontinue the use of stereotypes and overly simplistic theories.
- Eradicate the use of stereotypical punitive policies and inhumane practices.
- Stop ignoring girls' essential requirements for survival, safety, and well-being.

Attending to demographic intersections means not placing Aboriginal girls in centres thousands of miles from home and culture. It means radically changing correctional practices to reflect Aboriginal respect for spirit and land (Monture-Angus 2000). It means not charging one in three Canadian girls for administrative offences. It means rescinding the ineligibility of youth for welfare or time limits on assistance. It also means closing correctional beds and boot camps, and changing the 'three-strikes and you get adult time' provisions regarding presumptive offences in the new YCJA. Research demonstrates that harsh punishment is ineffective and inefficient (e.g., Green and Healy 2003, p. 139). Moreover, punitive approaches are inhumane and violent and merit no place in a civil society.

Girls, like boys, are not responsible for the family, race, class, or neighbourhood into which they are born. In youth forums for policy debates, girls argue that 'poverty, pollution and discrimination had effects as devastating as drug usage' (Meucci and Redmon 1997, p. 146). Whether they commit major or minor crimes or none at all, girls are entitled to the requirements for well-being: economic survival, clean air and water, good education, adequate health services and housing, and safety from violence inside and outside homes. These requirements are necessary so girls do not trade the dangers and hurt of insecure or violent families for dangerous streets and networks (Joe-Laidler and Hunt 1997). Research indicates that access to quality education, apprenticeship, income assistance, and housing programs that meet the essential requirements of convicted girls are more effective in reducing recidivism and in increasing their well-being than the general, short-term counselling for primarily emotional, cognitive, or family problems (e.g., Baines and Alder 1996; Chesney-Lind and Pasko 2004).

One simple intervention that prevents reducing persons into behaviours is to stop using short-hand phrases such as 'violent girl' as the words reinforce inaccurate, hurtful, static stereotypes. The alternative phrase, 'a girl who acted violently when . . .' suggests there is an interaction between context and behaviour, and that change and growth are possible. Every girl is a complex person, struggling against restrictive stereotypes, including pervasive messages that boys are more important than girls. Every girl lives her life at the nexus of several intersecting factors, including biology, psychology, and social dynamics. She cannot be placed in stereotypical, generalized categories according to a single factor or in accordance with crime typologies but instead must be recognized as an individual. Gaarder and Belknap (2002) speak about the value of 'blurred boundaries' as girls are often both victims and offenders. They found that girls convicted of serious violent offences may never have been allowed to be young and yet are expected to act like responsible, rational adults. Abolishing the simplistic stereotypes and 'one size fits all' intervention frees up energy to develop individualized, flexible approaches.

Expanding Practices Based on Intersectionality

Research and experience provides extensive guidance on interventions that do work with specific groups of girls. These include the promotion of complex forms of **differential intervention** and **differential treatment** and **compensatory interventions** for girls and their communities.

In differential intervention, as with compensatory practices, the focus is on client strengths. Individual variation is key to a differential approach; thus, those who deliver the intervention must be able to draw from multiple theoretical explanations for particular issues and conditions and must be able to match need to approach rather than asking that clients fit a single cookie-cutter-type program.

Differential intervention has an established tradition of matching youth to their environment and is most developed in the arena of correctional treatment for convicted girls. Sophisticated differential-treatment systems, including conceptual level matching, where female offenders are matched to positive correctional environments and teaching styles on dimensions of complexity, autonomy, and organization, have been positively evaluated (Palmer 1995; Reitsma-Street and Leschied 1988; Stoppard and Henri 1987). Thus far results have shown promise, especially when programs are sustained over time as they are in the long-term, coordinated, multi-systemic therapy for youth convicted of serious offences and their families (Henggeler, Melton, and Smit 1992). For girls convicted of an offence and who live with serious mental illness, trauma from abuse, and heavy substance use, dialectical behavioural therapy (DBT)—a collaborative, therapeutically based intervention that assists clients to achieve cognitive and emotional self-knowledge and self-regulation and strengthens their ability to deal with stress and trauma—seems to be especially effective. DBT was first developed by Linehan (1993a and b) and further developed and applied by Linehan, Head, and Armstrong (1993); Linehan, Schmidt, Dimeff, Craft, Kanter, and Comtois (1999); Linehan, Dimeff, Reynolds, Comtois, Welch, Haggerty, and Kivlahan (2002); and others (see Trupin, Boesky, McClurg, Beach, Hormann, and Baltrusis 1999; Verheul, van den Bosch, Koeter, de Ridder, Stijnen, and van den Brink 2003; McDonagh, Taylor, and Blanchette 2009). DBT has been extensively researched and well established as a positive intervention, especially because it is based on a strong alliance between client and therapist and on the principle that clients are capable of understanding their own processes and participating in the creation of their own well-being.

Differential treatment, as with differential intervention, takes individual differences fully into account. Treatment is individually designed and flexible enough to allow for the need for variation as this need emerges.

Compensatory interventions assume that girls require differential, matching treatment. These interventions are typically designed to make up for something that is absent, especially in the learning and social environment, by supporting people in their current state, identifying their strengths and abilities, assisting them with identifying what they want to improve on and change, involving them in planning how they will make these improvements and changes, and helping them to learn what they need to know to achieve their goals. Examples of such programs are the High/Scope Perry PreSchool Project, the Abecedarian Early Intervention Project, and Head Start.

But compensatory interventions also take seriously the strains that racism, chronic violence or illness, and inadequate schooling inflict on girls who are poor, disabled, and of marginalized groups. Compensatory practice acknowledges the damage and aims to repair the destruction. These interventions can be family based (e.g., Moretti, Holland, Moore, and McKay 2004), school based (e.g., Artz and Nicholson 2010), group-home based (e.g., Brown 2010), and neighbourhood based (e.g., Jones 2010; Morash, Park, and Kim 2010). Expanding these types of interventions means fostering community practices and social policies that focus directly on one or more aspects of the well-being requirements for all children and youth in a family, school, neighbourhood, or province.

---

differential intervention

Takes into account that people do not come in one-size-fits-all packages and therefore refrains from applying the same approach to each person involved in a class, program, or other form of group-based change process.

differential treatment

An approach to treatment that takes individual differences fully into account. Treatment is individually designed and flexible enough to allow for variation as this need emerges.

compensatory intervention

An intervention designed to make up for something that is absent, especially in the learning and social environment of young people.

Such approaches can also go beyond targeting high-risk girls or multi-problem families, and can be adapted to invite all in a particular classroom or community to use the teen centre, the well-baby clinics, quality child care, housing, food, health services, education, or violence-prevention programs (Reitsma-Street and Neysmith 2000). The orientation to well-being or strengths abolishes the limited focus on professionals' definitions of the girls' problem behaviours, criminal thinking, or mental illness. Whole school programs, for example, that involve teachers, students, and parents working together to raise the level of social consciousness in schools and communities have proven to be the most effective violence prevention approach (see Shariff 2000).

Mobilizing Political Change Around Equity and Human Rights

The intersectional approach to girls and crime offers the potential to make important changes to policy (Daly 2008), including the following:

- Institute policies and practices to reverse systemic and personal discrimination.
- Demand gender and racial parity in resources.
- Keep neo-liberal and neo-conservative crime-control policies in check.

In recent history, girls, especially those of Aboriginal or visible minority status, have been treated more harshly than boys, particularly for minor illegal, status, or 'unfeminine' behaviours (see Parent 1986). Some argue gender discrimination may no longer be obvious, and in Canada status offences have been decriminalized (De Como 1998; Kowalski and Caputo 1999). Yet the reduction of gender or racial discriminatory practices is illusory. As mentioned earlier, despite changes to youth justice policy, evidence still shows that girls are disproportionately charged with 'status-like' administrative charges (Sprott and Doob 2009), with even higher charge rates for Aboriginal girls.

Girls who are charged or convicted of crimes have hopes similar to those not charged. They want to stop violence and the destruction of their bodies, health, spirit, and community; they want to get a good education and job; they want to love and care for people; and they want fun and adventure (Nicholson and Artz 2003; Reitsma-Street and Offord 1991). If we take seriously what girls (and boys) say, we then need to ask how particular interests are served by ignoring what girls, their families, and communities tell us. What was the benefit of forcing Aboriginal girls to attend residential schools against the wishes of children and parents? Who profits from the increased use of administrative charges or custody sentences? Why are services to girls so inadequate and minimalist? What privilege makes possible the systematic abuse of girls such as those documented in the inquiry of Ontario Grandview Training School for Girls (Kershaw and Lasovich 1991)? Unmasking the injustice and the unequal access to decision-making helps to account for what is of benefit or not, and to whom, and clarifies the political, contested nature of policies and practices.

Mobilizing political change around equity and human rights goes beyond unmasking differences in power. It moves toward dismantling inequitable policies, such as ceasing to scrutinize and judge the sexual histories of girls but not boys. It means above all an insistence that funding and legislative resources for girls in the justice system are proportionate to their numbers and adequate for well-being, including funding required for compensatory, differential intervention (Bloom, Owen, Deschenes, and Rosenbaum 2002; Green and Healy 2003). Politicizing equity would mean that at least one-fifth of Canadian youth justice funds and resources are explicitly tied to girls and their well-being, and proportionately more to Aboriginal and Métis girls. But these funds should not be used to pay for longer custody sentences or more courts and police officers. Rather, we support the recommendations of the Canadian parliamentary committee and the Department of Justice that 80 per cent of correctional funding be used for community, compensatory, differential programs, thereby reversing the current formula that assigns the majority of funds to custody costs (House of Commons 1997; Department of Justice 1998).

The current climate of the federal government in relation to crime control has fostered an adherence to neo-liberal crime control policies that see crime prevention as synonymous with the punishment of aberrant individuals and that completely ignore the well-documented evidence that crime emerges in toxic contexts and circumstances that can be altered.

Summary

Girls are involved in all manner of anti-social, deviant, and criminal behaviours. But their criminal behaviour is infrequent despite fears that youth crime and violence by girls are increasing. Girls commit few serious crimes of violence—a trend that has been remarkably steady for decades. We argue that we need to study crime and our responses to girls and crime as a political project that reveals how social order and gender inequity are established, and how they can be changed.

Girls' minimal involvement in crime has led to theories about female crime and delinquency that, until the 1970s, largely overlooked girls' experiences. Alternatively, theories attempted to explain girls' criminal behaviour as an aberration of 'normal' femininity, or they proposed gender-neutral explanations that de-contextualized the complex reality of girls living in a gendered, racist, and unequal world. With the rise of feminism in academia and a concomitant groundswell in gender studies, more attention is being paid to the need for differential explanations of deviance, delinquency, and crime. Yet most research and practice continues to compare girls to boys and to adapt male-derived theories to account for female behaviours.

Some promising work, however, does exist. Theorists like Artz (1998), Chesney-Lind and Pasko (2004), Reitsma-Street (2004), Zahn (2009), and Chesney-Lind and Jones (2010) remind us that crime is not just a function of interactions within an established order (see Daly 1997; Katz 2000). We need to understand illegal and other behaviours as part of active struggles within a changing social order in which power and privilege are unequally distributed and frequently contested. In order to develop a fully delineated theory of girls' crime, we must resist applying the pervasive male standard to female behaviour. Rather, we need to examine our expectations of girls, and our fears and values in relation to them. This means we will question approaches to constructing knowledge about girls while paying close attention to the impact of different laws and regulations on girls and society. Most of all, we must be willing to attend to what girls themselves say if we are to learn more about girls' crime and to respond positively.

In previous iterations of this discussion, we pointed to differential intervention as a promising approach in that it invites the application of policies and practices premised on interactions between participants and their complex situations. The focus was on the behaviour and responsibilities of girls, adults, and the environment—before, during, and after crimes are committed. Research that examines the impact of differential intervention is encouraging: recidivism is reduced and life quality enhanced if differential intervention programs are adequately implemented and sustained. A few years ago, Reitsma-Street (2005) and Reitsma-Street, Artz, and Nicholson (2005) sketched a more encompassing approach, termed 'radical pragmatism', that includes but goes beyond differential intervention. Radical pragmatism encompasses abolishing inhumane, ineffective policies, expanding differential, compensatory practices, and politicizing equity and rights (Reitsma-Street 2005). In this chapter, we have extended this thinking and now see intersectionality as a promising theoretical and practical approach that will help to address the complex intersections in the gendered, racist world in which girls live, and aid policy-makers in building the just, humane, and effective possibilities that girls hope for.

Key Terms

administrative offences

biopsychosocial model

compensatory intervention

differential intervention

differential treatment

gender gap

gender role theories

intersectionality

power-control theory

Review Questions

1. Do official crime statistics support the claim that female crime is increasing? Can you ever know the 'truth' about crime rates?

2. What are administrative offences and why have they increased?

3. What are the prevailing themes about girls in the theories of female crime and delinquency? What do the theories not explain?

4. What is the intersectional approach to intervention and inquiry? What aspects of the intervention apply to boys? What are its strengths and limitations?

Critical Thinking Questions

1. How would you describe and explain the context in which girls commit minor crimes? Serious crimes? How is the context for girls different than for boys?

2. Imagine yourself to be a member of the opposite sex. The police have caught you breaking into a neighbour's house. How would you explain yourself to your family? To your friends? How do you think the police would respond to you? What do you believe should happen to you?

3. What research questions about girls, policies, and crime need to be studied?

4. Should girls who fail to comply with previous noncustodial dispositions under the YCJA be sentenced to custody? Debate this question in light of the case of M.B. discussed in Box 6.1.

Suggested Readings

Chesney-Lind, M. and Jones, N. (Eds.). (2010). *Fighting for girls: New perspectives on gender and violence* (pp. 13–32), New York: SUNY Press.

Sprott, J.B. and Doob, A.N. (2009). Justice for girls? Stability and change in the youth justice systems of the United States and Canada. Chicago: University of Chicago Press.

Zahn, M. (Ed.). (2009). *The delinquent girl*. Philadelphia: Temple University Press.

Suggested Weblinks

Canadian Association of Elizabeth Fry Societies

www.elizabethfry.ca

- An association that works with women and girls in the justice system.

Justice for Girls

www.justiceforgirls.org

- A non-profit organization seeking justice for teenage girls who live in poverty.

National Youth in Care Network
www.youthincare.ca
* An organization that works to improve services for youth in care.

References

Acoca, L. and Dedel, K. (1998). *No place to hide: Understanding and meeting the needs of girls in the California juvenile justice system.* San Francisco: National Council on Crime and Delinquency.

Adler, F. (1975). *Sisters in crime.* New York: McGraw-Hill.

Agnew, R. (1992). Foundation for a general strain theory of crime and delinquency. *Criminology, 30*: 47–87.

Agnew, R. (1995, Nov. 15–18). Gender and crime: A general strain theory perspective. Boston: Paper presented at the 1995 annual meeting of the American Society of Criminology.

Agnew, R. (2009). The contribution of 'mainstream' theories to the explanation of female delinquency. In M. Zahn (Ed.), *The delinquent girl* (pp. 7–29), Philadelphia: Temple University Press.

Artz, S. (1998). *Sex, power and the violent school girl.* Toronto: Trifolium.

Artz, S. and Nicholson, D. (2010). Reducing aggressive behavior in girls by attending to school climate. In M. Zahn (Ed.), *The delinquent girl* (pp. 149–74), Philadelphia: Temple University Press.

Artz, S., Nicholson, D., and Magnuson, D. (2008). Examining sex differences in the use of direct and indirect aggression. *Gender Issues, 25*(4): 267–88.

Baines, M. and Alder, C. (1996). Are girls more difficult to work with? Youth workers' perspectives in juvenile justice and related areas. *Crime and Delinquency, 42*(3): 467–85.

Bala, N., Carrington, P.J., and Roberts, J.V. (2009). Evaluating the Youth Criminal Justice Act after five years: A qualified success. *Canadian Journal of Criminology and Criminal Justice, 51*(2): 131–67.

Barron, C. and Lacombe, D. (2005). Moral panic and the nasty girl. *Canadian Review of Sociology and Anthropology, 42*(1): 51–69.

Beattie, S. (2009, October). Homicide in Canada, 2008. *Juristat, 29*(4). Ottawa: Statistics Canada Catalogue. No. 85-002-X.

Berger, M.T. and Guidroz, K. (2009). Introduction. In M.T. Berger and K. Guidroz (Eds.), *The intersectional approach: Transforming the academy through race, class and gender* (pp. 1–22). North Carolina: North Carolina Press.

Berger, R. (1989). Female delinquency in the emancipation era: A review of the literature. *Sex Roles, 21*(5/6): 375–99.

Binder, A., Geis, G. and Bruce, D. (1988). *Juvenile delinquency: Historical, cultural, legal perspectives.* New York: Macmillan.

Blackwell, B., Sellers, C. and Schlaupitz, S. (2002). A power-control theory of vulnerability to crime and adolescent role exits—revisited. *Canadian Review of Sociology and Anthropology, 39*(2): 199–218.

Bloom, B., Owen, B., Deschenes, E.P., and Rosenbaum, J. (2002). Improving juvenile justice for females: A statewide assessment in California. *Crime and Delinquency, 48*(4): 526–52.

Brantingham, P.J. and Faust, F.L. (1976). A conceptual model of crime prevention. *Crime and Delinquency, 22*(3): 284–96.

Broidy, L., and Agnew, R. (1997). Gender and crime: A general strain theory perspective. *Journal of Research in Crime and Delinquency, 34*(3): 275–306.

Brown, M. (2010). Negotiations of the living space: Life in the group home. In M. Zahn (Ed.), *The delinquent girl* (pp. 175–99). Philadelphia: Temple University Press.

Calverley, D. (2007). Youth custody and community services in Canada, 2004/2005. *Juristat, 27*(2), Ottawa: Statistics Canada Catalogue no. 85-002.

Calverley, D., Cotter, A., and Halla, E. (2010). Youth custody and community services in Canada, 2008/2009. *Juristat, 30*(1). Ottawa: Statistics Canada Cat no. 85-002-X.

Campbell, A. (1991). *The girls in the gang* (2nd ed.). New York: Basil Blackwell.

Cernkovich, S. and Giordano, P. (1987). Family relationships and delinquency. *Criminology, 25*: 295–321.

Cesaroni, C. and Bala, N. (2008). Deterrence as principle of youth sentencing: No effect on youth, but significant effect on judges. *Queen's Law Journal, 34*: 447.

Chesney-Lind, M. (2010). Jailing 'bad' girls: Girls' violence and trends in female incarceration. In M. Chesney-Lind and N. Jones (Eds.), *Fighting for girls: New perspectives on gender and violence* (pp. 57–79). New York: SUNY Press.

Chesney-Lind, M. and Irwin, K. (2008). *Beyond bad girls: Gender, violence and hype.* New York: Routledge.

Chesney-Lind, M. and Jones, N. (2010). *Fighting for girls: New perspectives on gender and violence.* New York: SUNY Press.

Chesney-Lind, M. and Okamoto, S. (2001). Gender matters: Patterns in girl's delinquency and gender responsive programming. *Journal of Forensic Psychology Practice, 1*(3): 1–28.

Chesney-Lind, M. and Pasko, L. (Eds.). (2004). *Girls, women and crime: Selected readings.* Thousand Oaks, CA: Sage.

Chesney-Lind, M. and Shelden, R. (1998). *Girls, delinquency and juvenile justice* (2nd ed.). Belmont, CA: West/Wadsworth.

Cloward, R. and Ohlin, L. (1960). *Delinquency and opportunity.* New York: Free Press.

Cohen, A. (1955). *Delinquent boys: The culture of the gang.* New York: Free Press.

Corrado, R., Odgers, C. and Cohen, I. (2000). The incarceration of female young offenders: Protection for whom? *Canadian Journal of Criminology, 42*(1): 189–207.

Cowie, J., Cowie, V., and Slater, E. (1968). *Delinquency in girls.* London: Heinemann.

Daly, K. (1997). Difference ways of conceptualizing sex/gender in feminist theory and their implications for criminology. *Theoretical Criminology, 1*(1): 25–51.

Daly, K. (2008). Seeking justice in the 21st century. In H. Ventura Miller (Ed.), *Restorative justice: From theory to practice.* Bingley, UK: Emerald Group.

Daly, K. (2010). Feminist perspectives in criminology: A review with Gen Y in mind. In E. McLaughlin and T. Newburn (Eds.), *The SAGE handbook of criminological theory* (pp. 225–246). Thousand Oakes, CA: SAGE.

De Como, R.E. (1998). Estimating the prevalence of juvenile custody by race and gender. *Crime and Delinquency, 44*(4): 489–506.

Dean, A.R. (2005). Locking them up to keep them 'safe': Criminalized girls in British Columbia: A systemic advocacy project conducted for Justice for Girls. Vancouver, BC: Justice for Girls. Retrieved 15 August, 2010, from http://www.justiceforgirls.org/publications/pdfs/jfg_complete_report.pdf

Department of Justice Canada (1998). *A strategy for the renewal of youth justice.* Ottawa: Department of Justice Canada.

Dionne, G., Tremblay, R., Boivin, M., Laplante, D., and Pérusse, D. (2003). Physical aggression and expressive vocabulary in 19-month-old twins. *Developmental Psychology, 39*(2), 261–73.

Dodge, K.A. and Pettit, G.S. (2003). A biopsychosocial model of the development of chronic conduct problems in adolescence. *Developmental Psychology, 29*(2), 349–71.

Doob, A. and Sprott, J. (1998). Is the 'quality' of youth violence becoming more serious? *Canadian Journal of Criminology, 40*(2), 165–84.

Durkheim, E. (1933). *The division of labor in society.* (G. Simpson, trans.) New York: Free Press.

Estrada, F. (2001). Juvenile violence as a social problem: Trends, media attention and societal response. *British Journal of Criminology, 41*: 639–55.

Fishbein, D., Miller, S., Winn, D.M. and Dakof, G. (2009). Biopsychological factors, gender and delinquency. In M. Zahn (Ed.) *The delinquent girl* (pp. 84–106). Philadelphia: Temple University Press.

Foster, H. and Hagan, J. (2007). Incarceration and intergenerational social exclusion. *Social Problems, 54*(4): 399–433.

Gaarder, E. and Belknap, J. (2002). Tenuous borders: Girls transferred to adult court. *Criminology, 40*(3): 481–517.

Giordano, P. (2009). Peer influences on girls' delinquency. In. M. Zahn, (Ed.). *The delinquent girl* (pp. 127–45). Philadelphia: Temple University Press.

Giordano, P. and Cernkovich, S. (1979). On complicating the relationship between liberation and delinquency. *Social Problems, 26*: 467–81.

Giordano, P., Cernkovich, S. and Pugh, M. (1986). Friendships and delinquency. *American Journal of Sociology, 91*: 1170–1202.

Green, R. and Healy, K. (2003). *Tough on kids: Rethinking approaches to youth justice.* Saskatoon, SK: Purich.

Grosser, G. (1951). Juvenile delinquency and contemporary American sex roles. Unpublished doctoral dissertation: Harvard University.

Hagan, J. (1988). *Structural criminology.* St. John, NB: Polity Press.

Hagan, J. (1990). The structure of gender and deviance: A power-control theory of vulnerability to crime and the search for deviant role exits. *Canadian Review of Sociology and Anthropology, 27*(2), 137–56.

Hagan, J., Gillis, A., and Simpson, J. (1985). The class structure of delinquency: Toward a power-control theory of common delinquent behaviour. *American Journal of Sociology, 90*: 1151–78.

Hagan, J., McCarthy, B. and Foster, H. (2002). A gendered theory of delinquency and despair in the life course. *Acta Sociologica, 45*: 37–46.

Hagan, J., Simpson, J. and Gillis, A. (1987). Class in the household: A power-control theory of gender and delinquency. *American Journal of Sociology, 92*: 788–816.

Henggler, S.W., Melton, G.B., Smith, L.D. (1992). Family preservation using multisystemic therapy: An effective alternative to incarcerating serious juvenile offenders. *Journal of Consulting and Clinical Psychology, 60*(6): 953–61.

Hirschi, T. (1969). *Causes of delinquency.* Berkeley, CA: University of California Press.

Holland, J., Ramazanoglu, C., Sharpe, S., and Thomson, R. (1998). *The male in the head: Young people, heterosexuality and power.* London: Tufnell Press.

House of Commons. (1997). *Renewing youth justice.* 13th Report of the Standing Committee on Justice and Legal Affairs, Shaughnessy Cohen, Chair. Ottawa: Queen's Printer.

Irwin, K. and Chesney-Lind, M. (2008). Girls' violence: Beyond dangerous masculinity. *Sociology Compass, 2*(3): 837–55.

Jensen, G. and Eve, R. (1976). Sex differences in delinquency. *Criminology, 13*: 427–48.

Joe-Laidler, K. and Hunt, G. (1997). Violence and social organization in female gangs. *Social Justice, 24*: 148–69.

Jones, N. (2010). 'It's about being a survivor . . .': African American girls, gender, and the context of inner-city violence. In M. Chesney-Lind and N. Jones, (Eds.), *Fighting for girls: New perspectives on gender and violence* (pp. 203–18). New York: SUNY.

Katz, R. (2000). Explaining girl's and women's crime and desistance in the context of their victimization experiences. *Violence Against Women, 6*(6): 633–60. Reprinted with permission in M. Chesney-Lind and L. Pasko (Eds.). (2004), *Girls, women and crime* (pp. 24–41). Thousand Oaks, CA: Sage Publications Inc.

Katz, R.S. (2004). Explaining girls' and women's crime and desistence in the context of the victimization experiences: A developmental test of revised strain theory and the life course perspective. In M. Chesney-Lind and L. Pasko (Eds.), *Girls, women and crime: Selected readings* (pp. 24–41). Thousand Oaks: Sage.

Kershaw, A. and Lasovich, M. (1991). *Rock-a-bye baby: A death behind bars.* Toronto: McClelland and Stewart.

Kong, R. (2009). Youth custody and community services in Canada, 2007/2008. *Juristat, 29*(2). Ottawa: Statistics Canada Cat no. 85-002-X.

Kong, R. and AuCoin, K. (2008). Female offenders in Canada. *Juristat, 28*(1). Ottawa: Statistics Canada Cat no. 85-002-XIE.

Konopka, G. (1966). *The adolescent girl in conflict.* Englewood Cliffs, NJ: Prentice-Hall.

Konopka, G. (1983). *Young girls: A portrait of adolescence.* New York: Hayworth Press.

Kowalski, M. and Caputo, T. (1999). Recidivism in youth court: An examination of the impact of age, gender and prior record. In T. Fleming, P. O'Reilly and B. Clark (Eds.). (2001), *Youth injustice: Canadian perspectives* (2nd ed.), (pp. 483–510). Toronto: Canadian Scholars' Press.

Kruttschnitt, C. and Giordano, P. (2009). Family influences on girls' delinquency. In. M. Zahn, (Ed.), *The delinquent girl* (pp. 146–63). Philadelphia: Temple University Press.

Lanctôt, N., Émond, C., and Le Blanc, M. (2004). Adjudicated females' participation in violence from adolescence to adulthood: Results from a longitudinal study. In M. Moretti, C. Odgers, and M. Jackson (Eds.), *Girls and aggression: Contributing factors and intervention principles.* Boston: Kluwer.

Laub, J., Nagin, D., and Sampson, R. (1998). Trajectories of change in criminal offending: Good marriages and the desistance process. *American Sociological Review, 63*: 225–38.

Linehan, M.M. (1993a). *Cognitive behavioural treatment of borderline personality disorder.* New York and London: The Guilford Press,

Linehan, M.M. (1993b). *Skills training manual for treating borderline personality disorder.* New York and London: The Guilford Press.

Linehan, M.M., Heard, H.L., and Armstrong, H.E. (1993). Naturalistic follow-up of a behavioral treatment for chronically parasuicidal borderline patients. *Archives of General Psychiatry, 50*: 971–74.

Linehan, M.M., Schmidt, H., Dimeff, L.A., Craft, J.C., Kanter, J., and Comtois, K.A. (1999). Dialectical behavior therapy for patients with borderline personality disorder and drug-dependence. *American Journal on Addiction, 8*(4): 279–92.

Linehan, M.M., Dimeff, L.A., Reynolds, S.K., Comtois, K.A., Welch, S.S., Haggerty, P., and Kivlahan, D.R. (2002). Dialectical behavior therapy versus comprehensive validation plus 12-step for the treatment of opioid dependent women meeting criteria for borderline personality disorder. *Drug and Alcohol Dependence, 67*(1): 13–26.

Males, M. (2010). Have 'girls gone wild'? In M. Chesney-Lind and N. Jones (Eds.), *Fighting for girls: New perspectives on gender and violence* (pp. 13–32), New York: SUNY Press.

McDonagh, D., Taylor, K. and Blanchette, K. (2009). Correctional adaptation of dialectical behaviour therapy (DBT) for federally sentenced women. Correctional Services of Canada Forum on Corrections Research: http://www.csc-scc.gc.ca/text/pblct/forum/e142/e142i-eng.shtml

Means, R. (2002). Decreasing the raise [sic] in female delinquency through gender specific program [sic] and proactive police involvement. Eastern Michigan University, Michigan: Unpublished Report. Department of Interdisciplinary Technology as part of School of Police Staff and Command Program.

Meucci, S. and Redmon, J. (1997). Safe spaces: California children enter a policy debate. *Social Justice, 24*(3): 139–51.

Miller, E. (1986). *Street women: The illegal work of underclass women.* Philadelphia: Temple University Press.

Miller, J. (2001). *One of the guys: Girls, gangs, and gender.* New York: Oxford University Press.

Miller, W. (1958). Lower class culture as a generating milieu of gang delinquency. *Journal of Social Issues, 14*: 5–19.

Ministry for Children and Families. (2000). Profile of young offenders, 1999–2000. Victoria: B.C. Justice Services.

Moffitt, T., Brammer, G., Caspi, A., Fawcett, J., Raleigh, M., Yuwiler, A., and Silva, P. (1998). Whole blood serotonin relates to violence in an epidemiological study. *Biological Psychiatry, 43*(6): 446–57.

Monture-Angus, P. (2000). Aboriginal women and correctional practice. In K. Hannah-Moffat and M. Shaw (Eds.), *An ideal prison?: Critical essays on women's imprisonment in Canada* (pp. 52–60). Halifax, NS: Fernwood.

Moretti, M., Holland, R., Moore, K. and McKay, S. (2004). An attachment-based parenting program for caregivers of severely conduct-disordered adolescents. *Journal of Child and Youth Care Work,* 19, 170–179.

Morash, M., Park, S., and Kim, J. (2010). In M. Zahn (Ed.), *The delinquent girl* (pp. 219–40). Philadelphia: Temple University Press.

Morris, R. (1965). Attitudes towards delinquency by delinquents, nondelinquents and their friends. *British Journal of Criminology, 5*: 249–65.

Naffine, N. (1987). Female crime: *The construction of women in criminology.* Sydney: Allen and Unwin.

National Council of Welfare. (2000). *Justice and the poor.* Ottawa, ON: Author.

Nicholson, D. and Artz, S. (2003). Preventing youthful offending: Where do we go from here? *Relational Child and Youth Care Practice, 16*(4): 32–46.

Nye, F. (1958). *Family relationships and delinquent behaviour.* New York: Wiley.

Öhrn, E. (2001). Marginalization of democratic values: A gendered practice of schooling? *International Journal of Inclusive Education, 5*(2/3): 319–28.

Palmer, T. (1995). Programmatic and nonprogrammatic aspects of successful intervention: New directions for research. *Crime and Delinquency, 41*(1): 100–31.

Parent, C. (1986). Actualités et bibliographies: La protection chevalresque ou les representations masculines du traitement des femmes dans la justice pénale. *Déviance et Société, 10*(2): 147–75.

Piquero, A. and Mazarolle, P. (2000). *Life-course criminology: Contemporary and classic readings.* New York: Wadsworth.

Pollack, O. (1950). *The criminality of women.* New York: Barnes.

Raine, A. (2002). Annotation: The role of prefrontal deficits, low autonomic arousal, and early health factors in the development of antisocial and aggressive behavior in children. *Journal of Child Psychology and Psychiatry, 43*: 417–34.

Reckless, W. (1961). *The crime problem* (3rd ed.). New York: Barnes.

Reiss, A. (1951). Delinquency as the failure of personal social controls. *American Sociological Review,* 16: 196–207.

Reiss, A. and Roth, J. (Eds.). (1993). *Understanding and preventing violence.* Washington: National Academy Press.

Reitsma-Street, M. (1998). Still girls learn to care; girls policed to care. In C. Baines, P. Evans, and S. Neysmith (Eds.), *Women's caring: Social policy in Canada* (revised ed.) (pp. 87–113). Toronto: Oxford University Press.

Reitsma-Street, M. (1999). Justice for Canadian girls: A 1990s update. *Canadian Journal of Criminology, 41*(4): 335–63.

Reitsma-Street, M. (2004). Connecting policies, girls, and violence. In M. Moretti, C. Odgers, and M. Jackson (Eds.), *Girls and aggression: Contributing factors and intervention principles* (pp. 115–30). Boston: Kluwer.

Reitsma-Street, M. (2005). Radical pragmatism: Prevention and intervention with girls. In M. L. Hoskins and S. Artz, (Eds.), *Working relationally with girls: Complex lives/ complex identities* (pp. 119–38). New York: Haworth Press.

Reitsma-Street, M., Artz, S., and Nicholson, D. (2005). Canadian girls and crime in the 21st century. In J.A. Winterdyk (Ed.), *Issues and perspectives on young offenders in Canada* (3rd ed.), (pp. 57–82). Toronto: Nelson.

Reitsma-Street, M. and Leschied, A. W. (1988). The conceptual-level matching model in corrections. *Criminal Justice and Behavior, 15*(1): 92–108.

Reitsma-Street, M. and Neysmith, S. (2000). Restructuring and community work: The case of community resource centres for families in poor urban neighbourhoods. In S. Neysmith (Ed.), *Restructuring caring labour: Discourse, state practice and everyday life* (pp. 142–63). Toronto: Oxford University Press.

Reitsma-Street, M. and Offord, D.R. (1991). Girl delinquents and their sisters: A challenge for practice. *Canadian Social Work Review, 8*(1): 11–27.

Rubinow, D. and Schmidt, P. (1996). Androgens, brain, and behavior. *American Journal of Psychiatry, 153*(8): 974–84.

Shariff, S. (2000). Identifying successful school and community programs for youth: An evaluation rubric and compendium of sources. Unpublished report. Youth Justice Education Partnerships. Retrieved 20 April, 2003, from http://www.extension.ualberta.ca/youthjustice/rubric.doc

Sharpe, G. and Gelsthorpe, L. (2009). Engendering the agenda: Girls, young women and youth justice. *Youth Justice, 9*(3): 195–208.

Simon, R. (1975). *Women and crime.* Lexington, MA: Lexington Books.

Spelman, E. (1988). *Inessential woman: problems of exclusion in feminist thought.* Boston: Beacon Press.

Sprott, J. and Doob, A. (2003). It's all in the denominator: Trends in the processing of girls in Canada's youth courts. *Canadian Journal of Criminology and Criminal Justice, 45*: 73–80.

Sprott, J.B. and Doob, A.N. (2009). *Justice for girls? Stability and change in the youth justice systems of the United States and Canada.* Chicago: University of Chicago Press.

Sprott, J.B. and Doob, A.N. (2010). Gendered treatment: Girls and treatment orders in bail court. *Canadian Journal of Criminology and Criminal Justice, 52*(4): 427–41.

Statistics Canada. (2002a). Adults and youths charged by sex and offence category, Canada 1999–2002, Table 1095009. Ottawa: Statistics Canada.

Statistics Canada. (2002b). Adults and youth charged by sex, using Uniform Crime Reporting Survey and estimates of population by age and sex for Canada. CANSIM II Series V12442.

Statistics Canada. (2002c). Youth court survey, number of cases by sex, major and minor assault, homicide and attempted. CANSIM II Series V21127.

Statistics Canada. (2006a). Adult criminal court survey, number of cases by sex of accused. CANSIM Table 2520044.

Statistics Canada. (2006b). Youth court survey, number of cases, by sex of accused, annually. CANSIM Table 2520048.

Steffensmeier, D., Schwartz, J., Zhong, H., and Ackerman, J. (2005). An assessment of recent trends in girls' violence using diverse longitudinal sources: Is the gender gap closing? *Criminology, 43*(2): 355–406.

Stoppard, J.M. and Henri, G.S. (1987). Conceptual level matching and effects of assertion training. *Journal of Counseling Psychology, 34*: 55–61.

Sutherland, E. (1939). *Principles of criminology.* Philadelphia: Lippincott.

Sutherland, E. and Cressey, D. (1978). *Criminology* (10th ed.). Philadelphia: Lippincott.

Tanner, J. (1996). *Teenage troubles: Youth and deviance in Canada.* Toronto: Nelson Canada.

Taylor-Butts, A. and Bressen, A. (2007). Youth crime in Canada, 2006. *Juristat, 28*(3). Ottawa: Statistics Canada Cat no. 85-002-XIE.

Thornberry, T. (1997). Some advantages of developmental and life-course perspectives for the study of crime and delinquency. In T. Thornberry (Ed.), *Developmental theories of crime and delinquency* (pp. 1–10). New Brunswick, NJ: Transaction Publishers.

Toby, J. (1957). Social disorganization and stake in conformity: Complementary factors in predatory behaviour in hoodlums. *Journal of Criminal Law, Criminology and Police Service*, 48: 12–17.

Tremblay, R. (2003). Why socialization fails: The case of chronic physical aggression. In B. Lahey, T. Moffitt, and C. Avshalom (Eds.), *Causes of conduct disorder and juvenile delinquency* (pp. 182–224). New York: Guilford.

Tremblay, R.E., Nagin, D.S, Séguin, J.R., Zoccolillo, M., Zelazo, P.D., Boivin, M., Pérusse, D., and Japel, C. (2005, February). Physical aggression during early childhood: Trajectories and predictors. *Journal of the Canadian Academy of Child and Adolescent Psychiatry, 14*(1): 3–9. http://www.ncbi.nlm.nih.gov/pmc/articles/PMC2538721/

Trupin, E., Stewart, D., Boesky, L., McClurg, B., Beach, B., Hormann, S., and Baltrusis, R. (1999, February). Evaluation of a dialectical behavior therapy with incarcerate female juvenile offenders. Tampa, FL: Paper presented at the 11th annual research conference, 'A system of care for children's mental health: Expanding the research base'.

Verheul, R., van den Bosch, L.M.C., Koeter, M.W.J., de Ridder, M.A.J., Stijnen, T., and Van den Brink, W. (2003). Dialectical behaviour therapy for women with borderline personality disorder: 12-month, random-ised clinical trial in the Netherlands. *British Journal of Psychiatry*, 182: 135–40.

Wilson, J. and Herrnstein, R. (1985). *Crime and human nature*. New York: Simon and Schuster.

Woolford, A. (2009). *The politics of restorative justice: A critical introduction*. Halifax, NS: Fernwood.

Zahn, M.A. (Ed.). (2009). *The delinquent girl*. Philadelphia: Temple University Press.

7 New Theoretical Perspectives on Youth Crime

Stephen W. Baron

Overview

This chapter will review five of the new theoretical perspectives that have emerged in the past two decades to explain youth crime. The chapter will examine each of these perspectives in the order in which they were developed, beginning with the general theory of crime and then moving to general strain theory, the age-graded theory of social control, control balance theory, and differential coercion theory. The examination of each perspective will begin by first outlining the main theoretical premises offered by the theorists. That is, we will scrutinize in some detail the way that the theorists of each particular perspective explain how youths become involved in crime. This will include how certain factors might lead to other factors, which in turn can lead to crime. It will also dedicate some discussion to the way that certain causal factors may work together with other factors, or require that other factors be present, before they will increase the risk that youths will become involved in illegal activities. After reviewing each theoretical perspective, we will examine the empirical status of that specific theory, paying particular attention to the research that has been undertaken on the theory to date. This overview will determine if each theory works as an explanation of youth crime, where future research is needed to clarify the causal mechanisms outlined in the particular perspective, and if theoretical revisions are required for the theory to better explain youth involvement in criminal activities.

Key Objectives

After reading this chapter, you should be able to:

- Identify and distinguish the new theoretical perspectives developed to explain youth crime.
- Better understand the way different theoretical concepts can be integrated to better understand youth crime.
- Appreciate the complexity required to understand youth crime.
- Recognize some of the empirical weaknesses of theoretical approaches offered to explain youth crime.

Introduction

In this chapter we examine a number of the more recent theoretical perspectives that have been offered to help explain and understand youth crime. Until quite recently, explanations of youth crime were dominated by theoretical perspectives developed prior to the 1970s (e.g., strain, differential association, social control, labelling). Researchers exploring these perspectives, however, discovered that these traditional explanations of crime provided only a limited account of the behaviour under examination. This lack of empirical support suggested that additional thinking was required to understand how youths became involved in crime. In response, the past two decades have seen a growth in the number of, and complexity in, explanations for youth crime. Here we will review five of the newly offered theoretical perspectives in the historical order in which they emerged. Contained in our assessment will be the general theory of crime, general strain theory, the age-graded theory of social control, control balance theory, and differential coercion theory. Some of these perspectives build on past perspectives that have already been examined, while others attempt to put together, or integrate, a number of the previously examined perspectives with innovative, new causal concepts to create novel explanations of criminal behaviour. Our goal is to explore the main causal factors that each perspective outlines as leading to criminal behaviour. We will also be interested in the more indirect and less obvious ways that these factors may lead to crime. We will be following the causal trail of each perspective, investigating how certain factors lead to other factors, which in turn lead to crime. Further, we will be paying attention to the role that combinations of factors play together in helping us to understand crime. Here we want to be aware of how the central causal factor may work better when other factors are also present. As our agenda suggests, these recent theoretical developments can be both simple and sophisticated, reflecting the evolution of the understanding of crime.

The General Theory of Crime: Self-Control

The general theory of crime, as outlined by Michael Gottfredson and Travis Hirschi (1990), focuses on the key concept of self-control. Self-control refers to the ability to restrain oneself from momentary temptations. People who develop self-control are said to be less likely to engage in criminal activities. In contrast, the failure to develop this characteristic leaves one more at risk to engage in crime and also increases the likelihood of involvement in other negative activities as well. While viewed as an overarching concept, **low self-control** is argued to be made up of six different characteristics. While these six elements are distinct, Gottfredson and Hirschi argue that they tend to come together in the same people, operate in tandem, and persist over the lifespan to produce a stable, coherent construct (see Figure 7.1).

low self-control
A trait made up of impulsivity, short-sightedness, risk-taking, physicality, insensitivity, and low frustration tolerance, which leaves individuals less able to refrain from activities that provide short-term pleasure or gain.

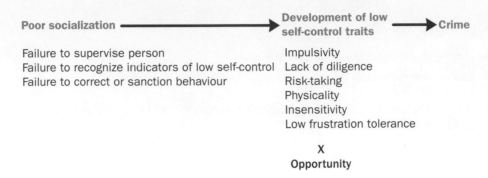

Figure 7.1 The General Theory of Crime

Characteristics of Low Self-Control

Impulsivity

The first characteristic of those who lack self-control is the tendency to be impulsive. Impulsivity can be summarized as the inability to defer gratification or to control impulses as well as the inclination to focus on events that are taking place in the here and now. For those who are impulsive, criminal activities can serve to satisfy various personal desires easily and immediately. For example, crime can lead to the quick acquisition of property without putting in the effort to secure resources to purchase the desired goods. Crime allows quick revenge against others without waiting for resolution through the courts or for intervention of others. And for those who wish to obtain sex without going through the effort of courtship, crime potentially provides a simple and quick method to satiate these desires. According to the theory, impulsivity comes naturally and is therefore something to be controlled. It requires effort to consider the consequences of various behavioural options and to gratify desires in an intentional, purposeful manner. For those who develop this capacity, the likelihood of engaging in crime is diminished.

Lack of Diligence

The second characteristic outlined to be indicative of a deficiency in self-control focuses on the lack of diligence. Those who have developed self-control are thought to have developed the tendency to be persistent, industrious, and tenacious in a course of action. The theory suggests that people naturally wish to accomplish their goals through the simplest, easiest means possible. People who lack diligence will choose the quickest path to satisfy their desires even if the long-term consequences are negative. The more complicated the path required to reach a goal and the more effort necessary to accomplish the desire, the more problematic the satisfaction of the goal for those with low diligence. Crimes allow people to satisfy desires more easily with minimal effort and to bypass some of the more complicated methods of reaching goals through more conventional avenues. In contrast, those with higher self-control will be more willing to undertake difficult tasks and exert the effort and discipline required to successfully reach the tasks; therefore, they will be less likely to engage in crime to satisfy their desires.

Risk-Taking

The third element of low self-control is the tendency to be a risk-taker. People with low self-control enjoy engaging in activities that provide adventure, thrills, and excitement. Criminal acts involve elements of excitement and risk. Breaking into a house, stealing a car, and/or getting into a fight all provide exciting adventures that are appealing to those with low self-control. Those who have high self-control are more likely to be risk averse and more cautious and careful in their behaviour, all of which discourage involvement in criminal activities.

Physicality

The fourth characteristic of low self-control is the tendency to be physical as opposed to valuing or possessing cognitive or academic skills. Gottfredson and Hirschi note that most crimes do not require much skill or training, nor do they entail elaborate planning. Instead, the cognitive requirements for crime are argued to be slight. Most criminal acts simply entail physically hurting others or taking their property and are undertaken impulsively based on in-the-moment decisions. Thus, crime becomes an attractive pursuit for those who do not wish to be challenged cognitively, particularly if the deviant action involves physical activity.

Insensitivity

The fifth element of self-control focuses on the degree of a person's self-centredness or insensitivity. Those who lack self-control are egotistical and unconcerned about the needs of others. Gottfredson and Hirschi argue that people are naturally selfish and are more concerned about their own individual needs. Criminal acts often leave victims in pain if physically harmed, or feeling violated if their property has been stolen. Individuals who consider the feelings of others prior to their actions, and adjust their behaviour to minimize hurting others, are deemed to have higher levels of self-control, reducing the potential for involvement in criminal behaviour.

Low Frustration Tolerance

Finally, Gottfredson and Hirschi argue that those with self-control are able to control their frustrations when faced with difficult circumstances. In contrast, those with low self-control have low frustration tolerance and respond negatively to events that they interpret as irritating. Thus, slights from people can lead to assaults, frustrating tasks can lead to property damage, and difficult interpersonal interactions can lead to violence rather than verbal resolution. In contrast, those people with self-control have the ability to cope with frustrating situations and respond to interpersonal conflicts with verbal tactics rather than physical responses.

Convenience and Opportunity

Although low self-control leaves one more likely to commit crime, a person also requires the convenience and opportunity to commit crime. Gottfredson and Hirshi argue that criminal events contain features that appeal to persons with low self-control. They suggest that it is the interaction between the person with low self-control and opportunity that increases the probability that a criminal act will take place. In effect, they argue that self-control constitutes a disposition to act in a certain way, triggered by circumstance.

While Gottfredson and Hirschi propose that lack of self-control is the main cause of crime, they also suggest that it is linked to a range of other behaviours and life outcomes. They argue that, in addition to crime, low self-control influences involvement in behaviours whose nature is analogous to crime. These analogous behaviours are often viewed as deviant and, like criminal acts, require little planning, provide immediate gratification, and offer a great deal of excitement. Self-control, therefore, will leave one more likely to smoke, to drink, to not wear a seat belt, to drive a vehicle too fast, and to be involved in more traffic accidents. People with low self-control will gamble, have illicit sex, and have children out of wedlock. Further, Gottfredson and Hirschi argue that low self-control has 'social consequences' that shape people's ability to succeed in social institutions and to form **social bonds**. Thus, those lacking self-control will have more problems completing

social bonds
The degree to which individuals, through socialization, have connections to people and institutions in a society and believe in the rules of the society. These connections serve as restraints against criminal opportunities and behaviour.

their education, becoming involved in stable relationships, and securing stable employment. They will be more likely to become divorced, to be unemployed, and to drop out of school. In fact, Gottfredson and Hirschi argue that the relationship between social failure and crime outlined in other theoretical perspectives is spurious rather than causal. In other words, the cause of various social failures and crime is low self-control; the social failures themselves actually have no causal impact on crime. Thus, the negative impact that low self-control has on people's lives is extremely broad.

Causes of Variation in Self-Control

How does someone end up with low self-control? Gottfredson and Hirschi argue that low self-control is the result of an absence of training or ineffective or incomplete socialization. While Gottfredson and Hirschi admit that there will be variations in the degree to which children demonstrate the traits associated with low self-control, they note that effective socialization to develop self-control is always achievable regardless of the constitution of individual traits. So how do we ensure effective socialization? Teaching self-control requires that caregivers (1) monitor a child's behaviour; (2) recognize the characteristics of low self-control, demonstrated in the forms of impulsiveness, lack of diligence, risk-taking, physicality, insensitivity, and low frustration tolerance, when they are exhibited; and (3) sanction and correct those behaviours indicative of low self-control. This child-rearing strategy will increase the child's capabilities in delaying gratification, develop his or her sensitivity to the feelings and wishes of others, create more tolerance for frustration, promote diligence and focus on cognitive development, and build an aversion toward risky, dangerous activities.

Gottfredson and Hirschi note, however, that this child-rearing process can be undermined in a number of ways, including situations where there is a lack of emotional attachment between the parents and the child and/or where the parents lack the time or resources to supervise the child's activities and conduct. Gottfredson and Hirschi also note that parents may not recognize the characteristics of self-control, nor make a connection between these traits and later problematic behaviour and therefore may not view the behaviours negatively. Gottfredson and Hirschi stress that without proper socialization, low self-control becomes difficult to alter and between the ages of 8 and 10 becomes relatively stable and will influence behaviour across the life course.

Current Empirical Research into the General Theory of Crime

The general theory of crime has generated a great deal of controversy and a considerable amount of empirical research. Empirical research has generally been supportive of the perspective, finding that those with low self-control tend to engage in crime and analogous behaviours (Pratt and Cullen 2000). There is also work that suggests that low self-control is predictive of negative social consequences, such as unemployment, homelessness, accidents, criminal associates, and criminal victimization (Baron 2003; Miller, Schreck, and Tewksbury 2006). However, the theory has not necessarily been shown to be a general theory of crime, nor has it been shown to be the only possible explanation of crime. For example, the theory has shown little success in explaining white-collar offending (Miller, Schreck, and Tewksbury 2006), and studies that include other theoretical perspectives in addition to low self-control in their analysis often find that these perspectives add to our understanding of crime. In particular, the role of differential association/social learning perspectives and strain perspectives appear to remain important predictors of crime when included in models testing the explanatory power of low self-control (Baron 2003). There is also evidence that a number of the social consequences associated with low self-control that Gottfredson and Hirschi argue have spurious relationships with crime (relationships that disappear once self-control is accounted for because they are generated by low self-control) do in fact appear to have direct relationships with crime (Baron 2003). There has also been considerable debate regarding the stability of low self-control and the degree to which levels of self-control can shift over the life course (Piquero and Turner 2002).

The unidimensionality of low self-control has also been questioned. Some research suggests that the six characteristics of low self-control do not come together as one measure of self-control; rather, they remain separate, distinct indicators of impulsivity, lack of diligence, risk-taking, physicality, insensitivity, and low frustration tolerance. This is important because some work suggests that some of the individual components are better predictors of certain behaviours. For example, low frustration tolerance appears to have a strong link to violent offending while risk-taking has been linked to property offending (Baron, Forde, and Kay 2007). In sum, while there is general support for the link between low self-control and crime, the theory has generated a great deal of debate and will no doubt provide a fruitful ground for further research.

General Strain Theory

Robert Agnew (1992, 2001) provides a theory that focuses on how a broad number of negative situations can lead to criminal behaviour. He focuses on emotional reactions to negative situations or **strains** and details how other factors can influence people in their choice to cope with strain through either criminal or noncriminal means. The general strain theory, or what is commonly referred to as GST, focuses squarely on people's negative relationships with others. These are situations where people do not like the way that they are being treated and it is this experience that pressures people into committing crime as a means of coping with the strain. In his perspective, Agnew outlines three broad areas of strain that are thought to lead to crime (see Figure 7.2).

strain
Experiences or situations that individuals perceive as being negative, creating a negative emotional reaction that provides the possible incentive for using crime as a coping mechanism.

Types of Strain

Failure to Achieve Goals

The first broad area of strain outlined in the general strain perspective is the failure to achieve positively valued goals. Within this broad area are three sub-areas that Agnew summarizes can possibly lead to criminal behaviour. The first form of strain encompasses the disjunction between aspirations and expected achievements and is similar to the version of strain that Merton outlines in his

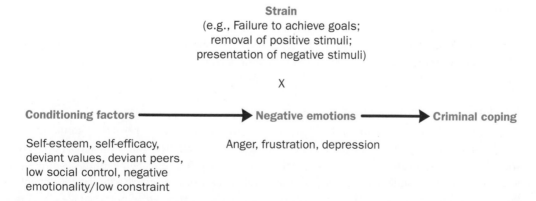

Figure 7.2 General Strain Theory

classic perspective. Here the gap between what people desire and what people expect to achieve leads to unpleasant feelings, pressuring them to utilize criminal means to achieve those aspirations. Thus, if someone aspires to extreme wealth but expects more modest success then this can lead people to adopt crime as a potential avenue to success.

The second type of strain outlined by Agnew under the rubric of the failure to achieve positively valued goals is the disjunction between expected achievements and actual achievements. This form of strain moves away from focusing on aspirations (e.g., acquiring a fortune), which are sometimes unrealistic. Instead, it centres on people's expectations of achievement, which are formed from their past achievement experiences and/or their observations of similar others' achievements. Thus, expected achievements can be viewed as more realistic in terms of accomplishment than are aspirations. If there is a gap between these more realistic expectations for achievement and what is actually achieved, this failure motivates individuals to turn to crime as a method of addressing this gap.

The third form of strain Agnew outlines under the category of the failure to achieve positively valued goals is the disjunction between just or fair outcomes and actual outcomes. In contrast to the two previous forms of strain, some individuals may not necessarily have specific expectations regarding outcomes when they enter into a situation. Instead, they may enter into circumstances believing that rewards will be allocated fairly. When the actual outcome in a situation is different than what people believe to be a fair or just outcome, then crime may be one response to attempt to adjust their outcomes. Crime can be viewed as a method where people can gain more rewards for themselves and decrease the rewards for others, meaning the allocation of outcomes can be shifted to where the individual perceives them to be more equitable. Thus, an individual who gets a poorer grade than a classmate who puts in less effort may steal from, or assault, the classmate or the teacher who distributed the outcomes in an attempt to alter outcomes.

Removal of Positive Stimuli

The second broad source of strain that Agnew outlines is the removal of positively valued stimuli. This removal can be actual or it can be anticipated. In other words, people may react to events they believe will happen in the future as well as to negative events that have already happened. There are a range of positively valued stimuli that can cause individuals to turn to crime if they are removed, including property and relationships, which may be terminated through breakup, death, or a change in residence. Agnew outlines that there are a number of potential responses to these types of losses. In some cases people may try to prevent the loss of the valued item, for example, by defending themselves and their property if being robbed. Second, the person who loses a positively valued item might seek revenge against those who stole their property by assaulting the guilty party. Third, those who lose positively valued stimuli may attempt to recover or reclaim the lost stimuli, or perhaps search out a replacement for the stimuli. They may steal back their property or engage in theft to gain an item similar to what they lost. Finally, Agnew notes that losing positively valued stimuli can generate negative emotions, and these emotions may be addressed through the use of alcohol or drugs.

Presentation of Negative Stimuli

The third broad source of strain outlined in the GST is the presentation of negative stimuli. Again, either the anticipation of a negative experience or the actual experience with some sort of negative stimuli can lead individuals to cope by resorting to a criminal response. Some examples of negative stimuli might include criminal victimization, child abuse, and a negative school environment. Similar to the removal of positively valued stimuli, there are a number of potential avenues for coping with this form of strain. First, individuals who experience negative stimuli may attempt to avoid or escape from the source of the stimuli. For example, a person who dislikes school or is being abused at home may become truant or run away from home. Second, that person may seek revenge against the source of the negative stimuli or against a displaced target that represents the source of the negative stimuli. For example, such individuals may assault the teacher if they dislike school or the parent who is abusing them. Third, individuals experiencing negative stimuli may attempt to bring an end to the source of the negative stimuli. Finally, the experience of negative stimuli will give rise to negative emotions, which can be dealt with by using drugs and/or alcohol.

Overlapping Strains

While these types of strain outlined in the GST are theoretically distinct from one another, they may often be viewed as overlapping. School failure can lead to a gap between expectations and achievements, perceptions of unjust outcomes, and the presentation of negative stimuli. Further, there is a wide range of circumstances that can be contained within these broad categories of strain. Agnew notes that it is important to distinguish between what are referred to as 'objective strains' and 'subjective strains'. Objective strains are conditions, situations, or episodes that a majority of a given group will dislike while subjective strains allude to the conditions, situations, or episodes that are not liked by the individuals who are experiencing them or have experienced them in the past. Examples of objective conditions or events that most people dislike regardless of their group membership might include school failure, a lack of shelter and/or food, and violent victimization. However, we must recognize the possibility of group differences in measures of objective strain. Further, people differ in their subjective evaluation of the same objective strains. Thus, one person may find living in poverty, failing school, or being the victim of crime as more of a strain than another person. The subjective evaluation can be influenced by a number of factors, including values, social resources, and life circumstances. Therefore, we must consider not only the objective situations that individuals encounter but also their perceptions and interpretations of those situations.

Agnew also suggests that the impact of strain may vary depending upon the severity/magnitude, duration, recency, and centrality of the strain. Strains that are severe or high in magnitude influence actors' abilities to cope in a noncriminal manner by decreasing the perceived costs of criminal coping and increasing the disposition to engage in criminal coping. Strains that are of a long duration (chronic stressors) and/or high frequency are expected to have a greater negative impact on the individual. As well, more recent strains are expected to have a greater impact on judgments of magnitude than older strains. Yet here Agnew acknowledges that certain types of strain, including severe childhood strains, may have long-term effects and potentially contribute to later criminal behaviour. In terms of the 'centrality' of the strain, negative experiences, particularly extreme or severe traumatic events that jeopardize central values, goals, needs, identities, and activities, are argued to be more criminogenic in nature because they undermine the ability to cope in a noncriminal fashion.

Agnew also notes that strains associated with or caused by low social control can increase the probabilities of a criminal coping strategy because the costs of crime are reduced. Further, individuals who lack conventional commitments, conventional attachments, and conventional supervision are less likely to have access to the resources that promote noncriminal coping. Agnew also argues that strains that are viewed as unjust increase the probability of criminal coping because they are particularly conducive to creating anger. Agnew adds that certain forms of strain also produce some inducement, stimulus, or motivation to utilize crime as a method of coping. For example, certain strains (e.g., criminal victimization, peer abuse, and physical abuse) provide access to values or beliefs that support criminal coping strategies and models that reinforce criminal coping strategies. Further, in some environments the best, or perhaps lone, strategy to cope with strain is through criminal means.

Negative Emotions

The various forms of subjective and objective strain within the three broad categories of strain are thought to elevate the probability that the person experiencing the strain will react with a possible array of negative emotions. It is important to note that the emotional response to an event or condition is distinct from the type of strain experienced. Thus, violent victimization is distinct from the emotional response to violent victimization. The emotional response, however, will be closely linked to the strain experienced, particularly subjective strains, since these types of strain deal more directly with a person's evaluation of an event or condition. Nevertheless, people with similar levels of subjective strain may respond with different emotions or varying degrees of the same emotion in response to the strain.

Some of the possible emotions that strain might call forth include fear and depression. However, the critical emotion outlined in this perspective is anger. A person is more likely to respond to strain with anger when they blame the experiences on other people because anger amplifies a person's feeling of injury. It is an emotional response that generates a need for revenge or retaliation or some sort of corrective action. Anger can also invigorate a person to actually take some sort of action. At the same time, anger lowers inhibitions and reduces any fear of punishment for engaging in crime, in part because strained, angry individuals suppose that others will consider their response to strain as justified. Anger can also be seen to promote crime because it undermines cognitive processes that impede considering noncriminal options for coping. In addition, anger may lead individuals to ignore resources that might help change the circumstances causing strain, and it diminishes a person's capacity or facility to articulate injustices clearly in a nonconfrontational manner. In sum, those who respond to strain with greater levels of anger will be more likely to engage in crime. Crime, then, can be interpreted as a means of easing the negative emotions generated by strain as well as a method to alter the strain itself.

Conditioning Factors

Agnew notes that there are a number of different factors that will increase or buffer the effect of strain, influencing whether a person will adopt a criminal or noncriminal coping strategy in response to strain. First, Agnew notes the importance of levels of *self-efficacy*. He argues that self-efficacy will influence sensitivity and reaction to strain. In particular, he suggests that those high in self-efficacy will be more likely to feel they can cope with strain in a nondelinquent manner, leaving them less likely to use criminal coping. Those lacking self-efficacy will be more sensitive to events and believe that they will be unable to alter those events through the use of noncriminal means. Second, *self-esteem* will influence individuals' sensitivity to strain and their ability to engage in various coping strategies. High self-esteem will buffer individuals from strain, leaving them less likely to use criminal coping strategies. Third, those who associate with deviant criminal peers and hold values supportive of deviant behaviour are more likely to react to strain with illegal behaviour. Deviant peers may strengthen the link between strain and delinquency by providing definitions for certain situations to be interpreted as strain, supplying support for criminal behaviour, modelling criminal behaviour, defining certain deviant activities as appropriate responses to strain, and serving as instigators of criminal behaviour. Moral values against crime may dampen the effect of strain on crime while deviant attitudes that support criminal coping may increase the effect of strain on crime. Fourth, Agnew argues that people are more likely to engage in crime when they blame their adversity on others. External attributions are more likely to lead to anger, which increases individuals' feelings of injury, creating the desire for revenge and justification for criminal coping. Fifth, the availability and quality of social support that people have at their disposal will also influence whether they deal with strain in a criminal or a conventional fashion. Social support may come in the form of financial assistance, guidance, and emotional support—all resources that steer strained individuals clear of crime. What is also important here is that the social support comes from conventional rather than deviant sources. In contrast, those without conventional, instrumental, and social support are more likely to adopt criminal coping strategies. Criminal coping is also more likely when the benefits of utilizing crime are great and the costs of utilizing criminal coping are low. The calculation of the costs and benefits of crime will be influenced by situational factors, including the absence of conventional adults, the presence of an attractive target (human or property) against which to offend, and the presence of criminal peers.

Finally, Agnew argues that the personality traits of negative emotionality and low constraint will influence whether an individual deals with strain through criminal or noncriminal means. Individuals with negative emotionality are easily upset and angered and tend to have aggressive interaction styles. Those with low constraint tend to be impulsive risk-takers, with little empathy for others. These characteristics are likely to increase the relationship between strain and crime because individuals with low constraint and negative emotionality are more likely to be sensitive to strain, to interpret situations as strain, and to view situations as unjust. Agnew argues that individuals with these characteristics care little about the reactions of others and give little thought to the consequences of their actions, leaving them more likely to adopt criminal coping strategies. The aggressive interaction style and proneness for risk that characterizes individuals with these traits also increase the likelihood of an illegal response in reaction to strain. In sum, those individuals who experience a strain when they have low self-efficacy, low conventional social support, greater access to deviant peers and deviant values, and greater negative emotionality/low constraint, and who see the costs of criminal coping to be minimal and who blame the strain on others will be more likely to engage in crime. Box 7.1 provides an example of how criminologists are using Agnew's general strain theory to further develop and test integrative theories aimed at explaining more serious forms of juvenile delinquency and youth crime.

Current Empirical Research into General Strain Theory

General strain theory has generated a great deal of research. There is much support for linkages between various negative experiences and criminal coping (Agnew 2006). Much of the early research utilized measures incorporating a number of different types of strain, making it difficult to determine which types of strain were actually linked to criminal behaviour. Later research, following the guidance of Agnew, has been focused on exploring links between more specific forms of strain and criminal coping. This more strain-specific approach suggests that a number of negative experiences are associated with criminal coping, including the following:

- The failure to achieve core goals that can easily be achieved through crime (including quick money, masculine status, and autonomy)
- Parental rejection
- Emotional and physical abuse in various settings (including the family, school, and criminal justice system)
- Negative school experiences
- Poor employment conditions (that involve unpleasant, physically demanding, and repetitive work; minimal autonomy; low wages; absent benefits; and limited prospects for advancement)
- Abusive peer relationships
- Criminal victimization
- Youth homelessness (Agnew 2006; Baron 2004)

Box 7.1   Youth Justice in Action

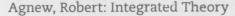

Agnew, Robert: Integrated Theory

The beginning of the 21st century was an exciting period in which to study the causes of crime. Violence in the United States, particularly among juveniles, had dropped precipitously from its levels in the early 1990s and criminologists vigorously sought an explanation. Data with which to test classic theories such as social disorganization theory had recently become available for the first time and were generating empirical support for ideas that had not previously been tested. Recent revisions of learning theory and control theory had sparked heated debate about both the causes of crime and the most effective methods with which to identify those causes empirically. Strain theory had begun a major resurgence in the literature and was generating renewed research in its own right.

However, while these and other such developments generated new interest in the causes of crime, it was becoming increasingly difficult for practitioners to keep up with the latest literature, for academics to summarize it in a coherent way, and for students to leave criminology courses with a straightforward answer to a seemingly simple question: Why do criminals offend? Robert Agnew's *general theory of crime* represents a leading effort to integrate prior theory and research for the purpose of answering this question in a manner that is relatively succinct but simultaneously complete.

The Goals of Agnew's General Theory

Although it may seem counterintuitive, different criminological theories sometimes attempt to explain different phenomena. This occurs for two reasons. First, different theories define crime in different ways. For example, although Michael Gottfredson and Travis Hirschi refer to their influential control theory as a 'general theory of crime', they seek to explain any behavior that serves to satiate an individual's short-term self-interest at the expense of long-term well-being. While such behaviors certainly include acts of force or fraud for which there exist codified legal sanctions, they also include legal behaviors, like promiscuous sex or smoking, that are 'analogous' to crime insofar as they satiate the perpetrator's immediate desires at the expense of long-term well-being. In contrast to Gofredson and Hirschi's theory, Agnew's (2005, p. 12) integrated theory is designed specifically to explain *'behaviors that are generally condemned* and that *carry a significant risk of sanction* by the state if detected'* (emphasis in the original).

Source: Rebellon, Cesar J. 'Agnew, Robert: Integrated Theory.' *Encyclopedia of Criminological Theory*. 2010. SAGE Publications. 3 May, 2011.

There is also evidence for the link between these negative experiences and negative emotions, such as anger. In turn, there is some evidence that anger is related to criminal coping, particularly for more aggressive forms of offending. Some debate has emerged here regarding the type of anger that has been explored, which has often been more of a measure of trait anger (a stable personality trait) than of state anger (an emotion generated by the situation) (Agnew 2006). The minimal research conducted so far suggests that there may be differences. There is also some debate regarding whether the effects of strain leading to crime should flow primarily through anger or whether they have some independent impact (Agnew 2006). Finally, there are now calls for work to explore other types of emotions, for example depression, and to determine which types of strain may generate these emotions and which types of coping these alternative emotional reactions might generate (Agnew 2006).

The work exploring the role of the conditioning factors has generated more uneven results. Overall, there is limited support for the moderating roles of self-efficacy, self-esteem, social control, deviant values, deviant beliefs, negative emotionality/low constraint, external attribution, and low risk of apprehension. However, the results often vary across studies, populations examined, the type of strain examined, and the form of crime to be explained (Agnew 2006; Baron 2004). Overall, this sporadic support beyond the basic relationships between various forms of strain and crime suggests that more work is required to more accurately specify which type of conditioning factor and emotion will work with which form of strain, and within which type of population.

Age-Graded Theory of Social Control

Sampson and Laub (1993 and Laub and Sampson 2003) offer an age-graded theory of **informal social control**. It is a theory that seeks to explain how people become involved in offending in the first place (the onset of offending), why people keep offending (continuity in offending), and later changes that lead individuals to move from offending to non-offending (desistance), or from non-offending to offending. The theory focuses on the manner in which informal social controls at different stages of a person's life influence continuity and change in offending behaviour as a person moves from childhood to adolescence to young adulthood and beyond (see Figure 7.3).

Mechanisms of Adolescent Informal Social Control

The theory begins by identifying three mechanisms of informal social control within the context of the family: attachment to the family, monitoring, and consistent discipline. The degree to which the child is connected to the family inhibits or allows for delinquency. These three methods of informal control can buffer youth from participating in delinquency through the presence of strong emotional bonds or by means of the more direct control influence of supervision and punishment. The school provides an additional significant socializing institution where the degree of attachment as well as academic performance reduces or allows for participation in delinquency.

Social Structural Factors

The age-graded theory suggests that social structural factors influence the quality and levels of these social bonds. That is, socio-economic status, unemployment, family dissolution, and residential mobility can undermine social bonds. In fact, Sampson and Laub suggest that these types of factors affect the probability of delinquency through social bonds rather than having any direct link to crime. For example, socio-economic disadvantage may have a negative impact on parents,

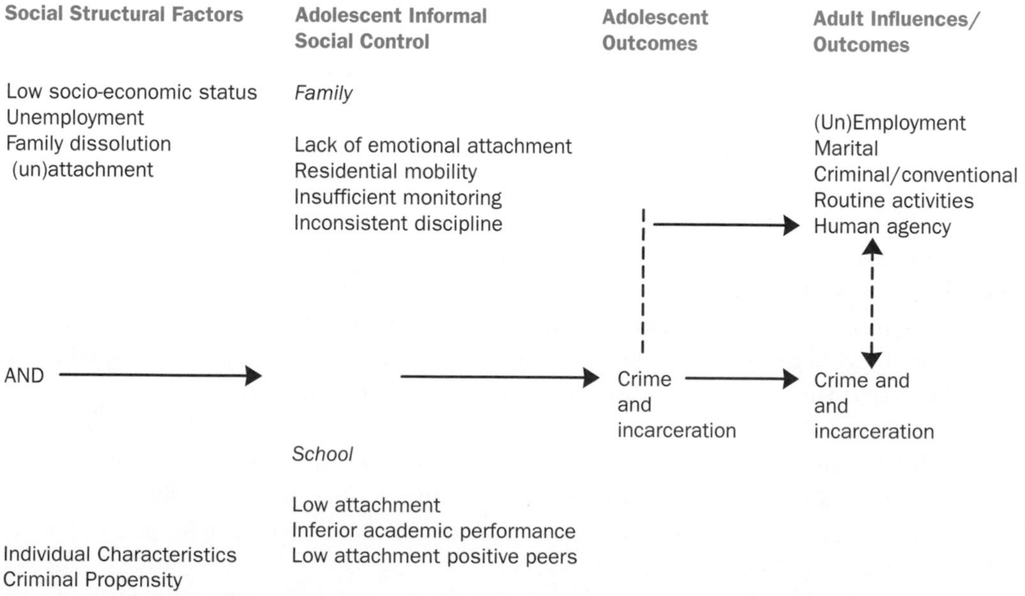

informal social control

The control over people's behaviour that develops as a result of relationships and attachments to significant others and investments in conventional activities that could be damaged by engaging in illegal activities.

Social Structural Factors	Adolescent Informal Social Control	Adolescent Outcomes	Adult Influences/ Outcomes
Low socio-economic status Unemployment Family dissolution (un)attachment	*Family* Lack of emotional attachment Residential mobility Insufficient monitoring Inconsistent discipline		(Un)Employment Marital Criminal/conventional Routine activities Human agency
AND ⟶	⟶	Crime and incarceration ⟶	Crime and incarceration
	School Low attachment Inferior academic performance Low attachment positive peers		
Individual Characteristics Criminal Propensity			

Figure 7.3 Age-Graded Theory of Social Control

increasing the likelihood of parental difficulties in coping and impeding parenting behaviour that facilitates social control. The stress associated with living in poverty and dense households may undermine the attachment between the child and the parent, reducing emotional social control, while the attraction of the less crowded streets can interrupt monitoring.

Disrupted social control can destroy attachments to school and, along with the lack of monitoring and supervision where homework is checked and attendance confirmed, can lead to educational deficits. In turn, it is the lack of connection to the school and the lack of social bonds in the family that have a direct effect on crime in youth, mediating the impact of poverty and social disadvantage.

Social bonds can also be undermined by individual differences in criminal propensity. These individual differences can be characterized by early conduct disorder, difficult temperaments, and persistent tantrums. Positive parenting styles are disrupted by the child's anti-social behaviour. Displays of anti-social behaviour can provoke angry and hostile reactions from parents and inhibit or destroy social bonds, creating additional negative behaviour from the child. Similarly, poor school attachment can be a consequence of misbehaviour as well as a cause. Teachers may react negatively to difficult and disruptive children, leading to damaged student/teacher relationships. These damaged relationships can lead to a decreased attachment to the school and potentially undermine the child's academic performance, thereby increasing the potential for criminal activities. Displays of anti-social characteristics can also lead to rejection from more conventional peers. Peer rejection means another potential source of positive socialization is destroyed as those with negative traits move into groups containing others who display similar anti-social characteristics.

Sampson and Laub suggest that adult crime can be understood in terms of **cumulative continuity**, where behaviour is sustained by the process of its consequences. According to Sampson and Laub, weak social bonds account for continuity in criminal activities beyond childhood and into adolescence and adulthood. Early negative behaviours, such as crime and the anti-social characteristics outlined in the previous section, are associated with negative adult behaviours, including participating in crime and using drugs. Further, criminal behaviour persists into adulthood because such behaviour affects prospective life chances and undermines adult social control. Negative life experiences associated with earlier criminal participation, arrest, conviction, and incarceration may lead to school failure and unemployment, thereby decreasing future opportunities. Further, previous criminal involvement can also jeopardize informal social bonds with family, friends, and school and make vulnerable the creation and progress of adult social bonds. Thus, childhood criminal behaviour leads indirectly to adult criminal behaviour by undermining adult social bonds.

Adult Influences/Outcomes

While Sampson and Laub argue there is continuity in criminal behaviour as a result of the link between crime and social control, they also stress that socialization experiences and significant life events in adulthood can offset or neutralize the sway of earlier life events and experiences. The theory outlines **life-course turning points**, such as employment and marriage, that can modify and shift life **trajectories**. In particular, the theory outlines that these transitions potentially contain social ties, monitoring, and social support that can supply social control that alters a person's trajectory from offender to nonoffender. Alternatively, transitions that destroy these sources of social control may lead a person to move from nonoffender to offender. In either case, individual pathways to both crime and conformity, independent of prior criminal propensity, can be modified by key social control institutions.

Laub and Sampson (2003) have recently revised their perspective, identifying a number of additional causal factors, including structured routine activities and human agency, to help understand desistance from crime in adulthood as well as continuity. Laub and Sampson argue that the type

---

disrupted social control
Events or life circumstances that weaken or destroy the relationships, attachments, and activities that provide barriers to engaging in criminal activities.

cumulative continuity
A developmental model that outlines how crime in adolescence has negative consequences for future life chances, including education, relationships, and employment, and increases the likelihood that criminal behaviour will continue into adulthood. These in turn undermine further life chances, escalating the probabilities of continued, persistent criminal behaviour.

life-course turning points
Events such as marriage/divorce or employment/unemployment that serve to direct an individual's developmental criminal career path toward either desistance or onset.

trajectories
Paths or avenues of development throughout the lifespan. These are long-term patterns of behaviour that often consist of marriage, parenthood, employment, and involvement in criminal activities.

of routine activities that individuals engage in will influence their involvement in crime. Different routines influence the behavioural choices available to individuals. For example, spending time out on the street at night with other offenders increases the likelihood that someone will become involved in crime. In contrast, spending time with extended family or spending significant amounts of time at work, where an individual is monitored, might be expected to decrease behavioural choices that involve crime. Thus, having a family and/or employment creates structured routine activities that promote desistance from crime, even if the individual in question has a history of prior offending. Those who persist in offending are likely to be in circumstances where there is a continued lack of structured routine activities and social controls. Individuals whose social controls become damaged or undermined in adulthood are likely to have changes in their routine activities, increasing their likelihood of anti-social behaviour.

Human agency is the last factor offered to shape offending trajectories across the life course. This concept suggests that individuals are actively involved in actions to transform their situations. Here Sampson and Laub introduce the idea of **situated choice**. People make choices to get involved in certain relationships, be they work or personal, but these choices are situated under certain structural and historical conditions. At the same time, the choices that people make under these conditions will influence their behaviour. Thus, people make decisions regarding offending or desistance, and in turn those decisions influence outcomes. These outcomes, however, according to the theory, are not necessarily predictable. Nevertheless, Sampson and Laub offer a perspective showing how independent of prior criminal propensity (e.g., low self-control), behaviour can negatively influence people's future outcomes but can still be modified across the life course by the availability of social control and alternative routine activities associated with social control and choice.

situated choice
The choices individuals make to become involved in certain relationships, be they work or personal, that are situated under certain structural and historical conditions and that can influence future behaviour.

Current Empirical Research into the Age-Graded Theory of Social Control

The original version of the theory, and to a lesser extent its recent revision, have been subject to theoretical verification through both prior and new research. The empirical work exploring deviance in childhood and adolescence provides a great deal of support for the association between family and school bonds and youth crime (Laub, Sampson, and Sweeten 2006; Sampson and Laub 1993). Furthermore, there is work that outlines the negative impact that social structural factors have on these social bonds, and the largely indirect relationship to crime these larger structural factors have through their destruction of social bonds (Laub et al. 2006; Sampson and Laub 1993). There is also considerable support for the argument that criminal behaviour continues from adolescence into young adulthood and beyond. Part of this is explained by the continuing effect of a previous anti-social propensity, such as low self-control. But research has also detailed the indirect effects this propensity and other anti-social behaviours have on undermining adult social bonds. Moreover, there is evidence that offending in adolescence undermines adult opportunities. Researchers have called this cumulative continuity, where offending cuts off opportunities and channels offenders into a continuing offending lifestyle. Thus, the empirical evidence shows to some degree that anti-social behaviour in childhood and adolescence is associated with a number of negative adult outcomes and is relatively stable across stages of the life course, supporting the perspective (Laub et al. 2006; Sampson and Laub 1993).

There is also support for the arguments regarding changes in behaviour. Tests of the age-graded theory do show that important life events that create social bonds in adulthood can lead to desistance from criminal activities. In particular, getting married (where an attachment bond is formed) or having a stable job (that establishes a social bond) leads to changes from criminal to noncriminal behaviour, even if the person has a criminal history and criminal propensity (Laub et al. 2006; Sampson and Laub 1993). While less direct work has been undertaken on the elaborated perspective, Laub and Sampson (2003; Laub et al. 2006) themselves provide supportive evidence of the importance of routine activities and agency, as have researchers working more specifically with these issues. Thus, the growing literature on routine activities shows that those who are involved in such activities will be less likely to become involved in anti-social behaviour. In addition, social control relationships offer routine activities that reduce opportunities for criminal offending. Finally, the limited work on the agency component of the perspective suggests that people make decisions to desist or persist in offending and that these decisions are often influenced by outside factors, of which the individual is unaware (Laub and Sampson 2003; Laub et al. 2006).

Control Balance Theory

control balance

The degree of control individuals perceive that they have over their environment relative to the degree of control they perceive their environment has over them.

Charles Tittle (1995, 2004) offers a theory where the central concept is 'control'. The idea of *being controlled* focuses on how an individual's behavioural choices are restricted to some degree by some other person or group of people who have the power or resources to impede or assist that individual in achieving his or her goals or in satisfying his or her motivations. Being controlled can also include the degree to which physical or social structural arrangements make attaining one's goals more problematic. *Exercising control*, in contrast, focuses on how individuals, alone or with others, escape the limitations of the behavioural restrictions imposed by others. Exercising control also refers to individuals' capacity to overcome structural or physical obstacles in order to realize their personal goals. It can also include the ability to help or impede others in individuals' quest to reach their goals.

The amount of control that a person experiences relative to the amount of control a person can exercise is referred to as a control ratio. This ratio influences whether a person will engage in deviance and what form of deviance they might engage in. People are said to have a number of specific control ratios associated with their various roles, statuses, and environments, in addition to a general control ratio reflecting their overall ability to control and be controlled. Thus, people can have a control ratio for their friendships, jobs, school, and family, as well as a general control ratio that encompasses all of these various situations (see Figure 7.4).

When the amount of control that individuals exercise is equal to the amount of control they experience, their control ratio is balanced, which is unlikely to lead to deviance. In contrast, control ratio imbalances, which can take two forms, leave individuals more likely to consider deviance as a method of altering that imbalance. Individuals will have a *control surplus* when the amount of control they exercise is greater than the amount of control they experience. Therefore, if you perceive that you have more control over your friendships than they have over you, then you would have a control surplus in that domain. *Control deficits* arise where the amount of control that a person experiences exceeds the amount of control exercised. For example, if you felt that school had greater control over you than you had over it, you would have a control deficit for that domain. The two types of control imbalance predispose a person to undertake deviance to improve control ratios. However, this predisposition will only transform into a motivation for deviance under

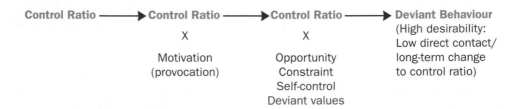

Figure 7.4 Control Balance Theory

circumstances where people experience a provocation that reminds them, or makes them aware, of their control imbalance. For example, homeless youths may experience verbal slights from passersby that remind them that their poverty has greater control over them than they have over it. These provocative reminders create negative emotions like humiliation and debasement. The greater the control ratio imbalance, the higher the likelihood that people will feel debased or humiliated when faced with provocation. In turn, the experience of humiliation focuses the individual on deviance as a potential solution that might serve to alter the control ratio imbalance.

Once motivation is created by control ratio imbalances and provocation, it will only lead to criminal activity if there is opportunity to carry out criminal activity. The person cannot, for example, break into a car or assault someone when there are no vehicles or human targets present. The theory suggests that, given motivation and opportunity, individuals will review a range of deviant acts, including those that they perceive will lead to the greatest change in their control ratio. Many of these behaviours, however, are also likely to be viewed as serious and bring about counter-controlling reactions, such as police intervention and incarceration. Therefore, the most serious acts may not serve as viable options for altering a control ratio imbalance, forcing individuals to choose other forms of deviance from their available options. The act that the individual actually chooses will be influenced by *constraint*.

Constraint is a complex variable that represents the seriousness of the act being considered and situational risk. Seriousness is related to the amount of counter-control that the act might elicit. Those acts that are thought to lead to greater punishment will be viewed as more serious. Situational risk is the concern about being caught engaging in the act and actually experiencing the counter-controlling reactions. Thus, individuals will be sensitive to constraint when reviewing possible avenues to address imbalances and are more likely to choose those acts where the probabilities of detection are lower and the penalties less severe.

The causal process summarized above is argued to work as outlined when a person has high self-control. Low self-control makes people vulnerable to provocation, leaving them more apt to become motivated for crime, more likely to react instantly, less likely to consider the counter-control associated with their acts, and less likely to consider gains. In contrast, those high in self-control can restrain themselves from taking instantaneous actions, leaving them more likely to consider different types of acts than those with low self-control. These acts may have more impact on altering control balance ratios.

Contingencies

The causal process of the theory may also be influenced by various contingencies, including moral beliefs, self-efficacy, prior deviant experience, and subcultural involvement. While not required for the control balance variables to impact on deviance, and not having significant independent causal impact, contingencies can modify the control balancing process. For example, moral beliefs may disturb the impact of an imbalanced control ratio on crime. Thus, thinking certain criminal activities are wrong will mean that there is less likelihood that a control imbalance will be addressed through illegal activities. In contrast, when facing control imbalance, higher self-efficacy may leave a person more likely to confront controls and/or take advantage of deviant opportunities that others would find risky. Prior experience with deviance can also act as a contingency because people can recall previous successes in altering control imbalances through crime and recognize the low potential for counter-control. Similarly, subcultural involvement may produce motivations for deviance beyond those stemming from imbalanced control ratios as people are exposed to various forms, excuses, rationalizations, and expectations of deviance.

Risk, an important component of constraint, can also act as contingency. The link between control imbalance and deviance should be greatest when actors perceive the risk of detection and punishment to be minimal. The benefits or perceived rewards represented in the motivation variable can also be used as a contingency variable. Here, the greater the benefits, including the perceived pleasure of the act, the greater the impact of an imbalanced control ratio on crime.

Tittle notes that control balance is highly dependent on life-cycle stages. He suggests that as people age they typically gain more ability to control as well as to escape control. Furthermore, individuals' perceptions of risk, feelings of debasement, and the other contingencies outlined in the theory can be altered by experience and change throughout the life cycle. Tittle observes that young people are controlled by adults, by peers, by political structures, by organizations, and generally by the environment. He suggests that, as a result, individuals potentially suffer from extreme control deficits. However, Tittle also acknowledges that some youth, through subcultural participation, can escape adult control, especially school authorities and parents, allowing these youth greater control over their environment.

Types of Deviance

In the revised version of the theory, Tittle (2004) argues that different types of control imbalance will lead to different forms of deviance that are distinguished by their *control balance desirability*. Control balance desirability is made up two components. The first surrounds the potential long-term change in the control ratio that may result from the act. The second focuses on the degree to which the offender needs to be personally or directly involved with the victim. Acts with little direct contact with victims and that allow for long-term changes in control balance ratios have the greatest control balance desirability. Acts that involve direct contact and have shorter-term impact on control balance ratios are seen to have less control balance desirability. Tittle suggests that acts can be sorted on a continuum based on these characteristics. He argues, however, that the theory does not permit the precise estimate of particular behaviours; rather, he claims it can help explain the choosing of a certain act from behaviours with similar control balance desirability scores.

Actors with substantial control surpluses, high in self-control, who are presented with opportunities and few constraints will be most likely to undertake behaviours high in control balance desirability (for example, committing a sophisticated white-collar crime or leading an organized crime syndicate). In contrast, acts low in control balance desirability are more likely to be accessed by people who have small to medium control deficits, who are low in self-control, and who face constraints on committing acts high in control balance desirability but have opportunities for the low desirability acts (for example, assaulting a boss or robbing a convenience store). Acts around the middle of the desirability continuum may point toward various levels and amalgamations of the causal variables. Those with surpluses or small deficits, a range of self-control, and a range of constraint could engage in acts of medium control balance desirability as long as opportunities present themselves (for example, embezzlement or shoplifting). Those with extreme deficits, however, are most likely to resort to *submission,* which will include passive rather than active responses and, therefore, are not included on the continuum (see Figure 7.4). Tittle argues that the sense of autonomy of those with extreme deficits is destroyed to the point where they are unable to imagine options to their situations. As a result, individuals in these situations are likely to be subjected to various acts of degradation, including chronic victimization.

Current Empirical Research into Control Balance Theory

Most of the limited number of available empirical tests on the control balance perspective have found that both control balance deficits and control balance surpluses were related to a range of deviant behaviours, including assault, theft, drug and alcohol use, deviant sexual practices, eating disorders, using others' school work, cheating, and criminal victimization (Baron and Forde 2007; Tittle 2004). The bulk of the research, however, has taken place prior to Tittle's (2004) refinement of the theory, so there has been little focus on the relationships between control ratio imbalances and different behaviours that might have different control balance desirability (Baron 2010; also see Box 7.2). Limited research has also examined the moderating effects of the contingency variables. This research shows mixed support for the argument that control surpluses and deficits will have a greater impact at lower levels of self-control. The findings on the moderating impact of constraint on the control balance ratio have also been mixed, as have the results focusing on risk. Limited research has indicated that the impact of control imbalances on deviance is greater at higher levels of deviant peer association. Generally, support for the contingency variables depends on the sample used and the offence being examined (Baron and Forde 2007). Further, the research often shows that rather than influencing the impact of the control balance ratios, the contingency variables appear instead to be direct causes of crime (Baron 2010). Thus, a review of the research suggests that while the basic, direct causal process appears related to deviance, as a new emerging perspective with a number of potential avenues for research, support for the more nuanced causal process is still yet to be determined.

Box 7.2 Youth Justice in Action

Tittle, Charles R.: Control Balance Theory

After reviewing and critiquing extant criminological theories, Charles R. Tittle concluded that most fail as general theories of crime and deviance because they do not offer breadth, comprehensiveness, precision, or depth. These limitations do not mean that these theories are inadequate explanations of crime phenomena. In fact, each adds to the understanding of deviant and criminal behavior by focusing on a particular causal factor, and more importantly, each has generated at least modest support. This sentiment, however, does imply that existing theories are both restricted and incomplete. Tittle proposed an integrated criminological theory drawing from learning, anomie, conflict, social control, labeling, utilitarian, and routine activities theories. As such, **control balance** theory is a general theory that not only is designed to explain all forms of deviant behavior but also to account for conforming behaviors.

Original Theory

In the original formulation of control balance theory, deviance is defined as 'any behavior that the majority of a given group regards as unacceptable or that typically evokes a collective response of a negative type' (Tittle 1995, p. 124). Deviance can be divided into six different categories: predation, exploitation, defiance, plunder, decadence, and submission. Predation involves direct acts of physical violence, manipulation, or property theft, which benefit the perpetrator and have no regard for the well-being of the victim. Exploitation is indirect predation where others or the situational context is used to coerce, manipulate, or steal from a victim for the benefit of the exploiter. Defiance refers to the indifference of individuals toward an individual, a group, or norms and values of a designated individual or group. Plunder is the pursuit of one's own goals with little regard for the effects of one's own actions on others and is considered especially heinous. Decadence deals with unpredictable and impulsive acts that have no rational motivation but instead deal with the whims of the moment. Submission is passive obedience toward others.

Source: Piquero, Nicole Leeper. 'Tittle, Charles R.: Control Balance Theory.' *Encyclopedia of Criminological Theory.* 2010. SAGE Publications. 3 May, 2011.

Differential Coercion Theory

Mark Colvin (2000) has offered a theory that integrates several of the perspectives outlined in the book and in this chapter, including social control theory, social learning theory, general strain theory, the general theory of crime, control balance theory, as well as Marxist perspectives explaining youth offending. Central to the perspective are two dimensions of control. The first surrounds **coercion**, which can range from extremely coercive to completely noncoercive. Coercion is viewed as punitive because of the emotional and/or physical pain it can cause and because it can take away vital sources of instrumental and social support. The second dimension of control is the consistency with which it is delivered. Consistency can range from highly erratic to extremely consistent (see Figure 7.5).

coercion
A personal or impersonal force that compels or frightens individuals to behave in a certain way.

Direct and Indirect Coercion

When examining these dimensions, it is also important to recognize that coercion can be either direct or indirect. For example, control developing from a tangible interpersonal relationship (e.g., the family) would be direct coercion. Control emerging from forces beyond an individual's control can be viewed as indirect coercion. Economic conditions, for example, might force individuals to remain in coercive family or work relationships or to take employment that they do not like in a location where they do not want to live.

Both direct and indirect coercion can be consistent or erratic. For example, a parent who punishes a child for every single infraction no matter how minor can be seen to be engaging in consistent direct control. The parent who sanctions irregularly is engaging in inconsistent direct control. Broad labour market conditions that move an individual in and out of employment are erratic and indirect. Those that provide long-term or permanent exclusion from the labour market can be seen as more consistent and indirect.

There can be ties between interpersonal and impersonal forms of coercion. The ability to escape coercive *interpersonal* relationships may depend on the nature of *impersonal* coercive relationships. For example, individuals' ability to leave their family or their undesirable employment might be disrupted by poor labour markets and the lack of employment. Therefore, impersonal economic forces can emerge as coercive in and of themselves when they have an impact on the interpersonal coercive forces.

Colvin observes that coercion has numerous sources—including the family, peers, criminal justice and social service agencies, as well as the broader economy. In these settings, individuals are

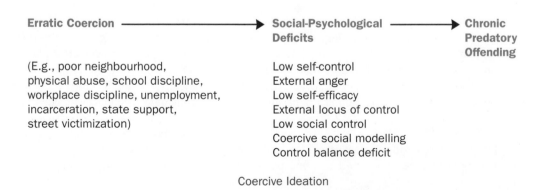

Figure 7.5 Erratic Coercion and Chronic Predatory Offending

said to differ in the degree to which they experience coercion (ranging from no coercion to extreme coercion). In families where force, intimidation, and threats are used with some frequency to gain compliance, children are understood to experience coercion. Individuals who participate in peer groups where they continually encounter violent victimization and verbal degradation and disparagement at the hands of others are also viewed as suffering coercion. Impoverished individuals under the formal supervision of state agencies who can remove or threaten to remove financial support and threaten or impose sanctions are exposed to coercion. Being incarcerated, since it entails being held in a confined space against one's wishes by force, is viewed as coercive. Finally, poverty and economic necessity and the stress and desperation that surfaces from economic pressure are thought to be extremely coercive. Colvin notes that often individuals experiencing coercion in one setting move to other settings where they again experience coercion.

Types of Control Structures

Colvin argues that four types of control structures can be identified based on the degree of coercion (coercive/noncoercive) and the consistency (consistent/erratic) with which the coercion is delivered. The different types of control structures influence the development of a number of social-psychological mechanisms. The extent of coercion and the degree of consistency in its delivery will impact on levels of social bonds, self-efficacy, locus of control, self-control, anger, the social learning of behaviour, and control balance deficits. In turn, the type of control experienced and the type of psychological mechanisms developed will influence whether an individual will become involved in crime and in what type of crime that person will likely become involved.

A Consistent, Noncoercive Environment

The first type of control structure outlined by Colvin is one where the individual experiences a consistent, noncoercive environment. Here, any sort of control is applied in a manner that is firm and fair and will be accompanied by explanations that outline the reasoning for the application of control. Further, instrumental means, like offers of money or gifts, to gain compliance is avoided. This type of environment offers no opportunities to observe aggressive models and, because of the fairness in applying control, is unlikely to generate anger or to provide any sort of provocation to remind people that they have a control imbalance. However, because of the bonds that are developed by using this form of control, this type of environment does lead to higher levels of social control, self-control, self-efficacy, and an internalized locus of control. As a result, people who experience this type of control structure will show an inclination toward pro-social behaviours, leaving them less likely to become involved in criminal activities.

An Erratic, Noncoercive Environment

In contrast, the second type of control structure that Colvin outlines is referred to as erratic and noncoercive. This form of control can best be described as lenient, negligent, or weak. The controller tends to exhibit an indifference or detached involvement with the individual who is being controlled. In light of this, when the controller does intervene, the control is weak as well as inconsistent or erratic. The lack of interest on the part of the controller results in intermittent emotional social support at best. There may be somewhat more instrumental support as controllers may attempt to influence the subject's actions through the use of money and other incentives, but this support still will take place erratically. Again, because this type of control does not involve coercion it will not generate anger; nor will it provide any sort of provocation that will remind people of imbalanced control ratios. In this particular situation, individuals may have a control balance surplus since the person who is controlling rarely exerts control. Furthermore, these individuals are likely to develop high levels of self-efficacy and an internal sense of control. The failure of consistent emotional support to develop and the erratic recognition and correction of anti-social behaviour means that people under this control regime will, however, have low social control and low self-control. The lack of social control and self-control along with the sense of self-efficacy will, Colvin argues, lead to a greater likelihood for individuals to experiment with pleasurable deviant activities, such as drinking, drug use, and illicit sex. Further, due to their history of exchanging compliance for instrumental rewards they will have the tendency to lie to and manipulate authority figures. Finally, because their control history does not involve anger-generating coercion, such individuals are more likely to engage in minor forms of street crime rather than in more serious predatory street offending. Colvin argues that this type of control structure and the types of offending it produces accounts for the majority of offenders.

A Consistent, Coercive Environment

The third type of control structure that Colvin outlines is referred to as consistent coercive control. This is a pattern of control that is regularly and repeatedly delivered and highly coercive, creating a relationship between the controller and the object of control that is highly punitive. These types of relationships usually lack emotional support and guidance as well as instrumental support. To any extent that emotional and instrumental social supports are available, they are continuously in danger of being eliminated or taken away as an additional method of coercion. This type of consistent, coercive control relationship incites a control ratio deficit—often, to such an extent that the subject of control will become resigned to his or her negative situation. Additional fallout from these experiences includes a low sense of self-efficacy and an external locus of control. Furthermore, the coercion involved incites anger, but because the coercion is consistent, and any external reaction to coercion is punished, the anger is self-directed. The coercion also provides a model for the social learning of coercive behaviour. Finally, since the social supports are weak and constantly under threat of removal, the social bonds that develop are moderate and calculative, and the consistent supervision and discipline lead to high self-control.

Consistent, coercive control limits the probability of criminal behaviour but its nature also leads to a low probability of pro-social behaviour. The highly restrictive environment does not allow for deviance, and fear of the consequences resulting from the failure to comply leads to highly self-monitored behaviour. Highly self-monitored behaviour inhibits the initiative, creativity, or development that are necessary for success in education and other pursuits. Instead, consistent, coercive control leads to an increased likelihood of mental-health problems, including chronic depression. Moreover, Colvin suggests that it is possible that in situations where the consistent constraints are loosened or removed from these individuals, then the self-directed anger may be rerouted externally, leading to violent behaviour.

An Erratic, Coercive Environment

The final type of control structure outlined by Colvin is the erratic, coercive type. In this type, control takes the form of irregular punitive responses to transgressions. On occasions, serious misbehaviour is overlooked while minor misconduct is severely punished. There may be other circumstances where punishment is meted out when no violation has occurred. The experience of erratic and what appear to be arbitrary punishment practices lead youth to develop feelings of injustice and externally directed anger. Furthermore, the erratic nature of the coercion leads to low self-efficacy and an external locus of control. The inconsistent nature leaves these youth feeling that events are beyond their control, unrelated to their behaviour, and that they have little chance of changing the circumstances. The erratic coercion allows intermittent periods of reprieve that leaves victims feeling humiliated and debased. The experience leads to such individuals recognizing control balance deficits or to feelings that they have less control than they are subject to, which fuels deviant motivation. The inconsistent nature of the punishment also means that self-control fails to develop, allowing negative traits such as risk-taking, temper, and impulsiveness, to be exhibited unfettered. The coercive experience also provides extreme avenues for learning coercive behaviour. Here, youth learn how to use coercion themselves as a method for controlling and gaining the compliance of others. Finally, since in these situations emotional and instrumental social support tends to be minimal or completely absent, there is little opportunity for social bonds to develop. In fact, any bonds that do develop are negative.

Taken together, the experiences of coercion along with the social-psychological deficits—i.e., negative social bonds, low self-control, low self-efficacy, external locus of control, coercive behaviour modelling, and control balance deficits—lead to the generation of *coercive ideation* (see Figure 7.5). Coercive ideation is where the individual comes to interpret the world as an environment enveloped in coercion and the only method to combat the coercion that the individual experiences is through the use of coercion. Individuals who develop coercive ideation will come to see the broader world as cruel, callous, and nasty.

Colvin argues that the psychological ramifications that emerge from erratic coercion increase the likelihood of chronic involvement in predatory street crime, the intimidation and coercion of others, and hostility and defiant behaviour directed toward those in authority. Colvin argues that offenders drawn from the erratic/coercive control structure begin their offending at an early age and are more likely to become involved in violent offending due to their exposure to coercive modelling and to their coercive ideation. Colvin notes that individuals who have experienced erratic and extreme coercion are often drawn to the street and the culture it offers, which tends to match the social-psychological deficits that are produced by inconsistent coercion.

Current Empirical Research into Differential Coercion Theory

As a new perspective, differential coercion theory has been subjected to limited empirical research to date—all of which has focused on the crime-causing impact of erratic coercive control. This research is extremely supportive of the perspective. It shows that different forms of coercion, including parental coercion, a coercive school environment, coercive neighbourhoods, incarceration, state support, and street victimization, are related to crime generally and to violent offending specifically (Baron 2009; Unnever, Colvin, and Cullen 2004). However, this research also shows that coercion that is delivered more to the consistent end of the erratic continuum is related to these behaviours, suggesting that further theoretical refinement is required. The social-psychological deficits of social control, low self-control, trait anger, control imbalances, coercive social models, and coercive ideation have also been shown to be related to crime (Baron 2009; Unnever, Colvin, and Cullen 2004). Limited work also reveals that erratic coercion toward the more consistent end of the continuum is related to the development of low self-control, anger, coercive modelling, and coercive ideation. In contrast, erratic coercion does not appear to be related to the development of control imbalances (Baron 2009).

While generally supportive, there is still room for work exploring the other types of control structures and their relationships with social-psychological deficits and together how these are related to other forms of behaviour. Theoretical work is already being extended to include the idea of social supports and the degree to which they are offered in a consistent or erratic fashion. Thus, future empirical work will need to explore the role of social support in tandem with the degree and erratic or consistent nature of coercion. Such research will also have to investigate the relationships of these various combinations with different forms of behaviour, including crime (Colvin, Cullen, and Vander Ven 2002).

Summary

Our review of emerging theoretical perspectives to understand youth crime has provided us with a breadth of possible explanations. The general theory of crime outlines how low self-control leaves individuals unable to refrain from temptation, increasing their risk for crime when opportunities present themselves. The general strain perspective focuses on how not being treated the way a person would like to be treated leads to negative emotions, which encourage people to engage in crime to address these emotions. Such experiences are more likely to lead to crime when they are accompanied by various characteristics, including deviant values, deviant peers, negative emotionality/low constraint, low self-esteem, and low self-efficacy. The age-graded theory of social control focuses on the manner in which informal social controls at different stages of a person's life influence continuity and change in offending behaviour. This theory outlines how structural conditions and early anti-social propensities impact upon social control factors in the family and school, leading to crime. This theory also explains how criminal participation in youth undermines social control mechanisms in adulthood, leading to continuity in crime. The age-graded theory of social control also delineates how, through concerted efforts and employment and marriage, individuals can re-establish social control and alter criminogenic routine activities, leading to a desistance from illegal activities. The control balance perspective cues us to the importance of having a sense of control over various domains in our lives. When we have too much or too little control, we are more likely to engage in crime when we are reminded of our situation, and when we encounter the proper opportunity. The type of crime we pick and its impact on our sense of control will be influenced by the way deviant values, deviant peers, low self-control, self-efficacy, and perceptions of risk of apprehension shape our perceptions of control. Finally, the differential coercion perspective outlines how personal and impersonal forces of coercion that are delivered in different ways can lead to a variety of social-psychological mechanisms that lead to crime. More erratic coercion will lead to the development of low self-control, low social control, anger, values supporting coercion, an external locus of control, and low self-efficacy, which in turn increase the likelihood of offending.

Our review of some of the more recent theoretical developments in youth crime shows the variety of ways that scholars have approached the topic. Some, such as the general theory of crime, have focused on a monocausal approach. Others have outlined perspectives that incorporate a broader range of factors that attempt to more clearly specify how the central factor will lead to crime and under what conditions. Further, some of these approaches have adopted a strategy for theoretical development whereby they attempt to bring in useful pieces of other theoretical perspectives. Rather than viewing different theoretical perspectives as competitors, there is a recognition that to successfully understand youth crime, we must recognize and include ideas not normally viewed as complementary. These ideas need to be brought in and incorporated in the causal process, allowing for a more complex and nuanced understanding of how youth crime emerges and evolves. This strategy enables researchers to establish various possible entry points for youths to explore crime and also establishes that there may be more than one possible causal path to crime. As we think about youth crime, we must provide a number of possible answers to the many questions we might pose. Then, theories provide a number of insights into how we might answer such questions.

Key Terms

coercion

control balance

cumulative continuity

disrupted social control

informal social control

life-course turning points

low self-control

situated choice

social bonds

strain

trajectories

Review Questions

1. Gottfredson and Hirschi's argument suggests that low self-control leads not only to crime but also to analogous acts. Why would this be the case?

2. Using general strain theory, outline the type of young person who would most likely turn to criminal activities in an attempt to cope with his or her strain.

3. Tittle argues that a number of conditions must converge for an imbalanced control ratio to lead to crime. Review these conditions and outline why the individual's control ratio will be central to these conditions.

4. Outline the main causal process that could lead a youth to desist from crime, according to the age-graded theory of social control.

5. Summarize Colvin's four types of control and discuss which of the four types is most likely to lead to serious offending and for what reasons.

Critical Thinking Questions

1. In Colvin's theory of crime and coercion, a number of social-psychological deficits are identified. How do these deficits relate to some of the other perspectives that we have read about or discussed in class? Do we benefit from including various perspectives together?

2. Gottfredson and Hirschi's general theory of crime sees self-control as a trait that is relatively stable and unchangeable, leading to a life of participation in crime and other negative activities. Compare this with how Sampson and Laub might view this issue.

3. Explore the possibilities that different types of contingency variables (e.g., peers, values, self-efficacy) may be more important in moderating the impacts of certain forms of strain on crime than others.

4. Tittle argues that different criminal acts will have different levels of control balance desirability. Explore which types of acts you think will fall along the continuum of control balance desirability and which types of individuals will be more likely to commit these types of acts.

Suggested Readings

Agnew, R. (2006). *Pressured into crime: An overview of general strain theory.* Los Angeles: Roxbury.

Colvin, M. (2000). *Crime and coercion: An integrated theory of chronic criminality.* New York: St. Martin's Press.

Gottfredson, M.R. and Hirschi, T. (2000). *A general theory of crime.* Stanford: Stanford University Press.

Laub, J.H. and Sampson, R.J. (2003). *Shared beginnings, divergent lives: Delinquent boys to age 70.* Cambridge: Harvard University Press.

Tittle, C.R. (1995). *Control balance: Toward a general theory of deviance.* Boulder: Westview.

Suggested Weblinks

Everyday Sociology Blog

http://nortonbooks.typepad.com/everydaysociology/2008/11/gottfredson-and.html

- 'Gottfredson and Hirschi's Low Self-Control Theory; or why kids feed lizards to crocodiles.'

Everyday Sociology Blog

http://nortonbooks.typepad.com/everydaysociology/2008/12/sampson-laubs-a.html

- 'Sampson and Laub's Age-Graded Life-Course Theory of Crime.'

College of Criminology and Criminal Justice, Florida State University

http://criminology.fsu.edu/crimtheory/agnew.htm

- 'Robert Agnew's General Strain Theory.'

Division on Critical Criminology: American Society of Criminology

http://critcrim.org/critpapers/barak_integrative.htm

- 'Integrative Theories, Integrating Criminologies': A discussion of recent efforts made to develop integrative theories of crime.

References

Agnew, R. (1992). Foundation for a general strain theory of crime and delinquency, *Criminology, 30*(1): 47–87.

Agnew, R. (2001). Building on the foundation of general strain theory: Specifying the types of strain that most likely lead to crime and delinquency. *Journal of Research in Crime and Delinquency, 38*(4): 319–61.

Agnew, R. (2006). *Pressured into crime: An overview of general strain theory.* Los Angeles: Roxbury.

Baron, S.W. (2003). Self control, social consequences, and criminal behavior: Street youth and the general theory of crime. *Journal of Research in Crime and Delinquency, 40*(4): 403–25.

Baron, S.W. (2004). General strain, street youth and crime: A test of Agnew's revised theory. *Criminology, 42*(2): 457–83.

Baron, S.W. (2009). Differential coercion, street youth, and violent crime. *Criminology, 47*(1): 239–68.

Baron, S.W. (2010). Street youths' control imbalance and soft and hard coming drug use. *Journal of Criminal Justice, 38*: 903–12.

Baron, S.W. and Forde., D.R. (2007). Street youth crime: A test of control balance theory. *Justice Quarterly, 24*(2): 335–55.

Baron, S.W., Forde, D.R., and Kay, F.M. (2007). Self control, risky lifestyles, and situation. The role of opportunity and context in the general theory. *Journal of Criminal Justice 35*(2): 119–36.

Colvin, M. (2000). *Crime and coercion: An integrated theory of chronic criminality.* New York: St. Martin's Press.

Colvin, M., Cullen, F.T., and Ven, T.V. (2002). Coercion, social support, and crime: An emerging theoretical consensus. *Criminology, 40*(1): 9–42.

Gottfredson, M.R. and Hirschi, T. (2000). *A general theory of crime.* Stanford: Stanford University Press.

Laub, J.H. and Sampson, R.J. (2003). *Shared beginnings, divergent lives: Delinquent boys to age 70.* Cambridge: Harvard University Press.

Laub, J.H., Sampson, R.J., and Sweeten, G.A. (2006). Assessing Sampson and Laub's life-course theory. In F.T. Cullen, J.P. Wright & K.R. Blevins (Eds.), *Taking stock: The status of criminological theory. Advances in criminological theory* (Vol. 15, pp. 313–33). New Brunswick, NJ: Transaction Publishers.

Miller, J.M., Schrek, C.J., and Tewksbury, R. (2006). *Criminological theory.* Toronto: Pearson.

Pratt, T.C. and Cullen, F.T. (2000). The empirical status of Gottfredson and Hirschi's general theory of crime: A meta-analysis. *Criminology, 38*(3): 931–64.

Sampson, R.J. and Laub, J.H. (1993). *Crime in the making: Pathways and turning points through life.* Cambridge: Harvard University Press.

Tittle, C.R. (1995). *Control balance: Toward a general theory of deviance.* Boulder: Westview.

Tittle, C.R. (2004). Refining control balance theory. *Theoretical Criminology, 8*(4): 395–428.

Turner, A.R. and Piquero, A.R. (2002). The stability of low self-control. *Journal of Criminal Justice, 30*(6): 457–71.

Unnever, J.D., Colvin, M., and Cullen, F.T. (2004). Crime and coercion: A test of core theoretical propositions. *Journal of Research in Crime and Delinquency, 41*(3): 244–68.

8 Critical Criminology and Youth Justice in the Risk Society: Issues of Power and Justice

Bryan Hogeveen and Joanne C. Minaker

Overview

This chapter highlights the importance of critical criminology for the study of youth justice and attends to important questions concerning social (in)justice, choice, and power. We encourage readers to think critically about youth justice issues and engage in what Minaker and Hogeveen (2009, p. 5) call 'social justice praxis'. Critical scholarship attends to the systemic inequality, marginalization, and social exclusion that underpins and is often at the centre of young people's encounters with the law. Toward attending to what might constitute justice for young people and meaningful societal changes, the chapter draws heavily on the theoretical work of scholars like Jacques Derrida and Michel Foucault. At the same time, it encourages students to ask themselves some questions: *What is to be done? What is my responsibility to this end?* Critical criminology offers a unique location from which to consider what a humane, hospitable, and just Canadian society might entail.

Key Objectives

After reading this chapter, you should be able to:

- Explain what it means to be critical.
- Explore how young people, especially indigenous peoples, are marginalized in Canada.
- Highlight the political dimensions of space.
- Describe Jacques Derrida's understanding of deconstruction and hospitality as it relates to critical criminology.
- Highlight Foucault's unique understanding of power.
- Describe the 'risk society' and the place of young people therein.
- Illustrate cultural criminology and its contribution to critical scholarship.

Introduction

> We are not content to teach our students about the social world—to pass on knowledge claims about what is—without also encouraging a process of critical reflection and social engagement about what *could* be.
>
> — Minaker and Hogeveen 2009, p. 5

Youth, crime, and justice are contentious; we seem to lack definitive answers to these pressing concerns. Nevertheless, newspaper headlines and nightly news stories caution about 'troubling kids' and advocate punishment as the solution. Obscured from this picture are the inequalities, discrimination, abuse, and neglect that characterize the life histories of a vast majority of the young people who make their way into the youth justice system.

While mainstream criminology does its part to examine the causes, consequences, and control of youth crime, **critical criminology** begins from a very different perspective. One strand of critical scholarship takes contemporary criminal justice processes to task for their part in contributing to structural inequalities that marginalize young people. Others presume that Canadian society is organized in hierarchies of age, gender, race, ethnicity, class, sexuality, and ability. Recognizing the impact of difference and disadvantage under law has been the passion of feminist writers like Carol Smart (1989). Since the 1960s, feminist scholars have clearly articulated the disadvantaged social position of women and girls in the justice system and in society. In more recent decades their analyses have extended beyond the singular emphasis on gender. They have examined how criminology as a 'decidedly male-centred enterprise' considers girls and women involved in crime as 'monsters, misfits and manipulators' (Balfour and Comack 2006, p. 22).

Like feminist scholarship, critical criminology begins from the perspective that the lives of the most marginalized in contemporary society are lived out in circumstances not of their own choosing. They are thrown into a world that is discriminatory, racist, and sexist. These conditions structure the life chances of the marginalized other—Aboriginal youth, the poor, and racial minorities—and translate into overrepresentation in the contemporary youth justice system. This chapter will explore the unique insights of such scholars as Lefebvre, Derrida, and Foucault, and of cultural criminologists. We encourage you to think critically about the issues presented. Minaker and Hogeveen (2009, p. 5) suggest this kind of inquiry is a first step toward 'social justice praxis', which is aimed at 'addressing the systemic conditions of **marginalization**, exclusion and social inequality that lead to the involvement of youth in crime in the first place'. Critical criminology is

critical criminology
Scholarship on crime and justice that seeks to examine and alter inequalities, marginalization, and social exclusion.

marginalization
The exclusion of certain groups from mainstream society who routinely suffer as the result of gross inequalities.

dedicated to making meaningful changes to improve the life chances of young people. It asks, *What is to be done?* and *What is my responsibility to this end?* As you will see, critical criminology offers unique opportunities to envision a more just, humane, hospitable and inclusive society.

What Does It Mean to Be Critical? Why Is It Important?

> To say all this is deconstructable does not amount to disqualifying, negating, disavowing, or surpassing it, of doing the critique of critique (the way people wrote critiques of the Kantian critique as soon as it appeared), but of thinking its possibility from another border, from the genealogy of judgment, will, consciousness or activity, the binary structure, and so forth.
>
> — Derrida 1995, p. 357

What does it mean to be critical? Criticism routinely appears as negative judgment. From this broad perspective, in one way or another, all of us are critical. Recently, the federal gun registry has been the subject of scorn among some Canadians. Others have condemned the massive destruction of land and water by excavation in the Alberta oil sands. We need look no further than our own daily lives for 'critiques': 'This traffic light takes far too long to change colour'; 'The dress she is wearing is far too short'; Britney Spears should invest in some singing lessons'; 'This professor gives far too much homework'. Critique and criticism, it seems, is all around us. And one group never far from criticism is young people, particularly criminalized youth.

If critique is something we all do, what sets critical scholars apart? Put another way, how are critical criminologists distinct in their critiques? Some strands of criminology and criminal justice studies are concerned with criticizing government policy and suggesting alternative approaches that might better respond to youth crime, to offenders, and to victims. In recent years, for example, restorative justice advocates have successfully argued that traditional youth justice processing fails victims of crime and alienates communities from the process (Minaker and Hogeveen 2009). Restorative justice scholarship calls traditional and existing governmental process into question and proposes (perhaps) a more effective alternative (e.g., circle sentencing). At a more practical level is the Edmonton- and Ottawa-based Youth Restorative Justice Project, or YRAP. A diverse group of young people (ages 14 to 24) grew concerned that young people were silent in youth justice matters and were otherwise alienated from the process. In response, YRAP administers the world's first restorative justice committee for and by youth and challenges the Western status quo whereby adults alone are responsible for delivering and administering justice (Hogeveen 2006).

YRAP and other restorative justice groups who oppose traditional criminal justice orthodoxy are certainly critical in the conventional sense of casting judgment upon existing programs and suggesting the object of criticism falls somewhat short of an established ideal. Nevertheless, youth justice officials can comfortably incorporate this flavour of critique (critique as modification) within existing processes without much concern that its established infrastructure will crumble to the ground. Indeed, without fear of significantly altering their contemporary mandate and with the goal of streamlining existing practices, many youth justice systems encourage this form of intervention.

In our contemporary ethos, judgment is most closely associated with critique. Such judgmental criticism derives its meaning and its efficacy from an established mean or aesthetic. Consider, for example, current television programming, such as *American Idol*, *Dancing with the Stars*, *America's Got Talent*, and, but not limited to, *So You Think You Can Dance*. All are premised upon a (supposed) expert's offering of sage banter in the wake of a competitor's performance. Much to the delight of the viewing audience, the expert stands before this group conferring witty and (often) acrimonious critique upon the performer. The program would be rather dull without the expert's judgments, which make the show a success. How many regular viewers of *American Idol* can remember the winner of each season? By contrast, how many people, whether viewers or not, would recognize the name *Simon Cowell* as one of the show's judges? We speculate that many more would answer the latter correctly. What does it say about our society when the judges who often heap lamentable criticism on unwitting contestants are the 'real' stars?

Criterion provides the impetus for judgment and suggests that we make an assessment of something (i.e., a performance, beauty, or youth justice programming) against a normative standard that has been put forth as the ultimate by which those things should be measured. For example, the *Mona Lisa*, Wayne Gretzky, Luciano Pavarotti, and Michael Jordan are routinely considered the criterion upon which all else in their particular field is measured. Youth justice officials, too, employ normative standards to judge programming and the behaviour of criminalized youth. Recidivism rates are seemingly objective measures of a program's success. Whether a subject who has been adjudicated by YRAP, for example, has re-offended is an ostensibly even-handed means through which to determine this Youth Justice Committee's (YJC) effectiveness. Two problems become immediately evident, however. On the one hand, other favourable outcomes may not be readily observable in re-arrest rates. Indeed, a young person may acquire a skill set in the adjudication process that will keep them off the streets. On the other hand, police administrative policies and severity of the offence of record for entry into the program tend to affect recidivism rates. For example, compared to other youth justice committees, YRAP tends to deal with more serious offenders (Hogeveen 2006). As a result, the recidivism rates for this program are artificially higher than for more traditional YJCs. Employing standardized criterion often leads to overlooking programmatic nuances that may qualitatively and positively impact the young person. Consider, for instance, a street-entrenched youth who finds secure housing and a stable job through the assistance of YRAP but misses a court appearance because her employer insists she work a shift. The young person may be charged with 'failure to appear'. In this instance the case would be logged as a failure because it resulted in a new charge. Such an approach to determining the success of a program misses how the young person was unquestionably impacted by her/his involvement with YRAP.

Critical criminology stands in stark contrast to those forms of critique that seek to improve the functioning and efficacy of the existing youth justice system. Instead of chasing down programming that will work effectively within contemporary justice processes, critical criminology seeks 'to take the system to task rather than tinker with its parts' (Ratner 1971). Since Ratner's keen insight, which differentiated a critical brand of Canadian criminology some 40 odd years ago, much debate has emerged concerning what counts as pushing the system hard enough or long enough or what kind of critique qualifies as doing more than merely criticizing the system for reinforcing race, class, gender, age, and other hierarchies. A critical approach examines systemic issues of power and justice vis-à-vis youth crime and society. Critical scholars reject traditional assumptions of mainstream criminological theory (i.e., emphasis on crime control, law and order, and state-centredness) and direct their gaze at structural inequalities within and outside of the criminal justice system. As we hope you will come to see, critical scholars are concerned with more than exposing systemic conditions of marginalization. They are dedicated to opening up more ethical ways of being with others and are not content with the social world as it is. Instead, they encourage critical and serious reflection about how things could be otherwise. Critical criminology engages 'with the challenges and contradictions involved in making ameliorative changes in our social world that offer hope instead of despair, compassion instead of intolerance, and justice instead of marginalization, exclusion, and suffering' (Minaker and Hogeveen 2009, p. xiii).

Critical criminology attempts to avoid the trap of collusion with criminal justice processes that serve only to further marginalize the least powerful in society. Bryan Hogeveen and Andrew Woolford (2006) encourage scholars to become intensely creative in their approaches and to conjure up alternatives that will push beyond established limits of youth justice orthodoxy. It is this reticence to avoid the trap of complicity with contemporary systems of governance, no matter how auspicious, that sets critical criminology apart. Drawing on the scholarship of Jacques Derrida, Michel Foucault, Giorgio Agamben, and cultural criminology, critical criminology clamours for interventions that push beyond established hegemony. Instead of well-worn strategies, these scholars and their interlocutors promise an art of critique that unsettles, disrupts, or otherwise challenges contemporary relations (both inside and outside the CJS) in the name of justice and amelioration to come. They suggest more just ways of being with others in a world bent on racism and exclusion toward the marginalized other.

Marginalization and Aboriginal Youth Crime

Lost among sensational headlines concerning the recalcitrance of young people today and efforts by the federal government to get tough on youth crime by overhauling contemporary legislation is the number of young people who suffer crime's ill-effects. Media images colour our understanding of crime and criminals. Television shows, such as *Law and Order* and the evening news, would have us believe that the average young offender is a gun-toting gangbanger who preys on the unwitting. Many in Western society would be surprised to hear that the majority of reported crime is property related and nonviolent in nature. But this misperception is not surprising given that for the vast majority of Canadians the media are their primary sources of crime information (Sprott 1996). When the conception of youth crime and young offenders is stockpiled with violent images, intrusive and carceral solutions are most often proposed as the only viable alternatives to the violent young offender (see, e.g., Harper 2008; see also Box 8.1).

According to a recent Statistics Canada report, young people were the most likely group to divulge violent victimization during the previous 12 months. Indeed, individuals between the ages of 15 and 24 were almost '15 times more likely than those aged 65 and older to report being a victim of violent' crime (Perreault and Brennan 2010). More disconcerting is how Aboriginal peoples, especially Aboriginal women, are disproportionately represented as victims of crime. Consider, for example, that indigenous peoples were three times more likely to be victims than non-Aboriginals and five times more likely than other Canadians to have been the victim of sexual offending (Mihorean et al. 2001; Hylton 2002; Chartrand and McKay 2006). Indeed, Chartrand and McKay (2006) report 'while victimization of Aboriginal people is much higher than non-Aboriginal people, statistics demonstrate that it is Aboriginal women and children who are largely bearing the burden of victimization'. In *Black Eyes All of the Time: Intimate Violence, Aboriginal Women, and the Justice System*, McGillivray and Comaskey (1996) maintain that the violence experienced by Aboriginal women is appalling. Further, the past two decades have witnessed over 500 Aboriginal women go missing, and most are presumed dead (Amnesty International 2009).

Why is it that violence disproportionately affects Aboriginal peoples? While a full accounting of the conditions that have given rise to this lamentable situation is beyond the scope of this chapter, we can consider the impact of colonialism on contemporary indigenous life. Systemic racism is conspicuous in the gross overrepresentation of indigenous young people in Canadian carceral institutions. Donna Calverley (2007) reports that in 2004 and 2005 Aboriginal young people made up approximately 5 per cent of the entire Canadian population yet constituted 25 per cent of young people admitted to custody. This is an egregious situation with no sign of abating.

The Canadian state has a long history of confining Aboriginal peoples. They have been held captive on reserves through a shameful pass system and in residential schools where the tutelage they

Box 8.1 Youth Justice in Action

Winnipeg Free Press, Tuesday, 1 March, 2011

Young Mother Spent Life Battling Vices
Struggled after conviction in homicide

By Mike McIntyre

Kami Pozniak spent less than two years in prison for her role in the headline-grabbing homicide of Joseph 'Beeper' Spence. But the troubled young woman spent a lifetime battling the demons believed to have contributed to her own demise.

Pozniak, 32, died suddenly on Feb. 20, survived by two young children. Family members are asking for privacy and for donations in her name to be made to any provincial addictions foundation. Sources told the *Free Press* Pozniak had continued to struggle with the vices that had plagued her since childhood.

Pozniak is no stranger to the criminal justice system and made headlines in 1995 when she was involved in the drive-by shooting that left the 13-year-old dead on a North End Street. Pozniak—just 16 at the time—was driving the vehicle that pulled up beside the teen, believing he was a member of a rival street gang. Conrad Johnson, 17, fired the shotgun blast that killed Beeper.

The slaying made headlines across Canada and sparked calls for tougher penalties for young offenders and tougher laws for gangs. The murder was also one of the first signs that Winnipeg had a major street gang problem.

Pozniak eventually pleaded guilty to manslaughter and was sentenced to two years behind bars after agreeing to be raised to adult court. Johnson admitted to second-degree murder and was released on day parole in 2008. A third teen accused, Fabian Torres, also admitted to manslaughter for encouraging the deadly attack inside the vehicle. He was given 14 years in prison and was released on parole in 2007.

'My client is not a monster,' defence lawyer Evan Roitenberg told court at Pozniak's sentencing hearing. He suggested Pozniak had just been in the wrong place at the wrong time and made poor choices about her peers and lifestyle. Hope was expressed that some time behind bars would give her the chance to escape the past and move forward on a brighter future.

Unfortunately, Pozniak continued to go through the revolving door of justice upon her release. Court records obtained by the *Free Press* show she had been convicted of more than a dozen separate offences—including drugs, prostitution and failing to comply with court orders—since 2003 alone. Pozniak was also getting into violent disputes with other inmates and guards that had landed her in segregation.

In 2000, Pozniak appeared before a parliamentary standing committee in Ottawa that was exploring possible changes to the Youth Criminal Justice Act. One of the big issues then was whether youth criminals who are raised to adult court should be named in public, as Pozniak was.

'Every day when I go out, lots of people recognize my name when I get introduced to people. I have a hard time getting a job. When I attended school, the teachers knew who I was, and my law teacher knew who I was,' Pozniak told federal lawmakers, including Peter MacKay, who is now the defence minister. 'I find it very difficult to be known just as that instead of being known as me, being known as something I was labelled for in the past. It still reflects in my face every day I live out in the community.'

Kim Pate, executive director of the Elizabeth Fry Society, described Pozniak at the time as a 'young aboriginal woman who is struggling to complete school . . . is basically struggling to get back on her feet after that.'

Pate told the committee Pozniak had attempted suicide on multiple occasions and frequently found herself in segregation.

'She unfortunately has had some of the worst experiences of our system and some of the worst experiences of the current system,' said Pate. Pozniak also told MacKay she hoped to one day meet with Beeper's family.

'I've always wanted to meet with them. At my sentencing I apologized to the family for my responsibility in taking part in it. But the family isn't ready for me, I guess, so I'm just waiting until that perspective comes,' she said.

It's a meeting that never occurred. Pozniak's funeral service will be held on Thursday.

Kami Pozniak's case dramatically and sadly demonstrates the blurred boundaries between youthful offending and victimization. Her struggles with violence, addictions and poverty characterize the lives of many young, Aboriginal females and their counterparts serving time in women's correctional facilities. Notice the intersection of marginalization (economic, racial and gender) that contoured Kami's life.

received inculcated Euro-Canadian norms and mores. Residential school officials, most often with religious ties, forcibly removed Aboriginal children from their parents and cultural milieu for years at a time while they attempted to indoctrinate Euro-Canadian ideals (Miller 1996). The effects were devastating and predictable. Removed from their communities and obliged to renounce their former selves in favour of alien values and symbols, residential school survivors never fully recovered. Torn from their parents and elders and forced to live at some distance from their traditional lands, their manner of being in the world was almost completely shaped by residential school officials, who were notoriously physically violent and sexually abusive. Aboriginal authors, such as Fournier and Crey (1997), maintain that the intergenerational impact of residential schools, particularly as it relates to sexual and physical abuse, has collectively contributed to high rates of alcohol and drug abuse among Aboriginal peoples, and is manifested in countless social, health, and psychological problems (Royal Commission on Aboriginal Peoples 1996; Aboriginal Healing Foundation 2003).

The Aboriginal Healing Foundation argues in its report on domestic violence that

> The legacy of the residential school experience has been well documented and is clearly linked to symptoms of post traumatic-stress disorder, as well as to a wide range of social problems, including addiction and physical and sexual abuse . . . In general, this body of research, theories and models all point to the same general conclusion—family violence and abuse in Aboriginal communities has its roots, at least in part, in historical trauma and in the social realities created by those historical processes. (2003, p. 22)

It is into this ethos of violence conditioned by a dismal colonial heritage that many Aboriginal people are born. A recent review by the Aboriginal Healing Foundation (2003) found that colonialism, specifically the residential school system, bears much of the burden for the economic, cultural, and political inequalities faced by Aboriginal people today.

Buttressing this tragic condition are the dire levels of poverty experienced by this group. Despite increasing and growing demand, social welfare rates and services have not kept pace. Aboriginal groups are increasingly in need of social service support (i.e., housing, health care, social services, etc.) only to find what they need harder to access. While poverty and homeless rates among indigenous peoples are snowballing, the social welfare net that has traditionally been in place to cushion the blow of unemployment and homelessness has been repeatedly stripped away (Scott 2003). Cuts to social welfare are a recurrent theme in the contemporary ethos. Indeed, a burgeoning group of homeless Aboriginal peoples are being forcibly moved to the back of social assistance lines while industries that the government deems as having more pressing needs (i.e., horse racing) get their cut (Hogeveen 2007).

The Aboriginal population is today much younger than the Canadian average. The Canadian Council on Social Development claimed in its 2003 report that the median age for Aboriginal groups was 24.7 years, which is much younger than the 37.7 years for non-Aboriginals. Moreover, children 14 and under made up 33 per cent of the Aboriginal population compared to just 19 per cent for non-indigenous peoples (Anderson 2003). Appallingly, this group is most likely to live in poverty. Campaign 2000 recently released its report card on child poverty in Canada for the 20-year period between 1989 and 2009 with egregious conclusions: especially as it reflects the conditions of Aboriginal life. While it is horrendous that 1 in 10 Canadian children live below the poverty line in this land of plenty, more intolerable still is that 1 in 4 Aboriginal children experience poverty's ill effects. Further, 49 per cent of Aboriginal children who are under age 6 and living off-reserve live in poverty, compared to just 18 per cent of non-Aboriginal children (Campaign 2000, 2009).

Not only is the Aboriginal population becoming younger, it is increasingly urban. According to a recent study by Chris Andersen (2009), between 2001 and 2006 population growth among

Aboriginal people in Edmonton far outpaced all other groups (25 per cent compared to 9 per cent). Most (60 per cent) live in the inner city where the space is run down and the community is overwhelmed by crime and disorder (Andersen 2009). Urban landscapes are not only marked geographically, but racially.

Outcast Spaces

In Canada, an Aboriginal is more likely to be detained in state institutions of control and, at the same time, to be impoverished, homeless, and anchored in undesirable and outcast space (Minaker and Hogeveen 2009; Mallea 2010). Although Karl Marx was relatively silent on the question of space, Marx-inspired authors like Edward Soja, Henri Lefebvre, and David Harvey have drawn critical attention to its importance in class relations. Marx's relative silence on this issue may have been because cities were just beginning to take on their current configuration during his lifetime (Elden 2007). Lefebvre (1996) famously took up this gap in Marx's work and argued that space is political. He maintains that city spaces become divided up in very definite ways that betray their ethos. That is, space is socially constructed rather than being naturally constituted. This condition dramatically impacts the actors living out their lives in particular areas. Social space, Lefebvre suggests, is allocated along class lines such that city planning reproduces and buoys the existing class structure. It follows that the quality of space allotted provides obvious clues as to its owners (Elden 2007). The inner-city spaces and core areas of town, such as Winnipeg's North End, are older, crowded, and often abandoned, yet are also over-policed. By contrast, sprawling suburbs complete with white picket fences and open 'green' spaces are reserved for the more affluent. Whereas children growing up in suburbia enjoy new schools and growing recreational centres, the 'playground' for poor children and their families looks more like a grey concrete mass and is shared with the mentally ill, the criminal, and the drug user. David Harvey (1989, p. 237) maintains that the history of capitalism is the history of a struggle for the command of space: '[T]he whole history of territorial organization, colonialism and imperialism, of uneven development, of urban and rural contradictions, as well as of geopolitical conflict testifies to the importance of such struggles within the history of capitalism.'

All are contained in their space so as to better facilitate rule and control of the recalcitrant and marginalized other. Consider how space is allocated and lived in Edmonton, Alberta. Rather than containing open spaces where strangers may intersect and interact, Edmonton's city planners have seemed to sweep away and confine the poor into spaces of disorder. As 'blots' on the otherwise serene and tranquil city, the impoverished roam the streets and are routinely shooed and shunted into the least coveted and most dangerous places. Most people never see where the truly marginal live as they are tucked away in spaces long forgotten and out of the way of the business classes who scurry back to the suburbs hopeful the disorder will not touch their lives.

Even when the capitalist state seeks to ameliorate the marginalized other's suffering, any programs are carried out not in the centres of affluence but in the most downtrodden and overburdened areas of the city. Following the lead of Calgary and Seattle, Edmonton is in the midst of a 'Housing First' initiative. Under this plan the chronically homeless are allotted housing for a one-year period, during which they are provided with a residence and a limited amount of support to help manage and deal with their addictions and other social problems (see Edmonton Committee to End Homelessness 2009). What will happen to these residents after the time limit runs out has yet to be determined. However, units to house the marginalized—including but not limited to street-involved youth who have left home to escape abuse, former inmates who have left prison and who have no family or work to go to, and drug-addicted clients no longer welcome in detoxification centres—are not evenly spread throughout the city. Indeed, there are no group homes for the homeless and drug-addicted in affluent neighbourhoods. Instead, the city has dumped these units in the city's most economically depressed spaces. What's more, even before the Housing First initiatives, these outcast spaces were already saturated with social services, as well as crime, disorder, drug addictions, and homelessness (Kleiss 2010). It seems the city is willing to help provided doing so does not upset the tranquility of suburban space.

Jacques Derrida and Justice

So far we have spent much time discussing and contemplating (in)justices facing young people today, especially as they pertain to Aboriginal peoples. Clearly, marginalized populations are excluded from full and meaningful participation in contemporary Canadian society. Quite simply, racial divisions are reflected spatially and assist in underwriting patterns of exclusion (Herbert and Brown 2006). What is to be done about this egregious condition? Instead of shunting the marginalized other into cities' least desirable spaces, we should welcome them instead. Toward this end, we suggest the deconstructive work of Jacques Derrida (2005, 2002, 1999; Derrida and Dufourmantelle 2000) and maintain that his understanding of **justice** and **hospitality** has considerable relevance.

Our insistence on Derrida's work will come as some surprise to those who have relegated his work to the postmodern trash heap. It would be fair to say that Derrida is one of the twentieth century's most influential philosophers. His name is spoken alongside such monumental figures as Heidegger, Husserl, Levinas, and Foucault (whom we will discuss later). It would be fair to suggest that Derrida is one of the most controversial, as the 'Cambridge Affair' clearly demonstrates. In 1992 Cambridge University was about to award Derrida an honorary doctorate when leading philosophers from around the United States and Europe who were adherents of a competing philosophical tradition set about to intervene by writing a letter (Smith 2005). In the letter, the group—which included such notable scholars as René Thom and Willard Van Orman Quine—claimed that Derrida's work not only lacked sufficient rigour worthy of such a designation but contained nothing but tricks and gimmicks. The letter also suggested that French academics only saw in Derrida a cause for 'silent embarrassment' (Smith et al. 1992). Despite the protests, Derrida was awarded the degree.

Although Derrida has become widely known as the philosopher of **deconstruction**, he was rather reticent when it came to spelling out its nuances. In fact, the word *deconstruction* rarely appears in his many works. Deconstruction is not synonymous with destruction; despite claims and criticism to the contrary, Derrida was not interested in demolition. Rather, he was concerned with opening words and works that were previously taken for granted to intense scrutiny. He argued that 'deconstruction, if such a thing exists, should open up' (Derrida 1987, p. 261). Thus, if there is such a thing as deconstruction it is intended to 're-construct, re-constitute or re-affirm' a given word structure (Bradley 2008). Deconstruction works to unbolt language and reveal its silent, hidden, or repressed elements that lend meaning to the thing itself. On the rare occasion where Derrida did articulate a meaning for deconstruction he maintained that it represented the 'undoing, demolition and de-sedimenting of structures [so as to] understand how an "ensemble" was constituted' (Derrida 1985).

To understand what is going on at the heart of language, Derrida maintains that we must comprehend the **trace**, which refers to the silent components of our language that assign meaning. However, this quiet element is tremendously slippery and difficult to grab a hold of. Trace is present in all flows of conversation and in all language, but is constantly deferred and silent. Each sign (word) must always already contain traces of other signs through which the original sign derives meaning. For Derrida, everything that is present before us contains traces of other elements that are ostensibly absent (Bradley 2008). Derrida claims that all things oscillate between being present and absent without ever being wholly at hand or wholly silent.

justice (Derrida)
For Derrida, justice is a messianic promise of a more just future 'to come'.

hospitality
An unrestrained welcome to a stranger. It calls for open spaces that welcome the other as they arrive.

deconstruction
Involves opening up words to their hidden or closed-off possibilities in an attempt to reveal what is going on behind language.

trace
The silent elements that provide words with their essential meaning (Spivak 1976) and that underlie all language.

Let us consider deconstruction at work or what happens when we open up language. Consider, for example, the term *hospitality*. It might conjure images of welcome mats, dinner parties, or a weekend guest who is visiting from out of town. In the West, we often invite people into our places of residence with the greeting 'make yourself at home'. We do not, for the most part, mean this in the literal sense. Not immediately evident in this seemingly gracious term is an inalienable tension—between a welcome to a stranger and an uncertain hostility concealed within that welcome. Quite simply, the welcome itself already assumes a stranger in its very utterance. Fashioning the other as 'other' in the instance of the welcome sets in motion and entrenches relations of dominion over space. Anyone who has hosted particularly odious houseguests can begin to understand the duality endemic to hospitality. A guest who has overstayed his or her welcome becomes a stressor for the host. Welcoming a guest into one's home is conditional upon the guest's accepting and attending to established rules of decorum. When I say, 'Welcome, please make yourself at home', I am actually commanding my guest to be comfortable in a space that belongs to me and over which I am sovereign. Hospitality, as we know and practise it in the West, contains a trace of restraint and hostility that 'preserves the distance between one's own and the stranger, between owning one's own property and inviting the other into one's home. So, there is always a little hostility in all hosting and hospitality' (Derrida and Caputo 1997, p. 110).

Opening language to its silent but essential elements is at deconstruction's core. Deconstruction may lead us to think more clearly and critically about justice. In the contemporary ethos where marginalized young people are shunted into the most deleterious and pejorative spaces of the city, justice and hospitality for and to the other is necessary. That is, we must welcome 'the other' free of the hostility that is a fundamental part of encounters with strangers.

surveillance

The direct or indirect observation of conduct, which is intended to produce a desired outcome (i.e., conformity).

Over the summer months of 2010 the Edmonton Police Service (EPS) increased its **surveillance** and presence in Churchill Square, which is situated firmly within the city's downtown core and is also the site of countless festivals that attempt to attract the affluent and their dollars. Marginalized young people, as you might imagine, were not similarly welcomed into this site. Instead, police officers stationed around the square were instructed to stop, question, and search any 'suspicious-looking' young people (read: Aboriginal). With their rather unkempt appearance and lack of surplus income, these youth were unwelcome in Churchill Square and were constituted as 'other' to the affluent suburbanites that city officials were attempting to attract (Hogeveen and Freistadt, forthcoming).

What would a politics of hospitality look like? Hospitality without the trace of hostility and exclusion would push out beyond established limits and work toward welcoming the other without limit and would encourage 'the other' to be as they are and as they arrive (Derrida 2005, p. 66). Hospitality demands acts of total munificence and an opening of space to an unknown and unknowable other (Carroll 2006): 'It is a politics that does not accept limits imposed upon itself, but always asks "what's next?" and in response relentlessly pushes against established exclusionary boundaries of being' (Carroll 2006). Such a way of being in the world is founded in a reverence for the other who appears at a person's threshold and may be dangerous. In the case of Churchill Square, and in the spirit of hospitality, the city might open the square to the marginalized other and establish venues that encourage their unique interests. Instead of closing down in the face of the other and employing the EPS to repress and choke their manner of expression, such a welcome would open out to them and invite these youth to share the space on their own terms.

Opening up of things to what lies beyond encourages adherents of deconstruction to think outside of current ontological being in the world and toward more just ways of being with others. If that is what we are after, should we now deconstruct or open up 'justice'? It would be extremely profitable and intellectually expedient if this were indeed possible, but Derrida insists that justice is impossible. It does not exist. It is always to come (Derrida 2002). If justice does not indeed exist, why does Canada have a youth justice system, justices of the peace, and the YCJA? Surely, these are all instances of justice. Hardly—these are instruments of vengeance and are what counts as justice today (Hogeveen and Woolford 2009). That is, the youth justice system is authorized under the YCJA to deliver pain to juvenile offenders as payment for this or that harm caused. Jails and penitentiaries are run based on this misguided logic. Justice that finds its end in retribution is not just—it is a form of revenge, which is fully at odds with the logic and spirit of justice. Further, it is the marginalized other who is typically on the receiving end of this brand of vengeance, masquerading as justice. What we have, then, is a so-called justice system predicated on punishing the poor and marginalized.

Derrida has something much different in mind. He understands justice to be a 'promise' that is 'beyond law, and is itself incalculable, infinite and undeconstructable' (Pavlich 2007, p. 989). For Derrida, justice is not present and no one can seriously claim to be just. Maintaining that our system of punishment is just would be to claim that all of our hard work is done. Understood from Derrida's perspective, justice becomes an ideal that exists beyond current ontological limits and must be doggedly pursued. Suggesting that the youth criminal justice system is just because it administers the laws of Canada would be to deny the suffering of the indigenous other who is overrepresented at all stages of the system. There is much to be done.

Michel Foucault and Power

Like Derrida, Michel Foucault (1926–1984) was a highly influential French philosopher. His many books include *The History of Sexuality* (three volumes), *Power/Knowledge*, and the *Archaeology of Knowledge*. Given his disdain for the discipline, it may seem odd to include a section on Foucault in a book on youth crime and criminology. Foucault thought criminology to be replete with 'garrulous discourse' and 'endless repetition' and was convinced that the discipline's primary and perhaps only function was to relieve criminal justice officials of their guilt for delivering pain and suffering upon the other (Foucault 1980, p. 47). That is, he was certain that criminology only served to make judges, for example, feel better about sending young people away from their families and communities because doing so was for 'their own good' and a protection for society. Nevertheless and despite Foucault's distaste for criminology, scholars interested in the subject have successfully drawn on his voluminous work to render contemporary systems of governance intelligible. Foucault's book *Discipline and Punish* and his series of articles on governmentality have been particularly influential.

Foucault's work has been prominent in several studies that attend to how young people are governed and disciplined. As we have seen already, youth, and particularly recalcitrant and marginalized young people, are increasingly the targets of surveillance. Ericson and Haggerty (1999) have examined this phenomenon through a governmentality lens. They argue that 'governance is organized in terms of risk management technologies that identify dangers' and maintain that police collaborate with other agencies to provide knowledge about youth (i.e., using street-stop recording systems and missing persons registries) (Ericson and Haggerty 1999, p. 163). The authors maintain that police function as 'the fulcrum of risk communication systems for governing the young' (Ericson and Haggerty 1999, p. 164). Predictably it is marginalized youth and those identified as having the highest levels of **risk** that are subjected to the most intensive surveillance.

We can see from this brief example that scholars have been particularly drawn to Foucault's unique understanding of **power**. Prior to Foucault's interdiction, many writers were convinced that power was concentrated in the hands of a few. By contrast, Foucault maintains that power extends beyond a particular class or state and is evidenced only when it is exercised. From this view, power is not something that can be held, accumulated, or stored up for later use. It is only ever evident when it is being put to use. Think about this for a minute. Can you show me power? Can you hold it in your hands and bring it to me? Money as power is a common theme in contemporary music.

risk
The calculated probability of an event or circumstance. Risks are calculated and managed through class, gender, age, and race categories.

power (Foucault)
Rather than as a quantity held or possessed by the state, Foucault understood power to be relational, positive, and exercised.

Consider, for example, the song *Money, Power and Respect* by Lox (featuring Lil' Kim and DMX) (www.youtube.com/watch?v=YAOgWDLo--w). In the song, the artist makes it clear to the listener that becoming powerful is dependent on first acquiring money. For this group, 'it's the key to life'. Foucault disagrees with Lox's assessment. For Foucault, money becomes power only when it is spent; it has no power in and of itself.

Foucault (1991, 1980, 1977) was deeply interested in how power shaped the conduct and lives of those subjected to its disciplinary effects. In his classic work on the rise of the prison and punishment, Foucault (1977) traces the emergence of a new economy of discipline that continues to dominate our thinking about how best to govern and train human beings. He was convinced that discipline was characterized by micro-powers that shaped human subjects in preferred ways. These micro-powers, Foucault argues, operate at the minutiae of our existence but are nevertheless momentous in their effects. Every bit of our being is shaped through the exercise of this kind of micro-power. All things, from holding a pencil, to martial arts, to riding a bike, are taught to us through an exacting discipline. Instead of punishing the body via capital punishment or the stock and pillory for that matter, discipline takes hold of the soul and shapes it in ways that are functional and desirable. Thus, rather than seeing power as being repressive or negative, Foucault suggests that power is creative and positive: not in terms of being good or exceptional but in terms of producing some desirable behaviour or outcome. He argues that '. . . we must cease once and for all to describe the effects of power in negative terms . . . In fact, power produces; it produces reality; it produces domains of object and rituals of truth' (Foucault 1979, p. 194). In this way, Foucault urges scholars to avoid the trap of examining how power dismantles social relations and instead consider what is created through power's exercise.

Foucault was convinced that these micro-powers are not confined to the prison but have been diffused into the larger social world. Following Foucault (as well as David Garland 1985), Dorothy Chunn (1992) has demonstrated how disciplinary powers were disseminated throughout early twentieth century Canadian society to create a dense and interlocking web of surveillance intended to discipline the working classes. We encourage you to think about your everyday lives. What forms of discipline are acting upon you? What forms of surveillance are encouraging you to act appropriately? Are there closed-circuit television cameras at your college or university? Will you pass a photo radar vehicle on your way home? How does your behaviour change as a result?

Foucault's work has been routinely challenged for conceptualizing human subjects as 'docile' bodies who are the subject of discipline without at the same time resisting incursion into their lives. Foucault addresses this criticism in a 1982 essay entitled 'The Subject and Power', where he argues that power operates on individuals so long as they are free. For Foucault (1982) power operates on the actions and behaviour of others, which implies that power can only ever work on a subject who is capable of action and who is (relatively) free. Power seeks to structure subjects' choices in ways that bring their behaviour in line with the needs and desires of governors. For example, during their trip to Disney World, Clifford Shearing and Phillip Stenning (1984) noticed that, despite the hordes of people and without overt signs of discipline and control, the amusement park seemed to function like clockwork. They found that 'designed-in' features, like carefully marked roadways and smiling employees (even Donald Duck is in on the action), control and shape behaviour in ways conducive to good order at the park. One does not have to travel to Florida to witness similar effects. The first author of this chapter recently visited IKEA to purchase an item for his home. When he arrived he knew exactly what he wanted and where he could find it (in the warehouse). Despite this knowledge, the configuration of the store shaped his actions such that he was 'encouraged' by the partition separating the entrance (on one side) from the warehouse (on the opposite side) to venture through the entire store. Those familiar with the massive size of IKEA can imagine his frustration. Foucault's work assists crime scholars to understand modern configurations of power by alerting them to how the behaviour of active subjects is shaped and contoured in ways often hidden from view, but with very real effects.

Risk and the Risky Society

Risk is seemingly ubiquitous today. Consider, for example, how the University of Alberta boasts a department of Risk Management Services (RMS). Campus security, emergency management, and insurance and risk management all fall under the RMS rubric. The very existence of this unit suggests that there are numerous risks at the university and that they require some form of regulation. According to its website, the RMS's 'vision is to make risk management an integral part of all decision making, at all levels, across the University'. It seems that managing risk is such a fundamental part of the contemporary ethos at the university that all decisions require an assessment of risk levels.

It is not only at universities that discourses concerning risk have become omnipresent. It seems that almost everything we do can be understood in risk terms. A quick search of the internet returns countless websites dedicated to providing information on all manner of diseases. Not only does such a site provide knowledge about the problem, it is also an instrument for you to ascertain your individual level of risk for such calamities as heart disease, sexually transmitted diseases, stroke, breast cancer, and, but certainly not limited to, diabetes. There is nothing inherently risky about having sexual intercourse or eating a diet rich in fat. Rather, it is only when these problems are translated into statistics via actuarial techniques for determining probability that they become risky. That is, only when we are able to accumulate sufficient data on a problem and then assemble that data into a form amenable to calculation do seemingly random events become constituted into the language of risk. Patterns of probability emerge when incidents are tabulated across time and across space. Without this ability to translate events and actions into probabilities, events would only be as they are or as we encounter them.

Awareness of predictable crime patterns often shapes our decision-making processes. How many readers, or parents of readers, of this chapter have purchased a burglar alarm for their homes? What prompted this decision? Or, how many have altered their diet because of the latest research tying cancer to this or that food category? Francois Ewald (1991, p. 199) maintains that there is nothing in our world that is in and of itself a risk; rather, 'it all depends on how one analyses the danger, considers the event'. Thus, the invention of instruments that calculate risk orders our social world through technologies that render risk knowable and thus governable. That is, if we know that having a burglar alarm, trimming the hedges around our homes, purchasing solid and quality locks, and turning on lights at night reduce our risk of victimization, we can take steps to predictably lower the probability that our home will be targeted.

Risk is the probability of an event or an action occurring (Ewald 1991). Insurance agents ask a number of probing questions that are intended to determine a person's level of risk and that are used to provide a quotation for their services: *How old are you? What gender? Have you ever had an 'at fault' accident? How many traffic tickets?* By comparing your answers to data aggregated across time (i.e., accident reports and police statistics), insurance companies determine your level of risk and the probability that they will be called upon to pay a claim on your behalf. Young, unemployed, and undereducated males with several traffic tickets are likely to pay much more for their coverage than married women with no blemishes on their driving records. Calculating risk in this way orders seemingly random occurrence in a form that can be used to definite ends (Dean 1999).

Contemporary calculations of risk are not the exclusive domain of the insurance industry, however. Indeed, they are widely applied to and available in the youth justice system. And because of their seeming ability to efficiently and accurately match disciplinary practice to offender characteristics, these technologies of governance have become ubiquitous (Simon 1988; O'Malley 1996). Youth, it seems, are at risk for a greater number of predicaments and misadventures than any other segment of the Canadian population (Health Canada 1998). Studies of young people have revealed a series of risk factors that may increase their probability of being victimized or of developing behavioural problems that may then lead to crime and other anti-social behaviour (Howell 2005; Hawkins and Pollard 1999; Shader 2003; Wyrick and Howell 2004). Canada's National Crime Prevention Centre (2007) has identified a variety of risk factors that may lead to gang involvement. Based on accumulated knowledge and data, the centre argues that the following are predictive of gang involvement: over-reliance on anti-social peers, poor parental supervision, prior delinquency, aggression, and, but not limited to, early or precocious sexual activity. Risk factors such as these do not stand alone but are often combined toward a variety of ends. For example, Hoge and Andrews (2010) have aggregated risk factors into the latest incarnation of the Youth Level of Service/Case Management Inventory (YLS/CMI), which, they maintain, now takes into account gender and cultural factors. Hoge and Andrews (2010, para. 1) argue that the 'YLS/CMI helps probation officers, youth workers, psychologists, and social workers identify the youth's major needs, strengths, barriers, and incentives; select the most appropriate goals for him or her; and produce an effective case management plan'.

Risk has come to order our social world to such an extent that social theorist Ulrich Beck (1992) has deemed our contemporary ethos the **risk society**. Whether through advertising, television programming, or word of mouth, citizens in the West are increasingly made aware of their risks for all manner of calamity and are taking steps to remedy these seemingly inevitable ends. For Beck (1992) and others (Giddens 1990), this practice is very much characteristic of a reflexive modern society that is consistently reflecting back upon itself with a wary eye toward the future. Whereas previous societies were constantly looking backward and were reactive, the risk society is preoccupied with allaying future harms. Because contemporary citizens are very much aware of looming risks, they trim their hedges, install burglar alarms, remove all of the valuables from their vehicles, avoid the wrong part of town, and eat a diet free of harmful pesticides and hormones. However, Beck (1992) does not argue that contemporary society is any more at risk than at any other point in history. Rather, insurential technologies have organized our lives according to risks that are seemingly ubiquitous.

Because risk has become increasingly pervasive in contemporary society, it has also become a subject of and for critical scholars (Hannah-Moffat 2001). And while risk orders our contemporary manner of being in the world, there are inherent problems intrinsic to such an ontology. In particular, when risk structures our thinking about social problems (i.e., poverty, drug use, violence, youth crime, and punishment), these unfortunate conditions cease to be obstacles to the more just ordering of the social world. Instead, such issues become constituted as risks that require management (Hogeveen and Woolford 2009). For example, a 10-year-old Aboriginal boy living in poverty is determined to be at risk for joining a gang because of his family history of crime and his low birth weight, and because he lives in poverty is doing poorly in school. When risk is calculated without consideration for structural conditions that buoy marginality, poverty (for example) is constituted as a risk factor rather than as an intolerable condition that demands redress and amelioration (Minaker and Hogeveen 2009).

Cultural Criminology

Beck (1992) and Giddens's (1990) work alerts us to the growing importance and seeming omnipotence of risk in contemporary societies. However, this scholarship does little to help criminologists understand and conceptualize how young people on the ground experience and understand this phenomenon. Evidence suggests that young people today are engaging in and enjoying more risky behaviours simply because they are constituted to do so (Hunt, Evans, Moloney, and Bailey 2009; Sanders 2005). Sean Morrissey (2008), in his examination of voluntary risk-taking behaviour among a Scottish dance education company, suggests that young people find risk taking to be particularly alluring. He argues that transgressive conduct is particularly tempting in societies of caution, where young people are heavily surveilled and policed (Morrissey 2008). Indeed, risk-taking behaviour among young people is evident in a number of divergent and diverse domains of

risk society
This refers to a break with modernity into an emerging societal form characterized by the production of risks and tools for their management. In contrast to the view that social problems are to be solved, issues in the risk society (i.e., crime) are risks to be managed.

youth culture from BASE jumping (using a parachute to jump from buildings, antennas, spans, and earth) to ecstasy use in the rave scene.

Contemporary criminological theories have difficulty accounting for these seemingly absurd and baseless choices. Rational choice theory, for example, is among the most prominent perspectives in criminology for understanding youthful offending. It posits that young people are rational actors who make informed and rational decisions about rule breaking. While criminologists have widely applied this theory in the context of crime, other scholars have attended to how almost all behaviour (i.e., purchasing a television) can be understood in relation to how we understand perceived costs and benefits. Nevertheless, such a perspective does little to account for the emotional and visceral elements of crime and deviance. Cultural criminology, by contrast, is attentive to what renders 'transgression and the consumption of transgression so seductive' (Hayward 2002). Cultural criminologists are less concerned with state definitions of crime and the pragmatism of crime control than with the adrenaline surge and emotion that accompanies the commission of crime. Fenwick and Hayward (2000) suggest that this insight challenges one of the most widely held and central assumptions of criminology: that crime is 'routinized' and rather 'banal'. They maintain that this 'is undoubtedly the case if one adopts the perspective of the police . . . however, it is not necessarily true for those participating in criminal activity, for whom the most innocuous transgression may well represent an exhilarating form of experience' (Fenwick and Hayward 2000, p. 36). Thus, home invasion may not make rational sense to the average crime scholar; however, cultural criminologists may argue that this crime is more often the result of the adrenaline rush emerging from the commission of the crime than from reasoned aforethought.

Cultural criminology enjoys considerable intellectual momentum at present (Ferrell and Young 2004). This group of scholars, who are critical of the methods and inability of orthodox criminology to conceptualize the adrenaline and emotions intrinsic to offending, interweave a number of intellectual threads. These include cultural studies, postmodern theory, critical theory, textual/media analysis, and ethnographic methodologies (Ferrell 1999). Considered more broadly, the very notion of cultural criminology indexes the increasing attention crime scholars lend to popular culture constructions of crime and its control (McCormick 2010; Ferrell 1999). Through innovative theoretical and methodological precepts, cultural criminologists aim to expand and enliven the discipline (Ferrell and Sanders 1995, p. 17).

Innovative methodologies provide cultural criminologists with unique insight into the visceral nature of crime and deviance. According to Stephanie Kane (2004, p. 303) 'participant observation remains the methodological touchstone for the culture-worker'. Ethnographic research is particularly appropriate for the subject of cultural criminology. This method attends to the 'nuances of meaning within particular cultural milieux' (Ferrell 1999, p. 399). Deep immersion in criminal or deviant fields encourages researchers to formulate pithy and textured descriptions of these worlds, which are often hidden from view. However, cultural criminologists do not only employ participant observation to their academic ends. Maggie O'Neill (2004), for example, uses a method she calls 'ethno-mimesis' to capture the complexity of lived reality. For example, she had sex workers use art and prose to detail not only their life experiences but their ideas for social change (O'Neil 2004).

Cultural criminology possesses much potential for transgression. Like the other critical projects discussed in this chapter, cultural criminology unflaggingly challenges taken-for-granted assumptions about crime and its study so as to expose how these are 'culturally constructed and delimited by a particular world view' (Hogeveen and Woolford 2009, p. 354; Morrison 2004). Jock Young (2004, p. 1) maintains that, because we are 'confronted at this moment with an orthodox criminology which is denatured and desiccated', the need for a cultural criminology that captures the phenomenology of crime—'its adrenaline, its pleasure and panic, its excitement, and its anger, rage and humiliation'—has never been more pressing.

Summary

Critical criminologists direct attention to the structural inequalities within and outside of the criminal justice system. They advocate social engagement in ways that would transform marginalization and bring about justice for the other. Critical criminologists recognize that Canadian young people are marginalized by age, class, gender, and race. While marginalization is widespread, the situation facing Aboriginal youth is particularly egregious, which is evident in incarceration rates and homelessness, and in the tragic history and impact of colonialism that continues unabated in contemporary society.

Deconstruction, as understood by Derrida, opens language to its hidden and its silent elements. While almost all language can be deconstructed, justice resists our attempts as it is forever 'to come'. Considered in this way, justice encourages tireless ameliorative efforts on the behalf of marginalized others.

Foucault's impact on critical scholarship is particularly significant. He attuned scholars to new ways of thinking about and understanding power. Instead of seeing power as solely repressive, he thought it was creative and productive. Rather than being housed in some place or entity (i.e., the state), Foucault argued that power is evident only in its exercise. Through discipline, surveillance, and governmentality, Foucault maintained that power shapes individuals in ways that render them more amenable to governance.

Critical criminologists have also made us of the concepts of risk, actuarialism, and the risk society to critically examine contemporary society's preoccupation with insurance-like predictions of potential harm. Because of their age, level of maturity, and propensity for precarious behaviour, young people are particularly likely subjects of such forms of calculation. Critical scholarship attends to the social contexts that produce the risk society and encourages academics to draw attention to how marginalization is camouflaged in risk-management approaches to juvenile justice. Similarly, cultural criminology is critical of contemporary scholars who reject crime as a visceral phenomenon. Scholars working in this tradition direct academic attention to crime as a lived experience that can best be understood through **ethnography**.

ethnography
A form of participatory research that involves immersion in the field of study. Because it allows for rich and descriptive findings on areas that are often hidden from view, ethnographic research is fundamental to cultural criminology.

Key Terms

critical criminology
deconstruction
ethnography
hospitality
justice (Derrida)
marginalization

power (Foucault)
risk
risk society
surveillance
trace

Review Questions

1. Explain how critical criminologists understand and operationalize critique.

2. Highlight and provide examples of how colonialism has contributed to social suffering and to the marginalization of Aboriginal people.

3. Describe and provide examples of how cultural criminology is critical.

4. Explain and provide an example of deconstruction (pay particular attention to the trace).

5. Explore why Derrida claims justice is not deconstructable.

Critical Thinking Questions

1. Explain what being critical means to you. Discuss the differences and similarities between your understanding of being critical and that of critical criminology.

2. Marginalization of the other is found in every Canadian city. Discuss what responsibility, if any, you might have to ameliorate the suffering experienced and lived by the other.

3. How might the insights of the various scholars outlined in this chapter be implemented in the real world?

4. Recall Foucault's understanding of power. How does this conception differ from more widely held beliefs about power in Western society? Explore how your everyday behaviour is disciplined, is the subject of surveillance, and is governed. To what ends is this governance exercised?

Suggested Readings

Derrida, J. and Caputo, J.D. (1997). *Deconstruction in a nutshell: A conversation with Jacques Derrida.* New York: Fordham University Press.

Ferrell, J., Hayward, K., Morrison, W., and Presdee, M. (Eds.). (2004). *Cultural criminology unleashed.* London: Glasshouse.

Hogeveen, B., Martel, J., and Woolford, A. (Eds.). (2006). 'Law, crime and critique' a special issue of the *Canadian Journal of Criminology and Criminal Justice, 48*(5).

Minaker, J. and Hogeveen, B. (2009). *Youth, crime, and society: Issues of power and justice.* Toronto: Pearson Prentice Hall.

Muncie, J., Hughes, G., and McLaughlin, E. (2002). *Youth justice: Critical readings.* London: Sage.

Pavlich, G. (2000). *Critique and radical discourses on crime.* Dartmouth: Ashgate.

Suggested Weblinks

Amnesty International
www.amnesty.org
* The homepage of this human rights organization.

Critical Criminology
www.critcrim.org
* Information and resources on critical criminology.

Cultural Criminology
www.culturalcriminology.org
* The website of the cultural criminology team at the University of Kent, UK.

iHuman
www.ihuman.org
* An organization that helps Edmonton youth through the arts.

The Youth Restorative Action Project
www.yrap.org
* 'A Youth Justice Committee founded and run by Edmonton youth.'

References

Aboriginal Healing Foundation. (2003). *Aboriginal domestic violence in Canada*. Ottawa: Anishinabe Press.

Amnesty International. (2009). *No more stolen sisters: The need for a comprehensive response to discrimination and violence against Indigenous women in Canada*. London: Amnesty International Publications.

Andersen, C. (2009). *Aboriginal Edmonton: A statistical story—2009*. Edmonton: City of Edmonton Aboriginal Relations Office.

Anderson, J. (2003). *Aboriginal children in poverty in urban communities*. Ottawa: Canadian Council on Social Development.

Balfour, G. and Comack, E. (2006). *Criminalizing women: Gender and (in)justice in neoliberal times*. Halifax: Fernwood.

Beck, U. (1992). *Risk society: Towards a new modernity*. London: Sage.

Bradley, A. (2008). *Derrida's Of grammatology*. Bloomington: Indiana University Press.

Calverley, D. (2007). Youth custody and community services in Canada, 2004/2005. *Juristat, 27*(2).

Campaign 2000. (2009). *2009 report card on child and family poverty in Canada, 1989–2009*. Toronto: Campaign 2000.

Carroll, D. (2006). 'Remains' of Algeria: Justice, hospitality, politics. *Modern Language Notes, 121*(4): 808–27.

CBC News Online. (2008, September 2). Conservatives vow to toughen youth justice act: Youth 14 and over would be named when convicted of serious crimes. *CBC News Online*. Retrieved from http://www.cbc.ca/news/canadavotes/story/2008/09/22/harper-elxn.html

Chartrand, L. and McKay, C. (2006). *A review of research on criminal victimization and First Nations, Métis and Inuit People, 1990 to 2001*. Ottawa: Department of Justice.

Chunn, D. (1992). *From punishment to doing good: Family courts and socialized justice in Ontario, 1880–1940*. Toronto: University of Toronto Press.

Dauvergne, M. (2008). Crime statistics in Canada, 2007. *Juristat, 29*(7).

Dean, M. (1999). *Governmentality: Power and rule in modern society*. London: Sage.

Derrida, J. (1985). Letter to a Japanese friend. In D. Wood, and R. Bernasconi (Eds.), Derrida and différance (pp. 1–6). Warwick: Parousia.

Derrida, J. (1987). Some questions and responses. In N. Fabb, D. Attridge and C. MacCabe (Eds.), *The linguistics of writing: Arguments between language and literature* (pp. 252–64). Manchester: Manchester University Press.

Derrida, J. (1995). In Weber E. (Ed.), *Points—interviews, 1974–1994* (P. Kamuf, Trans.). Stanford: Stanford University Press.

Derrida, J. (1999). Hospitality, justice and responsibility: A dialogue with Jacques Derrida. In R. Kearney, and M. Dooley (Eds.), *Questioning ethics: Contemporary debates in philosophy* (pp. 65–83). New York: Routledge.

Derrida, J. (2002). Force of law: The 'mystical foundation of authority'. In G. Anidjar (Ed.), *Jacques Derrida: Acts of religion* (pp. 229–98). London: Routledge.

Derrida, J. (2005). *The principle of hospitality. Paper machine* (R. Bowlby, Trans.). (pp. 66–69). Stanford: Stanford University Press.

Derrida, J. and Caputo, J. D. (1997). *Deconstruction in a nutshell: A conversation with Jacques Derrida*. New York: Fordham University Press.

Derrida, J. and Dufourmantelle, A. (2000). *Of hospitality*. Stanford, CA: Stanford University Press.

Edmonton Committee to End Homelessness. (2009, January 29). *Edmonton Committee to End Homelessness releases 10-year plan*. Edmonton Committee to End Homelessness News Release. Retrieved from http://www.endedmontonhomelessness.com/docs/mediapackagewithgoals.pdf

Elden, S. (2007). There is a politics of space because space is political: Henri Lefebvre and the production of space. *Radical Philosophy Review, 10*(2): 101–16.

Ericson, R. and Haggerty, K. (1999). Governing the young. In R. Smandych (Ed.), *Governable places: Readings on governmentality and crime control* (pp. 163–90). Aldershot: Ashgate.

Ewald, F. (1991). Insurance and risk. In G. Burchell, C. Gordon and P. Miller (Eds.), *The Foucault effect: Studies in governmentality* (pp. 197–210). Chicago: University of Chicago Press.

Fenwick, M. and Hayward, K. (2000). Youth crime, excitement and consumer culture: The reconstruction of aetiology in contemporary theoretical criminology. In J. Pickford (Ed.), *Youth justice: Theory and practice* (pp. 31–50). London: Glasshouse.

Ferrell, J. (1999). Cultural criminology. *Annual Review of Sociology, 25*(1): 395–418.

Ferrell, J., Hayward, K., Morrison, W., and Presdee, M. (Eds.). (2004). *Cultural criminology unleashed*. London: Glasshouse.

Ferrell, J. and Sanders, C. (1995). *Cultural criminology*. Boston: Northeastern University Press.

Ferrell, J. and Young, J. (2004). Cultural criminology: Some notes on the script. *Theoretical Criminology, 8*(3): 259–73.

Foucault, M. (1977). *Discipline and punish*. New York: Vintage.

Foucault, M. (1979). *The history of sexuality*. New York: Vintage.

Foucault, M. (1980). *Power/knowledge: Selected interviews and other writings*. New York: Pantheon.

Foucault, M. (1982). The subject and power. In H. Dreyfus, and P. Rabinow (Eds.), *Michel Foucault: Beyond structuralism and hermeneutics* (pp. 208–26). Chicago: University of Chicago.

Foucault, M. (1991). Governmentality. In G. Burchell, C. Gordon and P. Miller (Eds.), *The Foucault effect: Studies in governmentality* (pp. 87–104). Chicago: University of Chicago Press.

Fournier, S. and Crey, E. (1997). *Stolen from our embrace: The abduction of First Nations children and the restoration of Aboriginal communities*. Vancouver: Douglas and McIntyre Inc.

Garland, D. (1985). *Punishment and welfare: A history of penal strategies*. London: Gower.

Giddens, A. (1990). *The consequences of modernity*. Cambridge: Polity Press.

Hannah-Moffat, K. (2001). *Punishment in disguise: Penal governance and federal imprisonment*. Toronto: University of Toronto Press.

Harper, S. (2008). Prime Minister Stephen Harper delivers remarks at the 6th Annual Gala and Fundraiser for the Canadian Crime Victims Foundation. Retrieved 24 November, 2010, from http://pm.gc.ca/eng/media.asp?id=2145

Harvey, D. (1989). *The condition of postmodernity: An inquiry into the origins of cultural change*. London: Blackwell.

Hawkins, D. and Pollard, J. (1999). Risk and protective factors: Are both necessary to understand diverse behavioural outcomes in adolescence? *Social Work Research, 23*(3): 145–58.

Hayward, K. (2002). The vilification and pleasures of youthful transgression. In J. Muncie, G. Hughes and E. McLaughlin (Eds.), *Youth justice: Critical readings* (pp. 80–93). London: Sage.

Health Canada. (1998). *Meeting the needs of youth-at-risk in Canada: A summary of the learnings*. Ottawa: Health Canada.

Herbert, S. and Brown, E. (2006). Conceptions of space and crime in the punitive neoliberal city. *Antipode, 38*(4): 755–77.

Hoge, R.D. and Andrews, D.A. (2010). YLS/CMI: Youth level of service/case management inventory 2.0. Retrieved 24 November, 2010, from http://www.mhs.com/product.aspx?gr=safandprod=yls-cmiandid=overview

Hogeveen, B. (2006). Unsettling youth justice and cultural norms: The Youth Restorative Action Project. *Journal of Youth Studies, 9*(1): 47–66.

Hogeveen, B. (2007). Is there justice for youth? In G. Pavlich, and M. Hird (Eds.), *Questioning sociology: Canadian perspectives* (pp. 210–25). Don Mills, Ontario: Oxford University Press.

Hogeveen, B. and Freistadt, J. (Forthcoming). Youth justice and hospitality: Overcoming 'scarecrow policing'. In R. Jochelson, and K. Gorkoff (Eds.), *Theorizing justice: Interdiscipling the divide—A reader*. Halifax: Fernwood.

Hogeveen, B., Martel, J., and Woolford, A. (Eds.). (2006). 'Law, crime and critique' a special issue of the *Canadian Journal of Criminology and Criminal Justice, 48*(5).

Hogeveen, B. and Woolford, A. (2006). Critical criminology and possibility in the neoliberal ethos. *Canadian Journal of Criminology and Criminal Justice, 48*(5): 681–702.

Hogeveen, B. and Woolford, A. (2009). Contemporary critical criminology. In R. Linden (Ed.), *Criminology: A Canadian perspective* (6th ed.) (pp. 339–70). Toronto: Pearson Education Ltd.

Howell, J. (2005). Moving risk factors into developmental theories of gang membership. *Youth Violence and Juvenile Justice, 3*(5): 334–54.

Hunt, G., Evans, K., Moloney, M., and Bailey, N. (2009). Combining different substances in the dance scene: Enhancing pleasure, managing risk and timing effects. *Journal of Drug Issues, 39*(3), 495–522.

Hylton, J. (2002). *Aboriginal sex offending in Canada*. Ottawa: Aboriginal Healing Foundation.

Kane, S. (2004). The unconventional methods of cultural criminology. *Theoretical Criminology, 8*(3): 303–21.

Kleiss, K. (2010, October 11). Housing dollars fuel social chaos: residents. *Edmonton Journal*. Retrieved from http://www.edmontonjournal.com/business/Housing%20+dollars+fuel+social+chaos+residents/3653120/story.html

Lefebvre, H. (1996). *Writing on cities*. London: Blackwell.

McCormick, C. (2010). *Constructing danger: Mis/Representation of crime in the news*. Halifax: Fernwood.

McGillivray, A. and Comaskey, B. (1996). *Black eyes all the time: Intimate violence, Aboriginal women and the justice system*. Toronto: University of Toronto Press.

McIntyre, M. (2011, March 1). 'Young mother spent life battling vices: Struggled after conviction in homicide.' *Winnipeg Free Press.*

Mallea, P. (2010). *The fear factor: Stephen Harper's 'tough on crime' agenda.* Ottawa: Canadian Centre for Policy Alternatives.

Mihorean, K., Besserer, S., Hendrick, D., Brzozowski, J., Trainor, C., and Ogg, S. (2001). *A profile of criminal victimization: Results from the 1999 General Social Survey.* Ottawa: Canadian Centre for Justice Statistics.

Miller, J.R. (1996). *Shingwauk's vision: A history of Native residential schools.* Toronto: University of Toronto Press.

Minaker, J. and Hogeveen, B. (2009). *Youth, crime, and society: Issues of power and justice.* Toronto: Pearson Prentice Hall.

Morrison, W. (2004). 'Reflections with memories': Everyday photography capturing genocide. *Theoretical Criminology, 8*(3): 341–58.

Morrissey, S.A. (2008). Performing risks: Catharsis, carnival and capital in the risk society. *Journal of Youth Studies, 11*(4): 413–27.

Muncie, J., Hughes, G., and McLaughlin, E. (2002). *Youth justice: Critical readings.* London: Sage.

National Crime Prevention Centre. (2007). *Youth gang involvement: What are the risk factors?* Ottawa: National Crime Prevention Centre of Public Safety Canada.

O'Malley, P. (1996). Risk and responsibility. In A. Barry, T. Osborne and N. Rose (Eds.), *Foucault and political reason: Liberalism, neoliberalism and rationalities of government* (pp. 189–208). Chicago: University of Chicago Press.

O'Neill, M. (2004). Crime, culture, and visual methodologies: Ethno-mimesis as performative praxis. In J. Ferrell, K. Hayward, W. Morrison and M. Presdee (Eds.), *Cultural criminology unleashed* (pp. 219–29). London: Glasshouse.

Pavlich, G. (2000). *Critique and radical discourses on crime.* Aldershot: Ashgate.

Pavlich, G. (2007). Deconstruction. In G. Ritzer (Ed.), *Blackwell encyclopedia of sociology* (pp. 986–89). Malden: Blackwell.

Perreault, S. and Brennan, S. (2010). Criminal victimization in Canada, 2009. *Juristat, 3*(2).

Ratner, R. (1971). Criminology in Canada: Conflicting objectives. Unpublished manuscript.

Royal Commission on Aboriginal Peoples. (1996). *Report of the Royal Commission on Aboriginal Peoples.* Ottawa: Indian and Northern Affairs Canada.

Sanders, B. (2005). In the club: Ecstasy use and supply in a London nightclub. *Sociology, 39*(2): 241–58.

Scott, K. (2003). *Funding matters: The impact of Canada's new funding regime on nonprofit and voluntary organizations.* Ottawa: Canadian Council on Social Development.

Shader, M. (2003). *Risk factors for delinquency: An overview.* Washington: Office of Juvenile Justice and Delinquency.

Shearing, C. and Stenning, P. (1984). From the panopticon to Disney World: The development of discipline. In A. Doob, and E. Greenspan (Eds.), *Perspectives in criminal law* (pp. 335–49). Toronto: Aurora.

Simon, J. (1988). The ideological effects of actuarial practices. *Law and Society Review, 22*(4): 772–800.

Smart, C. (1989). *Feminism and the power of law.* London: Routledge.

Smith, B. et al. (1992, May 9). Open letter against Derrida receiving an honorary doctrate from Cambridge University. *The Times* (London). Retrieved from http://courses.nus.edu.sg/course/elljwp/againstdsdegree.htm.

Smith, J. (2005). *Jacques Derrida: Live theory.* London: Continuum.

Spivak, G. (1976). Translator's preface. In J. Derrida, *Of grammatology* (G. Spivak, Trans.) (pp. ix–lxxxvii). Baltimore: John Hopkins University Press.

Sprott, J.B. (1996). Understanding public views of youth crime and the youth justice system. *Canadian Journal of Criminology, 38*(3): 271–90.

Wyrick, P. and Howell, J. (2004). Strategic risk based response to youth gangs. *Juvenile Justice Journal, 9*(1): 20–29.

Young, J. (2004). Voodoo criminology and the numbers game. In J. Ferrell, K. Hayward, W. Morrison and M. Presdee (Eds.), *Cultural criminology unleashed* (pp. 13–27). London: Glasshouse.

Part III
At-Risk and Criminalized Youth in Canada: Selected Types and Problems

When the subject of delinquency, criminalized youth, or youth at risk is discussed, most conversations inevitably shift toward specific subject areas (e.g., Aboriginal youth, substance abuse, gangs, violence, bullying, etc.). This shift is seen as a natural progression due to the imprecise meaning of the concept of young offenders or delinquency. Furthermore, any discussion about the different expressions of youth at risk, or criminalized youth, can be examined from a variety of different perspectives—generally reflecting the complexity of delinquency and the multidisciplinary nature of the study of youth crime. Practical constraints do not allow us to cover all the key topics that we might want to address in a book of this nature. Therefore, in this section we focus on five different types of delinquent behaviour and/or phenomena. Collectively, the chapters serve to illustrate not only that young persons' behaviour is complex but that any efforts to prevent, control, treat, or otherwise respond are both challenging and fraught with varying degrees of controversy. The topics covered in this section also serve to illustrate that we cannot rely on blanket solutions, programs, or treatment techniques to solve youth crime.

The themes and topics included in Part Three tend to reflect themes and topics that have dominated the youth crime and youth justice literature for several generations now. In fact, entire books have been written on each of the topics presented. Therefore, while we do not profess to provide a comparable level of depth of analysis, each of the chapters offers a concise and yet enriched and enlivened overview of the subject matter being addressed.

The first chapter by Jordon Diplock and Darryl Plecas (Chapter Nine) provides an engaging discussion on the topic of substance abuse and related crime in adolescence. In addition to spending the first part of their chapter providing some factual details around the extent and nature of adolescent substance use among Canadian youth, the authors also attempt to provide a contextual framework as to why young people experiment with and/or use drugs, and they discuss a range of the risks (e.g., health, psychological health). Diplock and Plecas then succinctly describe how substance use and abuse is related to various youth crimes as a result of such risk factors as impaired judgment, social pressure, and the lure of 'fast money', etc. In recognizing the varied harms of substance use and abuse, Diplock and Plecas then examine a range of formal and informal intervention and prevention strategies (most of which are school-based) that have been successfully used to prevent youth from ever experimenting and to 'just say no'. The authors conclude by reiterating that while in recent years there appears to have been a general decrease in substance use and abuse among young people across Canada, the topic remains complex and one that requires us to 'build upon existing knowledge' to better inform prevention strategies.

The next chapter (Chapter Ten) in Part Three was written by Hirsch Greenberg, Jana Grekul, and Rhonda Nelson. The focus of the chapter is on Aboriginal youth, who, like other minority groups around the world, are overrepresented in the Canadian youth justice system. After providing some disheartening statistics of the nature and type of this overrepresentation, the authors move on to provide a sound historical context by which to understand how and why Aboriginal youth have become so closely aligned with youth crime. Through clear examples they show how 'specific historical policies and processes have contributed to intergenerational experiences of trauma' and overrepresentation in the youth criminal justice system. Then, by drawing on the Aboriginal perspective, Greenberg, Grekul, and Nelson show how using Aboriginal-based approaches to justice may better fit the needs and values of Aboriginal youth. The overarching approach that is expressed through this chapter may be referred to as a social justice–based approach. For readers not familiar with the contextual framework of Aboriginal youth, the authors present a critically compelling argument for major reforms in how we have traditionally dealt with young Aboriginal offenders.

In Chapter Eleven, Mark Totten tackles the topic of gang-involved youth in Canada. While a topical and controversial subject matter, 'youth gangs' are generally not well understood due to their nature and complexity. Couched within the context that there is very limited reliable data on the actual nature and number of gangs in Canada, Totten begins by describing the three major types of gangs that exist in Canada: street gangs, mid-level gangs, and organized crime groups. Among other elements, by referring to specific type of gangs, he provides a clear examination of their structure, history, prevalence across Canada, and criminal activity. Based on available information, Totten provides a descriptive overview of such topics as recruiting and exiting, and criminal activity. He then goes on to point out that while the legislation (i.e., Bill C-24, which came into effect on 1 February, 2002) has attempted to define gang-related activity, it 'has not been successfully applied in many cases'. Totten then explores a range of theories that have been used to explain gang engagement and provides an overview of certain key risk factors such as family, school peer group, and community, which can all contribute to predisposing a young person to joining a gang. The final section of the chapter summarizes some of the intervention and prevention programs that have been introduced across Canada to combat youth gangs or deter young people from joining gangs. Yet in spite of the image many might have of gangs or gang members, Totten reminds the reader that for many it is not a lifestyle choice and that they are often 'troubled youth' in need of support.

Bruce MacLaurin and Catherine Worthington co-authored Chapter Twelve, which focuses on street-involved youth in Canada. Although regularly overlooked, or given only passing attention in most books on young offenders, the authors offer clear insight into the important relationship between street-involved youth and youth crime. Through their careful review of the different typologies of street involvement, they identify the various risk factors (i.e., pathways) that may result in street youth turning to delinquent behaviour for myriad reasons. In addition to discussing the impact of street involvement on the education system and on child welfare, MacLaurin and Worthington include an examination of the impact of street involvement on the criminal justice system. And, as with all the chapters in this section, they discuss intervention and prevention strategies but point out that such services are underutilized. However, drawing on their related work they offer some examples that have proven promising. The chapter concludes by reiterating that not only are street youth a marginalized group, they are also a diverse and complex group of young people, who, despite being resilient, have their own unique challenges that deserve careful attention.

The final chapter in this section (Chapter Thirteen) was prepared by Susan McIntyre. McIntyre addresses a longstanding concern but from a unique perspective. While there exists a rich body of literature on female adolescent prostitution, McIntyre instead directs her attention to sexual exploitation of young men. As reflected in the title to her chapter, it is a topic that has remained largely 'under the radar'. Yet over the years McIntyre has accumulated the most comprehensive data set of its kind in Canada. She uses the data set to provide a detailed and expansive overview of sexually exploited young men. Most of the data used is based on first-person accounts of sexually exploited males rather than relying on service-provided insight/feedback. Her discussion shows that the nature, extent, and characteristics of sexually exploited young men are different than those of their female counterparts. McIntyre's discussion also shows that the risk factors for young males also differ from those of their female counterparts, and hence require different intervention and prevention strategies. For example, males are more likely to be victims of gay bashing and violence. The chapter concludes by pointing out that, as with most types of youth crime and problems, young males do not enter the sex trade by choice but, once involved, 'it is not easy to leave the trade'. In fact, McIntyre notes that 'comparatively nothing has been done for young males'.

9 Issues of Substance Abuse and Related Crime in Adolescence

Jordan Diplock and Darryl Plecas

Overview

This chapter provides an overview of some of the major issues surrounding substance use and abuse among youth in Canada. To provide background for these issues in Canada, the first half of the chapter presents information on the nature and extent of adolescent substance use, the reasons young people use drugs and alcohol, and the potential harms of substance use for adolescents. The chapter then discusses in more depth how adolescent substance use and abuse relates to crime in this age group. The sections focus specifically on the theories and evidence suggesting a link between substance use and crime, the nature and extent of adolescent participation in drug-specific crimes, and the strategies used to prevent adolescents from getting involved in substance abuse and related criminal activity. This chapter allows students to critically assess the current situation surrounding substance use among youth in Canada to inform their opinions about the future steps that policy-makers, researchers, and law-enforcement officials should take to deal with these many issues.

Key Objectives

After reading this chapter, you should be able to:

- Identify the most common substances used by young people in Canada, and argue the degree to which the rates of usage of those substances should be of concern to Canadians.
- Identify the challenges inherent in conducting research studies on the prevalence of youth substance use and abuse.
- Recognize some of the reasons youth become involved with drugs, and have an understanding of the issues surrounding this topic.
- Identify the main potential negative consequences of various types of drug use.
- Discuss the link between adolescent drug use and criminal behaviour.
- Explain the role drug markets play in providing opportunities for youth to become involved in criminal activity.
- Critically assess current anti-drug strategies targeted at youth.
- Consider viable alternatives to current anti-drug strategies to reduce rates of or limit the harm associated with adolescent substance abuse.

Introduction

The use and abuse of licit and illicit substances has become a part of the social landscape in Canada, as it has in other parts of the world. For example, although there has been considerable success in reducing rates of smoking across Canada (a decrease of 7 per cent from 1999 to 2009), nearly one-fifth (18 per cent) of Canadians over the age of 15 were current smokers in 2008 (Health Canada 2010b). Alcohol consumption represents a major component of Canadian leisure-time culture, with Canadians ranking among the world's top 50 in per capital alcohol consumption (World Health Organization 2004). In addition to legal substance use, illegal drugs have become a serious concern in Canada. In recent years, the United Nations has named Canada (UN Office on Drugs and Crime 2010) as a source country for the exportation of both marijuana and designer drugs such as methamphetamine and ecstasy through large and increasingly sophisticated production operations (Diplock, Kirkland, Malm, and Plecas 2005; Plecas and Diplock 2007; Plecas, Malm, and Kinney 2005). The country is also home to more than 100 000 intravenous drug users, many living in urban areas such as Vancouver's infamous Downtown Eastside (Urban Health Research Initiative 2009). These issues have occurred concurrently with a general increase in the number of Canadians who believe that marijuana possession should no longer be illegal (Millhorn et al. 2009). This current reality inevitably exposes young Canadians to these substances, and contributes to the ongoing concern that youth in this country will face serious life problems related to **substance abuse**.

Generally, there are many reasons substance abuse among youth is a serious concern for Canadians. Paramount among them is that substance abuse in adolescence may be detrimental to a young person's future. Whether that is a result of negative health consequences, the development of mental illness, implications for academic and career success, the link to other drugs, addiction, or involvement in criminal behaviour, there may be substantial costs to individuals, to their families, and indeed to all Canadians. Estimates based on figures from 2002 suggest the costs of substance abuse totalled $39.8 billion (Rehm et al. 2006). While the majority of these costs are not likely the direct result of substance abuse by youth, there is a prevailing belief that early prevention can reduce the future harms and social costs of substance abuse (Lubman, Hides, Yucel, and Toumbourou 2007). The continued efforts from the various levels of government across the country to reduce rates of tobacco, alcohol, and illicit substance use, specifically within the youth population,

substance abuse
Excessive, unhealthy use of a substance such as alcohol, tobacco, or illicit drugs.

demonstrate official recognition that these behaviours can and do place considerable burdens on Canadians, primarily with respect to loss of productivity, enforcement and criminal justice, health care, and other social-welfare systems. Even with this recognition and the accompanying efforts and funding to address substance abuse in Canada, properly addressing this issue remains a considerable challenge amid the perceived ubiquity of drugs and alcohol in the country (see Fischer, Rehm, and Hall 2009; Saewyc 2009).

The most recent National Anti-Drug Strategy from the Government of Canada (2007) was unveiled in 2007 and has a strong focus on youth substance abuse. One initiative is a national awareness campaign, 'drugsnot4me', which includes television commercials and websites with information targeting young people and their parents with the focus of discouraging drug use and experimentation (Health Canada 2009). Accompanying the awareness campaign is increased funding for drug treatment as well as enforcement and intervention for youth struggling with substance abuse (Government of Canada 2007). Such a national strategy and the millions of dollars in funding (Department of Justice Canada 2010) in addition to private and government websites, programs, and other information resources indicate that substance abuse among youth is a priority issue in Canada.

Is all this concern over substance abuse among youth in Canada warranted? Are the hundreds of millions of dollars spent annually across the country on prevention initiatives, research, policing, courts, and corrections in hope of discouraging youth from starting or continuing drug and alcohol use going toward appropriate policy decisions? Or, conversely, is more emphasis needed on youth substance abuse issues, with increased enforcement powers, more and better treatment options, and more pervasive educational programs? This chapter will provide the reader with some of the information to begin to answer these and other related questions.

The chapter begins with an overview of the situation of adolescent substance use in Canada: the types of drugs that are most commonly used by those within this age group, the rates of use of school and college-aged youth, as well as some of the challenges of gathering an accurate picture of the true extent of substance abuse among youth. The overview is followed by a section that investigates the reasons youth use drugs; having an understanding of these underlying reasons for drug use is important for judging the necessity and potential efficacy of current and alternative policy options. Subsequently, the chapter presents information on the negative effect that substance abuse can have on young people, focusing specifically on issues of impairment, negative general and mental health consequences, and addiction. The chapter continues with a focus on crime, with sections discussing the link between youth substance abuse and consequent criminal behaviour, and youth involvement in drug crimes such as possession of illicit substances, drug dealing, and participation in drug production and trafficking networks. The chapter then explores existing strategies to prevent youth substance abuse and drug crime, specifically focusing on the most common programs and potential alternatives. Finally, a summary emphasizes the important issues from the chapter and suggests next steps for future learning and making positive contributions to ongoing discussions of what to do about youth substance abuse.

Substance Abuse among Canadian Youth

Some commentators have suggested that drug use among youth is at or near an 'epidemic' level in Canada (Teed 2009). Statistics from provincial and national surveys support the conclusions that substance use of one type or another is common among youth, with alcohol, marijuana, and tobacco being the most commonly used substances (Paglia-Boak and Adlaf 2007). However, for most drug categories, use among youth has been decreasing in recent years (Centre for Addiction Research in BC 2008; Health Canada 2010a). While some may hold the view that any use is too much when it comes to young people in this country, the fact remains that the majority of those in the general youth population between the ages of 15 and 24 do not report the use of illicit drugs, of tobacco smoking, or of frequent, heavy alcohol consumption (Health Canada 2010a).

Recent survey results from students in grades 7 to 12 in British Columbia (Centre for Addictions Research in BC 2009) and Alberta (Alberta Health Services 2008) indicate that apart from alcohol (54 per cent in BC; 52 per cent in Alberta), tobacco (26 per cent in BC; 30 per cent in Alberta), and marijuana (30 per cent in BC; 21 per cent in Alberta), the only other category of drugs that had a rate of life-time use greater than 10 per cent was that of prescription drugs (15 per cent in BC; 17 per cent in Alberta). Generally, there has been little variation in substance abuse rates among youth between provinces (Leslie 2008), although there may be specific youth populations that exhibit unique issues related to substance abuse. In Ontario, one study (Brands, Paglia-Boak, Sproule, and Leslie 2010) found it was much more common for students to have used prescription painkillers (i.e., opioid analgesics) for non-medical reasons (20 per cent used in the previous year). Typically, substance abuse increases with age during adolescence (Leslie 2008), and therefore, the overall figures indicated above are higher than the rates of life-time use for students in the lower grades and lower than the actual rates for students in the higher grades.

Alcohol Use

The history of alcohol use dates back to around 10 000 BCE; it has been commonly used for nutrition, medicine, relaxation, pleasure, and religious worship (Hanson 1995). It is the most common substance used by youth, with three-quarters of people between ages 15 and 24 having consumed alcohol at least once in the year prior to the 2009 survey (Health Canada 2010a). While alcohol is a legal substance, there are age restrictions and other regulations to control its use in Canada. The legal minimum age to purchase and consume alcohol is 19 in all provinces other than Alberta, Manitoba, and Québec, where the legal minimum age is 18.

Alcohol acts as a nervous system depressant, initially producing feelings of relaxation and diminished inhibitions; then, depending on the dose and rate of drinking, it can lead to intoxication, including a loss of balance, delayed reactions, impaired vision and other senses, confusion, impaired memory, dizziness, vomiting, and unconsciousness. The initial effects of alcohol that increase sociability along with the social culture of alcohol that is perpetuated through marketing (American Academy of Pediatrics [AAP] 2010) and misperceptions about the alcohol consumption of peers (Martens, Page, Mowry, Damann, Taylor, and Cimini 2006) make it a popular drug for youth and as well as adults.

Tobacco Use

While much less common than drinking alcohol, tobacco smoking is one of the most commonly used substances by youth. Yet until a little more than a decade ago, 'comparatively little attention or concern [was] directed towards tobacco use among young people' (McDougall, Vajushi, and Winterdyk 2005, p. 162). Those young people who smoke tobacco often begin in early adolescence (Health Canada 2006). Of the grades 7 through 12 students in Alberta who responded to a survey in 2008, less than 5 per cent had smoked tobacco in the 30 days prior to the survey, but of those who had ever tried smoking, more than 80 per cent had smoked their first cigarette at age 15 or younger (Alberta Health Service 2008). Much like alcohol, each province has a minimum age of 18 or 19 to buy tobacco products. Although tobacco use among Canadians appears to be declining (Health Canada 2010), the addictive quality of nicotine, the stimulant drug within tobacco, and the numerous negative health consequences associated to long-term cigarette smoking make its use among youth a major concern in Canada.

Illicit Drug Use

With the exception of marijuana use, illicit drug use is not common within the general youth population in Canada. Indeed, in the most recent 2009 Canadian Alcohol and Drug Monitoring Survey (Health Canada 2010a), 26 per cent of youth and young adults between ages 15 and 24 reported using marijuana (also referred to as the 'gateway drug'; street names include 'dope', 'grass', 'pot', or 'weed') in the past year, while only 6 per cent of those from the same age group indicated using any one of cocaine ('rock', 'snow', 'C', or 'coke'); heroin ('junk', 'smack', 'H', or 'horse'); inhalants (gasoline and other solvents, aerosol sprays, commercially available gases, and nitrites); methamphetamines ('crank', 'jib', 'ice', 'crystal meth', or 'meth'); amphetamines ('speed'); club drugs, such as ecstasy ('MDMA', 'X', 'XTC', or 'hug drug'), ketamine, and GHB; or other hallucinogens in the past year. Both of these figures were substantially higher than the previous-year usage rates for adults over the age of 25 (almost four times higher for previous-year marijuana use and almost five times higher for previous-year use of other drugs) (Health Canada 2010a). Simultaneous polysubstance use—the use of a combination of two or more substances concomitantly—is also common among some adolescent drug-using populations, with alcohol, marijuana, and tobacco the most commonly mixed substances (Barrett, Darredeau, and Pihl 2006). Perhaps the higher rates of marijuana use are the product of an ongoing debate over its legal status 'characterized by selective reporting or the misuse or misinterpretation of available information' (Diplock, Cohen, and Plecas 2009, p. 1), a debate that has, as of yet, not been taken up for other illicit drugs.

Given the wide array of effects of these other illicit drugs, their illegal status, and a general lack of acceptance in mainstream society, it is not surprising that the usage rates of these drugs among youth are low compared with alcohol, tobacco, and marijuana, just as they are for adults. Given the general decrease in youth illicit substance use and the concurrent decreases or stabilizing of adult rates (Health Canada 2010a), perhaps what the comparison of previous-year usage rates between youth and adults indicates is that greater experimentation occurs during adolescence, but that the majority of illicit drug–using youth abstain later in adulthood.

Table 9.1 Changes in Past-Year Substance Use among Canadian Youth* from 2004 to 2009

Substance	% Past Year Use (2004)	% Past Year Use (2009)	% Change	
Alcohol	82.9	75.5	–7.4	↓
Cannabis	37.0	26.3	–10.7	↓
Tobacco				
15–19 yrs	18.0	13.0	–5.0	↓
20–24 yrs	28.0	23.0	–5.0	
Cocaine/Crack	5.5	3.0	-2.5	↓
Ecstasy	4.4	3.6	–0.8	↓

*Age 15–24

Source: Health Canada. (2010a). Canadian alcohol and drug use monitoring survey. Retrieved September 13, 2010, from www.hc-sc.gc.ca/hc-ps/drugs-drogues/stat/_2009/summary-sommaire-eng.php; Health Canada. (2010b). Canadian tobacco use monitoring survey: Smoking prevalence 1999–2009. Retrieved September 14, 2010, from www.hc-sc.gc.ca/hc-ps/tobac-tabac/research-recherche/stat/_ctums-esutc_prevalence/prevalence-eng.php

Inherent Challenges of Measuring Adolescent Drug Use

Drug and alcohol surveys are inherently unable to procure information from the entire youth population. The information obtained through these types of surveys typically comes from the general youth population; in other words, from youth who attend public schools or from youth who can be contacted through telephone surveys, and who agree to participate in the surveys. In addition to a wide array of potential methodological problems with these types of self-report surveys—such as **social desirability effects**, errors in memory, exaggeration, and deception (Palys 1997)—the selection biases necessarily exclude the drug use of those youth who do not attend school or rarely attend school, and those youth who are homeless or otherwise marginalized. In Canada, estimates of the number of **street-involved youth** have been cited at 150 000 (Public Health Agency of Canada 2006; also, see Chapter 12 in this textbook). While these adolescents do not comprise a substantial portion of the age group, researchers who have studied these populations have found that they are at greater risk than mainstream youth to use both non-injection and injection drugs and to engage in unsafe sexual behaviour, and that they suffer from various health problems and mental illnesses (Werb, Kerr, Li, Montaner, and Wood 2008).

Without obtaining information from these marginalized youth, the official rates of national drug use likely underestimate to some degree the true extent of adolescent usage. Perhaps, as some commentators (see Saewyc 2007) have suggested, focusing on measuring and discouraging substance abuse in mainstream youth is misguided, as most of the problems related to substance abuse will manifest within the most at-risk populations: populations that are currently difficult to study and that are targeted by law-enforcement anti-drug measures while being largely ignored by anti-drug awareness campaigns.

social desirability effects
Biases in research caused by respondents' desire to provide what they feel is the socially acceptable response or 'what the researcher wants to hear'.

street-involved youth
A heterogeneous population of youth between ages 12 and 24 who lack adequate shelter and are considered to live outside the mainstream youth population.

Reasons Youth Use Drugs and Alcohol

With the exception of rare cases, initiation of substance use requires adolescents to make the decision to use. And, given the restrictions in place to prohibit youth access to alcohol, tobacco, and illicit drugs, adolescents have to make this decision in defiance of official opposition and the potential consequences of such defiance. Therefore, as part of understanding the issue of adolescent substance abuse, it is important to consider those factors that overcome the messages that discourage drug and alcohol experimentation and use.

For Pleasure

One key rationale that adolescents offer for substance use in self-report surveys is enjoyment (Terry-McElrath, O'Malley, and Johnston 2009). Such enjoyment is generally equated with increasing positive experiences while at parties or during other social events. While there may be other underlying reasons, such as a lack of enjoyable pro-social alternatives, many young people are drawn to the promise of pleasure offered by drugs. Perceptions can compound this, as research has demonstrated that youth regularly overestimate the prevalence of alcohol and drug use among their peer group (Martens et al. 2006), and that users may downplay the negative aspects of their drug use experiences (Hayaki, Hagerty, Herman, Dois, Anderson, and Stein 2010). Since adolescents may perceive substance use as a normative method of enjoyment, the role of pleasure within the context of youth drug use should not be overlooked by assuming that all substance abuse necessarily stems from an underlying pathology (Hunt, Moloney, and Evans 2009).

As a Result of Peer Pressure

Researchers generally accept that young people are influenced by their peer group as they seek to establish their identity, and that much socialization occurs within these groups (Harris 1995).

Feeling pressure from drug- and alcohol-using peers is often emphasized as a reason for adolescent substance use. With the inaccurate perceptions adolescents hold with regards to the prevalence and regularity of their peers' drug and alcohol use (Martens et al. 2006), peer pressure, or the perception of peer pressure, may play a role in substance use despite existing prohibitions. If drug and alcohol use is perceived as normative, young people may view the social consequences of not partaking as more detrimental than the consequences prescribed by the law or others in authority. This may be more relevant for explaining early experimentation with substance use, as adolescents may perceive substance use as a social developmental milestone or rite of passage within their peer group (Bonomo 2005).

Social factors may, however, be less important to continuation than the perceived psychological and physical effects of the drug (Bailey, Flewelling, and Rachal 1992; Cooper, May, Soderstrom, and Jarjoura 2009), as those youth who do not enjoy their first experience are likely to make the choice to discontinue. While it is common that youth with friends who use alcohol and drugs also tend to be involved with these substances, it is also true that youth who abstain tend to associate with peers who also abstain (Bauman and Ennett 1996). Therefore, while peer pressure may influence a young person's decision to try alcohol and other drugs, the interplay between social factors and personal choices becomes more complex as youth decide whether or not to continue using by considering the preferences of their peers and their own perceptions of the benefits and risks involved.

As a Means of Coping

Adolescence is a time of transition and experimentation, often causing a number of struggles for youth as they navigate the changes (Wolfe, Jaffe, and Crooks 2006), and some adolescents turn to drug use as a coping mechanism for other difficulties in their lives (Terry-McElrath et al. 2009). While perhaps less likely than experimenting with drugs and alcohol for excitement and social approval, difficulty coping with life stressors could be related to initiation of substance use. In fact, it may be the promise of excitement and social approval that leads some adolescents to believe that drugs and alcohol will help them to cope with their life stressors. Some youth struggling with a difficult home life, poor school performance, mental illness, or any number of other issues may perceive drugs and alcohol as an escape by witnessing other youth experiencing enjoyment and social rewards. Coping may also be a potential reason for continuation of substance use because even if a young person first tries drugs for excitement or as a result of peer pressure, he or she may eventually begin to equate the positive feelings associated with alcohol and drug use as a method to cope with life stressors that arise after initiation. Perhaps predicting if adolescent substance abuse will become problematic in the future can be aided by knowing the reasons behind the initiation and continued use before such problems occur.

Potential Negative Effects of Adolescent Substance Abuse

Consequences of Impairment

While youth may consume drugs to experience a 'high' for reasons of enjoyment or escape, there is certainly a risk of serious negative consequences due to impairment and intoxication. Accidents and self-induced injuries were among the most common causes of alcohol- and illegal-drug-related hospitalizations and death in Canada in 2002 (Rehm et al. 2006). While injuries due to alcohol alone or in combination with drugs represented only a small proportion (0.6 per cent of all visits for youth under age 25) of overall visits to Canadian emergency rooms for young people between

2000 and 2003, the rates increased with age, and increased annually for all age groups (Lea, Black, and Asbridge 2009). While not a prolific cause of injury among youth, according to official medical documentation, injuries can arise as the result of either the injured person's own impairment or the impairment of another person.

In addition to injuries, young people often experience other potentially negative consequences of drugs and alcohol. Substance use may result in unplanned, unwanted, or unprotected sexual activity; a drive in a car driven by an intoxicated driver; an inability to remember events; passing out; arguing with family; and committing criminal acts (Centre for Addictions Research in BC 2009; Leslie 2008). Therefore, even if the intention of consuming drugs and alcohol is to have fun, youth run the risk of engaging in behaviours that can have immediate and long-term negative repercussions.

General Health Risks

Depending on the type of substance used and the **method of administration**, substance abuse can have serious adverse effects on the health of users young and old. The most serious potential harm of drugs and alcohol use is death, which occurred in 8103 cases related to alcohol, in 1695 cases related to illegal drugs, and in 37 209 cases related to tobacco use in Canada in 2002 (Rehm et al. 2006). In terms of death as a result of consequences to a person's general health (as separate from those resulting from accidents and suicides), alcohol-related deaths were most commonly linked to cirrhosis of the liver (1246), esophageal cancer (501), and cardiac arrhythmias (449). Tobacco-related deaths were typically caused by the effects of smoking, namely cancers (most commonly lung cancer, 13 401), cardiovascular diseases (most commonly ischemic heart disease, 5343), and respiratory diseases (most commonly chronic obstructive pulmonary disease, 7533). More than half of all deaths related to illegal drug use were as a result of overdose (958), while hepatitis C (165) or HIV (87) was also a major cause of death (Rehm et al. 2006).

While death is the most serious potential consequence to the health of drug and alcohol users, there are other negative health conditions linked to substance abuse, ranging from debilitating to inconvenient. The chemicals themselves can have damaging effects on the body. For example, the nicotine in tobacco can cause the narrowing of arteries, reducing the blood supply to the heart and making it work harder (Benowitz 2009). Cocaine and other stimulants produce a similar effect on the cardiovascular system and can lead to increased respiration, rapid and irregular heartbeat, increased blood pressure, and hyperthermia (NIDA 2010). These symptoms increase the risk of heart attack and stroke (Coombs 2007; Treadwell and Robinson 2007). Heroin and other opioids, such as codeine, morphine, and oxycodone, can slow respiration to dangerous levels (NIDA 2010). And heavy alcohol use, or **binge drinking**, typically defined as five or more drinks on a single occasion, has also been linked to liver and kidney diseases, various cancers, heart disease, and malnutrition (Rehm, Giesbrecht, Popova, Patra, Adlaf, and Mann 2006).

The method of administration of the drug can also be a factor in the negative health consequences of consumption. For substances administered through smoking combusted plant matter, such as tobacco or marijuana, the majority of the harm stems from the introduction of chemicals into the lungs. Smoking can lead to symptoms of obstructive pulmonary disease, lower respiratory tract infections, and cancers, although this has not been substantiated for marijuana use (Diplock and Plecas 2009). Intravenous injection of drugs such as heroin, cocaine, and methamphetamine can not only be damaging to the veins, but also puts the user at a greatly increased risk of contracting illnesses such as hepatitis B and C, HIV, and other infections (Thorpe et al. 2002). Intranasal administration, or snorting, can cause irritation to the nasal lining, chronic running or bleeding nose, loss of smell, and difficulty swallowing (Centre for Addiction and Mental Health [CAMH] 2003). Therefore, while it is important to stress the negative health consequences of the drugs themselves

method of administration
The path by which a drug or other substance is brought into contact with the body. Common methods include smoking, ingestion, injection, and intranasal inhalation.

binge drinking
Heavy alcohol consumption over a short period of time for the purpose of becoming intoxicated. Generally, the concept is operationalized as the consumption of five or more drinks on one occasion (four or more for females).

to discourage use among adolescents, it is equally as important to disseminate information about the harms associated with particular methods of consuming those drugs and to offer alternatives that will reduce the potential for harm caused by the method of administration.

Psychological Health Risks

Drug and alcohol use can lead to serious negative consequences to a person's mental health. This may be especially true for adolescent users, as the developing adolescent brain may be more vulnerable to effects of these substances (Lubman, Yucel, and Hall 2007; Vaccarino 2007). Recent research has suggested that substance use in adolescents can lead to abnormalities in brain functioning (Squeglia, Jacobus, and Tapert 2009). However, because few adolescent drug users do not also use alcohol, challenges arise in separating the effects of various substances on adolescent brain development (Squeglia et al. 2009). Thoma et al. (2010) found that, consistent with the body of literature relating to the effects of substance abuse on rodent brain development, heavy alcohol use and marijuana use in human adolescents leads to reduced attention and executive functions and to memory detriments, respectively. While further research is necessary, these changes to the structure and processes in young developing brains may put early onset substance users at greater risk of acquiring long-term cognitive impairment, mental illness, and addiction.

In 2002, substance abuse led to 2058 alcohol-related and 1517 illegal-drug-related psychiatric hospitalizations in Canada (Rehm et al. 2006). Psychoses were the most common causes of psychiatric hospitalization related to illicit drug use (Rehm et al. 2006). There is some evidence that the use of stimulants—such as cocaine, amphetamines, and methamphetamine—can also cause **psychosis** (Dore and Sweeting 2006). Furthermore, marijuana use might also trigger the onset of psychosis in those people with an existing predisposition (Degenhardt and Hall 2006). In other cases, prolonged or heavy substance use can result in what is known as drug-induced psychosis, a condition where the user exhibits psychotic symptoms, such as hallucinations, delusions, memory loss, and confusion, for a temporary period (CAMH 1999). Adolescent drug use, particularly exposure at an earlier age, may put users at a greater risk of developing psychosis resulting from or triggered by substance abuse (Konings, Henquet, Maharajh, Hutchinson, and van Os 2008; Smith, Thirthalli, Abdallah, Murray, and Cottler 2009).

As is the case with psychosis, studies have found high levels of **co-morbidity** of substance abuse and mental health problems among adolescents similar to levels among adults (Chan, Dennis, and Funk 2008). Other mental health problems co-occurring with substance abuse include depression and anxiety (Chan et al. 2008). However, trying to determine whether substance abuse is a causal factor in mental illness presents researchers with a considerable challenge. Studies are often limited because it is difficult to determine if substance abuse caused a change to brain functioning that in turn led to mental illness, or if the onset of mental illness was a factor in the initiation of drug use (Degenhardt, Hall, and Lynskey 2002). While the sequence of events that explains the link between substance abuse and mental illness requires continued study, there is evidence to suggest that some substances may trigger mental illness in those already predisposed and may exacerbate, or prolong, symptoms in those already experiencing mental health illness (Grech, van Os, Jones, Lewis, and Murray 2005).

Addiction

Because the adolescent brain is in a stage of development, some researchers believe that substance abuse during this period may put the user at a greater risk of changes to brain structure and functioning that could lead to addiction (Lubman et al. 2007; Squeglia et al. 2009; Vaccarino 2007). Addiction, also called **dependence**, generally refers to either psychological or physical dependence

psychosis
A symptom of mental illness involving a substantial alteration to an individual's personality and a loss of contact with objective reality.

co-morbidity
Two or more independent and coexisting medical conditions.

dependence
When an individual feels that use of a substance is necessary for normal daily functioning or when substance use leads to tolerance. Abruptly stopping use may lead to symptoms of withdrawal.

on a substance. According to the Centre for Addiction and Mental Health (CAMH 2009), psycho-logical dependence exists when a substance abuser feels that he or she needs the drug in order to function or feel normal. Physical dependence occurs when a substance abuser's body has developed a tolerance, meaning that a higher dose of the drug is necessary to get the same effect. Furthermore, when substance abuse stops, the user may feel symptoms of withdrawal (CAMH 2009). In some research, behaviours considered necessary to meet the established criteria for being classified as drug dependent include tolerance, withdrawal, taking the drug for longer periods of time or in lar-ger doses than intended, an inability to stop or reduce use, an increase in the time spent obtaining the drug and recovering from its effects, ignoring other important activities, and continuing use despite undesirable consequences (Looby and Earlywine 2007).

Dependency is not the reality for the majority of Canadians. In fact, only 8.8 per cent of Canadians age 15 and over were considered 'probable' or 'highly probable' for alcohol dependence, and only 0.8 per cent were considered dependent on illicit drugs (Statistics Canada 2002). The nicotine in tobacco has been known for years to be very addictive, and while smoking in Canada is becoming less com-mon, current smokers use an average of 16 cigarettes per day and often experience serious difficulties quitting due to withdrawal symptoms (CAMH 2009). Despite the low rates of dependence in Canada, addiction is a serious concern. The compulsive drug seeking that accompanies addiction, in concert with or as a result of an increased tolerance to the effects of the drug, compels the addicted substance abuser to use more and to continue to use despite negative experiences (Friedman 2009). As a result of a decreased ability to make proper decisions and judge consequences, the compulsive drug seeking can put the substance user in potentially harmful situations, and can preoccupy his or her thoughts and behaviours to the detriment of other important aspects of life (Friedman 2009). Furthermore, continued drug use puts the user at greater risk of developing the health and mental health afflictions discussed earlier. These consequences are exacerbated by the social **stigma** surrounding drug abuse— a stigma fuelled by the self-destructive, burdensome, and victimizing behaviour that can result from addiction (Room 2005). Therefore, while addiction may be uncommon, the consequences are dire because it is a condition where the drug user may require a great deal of support and yet be separated or marginalized from the mainstream sources of that support (Mooney 2005).

stigma
A behaviour or attribute that causes an individual to be discredited, rejected socially, or negatively stereotyped.

Adolescent Substance Abuse and the Link to Criminal Behaviour

The link between substance use and crime has been explored on an ongoing basis in criminology. Generally, this discussion has excluded the link between crime and tobacco smoking, although tobacco smoking is common among offender populations (Donahue 2009) and often plays a role in prison culture (Richmond, Butler, Wilhelm, Wodak, Cunningham, and Anderson 2009). Further-more, tobacco smuggling to avoid taxation has also become an emerging criminal problem in Can-ada (Kelton and Givel 2008). However, as tobacco crimes and the link between tobacco smoking and crime are typically outside of the general discussion on the drug–crime relationship, the focus of this section and the subsequent section will be on alcohol and illicit drugs.

In Canada, data on federal and provincial inmates, as well as on arrestees, indicated that more than half of offenders from each of these groups were intoxicated by illicit drugs, alcohol, or both during the commission of the most serious crimes (Pernanen, Cousineau, Brochu, and Sun 2002). This study did not provide the proportions for young offenders alone, but it is not uncommon for adolescents to commit crime while impaired by drugs or alcohol (Brunelle, Brochu, and Cousineau 2000). While evidence suggests that approximately half of the offenders involved in crime are sub-stance abusers, according to data from the United States, the vast majority of those who use illicit drugs or alcohol do not become negatively involved with the law (Office of National Drug Control Policy 2000). This supports the conclusions of others (Harrison, Erickson, Adlaf, and Freeman 2001) that although there is a strong relationship between adolescent substance abuse and crime, there are likely other underlying factors that contribute to both.

The explanations for the link between substance abuse and crime have typically relied on the tripartite drug-crime model first discussed by Goldstein (1985), suggesting that drug use causes crime through three distinct modes: (1) psychopharmacological, (2) economic compulsive, and (3) systemic. The first, psychopharmacological, refers to the idea that the intoxicating effects of the substances change a person's behaviour in such a way that causes that person to act out and break the rules. A person may also use the drug to inhibit feelings of nervousness or fear in order to partake in crime (Brunelle et al. 2000). The second mode, economic compulsive, posits that some drug users commit crime in order to obtain the money to support expensive drug use. Finally, the third mode, systemic, suggests that the nature of the drug market requires those involved to commit crime, generally violent crime, to protect territory, maintain supply, and retrieve debts. According to the work of Brunelle et al. (2000), only the first two modes of the tripartite drug-crime model appear to be relevant to discussion on crime committed by adolescent substance users. However, even with these explanatory linkages between drug use and crime, the relationship is a complex one (Casavant and Collin 2001).

Adolescent Crime Caused by Impairment

Crimes such as property damage, public disorder, violent offences, shoplifting and other thefts, and driving offences are some of the most common offences committed by adolescents and adults under age 25 (Diplock and Plecas 2010). These offences are also those that are commonly linked to alcohol and drug use (Bromley and Nelson 2002; Felson, Salvolainen, Aaltonen, and Moustgaard 2008), which could be an indication that substance use among adolescents leads to participation in criminal behaviour and other rule-breaking activities. As we noted previously, some believe that the impairment caused by substance use results in a change in behaviour, sometimes manifesting as crime. This argument is generally more applicable to substances, such as alcohol, that have a disinhibiting effect. For example, research has found that rates of alcohol use were statistically significantly related to rates of violent offending but the same was not true for rates of cocaine use (Martin, Maxwell, White, and Zhang 2004). Moreover, the same study (Martin et al. 2004) found that neither cocaine use nor alcohol use was statistically significantly associated to property crime. Other research (Harrison et al. 2001) found significant relationships between aggregate use of all substances and violent behaviour among their adolescent samples from both Canada and the United States, but concluded that the relationships were best explained as spurious. Therefore, while the psychopharmacological argument suggesting substance use causes crime may make sense, there are likely confounding variables that explain both the criminal behaviour and the substance abuse of these youth independently.

Of course, there are specific offences that do involve the use of a substance as a major component of the offence. The most obvious example is impaired driving, which generally necessitates the consumption of alcohol or drugs. In a recent roadside survey of British Columbian drivers, results indicated that 8.1 per cent and 10.4 per cent had been drinking or using drugs, respectively (Beirness and Beasley 2009). While no one aged 16 through 18 was found to be drinking, the rates of drug use among drivers was comparable across all age groups, with 9 per cent of those age 16 to 18 and 10 per cent of those age 19 to 24 having consumed drugs prior to driving. Among those cases where drug use was found, marijuana was the most frequently used, followed by cocaine, and then opiates (Beirness and Beasley 2009). As there are maximum legal limits for BAC (blood alcohol concentration), above which is legally prohibited by the Canadian Criminal Code, low levels of BAC may not constitute impaired driving; however, in many adolescent drivers' licensing regimes, any alcohol consumption represents an infraction. Given the lack of consensus on how drug concentrations in the body relate to impairment, there is no legally prescribed limit for drug consumption prior to driving, but recent changes to impaired driving legislation have given police the power to perform **drug recognition expert (DRE) evaluation** to test potentially impaired drivers for signs of drug intoxication (Department of Justice 2009). In 2009, over 1400 incidents of drug-impaired driving were reported by police, making up 2 per cent of all impaired driving incidents (Dauvergne and Turner 2010).

Drug and alcohol impairment may also lead to crime in another way: youth may become easier targets of violence, thefts, and sexual assaults when they are impaired by substance use. According to research by McClelland and Teplin (2001), alcohol intoxication contributes substantially to violent offending, particularly increasing the risk to those who would otherwise be unlikely victims, such as non-minorities, males, and people of higher socio-economic status. Another study (Shepherd, Sutherland, and Newcombe 2006) found a similar finding among a sample of adolescents, suggesting that alcohol use, independent of other factors, increased the vulnerability to victimization. Alcohol intoxication is also a major contributing factor in rapes of young college women (Testa and Livingston 2009). While drug use is also related to victimization, other factors such as heavy drinking are also often present, which perhaps influence the relationship more than drug use alone. Still, research suggests that while heavy drinking puts young males at a greater risk of victimization than young females, young female illicit drug users may be at a greater risk of victimization as a result of their substance abuse than their male counterparts are (Wells and Thompson 2009).

Adolescent Crime Resulting from the Search for Drugs

The second explanatory link in Goldstein's (1985) often-cited model, economic compulsion, posits that substance abusers commit crimes to obtain money to get drugs. These types of crimes may be simple thefts of money or may include activities such as stealing items to sell to obtain drugs, stealing items to save legitimate money for drugs, or engaging in illegal money-making activities such as prostitution or selling drugs (Bennet and Holloway 2009). Brunelle et al. (2000) suggest that the economic powerlessness of adolescents is a factor that might push them toward crime in order to consume even less expensive drugs. Youth have fewer opportunities to make money through work, unemployment insurance, social welfare, or by selling possessions and, therefore, may be more likely to resort to crime to gain access to money. However, this option appears to be more likely for those youth already comfortable with delinquent behaviour or for those who are compulsively seeking the drug, potentially as a result of addiction or to avoid withdrawal (Bennet and Holloway 2009; Brunelle et al. 2000). This assertion is supported by Canadian research on inmate populations, which found that nearly half of drug- or alcohol-dependent inmates committed their most serious crime in order to get drugs compared to less than 10 per cent of non-dependent inmates (Pernanen et al. 2002).

Youth Involvement in Drug Crimes

In addition to the commission of criminal acts as a result of being impaired by or in search of drugs, many of the activities involved in the use of drugs are illegal, as outlined in Canada's Controlled Drugs and Substances Act (CDSA 1996). The possession, production, distribution, importation, and exportation of specifically scheduled substances are prohibited, each having its own criminal sanctions, which vary by the type (or schedule) of the substance. According to the law, it is illegal to be in possession of or to seek to obtain controlled drugs for personal use without proper authorization, just as it is to distribute those drugs or possess the drugs for the purpose of distributing them

drug recognition expert (DRE) evaluation
A standardized procedure performed by a trained drug recognition expert—involving visual cues, vital signs, questioning, and the provision of bodily fluids by the potentially impaired driver—that is used for determining impairment by drugs or a drug in combination with alcohol.

to others. It is also illegal to import and export controlled substances between Canada and other countries or to produce the drugs within Canada, by cultivating plants that are or that contain controlled substances or by manufacturing the substances through chemical processes. For some offences, such as trafficking, importation or exportation, and production (again depending of the schedule of the substance), the maximum penalty is imprisonment for life (CDSA 1996).

Approximately 98 000 incidents of drug crimes occurred in Canada in 2009 (Dauvergne and Turner 2010). According to data from Statistics Canada (2009), the most common offences involved the possession of an illegal substance, followed by trafficking, and then production and importation/exportation offences. The vast majority of drug offences are related to marijuana, mainly resulting from possession (Dauvergne 2009). Of course, a substantial proportion of actual offences go undetected because few of the people involved would consider themselves 'victims' and would therefore not report the offences to police. Therefore, drug offences tend to be the result of **proactive police work**, and the rates and types of offences dealt with are a product of the direction of that police work (Warner and Wilson-Coomer 2003).

proactive police work
Enforcement activities that are police initiated, rather than in response to a call for service.

In 2007, of the over 90 000 people accused of drug offences in Canada, approximately 19 per cent were youth (ages 12 to 17) (Dauvergne 2009). As is often the case with the age–crime relationship in general (Diplock and Plecas 2010), those between the ages of 15 and 25 have much higher rates of involvement in drug offences than those of other age groups (Dauvergne 2009; Desjardin and Hotton 2004). For youth, this trend is most prominent for marijuana-related drug crimes, as youth represented 24 per cent of accused offenders for marijuana offences compared to only 5 per cent of those accused of cocaine offences (Dauvergne 2009). Of all adolescents accused, only 38 per cent of the files went forward with charges, demonstrating an effect of Canada's Youth Criminal Justice Act (YCJA), which encourages police to make a concerted effort to divert youth involved in drug offences away from charges toward extrajudicial measures (Dauvergne 2009).

Possessing Drugs and Alcohol

As is the case for every Canadian, it is an offence for youth to be in possession of a controlled substance without a valid authorization. Although alcohol is available for legal purchase and is regulated by the provinces, the possession of alcohol is prohibited for those under the legally prescribed minimum age. Therefore, in the case of adolescent substance use, simply possessing drugs and alcohol constitutes a violation and therefore necessarily implicates the youth in criminal or delinquent behaviour. While possession alone may seem like a minor offence, it can be accompanied by other related rule breaking and deviant behaviour, such as using fake identification, stealing from family or friends, hiring bootleggers, or buying from people involved in the criminal lifestyle. Also, since possession is likely to lead to use and intoxication, possession offences can be seen to be linked to the predatory crimes that may result.

Although there are reported rates for observed possession offences, as noted previously, police can detect only a fraction of the actual offences. Based on the rates of self-reported youth drinking, smoking, and drug use, adolescents clearly are regularly in possession of prohibited substances or at least collaborating together to have these substances available. Although the rates of drug possession charges are driven by police behaviour, they generally reflect the overall patterns of adolescent substance abuse; as rates of substance use rose over previous decades, so too did the rates of youth accused of drug possession offences (Dauvergne 2009). Police often rely on visual cues and random checks when enforcing age limits in drinking establishments (Schafer 2005), and typically come across incidents of illicit drug and underage alcohol possession through traffic and street stops in response to other observed suspicious behaviour.

Selling Drugs

The fact that adolescents have a higher likelihood of using illicit drugs than adults do (Health Canada 2010a) provides an opportunity for some youth to get involved in the distribution of these drugs to other youth. While most youth access illicit drugs through social sources and very few exclusively buy their own drugs, a majority of youth who use drugs have bought drugs from people they know (Harrison, Fulkerson, and Park 2000). According to research samples of Montreal and Toronto youth (Harrison, Erickson, Korf, Brochu, and Benschop 2007), while most students either do not use illicit drugs or never buy them, of those who do buy drugs, they most often obtain them through friends. Very few students get drugs from people they do not know or from non-friends from school. However, for those youth who are dropouts or were detained awaiting trial, the majority purchase drugs themselves and relatively few access drugs through sharing with friends (Harrison et al. 2007). Students reported obtaining marijuana most frequently at school or outdoors and less frequently in a house or apartment. This was in contrast to the dropouts and detainees, who more regularly bought marijuana at houses and apartments, then outdoors, and very rarely at schools (Harrison et al. 2007). Most commonly, youth reported paying around 10 Canadian dollars for a gram of marijuana.

Given the existence of a youth drug market and the preference of mainstream youth to buy from friends, there are opportunities for youth to sell drugs to their peers. However, even though the mainstream youth population presents a large potential market for selling drugs, opportunities appear to be dependent on close peer connections and are largely limited to marijuana (Harrison et al. 2007). Dealing in 'harder' drugs or dealing outside of the close peer group is more common among youth who are more entrenched in drug cultures and already involved in criminal activity. In street-level dealing as well as selling to mainstream youth, those youth who sell drugs are generally also drug users (Floyd, Alexandre, Hedden, Lawson, Latimer, and Giles 2010). Among a sample of young offenders in Calgary, drug selling was common among those youth who were considered chronic or habitual offenders, all of whom had been illicit drug users (MacRae, Bertrand, Paetsch, and Hornick 2008). In a study of Vancouver's street-involved youth (Werb, Kerr, Li, Montaner, and Wood 2008), over half were involved in street-level drug dealing. They most commonly sold marijuana, crack cocaine, and crystal methamphetamine, with the majority also using crack cocaine in addition to being homeless, impoverished, and suffering from illnesses (Werb et al. 2008). Although there is some research to suggest that improving access to legitimate job opportunities would effectively reduce levels of drug dealing among youth (Ihlanfeldt 2007), since many drug dealers are also drug users, addressing issues of addiction and other substance abuse problems among adolescent drug dealers may also be necessary (Floyd et al. 2010; Werb et al. 2008).

Producing and Trafficking Drugs

Because drug markets are typically controlled by adult offenders, adolescent participation in drug distribution markets is largely dependent on whether they are needed (Bouchard, Alain, and Nguyen 2009). Youth fill a niche in markets that are either inaccessible to adults, such as schools, or where the market exceeds the capacity of adult drug offenders, sometimes the result of law enforcement efforts (Bouchard et al. 2009). In Canada there are large illegal drug industries that both produce and distribute drugs on a mass scale. For example, estimates of the number of illegal marijuana growing operations in the province of British Columbia alone are between 10 000 (Plecas, Diplock, Garis, Carlisle, Neal, and Landry 2010) and 17 500 (Easton 2004). Similarly, estimates for Québec have been around 13 000 (Bouchard 2007). The large number of growing operations in particular parts of the country have provided opportunities for high-school aged youth to enter into a potentially lucrative illegal industry as labourers for adult growers or as operators of their own operations (Bouchard et al. 2009).

Organized criminals are often major players within the illegal drug production and trafficking industry (Royal Canadian Mounted Police 2007). These organized criminal groups can use youth to sell drugs to their peers, to work as **sitters** or labourers in drug production operations, and to smuggle drugs, alcohol, and contraband tobacco across provincial or international borders (Richter-White 2002). For these youth, this involvement may seem like an opportunity to make money, while for adult organized criminals it is an opportunity to increase profits and reduce personal risk through low-cost and convenient labour (Bouchard et al. 2009). We might expect that the children of adult drug traffickers and those youth who are otherwise heavily involved in criminal activity would gravitate toward the lure of the easy profits and status promised by gang and organized criminal involvement in drug production and trafficking. However, many labourers employed by marijuana growing operations have been described as otherwise conventional youth, and many (i.e., 42 per cent) are female (Bouchard et al. 2009).

As was the case with selling drugs, the majority of youth who made up the sample of growers were also drug users (Bouchard et al. 2009). Adolescents may be involved in the drug industry partially because it helps to support their expensive drug use and because they do not perceive the drugs or the illegal activity as particularly harmful. This is most likely the case for youth who become involved in the large marijuana industry in Canada. Their perceptions of the harms may be formed based on decreasing support for the criminalization of marijuana possession (Millhorn et al. 2009), on misinformation arising from the prohibition–legalization debate (Diplock and Plecas 2009), or on a general confusion about the legal status of marijuana in the country (MacCoun, Pacula, Chriqui, Harris, and Reuter 2009), especially after proposed decriminalization legislation and several court rulings in 2003 (Dauvergne 2009). The inconsistent messages, and even terms of differentiation such as 'soft' and 'hard' drugs, likely combine with their own short-term experiences with drugs to minimize their perceptions of the harms of their illegal activity. This is unfortunate given the numerous harms associated with drug production and organized criminal involvement in drug markets, including property damage and devaluation, fire and electrical hazards, contamination of houses and properties, increased gang violence and predatory home invasions, and environmental damage (Plecas, Diplock, and Garis 2011; Garis 2008; Richter-White 2002). Again, maybe youth lack enough of what they perceive to be good, legitimate opportunities for work at their age, which makes illegal drug crime an appealing option. However, in addition to improving employment opportunities (Ihlanfeld 2007) for these youth, there may be a need for more consistent messaging about not just the negative effects of drug use but also about the societal impact of the entire drug industry.

Strategies to Prevent Adolescent Substance Abuse

Since there is strong research evidence and a prevailing belief that substance abuse among adolescents contributes to poor decision making, unhealthy lifestyles, criminal behaviour, injuries, illnesses, addictions, and deaths, governments and other concerned individuals have put effort and money toward preventing experimentation and substance use. Because most adolescents go through school systems, many of the strategies to prevent substance abuse and related crime are delivered during school. These programs tend to adopt the stance that substance abuse problems can happen to anyone, and that everyone is at equal risk (Saewyc 2007). Therefore, the overarching goal is to prevent youth from ever experimenting, to 'just say no'. While early education programs reach nearly all children, programs targeted at high school–aged youth appear to neglect those most at risk: those outside of the mainstream student population (Saewyc 2007). There is a need for both

sitters
Individuals who are paid to tend to and protect the plants in a marijuana growing operation. Sitters may also appear to legitimately occupy a residence to avoid drawing suspicion.

early education and intervention with regard to substance abuse (Lubman et al. 2007), while at the same time focusing attention on those who are most in need (Saewyc 2007).

There are many substance abuse prevention programs that have shown varying levels of success (Roberts et al. 2001). Some effective programs are universal, school-based programs, while others focus specifically on those at higher risk or those who are already involved heavily in drugs. According to the CCSA's Compendium of Best Practices (Roberts et al. 2001), keys to effective substance abuse prevention programs include building a strong framework, striving for accountability, understanding and involving young people, and creating an effective process. These components emphasize the need for the message to be credible and based on accurate information that recognizes adolescent development and perceptions. Also, since many programs rely on teachers, student leaders, law-enforcement officers, and other professionals to take part as facilitators, those who lead or facilitate the programs must be competent, credible, empathetic, and able to interact well with youth (Roberts et al. 2001). More recently, the CCSA (2010) published a set of 18 standards for community-based adolescent substance abuse prevention. These standards focus on assessing the community's situation, building capacity, planning for sustainability, coordinating and building upon evidence-based activities, and evaluating the work done. Importantly, substance abuse prevention efforts should involve many facets of the community in a coordinated approach (Mangham and Nicholson 2009).

School-Based Interventions

Since most eventual drug users and those with substance abuse problems started their substance abuse before adulthood and because early initiation is a risk factor for later problems (Lubman et al. 2007), school age is an appropriate time to implement substance abuse prevention. Schools present an ideal setting to guarantee that nearly all children receive the intended message of substance abuse prevention programs. However, with substance use—particularly of alcohol, tobacco, and marijuana—being common among adolescents, there is inevitably the question of whether or not these programs work. The effectiveness of Drug Abuse Resistance Education (DARE), probably the most prevalent and well-known school-based program in Canada (Mangham 2007; National Crime Prevention Centre 2009), has been the subject of numerous evaluations, and the results have been inconsistent. Taken together, the many evaluations suggest that the program has a very small effect on reducing drug use among youth (Pan and Bai 2009). However, other programs such as Life Skills Training and Project ALERT have been found to be effective at reducing the levels of substance use, although not necessarily at preventing initiation (National Crime Prevention Centre 2009). The most effective type of school-based substance abuse prevention programs are skill-based, where youth are taught resistance skills and learn about the social influences of substance use while receiving other life-skills training (Faggiano, Vigna-Taglianti, Versino, Zambon, Borraccino, and Lemma 2008; National Crime Prevention Centre 2009). Programs that focus purely on information and knowledge about the harms of drugs are largely ineffective.

Anti-Drug Media Campaigns

The message of substance abuse prevention is often spread through mass media campaigns. As mentioned earlier, the 'drugsnot4me' campaign (Government of Canada 2007; Health Canada 2009) involves television commercial and websites targeted at both youth and their parents. These media campaigns are intended to reach a wide audience and present messages that will resonate with youth as well as with adults. Mass media campaigns have traditionally involved television and print ads but have expanded by incorporating other media and technology such as websites, social networking websites, and cell phones. While there may be potential for mass media campaigns to effectively change the beliefs and behaviours of youth, improperly guided campaigns could simply be wasting resources (Palmgreen and Donohew 2003). Based on an understanding of the characteristics of youth who are most likely to use illicit drugs, anti-drug media campaigns may be more effective if they appeal to sensation-seeking youth by having novelty or 'shock value' (Palmgreen and Donohew 2003).

In the 1990s and 2000s, tobacco smoking was the focus of large mass media campaigns in Canada as well as elsewhere. Although the ads were criticized for being less effective than those in the United States (CBC 2002; Pechmann and Reibling 2000), tobacco use has decreased steadily in the last decade (Health Canada 2010b). Whether the reductions in smoking rates among Canadians has anything to do with media campaigns or even school-based anti-smoking programs is debatable, but in addition to lower smoking rates, numerous smoking bans and related legislation have been successfully implemented in all provinces and territories in Canada (CBC News 2009), suggesting changing norms in the acceptability of tobacco smoking.

Alternatives to Fear-Based Communication

fear-based communication
Messages used to frighten youth away from experimentation with substances by emphasizing the potential negative effects of use.

Researchers generally agree that **fear-based communication** is an ineffective approach to dissuading youth from using substances such as alcohol, tobacco, and marijuana (National Crime Prevention Centre 2009). The fear-based approach, although not untruthful in presenting information, overemphasizes the potential harms, highlighting worst-case scenarios and intentionally increasing the perceptions of the likelihood of harm. These messages contradict what the majority of youth will later or already know about the effects of substance abuse, potentially causing the messenger to lose credibility (Tupper 2008). Despite recognizing the ineffectiveness of fear-based communication, most current anti-drug messaging includes language that is consistent with this technique even when trying to be neutral and 'fact-based' (Tupper 2008). The challenge is in finding ways to dissuade problematic substance use among adolescents without resorting to strategies that rely on fear and on the condemnation of the substances and substance users.

As previously discussed, there is value in credible and well-designed substance abuse–prevention messages directed at youth through school-based and mass media programs. Perhaps rather than emphasizing what youth should not do, messages should instead focus on promoting healthy living in general. Tupper (2008) suggests that drug education should adopt the discourse of drugs as 'tools', which, when used properly and for the right reasons, may be very beneficial, but when misused, can be socially harmful. Ideally, messaging would change social norms among adolescents so that unhealthy behaviours are not 'just part of growing up'. A substantial part of changing social norms and attitudes toward alcohol, tobacco, and illicit drugs is to address perceptions by emphasizing that substance use is actually less normative that many youth perceive (Martens et al. 2006).

harm-reduction strategies
Any policies or programs that are designed to reduce the level of harm associated with substance use and abuse without requiring the cessation of use.

There is still a need to emphasize the potentially serious consequences of substance use, but these messages should be accompanied by a full complement of alternative approaches. Other approaches might include increased taxation of unhealthy substances, regulation to ensure appropriate use and deter unsafe use, and **harm-reduction strategies** to address factors that contribute to the negative consequences associated with substance abuse (Toumbourou, Stockwell, Neighbors, Marlatt, Sturge, and Rehm 2009). The overall goal of all prevention efforts should be to establish social norms that promote healthy lifestyles while providing the support necessary for those who are struggling with substance abuse issues. Of course, if there is an expectation that changes will occur among the younger members of society, the messages have to be consistent and non-ambiguous, and apply equally to adults. A society in which substance use among adults is portrayed as normative through advertising, entertainment, and actual consumption should expect that adolescents will follow suit (American Academy of Pediatrics 2010; Bonomo 2005).

Summary

Despite the perception that drug use among youth is rising 'out of control' (Saewyc 2009), there have recently been general decreases in rates of adolescent substance use across Canada (Health Canada 2010a). Is this evidence of effective drug prevention efforts, changing norms among young people away from unhealthy behaviours, or simply a predictable downturn after a rising trend in drug use from the mid-1990s through early 2000s? When considering these lower rates, we must not allow them to overshadow the fact that alcohol consumption and, to a far lesser but still notable degree, marijuana and tobacco use are common among adolescents, and that usage rates are substantially higher than those of adults (Health Canada 2010a). In fact, when considering adolescent populations outside the mainstream population, even the use of so-called 'hard' drugs is common (Public Health Agency of Canada 2006). While experimentation, coping with the struggles of adolescence, and generally fitting in all act together to produce 'past-year' adolescent substance use rates above those of adults, lifetime use of many substances is similar among adolescents and adults. Indeed, those substances with relatively higher 'past-year' usage rates among young people are generally the same substances that exhibit higher rates among adults (Health Canada 2010a). This suggests that not only will the majority of adolescents who experiment with substances abstain in the future but also that the substance use of adolescents is largely reflective of adult substance use, perhaps as a result of inconsistent messaging that portrays substance use as a rite of passage into normative adult behaviour.

Adolescent substance abuse, its consequences on the futures of Canada's young people, and its potential to create problems associated with crime and criminality are ongoing concerns in this country. Hundreds of millions of dollars are spent on law-enforcement efforts, education, research, and media campaigns to get youth to say that drugs and alcohol are 'not for me'. Students in the field of crime control, policing, and criminology must critically assess the direction of drug policies and other prevention strategies and work toward improving them where needed and forging new directions when existing ones prove inadequate, inappropriate, or counterproductive. In spite of the downward trend in adolescent substance use rates, it may seem easy to criticize drug prevention efforts. Much of the funding ultimately culminates in information revealing the substance use patterns of those at relatively low risk for serious problems. A great deal of the funding is used by police agencies to have their officers instruct children on the harms of drugs; on strategies to resist peer pressure; on television commercials emphasizing the dangers of choosing the wrong path; and on a high number of cases of adolescents coming in contact with police for possession offences, many of which are now being cleared without charge (Dauvergne 2009). At the same time, adolescents are being drawn into drug production and distribution networks (Bouchard 2009; Harris et al. 2007), while ongoing debates over the appropriate legal status of drugs are spreading misinformation (Diplock et al. 2009), and research is concluding that the relationship between substance use and crime is 'spurious' (Harrison et al. 2001) and 'complex' (Casavant and Collin 2001). However, the goal is to be more than critical, and to build upon existing knowledge and promising practices to determine whether alternatives, such as addressing adolescent perceptions, improving employment opportunities, reframing drugs as 'tools', regulating substances, increasing taxation, removing stigma, and implementing harm-reduction strategies, are any more likely to be the answer.

Key Terms

binge drinking

co-morbidity

dependence

drug recognition expert (DRE) evaluation

fear-based communication

harm-reduction strategies

method of administration

proactive police work

psychosis

sitters

social desirability effects

stigma

street-involved youth

substance abuse

Review Questions

1. In your experience, what are the main differences between youth who use drugs and those who do not?

2. Most people recognize that marijuana is not a 'gateway drug' in the sense that its use does not lead directly to the use of other drugs. Do you think, though, that marijuana use is a potential gateway to other drug use in any other sense?

3. Consider Goldstein's tripartite drug-crime model. Which, if any, of the three modes do you feel best fits the relationship between adolescent substance use and criminal behaviour?

4. As was discussed in this chapter, some Canadian youth become involved in drug crime beyond 'simple' possession (drug dealing, working in marijuana growing operations, joining gangs who traffic in drugs, etc.). What factors might lead young Canadians to engage in this type of criminal behaviour? Do you think these are the same factors that lead young Canadians to use drugs?

Critical Thinking Questions

1. Many schools and law-enforcement agencies in Canada work in concert to provide drug prevention information to children and adolescents with police officers taking on the role of drug-prevention educators. What might be some advantages and disadvantages of police officers' taking on this role in substance use prevention?

2. If you were responsible for designing a program in your community to dissuade youth from impaired driving, what would you focus on?

3. How do you feel the existing ways that alcohol and tobacco are regulated in your province (minimum age limits, rules surrounding advertising, licensing of drinking establishments, anti-smoking regulations, etc.) reduce adolescent substance use or make it less harmful? In what ways do you feel these regulations inadvertently contribute to adolescent substance use or make it more harmful?

4. As a result of the association between substance use/abuse and crime, substance use issues become a concern for health-care and criminal justice systems, among others. What do you think would be the ideal balance between the health-care and criminal justice systems to reduce and prevent the harms associated with substance use?

Suggested Readings

Bouchard, M., Alain, M., and Nguyen, H. (2009). Convenient labour: The prevalence and nature of youth involvement in the cannabis cultivation industry. *International Journal of Drug Policy*, 20(6): 467–74.

Brunelle, N., and Cousineau, M. (2000). Drug-crime relations among drug-consuming juvenile delinquents: A tripartite model and more. *Contemporary Drug Problems, 27*: 835–66.

Canadian Centre on Substance Abuse. (2010). *Stronger together: Canadian standards for community-based youth substance abuse prevention*. Ottawa, ON: Author.

Harrison, L.D., Erickson, P.G., Adlaf, E., and Freeman, C. (2001). The drugs-violence nexus among American and Canadian youth. *Substance Use and Misuse, 36*(14): 2065–86.

National Crime Prevention Centre. (2009). *School-based drug abuse prevention: Promising and successful programs*. Ottawa, ON: Author. Also available online at http://www.publicsafety.gc.ca/res/cp/res/2009-01-drg-abs-eng.aspx

Suggested Weblinks

National Anti-Drug Strategy drugsnot4me Youth Drug Prevention
www.not4me.ca
- This site provides the Government of Canada's most recent anti-drug messages to young people.

Canadian Centre on Substance Abuse
www.ccsa.ca
- CCSA provides national leadership, evidence-informed analysis, and advice on substance abuse issues.

References

Alberta Health Service. (2009). *The Alberta youth experience survey: Highlights report*. Edmonton, AB: Author.

American Academy of Pediatrics. (2010). Policy statement—Children, adolescents, substance abuse, and the media. *Pediatrics, 126*(4): 791–9.

Barrett, S.P., Darredeau, C., and Pihl, R.O. (2006). Patterns of simultaneous polysubstance use in drug using university students. *Human Psychopharmacology: Clinical and Experimental, 21*: 255–63.

Bauman, K.E. and Ennett, S.T. (1996). On the importance of peer influence for adolescent drug use: Commonly neglected considerations. *Addiction, 91*(2): 185–98.

Beirness, D.J. and Beasley, E.E. (2009). *Alcohol and drug use among drivers: British Columbia roadside survey 2008*. Ottawa, ON: Canadian Centre on Substance Abuse.

Bennett, T. and Holloway, K. (2009). The causal connection between drug misuse and crime. *British Journal of Criminology, 49*: 513–31.

Benowitz, N.L. (2009). Pharmacology of nicotine: Addiction, smoking-induced disease, and therapeutics. *Annual Review of Pharmacology and Toxicology, 49*: 57–71.

Bonomo, Y.A. (2005). Adolescent alcohol problems: Whose responsibility is it anyway? *Medical Journal of Australia, 183*: 430–32.

Bouchard, M. (2007). A capture-recapture model to estimate the size of criminal populations and the risks of detection in a marijuana cultivation industry. *Journal of Quantitative Criminology, 23*: 221–41.

Bouchard, M., Alain, M., and Nguyen, H. (2009). Convenient labour: The prevalence and nature of youth involvement in the cannabis cultivation industry. *International Journal of Drug Policy, 20*(6): 467–74.

Brands, B., Paglia-Boak, A., Sproule, B.A., Leslie, K., and Adlaf, E.M. (2010). Nonmedical use of opioid analgesics among Ontario students. *Canadian Family Physician, 56*: 256–62.

Bromley, R.D.F. and Nelson, A.L. (2002). Alcohol-related crime and disorder across urban space and time: Evidence from a British city. *Geoforum, 33*: 239–54.

Brunelle, N. and Cousineau, M. (2000). Drug-crime relations among drug-consuming juvenile delinquents: A tripartite model and more. *Contemporary Drug Problems, 27*: 835–66.

Canada. Department of Justice. (2010). National anti-drug strategy implementation evaluation, final report. Retrieved 14 September, 2010, from http://www.justice.gc.ca/eng/pi/eval/rep-rap/10/nasie-snaef/index.html

Canada. Government of Canada. (2007). *National anti-drug strategy: Speech for the Right Honourable Stephen Harper, Prime Minister*. Retrieved 13 September, 2010, from http://www.nationalantidrugstrategy.gc.ca/sp-dis/2007_10_04.html

Canadian Centre on Substance Abuse. (2010). *Stronger together: Canadian standards for community-based youth substance abuse prevention.* Ottawa, ON: Author.

Casavant, L. and Collin, C. (2001). *Illegal drug use and crime: A complex relationship.* Ottawa, ON: Library of Parliament, Parliamentary Research Branch. Retrieved 30 September, 2010, from http://www.parl.gc.ca/37/1/parlbus/commbus/senate/com-e/ille-e/library-e/collin-e.htm

CBC News. (2002, August 20). Canada's anti-smoking campaigns 'ineffective': Health groups. Retrieved 14 October, 2010, from http://www.cbc.ca/news/story/2002/08/19/smoking_ads020819.html

CBC News. (2009, October 7). Global anti-smoking efforts. Retrieved 14 October, 2010, from http://www.cbc.ca/health/story/2009/09/29/f-smoking-bans-tobacco.html

Centre for Addiction and Mental Health. (2009). *Do you know . . . tobacco.* Retrieved 13 October, 2010, from http://www.camh.net/About_Addiction_Mental_Health/Drug_and_Addiction_Information/tobacco_dyk.html

Centre for Addictions Research BC. (2009). *Adolescent substance use and related harms in British Columbia.* Victoria, BC: Author.

Chan, Y., Dennis, M.L., and Funk, R.R. (2008). Prevalence and co-morbidity of major internalizing and externalizing problems among adolescents and adults presenting to substance abuse treatment. *Journal of Substance Abuse Treatment, 34*(1): 14–24.

Controlled Drugs and Substances Act, S.C., c.19 (1996). Retrieved from http://laws-lois.justice.gc.ca/eng/acts/C-38.8/FullText.html

Coombs, M. (2007). Cocaine-induced myocardial infarction. *Nursing in Critical Care, 12*(4): 176–80.

Cooper, K., May, D., Soderstrom, I., and Jarjoura, G.R. (2009). Examining theoretical predictors of substance use among a sample of incarcerated youth. *Journal of Offender Rehabilitation, 48*(8): 669–95.

Dauvergne, M. (2009). Trends in police-reported drug offences in Canada. *Juristat, 29*(2). Retrieved 28 September, 2010, from http://www.statcan.gc.ca/pub/85-002-x/2009002/article/10847-eng.pdf

Dauvergne, M. and Turner, J. (2010). Police-reported crime statistics in Canada, 2009. *Juristat, 30*(2). Retrieved 13 October, 2010, from http://www.statcan.gc.ca/pub/85-002-x/2010002/article/11292-eng.pdf

Degenhardt, L. and Hall, W. (2006). Is cannabis use a contributory cause of psychosis? *Canadian Journal of Psychiatry, 51*: 556–65.

Degenhardt, L., Hall, W., and Lynskey, M. (2002). Testing hypotheses about the relationship between cannabis and psychosis. *Drug and Alcohol Dependence, 71*: 37–48.

Desjardins, N. and Hotton, T. (2004). Trends in drug offences and the role of alcohol and drugs in crime. *Juristat, 24*(1). Retrieved 29 September, 2010, from http://dsp-psd.communication.gc.ca/Collection-R/Statcan/85-002-XIE/0010485-002-XIE.pdf

Diplock, J., Cohen, I., and Plecas, D. (2009). A review of the research on the risks and harms associated to the use of marijuana. *The Journal of Global Drug Policy and Practice, 3*(2). Available from http://www.globaldrugpolicy.org/3/2/3.php.

Diplock, J., Kirkland, S., Malm, A., and Plecas, D. (2005). *Clandestine drug laboratories in British Columbia.* Abbotsford, BC: International Centre for Urban Research Studies, University College of the Fraser Valley.

Diplock, J. and Plecas, D. (2009). *Clearing the smoke on cannabis: Respiratory effects of cannabis smoking.* Ottawa, ON: Canadian Centre on Substance Abuse.

Diplock, J. and Plecas, D. (2010). Revisiting age and crime. *Journal of Criminal Justice Research, 1*(2).

Donahue, J.J. (2010). Tobacco smoking among incarcerated individuals: A review of the nature of the problem and what is being done in response. *Journal of Offender Rehabilitation, 48*(7): 589–604.

Dore, G., and Sweeting, M. (2006). Drug-induced psychosis associated with crystalline methamphetamine. *Australasian Psychiatry, 14*(1): 86–9.

Easton, S.T. (2004). *Marijuana growth in British Columbia.* Vancouver, BC: Fraser Institute.

Faggiano, F., Vigna-Taglianti, F.D., Versino, E., Zambon, A., Borraccino, A., and Lemma, P. (2008). School-based prevention for illicit drugs use: A systematic review. *Preventive Medicine, 46*: 385–96.

Felson, R., Salvolainen, J., Aaltonen, M., and Moustgaard, H. (2008). Is the association between alcohol use and delinquency casual or spurious? *Criminology, 46*(3): 785–808.

Fischer, B., Rehm, J., and Hall, W. (2009). Cannabis use in Canada: The need for a 'public health' approach. *Canadian Journal of Public Health, 100*(2): 101–3.

Friedman, D.P. (2009). Drug addiction: A chronically relapsing brain disease. *North Carolina Medical Journal, 70*(1): 35–37.

Garis, L. (2008). *Eliminating residential hazards associated with marijuana grow operations and the regulation of hydroponics equipment: A brief on British Columbia's Public Safety Electrical Fire and Safety Initiative.*

Available from http://www.nlafcff.nf.ca/pdf/FCABC%20Brief%20on%20BC's%20Public%20Safety%20 Electrical%20Fire%20Safety%20Initiative.doc.pdf.

Goldstein, P.J. (1985). The drugs-violence nexus: A tripartite conceptual framework. *Journal of Drug Issues, 15:* 493–506.

Grech, A., Van Os, J., Jones, P.B., Lewin, S.W., and Murray, R.M. (2005). Cannabis use and outcome of recent onset psychosis. *European Psychiatry, 20:* 349–53.

Hanson, D.J. (1995). *Preventing alcohol abuse: Alcohol, culture, and control.* Westport, CT: Praeger Publishers.

Harris, J.R. (1995). Where is the child's environment? A group socialization theory of development. *Psychological Review, 102*(3): 458–89.

Harrison, L.D., Erickson, P.G., Adlaf, E., and Freeman, C. (2001). The drugs-violence nexus among American and Canadian youth. *Substance Use and Misuse, 36*(14): 2065–86.

Harrison, L.D., Erickson, P.G., Korf, D.J., Brochu, S., and Benschop, A. (2007). How much for a dime bag? An exploration of youth drug markets. *Drug and Alchol Dependence, 90S:* S27–S39.

Harrison, P.A., Fulkerson, J.A., and Park, E. (2000). The relative importance of social versus commercial sources in youth access to tobacco, alcohol, and other drugs. *Preventive Medicine, 31:* 39–48.

Hayaki, J., Hagerty, C.E., Herman, D.S., de Dois, M.A., Anderson, B.J., and Stein, M.D. (2010). Expectancies and marijuana use frequency and severity among young females. *Addictive Behaviours, 35:* 995–1000.

Health Canada. (2006). *Youth and tobacco.* Retrieved 13 October, 2010, from http://www.hc-sc.gc.ca/hc-ps/pubs/tobac-tabac/youth-jeunes/intro-eng.php

Health Canada. (2009). *Not4Me: Youth drug prevention.* Retrieved 14 September, 2010, from http://www.hc-sc.gc.ca/hc-ps/drugs-drogues/youth-jeunes/index-eng.php

Health Canada. (2010a). *Canadian alcohol and drug use monitoring survey.* Retrieved 13 September, 2010, from http://www.hc-sc.gc.ca/hc-ps/drugs-drogues/stat/_2009/summary-sommaire-eng.php

Health Canada. (2010b). *Canadian tobacco use monitoring survey: Smoking prevalence 1999–2009.* Retrieved 14 September, 2010, from http://www.hc-sc.gc.ca/hc-ps/tobac-tabac/research-recherche/stat/_ctums-esutc_prevalence/prevalence-eng.php

Hunt, G., Moloney, M., and Evans, K. (2009). Epidemiology meets cultural studies: Studying and understanding youth cultures, clubs and drugs. *Addiction Research and Theory, 17*(6): 601–21.

Ihlanfeldt, K.R. (2007). Neighborhood drug crime and young males' job accessibility. *The Review of Economics and Statistics, 89*(1): 151–64.

Kelton, M.H. and Givel, M.S. (2008). Public policy implications of tobacco industry smuggling through Native American reservations into Canada. *International Journal of Health Services, 38*(3): 471–87.

Lea, S., Black, K., and Asbridge, M. (2009). An overview of injuries to adolescents and young adults related to substance abuse: Data from Canadian emergency departments. *Canadian Journal of Emergency Medicine, 11*(4): 330–36.

Leslie, K. (2008). Youth substance use and abuse: Challenges and strategies for identification and intervention. *Canadian Medical Association Journal, 178*(2): 145–48.

Lubman, D.I., Hides, L., Yucel, M., and Toumbourou, J.W. (2007). Intervening early to reduce developmentally harmful substance use among youth populations. *Medical Journal of Australia, 187:* S22–S25.

Lubman, D.I., Yucel, M., and Hall, W. (2007). Substance abuse and the adolescent brain: A toxic combination? *Journal of Psychopharmacology, 21*(8): 792–94.

MacCoun, R., Pacula, R.L., Chriqui, J., Harris, K., and Reuter, P. (2009). Do citizens know whether their state has decriminalized marijuana? Assessing the perceptual component of deterrence theory. *Review of Law and Economics, 5*(1): 347–71.

McDougall, D., Vajushi, S., and Winterdyk, J.A. (2005). Adolescent substance abuse and criminal behaviour. In J.A. Winterdyk (Ed.), *Issues and perspectives on young offenders in Canada* (3rd ed.). Toronto: Nelson Education.

Mangham, C. (2007). *The effectiveness, appropriateness and fit of DARE in Canadian schools: Responding to criticisms about the program.* Retrieved 30 September, 2010, from http://www.dare.com/home/Resources/documents/DAREpaper.doc.

Mangham, C. and Nicholson, D. (2009). *Characteristics and evidences of effectiveness of the Community Prevention Education Continuum.* Unpublished manuscript.

Martens, M.P., Page, J.C., Mowry, E.S., Damann, K.M., Taylor, K.K., and Cimini, M.D. (2006). Differences between actual and perceived student norms: An examination of alcohol use, drug use, and sexual behaviour. *Journal of American College Health, 54*(5): 295–300.

Martin, S.E., Maxwell, C.D., White, H.R., and Zhang, Y. (2004). Trends in alcohol use, cocaine use, and crime: 1989–1998. *Journal of Drug Issues, 4*(2): 333–60.

McClelland, G.M. and Teplin, L.A. (2001), Alcohol Intoxication and Violent Crime: Implications for Public Health Policy. *The American Journal on Addictions, 10*: s70–s85. DOI: 10.1080/10550490150504155.

Milhorn, M., Monaghan, M., Montero, D., Reyes, M., Roman, T., Tollasken, R., et al. (2009). North Americans' attitudes toward illegal drugs. *Journal of Human Behaviour in the Social Environment, 19*(2): 125–41.

Mooney, G.H. (2005). Addictions and social compassion. *Drug and Alcohol Review, 24*: 137–41.

National Crime Prevention Centre. (2009). *School-based drug abuse prevention: Promising and successful programs.* Ottawa, ON: Author.

Office of National Drug Control Policy. (2000). Drug-related crime. Retrieved 30 September, 2010, from http://www.whitehousedrugpolicy.gov/publications/pdf/ncj181056.pdf

Paglia-Boak, A. and Adlaf, E. (2007). Substance use and harm in the general youth population. In *Substance abuse in Canada: Youth in focus.* Ottawa, ON: Canadian Centre on Substance Abuse.

Palmgreem P. and Donohew, L. (2003). Chapter 2: Effective mass media strategies for drug abuse prevention campaigns. In Z. Sloboda and William J. Bukoski (Eds.), *Handbook of drug abuse prevention: Theory, science, and practice.* New York: Kluwer Academic/Plenum Publishers.

Pan, W. and Bai, H. (2009). A multivariate approach to a met-analytic review of the effectiveness of the DARE program. *International Journal of Environmental Research and Public Health, 6*: 267–77.

Pechmann, C. and Reibling, E.T. (2000). Anti-smoking advertising campaigns targeting youth: Case studies from USA and Canada. *Tobacco Control, 9*(Suppl II): ii18–ii31.

Pernanen, K., Cousinea, M., Brochu, S., and Sun, F. (2002). *Proportions of crimes associated with alcohol and other drugs in Canada.* Ottawa: Canadian Centre on Substance Abuse.

Plecas, D. and Diplock, J. (2007). *Marijuana growing operations in Alberta, 1997–2004.* Abbotsford, BC: Centre for Criminal Justice Research, University of the Fraser Valley.

Plecas, D., Diplock, J., and Garis, L. (2011). Commercially viable marijuana growing operations: What makes them such a serious issue? *Journal of Criminal Justice Research, 1*(1).

Plecas, D., Malm, A., and Kinney, B. (2005). *Marijuana growing operations in British Columbia revisited, 1997–2003.* Abbotsford, BC: University College of the Fraser Valley.

Public Health Agency of Canada. (2006). *Street youth in Canada: Findings from enhanced surveillance of Canadian street youth, 1999–2003.* Ottawa: Author.

Rehm, J., Baliunas, D., Brochu, S., Fischer, B., Gnam, W., Patra, J., et al. (2006). *The costs of substance abuse in Canada 2002.* Ottawa: Canadian Centre on Substance Abuse.

Rehm, J., Geisbrecht, N., Popova, S., Patra, J., Adlaf, E., and Mann, R. (2006). *Overview of positive and negative effects of alcohol consumption-implications for preventive policies in Canada.* Toronto: Centre for Addiction and Mental Health.

Richmond, R., Butler, T., Wilhelm, K., Wodak, A., Cunningham, M., and Anderson, I. (2009). Tobacco in prisons: A focus group study. *Tobacco Control, 18*: 176–82.

Richter-White, H. (2002). The direct and indirect impacts of organized crime on youth, as offenders and victims. *Trends in Organized Crime, 7*(4): 79–111.

Roberts, G., McCall, D., Stevens-Leavigne, A., Anderson, J., Paglia, A., Bollenbach, S., et al. (2001). *Preventing substance use problems among young people: A compendium of best practices.* Ottawa: Canadian Centre on Substance Abuse.

Room, R. (2005). Stigma, social inequality and alcohol and drug use. *Drug and Alcohol Review, 24:* 143–55.

Saewyc, E.M. (2007). Substance use among non-mainstream youth. In *Substance abuse in Canada: Youth in focus.* Ottawa: Canadian Centre on Substance Abuse.

Saewyc, E.M. (2009). Alcohol and other drug use among BC students: Myths and realities. *Visions Journal, 5*(2): 8–9.

Schafer, J.A. (2005). Negotiating order in the policing of youth drinking. *Policing: An International Journal of Police Strategies and Management, 28*(2): 279–300.

Shepherd, J.P., Sutherland, I., and Newcombe, R.G. (2006). Relations between alcohol, violence and victimization in adolescence. *Journal of Adolescence, 29*: 539–53.

Squeglia, L.M., Jacobus, J., and Tapert, S.F. (2009). The influence of substance use on adolescent brain development. *Journal of Clinical EEG and Neuroscience, 40*(1): 31–38.

Teed, R. (2009, February 26). Adolescent use of drugs, liquor nears epidemic. *Star-Phoenix.* Retrieved 17 September, 2010, from Canadian Newsstand.

Terry-McElrath, Y.M., O'Malley, P.M., and Johnston, L.D. (2009). Reasons for drug use among American youth by consumption level, gender, and race/ethnicity: 1976–2005. *Journal of Drug Issues, 39*(3): 677–714.

Testa, M. and Livingston, J.A. (2009). Alcohol consumption and women's vulnerability to sexual victimization:

Can reducing women's drinking prevent rape? *Substance Use and Misuse, 44:* 1349–76.

Thoma, R.J., Monnig, M.A., Lysne, P.A., Ruhl, D.A., Pommy, J.A., Bogenschutz, M., et al. (2010). Adolescent substance abuse: The effects of alcohol and marijuana on neuropsychological performance. *Alcoholism: Clinical and Experimental Research.* DOI: 10.1111/j.1530-0277.2010.01320.x

Thorpe, L.E., Ouellet, L.J., Hershow, R., Bailey, S.L., Williams, I.T., Williamson, J., et al. (2002). Risk of hepatitis C virus infection among young adult injection drug users who share injection equipment. *American Journal of Epidemiology, 155*(7): 645–53.

Toumbourou, J.W., Stockwell, T., Neighbors, C., Marlatt, G.A., Sturge, J., and Rehm, J. (2009). Interventions to reduce harm associated with adolescent substance use. *Lancet, 369*: 1391–1401.

Treadwell, S.D. and Robinson, T.G. (2007). Cocaine use and stroke. *Postgraduate Medical Journal, 83*: 389–94.

Tupper, K.W. (2008). Drugs, discourses and education: A critical discourse analysis of a high school drug education text. *Discourse: Studies in the Cultural Politics of Education, 29*(2): 223–38.

United Nations Office on Drugs and Crime (2010). World Drug Report 2010. Retrieved 14 September, 2010, from http://www.unodc.org/unodc/en/data-and-analysis/WDR-2010.html

Urban Health Research Initiative. (2009). *Drug situation in Vancouver.* Vancouver, BC: British Columbia Centre for Excellence in HIV/AIDS.

Vaccarino, F. (2007). Drug abuse, addiction and youth: A neuroscience perspective. In *Substance abuse in Canada: Youth in focus.* Ottawa: Canadian Centre on Substance Abuse.

Warner, B.D. and Wilson-Coomer, B. (2003). Neighborhood drug arrest rates: Are they a meaningful indicator of drug activity? A research note. *Journal of Research in Crime and Delinquency, 40*(2): 123–38.

Wells, S. L. and Thompson, J.M. (2009). Alcohol-related victimization among young adult Canadian drinkers: The explanatory roles of hazardous drinking and illicit drug use. *Canadian Journal of Public Health, 100*(1), 55–59.

Werb, D., Kerr, T., Li, K., Montaner, J., and Wood, E. (2008). Risks surrounding drug trade involvement among street-involved youth. *The American Journal of Drug and Alcohol Abuse, 34*: 810–20.

Wolfe, D.A., Jaffe, P.G., and Crooks, C.V. (2006). *Adolescent risk behaviours: Why teens experiment and strategies to keep them safe.* New Haven, CT: Yale University Press.

World Health Organization. (2004). Global status report on alcohol 2004. Geneva: Author.

10 Aboriginal Youth Crime in Canada

Hirsch Greenberg, Jana Grekul, and Rhonda Nelson

Overview

This chapter explores historical policies as well as some of the individual and community issues influencing Aboriginal youth crime and youth justice in Canada. It briefly sets out the historical relationship between Aboriginal and non-Aboriginal peoples and discusses intergenerational effects of this relationship on Aboriginal youth. The chapter is based in an understanding of Aboriginal youth crime as influenced by specific historical policies and processes that have contributed to intergenerational experiences of trauma. These influences are expressed as loss of identity, family dysfunction, substance abuse, violence, lack of education, unemployment, poverty, experiences of racism and discrimination, gang involvement, and overrepresentation in the criminal justice system. Furthermore, this chapter draws on Aboriginal authors and representations to explore the possibility and value of using Aboriginal-based approaches to justice that more appropriately fit with and address the issues that lead to criminal behaviours in the first place.

Key Objectives

After reading this chapter, you should be able to:

- Understand the complexities of youth and crime in an Aboriginal context.
- Contextualize Aboriginal youth crime based on individual risk factors, protective factors, and social environmental factors.
- Understand complex Aboriginal youth crime behaviours from individual, community, and historical perspectives.
- Review Canadian judicial responses to Aboriginal youth crime.
- Compare mainstream responses with alternative justice approaches.
- Identify future avenues for intervention that are culturally sensitive, socially responsible, and individually accountable and that can positively affect Aboriginal youth.

Introduction

Crime, whether youth or adult, is often reported by mainstream media as ubiquitous. Criminals are constructed as faceless strangers invading our communities. Media reports neglect to mention that criminals are members of communities and are a product of communities (see Box 10.1). Crime is everywhere—or maybe it just appears that way.

This approach drives a wedge between 'law-abiding citizens' and those who 'choose' to commit unlawful acts—the wedge is punishment, and many consider a 'get tough' approach to be the definitive answer to crime.

Yet many who break the law experience significant human and personal costs. We know that victims suffer; their suffering and victimization is more obvious, or apparent. But many offenders, too, suffer: many feel they do not or cannot meet the expectations of society. These individuals can be recognized by their disengagement, confusion, and detachment from acceptable social engagement. Punishment in the form of incarceration confirms their world view that social acceptance is biased and unjust, that they are outsiders and unworthy of belonging. While 'getting tough' on offenders is a popular approach to dealing with crime, Dietrich Bonhoeffer, a Lutheran minister

Box 10.1 Youth Justice in Action

Crime Is Everywhere
Vancouver Sun, December 29, 2010

I'm done with my life of crime. All those murderers, drug dealers, rapists, serial killers. Sure, in the end justice is usually done, but I'm finished with that as well.

Crime crept so stealthily into my life that I scarcely noticed it.

But I've had it.

No more *Mentalist*. No more *CSI*, regardless of the location. No more *Blue Bloods*, *Hawaii Five-O*, *Lie to Me* or any of those others. I don't have to give up *Dexter* because even at my worst, I could never bear even the idea that a psychopathic serial killer could be a 'hero.'

Television is so stuffed with blood, guts, murder, torture, gang fights, rapes and all manner of evil. Crime has become a prime source of all entertainment, even though most is nearly devoid of the mystery that makes whodunits so appealing. . . .

Source: Retrieved 3 February, 2011, from www.canada.com/vancouversun/news/westcoastnews/
story.html?id=07267aa8-7f9f-4282-8de0-e82c3d8f124a

whose experiences emerged from the concentration camps of World War II, suggests a different response: 'We must learn to respond to people less in the light of what they do or omit to do, and more in the light of what they suffer' (in Braswell et al. 2005, p. 447).

Aboriginal
Includes individuals who identify as First Nations, Métis, or Inuit.

The approach taken in this chapter is to understand **Aboriginal** youth crime, in part, as an outcome of historical policies, practices, and processes that have resulted in severe and entrenched trauma among generations of Aboriginal peoples in this country. This chapter presents the view that the underlying contributing factors to Aboriginal youth crime are varied and crisscross a complex web of historical and existing conditions that in some ways set these actions apart from other criminal events: a 13-year old Aboriginal youth—whose home and other socio-economic environments are unhealthy—who steals a car is not equivalent to a 56-year old, white, middle-class male income earner committing the same criminal offence.

As we explore the issues raised in this chapter, we will observe that for some Canadians crime, as it affects offenders and victims, is not about an act committed against the Queen or about a law broken (see Chapter 2) but, rather, about harm and harmed relationships. Often these harms or criminal offences are heavily influenced by relationships between individuals, families, and communities and intersect with broader societal processes. These behaviours and harmed relationships, often circumscribed as criminal by Western judgment, are an expression of the traumatization and victimization experiences of Aboriginal peoples and Aboriginal youth in particular. They are expressions of anomie, strain, or normlessness: in other words, feelings of being lost. **Values** from Aboriginal knowledge and experience inform us that expressions of anomie are essentially about broken relationships, a consistent theme throughout Aboriginal justice perspectives. If we take this approach to understanding youth misbehaviour, it becomes more difficult to accept 'get tough' approaches to crime and easier to explore alternatives to dealing with the problem of crime. Understanding the offender and the context within which he or she has 'chosen' to commit an offence leads us to consider the value of a healing perspective in dealing with such offenders, one that focuses on repairing harms done instead of exacerbating already damaged relationships.

values
A collective conception of what is considered proper, desirable, and good—or improper, undesirable, and bad—in a culture.

Who is an offender? An offender is someone who shows little regard for right relationships and who has little respect for others. Navajos say of such a person, 'He acts as if he has no relatives'. So, what do you do when someone acts as if they have no relatives? You bring in the relatives (Chief Justice Robert Yazzie, Navajo First Nation, in McCaslin 2005, p. 85).

How we define crime—by a law or by a relationship harmed—determines the path we take toward understanding, explaining, intervening, and resourcing solutions. We are reminded of an Aboriginal youth who shared his story with the first author when he was apprehended with a weapon while attending school. 'Why do you have a weapon?' I asked. 'For protection!' the youth responded. 'Protection from what?' I responded quizzically. 'Someone wants to beat me up,' stated the youth. 'Why?' I asked. 'Because my brother beat him up!' Pursuing his logic, I explored the story further: 'Why did your brother beat him up?' 'Because,' said the youth, 'he stole my brother's bike!' Pausing, I thought about the youth's responses. 'So, why is the boy going after you, and not your brother?' (I thought there was a hole in his story.) 'Because my brother is bigger than he is!' he argued. Ah . . . retribution, I thought. I asked, 'Who do you think is winning this fight, you, the boy who is after you, or your brother'? 'My brother! Because he beat up the boy who stole his bike.' 'Yes, I can see that,' I said, 'but your brother doesn't have a bike!' The youth was silent.

In this anecdote, the three Aboriginal youth did not turn to any legal or school authority, or even to an adult with their problem. They simply took matters into their own hands. We can speculate as to how many times this story plays out among Aboriginal youth. Cousins reflects that before the 'Great Law' was introduced, the Haudenosaunee lived pretty much as these three youth: engaged in blood feuds and revenge, and repeating the cycle of vengeance. In response to this internal violence and strife, the Creator sent the Peacemaker to convince the Haudenosaunee to accept the Great Law of Peace and to establish one of the most powerful political alliances on the North America continent (as cited in McCaslin 2005, p. 145).

Injustices in the lives of young Aboriginals beckon redress but, with nowhere to turn, retribution, either against each other or against those with more social privilege, seems the only answer. This is an outcome of processes set in motion centuries ago and is reflective of the destruction of social, cultural, and economic well-being since contact with Europeans. What happened to this once flourishing and rich social fabric comprised of 'a variety of languages, cultures and social traditions' (Report of the Royal Commission on Aboriginal Peoples 1996, p. 6), existing in social cohesion and characterized by group conformity, reverence for nature and community, and awareness of the Creator (Dumont, in the Canadian Criminal Justice Association 2000, p. 6)?

Understanding the Complexities of Aboriginal Youth Crime

> This report is for Lawrence Wegner, Rodeny Naistus, Pamela George, Leo La Chance, and the many unnamed Aboriginal men and women who have paid the ultimate price for ignorance and neglect . . . While these men, and women, who were sons, daughters, fathers and mothers, are gone . . . they are not forgotten.
>
> — Commission on First Nations and Métis Peoples and Justice Reform, 2003–04. Final Report, Vol. II, 2003, pp. 1–1

The complexities of Aboriginal youth crime interlace two main features. First is the shared experience of Aboriginal peoples—historically, culturally, socially, and economically—as defined by relations with the settlers. These relations include racism, broken treaties, assimilation attempts, and domination. A second feature is intergenerational trauma, the repercussions of which are felt in the daily lived experiences of Aboriginal youth. Effects include poverty, underemployment, family violence, high rates of substance abuse, poor health, overrepresentation in the criminal justice system, and experiences of racism and discrimination.

The common experience and the resulting individualized traumatic experiences are so tightly woven together in the life stories of Aboriginal communities and individuals that they should be observed as one. This has been a failing of intervention strategies, which are mostly 'programming' approaches to 'fix' the problem of crime while ignoring root causes of such behaviours. Margaret Wheatley writes this: 'When we start a conversation by asking, "What's wrong and how can we fix it?" we spark criticism, and not necessarily of the healthy sort. . . . When we ask questions like, "Who cares and what is possible?" we immediately open ourselves to one another' (as cited in Borne 2008, p. 49). Shared community and individual healing must occur concurrently (we will discuss this later in the chapter). First, we briefly discuss the historical context critical to understanding the **criminalization** of Aboriginal youth.

> **criminalization**
> The process whereby individuals are assigned the label of 'criminal'.

Historical Context

Broken Relations and Promises

The historical context illustrates the link between Aboriginal youth's common experience, traumatization, victimization, and criminalization. Relationships between Aboriginal and non-Aboriginal (settlers) peoples are marred by broken relations and promises. After some 500 years of a relationship that has swung from partnership to domination, from mutual respect and co-operation to paternalism and attempted assimilation, Canada must now work out fair and lasting

Provincial/Regional	Title
1989	The Royal Commission on the Donald Marshall Inquiry
1990	The Osanburgh/Windigo Tribal Council Justice Review (Northern Ontario)
1991	Report of the Aboriginal Justice Inquiry of Manitoba
1991	The Task force on the Criminal Justice System and Its Impact on the Indian and Métis People of Alberta
1991	Policing in Relation to the Blood Tribe (Southern Alberta)
1992	Indian Justice Review Committee and Métis Justice Review Committee (Saskatchewan)
1993	The Caribou Chicoltin Justice Report (Interior British Columbia)
1995	Report and Recommendations of the Advisory Committee in the Administration of Justice in Aboriginal Communities (Québec)
Federal	
1969	Statement of the Government of Canada on Indian Policy (The White Paper)
1990	Indian and Northern Affairs Canada: Indian Policing Policy Review
1991	Correctional Services Canada: Task Force on Federally Sentenced Women
1991	Law Reform Commission of Canada: Aboriginal Peoples and Criminal Justice
1996	Royal Commission on Aboriginal Peoples: Bridging the Cultural Divide

Figure 10.1 Justice Inquiries and Commissions

Source: Chartrand, L. and McKay, C. (2006).

terms of co-existence with Aboriginal people (Report of the Royal Commission on Aboriginal Peoples 1996, p. 4).

There can be little doubt that there is a relation problem between Canadians of European ancestry and the first peoples of North America (Turtle Island). Figure 10.1 provides a brief chronology of attempts to redress this relationship. These broken relations and promises included policies of domination and assimilation. The establishment of reserves isolated and impoverished Aboriginal peoples: '[The Indian Act] has ... deprived of us of our independence, our dignity, our self-respect and our responsibility', stated Katherine June Delisle of Kanien'kehaka First Nation, Kahnawake, Québec, to the Royal Commission on Aboriginal Peoples (1996, p. 10). Ceremonies such as potlatch—giveaways or gifting—were outlawed; a pass system for reserves was instituted, forbidding outsiders from doing business with Aboriginal peoples without permission of the Indian Agent; and in 1849 residential schools were created to deal with Aboriginal independence and 'savagery' (Report of the Royal Commission on Aboriginal Peoples 1996, p. 11). Along with imposed poverty and economic, social, cultural, and linguistic marginalization, noncompliant behaviours were defined as illegitimate. For example, Aboriginal students in residential schools were forbidden to speak their own language and grow their hair long (an important self-identity for Aboriginal males).

Indeed, from a historical analysis of Aboriginal Peoples and the Criminal Justice System, the Canadian Criminal Justice Association (CCJA) (2000) summarizes its findings:

the historical problems of many Aboriginal peoples stem directly from assimilation, which fundamentally changed the economic, political, and social life—indeed the very culture—of First Nations people. Assimilation policies were based partly on the European belief that Aboriginal people were uncivilized and incapable of governing themselves. As a result of the devaluation of their language, traditions, and customs after this experience, Aboriginal people began to suffer cultural uncertainties. This cultural crisis can be linked to specific internal problems that currently plague Aboriginal communities, including disproportionate levels of Aboriginal incarceration, poverty, unemployment, alcohol abuse, domestic violence, and an absence of economic self-sufficiency and business infrastructure. (p. 3)

For Aboriginal youth, the intergenerational effects of **colonization** are felt to this day. Robert Yazzie, a Chief Justice Emeritus of the Navajo Supreme Court writes, 'In time of legend, Navajos slew monsters. Today, Navajos [youth] face new monsters . . . domestic violence, child abuse, and neglect . . . alcoholism . . . These problems are today's monsters . . . which get in the way of success, (Yazzie, in Boyes-Watson 2008, p. 23).

Historical policies aimed at 'civilizing' and 'assimilating' Aboriginal peoples have created a legacy wherein Aboriginal youth are confronted with 'violence, fear, abandonment, loss, neglect, economic hardship, discrimination and displacement, (Boyes-Watson 2008, p. 23). As Youngblood Henderson writes, these disadvantages create self-identity issues and frustration for Aboriginal youth: 'In the perplexing context of settler states [Canada] and their concept of legal systems, the implementation of human rights and fundamental freedoms will not come easy' (Youngblood Henderson 2008, p. 95).

Traumatization

Lack of freedom to gain independence (i.e., constrained by poverty), powerlessness to engage in healthy choices because of a lack of decent housing, safety, clothing, and diet, as well as the absence of a sense of belonging (intergenerational violence and substance abuse, lack of family cohesion) create an overwhelming sense of oppression. Judith Herman explains:

> Traumatic events call in question basic human relationships. They shatter the construction of the self that is formed and sustained in relation to others [crime behaviour for example]. They undermine the belief systems that give meaning to human experience. They violate the victim's faith in natural or divine order and cast the victim into a state of existential crisis. (Herman 1997, p. 51)

Linking traumatic experiences to history is essential to understanding the issues Aboriginal youth face today. Five-and-a-half centuries after the European arrival in the Americas 'Indigenous populations [today] are characterized by poverty, subsistence holdings [reserves] . . . ' (Youngblood Henderson 2008, p. 28). Such conditions have undermined indigenous culture, languages, self-governance, and relations (e.g., residential schools) with the end result being a profound sense of loss about how the indigenous world should work. Positive self-identity has been diminished by colonialism; racism has made acceptance within the larger social and cultural space challenging and has had an impact 'not only on individual psychological structures of the self (e.g., Aboriginal youth who commit crime) but also on the systems of attachment and meaning that link individual and community' (Herman 1997, p. 51). Various policies, programs, and activities that the government implemented over the history of colonization have undermined Aboriginal traditions, identity, and social cohesion:

colonization
Refers to historical and ongoing processes that began with the arrival of Europeans to the country and that include attempts to dominate and assimilate indigenous peoples.

. . . It becomes clear when considering various sources of trauma, that the eventual impact of trauma originating from outside Aboriginal communities was to generate a wide range of dysfunctional and hurtful behaviours (such as physical and sexual abuse) which then began to be recycled generation after generation inside communities. (Lane et al. 2002, p. 3, in Chartrand et al. 2006, p. 15)

There is a long history of deliberate disenfranchisement of a great proportion of Aboriginal people in Canada, resulting in not only barriers to prosperity but post-colonial stress expressed through addiction, depression, health problems, suicide, and violence (Episkenew 2009): 'Because those steeped in imperial ideology believed without question in their superiority over the Indigenous people, neither the regime nor colonial society in general was willing to welcome the Indigenous peoples into its midst. To do so would have required tolerance of difference, and the colonizers interpreted difference as evidence of inferiority' (Episkenew 2009, p. 25).

Furthermore, in urban settings, the experience of Aboriginal persons involves inadequate housing, limited education, lack of cultural awareness, unemployment, alcohol abuse, and discrimination (Wente 2000). Such underlying social issues cannot be solved through a more punitive criminal justice system.

Educational and Socio-economic Implications of Crime

For youth and young adults who are of First Nations heritage, historical and current societal power structures have predisposed them not only to pervasive disadvantage but to a suppression and repression of personal value, which is apparent across many contexts, one of which is the experience of 'schooling'.

Individuals' experience of school varies greatly according to a two-pronged set of factors. Personal characteristics, including gender, social class, religious creed, and ethnicity, affect students' objective chances of academic success. They also impact on the subjective experience of school, including attitudes toward the institution. Second, education systems differ according to the context and culture in which they are located (Raveaud 2005, p. 460). Essentially, educational institutions are based on academic or vocational streams around Judeo-Christian values. There is a vacuum, generally speaking, in these institutions that can address the personal characteristics and subjective experiences of Aboriginal children and youth. For example, impoverishment and racism can affect learning.

Aboriginals are also disadvantaged socio-economically. The Aboriginal population is younger on average than other groups in Canada and Aboriginals have higher unemployment rates than other ethnic groups in Canada. They are more likely to live in crowded conditions and have higher residential mobility, and their children are more likely to be members of a lone-parent family. In addition, they have lower levels of education (Mercredi 2000; Statistics Canada 2006; Deane et al. 2007; Kelly and Caputo 2007). For policy-makers, focusing on crime (managing the symptom) may be more practical than addressing the social problems, including the **marginalization** of people on economic and racial grounds (the causes), from which crime emerges. Band-aid solutions (i.e., 'getting tough on crime') are quick fixes that divert attention from the broader issues that require more sustained attention, more critical analysis, more resources, and more comprehensive social change.

Contemporary Context

Victimization: A Statistical Profile

Trauma and **victimization** characterize Aboriginal populations yet observers point to a noticeable lack of information on Aboriginal victimization. Research shows that the link between victimization

marginalization
The partial exclusion from mainstream society, and the social inequalities that accompany it, experienced by certain social groups.

trauma
The community-level and individual-level damage, pain, and suffering of indigenous peoples—physically, spiritually, emotionally, and psychically—as a result of the historical and current processes of colonization.

victimization
The experience of being a victim, which can be linked to future criminalization.

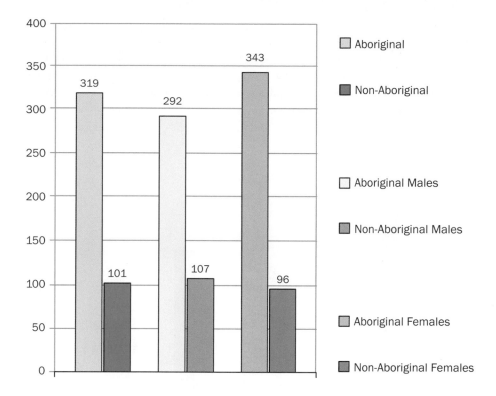

Figure 10. 2 Aboriginal People More Likely To Be Victims of Violent Crime, 2004[1,2]

1. Includes incidents of spousal physical and sexual assault.
2. Includes sexual assault, assault, and robbery.

Source: Statistics Canada, General Social Survey, 2004.

and future criminalization is a significant one (Minaker and Hogeveen 2009). Although a person can be a victim one day and an offender the next, most reports focus on the role of Aboriginal youth as offenders rather than as victims (Chartrand et al. 2006, p. 20) (see Figure 10.2).

Chartrand et al. (2006, pp. 25–32), for example, report the lack of comprehensive data on Aboriginal youth victimization. Further, Kingsley and Mark (2000, p. 42) and Elliot (1997) caution 'that historical, cultural and economic factors experienced by Aboriginal children and youth are different and unique and that "these factors limit application of the non-Aboriginal research, programs and policy to Aboriginal youth-at-risk"' (in Chartrand et al. 2006, p. 31). As Chartrand et al. (2006) explain: '. . . while Aboriginal youth often become engaged in criminality [gangs, sex trade, etc. . . .], their involvement is often a component of their continued victimization' (p. 32).

Figure 10.2 illustrates the relative victimization of Aboriginal peoples compared to non-Aboriginal peoples. While there are no specific studies we are aware of that focus on comparative Aboriginal youth victimization, it is clear from Figure 10.2 that Aboriginal youth victimization is likely similar to that of their families.

Criminalization: A Statistical Profile

Victimization in the form of family violence and abuse, bullying, and other types of assault is far too common in the lives of far too many Aboriginal youth. And the link between victimization and criminalization means many of these victimized youth are at risk for criminal behaviours.

While youth 12 to 17 years old who self-identified as Aboriginal represent 6 per cent of the Canadian population, in 2008/2009 they made up about 24 per cent of youth admitted to remand, 36 per cent of youth admitted to custody, and 24 per cent of youth who received probation (Calverley et al. 2010, p. 12). Figure 10.3 illustrates that Aboriginal youth are more likely to receive sentences that are restrictive and that they are overrepresented in custody dispositions (Calverley et al. 2010). As Figures 10.4 and 10.5 show, female Aboriginal youth are also overrepresented in the system compared to non-Aboriginal female youth, and they experience greater overrepresentation than their male counterparts (Calverley et al. 2010, p. 13).

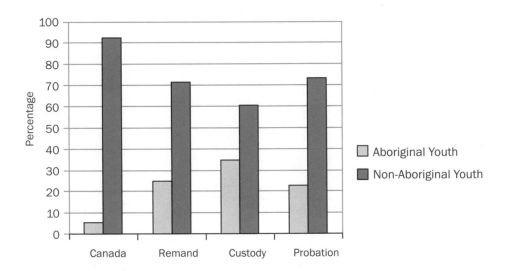

Figure 10.3 Aboriginal and Non-Aboriginal Youth in Canada and in the Youth Justice System

Source: Calverley, Cotter, and Halla 2010.

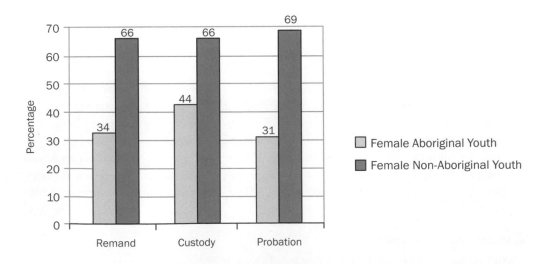

Figure 10.4 Relative Percentage of Female Youth in the Youth Justice System

Source: Calverley, Cotter, and Halla 2010.

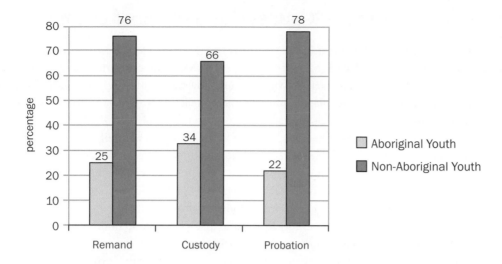

Figure 10.5 Relative Percentage of Male Youth in the Youth Justice System
Source: Calverley, Cotter, and Halla 2010.

The disturbing number of Aboriginal youth coming into conflict with the law occurs even though certain 'rights' are constitutionally guaranteed: 'Section 15: (1) every individual is equal before and under the law . . . without discrimination and, in particular, *without discrimination based on race* [author's emphasis], national or ethnic origin, colour, religion, sex, age, or mental or physical disability' (Roberts and Doob 1997, p. 471). The disproportionate representation of Aboriginal youth in the youth justice system is likely to be a consequence of some combination of the following: higher rates of offending by the Aboriginal population, higher use of the criminal justice system in some Aboriginal communities to deal with certain types of crime, direct and indirect discrimination by the criminal justice system, and the *socially disadvantaged role occupied by Aboriginals* in Canadian society [author's highlight] (Roberts and Doob 1997, p. 482). Indeed, the problem is systemic, as the Canadian Criminal Justice Association (2000) reports:

1. Aboriginal accused are more likely to be denied bail;
2. More time is spent in pre-trial detention by Aboriginal people;
3. Aboriginal accused are more likely to be charged with multiple offences and often for crimes against the system [failing to appear];
4. Aboriginal people are more likely not to have representation at court proceedings;
5. Aboriginal clients, especially in northern communities, where court party flies in the day of the hearing, spend less time with their lawyers;
6. Aboriginal offenders are more than twice as likely to be incarcerated than non-Aboriginal offenders;
7. Aboriginal Elders, who are the spiritual leaders, are not given the same status as prison priests and chaplains, in all institutions; and
8. Aboriginal people often plead guilty because they are intimidated by the court and simply want to get the proceedings over with.

Aboriginal youth crime must, then, be explained within and under historical, social, cultural, and economic conditions—indeed, these realities must be the prima facie conditions under which we examine, and understand, the victimization and criminalization of Aboriginal youth.

Understanding the Causes/Influences of Crime

There is resistance to consider offenders as victims as well. Yet the link between victimization and criminalization is well established (Minaker and Hogeveen 2009). We can perhaps understand this link more clearly if we consider the following question: how much suffering does one individual have to suffer before he or she retaliates against another human being (Gilligan 1996, p. 50)? Gilligan, an experienced psychiatrist, reports that he has not encountered an individual who has harmed another who was not first him- or herself a victim of harm: 'Children who fail to receive sufficient love from others fail to build those reserves of self-love and mostly feel numb, empty, and dead' (Gilligan 1996, p. 50). Feelings of low self-worth often lead to a sense of shame. 'The shame that oppressed Indigenous minorities . . . is central to understanding the persistence of their domination' (Ahmed et al. 2001, p. 4). This shame, according to Brené Brown (2006), is a sense of not fitting in. Aboriginal youth, lacking a cohesive socio-cultural history, retreat to finding 'worth' where it is available. And since marginalization and disenfranchisement mean there are limited options for finding self-worth, Aboriginal youth turn to criminal behaviours and gang involvement to provide such an option.

Identity, Self-esteem, and Risk-Protective Factors

Part of the attraction of gangs is the sense of belonging and identity they promise to provide their members. Identity is a life story or a set of stories that an adult has internalized in order to make sense of his or her life to self and others. Youth are expected to develop a core identity that is reasonably stable and sustainable while living within a society that is characterized by change. This is an enormous task that has the added complexity of 'selective understanding' in which the previous generation still has in its memory, and therefore its focus, the challenges applicable to their day and time. The current adolescent generation, however, faces challenges that may carry the history but reflect a different dynamic (Kegan and Lahey 2001). Aboriginal youth today inherit the legacy of residential school experiences of previous generations, as well as the intergenerational trauma that is the legacy of colonization.

Identity issues have implications for self-esteem. Recent reports find strong connections between low self-esteem and problems such as aggression and antisocial behaviour (see Donnellan, Trzesniewski, Robins, Moffitt, and Caspi 2005; Ybrandt 2008). The term *at risk* has come to be a general descriptor of young people who are considered to be '. . . on a trajectory toward a myriad of problems that threaten their present and future adjustment' (Schonert-Reichl 2000, p. 3). Previously, the word *disadvantaged* described factors that were considered to play a critical role in placing young people in jeopardy: poverty, ethnic minority status, community or family characteristics (i.e., single-parent family), parents' education, inadequate housing, child abuse, home–school breakdown, inadequate knowledge of the country's official language(s), and the type and geographic location of schools (Wotherspoon and Schissel 2001).

While the meaning of *at risk* appears to have multiple forms and inconsistent applications, there are common threads in that the term represents 'a set of presumed cause-and-effect dynamics that place the child or adolescent in danger of negative future events' (McWhirter 1998, p. 7). These dynamics include learning difficulties, poverty, social relationships, and family and school contexts. Youth who are described as 'at risk' are those who may be experiencing one or more life conditions, such as exposure to perinatal stress, lack of basic needs, abuse, death of a parent, school failure, teenage pregnancy, and juvenile delinquency (Schonert-Reichl 2000; Volpe 2000). While the very conception of the term *at risk* rests on the premise of deficit, various interpretations of what comprises that deficit exist. Considering the historical and contemporary life circumstances of many Aboriginal youth, the validity and applicability of the 'at risk' label is worth exploring. But 'risk-protective' factors are not solely about risk. Protective factors refer to those elements in a young person's life that offer insulation against negative influences: a healthy family situation, a positive role model, pro-social friends, involvement in positive activities, and positive educational experiences. For many Aboriginal youth, the situation is such that risk factors tend to outweigh the protective factors. One particularly salient risk factor that Aboriginal youth face is the trauma we have referred to throughout this chapter.

Much has been acknowledged about the trauma of Aboriginal youth as a result of their common experience. Joe Solanto, a faculty member of the Justice Institute of British Columbia, lectures widely on intergenerational trauma and healing. In his presentation to the Public Business and Law Institute Aboriginal Justice Forum (2008), he lays out how trauma not only is experienced by those who were in residential schools but becomes the shared experience of family and community for those who never attended residential schools. The violence becomes a shared experience as it is passed on from parents to children and grandchildren. Substance abuse is an attempt to nullify the pain of the residential school experience and is a learned behaviour to cope with poverty, violence, and family breakdown.

This intergenerational experience contributes to the insidiousness of symptoms that contribute to higher rates of risk among Aboriginal youth. A speaker from the Saskatchewan First Nations Women's Council, in a presentation to the Commission on First Nations and Métis Peoples and Justice Reform, describes the intergenerational experience: 'When some parents feel their lives are spiraling out of control, that parent is more likely to direct a form of violence, verbal, emotionally, physical, sexual, neglect or abandonment towards their child. This form of adult bullying can transfer down to sibling abuse and parental attack' (Commission Vol. I 2003, 3-2).

Kelly and Totten (2002) present a summary of youth violence risk factors, including individual factors, family factors, school factors, peer-related factors, and community and neighbourhood factors (See Chapter 11 in this volume). There are, then, numerous dimensions and layers to issues of crime and criminalization. Up to this point we have emphasized the role of history and social processes that have contributed to the marginalization of Aboriginal youth and have attempted to show how the line between victimization and criminalization is a porous one. We have discussed the importance of discriminatory policies and practices, which have created a context within which criminal behaviour become a viable 'option' for some youth, and we have showed how the criminal justice system is more apt to label Aboriginal youth as offenders and treat them more harshly than their non-Aboriginal counterparts. Rhonda Nelson, in her soon-to-be-completed Ph.D. dissertation on transformative learning as a change agent for youth involved in the criminal justice system, writes this:

> Through an exploration of a portion of the ample literature base, it is clear that, as human beings, we are far more complicated than simply our biology, our environment or our psychology. It is the complex interaction of factors within us and outside of us mixed with the intangible of human agency that makes accurate predictions of human behaviour difficult. (Nelson 2011, p. 5)

Nelson explores a number of theories that take into account other influences on behaviour. We turn, now, to a brief discussion of these other theories.

Biological/Genetic Influences

There is a wide assortment of behavioural problems, personality disorders, and mood disorders that have been determined to be influenced by genes, many of which are related to criminal behaviour.

Intellectual functioning, personality characteristics (for example, negativity), and temperamental factors (for example, impulsivity) all have genetic roots. Behavioural precursors to delinquency and crime (e.g., attention deficit hyperactivity disorder [ADHD]) have also been traced in the behavioural genetics research (Wright, Tibbetts, and Daigle 2008; Cottle, Lee, and Heilbrun 2001). While there is substantial importance attached to what is inherited, genes do not operate in isolation. The environment into which a child is born holds considerable sway as well.

Psychological Influences

From a psychological perspective, it is critical how you perceive who you are, how you understand what you experience and the meaning you place on that experience within the context of your life, and how valued you feel as a person (Spencer, Dupree, and Hartmann 1997). We seek to understand why some people do terrible things to other people, what makes violent people different from 'us'. Classifications have been created to distinguish one type of offender from another and to make sense of the statistics that show that crime is more often located in one group than another. These classifications may be based on characteristics that lead to stereotypical depictions of who is, and who is not, a criminal (Hollin 2007).

Socio-cultural Influences

Explanations for criminal behaviour that rest on social control look outside the individual to the social systems that surround him or her. From this perspective delinquent behaviour results from the failure of personal and social controls to produce behaviour that conforms to the norms of the social system. Delinquency occurs when those norms have not been internalized (e.g., due to marginalization, anomie, etc.). The common thread among the socio-cultural explanations for criminal behaviour is the critical importance of the interaction between an individual and others in his or her immediate and extended social world. Children with peer relationship difficulties are at an increased risk for aggression, academic problems, anxiety, depression, and loneliness, all of which can contribute to delinquent or criminal behaviour (Ooi, Ang, Fung, Wong, and Cai 2006; Haynie 2002; Matsueda and Anderson 1998) and can lead to membership in gangs due to a desire for social belonging and social identity (White 2008). (Also, see Chapter 6 in this volume for further discussion.)

Demographic Influences

The influence of the interrelationship between demographic variables, such as poverty, race, and neighbourhood, has also been explored (Anderson 1994; Anderson and Hughes 2009; Gilbert and Settles 2007; Spano, Rivera, Vazsonyi, and Bolland 2008; Vaughn, Wallace, Davis, Fernandes, and Howard 2008). The sense of physical and social disorder that can be characteristic of neighbourhoods that house large numbers of poor, marginalized people has been shown to exert damaging influences on an individual's social, physical, and psychological health (Weyers, Dragano, Mobus, Beck, Stang, Mohlenkamp et al. 2008; Reyes, Robles, Colon, Negron, Matos, Calderon et al. 2008; Parker and Reckdenwald 2008; Kuo and Sullivan 2001; Farrington 2007). With poverty restricting people's access to supports, their present is compromised and their future is uncertain. Such absence of resources has been implicated in the likelihood of criminalization (Aber, Bennett, Conley, and Li 1997; Spano, Rivera, Vazsonyi, and Bolland 2008; Liddle, Rowe, Dakof, and Lyke 1998; Reiman 2007; Weyers, Dragano, Mobus, Beck, Stang, Mohlenkamp, Jockel, Erbel, and Siegrist 2008).

Fetal Alcohol Spectrum Disorder (FASD)

One group of individuals that is at a higher risk of criminalization includes individuals diagnosed as having **fetal alcohol spectrum disorder** (FASD). FASD provides a poignant example of the ways in which biological, psychological, and social influences coalesce in such a manner as to heighten the risk of both victimization and criminalization. For Aboriginal youth, histories marred by neglect, abuse, and violence exemplify the victimization–criminalization connection. And FASD serves to complicate the situation and increase the risk of both. FASD is the result of maternal alcohol consumption during pregnancy. The degree to which prenatal exposure to alcohol affects the fetus is dependent on a number of factors, including genetics, maternal characteristics, nutrition, duration and exposure to alcohol, as well as a number of other factors. FASD can affect an individual's physical, cognitive, behavioural, and social functioning.

The diagnosis of FASD is challenging. This is partly because it is a relatively new disorder, having only been identified in the early 1970s, and also because not all physicians are trained in the area. Assessments ideally involve a team of specialists, including a geneticist or pediatrician experienced with FASD, a clinical psychologist, a speech-language pathologist, and a school or social worker (Chudley et al. 2005). The specialized nature of the diagnosis process means that the availability of such diagnosis is lacking. To complicate matters, provincial health-care plans do not cover the cost of the assessment, which is about $2000 (Fraser 2010). Given the prevalence of family violence in Aboriginal communities, diagnosis in these communities is further complicated by the overlap of FASD symptoms with post-traumatic stress disorder symptoms (see Table 10.1).

> **fetal alcohol spectrum disorder (FASD)**
> Refers to a medical diagnosis of fetal alcohol syndrome (FAS), partial fetal alcohol syndrome (PFAS), or alcohol neurodevelopmental disorder (ARND), all of which refer to some degree of permanent central nervous system damage to a fetus as a result of maternal alcohol consumption during pregnancy.

Table 10.1 Examples of How the Cognitive and Behavioural Characteristics of FASD Apply to Offenders, Victims, and Witnesses in Court[a]

Category	Characteristic	Difficulty in Court
Intellect	Do not learn from previous experiences	Difficulty understanding legal terms
	Difficulty generalizing from one event to another	Confused by sarcasm or abstract examples used by lawyers
Attention	Restless	Distracted by others entering and leaving courtroom
		Unable to focus on questions being asked
		Easily frustrated or overwhelmed in court setting
Memory	Impaired short- and long-term memory	Forgetful of time of day
		Difficult recollecting events
		Unsure of time frames or duration of events
		Unknowingly adding false statements when trying to remember events
Language	Speech difficulties	Unable to articulate thoughts effectively
Social Communication	Social cues	Going along with whatever argument the Crown, police, or lawyer is saying in order to please them
	Shy	Easily agreeing to leading questions

[a] The information in this table was adapted from 'Victims and Fetal Alcohol Spectrum Disorder (FASD): A Review of the Issues' by Charlotte Fraser, *Victims of Crime Research Digest*. Retrieved from www.justice.gc.ca/eng/pi/rs/rep-rap/rd-rr/rr07_vic4/p4.html

Estimating the incidence and prevalence of FASD is difficult, largely because of difficulties with diagnosis; it is likely, therefore, that the disorder is highly under-diagnosed. There is, however, some indication that rates of FASD are higher in Aboriginal populations. One recent estimate is that the incidence of FASD within the Canadian Aboriginal population ranges from 25 to 200 per 1000 births compared to the estimated incidence rate of 1 to 10 per 1000 births in the general Canadian population (Adler et al. 2009). What appears to be more clear is the link between FASD and criminalization. Recent studies in Saskatchewan and Manitoba report that at least 50 per cent of young offenders were born with FASD. Another in British Columbia found that of 415 individuals with FASD, 60 per cent aged 12 and over had been in trouble with the law (Adler et al. 2009).

FASD, however, also appears to increase the risk of victimization. Because of the nature of the disorder and the problems associated with it, individuals with FASD are particularly vulnerable to be taken advantage of, especially by family members and friends. Complicating matters is the fact that some victims with FASD may not realize that certain behaviours are wrong (i.e., sexual advances and inappropriate touching), may not fully understand what it means to be a victim of crime, and may have difficulty navigating through the court process as a victim or witness (see Table 10.1). Researchers, professionals, and communities alike emphasize the need for more research on FASD and its impact on individuals. Also required is more support for prevention programming and diagnostic assessment. An emerging concern is that gangs have begun to target youth with FASD because those youth are vulnerable, eager to please, and easily influenced.

Investigating the Aboriginal Youth Gang Phenomenon

The average age of a drug dealer in Hobbema[1] is 11.
— Edmonton Police Service Gang Unit police officer

Many of the risk-protective factors discussed thus far manifest themselves in criminal behaviours, but they also can lead to the formation of gangs. Gangs in turn contribute to further criminal behaviours. Risk of victimization within these groups at the hands of rival gang members and members of one's own gang is extremely high. Recent years have witnessed a growing concern with Aboriginal youth gangs, in part because of the perceived growth in these groups, and the increasingly violent nature of their activities. Aboriginal over-incarceration has also led to the strong connection that exists between street and prison gangs for this population. This is not to suggest that all Aboriginal youth are gang-involved, nor is it meant to suggest that all Aboriginal youth crime is gang-related. Investigating the gang phenomenon, however, provides an opportunity to explore the complex ways in which risk and protective factors combine with social, cultural, and historical processes to influence the formation of this type of response to community-level and individual-level issues and problems.

Part of the attraction to gangs for young people from all ethnic groups is based on the media sensationalization of these groups. Movies, music, and internet representations present a glamorous 'gangsta' lifestyle that appears to provide an endless supply of money, drugs, women, sex, and status to its members. The fact that many gang-involved Aboriginal youth strive to imitate their African-American 'gangsta bro's' in terms of dress, behaviour, language, and music is a testament to the power of media to promote a particular lifestyle. As Grekul and LaBoucane-Benson (2008) report, when Aboriginal youth 'choose to take on a personae generated by African-American gangs, they lose their connection to their people and their identity as a Cree, Blackfoot, Lakota, Dene, Metis, etc.' (p. 66). Arguably this search for identity is one of the main underlying causes of gang association for Aboriginal youth, who as we saw earlier, have lost an important part of their identity—their culture—as a result of historical and current discriminatory processes. This element of gang membership may be particularly influential for a group who is defined by cultural identity. In other words, for Aboriginal groups whose culture is integral to 'who they are', experiencing cultural loss has forced some members to seek an alternative source of cultural identity. Gangs may serve that function.

Gangs serve other functions for youth as well. Again, while they are functional for youth of all ethnic groups, the particular configuration of risk factors evident in Aboriginal communities may in fact come together in such a way as to make gangs a viable option for youth experiencing multiple risk factors. For example, a middle-class Caucasian youth who is doing well in school and has friends and a relatively stable family may become involved with a gang mainly to make more money than his part-time job will permit him to make. On the other hand, a young Aboriginal male who has dropped out of school and cannot find a job, and whose family is marred by domestic violence and substance abuse may join a gang as a way to deal with multiple issues. The point is that based on the type of social structural disadvantage discussed earlier, chances are great that an Aboriginal young person will experience multiple risk factors and will be less likely to have protective factors to insulate him/her from what might seem the 'functional utility' of gang involvement (also, see Chapter 11 in this volume).

We have mentioned a number of risk factors that can lead to gang involvement among youth. The gang promises to serve as a substitute family for its members. It promises to provide money and excitement, and it serves as a source of prestige and status for members. For young Aboriginals, many of whom experience violence inside and outside the home, gangs promise protection and loyalty ('we've got your back'; 'we'll back your play'). Protection as a reason for joining a gang becomes more significant for incarcerated youth. Some research suggests that many Aboriginal youth first join a gang inside prison, as a means of protection (Grekul and LaBoucane-Benson 2008). Over-incarceration of Aboriginal youth, then, becomes additionally problematic in that it ostensibly contributes to growth in gangs.

Also related to the unique configuration of social-structural and individually based factors that contribute to gang involvement among Aboriginal youth is recruitment by family members (Grekul and LaBoucane-Benson 2008). Aboriginal gangs were first identified as a growing concern in the early 1990s in Manitoba. Now, 20 years later, and as a result of official government and correctional policies which resulted in the flourishing of these groups in the prairie provinces, Aboriginal communities are witnessing intergenerational gang involvement.

In some cases, youth are even expected to follow in the footsteps of gang-involved parents, uncles, or family members and become members. In one case, for example, a gang-member father involved his two teenage sons in a conspiracy to commit murder. The sons ended up going to jail (as young offenders) for the offence (but the father did not). Out of jail now, the two boys have Facebook pages proudly stating their gang affiliation. In other cases, reports exist of babies being welcomed into their father's gang. Nimmo (2001), in her study on the role of females in Winnipeg's Aboriginal gangs, found that 'blessing-in ceremonies' were an important ritual in some groups. Along similar lines, 'a Native Syndicate member has a picture of his child with a Native Syndicate "dew rag" done up in the knot—the Native Syndicate-style knot—on Facebook as his profile picture' (Interview with gang unit detective). In the words of a gang unit detective, 'you have Native Syndicate members tattooing six-month old babies and they come into the hospital with an infection because they have a Native Syndicate tattoo' (Interview).

The intergenerational element is perhaps a sign of the entrenchment of gangs in some Aboriginal communities and in the lives of some Aboriginal families. The suggestion is that this entrenchment is occurring as a result of the 'almost-institutionalization' of the issues faced by Aboriginal communities. Social structural problems of the type discussed earlier have led to social structural responses that have become long-term and enduring. A gang unit detective (whose father and brother are also police officers) who works closely with these groups explains:

> You have a guy like [name] of the Redd Alert sitting there with his kid in a red bandana
> showing the gang sign in pictures . . . I have pictures of me and my brother wearing police
> hats when we were 10 and 8, or 5 and 3 and it's the same thing. We've allowed this thing
> to get to the level of where you have generational gang membership.

The gang unit detective goes on to explain the significance of this, not only as a commentary or reflection on the entrenched nature of social structural factors, but in terms of ways of addressing the gang issue: 'Intervention strategies on generational gang membership aren't going to work . . . you're not going to get to those youth before anyone else gets to them because they're being taught from a young age: police are bad, gangs are good, this is what you're in.' The implication is that band-aid solutions—programs or policies that target individual-level issues and risk factors—cannot operate successfully without efforts to address the structural-level or broader factors that contribute to the general social-structural disadvantage faced by Aboriginal communities and that manifest themselves in gang involvement.

Members of Aboriginal communities and researchers are increasingly turning to an understanding of intergenerational trauma as a framework for contextualizing the social-structural and individual-level risk factors we have been discussing. The suggestion is that a root contributing factor to youth crime and gangs in Aboriginal communities is based in the generational 'piling up' of trauma and grief, originating centuries ago with the arrival of the colonizers. But this kind of thinking is somewhat at odds with the approach to justice currently informing our criminal justice system.

Attribution of Responsibility: The Youth Justice System

We live in a society where there is personal attribution of responsibility for criminal action according to the law: 'You do the crime, you do the time.' However, the personal attribution of responsibility is not only for the criminal action itself but also the conditions and the response to the conditions that gave rise to the criminal behaviour in the first place: 'Criminal law rests on the notion of attributing personal responsibility for the crime . . . consequently the social, political and cultural context in which the problem occurred disappears into the background' (Law Commission of Canada 2003, p. 13).

There are a multitude of factors and influences that can place an Aboriginal youth at risk and promote negative outcomes, one of which is incarceration. The desire to understand why youth become disengaged and involved in delinquent and criminal activity has propelled inquiry into the situation. As we saw earlier, research into criminal behaviour has provided a variety of causal interpretations. These causal interpretations stem either from a belief that factors internal to the individual or external to the individual play a greater role in determining outcomes. Biological/genetic, psychological, socio-cultural, and demographic conditions exist that have been correlated with an increased likelihood that a child growing up and experiencing a combination of these conditions, each weighing in differentially, will be vulnerable to engaging in criminal behaviour (Wolfgang et al. 1987; Kirby and Fraser 1997; Walsh and Beaver 2009).

Researchers may find it highly desirable to 'find' the critical element(s) that promote criminal activity with an aim of significantly reducing the occurrence of criminal activity by changing those elements. However, to focus only upon the influence that certain experiences, conditions, or substances have on promoting criminal behaviour ignores the added complexity brought by one's own perceptions, motivations, and beliefs in the outcomes of one's life. The range of potentially critical influences that adolescents and young adults will have been exposed to, or currently have active, within their life and the accompanying experiences those influences will have brought with them are mediated by how that person perceives and interprets them in relation to him- or herself. It is this incredibly intricate and individualized interrelationship that provides a basis for attaching considerable significance to a process that, instead, affirms their life journey.

Healing: A More Appropriate Alternative to Aboriginal Youth Crime?

There has been a focus in the literature on causality of crime, on the characteristics of those who get involved in criminality, on the success or failure of interventions, and on the identification of educational needs of youth involved in criminal activities. Some studies look at the problems of youth coming out of custody from the perspective of those youth (Mazzotta 2004) or consider the societal perceptions of race, class, and gender that engender inadvertent bias towards youth who are at risk (Crenshaw 2005). Rarer are studies that seek to understand through the voices of youth and young adults how they perceive themselves as learners within the socially constructed experience of 'schooling' (Duke 1977) and how a change or shift in one's self-perception as 'learner' may be facilitated. What appears to be under-explored is how a sense of 'self as learner' could potentially be enhanced through recognition of past experiences and the learning that has resulted. It is within that gap that we now turn our attention to some Aboriginal perspectives and explanations.

Aboriginal Perspectives

The destruction of Aboriginal peoples' way of life changed their relationships with each other and with the larger society. We have presented how the lives of Aboriginal youth are affected by both historical conditions and contemporary insights. From Aboriginal perspectives—especially those of Aboriginal youth—in order to take a vibrant and meaningful step toward healing, the dominant culture must break down the barriers it has created.

   The most unfruitful response, from a healing perspective, would be for non-Native readers to dismiss or refuse to deal with what Aboriginal youth have expressed. It is this particular sense of white privilege that has contributed to such a gap in awareness in the first place. The fact that Natives often 'speak the truth' in these ways and that non-Natives often are unfamiliar with this level of truth-telling suggests where the healing process might start—namely, with listening to voices and views that are often not heard (Breton, in McCaslin 2005, p. 19). In this sense, the Royal Commission on Aboriginal Peoples (1996) strikes a chord for the future: 'The starting point is recognition that Aboriginal people are not as some Canadians think, an inconsequential minority group with problems that need fixing and outmoded attitudes that need modernizing. They are unique political entities, whose place in Canada is unlike that of any other people' (1996, p. 67).

   The number of Aboriginal perspectives, values, and beliefs is far too great and rich to discuss in this chapter. However, some shared beliefs and values include the following:

- A connection to nature and to each other
- The importance of circles and ceremonies
- 'Resisting justice as force'
- Healing broken relations with mainstream society
- Peacemaking and respecting community

James Dumont (1990) contrasts Aboriginal values with non-Aboriginal values (see Table 10.2) and emphasizes the importance of understanding and respect.

Table 10.2 Contrasting Values

Aboriginal Values	Non-Aboriginal Values
Gets along with group (conformity)	Gets ahead; or on top of the group
Gets ahead for the group	Gets ahead for oneself
Focuses on the present	Focuses on the future
Does not show fear when faced with difficult situations	Does not always face difficult situations with an impassive face
Uses nature and maintains reverence for it (has respect for and relationship with the land)	Uses nature for personal use
Awareness of the Creator	Spirituality is often in the background of one's life
Acts of religion are spontaneous and can occur at any time	Religion is compartmentalized (e.g., religious acts are restricted to certain days of the week)

Source: Dumont in Canadian Criminal Justice Association (2000).

Rupert Ross, Canadian Crown prosecutor and author of 'Returning to the Teachings: Explorations in Aboriginal Justice', learned that he was routinely misinterpreting the behaviour of Aboriginal victims, witnesses, and offenders, both in and out of court. He discovered that he regularly drew incorrect conclusions when he encountered witnesses who would not make eye contact, victims who would not testify in the presence of the accused, and parents who showed great reluctance to interfere in their children's offending behaviour. With the assistance of Aboriginal teachers, he began to see that behind such behaviour lay a complex web of coherent cultural commandments that he had never suspected, much less understood (2006, p. 5).

What Ross learned is well described in the Bulletin of the Canadian Criminal Justice Association and supports the premise discussed in this chapter that trauma is a fundamental experience of Aboriginal peoples, and importantly, of Aboriginal youth. For example, Ross '. . . found that Aboriginal witnesses often describe traumatic events in flat emotionless fashion' (2006, p. 4). The resulting perception is that Aboriginal youth are unresponsive, do not care, and are cavalier about the criminal justice process. Former deputy minister of justice and attorney general of Saskatchewan Robert Mitchell mentioned, after attending the Royal Commission on Aboriginal Issues in the early 1990s, that Aboriginal peoples are less concerned with who committed the crime (guilt) and more concerned with how to repair the harm. The concern is not really with punishment (personal communication). Table 10.3 offers a comparison of the manner in which Western society and traditional Aboriginal cultures understand and approach 'justice'.

The barriers Aboriginals encounter—poverty, substance abuse, family violence, limited education and recreational opportunities—almost guarantee hopelessness, despair, and boredom and certainly contribute to criminal offences (CCJA 2000, p. 6). In the first author's contact with the closed and open custody facilities in Regina, Saskatchewan, many staff reported that Aboriginal youth will commit crimes just to escape the harsh realities of their world on the outside or will commit a breach within the institutions, such as running away during an outing just prior to their release date, to extend their stay. At least then the Aboriginal youth will have a warm, safe place, a school, food, and a sense of positive relationships—with staff.

Table 10.3 Western Justice vs. Traditional Aboriginal Justice

	Western Justice	**Traditional Aboriginal Justice**
Justice system	Adversarial	Nonconfrontational
Guilt	Europe concept of guilty/not guilty	No concept of guilty/not guilty
Pleading guilty	The accused has the right against self-incrimination. Thus it is not seen as dishonest to plead not guilty when one has actually committed the offence.	It is dishonest to plead not guilty if one has committed the crime
Testifying	As part of the process witnesses testify in front of the accused.	Reluctance to testify. It is confrontational to testify against the accused while in his/her presence.
Truth	Expectation to tell the 'whole truth'	It is impossible to know the 'whole truth' in any situation
Witnesses	Only certain people are called to testify in relation to specific subjects	Everyone is free to give their say (witnesses do not want to appear adversarial and often make every attempt to give answers that please counsel, thus often change their testimony).
Eye contact	Maintaining eye contact conveys that one is being truthful	In some Aboriginal cultures, maintaining eye contact with a person of authority is a sign of disrespect
Verdict	Accused is expected to show, during proceedings and upon a verdict of guilty, remorse and a desire for rehabilitation	Accused must accept what comes to him/her without a show of emotion
Incarceration/probation	Means of punishing/rehabilitating offender	Completely absolves Aboriginal offender of responsibility of restitution to victim
Function of justice	Ensure conformity, punish deviant, and protect society	Heal the offender; restore peace and harmony to the community; reconcile the offender with victim/family that has been wronged; punishment is not the objective

Source: Canadian Criminal Justice Association (2000, pp. 5–6)

We have briefly discussed and made a case for understanding the complexities of Aboriginal youth crime. The historical context illuminates the policies of domination and assimilation, phrases we have termed as broken relationships and promises. We suggested that to address Aboriginal youth crime, any intervention must be constructed with elements to address poverty, racism, and self-determination. Further, interventions must include family and community as part of the process.

We have also discussed a number of approaches to understanding the contributing factors to criminal behaviour and criminalization, including those based in biology, sociology, and psychology. We suggest that the criminalization of 'deviant' Aboriginal youth behaviours is largely a result of victimization at individual and social structural levels. Finally, our conclusion is that any effort to effectively deal with the issues facing Aboriginal youth and Aboriginal offenders must be based in an understanding of Aboriginal culture, values, and justice if they are to be effective. Ultimately, any approach to reducing the criminalization of Aboriginal youth must be situated against a backdrop where social structural issues are also addressed.

Summary

> When it comes to moving health-care practices forward efficiently, Canada is a country of perpetual pilot projects. We seldom move proven projects into stable, funded programs, and we rarely transfer the outcomes of pilot projects across jurisdictions. This approach is not serving our health-care system well. (Bégin et al. 2009, p. 1185)

Nils Christie writes, 'My suspicion is that criminology to some extent has amplified a process where conflicts [criminal offences] have been taken away from the parties directly involved and thereby have either disappeared or become other people's property [professionals, researchers]. In both cases a deplorable outcome' (1977, p. 1). The sentiment of both these scholars, Bégin and Christie, informs us of two problems with 'programs': (1) programs come and go as ideas wax and wane in popularity; and (2) programs are not owned by the participants but, rather, are owned by the professionals. In the case of the latter, an Aboriginal youth stated to the Commission on First Nations and Métis Peoples and Justice Reform (2004), 'In many instances I think we would have experiences of bureaucracies who want to maintain control and power over programs that are under various departments' (p. 2–1). Another youth addressing the Commission speaks to the former point:

> And we did a bit of play with words here and thought that maybe we could use, instead of saying crime prevention all the time, we could maybe start talking about community promotion and create a sense of that among our youth, and from an early age, so that from—whether we're talking about the far North, in a small community, or a large city, or your part of the city, that we could be promoting our part of the communities to our children, our youth, so that sense of pride and self esteem is attached to that. (2-1)

Many programs start with good intentions but end up with unintended consequences for Aboriginal youth. Sections 4 and 5 of the Youth Criminal Justice Act provide for alternative interventions. For the first author (a board member of an alternative measures program in Regina, Saskatchewan), it is of constant concern that the number of youth being referred is dropping and that fewer Aboriginal youth are being referred. From a national perspective, referrals to alternative measures have not been widely used in cases involving Aboriginal young offenders (CCJA 2000, p. 6).

There are many programs that can be identified across the country. If we draw on Hester and Miller's idea that there is no 'one true light' (1995, p. 1) explanation or effective response for substance abuse and we extrapolate this observation to broader issues, the implication is that successful interventions into the human condition require considerate and 'multivariate' explanations and responses. Dr Rod McCormick, an Aboriginal psychologist and mental-health consultant, speaks to this understanding: 'Not all strategies will work for everyone as each community is different. That is why it is necessary to explore different strategies and adapt and modify them so that it fits the needs of your [our] youth (McCormick in White and Jodoin 2007, p. ii). One approach that is particularly impressive and that confirms the belief that change is about ownership, resilience, self-esteem, community, and then individuals is found in the First Nations Community Justice Guidebook (2010), developed and published by the Restorative Justice Unit of the File Hills Qu'Appelle Tribal Council (a member of Treaty 4). The book states that the 'program' is 'A facilitated learning process [that] allows for the full and active involvement of all participants and so enriches learning, promotes community development and enables change' (2010, p. 9). The guide continues: 'The art of leading people through processes towards agreed-upon objectives in a manner that encourages participants, ownership and creativity by all those involved' (2010, p. 10). The guide is an important document as many of the Treaty 4 (Southern Saskatchewan and Western Manitoba) languages are incorporated as are important First Nation artwork by Lawrence (Henry) Shepherd. In the guide, 12 elements are presented in a circle and are equally represented at each hour of the clock (2010, p. iii):

- The Youth Criminal Justice Act (12:00)
- Policing and Peacekeeping (1:00)
- Community Justice Committees (2:00)
- First Nations Law (3:00)
- Nurturing Leadership (4:00)
- Wellness and Balance (5:00)
- Inherent Authority and Treaty Relationships (6:00)
- Lands and Resources (7:00)
- Ancestral Laws (8:00)
- Restoring Balance (9:00)
- Justice and Healing (10:00)
- The Legal System and Legislation (11:00)

Surrounding the clock are the nations of their community, written in English, and the language representing each nation. What the guide has successfully accomplished is the integration of history, mainstream thinking, expertise, and practices with a strong sense of community, harmony, the land, and their own knowledge, experience, and expertise. Punishment is not a response: 'In the Commission on First Nations and Métis Peoples and Justice Reform report, Willie Littlechild spoke of people who are "Champions of Change" in our communities who are true leaders' (2010, p. 3). It is not about a single successful program or one that failed; it is instead about developing the culture for change, working collaboratively across 'broken promises and relationships' to effectively reduce the social structural and individual level challenges faced by Aboriginal youth which contribute to their victimization and criminalization in this country.

Key Terms

Aboriginal

colonization

criminalization

fetal alcohol spectrum disorder

marginalization

trauma

values

victimization

Review Questions

1. What happened to once-flourishing First Nations societies that contributed to Aboriginal youth crime?

2. Aboriginal youth experience victimization in greater numbers than their non-Aboriginal counterparts. Explain.

3. Aboriginal youth experience criminalization in greater numbers than their non-Aboriginal counterparts. Discuss.

4. What are the arrays of influences or explanations that contribute to Aboriginal youth crime?

5. How do Aboriginal perspectives on justice differ from that of non-Aboriginal perspectives?

Critical Thinking Questions

1. If Aboriginal youth are to succeed in Canada and partake as full citizens in the economy and educational system, and reduce their undesirable position in the criminal justice system, what critical changes would you make to policies? To legislation? To public education?

2. With respect to the historical relationship of First Nations and Métis peoples to European settlers, there have been numerous federal and provincial inquiries and reports. Yet Aboriginal children and youth today remain disadvantaged in many ways. Can the harmed relationship between First Nations and Métis peoples and European settlers ever be healed? Is the criminal justice system the vehicle for such change?

3. What are the implications for Aboriginal youth programs based on Aboriginal values for Aboriginal youth? For non-Aboriginal youth?

4. Rather than look at Aboriginal youth crime as a conflict with the law, the chapter suggests that the 'conflict' arises out of the intergenerational trauma experienced by youth. Discuss.

5. Discuss how you would intervene if you overheard your friends or family make racist comments about Aboriginal peoples.

Suggested Readings

Ahmed, E., Harris, N., Braithwaite, J., and Braithwaite, V. (2001). *Shame management through reintegration.* Cambridge, UK: Cambridge University Press.

Commission on First Nations and Métis Peoples and Justice Reform. (2003). *Final report, volumes I and II.* Saskatchewan Justice.

McCaslin, W.D. (2005). *Justice as healing: Indigenous ways.* St. Paul, MN: Living Justice Press.

Pranis, K., Stuart, B., and Wedge, M. (2003). *Peacemaking circles: From crime to community.* St. Paul, MN: Living Justice Press.

Royal Commission on Aboriginal Peoples. (1996). *Highlights from the report of the Royal Commission on Aboriginal Peoples: People to people; nation to nation.* Ottawa: Indian and Northern Affairs Canada. Retrieved Jan. 2011 from www.ainc-inac.ca/ap/pubs/rpt/rpt-eng.asp.

Suggested Weblinks

Heartspeak Productions: A Healing River
www.heartspeakproductions.ca/a-healingriver
* A video on restorative justice values and principles.

YouTube
www.youtube.com/watch?v=qQiFfA7KfF0
* Dr Brené Brown: Empathy, Shame, and Vulnerability.

Dr. Joe Solanto: Victimization
http://pipl.com/directory/people/Joe/Solanto
* Joe Solanto has been associated with the Justice Institute of BC as an instructor for over 15 years. During this time, his reputation as both an expert in trauma and as an instructor has grown.

Endnote

1. Hobbema is comprised of four First Nations and is located about an hour's drive south of Edmonton, Alberta. The area witnessed seven homicides in 2008 alone; the drive-by shooting of a toddler sitting at her grandfather's dinner table brought the community of approximately 12 000 into the national spotlight.

References

Adler, F., Mueller, G.O.W., Laufer, W.S., and Grekul, J. (2009). *Criminology* (Canadian ed.). Toronto: McGraw-Hill Ryerson.

Ahmed, E., Harris, N., Braithwaite, J., and Braithwaite, V. (2001). *Shame management through reintegration.* UK: Cambridge University Press.

Bégin, M., Eggertson, L., and Macdonald, N. (2009, June). A country of perpetual pilot projects. *The Canadian Medical Association Journal, 180*(12).

Blatier, C., Corrado, R., and Freedman, L. (2011). The over-representation of children in care in the youth criminal justice system in British Columbia: Theory and policy issues. *International Journal of Child, Youth and Family Studies 1 & 2*: 99–118. Retrieved 2 February, 2011, from http://journals.uvic.ca/index.php/ijcyfs/article/download/5429/1907

Borne, P. (2008). *Community conversations.* Toronto: BPS Books.

Boyes-Watson, C. (2008). *Peacemaking circles and urban youth: Bringing justice home.* St. Paul, MN: Living Justice Press.

Braswell, M.C. (2005). Criminal justice: An ethic for the future. In M.C. Braswell, B.R. McCarthy, and B.J. McCarthy, *Justice crime and ethics.* Matthew Bender & Company.

Brown, B. (2006). Courage, compassion and connection: Deconstructing the elements of shame resilience. Unpublished. In review.

Calverley, D., Cotter, A. and Halla, E. (2010, Spring). Youth custody and community service in Canada, 2008/2009, *Juristat,* 30(1).

Canadian Criminal Justice Association. (2000). Aboriginal peoples and the criminal justice system. Ottawa: Special edition of the *Bulletin.*

Canadian Criminal Justice Association. (2008, Spring/Summer). *Youth Justice, 23*(2-3). Ottawa.

Chartrand, L. and McKay, C. (2006). A review of research on criminal victimization and First Nations, Métis and Inuit peoples 1990–2001. Policy Centre for Victim Services, Department of Justice Canada.

Christie, N. (1977). Conflict as property. *The British Journal of Criminology, 17*(1): 1–15.

Chudley, A.E., Conry, J., Cook, J.L., Loock, C., Rosales, T. and LeBlanc, N. (2005). Fetal alcohol spectrum disorder: Canadian guidelines for diagnosis. *Canadian Medical Association Journal, 172* (supplement 5): s1–s21.

Commission on First Nations and Métis Peoples and Justice Reform. (2004). *Legacy of hope: An agenda for change.* Final Report, Volume I. Saskatchewan.

Commission on First Nations and Métis Peoples and Justice Reform. (2003–04). *Submissions to the commission,* Volume II. Saskatchewan.

Dumont, J. (1990). Justice and Aboriginal people. Public Inquiry into the Adminstration of Justice and Aboriginal Peoples. Winnipeg, MA. In *The Bulletin,* Canadian Criminal Justice Association.

Elliot, D. (1997). Social and health-care pilot project for sex trade workers: Interim report. In L. Chartrand, and C. McKay, *A review of research on criminal victimization and First Nations, Métis and Inuit peoples 1990–2001.* Policy Centre for Victim Services, Department of Justice Canada.

Episkenew, J. (2009). Taking back our spirits: Indigenous literature, public policy and healing. Winnipeg, MB: University of Manitoba Press.

Fraser, C. (2010). Victims and fetal alcohol spectrum disorder (FASD): A review of the issues. Department of Justice, Government of Canada. Retrieved 22 January, 2011, from http://www.justice.gc.ca/eng/pi/rs/rep-rap/rd-rr/rr07_vic4/p4.html

Gilligan, J. (1996). *Violence: Our deadly epidemic and its causes.* New York: Gosset/Putman Books.

Grekul, J. and LaBoucane-Benson, P. (2008). Aboriginal gangs and their (dis)placement: Contextualizing recruitment, membership and status. *Canadian Journal of Criminology and Criminal Justice, 50*: 31–57.

Herman, J. (1997). *Trauma and recovery.* New York: Basic Books.

Hester, R.K. and Miller, W.R. (1995). *Handbook of alcoholism treatment approaches: Effective alternatives* (2nd ed.). Needham Heights, MA: Allyn and Bacon.

Kelly, K.D. and Totten, M. (2002). *When children kill: A social psychological study of youth homicide.* Peterborough, ON: Broadview Press Ltd.

Kingsley, C. and Mark, M. (2000). *Sacred lives: Canadian aboriginal children & youth speak out about sexual exploitation: Save the Children Canada.* http://publications.gc.ca/collections/Collection/RH34-12-2000E. pdf

McCaslin, W. (2005). *Justice as healing: Indigenous ways.* St Paul, MN: Living Justice Press.

McWhirter, P.T. (1998). Risk factors associated with adolescent alcohol, tobacco, marijuana, solvent inhalant and cocaine use. *National Institute on Drug Abuse Research Monograph 179*: 202.

Minaker, J.C. and Hogeveen, B. (2009). *Youth, crime, and society: Issues of power and justice.* Toronto: Pearson Prentice Hall.

Nelson, R. (2011). Reconstruction of a learner self: A phenomenological study with youth and young adults post-incarceration. Doctoral candidate, dissertation proposal in the Faculty of Education & Faculty of Graduate Studies and Research, University of Regina, unpublished.

Newman, D. (2009). *A duty to consult: new relations with Aboriginal peoples.* Saskatoon, SK: Purich Publishing Ltd.

Nimmo, M. (2001, June). *The 'invisible' gang members: A report on female gang association in Winnipeg.* Canadian Centre for Police Alternatives.

Restorative Justice Unit, File Hills Qu'Appelle Tribal Council. (2010). *First Nations community justice handbook.* Saskatchewan: File Hills Qu'Appelle Tribal Council.

Roberts, J. and Doob, A.N. (1997). Race, ethnicity and criminal justice in Canada. Crime and Justice, 21. Ethnicity, crime and immigration: Comparative and cross-national perspectives (pp. 469–522).

Ross, R. (2006). *Dancing with a ghost.* Toronto: Penguin Group.

Royal Commission on Aboriginal Peoples. (1996). Highlights from the report, *People to people, nation to nation.* Ottawa: Indian and Northern Affairs Canada.

Solanto, J. (2008) Aboriginal Justice Forum presentation: Intergenerational trauma and healing. Found on the National Day of Healing and Reconciliation, January 28, 2010. Forum organized by Pacific Business & Law Institute with support from the Aboriginal Directorate, Justice Canada. Retrieved 8 June, 2011, from http://ndhr.ca/wordpress/?s=solanto

White, J. and Jodoin, N. (2007). *Aboriginal youth: A manual of promising suicide prevention strategies.* Centre for Suicide Prevention, Canadian Mental Health Association, Alberta Division.

Youngblood, H.J. (Sa'ke'j). (2008). *Indigenous diplomacy and the rights of peoples: Achieving UN recognition.* Saskatoon, SK: Purich Publishing Ltd.

Yazzie, R. (1993). Life comes from it: Navajo justice concepts. Legal education series, alternatives in dispute resolution and traditional peace making (Petaluma, CA: National Indian Justice Centre. In W. McCaslin (2005), *Justice as healing: Indigenous ways.* St Paul, MN: Living Justice Press.

11 An Overview of Gang-Involved Youth in Canada

Mark Totten

Overview

This chapter will provide an overview of youth gangs in Canada, including three major types of gangs: (1) street gangs, (2) mid-level gangs, and (3) organized crime groups. The primary differences between these gangs include hierarchical structure, level of sophistication, degree of organization, seriousness of criminal activity, breadth of influence, and longevity. We will also discuss the different roles in gangs, along with gender issues. Many young women involved in gangs experience sexual exploitation and other forms of violence. In general, most young women play tertiary roles in gangs. In addition, this chapter will present a biopsychosocial model for understanding gang involvement. This model explores key risk and protective factors in the following areas: biological and genetic, psychological, family, peer group, and community. Finally, we will investigate quality prevention, intervention, and suppression strategies.

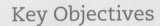

Key Objectives

After reading this chapter, you should be able to:

- Present an overview of the study of youth gangs.
- Examine internalized and externalized patterns of violence for gang-involved youth.
- Review Canadian judicial responses to gang crimes.
- Outline biopsychosocial explanations of gang involvement.
- Identify quality prevention, intervention, and suppression models.

Introduction

To understand and address youth involvement in gangs, we must examine pathways into and out of gang life. Qualitative research provides an excellent opportunity to hear the voices of young gang members. We begin this chapter by providing an overview of gang research in Canada. Next, we explore the differences between street gangs, mid-level gangs, and organized crime groups. We investigate why marginalized Aboriginal and minority young people are overrepresented in Canadian gangs and look at female involvement in gangs. Next, we examine a biopsychosocial model for understanding gang involvement. Finally, we explore quality prevention, intervention, and suppression approaches. Unfortunately, Canada's 'get tough' policies under the Conservative government do not work. We cannot incarcerate our way out of the gang problem.

Gang-involved youth are not born bad. Instead, they are trained by violent and unhealthy adults to engage in violent offending. When we take the time to sit down with gang members and hear their stories—what life has been like for them in early childhood, adolescence, and young adulthood—a clear picture emerges. Instead of just being 'gang members', we see that these young people have endured tremendous suffering and, despite this, have hidden talents and skills. Some are talented singers and rappers; others are poets and writers. Many have acute business savvy—skills that can be applied to the business world outside of gang life. Many are parents, struggling to raise children in impoverished and marginalized circumstances. Finally, most have tremendous health problems, such as brain damage, developmental delays, learning disabilities, and terminal illnesses. When we see the human face of gang-involved young people, it is much easier to develop quality strategies to prevent gang involvement, support exit from gangs, and implement effective criminal-justice-system responses.

Overview of Gang Research in Canada

How Many Are There?

It is difficult to find accurate data on the actual number of gangs in Canada. Police-based estimates are likely inflated for two main reasons: (1) there is no commonly accepted definition of a gang; and (2) levels of funding are in part dependent on how large the gang problem is (i.e., if police report high gang activity, they are likely to get an increase in funding). In addition, there is a lack of academic research focusing on prevalence across the country. Most studies have directed their attention to specific regions of Canada.[1] In addition to these problems, it is difficult to come up with a list of gang names and members because low-level street gangs are in a state of constant flux. Names and membership frequently change.

In 2006, the Criminal Intelligence Service of Canada identified 344 street gangs with 11 900 members. Three per cent of the identified gangs were organized crime groups. Most street gang members were between 21 and 30 years of age, and almost all had youth and adult members. Roughly 6 per cent were youth only—18 years and younger. These gangs were active in 166 urban, rural, and Aboriginal reserve areas. At that time, gangs were active in all parts of the country with the exception of PEI, Yukon, and Nunavut (CISC 2007). In 2010, the Criminal Intelligence Service of Canada reported that there could be as many as 900 gangs in Canada (CISC 2010). Although this may seem like a large increase in the number of gangs since 2006, we should interpret these figures with caution. It could be that new gangs are forming, but it could also be the case that police are counting gangs differently (for example, organized crime groups could be identified as street gangs, and cells from larger gangs could be identified as new gangs). As well, street gangs could break apart, forming smaller groups; and gangs could be changing names.

Western Canada has consistently had higher violent crime rates and gang activity compared to central and eastern Canada. This is likely due to pockets of high crime in cities such as Vancouver (the Downtown Eastside), Winnipeg (West End, West Broadway, Centennial, and North End neighbourhoods), Regina (the North Central neighbourhood), and Saskatoon (including Pleasant Hill and Riversdale communities).[2] These areas are populated by transient young men who are high school dropouts, by single-parent families with high rates of violence and abuse, and by addicts; the areas are characterized by high poverty, poor housing, and drug dealing.

Where Are They Located?

As we will illustrate in this section, gangs can be found throughout Canada, and their level of activity and membership varies by region.[3] Most street gangs are based in ethnically marginalized neighbourhoods and on reserves, and do not expand their territory outside of their turf or province. However, there are a few gangs that have higher levels of sophistication and have expanded to other parts of Canada or to the United States. Gangs with interprovincial connections include IP, NS, Crazy Dragons, UN, IS, Bo-Gars, and North Preston's Finest. Transnational gangs identified in Canada include MS-13 and the 18th Street Gang.

The Maritimes

One of the few active gangs in Newfoundland and Labrador is Street Fame. In Nova Scotia, there are roughly 10 gangs: Gaston Road Gang, G-Lock, Murda Squad, North End Dartmouth, Money Over Bitches, Wolf Pack, and the Woodside Gang. A small number of gangs have connections to other parts of Canada (such as North Preston's Finest), primarily involved in the sex trade. In New Brunswick, there are roughly seven gangs, including various factions of the Crips and the Bloods. Some of these also have links to gangs in other parts of Canada, including Ontario and Québec. Again, prostitution and trafficking of young women are the main criminal activities.

Québec

There are roughly 50 known gangs in Québec, most being Haitian, Jamaican, or Hispanic-based. Most gangs are ethnically homogenous and tend to be aligned with Red or Blue factions. Gangs that have a high degree of criminal sophistication and that are linked to outlaw motorcycle gangs or the Italian Mafia include Bo-Gars, Crack Down Posse, Syndicates, and the Wolf Pack. Most gangs in Québec are in the Montreal area, with the remainder based in Gatineau, Laval, Longueil, and Québec City.

Ontario

There are approximately 180 gangs in Ontario, with roughly 80 gangs in the Greater Toronto Area and 95 in York and most other major cities throughout Ontario as well as on Northern reserves.

Of these gangs, a handful are criminally sophisticated, highly organized, and linked to groups in other parts of Canada. They include the Slingers (Waterloo); the Québec-based Crack Down Posse (Niagara Falls) and Bo-Gars (Niagara Falls); Jamestown Crips, V.V.T., and Malvern Crew (Toronto); and the Ledbury-Banff Crips (Ottawa).

Manitoba

There are roughly 25 street gangs in Manitoba. A majority are Aboriginal, along with smaller numbers of African- and Asian-based groups. These latter gangs are primarily active in the Winnipeg area (including the Mad Cowz, African Mafia, and Asian Bomb Squad), whereas Aboriginal gangs are also based in Winnipeg (such as Native Syndicate and Indian Posse), and in rural areas and on reserves (including Manitoba Warriors, Indian Posse, Native Syndicate, and Native Syndicate Killers).

Saskatchewan

There are roughly 20 street gangs in this province, and almost all are Aboriginal. Indian Posse (IP) and Native Syndicate (NS) are the most sophisticated, with cells in Manitoba and Northern Ontario. The Hells Angels and their puppet club (the Freewheelers) have been in conflict with NS over the lucrative drug trade. Saskatoon, Regina, and Prince Albert have the highest number of active gangs, including Brown Premise, Crazy Cree, Crazy Dragons, Indian Mafia, Crips, Tribal Brotherz, and Scorpion Brothers, among several others. Fort Qu'Appelle, Yorkton, and many reserves also have gang activity.

Alberta

There are roughly 30 street gangs in Alberta. The Crazy Dragons is likely among the most sophisticated given its many cells across Alberta, in other provinces, and in the Northwest Territories. Most other gangs are Asian-based (such as Fresh Off the Boat and Fresh Off the Boat Killers) and Aboriginal (including IP, Redd Alert, and Alberta Warriors). Hobbema Reserve has a very high rate of gang activity, with a handful of gangs competing for control of the drug trade.

British Columbia

There are approximately 30 active gangs in this province, with most based in the Lower Mainland (including the 18th Street gang, Bloods, Crazy Dragons, Crips, MS-13). Some of these gangs have migrated to smaller cities, such as Prince George and Cranbrook. Aboriginal gangs are active on some reserves and in the Downtown Eastside of Vancouver. The most sophisticated gangs include the United Nations Gang (UN), Independent Soldiers (I.S.), and Red Scorpions. Many low-level gangs buy drugs from organized crime groups, such as Asian organized crime and the Hells Angels.

Northwest Territories

There is very little gang activity in the Territories, although cells of the Crazy Dragons, IP, Alberta Warriors, and RA have been active in Yellowknife. These gangs are primarily based in Alberta and have migrated north due to the lucrative drug trade.

Gang Typology in Canada

The multidimensional frameworks developed by Totten (2008a; 2009a, b) and Mellor et al. (2005) highlight the different types of Canadian gangs involving young adults.[4] Street gangs are visible, hard-core groups that come together for profit-driven criminal activity and often severe violence. Gang-related communication rituals and public displays of gang-like attributes are common, including tattoos (Totten 2000b, 2001; Gordon 2000). Gang involvement in Canada exists on a continuum and types of gangs can be conceptualized using a pyramid diagram (see Figure 11.1). The degree of organization in the gang is defined by the following:

- The gang's structure and hierarchical nature
- The gang's connection to larger, more serious organized crime groups
- The gang's sophistication and permanence
- The existence of a specific code of conduct or set of formal rules
- The gang's initiation practices
- The level of integration, cohesion, and solidarity among the gang's members (Totten 2008a; Mellor et al. 2005)

This integrated Canadian model allows for a general typology that can be applied and adapted to identify specific types of gangs. The common structure is very similar to that identified in the United States (Block and Block 2001), Europe (Klein 2002), and other countries (see Grennan et al. 2000). The continuum includes street gangs, mid-level gangs, and organized crime groups.

Street Gangs

Almost all youth gang members in Canada belong to street gangs. Following are some characteristics common to most street gangs:

- Street gangs are involved in serious crime and violence—this differentiates gangs from non-criminal youth groups.
- Street gangs have some stability over time, yet membership is fluid.
- Typically they claim an area/turf, which they protect from rival gangs. This may be a housing project or an area they claim to be their own for drug distribution.

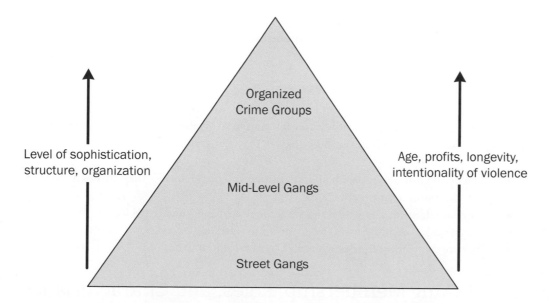

Figure 11.1 Gang and Organized Crime Group Typology

Source: Based on the work of Shinder Kirk, B.C. Integrated Gang Task Force*

* Verbal permission granted to use this diagram November 30, 2010.

- Members identify themselves through a common name, symbols, colours, signs, graffiti, clothing styles, bandanas, and hats.
- They rely on violent entry and exit rituals to protect the gang from outsiders.
- Marginalized ethnic and racial minorities including Aboriginal youth dominate membership. While some gangs have members mainly from a single ethnic group, an increasing number have a multi-ethnic membership. One key factor that differentiates those who become gang-involved from those who do not is the experience of severe poverty.
- Drug and alcohol abuse is common.

Mid-level Gangs

Mid-level gangs have characteristics of both street gangs and organized crime groups:

- These gangs can be multi-ethnic, although some groups in the Prairie provinces are exclusively Aboriginal.
- Members may come from different socio-economic backgrounds, but Aboriginal and African gang members have lived in extreme poverty.
- These gangs are frequently rooted in school, justice, and child-welfare settings—family blood lines and neighbourhoods are important.
- Compared to organized crime groups, mid-level gangs are made up of unstructured smaller groups or cells.
- Like street gangs, relationships with other groups are fluid and opportunistic—often organized around lucrative criminal opportunities.
- These gangs are involved in serious crimes: extortion, kidnapping, drug dealing and smuggling, homicide and extreme violence, and trafficking.
- Violence is often initiated in response to perceived threats from other groups, whether real or not.
- Members rely on violent entry and exit rituals to protect the gang from outsiders.
- Mid-level gangs are frequently sophisticated and disciplined (Totten 2010b).

Organized Crime Groups

According to the Criminal Intelligence Service of Canada,[5] organized crime groups have a number of common characteristics. It is relatively rare for teens to be involved in these sophisticated organizations. Typical features include the following:

- Organized crime groups are highly structured and hierarchical—they are often modelled after successful companies.
- They have flourished over time and are recognized, feared, and respected.
- Membership is exclusive and is based on family, race, and ethnicity.
- They are complex enterprises with rules, by-laws, and constitutions.

Street Gang Membership, Roles, and Characteristics

Who Is Involved in Street Gangs?

Youth gang membership can be conceptualized using a concentric circle diagram: wannabees/posers are on the outside, new recruits are in the outermost ring, and leaders are in the innermost ring (see Figure 11.2). The leadership structure is made up of the original founder and core members who started the gang. Membership commitment can be measured in a hierarchical ranking system within the gang (Totten and Dunn 2009a, b, c; 2010a, b, c). Often, there is not one person who directs other members, although older members have more influence compared to young members. Leaders (also called king pins, bosses, presidents, or captains) actively promote and participate in serious criminal activity. These males are generally in their mid-twenties or early thirties. Veterans (also called heavies or higher-ups) decide which criminal activities the gang will participate in and are considered to be faithful in their loyalty to the gang. Along with leaders, they are responsible for settling internal conflicts within the gang. These conflicts typically arise from members having friendships with rival gang members, those who engage in sexual relations with girlfriends of fellow gang members without their expressed consent, or those who steal money from criminal profits or illicit drugs. Consequences range from severe beatings to death. Core members (also called associates or affiliates) usually have been with the gang since it started and are experienced, proven members. Wannabees are at particularly high risk of being victimized by violence at the hands of legitimate gang members. These youth are looking for a sense of belonging and family,

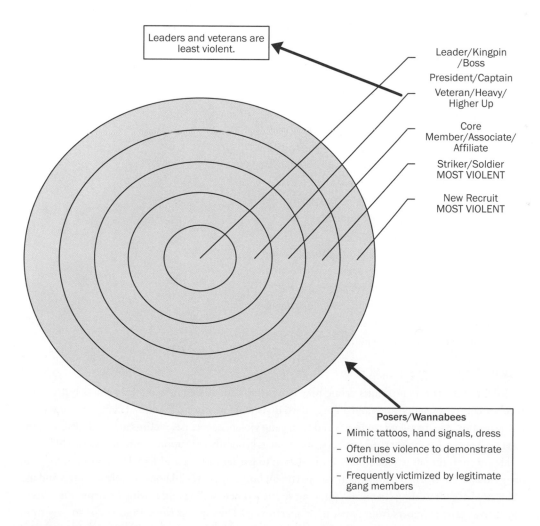

Figure 11.2 Roles in Street Gangs and Levels of Violence

Source: Totten 2010b.

and go to great lengths to mimic gang membership through tattoos, dress, display of colours, and hand signals.

There are some common indicators of membership. The more indicators there are, the greater the likelihood that a young person is gang involved. They include such indicators as: stylized dress and haircuts; jewellery; tattoos; gang slang; graffiti and drawings; monikers or nicknames; hand signs; claiming or repping (representing a gang using their dress, hand signals, graffiti, etc.); association with known gang members; burns and scars, particularly those which are stylized (such as cigarette burns in the form of a triangle); branding (including burning a gang tattoo off); gang photos on social media sites.

What Are the Primary Activities of Street Gangs?

Hanging Out

Contrary to popular belief, gang members spend the majority of their time hanging out, meeting basic needs such as food and shelter, partying, and being incarcerated (Totten 2010b). A primary activity is heavy drug and alcohol use and generally a withdrawal from mainstream social inter-action. Due to such drug use, property crimes and crimes of violence may result, often on an impulsive and senseless basis (Totten 2008a). Lori,[6] a 21-year-old female gang member, illustrates this life through her poetry:

> **The Hustle**
> *Hangin' on the corner time to slang another rock*
> *Watchin' for the pigs I keep my stash in my sock*
> *Feins[7] are actin' shady so I stay on my toe'z*
> *Careful not to slip and get caught up with the hoe'z*
> *Streets are gettin' drastic so I'm strappin' steel*
> *Hustlin' to make enough for my next meal*
> *My family's got to eat so I'm slangin' crack*
> *Paranoid as fuck hopin' I don't get jacked*
> *Bitche'z are always buggin' so they can get a cuff*
> *I know I can't five in cause I won't make enough*
> *Cops pullin' me over sayin' get on tha ground*
> *Reachin' for my socks knowin' it's a shake down*
> *Busted with some gags this shit is hell*
> *(name) your goin' back to jail.*

Making Profits from Serious Crime

Making money through serious crime may be episodic for disorganized street gangs but usually involves complex relationships and an organized division of labour for mid-level gangs and organized crime groups. As street-level robberies and rival gang violence increase, victims are made aware of the 'turf war' as gangs establish their territory. Street gangs generally prey upon communities in which they reside through threats, violence, and intimidation to garner respect and fear. It is common for rival gangs to take control of separate high-rise apartment buildings in social housing communities and use them as a base for dealing chemicals, pimping young women, selling and storing firearms, and shoot-ing at rival gang members from upper floor apartments. These gangs sometimes extort money from residents in return for protection from enemy gangs (Totten 2010b). As members become entrenched in violence and crime, the complexity of their behaviour increases and they assume a permanent place in specific geographic spaces. They come to acquire a steady supply of chemicals to sell (crack cocaine, crystal methamphetamine, ecstasy, heroin, etc.) and a sophisticated arsenal of guns to protect themselves and kill off rivals. The frequency and seriousness of violence and crime escalate over time, and by intimidating witnesses to their criminal activities, gang members enhance their status and increase their control over community residents and rivals, which we will discuss next.

Engaging in Severe Violence

Violence within and between gangs is associated with gaining social status and reputation. There is an emphasis on honour, personal integrity, and territoriality. Issues of self-esteem, gender identity, and self-protection help explain the onset and escalation of gang violence. Violence often occurs over seemingly insignificant incidents that are perceived as disrespectful by rival gang members, including crossing out a rival's graffiti or painting it upside down, and showing a rival's hand signs upside down or crossing out a rival's hand signs with another finger (Totten 2010b). There are numerous examples in Canada of street gangs splintering into different groups as a result of internal conflict. These groups then engage in severe violence, including murder, against each other (e.g., N.S. and Native Syndicate Killers; Fresh Off the Boat and Fresh Off the Boat Killers, etc.).

What Are the Distinguishing Characteristics of Gangs?

Hand Signals and Dress

The Bloods and Crips are two good examples of how different gangs use hand signals and dress to represent their gang. Each of these gangs has adopted specific cultural forms and public presentation of their attributes. Bloods' identifiers and symbols include the colour red, red bandanas ('rags'), crossed-out *C* in words as disrespect for Crips, and other disrespectful anti-Crips graffiti. Crips identifiers and symbols include the colour blue, blue bandanas, using the letter *C* in place of *B* in writing in disrespect for Bloods, and calling themselves 'Blood Killas' (BK).

Most Bloods gangs use one hand to form a variation of the lower-case letter *b* to represent or lay claim to their territory or faction. This form of 'repping' is used in many situations where other gang identifiers may not be possible or appropriate (such as graffiti), and it can also show that a gang member is in the area to conduct gang business as opposed to just passing through. These hand signs can also serve to relay more specific information, such as what faction gang members represent within a larger gang or in which activities they are currently taking part. Individual letters can be used to tell stories when flashed in rapid succession, each representing a word beginning with that letter. Some gang-related hand signals are similar to other common hand signs, which can result in confusion between gang members as well in individuals who are not affiliated with gangs. Sometimes the result is violent victimization.

Tattoos

Street gang members use tattoos for several reasons. Most gang members have numerous tattoos, particularly if they have spent time in young offender facilities, jails, or prison (Totten 2010b). Tattoos portray one or more symbols that the gang has adopted as something unique to represent the gang. Tattoos are also worn and used for intimidation. Members of violent gangs usually have the gang name tattooed in large, bold letters so that other persons or gang members will know what gang the person represents. Wearing an unauthorized tattoo typically results in the wearer being severely beaten or killed.

Crosses between the knuckles on both hands are meant to signify the number of years served in federal facilities (one cross is equivalent to one year served). Three dots or cigarette burn marks forming a triangle (usually near the thumb or wrist or next to one eye) signifies *mi vida loca* or 'my crazy life' (Knox 2000). Gang members in Canada report that the teardrop tattoo signifies to fellow gang members and rival gangs that the gang member killed a rival, had a member of his or her gang or family killed, or has served time. A primary function that young gang members attribute to this tattoo is to communicate the message that they are dangerous and must be respected (Totten 2010b).

Gang Recruitment and Exit

There are a handful of different routes into gang involvement for young people. Some members are 'born in', others are 'jumped in', some are actively recruited, some get 'sexxed in' or raped in, and yet others form their own gang (Original Gangster). Some of these routes are characterized by a high degree of motivation and choice; others involve no choice and are forced onto youth. For marginalized, abused, and vulnerable youth, there are many positive aspects of gang life. Many gang members talk about having a sense of family and belonging in their gangs, a safe place to hang out with friends, an identity, and a good source of income. For many youth who grow up in communities characterized by high unemployment, entrenched poverty, and violence, gang involvement is a rational choice (Totten 2009a). Gangs can also provide a shelter for young people who have suffered from racism, war atrocities, and the adverse effects of colonization (including having dysfunctional parents who suffered abuse in residential schools) to fight back against social injustice.

Recruitment refers to the process whereby youth are brought into a gang or how they gain access to gangs. The recruitment process is different depending on gang type. For example, in family-based gangs, there is no recruitment outside of the immediate family. Joining the gang is seen as a normal thing to do because prospective members are sometimes exposed to the gang by family members.

In other instances, street gangs and criminal organizations require recruits to perform specific tasks. Youth are required to prove themselves as worthy of being taken into the gang by committing acts of severe sexual and physical violence and/or serious crimes. Leaders are responsible for this. Tasks include armed robbery, aggravated assault, murder (often referred to as being 'murdered-in' and involves killing a rival when ordered to do so by a higher up), chemical dealing, and pimping (CISS 2005). There is a standard process for being recruited in each gang. Recruitment is common in young offender or adult facilities.[8]

Most youth gangs require prospective recruits to meet certain criteria and perform criminal acts before they are allowed into the gang. This is called 'crime-in'. Younger gang members are most likely to be involved in the most serious crimes of violence as they are in the process of being recruited into the street gang. These youth want to prove themselves and rise through the ranks; they often earn serious money for gangs. To gain entry, a recruit generally requires sponsorship. These members have their loyalty tested often by gang members and are 'put in work' by undertaking criminal activities when directed by leaders (Valdez 2000). Before a recruit is allowed entry into the gang she or he is often required to pass three initial tests:

1. Perform a series of criminal acts called *strikes* at the direction of superiors in the gang to prove their loyalty.
2. Produce *paperwork* (a copy of their criminal record) to members of the gang.
3. Endure a beating from the other gang members to prove their strength and loyalty (this is called *beating in*, *jumping in*, or *boot-fucking*).

Gender plays a crucial role in determining routes into gang involvement. Many female gang members get 'sexxed' in or raped in, where they are forced to endure sexual assaults by multiple gang members. The following example illustrates the unique ways in which young women become gang-involved. Julie, 21 years old, was the only female in an all-male street gang from the age of 15 to the age of 19. She had to show the male gang members that she was deserving of their respect and was tough. She also needed a strategy to avoid being forced to work in the sex trade and bring money into the gang. She resorted to pimping out a stable of anywhere from six to ten 15- to 17-year-old girls over a three-year period. She was widely feared on the streets due to her propensity to engage in severe violence. She continued this lucrative operation until she was charged and incarcerated for four years in both youth and adult facilities. She explained how treatment by her caregivers set the stage for gang membership:

> Coke and morphine. That's what I remember when I was young. Always lots of people coming and going, lots of girls and needles and alcohol. They all were slammin' (shooting up). My Dad was a dealer and a pimp—that's why there were always lots of girls and drugs around. That's how they took me (child protection). I brought a friend home when I was like five or six and my Dad and all those people were doing needles and then my friend went home and told her Mom and child welfare came to get me later that day. The cops picked my Dad up. My real Mom I don't like. She could never take care of me or my brother or sister. She's an addict. That day they picked up my Dad I got put in foster care. I've been everywhere—I've stayed in different places—until I went to jail—pretty much all my life . . . They took me from the ghetto and put me into a rich neighbourhood. I was the only Indian in an all-white school . . . Then I started to act out and went to (secure custody facility) lots.[9]

For many, the gang exit process can be just as difficult as, if not more difficult than, joining the gang. Methods of leaving can involve the following:

- *Blood out*: 'Doing minutes' (suffering a beating) at the hands of a couple of gang members.
- *Gang rape*: Being sexually assaulted by multiple gang members.
- *Getting pregnant, having kids, or getting married*: Many gangs purport to have honourable and romantic ideals, including permitting members to leave in order to start their families.
- *Gang exit program*: Joining a comprehensive program that supports leaving the gang. This can be dangerous because higher-ups do not want you to leave.
- *Death*: Unfortunately, being killed or committing suicide is a common way to end gang membership.

Legislation and Official Response to Gangs

Bill C-24 is the only section of the Criminal Code of Canada related to crimes committed by gangs and organized crime groups. The Criminal Code does not, however, make reference to 'gangs'. The legal treatment of gangs is covered by provisions for 'criminal organizations' (see Box 11.1). This section of the Criminal Code has not been successfully applied to many cases. However, there are an increasing number of young offenders who are being charged with organized crime. This is concerning because most youth gangs are not criminal organizations. Instead, they are loosely organized, nonhierarchical, and fluid groups that come together and dissolve quickly after profitable crimes have been committed (see Box 11.2).

Box 11.1 Youth Justice in Action

Legal Definition of a Criminal Organization

Bill C-24: A group, however organized, that:

- is composed of three or more persons, and
- has, as one of its main purposes or main activities, the facilitation or commission of one or more serious offences that, if committed, would likely result in the direct or indirect receipt of a material benefit, including a financial benefit, by the group or by any one of the persons who constitute the group.

(Section 467.1 C.C.C.)

In determining whether an accused participates in or actively contributes to any activity of a Criminal Organization, the Court may look at:

- If accused uses a name, word, symbol, or other representation of the Criminal Organization
- If accused frequently associates . . .
- If accused receives any benefit . . .
- If accused repeatedly engages in activities . . .
- If group has control over territory, either geographical or economic

Box 11.2 Youth Justice in Action

Criminal Intelligence Service Canada Street Gang Definition

'A group of persons consorting together to engage in unlawful activity.'

Criteria:

1. Reliable source of information (inside gang member/rival gang member, legitimate community resources).
2. Police information provided as a result of observed association with other known gang members (i.e., surveillance).
3. Admission of gang membership.
4. Involvement (direct/indirect) in gang-motivated crime.
5. Previous court findings that a person was a gang member.
6. Common and/or symbolic gang definition, (i.e., gang paraphernalia, tattoos, weapons, poems, induction rituals, clothing).

The minimum standard to be met when classifying persons as 'street gang members' is the fourth criteria, with any other two criteria.

Female Involvement in Gangs

Canada has few, if any, all-female gangs. Most youth gangs are male dominated, with a minority of female members. Gang-involved young women have unique and special risks, including a history of victimization (mainly physical, sexual, or emotional abuse); academic failure, truancy, or dropout; repeated running away and prostitution; unstable family life (lack of connectedness, isolation, other family members involved in justice system); a history of unhealthy, dependent relationships, primarily with older males; mental health issues; and a history of substance abuse. Compared to males, young women report having experienced significantly higher rates of physical and sexual violence and victimization in their childhood (Totten 2002a).

There are three categories of young women who are involved in gangs: (1) female members of all-women street gangs; (2) women who are affiliated with male-dominated gangs; and (3) street women in the sex trade (Moore 2007). Young women who are members of all-female gangs are not in the same social situation as those who are affiliated with male gang members. The latter group is more vulnerable. These are the girlfriends and partners of the male gang members. Their affiliation and status is defined by their 'man'. They are likely to experience extreme physical and sexual violence from their male partners and are dominated by them. If these women get rejected by their partners, they become the property of other male gang members. Often, these females monitor the behaviours of other affiliated women, ensuring that they are not intimate or flirting with their 'man'. They do not experience the same sense of belonging and family as members of all-female gangs. Gang-affiliated women are in a position of dependency and are very isolated. Because of the 'code of silence', they must demonstrate loyalty and cannot talk about their violent victimization.

Gang-affiliated young women play tertiary roles, such as being the lookout for the police, dealing drugs, or working in the sex trade (Totten 2009b). They are typically required to carry weapons and drugs because they have a lower chance of being searched by male police officers (Campbell 1990; Curry 1998), especially given the female anatomy (i.e., carrying drugs in the vagina). Women also are likely to also act as escorts, drivers, and intelligence gatherers. They are involved in debit- and credit-card scams. Some manipulate rival male gang members into thinking they want a romantic relationship, when in fact these women are gathering intelligence on the rival gang. Young women who do not have prior criminal records are particularly attractive for gangs because they are off the police radar (Totten 2009b).

On the other hand, young women who are members of all-female gangs report that they are relatively safe and free from violence, and belong to mutually supportive peer groups. Anne Campbell (1987, pp. 463–464) writes that 'Gang girls see themselves as different from their peers. Their association with the gang is a public proclamation of their rejection of the lifestyle which the community expects from them'. Girls in all-female gangs likely resist and negotiate their gender roles outside of traditional femininity; the gang provides a social space to do gender differently.

There are at least two types of all-female gangs: those that are auxiliaries to male-dominated gangs and those that are independent of other gangs. Canada has had very few members of either type. Both types of female gangs are likely to have their own hierarchy and status (Nimmo 2001). Examples include the Winnipeg-based Sisters in Action gang and Native Sistahs (reported to be related to N.S.). The Indian Posse Girls are reported to be the auxiliary to the Indian Posse Gang, and have exerted control of the Edmonton and Hobbema sex trade in the past. The Sisterhood Gang has been identified as affiliated with IP.

Unaffiliated street women/girls are by far the most vulnerable group of females. They are not respected or valued by the male gang members. These women hang out with gangs but do not have relationships with male gang members. Instead, they find themselves attracted to the gang and are treated as sex objects. They are often addicts and sex-trade workers, often referred to as 'party girls'. Some are wannabees or posers.

So far, we have provided an overview of the nature and characteristics of the different forms of youth gangs in Canada. Next, we will explore some of the explanations that have been used to describe and explain their actions.

A Biopsychosocial Theory of Youth Gangs

A **biopsychosocial** perspective (Santrock 2007; Frankel, Quill, and McDaniel 2003; Kelly and Totten 2002) addresses the multiple risk factors related to gang involvement. Pathways into gang life are best understood through an integration of biological, psychological, and social factors, including biophysiological and psychological characteristics, and family, school, peer, and social variables. Within each category, social inequalities such as poverty, gender, and race are significant risk factors that can lead to unhealthy child and adolescent development. Protective factors such as access

biopsychosocial model

An approach used to study the involvement of youth in gangs that addresses biological, psychological, and social risk factors related to gang involvement.

to quality health, recreation, education, and other social services and supports can improve the outcomes for children and youth who are vulnerable.

Children have different social, psychological, and familial experiences. They face different risks, and resiliency varies tremendously. Although all children have a right to an environment that is hospitable and nurturing, a significant minority grow up in one that is hostile and threatening. The playing field is far from level. Resilience is the ability of individuals living in adverse conditions to achieve positive outcomes (Howard et al. 1999; Luthar et al. 2000; Smokowski et al. 1999). It is through resilience that the combination of societal-level, institutional, and individual factors (Dekovic 1999; Gutman and Midgley 2000; Smokowski et al. 1999; Voydanoff and Donnelly 1999) to which young people are exposed result in positive and negative outcomes. It is important to recognize that diverse outcomes can be expected for young people living in similar negative life situations. The key is the ability of individuals, families, schools, and communities to mitigate the risk factors.

Biological and Genetic Factors

Biological and genetic factors can be key determinants of gang involvement. Children are born with different sets of abilities and potential as a result of these attributes in combination with other psychosocial factors. Factors such as resiliency, intelligence, cognitive functioning, physical ability, physical attributes, and body type are important protective factors in determining healthy child and adolescent development (see, generally, Santrock 2007). The presence of one or more of these attributes can go a long way in protecting a young person from involvement in gang life. Developmental problems, learning disabilities, and intellectual limitations, **fetal alcohol spectrum disorder (FASD)**, brain injuries, predisposition to mental-health problems, and certain personality traits are important risk factors that can lead to poor child and adolescent health in the absence of key buffers against these risks (Kelly and Totten 2002).

Personality traits that influence child behaviour are complex and the product of the co-occurrence of several genes (Plomin and Crabbe 2000). Temperament (whether children are fussy or calm, upset or happy) and other characteristics such as irritability, low self-control, and irresponsibility are moderately genetic (Moffitt et al. 2001). Children's capacity to learn the social use of language, to interact with others, and to regulate their emotions are influenced by genetic inheritance as well. These factors are directly influenced by a mother's behaviour when pregnant. For example, malnutrition, smoking, alcohol/drug consumption, and victimization by violence during pregnancy all contribute to negative health outcomes on the fetus. FASD, which results in infant brain damage to areas responsible for planning and self-control (Buxton 2004; Kyshan and Moore 2005), is a particular concern in Aboriginal communities. Risky behaviours during pregnancy are more common in low-income mothers. This is primarily due to a lack of education and other behavioural risk factors (Stark 2004).

It has been estimated that roughly 40 per cent of a child's antisocial behaviours may be related to genetic factors (Rhee and Waldman 2002; Moffitt 2005). However, genes interact with important environmental dynamics. For example, so-called bad genes inherited by a child (e.g., cognitive impairment and low intelligence) most likely will not negatively affect psychosocial functioning in the context of positive parenting, quality schooling, and a pro-social peer group.

In the preschool years, children with difficult temperaments, hyperactivity, impulsivity, oppositional and defiant behaviour, early onset aggression, and social difficulties are at high risk for serious and violent offending trajectories. Without comprehensive early intervention to address risk and protective factors, these children will likely grow into the 5 per cent of all adolescents who are responsible for committing over half of all serious youth crime (Shaw 2001; Sprott, Doob, and Jenkins 2001).

fetal alcohol spectrum disorder (FASD)

FASD is the umbrella term used to describe the entire continuum of disabilities, from most severe to least severe, of prenatal exposure to alcohol. It includes the related conditions of fetal alcohol syndrome (FAS), fetal alcohol effects (FAE), alcohol-related birth effects (ARBE), and alcohol-related neurodevelopmental disorder (ARND).

Psychology Factors

Certain psychological factors are key determinants of mental health. Intellectual and interpersonal abilities, positive self-esteem, personal responsibility, and pro-social behaviours are key protective factors that can shelter young people from the risks of gang involvement. However, risk factors such as poor mental-health status, low self-esteem and body image, learning disabilities, antisocial behaviours and attitudes, internalizing disorders (e.g., withdrawal, anxiety, eating disorders, and suicidal behaviour), and externalizing disorders (e.g., hyperactivity, concentration problems, and aggression) can compromise children's healthy development, particularly if they live in poverty and do not have protection from some of these risks. Children and youth with emotional and behavioural disorders (EBD) are significantly more likely to be involved in gangs (see Totten 2000b).

Family Factors

In the vast majority of cases, the seeds of violence and gang involvement are planted at home. Simply put, children with strong bonds to their parents have better mental and physical health (McCreary Centre Society 1999) and are highly unlikely to become involved in gangs.

In Canada, child maltreatment is a major public health epidemic (MacMillan 2000) that affects many more children than cancer or AIDS. Many maltreated kids have impaired physical, emotional, cognitive, and social functioning. Suffering serious and prolonged child maltreatment is strongly related to experiencing youth violence and mental-health problems (MacMillan et al. 1997; MacMillan 2000). All aspects of children's lives are affected when they grow up in violent homes. Domestic violence can make children less likely to succeed in school, more likely to suffer and commit violence, and more likely to face a host of health problems that can last throughout their lives (MacMillan 2000). Depression, low self-esteem, self-destructive and criminal behaviour, delayed cognitive development and poor school performance, and aggression are common (Trocme et al. 2001; Totten 2000b; MacMillan et al. 1997; Wolak and Finkelhor 1998). Severity, frequency, and duration of child abuse are crucial factors in the extent of emotional and behavioural difficulties these youth experience in their lives (Rae-Grant et al. 1989; and O'Keefe 1997). Children who witness and hear chronic and severely abusive behaviour between caregivers can show the same effects as children who directly experience such abuse (Sudermann and Jaffe 1999). In general, female victims internalize distress (substance abuse, eating disorders, self-mutilation, suicide attempts, and depression), and most male victims externalize distress. Boys have higher levels of conduct symptoms (i.e., destroying things, threatening others, and bullying and cruelty) and externalized violence (e.g., homicide, physical and sexual assaults, homophobia, racism, and bullying).

Twenty-three-year-old Michael, a long-standing street-gang member, was victimized by chronic and severe physical, sexual, and emotional abuse growing up. His poem is representative of the mental-health problems experienced by many gang members, resulting from untreated childhood **trauma**. He wrote this poem while incarcerated in a prison in Western Canada, halfway through a sentence for a serious crime of violence:

> *Suicide*
> *Thoughts of suicide once came into play*
> *Sobbing with pain holding the string*
> *Managed to tie,*
> *But just couldn't end my life,*
> *Reminiscence of family and friends,*
> *And how it could be the end,*

trauma
Experience that is psychologically painful, distressful, or shocking (such as suffering sexual abuse or witnessing serious violence) and that often results in long-term mental or physical effects (such as depression, anxiety, or insomnia).

Contaplating (sic) on taken (sic) the next step,
Towards an ending life feeling like thiers (sic) nothing left,
A childhood which wasent (sic) the greatest,
A ruined life I just couldn't take it,
With the noose around my neck,
And the tears dripping like sweat,
Really hoping somebody would help me,
To stop my pain and to stop all the misery,
Was dealt a cruel hand and lived my 22 years sad,
Reasons to live for, I wish I had.

Most maltreated children are not violent, however, and some violent youth have not experienced maltreatment as children. A key moderating variable in this link is the resiliency of abused children: their individual, familial, and community protective factors that offset the impact of child maltreatment. Key protective factors at the family level include strong attachment to parent(s) and caregivers, bonding with other adults, effective family management practices (positive reinforcement, consistent structure and discipline, good supervision), residential stability (adequate housing, few moves), and good health of parent(s) and caregivers (McCreary Centre Society 1999).

School Factors

School success and bonding (i.e., high commitment and educational aspirations), participation in extracurricular activities, and low delinquency rate of students at school are key protective factors for young people. These youth are highly unlikely to become gang-involved. Risk factors include academic failure, low literacy, frequent school transitions, truancy and dropping out of school, and high delinquency rate of students at school. These risks are linked to negative health outcomes in the absence of protective factors in other areas of a young person's life (Kelly and Totten 2002).

Staying in school provides structured daytime activities and supports a healthy socialization process. However, many gang members spend long periods of time outside of school: they are frequently suspended or expelled, have high rates of absenteeism, and frequently drop out.

Peer-Group Factors

Key protective factors at the peer group level that lead to positive health outcomes include pro-social siblings and peers and positive peer-group membership. Evidence suggests that most healthy peer networks are organized around hobbies, interests, and other activities shared by friends (Totten 2000b). Positive social support is related to lower rates of emotional and behavioural disorders, crime, and violence. Risk factors at the peer group level include delinquent siblings and peers and membership in anti-social peer groups. Researchers who have studied violence and youth crime in the social context of peer group processes argue that peers play a significant role in enabling and sustaining these anti-social behaviours (Pepler and Craig 2000; Salmivalli 1999; O'Connell et al. 1999). Associations with people who are violent role models can result in violent behaviour. These problems can interact and feed off genetic, biological, family, and school risk factors.

Community and Neighbourhood Factors

The risk factors at this level related to gang involvement include community disorganization (e.g., drug selling, gangs, poor housing, high unemployment, etc.), poverty, exposure to violence, and racial discrimination. Social infrastructures to promote inclusion and participation in quality health, social, and recreation services are minimal compared to those in more affluent neighbourhoods (Jackson et al. 2001). There are usually few social networks and ties, with a disproportionate number of single-parent families and individuals experiencing mental or physical health problems. These neighbourhoods tend to have low social capital. Immigrants, ethnic and visible minorities, and Aboriginal people make up a disproportionate share of many social housing communities. Protective factors include living in a community with mixed socio-economic backgrounds of families, organized and accessible community and social infrastructure (e.g., recreation facilities and activities, adequate housing, high employment), bonding to institutions outside of family and school, and strong cultural identity and racial harmony (Totten 2008a).

Roughly one in ten young people in Canada live in poverty. A large body of research on human development shows that health and well-being are linked to financial resources. Children and youth from low-income families are more vulnerable: they generally experience more physical, behavioural, and mental-health problems; they suffer more neglect and physical violence; and they do less well at school, are more likely to drop out, and experience less labour market success than people from more affluent family backgrounds.[10] The vast majority of gang members grow up experiencing severe poverty. The negative effects of poverty can be overcome with a positive family environment (good parenting skills, stable family unit, good mental health) positive community supports (e.g., regular involvement in structured, skill-building recreational activities that develop self-esteem; an adult mentor who provides unconditional support and models healthy behaviour) (Offord et al. 1998; Wolfe et al. 1995), access to quality health and social services, positive school experiences (e.g., high engagement, good grades, supportive teachers, development of future academic and vocational interests), or particular individual attributes (e.g., perseverance, determination).

Prevention, Intervention, and Suppression Approaches

What Doesn't Work?

Historically in Canada, gang suppression and community safety strategies have won out over evidence-based treatment and **prevention**. Unfortunately, scarce resources have been spent on 'get tough' approaches, where young gang members are incarcerated at huge financial cost. Ironically, the best gang **intervention** programs cost a fraction of the 'lock 'em up' approach yet have not been implemented in a systematic fashion across the country. Approaches described below are proven to be ineffective and should be stopped. They typically are not part of a broad continuum of integrated services. These include the following:

- *Curriculum-based prevention programs* targeting youth at risk for gang involvement, such as the American Gang Resistance Education and Training program (G.R.E.A.T.) and Drug Abuse Resistance Education (DARE) effect modest, short-term change. However, follow-up studies have found program participants to be as likely as nonparticipants to become gang members in the long term.
- *Traditional detached-worker programs*, which use social workers, youth and recreation workers, or Aboriginal leaders to outreach into gangs, are ineffective and can do more harm than good by increasing gang cohesion (Klein 1995). More modern detached-worker programs (such as the Broader Urban Involvement and Leadership Development) have included curriculum components addressing consequences of gang involvement, peer pressure, and substance abuse. These programs remain ineffective in preventing youth from joining gangs.

prevention
Approaches that prevent young people from joining gangs.

intervention
Approaches that address the needs of youth once they are involved in gangs.

suppression
Policing approach to
dealing with gangs.

- *Gang suppression program* evaluations have found mixed results. These programs are based on the prosecution and conviction of gang members, especially targeting gang leaders. Although effective in decreasing gang-related crime in the short term, gang **suppression** programs fail to address important psychosocial issues, such as child maltreatment, mental health, substance abuse, education, and employment. Suppression initiatives should only be utilized if other prevention and intervention programs have not been successful. Even then, suppression should be used to complement a range of interventions.
- *Incarcerating gang members* does not reduce future criminal behaviour (Aos, Miller, and Drake 2006). Studies in the United States demonstrate that locking up gang members can actually increase the chances of re-offending and staying in the gang (Benda and Tollet 1999; Olson, Dooley, and Kane 2004). Likewise, grouping early-onset, high-risk youth together can increase the negative bonding among members and lead to even more entrenched anti-social and criminal behaviour. In Canada, a comparison study of 1955 gang members and inmates who were not gang-involved found that the incarcerated gang members were more likely to re-offend (gang-related violent offences), have employability problems, associate with criminal peers, and be involved in assaults on prison staff and inmates and alcohol seizure (Nafekh 2002; Nafekh and Stys 2004).

What Does Work?

In Canada, about 1 per cent of all children and families with the most complex mental-health needs take up roughly one-third of all available human-services resources in traditional services (Offord et al. 1990). The long-term outcomes for these traditional, high-cost services (primarily residential and out-of-community) are poor in most cases (Burchard et al. 1993; Gutkind 1993; Lourie 1994; Duchnowski et al. 1998). These young people usually have early-onset aggression prior to age six years. If left untreated, most turn into serious and violent offenders and gang members. It is less costly and more effective to prevent youth from joining gangs than it is to support a member to exit a gang (Greenwood 2006). The programs that have the best outcomes are those that combine primary, secondary, and tertiary prevention in a multi-disciplinary and multi-systemic community approach. Some research indicates that positive outcomes depend more upon the individual young person compared to engagement in gang activities (see Aos, Miller, and Drake 2006).

Primary prevention focuses on the entire child and youth population at risk and the biological, personal, social, and environmental risk factors linked to criminal behaviour. Gang prevention focuses on awareness and education. It is assumed that if resiliency is enhanced and youth develop a capacity to recognize risky situations, then they may be better equipped to resist engaging in gang-related activity. Secondary prevention services target individuals and groups identified as being at greater risk of becoming gang members. Community assessments frame these strategies. The focus is on reducing risk factors rather than on variables that are not changeable (Offord and Bennett 2002). Both social problems and individual risk factors are targeted. Tertiary prevention targets gang members and recruits directly to rehabilitate or incapacitate youth, address the needs of victims, and provide exit strategies and support to leave and stay out of gangs.

The initiatives described next are proven to be effective in preventing membership in gangs and intervening with gang-involved youth.

Irving Spergel's Comprehensive Gang Model is a community-wide response to gangs that has been adopted by the Office of Juvenile Justice and Delinquency Prevention (OJJDP) across the US. This model consists of five core strategies that flow from an integrated and team-oriented problem-solving approach using secondary and tertiary prevention. The foundation of the model is that a lack of social opportunities and the degree of social disorganization in a community explain the youth gang problem. Contributing factors such as poverty, institutional racism, poor social policies, and a lack of or misdirected social controls are important. Each aspect of the model is described next:

1. *Community mobilization:* Mobilizing community leaders and residents to plan, strengthen, or create new opportunities or linkages to existing organizations for gang-involved or at-risk youth. Community organization around prevention of gangs in neighbourhoods with an emerging gang problem is one of the few approaches to gang interventions with a positive outcome (Spergel and Curry 1991; Spergel 1995).

2. *Social intervention:* Gang members are more likely to respond to programs taken directly to them as opposed to those they have to seek out themselves (Stinchcomb 2002). Teams of workers from different disciplines target specific youths, gangs, and social contexts to engage the gang in more pro-social activities or to influence members to exit. Detached workers take part in social activities (such as recreation) and provide social services such as tutoring, employment counselling, and advocacy work with the police and court, individual counselling, and family services (Howell 2000).

3. *Provision of academic, economic, and social opportunities:* Many gang intervention strategies have failed to implement an ecological framework to address educational and employment opportunities in the community (Huff 1990). These programs encourage members to stop or decrease participation in gang activities. Other social opportunities provided include programs to address poverty, malnutrition, and mental illness. Educational and vocational programming for high-risk youth is proven to result in lower crime rates (OJJDP 2006). School and employment bonding initiatives provide structured time and hope for the future for potential gang members. High-risk youth who graduate from secondary school are much more likely to be employed compared to school dropouts. Unemployment is one of the key predictors of youth crime (see, for example, see Greenwood 2006).

4. *Gang suppression:* Activities that hold gang-involved youth accountable, including formal and informal social control procedures of the justice systems.

5. *Facilitating organizational change and development:* To help community agencies better address gang problems through a team problem-solving approach, not unlike the community-oriented policing framework (Burch and Kane 1999).

Other programs that have demonstrated success include the following:

- Boston's *Operation Ceasefire* (Braga and Kennedy 2002), which engaged a broad array of local, state, and federal officials, as well as community and neighbourhood leaders, proved to be an effective and efficient response to youth violence and gangs.
- *Multi-systemic therapy* (MST) is highly effective with serious, violent, and chronic juvenile offenders (Henggeler 1997; Henggeler et al. 1992). It is a cost-effective program that provides gang members with intensive therapy, supervision, and monitoring. MST focuses on the multiple determinants of criminal and anti-social behaviour, and provides services in the youth's own neighbourhood. Offending is viewed as having many causes; therefore, interventions focus on the multitude of factors influencing anti-social behaviour. There is an average of 60 hours of contact with families over a four-month period.
- *Wraparound* is a complex, multifaceted intervention strategy designed to keep youthful offenders at home and out of institutions whenever possible. Rather than forcing young people to fit into categorical, inflexible therapeutic programs, a comprehensive continuum of individualized services and support networks are 'wrapped around' them (Portland State

University Research and Training Center 2003). Individual case management is a cornerstone (Burchard et al. 2002). Wraparounds conducted in Canada and the US have been effective in reducing the frequency of residential or institutional placement of children and youth, and in reducing recidivism and arrests of seriously violent youth (for example, see the Wraparound Surrey Project; Totten and Dunn 2010e; Kamradt 2000; Milwaukee County Behavioral Health Division 2003; Walker et al. 2004; Yoe et al. 1996; Northey et al. 1997; VandenBerg and Grealish 1996).

- The *California Repeat Offender Prevention Program* (ROPP, also referred to as the '8% Solution') is a multi-site early intervention program targeting young offenders at high risk of becoming serious repeat offenders and gang members. Originally developed by the Orange County, California probation department in the early 1990s, the program integrates intensive supervision with Wraparound services. Evaluations showed that control group youth significantly improved their academic performance and were twice as likely to complete probation orders compared to comparison group youth (State of California Board of Corrections 2002). Replication of the ROPP has had mixed results, largely due to failure to implement the program fully (Zhang and Zhang 2005; Schumacher and Kurz 2000; State of California Board of Corrections 2002).

- The *Philadelphia Youth Violence Reduction Partnership* (YVRP) targets offenders who are at high risk of being killed or of killing others. Youth-serving organizations and criminal-justice agencies collaborate to balance intensive supervision with comprehensive therapeutic support. YVRP provides youth with increased supervision and supports their access to relevant resources (employment, mentoring, school bonding, counselling, health care, and drug treatment). Street workers and police help probation officers supervise participants, resulting in almost daily contacts with seriously violent youth and smaller caseload sizes. Street workers mentor youth and broker in other services. A key goal is to stabilize the families of participants through such efforts as jobs for parents and locating housing. Analysis of youth homicide rates in Philadelphia suggests that the YVRP is effective (Fight Crime: Invest in Kids 2004; McClanahan 2004).

- *Warrior Spirit Walking Project (WSW)*, Prince Albert Outreach Program Inc. (PAOPI), is a Canadian leader in evidence-based prevention and intervention for gang-involved Aboriginal youth. The National Crime Prevention Centre (NCPC) provided rich funding for this project between 2007 and 2011. WSW also serves youth at high risk of gang involvement. It is nested within the broader PAOPI agency and serves youth aged 10 to 24 years in daily intensive services. Key programs include the Youth Activity Centre, the Won Ska Cultural School, intensive counselling, street outreach to youth in the sex trade, and court outreach. Evaluation data demonstrate statistically significant reductions in overall levels of risk for participants. In addition, statistically significant positive changes were found in levels of gang involvement, substance abuse, offending, and association with anti-social peers. The treatment sample of 150 youth was matched to a control group of 50 youth. Most participants were followed over a three-year period (Totten and Dunn 2010d).

- *Regina Anti-Gang Services Project (RAGS)*, North Central Community Association (NCCA), is a unique initiative for gang-involved Aboriginal youth and young adults aged 16 to 30 years living in the North Central neighbourhood of Regina. It is the only comprehensive gang exit project in Canada. NCPC provided rich funding for this project between 2007 and 2011. The program engages clients in intensive daily services aimed at reducing their involvement in gang life and facilitating their exit from gangs. The four core programs are life skills programming for young men; circle keeper program for young women; intensive gang exit counselling; and outreach to schools and institutions. Like the WSW Project, RAGS evaluation data demonstrate statistically significant reductions in overall levels of risk for participants. In addition, statistically significant positive changes were found in levels of gang involvement, substance abuse, and offending. The treatment sample of 66 young adults (15 of whom had been convicted of murder, attempted murder, or manslaughter) was matched to a control group of 20 high-risk gang members. Most participants were followed over a three-year period (Totten and Dunn 2010e).

Summary

The primary purpose of this chapter was to provide an overview of youth gangs in Canada. We differences between street gangs, mid-level gangs, and organized crime groups. The primary differences between these three types of gangs include hierarchical structure, level of sophistication, degree of organization, seriousness of criminal activity, breadth of influence (i.e., local, regional, provincial, national, international), and longevity. The chapter also provided a summary of gang activity across different provinces and the territories. A handful of gangs were identified as having high levels of sophistication and influence across different regions of Canada, including Indian Posse, Native Syndicate, Crazy Dragons, North Preston's Finest, Bo-Gars, Crack Down Posse, Wolfpack, Manitoba and Alberta Warriors, Independent Soldiers, United Nations, Red Scorpions, and various factions of the Crips and Bloods.

We discussed different roles in organized gangs, including new recruits, strikers and soldiers, associates and affiliates, captains and higher-ups, and leaders. Gender was identified as a key factor that influences young people's experiences in gangs. The sexual assault and objectification of young women is common in gangs. For the most part, female youth play tertiary roles in male-dominated gangs, and it is rare for women to occupy leadership positions. The chapter also investigated Canadian judicial responses to gang crimes, and addressed the problematic nature of the official definitions of street gangs and organized crime groups.

In addition, the chapter presented a biopsychosocial model for understanding gang involvement. This model explores how risk and protective factors at various levels impact on gang involvement. These factors are biological and genetic; psychological; family; school; peer group; and community/neighbourhood. Finally, the chapter identified quality prevention, intervention, and suppression strategies. The best models include all three strategies and address problems at various levels of the biopsychosocial framework.

Gang-involved youth have suffered greatly throughout their young lives. Although many have committed serious crimes and must be held accountable, we must not forget the human face of these troubled youth. They are much more than merely gang members: many have unique talents and skills that are often buried underneath their violence and anti-social behaviour.

Key Terms

biopsychosocial model

fetal alcohol spectrum disorder (FASD)

intervention

prevention

suppression

trauma

Review Questions

1. What are the main differences between street gangs, mid-level gangs, and organized crime groups?

2. What are some of the key risk and protective factors related to gang involvement?

3. What are some examples of quality prevention programs for youth?

4. What are some examples of quality intervention programs for youth?

Critical Thinking Questions

1. How does gender impact pathways into and out of gangs?

2. How does gender influence roles played in gangs?

3. Why are Aboriginal youth overrepresented in gangs?

4. Why are young people who come from war-torn countries susceptible to gang involvement?

5. Do suppression and correctional approaches work?

6. What do you think the implications are of official gang and organized crime definitions for the treatment of youth under the YCJA?

Suggested Readings

Chettleburgh, M.C. (2007). *Young thugs: Inside the dangerous world of Canadian street gangs*. Toronto: Harper Collins.

Pearce, J. (2009). *Gangs in Canada*. Ontario: Quagmire Press.

Totten, M. (2009). Preventing Aboriginal youth gang involvement in Canada: A gendered approach. In J. White and J. Bruhn (Eds.), *Aboriginal policy research: Exploring the urban landscape, volume VIII*. Toronto: Thompson Educational Publishing.

Totten, M. (2008). *Promising practices for addressing youth involvement in gangs*. British Columbia Ministry of Public Safety and Solicitor General End Youth Gang Violence Strategy. Vancouver: British Columbia Ministry of Public Safety and Solicitor General.

Totten, M. and Totten, D. (2012). *From children to outcasts: The tragic lives of Canadian gang members*. Toronto: James Lorimer.

Suggested Weblinks

Public Safety Canada
www.publicsafety.gc.ca/prg/cp/bldngevd/2007-yg-1-eng.aspx
• 'Youth Gangs in Canada: What Do We Know?'

Public Safety Canada
www.publicsafety.gc.ca/prg/cp/bldngevd/2007-yg-2-eng.aspx
• 'Youth Gang Involvement: What Are the Risk Factors?'

Public Safety Canada
www.publicsafety.gc.ca/res/cp/res/2007-yg-03-eng.aspx
• 'Addressing Youth Gang Problems: An Overview of Programs and Practices'

Public Safety Canada
www.publicsafety.gc.ca/prg/cp/ythgng/index-eng.aspx
* Much gang-related information available.

The American Office of Juvenile Justice and Delinquency Prevention.
www.ojjdp.gov/programs/antigang/index.html
* A wealth of American-based information on gangs and anti-gang strategies.

Mark Totten and Associates website
www.tottenandassociates.ca
* A host of gang-related information can be found here.

Endnotes

1. For example, Gordon 2000; Nimmo 2001; Totten 2009a, 2008a, 2000b.
2. For example, see Totten and Dunn 2010a, c; Totten 2009a.
3. These data on gang activity come from a number of sources, including interviews conducted by Totten with gang members across Canada; CISC and RCMP reports; and confidential interviews with municipal, provincial, and federal law-enforcement organizations.
4. Young adults are defined as those between 12 and 30 years of age.
5. For example, see CISC 2007.
6. Pseudonyms are used to protect the identity of participants.
7. *Feins* is street slang for 'jonesing' or a craving for drugs.
8. Although youth who are charged with a criminal offence under the age of 18 years are typically dealt with under the Youth Criminal Justice Act, a small number are transferred up to the adult system if they have committed very serious offences. If convicted, these latter youth usually serve their sentence in adult jails or prisons.
9. Permission granted by all participants to reproduce their narratives in publications by Totten.
10. For example, see Strohschein 2005.

References

Aos, S., Miller, M., and Drake, E. (2006). Evidence-based public policy options to reduce future prison construction, criminal justice costs, and crime rates. Olympia: Washington State Institute for Public Policy.

Benda, B. and Tollett, C. (1999). A study of recidivism of serious and persistent offenders among adolescents. *Journal of Criminal Justice 27*(2): 111–26.

Block, C. and Block, R. (2001). Street gang crime in Chicago. In Miller, Maxson and Klein (Eds.), *The modern gang reader.* Los Angeles: Roxbury.

Braga, A. and Kennedy, D. (2002). Reducing gang violence in Boston. In Reed and Decker (Eds.), *Responding to gangs: Evaluation and research.* Washington: National Institute of Justice.

Burchard, J., Bruns, E., and Burchard, S. (2002). *The wraparound process. Community-based treatment for youth.* Oxford: Oxford University Press.

Burch, J. and Kane, C. (1999). *Implementing the OJJDP comprehensive gang model.* Fact Sheet. Washington: US Department of Justice, Office of Justice Programs, Office of Juvenile Justice and Delinquency Prevention.

Buxton, B. (2004). *Damaged angels.* Toronto: Knopf Canada.

Campbell, A. (1987). Self-definition by rejection: The case of gang girls. *Social Problems, 34*: 451–66.

Campbell, A. (1990). *The girls in the gang* (2nd ed.). New Brunswick, NJ: Rutgers University Press.

Criminal Intelligence Services Saskatchewan. (2005). *2005 intelligence trends: Aboriginal-based gangs in Saskatchewan.* Saskatchewan: Author.

Criminal Intelligence Services Canada. (2007). Project spectrum: 2006 situational overview of street gangs in Canada. Ottawa: Author.

Criminal Intelligence Services Canada. (2010). *2010 annual report on organized crime.* Ottawa: Author.

Curry, D. (1998). Female gang involvement. *Journal of Research in Crime and Delinquency, 35*(1): 100–18.

Dekovic, M. (1999). Risk and protective factors in the development of problem behavior during adolescence. *Journal of Youth and Adolescence, 28*(6): 667–85.

Fight Crime: Invest in Kids. (2004). Caught in the crossfire: Arresting gang violence by investing in kids. Washington: Author.

Frankel, R., Quill, T., and McDaniel, S.. (2003). *The biopsychosocial approach: Past, present and future.* New York: Boydell and Brewer.

Gordon, R. (2000). Criminal business organizations, street gangs and 'wanna-be' groups: A Vancouver perspective. *Canadian Journal of Criminology,* Jan.: 39–60.

Greenwood, P. (2006). *Changing lives: Delinquency prevention as crime-control policy.* Chicago: University of Chicago Press.

Grennan, S., Britz, M., Rush, J., and Barker, T. (2000). *Gangs: An international approach.* Upper Saddle River, NJ: Prentice Hall.

Gutkind, L. (1993). *Stuck in time: The tragedy of childhood mental illness.* New York: Henry Holt.

Gutman, L. M. and Midgley, C. (2000). The role of protective factors in supporting the academic achievement of poor African American students during the middles school transition. *Journal of Youth and Adolescence* 29(2): 223–48.

Henggeler, S. (1997). The development of effective drug abuse services for youth. In J. Egertson, D. Fox, and A. Leshner (Eds.), *Treating drug abusers effectively* (pp. 253–79). New York: Blackwell Publishers.

Henggeler, S.W., Melton, G.B., and Smith, L. (1992). Family preservation using multisystemic therapy: An effective alternative to incarcerating serious juvenile offenders. *Journal of Consulting and Clinical Psychology, 60:* 953–61.

Howard, S., Dryden, J., and Johnson, B. (1999). Childhood resilience: Review and critique of the literature. *Oxford Review of Education 25*(3): 307–23.

Howell, J. (2000). *Youth gang programs and strategies.* Washington: US Department of Justice, Office of Justice Programs, Office of Juvenile and Delinquency Prevention.

Huff, C. (1990). Denial, overreaction and misidentification. In C. Huff (Ed.), *Gangs in America.* New York: Sage Publications Inc.

Jackson, A., Hanvey, L., Tsoukalas, S., Buckland, L., Roberts, E., and Perkins, N. (2001). *Recreation and children and youth living in poverty: Barriers, benefits and success stories.* Ottawa: CCSD.

Kamradt, B. (2000). Wraparound Milwaukee: Aiding youth with mental health needs. *Juvenile Justice Journal* 7(1):14–23.

Kelly, K. and Totten, M. (2002). *When children kill: A social psychological study of youth homicide.* Peterborough: Broadview Press.

Klein, M. (1995). *The American street gang.* New York: Oxford University Press.

Klein, M. (2002). Street gangs: A cross-national perspective. In C. Huff (Ed.), *Gangs in America III.* Thousand Oaks, CA: Sage.

Knox, G. (2000). *An introduction to gangs* (5th ed.). Chicago: New Chicago School Press.

Kyskan, C. and Moore, T. (2005). Global perspectives on foetal alcohol syndrome (FAS): Assessing practices, policies, and campaigns in four English-speaking countries. *Canadian Psychology, 46*: 153–65.

Lourie, I. (1994). *Principles of local systems of development.* Chicago: Kaleidoscope.

Luthar, S., Cicchetti, D., and Becker, B. (2000). The construct of resilience: A critical evaluation and guidelines for future work. *Child Development 72*(3): 543–62.

MacMillan, H. (2000). Child maltreatment: What we know in the year 2000. *Canadian Journal of Psychiatry 45*: 702–9.

MacMillan, H., Fleming, J., Trocme, N. et al. (1997). Prevalence of child physical and sexual abuse in the community: Results from the Ontario Health Supplement. *Journal of the American Medical Association 278*(2): 131–35.

McClanahan, W. (2004). *Alive at 25: Reducing youth violence through monitoring and support.* Philadelphia: Public/Private Ventures.

McCreary Center Society. (1999). Healthy connections: Listening to BC youth. Highlights from the Adolescent Health Survey II. Burnaby, BC: The McCreary Center Society.

Mellor, B., MacRae, L., Pauls, M., and Hornick, J. (2005). Youth gangs in Canada: A preliminary review of programs and services. Prepared for Public Safety and Emergency Preparedness Canada. Calgary: Canadian Research Institute for Law and the Family.

Milwaukee County Behavioral Health Division. (2003). Wraparound Milwaukee: 2002 annual report. Milwaukee, WI: Milwaukee County Behavioral Health Division, Department of Health and Human Services.

Moffitt, T. (2005). The new look of behaviour genetics in developmental pathology: Gene-environment interplay in antisocial behaviour. *Psychological Bulletin, 131*: 533–54.

Moffitt, T. et al. (2001). *Sex differences in antisocial behaviour.* Cambridge, UK: Cambridge University Press.

Moore, J. (2007). Female gangs. In J. Hagedorn (Ed.), *Gangs in the global city: Alternatives to traditional criminology.* Chicago: University of Illinois Press.

Morrison, G. and D'Incau, B. (1997). The web of zero-tolerance: Characteristics of students who are recommended for expulsion from school. *Education and Treatment of Children, 20*(3): 316–35.

Nafekh, M. (2002). *An examination of youth and gang association within the federally sentenced Aboriginal population.* Ottawa: Correctional Services Canada.

Nafekh, M. and Steys, Y. (2004). *A profile and examination of gang affiliation within federally sentenced inmates.* Ottawa: Correctional Services Canada.

Nimmo M. (2001). *The invisible gang members: A report on female gang association in Winnipeg.* Winnipeg: Canadian Centre for Policy Alternatives.

Northey, W., Primer, V., and Christensen, L. (1997). Promoting justice in the delivery of services to juvenile delinquents: The ecosystemic natural wrap-around model. *Child and Adolescent Social Work Journal, 14*(1): 5–22.

O'Connell, P., Pepler, D., and Craig, W. (1999). Peer involvement in bullying: Insights and challenges for intervention. *Journal of Adolescence 22.*

Offord, D. and Bennett, K. (2002). Prevention. In M. Rutter and E. Taylor (Eds.), *Child and adolescent psychiatry* (4th ed.) (pp. 881–99). Oxford, UK: Blackwell Science.

Offord, D., Boyle, M. and Racine, Y. (1990). *Ontario child health study.* Toronto: Queen's Printer.

Offord, D., Lipman, E. and Duku, E. (1998). *Which children don't participate in sports, the arts, and community programs?* Ottawa: Human Resources Development Canada.

OJJDP. (2006). *Juvenile offenders and victims: 2006 national report.* Washington: Office of Juvenile Justice and Delinquency Prevention.

O'Keefe, M. (1997). Predictors of dating violence among high school students. *Journal of Interpersonal Violence, 12*(4): 546–68.

Olson, D., Dooley, B., and Kane, C. (2004). The relationship between gang membership and inmate recidivism. *Research Bulletin, 2*(12). Chicago: Illinois Criminal Justice Research Authority.

Pepler, D. and Craig, W. (2000). Making a difference in bullying. Report #60.

Plomin, R. and Crabbe, J. (2000). DNA. *Psychological Bulletin, 126:* 806–28.

Portland State University Research and Training Center. (2003). Quality and fidelity in wraparound. *Focal Point.*

Rhee, S. and Waldman, I. (2002). Genetic and environmental influences on antisocial behavior: A meta-analysis of twin and adoption studies. *Psychological Bulletin, 128*(3): 490–529. Salmivalli, C. (1999). Participant role approach to school bullying: Implications for intervention. *Journal of Adolescence, 22:* 453–59.

Santrock, J. (2007). *A topical approach to human life-span development* (3rd ed.). St. Louis, MO: McGraw-Hill.

Schumacher, M. and Kurz, G. (2000). The 8% solution—Preventing serious repeat juvenile crime. Thousand Oaks, CA: Sage.

Shaw, M. (2001). Investing in youth 12–18: International approaches to preventing crime and victimization. Montreal: ICPC.

Smokowski P., Reynolds, A. and Brezruczko, N. (1999). Resilience and protective factors in adolescence: An autobiographical perspective from disadvantaged youth. *Journal of School Psychology 37*(4): 425–48.

Spergel, I. (1995). *The youth gang problem: A community approach.* New York: Oxford University Press.

Spergel, I., and Curry, D. (1991). *The national youth gang survey: A research and development process.* University of Chicago and Office of Juvenile Justice and Delinquency Prevention.

Sprott, J., Doob, A., and Jenkins, J. (2001). Problem behaviour and delinquency in children and youth. *Juristat 21*(4).

State of California Board of Corrections. (2002). *Repeat offender prevention program.* CA: State of California Board of Corrections.

Stark, J. (2004). Breaking the cycle: A community approach to prevention of low-birth weight babies. *Leadership in Health Services, 17*(4): 1–8.

Stinchcomb, J. (2002). Promising (and not so promising) gang prevention and intervention strategies: A comprehensive literature review. *Journal of Gang Research, 10*(1): 27–45.

Sudermann, M. and Jaffe, P. (1999). A handbook for health and social service providers and educators on children exposed to woman abuse/family violence. Ottawa: Minister of Public Works and Government Services Canada.

Totten, M. (2001, Summer). Legal, ethical and clinical implications of doing field research with youth gang members who engage in serious violence. *Journal of Gang Research 8*(4).

Totten, M. (2000b). *Guys, gangs and girlfriend abuse.* Peterborough, ON: Broadview Press.

Totten, M. (2002a). *The special needs of young women in Canada's youth justice system.* Ottawa: Prepared for Department of Justice Canada.

Totten, M. (2008a). *Promising practices for addressing youth involvement in gangs.* Vancouver: British Columbia Ministry of Public Safety and Solicitor General.

Totten, M. (2009a). Aboriginal Youth and violent gang involvement in Canada: Quality prevention strategies. *Institute for the Prevention of Crime Review.*

Totten, M. (2009b). Preventing Aboriginal youth gang involvement in Canada: A gendered approach. In J. White and J. Bruhn (Eds.), *Aboriginal policy research: Exploring the urban landscape, volume VIII.* Toronto: Thompson Educational Publishing.

Totten, M. and Dunn, S. (2009a). Annual evaluation report for the creating healthy Aboriginal role models (*CHARM*) gang project. Gatineau, QC: Totten and Associates, 2009.

Totten, M. and Dunn, S. (2009b). Annual evaluation report for the Prince Albert Outreach Program Inc. Warrior Spirit Walking gang project. Gatineau, QC: Totten and Associates.

Totten, M. and Dunn, S. (2009c). Annual evaluation report for the North Central Community Association Regina anti-gang services project. Gatineau, QC: Totten and Associates.

Totten, M. (2010a). Expert witness report on R. v. Osae.

Totten, M. (2010b). Use of the tear drop tattoo by young street gang members. Forthcoming in *Journal of Gang Research,* Winter 2011.

Totten, M. and Dunn, S. (2010a). Second annual evaluation report for the creating healthy Aboriginal role models (*CHARM*) gang project. Gatineau, QC: Totten and Associates.

Totten, M. and Dunn, S. (2010b). Second annual evaluation report for the Prince Albert Outreach Program Inc. Warrior Spirit Walking Gang Project. Gatineau, QC: Totten and Associates.

Totten, M. and Dunn, S. (2010c). Second annual evaluation report for the North Central Community Association Regina anti-gang services project. Gatineau, QC: Totten and Associates.

Totten, M. and Dunn, S. (2010d). Interim final evaluation report for the Prince Albert Outreach Program Inc. Warrior Spirit Walking gang project. Gatineau, QC: Totten and Associates.

Totten, M. and Dunn, S. (2010e). Interim final evaluation report for the North Central Community Association Regina anti-gang services project. Gatineau, QC: Totten and Associates.

Trocmé, N., MacLaurin, B., Fallon, B., et al. (2001). *The Canadian incidence study of reported child abuse and neglect: Final report.* Ottawa: Minister of Public Works and Government Services Canada.

Valdez, A. (2000). *A guide to understanding gangs.* San Clemente, CA: LawTech Publishing.

VanDenBerg J. and Grealish, E. (1996). Individualized services and supports through the wraparound process: Philosophy and procedures. *J Child Fam Studies* 5: 7–21.

Voydanoff, P. and Donnelly, B. (1999). Multiple roles and psychological distress: The intersection of the paid worker, spouse, and parent roles with the adult child role. *Journal of Marriage and the Family, 61*: 725–38.

Walker J., Bruns, E., Rast, J., et al. (2004). Phases and activities of the wraparound process. Portland, OR: National Wraparound Initiative, Regional Research Institute, Portland State University.

Wolak, J. and Finkelhor, D. (1998). Children exposed to partner violence. In J.L. Jasinski, L.M. Williams (Eds.), *Partner violence: A comprehensive review of 20 years of research* (pp. 73–112). Thousand Oaks, CA: Sage Publications.

Wolfe, D., Wekerle, C., Reitzal, D., and Gough, R. (1995). Strategies to address violence in the lives of high-risk youth. In E. Paled, P. Jaffe, and J. Edelson. (Eds.), *Ending the cycle of violence* (pp. 255–74). Thousand Oaks, CA: Sage.

Yoe, J., Santarcangelo, S., Atkins, M., and Burchard, J. (1996). Wraparound care in Vermont: Program development, implementation, and evaluation of a statewide system of individualized services. *Journal of Child and Family Studies, 5*: 23–39.

Zhang, S. and Zhang, L. (2005). An experimental study of the Los Angeles repeat offender prevention program: Its implementation and evaluation. *Criminology and Public Policy, 4*: 205–36.

12 Street-Involved Youth in Canada

Bruce MacLaurin and Catherine Worthington

Overview

This chapter provides an overview of street-involved youth in Canada. It focuses specifically on definitions and typologies of street involvement, pathways to the street from home or alternative care, key risk and protective factors associated with street-involvement, institutional experiences with education, child welfare, and juvenile justice systems, and street services and strategies for effective intervention.

Key Objectives

After reading this chapter, you should be able to:

- Discuss why there is such a significant number of street-involved youth in Canadian cities.
- Identify key risks and concerns for youths living on the streets.
- Describe why youth may become involved in street life.
- Outline types of services required by street youth.

Introduction

Street-involved youth are visible living on the streets of most major Canadian urban centres. This is not a recent phenomenon; nineteenth-century literature popularized Huckleberry Finn and Oliver Twist in stories of street children existing and surviving on their own. Street-involved youth may be more visible today, however, as newspapers during the past decade have consistently highlighted the lives of young street teens described as runaways, throwaways, panhandlers, squeegee kids, or teen parents (Abate 2001; Anonymous 2010a, 2010b; Carmichael 1997; Chase and Ketcham 1997; Derworiz 2010; Goar 2009; MacDonald 1997; McCarter 2010; Verma 1999). Despite this increase in recognition and awareness, the plight of street-involved youth arguably continues to worsen in Canada.

Street-involved youth are generally defined as individuals who are 25 years of age or younger who are either runaway, homeless, or underhoused (i.e., living in temporary or unreliable housing). A variety of typologies, or classifications, of street-involved youth have been developed to describe this population. This chapter will describe some of the typologies documented in current North American research to provide a comprehensive overview of street-involved youth. These typologies are based on the intent, or purpose, of the street involvement, the time spent on the street, the factors associated with street involvement, and whether there is a choice of returning home. In spite of some limitations, such as being too simple or vague, typologies can assist us in understanding this population and the specific risks that street-involved youth face on the street.

Street-involved youth experience a decrease in rights, opportunities, and social supports (Grover 2002; 2007; Worthington, MacLaurin, Huffey, Dittmann et al. 2008), which may exacerbate the risks associated with living on the streets. Street-involved youth are also at higher risk of developing mental-health problems, some of which can lead to suicide (Boivin, Roy, Hayel, and Galbaud du Fort 2005; Clatts, Goldsamt, Yi, and Gwadz 2005); becoming involved in survival or obligatory sex (Haley, Roy, Leclerc et al. 2004b); developing physical health concerns including contracting sexually transmitted diseases (Public Health Agency of Canada 2006a); getting involved in criminal and delinquent activity (Baron 2006); using and abusing drugs (Roy, Haley, Leclerc et al. 2002); and simply not meeting their basic physical needs for food, clothing, and shelter (Dachner and Tarasuk 2002). A review of the literature will illustrate how these risk factors have a significant impact on youth when on the streets.

Insufficient attention has been given to the service needs of street-involved youth. Services are needed that will support these youth while they are on the streets and when they try to leave the street life. This chapter describes effective forms of intervention available to street-involved youth in Canada as well as barriers to service utilization.

Defining Street-Involved Youth vs. Homeless Adults

As mentioned, the literature generally defines **street-involved youth** as being young people 25 years of age or younger who do not have a safe home or are underhoused (homeless); have been forced to

street-involved youth

Youth 25 years of age or younger who do not have a safe home or are underhoused; who have been forced to leave their families of origin; who have run away from their homes without the consent of their parent or guardian or who left foster or group-care placements; or who are not living on the street but who experiment and engage in street-involved activities and identify with street culture and street peer groupings.

leave their families of origin (**throwaway**); who have run away from their homes without the consent of their parent or guardian; or who left foster or group-care placements (runaway) (Hammer, Finkelhor, and Sedlak 2002; Kufeldt and Nimmo 1987b). These youth may be described as the most street entrenched; however, recent evidence indicates that there are additional youth becoming involved in street life who are less recognized or understood, who have significant and specific risks, and who would benefit from prevention and support services. Recent definitions of street-involved youth have expanded on the runaway and homeless definition to include youth who are not living on the street but who experiment and engage in street-involved activities and identify with street culture and street peer groupings (Worthington et al. 2008). In this chapter, the term *street-involved youth* will be used to describe this entire population.

Youth living on the streets present as a unique service population in comparison to the adult homeless population. Homelessness for adults is described first and foremost as a housing and poverty issue, which establishes the context in which individual risk factors can trigger a homeless episode (Burt 2001 as cited by Tutty et al. 2010). Four specific structural issues contribute to adult homelessness: (1) an increasing number of people are being priced out of the affordable housing market; (2) employment opportunities for those individuals with secondary education are dwindling; (3) institutional supports have been reduced for those people with severe mental health and addiction concerns; and (4) people are excluded from affordable housing due to racial, ethnic, and/or class discrimination (Burt 2001). Street-involved youth have experienced many of the same individual risk factors associated with the adult homeless population, including high rates of childhood maltreatment, child-welfare involvement, mental health concerns, incomplete education, and drug use; however, the factors that trigger their street involvement are different (Goering et al. 2002; Tutty et al. 2010; Worthington et al. 2008).

Typologies of Street-Involved Youth

A number of typologies have been developed in Canada and the United States over the past 30 years to help researchers and practitioners better understand the unique characteristics of youth who are involved in the street and to develop services designed to meet their current needs (Adlaf and Zdanowicz 1999; Kufeldt and Nimmo 1987b; Kufeldt and Perry 1989; Miller, Miller, Hoffman, and Duggan 1980; Zilde and Cherry 1992). Typologies generally include, but are not limited to, youth who experiment with street life by occasional running away or truancy, children who run from home to escape maltreatment and harm, and those young people who have spent years living on the streets and are firmly entrenched in the street lifestyle.

A recent ethnographic study based in San Francisco developed a **life-cycle model** that has proven to be useful in understanding the duration and range of street involvement that youth experience (Auerswald and Eyre 2002). This model proposes a series of stages that youth encounter on the street and includes an initial engagement in street life, a stage where youth become more comfortable with street life, and, finally, periods of crisis during which some youth may transition off the street. A cyclical pattern is noted, however, in that many youth who exit the street may become re-involved. The model describes key influences at each stage, including street mentors who provide youth with basic street survival skills and assist in understanding the culture of street life.

The Auerswald and Eyre (2002) life-cycle model, and other typologies, assist practitioners and researchers in understanding the Canadian street-youth population and the specific risks that are associated with the street lifestyle. These classification systems consider pathways to the street, the frequency and duration of street involvement, the level of individual choice for being on the street, and options for leaving the street. While these classifications provide an understanding of the range of street-involved youth, further work is required to test and validate these typologies (see Figure 12.1).

---

throwaways
Youth who are asked, or encouraged, to leave home by their parents/guardians, with the purpose of ending parental responsibility for the well-being of the youth.

life-cycle model
This model proposes a series of stages that youth encounter on the street and includes an initial engagement in street life, a stage where youth become more comfortable with street life, and, finally, periods of crisis during which some youth may transition off the street. A cyclical pattern is noted, however, in that many youth who exit the street may become re-involved.

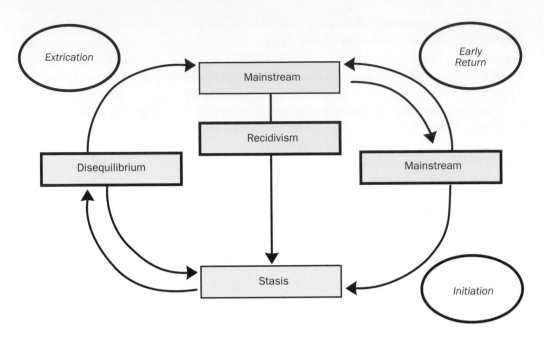

Figure 12.1 The Life-Cycle Model of Youth Homelessness
Source: Auerswald and Eyre 2002, p. 1501.

Numbers of Street-Involved Youth

To date, there are no accurate estimates for the Canadian street-involved youth population. It is difficult to estimate these numbers because of the challenges in defining street-involved youth, the unique differences within this population, and differential service use by subgroups of street-involved youth. Recent estimates based on the national incidence studies of missing youth in the United States suggest that more than 1.6 million youth in the US can be described as street involved (i.e., those who left home or were asked by a parent or guardian to leave the home) (Hammer et al. 2002). In 1999, it was estimated that 150 000 youth were homeless or street involved in Canada (DeMatteo et al. 1999). Gaetz, O'Grady, and Vaillancourt (1999) report that the Toronto Hostel Division estimated an average of 325 to 340 youth between the ages of 16 and 24 were living in shelters on any given night in Toronto in 1999; however, Toronto street surveys indicate that this figure was less than one-quarter of the total street-involved youth population in that city (Gaetz et al. 1999). This is supported by a recent US study that found that approximately 7 per cent of the street-youth population used shelters (Carlson, Sugano, Millstein, and Auerswald 2006).

Other cities in Canada face similar challenges when estimating the number of youth who are street involved. For example, in Calgary, **homeless youth** currently represent approximately 13 per cent of the entire homeless population (City of Calgary 2006). On May 10, 2006, there were 444 youth aged 13 to 24 staying on Calgary's streets, in emergency or transitional facilities, or at other non-shelter service agencies such as hospital emergency departments—a significant increase over the past 10 years (The City of Calgary 1996, 2006). However, this figure does not represent all street-involved youth in Calgary, including those who sleep in public areas, those who rely on friends for short-term accommodation (couch surfing), or those who engage in the street lifestyle only during the day. Conservative estimates of youth actively using street-youth services in Calgary are higher, ranging from 600 to 725 (Clarke and Cooper 2000; Kufeldt and Nimmo 1987a).

homeless youth
Youth who have either left or have been urged to leave home with the full knowledge or approval of legal guardians. They have no alternative home in which to live.

In Halifax, youth aged 16 to 19 made up 6.5 per cent of the 1252 homeless individuals using shelters in 2008, while those under age 16 comprised roughly 6 per cent (Community Action on Homelessness 2009). The current number of homeless youth may be higher, however, as the number of homeless individuals using shelters in Halifax increased to 1718 in 2009 (Community Action on Homelessness 2010). A study by the Halifax Regional Municipality (2005) reported that in 2004 youth under age 18 made up 12 per cent of homeless respondents and those aged 19 to 24 comprised 22 per cent. Seven per cent of youth under age 18 and 12 per cent of youth aged 19 to 24 lived in shelters, while 20 per cent of youth under 18 and 43 per cent of youth aged 19 to 24 lived on the streets.

Cross-sectional counts of those on the streets, in shelters, or in other service agencies do not capture the fluidity or diversity of the street-involved youth population, and the majority of street-involved youth report moving to large Canadian cities and spending time in different cities (Gaetz et al. 1999). Counts of the actual street-involved youth population in Canada will continue to be conservative estimates of this at-risk population. The range in the estimates of street-involved youth in Canada and the United States raises several questions about the accuracy of estimates. These variations can be definitely attributed to the methodological challenges of developing an accurate count and estimate (Peressini, McDonald, and Hulchanski 1995). Several critical issues to consider when planning an estimate or count of the number of street-involved youth include the following:

- What criteria determine street involvement? Definitions of who should be counted need to be established. For example, if runaway youth are included in the street-involved youth counts, should those who have run away but are staying with friends and not on the streets be included?
- How should street-involved youth be contacted? Some estimates of street-involved youth have used street counts at random periods over the course of a year (Kufelt and Nimmo 1987b), while other estimates were based upon counts submitted by service providers. Different methods of contact will run the risk of missing different types of street-involved youth.
- Should shelter numbers be used on which to base predictions of the uncounted street-involved population who do not access shelters or services? Estimates may be generated to include youth who do not use traditional street resources; however, the accuracy of these estimates remains unknown. This group would typically include youth involved in the formal sex trade, youth who access adult services, or highly transient youth who do not access any services.

Perspectives on Street-Involved Youth

The lens or perspective with which we view street-involved youth in Canada has a great impact on the way we respond to the needs of this population. The lens has shifted constantly over the past half century. Prior to the 1960s, youth on the street were seen as delinquents who were there as a result of their own individual pathology and deviant nature (Appathurai 1987). This position shifted during the 1960s as the counter-culture movement saw an increased number of middle-class teens living on city streets. Factors related to the family and school were primary areas of concern in the literature on street-involved youth in the 1970s, while maltreatment of children became a paramount concern for research and service delivery during the 1980s and early 1990s (McCormack, Janus, and Burgess 1986). With the end of the twentieth century and the beginning of the twenty-first century, structural factors now play an increasing role in understanding street-involved youth. The increase in HIV/AIDS (human immunodeficiency virus/acquired immunodeficiency syndrome), chronic poverty, inadequate housing, unemployment or under-employment, deinstitutionalization, and the challenged and overworked systems of child welfare are all critical factors that impact street-involved youth in Canada (Kufeldt and Burrows 1994; van der Ploeg and Scholte 1997; Worthington et al. 2008).

An ecological perspective has frequently been used as a theoretical framework for understanding the runaway and homeless phenomenon. The model described in this chapter was developed by Kufeldt and Burrows (1994), based on initial work by Bronfenbrenner (1974) and later expanded on by Garbarino (1982). Bronfenbrenner's influence was acknowledged in the author's description of the ecological approach: 'A child's development is influenced by a complex network of family, friends, school, community resources, and ultimately, by forces outside the child's immediate experience, such as government decisions and cultural or societal expectations' (Kufeldt and Burrows 1994, p. 13). This approach is useful for focusing the reader on the interaction of the individual with different systems (e.g., school, peers, and child welfare) and within the predominant values, attitudes, and philosophies of society (see Figure 12.2).

Pathways to the Street—The Vulnerable Population

Youth become involved with street life in a variety of ways. A significant proportion of street-involved youth identify that they initially left home as a result of family conflict, disruption, and maltreatment (Cauce 2004; Chen 2004; Hyde 2005; McLean 2005). In addition, many youth leave home because they were thrown out or forced to leave, or because they sought further independence (McLean 2005; Public Health Agency of Canada 2006b). Other youth become street-involved following early exit from or aging-out of the child-welfare system (Lenz-Rashid 2006).

Family Experiences

A large percentage of street-involved youth report a history of child maltreatment at the hands of their caregivers. The Enhanced Surveillance of Canadian Street Youth (E-SYS) is an ongoing project to monitor behaviours, risk determinants, sexually transmitted infections (STIs), and related infections in the Canadian street-youth population (Public Health Agency of Canada 2006b). The E-SYS reported that between 19 per cent and 28 per cent of street-involved youth left home because of physical abuse, sexual abuse, and/or emotional abuse. In addition, 30 per cent reported experiencing neglect in their homes.

Other North American studies report that rates of maltreatment range from 12 per cent to 50 per cent for sexual abuse, and 30 per cent to 90 per cent for physical abuse (Adlaf and Zhanowicz 1999; Cauce 2004; Chen 2004; Hyde 2005; Janus, Archambault, Brown, and Welsh 1995; MacLaurin, Worthington, Dittmann, and Kitt 2009b; Rotheram-Borus, Mahler, Koopman, and Langabeer 1996; Thrane, Hoyt, Whitbeck, and Yoder 2006; Worthington et al. 2008). The maltreatment experienced by street-involved youth is consistently reported to be chronic, extreme, and initiated at a young age (Cauce 2004; Janus et al. 1995; Tyler and Cauce 2002).

MacLaurin et al. (2009b) found that 71 per cent of street-involved youth surveyed in Calgary reported at least one type of maltreatment while living at home, including physical abuse (43 per cent), sexual abuse (20 per cent), neglect (29 per cent), and emotional maltreatment (52 per cent). And abuse among street-involved youth is rarely a one-time occurrence. Of this group, 61 per cent reported that the maltreatment had consisted of multiple events during a period of more than six months, while an additional 31 per cent reported multiple events occurring during six months or less. Only 8 per cent reported that the maltreatment had been a single event. In addition, 54 per cent of surveyed street-involved youth reported having witnessed domestic violence between their parents (MacLaurin et al. 2009b).

Children who experience maltreatment within their family may resort to running away from home as an alternative to the abuse or neglect. More than 11 per cent of children and teens who

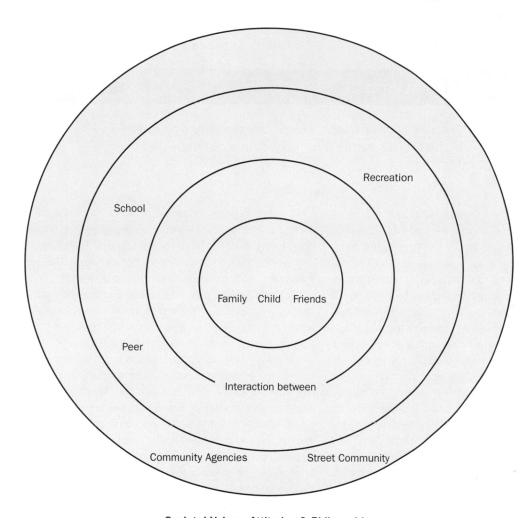

Societal Values, Attitudes & Philosophies

Microsystem	This is the immediate setting in which a person resides. For the street population, it can include family, school, child welfare placement, and the street culture itself.
Mesosystem	Represents the connections between the child's microsystems and exosystems. Risk and opportunity relate to the quality of connections and relationships and the congruencies of values within the microsystems.
Exosystem	Larger systems (school system, community agency) are exosystems in which policies and operations can enhance or detract from opportunities for homeless youth.
Macrosystem	Includes the culture and ideology of the society in which a person lives. The dilemma in leaving the street is the need to conform to predominant and straight culture without the means to incorporate and practise its values.

Figure 12.2 Ecological Framework

Source: K. Kufeldt and B. Burrows 1994, p. 14. Adapted from Bronfenbrenner 1979.

experienced substantiated maltreatment in Alberta in 2003 had a history of running away from home at the time of the child-welfare investigation, and the percentage of teens (ages 12 to 15) was significantly higher (MacLaurin et al. 2006) (see Box 12.1).

Box 12.1 Youth Justice in Action

Growing Up on Streets Trumps Dysfunctional Home Life; Family dynamics— Not Drugs or Alcohol—Is the Main Reason Why Thousands of Teens Choose to Run Away from Home

By Bronwyn McCarter

Christopher Brown, a 19-year-old homeless man, stood barefoot in a damp black hoodie, shivering, one bleak afternoon on Granville Street. His hard-luck story began, he said, when he was kicked out of his home at a young age. He spent days sitting on the steps of the Vancouver Art Gallery until the police found him and put him in foster care, he recalled in an interview. As he grew older, Brown said he tired of being shuffled from foster home to foster home, feeling that no one truly cared for him. At the age of 18, he turned to the streets. 'It's a hard life out here,' he said. Unfortunately, Brown isn't unique in feeling like the streets are the only place left to go. He is one of 65,000 homeless teenagers in Canada who struggle to find a safe, dry place to sleep each night. 'You don't know if you're gonna wake up in a car with a bag over your head, or with a knife to your throat,' said Brown, who mostly sleeps with a group of friends in various locations on Vancouver's sidewalks. On the streets, Brown said, teens make their own families. It is often hard to find someone to trust, but when that connection is made on the streets, he said, the relationships are strong and more meaningful than those he made at school.

Brown has been trying to get a job for more than three years. He began his search while in foster care, but now that he is homeless he said it [is] impossible to find employment. 'No one wants to hire someone like me,' Brown said. Employers don't want to hire a person who looks dirty, or doesn't have an address. They worry such an employee would turn away customers, and potentially hurt their businesses. That traps teens in a vicious cycle: They have nowhere to go except the streets, but they can't get jobs because they don't have stable families to live with, or easy access to showers and clean clothes. Money is by far the hardest thing to come by for homeless teens. While

food, used clothing, showers and laundry facilities can be found in downtown Vancouver, young people often start trying to collect money through pan handling— until desperation forces them to consider more drastic measures, such as prostitution and drug dealing.

For many people, dropping a couple of quarters into someone's hat is a difficult decision. They are unsure where the money will be spent: Will it go toward a new pair of shoes, an umbrella, or someone's next high? Directions Youth Services offers a job program that is Brown's personal favourite. The program is called Street Youth Job Action (SYJA), and allows young people to clean up the streets, do needle sweeps and leave at the end of the day with some cash in their pockets. Brown and other teens who sleep on Vancouver's streets applaud the SYJA program because they get a chance to give back to the community. Many people believe it is drugs or alcohol that bring young people to the streets. While that may be true for some, experts say it is often family dynamics that drive teens to the wet streets of Vancouver. Some are runaways from home; others are kicked out. Drugs often become the problem after they reach the streets.

Many homeless young people also have mental health problems and turn to drugs as a way of self-medicating, said Michelle Clausius, associate director of development and communications at Covenant House, a facility for youth on Drake Street. Jennifer Hanrahan, a manager at Directions Youth Services Centre, said crystal meth is one of the leading drugs causing addiction among young people. It is the cheapest drug on the market, and easily available. However, not all teens on the street are involved with drugs. A group of homeless teenagers on Granville recently told *The Vancouver Sun* they would never smoke anything more harmful than marijuana because becoming addicted to a stronger drug often means 'the drugs start doing you, you don't do the drugs'. Some of Brown's friends said their biggest dream is one day to get off the streets, and they believe that doing hard drugs could make it harder to get a roof over their heads.

Brown's two biggest goals, he said, are to find a home and go to college to study culinary arts. When asked what he thought would get him off the streets, he said that if he was given $125 more a month on his welfare cheque, he would be able to find a place to live. Then, he said, he could shower every day, feel safe sleeping, and try to pull himself together to get a job. Brown now gets the standard welfare rental rate of $375 a month for housing, but in Vancouver it is getting increasingly hard to find a place in which to live for that price. According to a recent report by the Carnegie Community Action Project, single-room occupancy hotel rooms in the Downtown Eastside rented at

welfare-friendly rates have gone down from 29 per cent of available rooms in 2009, to 12 per cent this year.

Helping homeless teens may seem like a hopeless task. How does society know where to start? Is it housing, food, and employment? Or just someone to believe in them and to encourage them along the way? People who work with homeless teens say the solutions vary. Hanrahan believes young people need the help of people who are non-judgmental and who will convey they are worth caring for, because sometimes they feel they have little self-worth. Every teen has potential, if given the chance. If a community can help one teen follow his or her dream, advocates say, it can become a win-win situation for society and, most importantly, for the young person on the street.

Bronwyn McCarter is a Grade 11 student at West Vancouver Secondary School.

Source: Bronwyn McCarter, *The Vancouver Sun,* Vancouver, BC: Nov 18, 2010. p. A17.

Child-Welfare Experiences

Children and youth who have experienced maltreatment and family conflict frequently become involved with child welfare and are referred to child-welfare care (MacLaurin and Bala 2004). Children in the care of child welfare (e.g., foster care, group homes, or treatment centres) are overrepresented in most street-youth populations (Biehal and Wade 2000; Duval and Vincent 2009; Fitzgerald 1995; Park 2005; Worthington et al. 2008). Worthington and MacLaurin et al. (2008) reported that 62 per cent of street-involved youth surveyed in Calgary reported that their family had a history of child-welfare involvement, and of this number 52 per cent had been placed in either foster or group care as a result of the involvement.

This overrepresentation may be a reflection of the number of youth who run away from current child-welfare care or of those youth who became homeless following emancipation from care (Lenz-Rashid 2006). Although less than 1 per cent of children in England were in foster care or group homes, more than 30 per cent of **runaways** reported as missing to the police were from care (Biehal and Wade 2000). This trend is also seen in Canada, with a high percentage of children reported missing to the police from institutional and foster care, and institutional care having the highest rate of repeat runners (Fisher 1989).

Child-welfare agencies have the mandate to effectively serve the transitional needs of youth as they prepare for independence following their in-care placements. Research focusing on the health and housing outcomes of youth aging out of the child-welfare system has identified that these young people are not consistently well served (Lenz-Rashid 2006). The percentage of youth emancipated from the care of child welfare who were described as homeless at the point of emancipation in the United States ranges from 25 to 66 per cent (Barth 1990; Courtney et al. 2001; California Department of Social Services 2002).

There are significant differences noted for youth who enter street life from foster or group care compared to those youth who enter the streets from home (Biehal and Wade 2000; Rees 1993). Rees

runaways

Youth who run away from their family or child-welfare placement, at least overnight, without parental or caretaker permission. They often leave as a result of family conflict or maltreatment.

(1993) found that street-involved youth who had left child-welfare placements were more likely to run repeatedly, more likely to run for longer periods of time, and more likely to be apprehended by police.

Life on the Streets

Once youth make the transition from home to the street, they enter a new world with its own culture, norms, and rules. As Auerswald and Eyre (2002) point out, this initial experience of the street is characterized by feelings of loneliness, disorientation, and the need to survive. Their study suggests that youth find street mentors and become acculturated to the street, including the street's resources, economy, language, and drugs. Victimization on the street is extremely common among street-involved youth, and can take the form of theft or robbery, sexual assault, physical assault, and assault with a weapon (Cauce 2004; Gaetz 2004). For minority groups like gay, lesbian, and bisexual youth, the level of victimization can nearly double (Whitbeck 2004). Furthermore, the mortality rate for street-involved youth is about 11 times the expected rate for the general youth population (Boivin 2005). Gaetz (2004) notes that a significant proportion of street-involved youth do not turn to anyone when they have experienced victimization on the street.

Social Support and Resilience

Street-involved youth develop social networks that can be a source of support (Johnson, Whitbeck, and Hoyt 2005; Milburn et al. 2005). Nearly 80 per cent of youth have relationships that were formed prior to their time on the streets, and 66 per cent have friends from home, indicating that these youth still value the ties from their past (Johnson et al. 2005). Furthermore, nearly one-third (31 per cent) of street-involved youth report family members as part of their social network, including siblings (Johnson et al. 2005; Kidd 2003). Weaker family ties are associated with youth who have externalizing behaviour problems; with gay, lesbian, and bisexual youth; and with those who experience caregiver abuse prior to leaving home (Johnson et al. 2005; Milburn et al. 2005). In a qualitative study by Kidd (2003), one-quarter of street-involved youth mentioned significant support from friends on the street who taught them the rules of street culture. Street acquaintances provide an element of family support for street-involved youth and are described as being there for personal, financial, and emotional support (Worthington, MacLaurin, Dittmann, and Kitt 2009c).

Street-involved youth are resilient in a number of ways. Kidd (2003) found that a large number of Canadian youth had a strong sense of confidence in their own abilities, security in their own beliefs, and a sense of self-worth. Other research supports these findings, and indicates that youth have both resource-related strengths (i.e., knowledge of the street environment and streetwise skills), and self-improvement skills (e.g., making healthier choices and gaining emotional maturity) (see Rew and Horner 2003). Beneficial coping mechanisms include having hope and goals for the future, having a sense of spirituality, having friends, having time alone to think, having positive thinking and humour, and hobbies (Kidd 2003; Worthington et al. 2009c). A major theme in Kidd's (2003) interviews with street-involved youth was their desire for more opportunities to increase their self-worth. These youth, despite their history and circumstances, continue to have a sense of hope for their future.

Risks Associated with Street Involvement

Substance Use and HIV Risk

Substance use is primarily used as a coping mechanism for life on the streets, stress, and early family abuse but can also be used for social or recreational purposes (Tyler and Johnson 2006). Substance use is common among street-involved youth, including use of tobacco, alcohol, marijuana, hashish, crack-cocaine, powder cocaine, heroin, lysergic acid diethylamide (LSD), mushrooms, crystal meth, speed, crank, ecstasy, and glue (Clatts, Goldsamt, Yi, and Gwadz 2005; Hagan and McCarthy 1997; Robert, Pauze, and Fournier 2005; also see Chapter 9 in this volume). The rate of substance use among street-involved youth varies by specific substance, with between 70 per cent and 94 per cent of youth overall reporting the use of any substance (Adlaf and Zhanowicz 1999; MacLaurin, Worthington, Dittmann, and Kitt 2009c). Specific levels of reported substance use include alcohol (67 per cent to 100 per cent), tobacco (96 per cent), and marijuana (43 per cent to 93 per cent), although several other substances are also used by the majority of street-involved youth (Ginzler 2003; Greene, Ennett, and Ringwalt 1997; Kipke, Unger, Palmer, and Edgington 1996; Thompson, Zittel-Palamara, and Maccio 2004; Tyler and Johnson 2006; Worthington et al. 2008). Brands, Leslie, Catz-Biro, and Li (2005) found that substance use among street-involved youth is not only common but also tends to be extreme.

Most studies report rates of injection drug use among street-involved youth from 20 per cent to 54 per cent (Clatts, Rees-Davis, Sotheran, and Atillasoy 1998; Gleghorn 1998; Leach, Wolitski, Goldbaum, Fishbein, and The AIDS Community Demonstration Projects 1997; Roy, Haley, Leclerc, Cedras, and Boivin 2002; Roy, Lemire, Haley, Boivin, Frappier, and Claessens 1998; Worthington et al. 2008). Furthermore, between one-quarter and three-quarters of youth who use injection drugs have shared drug-injection equipment (Clatts et al. 1998; Gleghorn 1998; Worthington et al. 2008).

Although some Canadian studies on street-involved youth have shown low risk of HIV infection through injection drug use, levels of injecting risk behaviours among street-involved youth require ongoing assessment. The majority of research shows that youth (defined as those under 30 years of age) who use injection drugs are at greater risk of HIV transmission than older users (Health Canada 2002b). This risk results from sharing contaminated needles, syringes, and other drug use equipment and the tendency to engage in unsafe sex, often under the influence of drugs (Diaz, Conover, Edwards, Monterroso, and Susser 1998; Elise et al. 1993; Hahn, Shafer, and Moss 1998; Kral, Lorvick, and Edlin 1999; Marshall 2010). Findings also indicate that youth who use injection drugs have a significantly higher rate of hepatitis C virus (HCV) (Boivin 2005).

Physical and Mental-Health Problems

Canadian research has consistently demonstrated that street-involved youth are a population at risk for physical and mental health problems. It has been suggested that street-involved youth face barriers to exercising their rights and opportunities of their citizenship (e.g., access to health care, to shelter, to mental-health support) while having the same basic needs as all Canadians, and that they are one of the most disenfranchised groups in our society (Bassuk, Rubin, and Lauriat 1984; Miller et al. 1980). A recent study of homeless Toronto **squeegee kids**, for example, suggests that the lives of this group of street-involved youth are characterized by a constant struggle to find safe, secure shelter, to generate income, and to find sufficient food (Dachner and Tarasuk 2002).

Study findings indicate a higher prevalence of mental-health problems for street-involved youth than for non-street-involved youth (Smart and Walsh 1993; Boivin 2005). Common mental-health problems in this population include conduct and oppositional disorder, anxiety disorders, dissociative symptoms, and depression (Booth and Zhang 1997; Robert et al. 2005; Thompson et al. 2004; Tyler, Cauce, and Whitbeck 2004). However, Ayerst (1999) found that most street-involved youth felt less depressed and stressed on the street than when they were living at home. Street-involved youth are at a higher risk for attempted and completed suicide, and suicidal ideation often follows completed suicides of street friends (Clatts et al. 2005; Molnar, Shade, Kral, Booth, and Watters 1998; Radford, King, and Warren 1991; Rotheram-Borus et al. 1992; Stiffman 1989; Yoder, Hoyt, and Whitbeck

squeegee kids

A group of street-involved youth who are resourceful in attempting to develop and maintain a livelihood and means of survival by offering to clean windshields at major intersections.

1998). Documented rates of attempted suicide range from 25 per cent to 46 per cent, with even higher rates noted for gay, lesbian, and bisexual youth (Adlaf and Zhanowicz 1999; Clatts et al. 2005; Greene and Ringwalt 1996; Kidd 2006; Whitbeck 2004; Worthington et al. 2009a). Mental health is a critical concern for all street-involved youth and specifically for select marginalized groups.

Given the lifestyle of street-involved youth, it is understandable that youth may not receive adequate health care and are frequently unable to obtain this care because of a lack of current health-care coverage (e.g., some may not have access to a health-care card) (Farrow, Deisher, Brown, Kulig, and Kipke 1992; Gaetz et al. 1999; Wright 1991). Health concerns reported by street-involved youth include upper-respiratory-tract infections, skin disorders (including scabies and lice), gastrointestinal disorders, genitourinary disorders, and foot problems (e.g., fungus and blisters) (Dachner and Tarasuk 2002; Wright 1991). A higher percentage of street-involved youth with a current or previous history of living on the street reported physical health conditions compared to youth who had never lived on the street (Worthington et al. 2009b). And chronic health concerns for street-involved youth may be twice as high compared to youth who are not street involved (Wright 1991). Additional health concerns are identified for street-involved youth who have children while they are living on the street (Pennbridge, MacKenzie, and Swofford 1991; Ray 1993). The literature highlights a relationship between the duration of street involvement and health outcomes for youth—the longer the duration, the greater the risk for tuberculosis, dental problems, viral and sexually transmitted diseases (STDs), HIV/AIDS, hepatitis B virus (HBV), and hepatitis C virus (HCV) (Kraus, Eberle, and Serge 2001).

Sexual Health—STIs and HIV Risk

According to findings from the Canadian E-SYS study (Enhanced Surveillance of Canadian Street Youth, initiated in 1998) street-involved youth are at high risk for contracting sexually transmitted infections (STIs) (Public Health Agency of Canada 2006a). Compared to the general youth population, street-involved youth included in the E-SYS study are 10 times more likely to have chlamydia, and 20 to 30 times more likely to have gonorrhea. Among youth included in the E-SYS study, between the years 1999 to 2003, approximately 2.3 per cent of street-involved youth had HBV, 3.6 per cent to 4.5 per cent had HCV, and 14.2 per cent to 18.8 per cent had herpes simplex virus-2 (HSV-2), associated with genital herpes.

Canadian and American incidence and prevalence data, in conjunction with surveillance data, reveal that street-involved youth are at very high risk of HIV infection (Boivin 2005; DeMatteo et al. 1999; Doherty et al. 1996; Hahn et al. 1998; Kipke, Montgomery, Simon, and Iverson 1996; Larke 2001; Roy et al. 2002; Roy et al. 2001; Roy et al. 1999; Sullivan 1996). The number of new HIV cases in youth between the ages of 15 and 19 years has remained relatively constant since 1999; however, the proportion of females among this group is growing (Health Canada 2002a, 2002b). Sexual activity is likely to present a major risk for HIV transmission among street-involved youth. St. Lawrence, Crosby, and O'Brannon (1999) found that the average age at first intercourse for street-involved youth is 12 years old, while the average number of times street-involved youth have sexual intercourse each week ranges from two to three times for casual sex, up to 13 times for paying sex (Public Health Agency of Canada 2006a). Studies report high percentages of youth with multiple sexual partners, and young men who have sex with men represent the most at-risk subgroup among street-involved youth, with an average of 45 lifetime partners (Booth and Zhang 1997; Leach et al. 1997; Public Health Agency of Canada 2006a; St. Lawrence et al. 1999).

Although young people are generally aware of HIV risks, research on sexual risk behaviours shows that youth are among the least likely to employ safer sex precautions. A large percentage of street-involved youth do not use condoms to protect themselves from HIV or other sexually transmitted diseases (STDs), with a low of 10 per cent of female street-involved youth who consistently use condoms (Clatts et al. 1998; De Rosa, Montgomery, Hyde, Iverson, and Kipke 2001; Haley 2004b; St. Lawrence et al. 1999; Weber 2002).

Pregnancy is also common among street-involved youth. Studies report that 42 per cent to 50 per cent of all female youth living on the street have been pregnant (Haley 2004a; Weber 2002; Worthington et al. 2009e). Greene and Ringwalt (1998) examined the relationship between pregnancy in street-involved youth and their level of street involvement, and found that youth currently living on the street were most likely to become pregnant and to experience multiple pregnancies. There are significant risks for youth who experience a pregnancy while living on the street, including drug use, access to prenatal and medical services, financial resources, and infant health (Thompson, Bender, Lewis, and Watkins 2008); however, there is evidence that pregnancies among street-involved youth may provide motivation for some youth to establish more stable housing (Hathazi, Lankenau, Sanders, and Bloom 2009).

Involvement in Survival or Obligatory Sex

Survival or obligatory sex involves the bartering of sex for money or other necessities, such as food and shelter. Studies reveal that up to 25 per cent of street-involved youth have traded sex at some point in their lives and that females may be at higher risk for involvement (Clatts et al. 1998; Haley 2004b; Public Health Agency of Canada 2006a; Weber 2002; Worthington et al. 2009e). Survival or obligatory sex may offer a way for street-involved youth to gain autonomy and independence while on the street. Many youth have left family or child-welfare situations in a manner that does not allow their return, and survival or obligatory sex and eventual involvement in the sex trade is a way of establishing some immediate financial independence and autonomy from their former living situations (McIntyre 1999; also see Chapter 13 in this volume). Street-involved youth may participate in unprotected sexual activity in order to receive a greater amount of money than that offered for protected sex or to secure a place to stay for the night (de Oliviera 1992; Slonim-Nevo, Ozawa, and Auslander 1991; Swart-Kruger and Richer 1997). Among Canadian street-involved youth involved in survival or obligatory sex, 44 per cent report not using a condom during their most recent obligatory sexual encounter (Public Health Agency of Canada 2006a; Swart-Kruger and Richer 1997).

Institutional Experiences of Street-Involved Youth

Education

Education for street-involved youth is a serious concern, as many of these youth may drop out of school or be expelled before finishing, or even reaching, high school. Without education, youth have difficulty finding and maintaining a steady job, making it even more difficult for them to transition off the street. This population also experiences a higher rate of learning difficulties (Barwick and Siegal 1996; Thompson et al. 2004). One study reported that more than half of all street-involved youth displayed evidence of a reading disability, nearly 30 per cent displayed evidence of arithmetic/written work disability, and 20 per cent were classified as 'normally achieving' (Barwick and Siegal 1996). School attendance declines as youth get older. Approximately 65 per cent of early-adolescent street-involved youth reported attending school within the past month compared to 27 per cent of older-adolescent street-involved youth (Unger et al. 1998). Reasons for not attending school are complex, but Thompson, O'Brannon, and Maccio (2004) identified that more than half of street-involved youth were either suspended or expelled from school. A survey of Calgary street-involved youth found that 69 per cent of respondents reported an incomplete high school education and 46 per cent reported having been kicked out of school (MacLaurin, Worthington, Dittmann, and Kitt 2009a).

Child Welfare

A high percentage of street-involved youth have had previous child-welfare experiences and foster-care placements (Clarke and Cooper 2000; Gaetz et al. 1999; Leslie and Hare 2000; Min Park 2005; Robert et al. 2005; Viner 2005; Worthington et al. 2008). In 2003, 42 per cent of Canadian street-involved youth in the E-SYS study reported having been in foster care, and 47 per cent reported having been in group homes (Public Health Agency of Canada 2006b). In addition, between 12 per cent and 38 per cent of youth transitioning out of foster care spend some time without a home shortly after discharge, either sleeping on the streets or in a homeless shelter (Cook 1994; Courtney 2001; Courtney and Dworsky 2006; Freundlich and Avery 2006; Reilly 2003). Recent studies reported that youth with child-welfare histories were two times more likely than other youth to be unable to pay their rent or utility bills, four times more likely to be evicted, and, overall, youth transitioning out of care reported feeling poorly prepared for independent living (Courtney 2001; Leslie and Hare 2000; Reilly 2003) (see Box 12.2).

Box 12.2 Youth Justice in Action

Street Kids' Toughness Only Skin Deep

By Carol Goar

A young, able-bodied panhandler asks you for spare change. Unless you're remarkably non-judgmental, your first thought is Why doesn't this kid get a job or go to school or at least do something useful? Raising the Roof, a national charity dedicated to ending homelessness, has spent the past three years seeking answers to those questions. It interviewed 689 street youth in three Canadian cities—Toronto, Calgary and St. John's—to find out where they came from, how they got there, why they stayed on the street and what kind of help they needed. Last week, it released its results. The 44-page report, entitled Youth Homelessness in Canada: The Road to Solutions, has two primary messages. Young people seldom choose to live on the streets. They end up there because they have no choice. These kids can become self-sufficient, with the right support. 'We know what is needed to guide youth toward the path of opportunity and independence,' the report says. 'The question is, are we committing adequate resources to be there at critical moments in a young person's life?' In any given year, an estimated 65,000 young people (aged 16 to 24) are homeless. Some stay in shelters, some couch-surf and some sleep on heating grates and park benches. To many Canadians, they look unkempt, defiant, probably drugged. There is some truth to that image. But there is a lot people don't see. The report fills in some of the gaps. Sixty-eight per cent of the kids in the survey had

previously been in foster care, group homes or a youth centre. Thirty-seven per cent had witnessed substance abuse in their families. Thirty-three per cent had mental health problems (which they hid because of the stigma). Twenty-four per cent had experienced sexual, physical or mental abuse. Aboriginal, gay, lesbian, bisexual and transgendered youths were overrepresented. These kids had made mistakes and they knew it. Seventy-one per cent reported brushes with the law. Sixty-two per cent had dropped out of school. Fifty per cent admitted drug and alcohol abuse. Twenty-one per cent had children, were pregnant or had a pregnant partner.

But most weren't willful rebels. They longed for the stability they'd never had. Here are some of the phrases they used to describe being homeless 'always afraid', 'lonely', 'no hope' and 'expect the worst'. The report acknowledges that it won't be cheap to give homeless youth a second chance. But the alternative—letting them fend for themselves—will be expensive too. It will drive up shelter costs, health-care costs, welfare costs, law enforcement costs and jail costs.

Raising the Roof recommends a three-pronged strategy: *Prevention*—Provide struggling families with the support they need to keep their kids off the streets. The risks are easy to spot. But the services are either absent or insufficient. *Emergency response*—Although youth-specific homeless shelters are not the answer, they offer kids a safe place to sleep and an access point to other services. *Long-term action*—Homeless young people with addictions, mental health problems, no job skills or no legitimate means of making money need a range of supports. The first imperative is affordable housing. A place to live gives them the stability to begin treatment, return to school, develop a healthy network of friends and train for a job.

The report calls on governments to show leadership, business leaders to lend a hand and educators, mental health workers, non-profit housing providers and social service agencies to look at the whole picture. Finally, it asks Canadians to shed their stereotypes. Street kids may look tough, but they feel vulnerable. They may want a handout, but they need a future.

Source: Carol Goar. *The Toronto Star*. Toronto, ON: November 23, 2009. p. A.13.

Criminal Justice System

Extensive work by Baron has shown how crime is related to several factors in the lives of street-involved youth (Baron 2003, 2004; Baron and Hartnagel 1997, 1998, 2006). These factors include monetary dissatisfaction; unemployment; deviant/criminal peers; being a victim of robbery, violence, or theft; perception of blocked opportunities; drug/alcohol use; low self-control; and high self-esteem. All of these factors interact to increase the risk of crime involvement in street-involved youth. As can be seen, criminal involvement among street-involved youth is a complex interaction of numerous factors, and cannot simply be explained as deviant behaviour.

Street-involved youth consistently report that selling drugs is a means of earning money while on the streets (Baron and Hartnagel 2006; Gaetz 2004; Hagan and McCarthy 1997). A significant proportion of street-involved youth are involved in some form of gang activity while on the street (Unger et al. 1998; Yoder, Whitbeck, and Hoyt 2003), while violent crime such as assault is also commonly noted in Canadian and US studies (Baron and Hartnagel 2006; Gaetz 2004). Other criminal involvement includes shoplifting, theft, and property offences (Baron and Hartnagel 2006; Gaetz 2004). A survey of Calgary street-involved youth found that 69 per cent of respondents reported that they had been charged with a crime at some point in their life, and of this group 79 per cent were charged under the juvenile justice system, 48 per cent were charged under the adult system, and 75 per cent had spent time in jail or detention as a result of these charges (Dittmann, MacLaurin, Worthington, and Kitt 2009).

It has been suggested that street-involved youth do not necessarily prefer to be delinquent or elect to become involved in criminal activities but, rather, become involved in response to the situational demands and challenges of living on the streets (Hagan and McCarthy 1997). For example, MacLaurin (1991) found that many of the juvenile charges laid against street-involved youth in Calgary were a result of nonpayment of transit fines for riding without a ticket. O'Grady and Green (2003) highlight that the more disadvantaged a homeless person becomes, the more likely that person may opt to be involved in criminal activity. This is especially critical when appropriate avenues for earning are limited or criminalized. During the late 1990s, there was a noted increase in the number of people involved in squeegee cleaning on the streets of many large Canadian cities. Squeegee cleaning, like panhandling, was an income-generating activity that was seen as the domain of street-involved youth and resulted in the term 'squeegee kids' (O'Grady and Bright 2002). The Safe Streets Act was enacted in Ontario in 2000 and resulted in the criminalization of squeegee cleaning as a means of income generation (Schneiderman 2002). O'Grady and Greene (2003) question the rationale of this move as research found that squeegee-cleaning street youth were less involved in criminal activity and reported lower levels of hard drug use and lower levels of psychological distress than that reported by street youth who did not participate in squeegee cleaning (O'Grady, Bright, and Cohen 1998).

Street Services and Intervention Strategies

Street-involved youth are not accessing services in all circumstances. In a sample of youth in Calgary without child-welfare status, McLean (2005) found that just over half of youth reported knowledge or use of community outreach services for homeless youth, and that young people primarily heard about these services from their friends. Of those surveyed in this study who used shelters, 29 per cent said they experienced difficulty accessing the service while 32 per cent said they had been turned away because they did not meet certain shelter criteria (McLean 2005).

One study in San Francisco examined differential service use for street-involved youth at different stages of street involvement and suggested that youth who were more entrenched in the street culture were less likely to access drug-related services while those attempting to leave the street were more likely to access medical services (Carlson et al. 2006). Regardless of the level of street involvement, 99 per cent of all street-involved youth in the study reported using at least one related service, 50 per cent used medical services, 45 per cent used outreach services, 21 per cent used drug-related services, and 7 per cent used shelters. This study demonstrated a high rate of service use overall but highlighted that the effectiveness of individual services truly differ for subpopulations (Carlson et al. 2006).

Worthington and MacLaurin (2008) report similar findings in Canada as use of specific services differed by type of street involvement. The three levels of street involvement included street-involved youth who were currently living on the street (Currently on Street); the second category included street-involved youth who were not currently living on the street but had a past history of living on the street (Not on Street—History); the third category included street-involved youth who were not currently living on the street and had no history of living on the street (Not on Street—No History). Youth currently living on the street reported higher use of shelters, drop-in centres, and outreach services while street-involved youth who had not lived on the street reported higher use of alternative educational services (Worthington et al. 2008) (see Table 12.1).

The majority of street-involved youth speak very positively about the services that are available to them—specifically those services that were flexible, that had employees with positive attitudes, that offered a comfortable atmosphere, and that provided a sense of safety and security (Worthington et al. 2008). A continued focus on quality assurance is needed, however, as street-involved youth continue to experience barriers in accessing timely and effective services. Karabanow (2004) provides an example of two Toronto-based shelters that have teamed with child-welfare organizations. While these programs were originally designed to provide emergency housing and services to street-involved youth, these organizations are now becoming long-term care facilities for young people experiencing difficulty with child-welfare services. Other barriers identified in the literature include inadequate program funding, unavailable programs and services, low salaries, insufficient and inexperienced staff, and government policy (Brooks, Milburn, Rotheram-Borus, and Witkin 2004; Worthington et al. 2008). According to Brooks et al. (2004), most of the issues identified by agencies as problem areas for street-involved youth are not well addressed by these agencies. Street-involved youth tend to respond best to service providers who are respectful, flexible, empathic, supportive, encouraging, and empowering (Thompson, McManus, Lantry, Windsor, and Flynn 2006).

Effective service development is not a simple prescription for filling the needs of street-involved youth. Given the diversity of street youth—as noted in the discussions of the life-cycle model of street involvement (Auerswald and Eyre 2002) and the level of street-involvement (Worthington et al. 2008), as well the inherent risks associated with street involvement—there is a critical need to establish a continuum of services to meet the diverse needs of street-involved youth. Services are required to assist young people at different points: before youth become regularly involved in the streets; during street involvement; during a transition from the street locale; and as a follow-up to

Table 12.1 Use of Street Services by Current Level of Street Involvement

| Services Used in the Past Three Months (N=333) | Current Level of Street Involvement | | | | | | | |
| | Not on Street— No History | | Not on Street— History | | Currently on Street | | Total | |
	%	#	%	#	%	#	%	#
Food Banks	22	14	38	43	33	50	32	107
Shelters*	19	12	32	36	72	111	48	159
Drop-in centres*	12	8	30	34	68	105	44	147
Medical clinics	35	23	45	51	40	61	41	135
Outreach services*	9	6	32	36	53	81	37	123
Financial aid	6	4	15	17	8	13	10	34
Employment services	23	15	21	24	29	44	25	83
Educational services	20	13	16	18	10	16	14	47
Counselling services*	15	10	26	30	10	16	17	56
No services used*	22	14	17	19	2	3	11	36
Total	Column totals not provided because participants could choose multiple responses							

Calgary Youth, Health and the Street — Final Report

Based on a sample of 333 responses with information about use of street services and current street involvement

* Significance level p ≤ 0.05

Source: Worthington, MacLaurin, Huffey, Dittmann, Kitt, Patten, and Leech 2008, p. 116.

street involvement (Kufeldt and Burrows 1994). Services at each of these points need to address the physical needs (food, clothing, shelter) of young people involved in street life as well as needs related to their physical and mental health, education, and employment (see Table 12.2). Studies advocate for a **youth-centric programming model** that allows youth to play a significant role in developing and evaluating programs, and in which the agencies continue to be flexible in adapting to the changing needs of street-involved youth (Baer 2004; Barry 2002; Whitmore and McKee 2001) (see Box 12.3).

youth-centric programming model

Youth play a significant role in developing and evaluating programs, and agencies continue to be flexible in adapting to the changing needs of street-involved youth.

Summary

Street-involved youth are a diverse, marginalized population that face multiple challenges and insufficient and fragmented support from institutions and services. Understanding the experience of street-involved youth and the risks associated with street involvement is critical in developing services to meet their needs at all stages of their involvement—from early contact with the street, during their extended time spent on the street, and following their decision to leave the street. Communities need to promote and support positive life choices among street-involved youth while respecting their independence. Research has shown that while street-involved youth are at higher risk for a variety of issues related to survival, safety, and health, these youth possess resilience and a strong desire to develop a future for themselves. A male street-involved youth eloquently described this hope for the future during a study interview in Calgary: 'It's not a dark road. I mean it's whatever I want to make of it. Wherever I want to go, I know I can get there. It's gonna to take work, it's gonna take discipline, it'll take a lot of things, but it's not unreachable. So, I'm not hopeless' (Worthington et al. 2008, p. iii).

Table 12.2 Continuum of Services for Homeless Youth: Stage of Homelessness and Type of Service Required

	Before the Street	On the Street	Transitional Services	Off the Street
Accommodation	– Affordable housing	– Emergency housing – Place to go during the day		– Affordable housing
Protection	– Community outreach – Child-welfare services	– Secure treatment – Safe, protected accommodation – Emergency child-welfare placements		
Food	– Adequate family income	– Daily meals		– Adequate income
Clothing	– Adequate family income	– Clothing – Storage and laundry facilities		– Adequate income
Health and hygiene	– Accessible, affordable health care	– Walk-in or mobile medical services – Showers	– Accessible, affordable health care	– Accessible, affordable health care
Mental health	– Crisis intervention counselling and/ or mental-health services	– Crisis intervention	– Supportive counselling	– Informal social supports
Substance abuse	– Information counselling and/or treatment	– Detoxification services	– Substance abuse treatment and follow-up	– Informal social supports
Education	– Drop-out prevention – Special ed programs	– Walk-in schooling	– Transitional school programs	– Regular schools – Adult upgrading
Income	– Adequate family income		– Social assistance	– Job
Employment	– Job or school		– Life skills training – Employment training – Job-finding help	– Job

Source: Kufeldt and Burrows 1994, p. 65.

Box 12.3 Youth Justice in Action

Youths Get Help to Leave Streets; 'Plan within a Plan' to End Homelessness

By Colette Derworiz

As the number of teens turning to shelters continues to grow, the Calgary Homeless Foundation is working on the country's first plan dedicated to ending youth homelessness. The blueprint, which would become part of Calgary's overall 10-year plan to end homelessness, will focus on ways to help youths between the ages of 12 and 24. 'We recognize that there are some very specific needs and we want to respond to those needs with a bit more emphasis than our original plan to end homelessness,' said Tim Richter, president of the Calgary Homeless Foundation, which oversees the local plan. 'It's a plan within a plan.' Officials from the foundation will work with the United Way and local service agencies dealing with homeless youths to develop the plan over the coming months, he said. Richter said it will be based on the foundation's draft discussion paper on youth homelessness in Calgary.

The paper, released in May 2009, called on the province's Children and Youth Services Department to develop a strategy to specifically address youth homelessness. It was supposed to be considered as part of a provincial review into youth homelessness, which was due to issue a report on its findings last fall. But the report has never been released publicly and no strategy has been developed. Children and Youth Services Minister Yvonne Fritz said she has yet to see the final report from the provincial review, but she commended the Calgary Homeless Foundation's efforts to start addressing the issue in Calgary. 'Youth homelessness is a community issue and I think it requires community solutions,' she said. 'None of us can address the issue alone.'

According to recent statistics, the problem of youth homelessness is substantial and continues to grow.

The city's 2008 homeless count identified 4,060 homeless Calgarians, including 355 people under the age of 18 and another 327 people between 18 and 24. In the same year, the Calgary Drop-In Centre reported serving 1,200 different youth between the ages of 16 and 24. Wood's Homes Exit Youth Shelter also housed 712 people between the ages of 12 and 17, and the Salvation Army Centre of Hope had 449 youth come through its doors. As a result, the homeless foundation suggested in its 2009 paper that the city's homeless youth population could be as high as 2,000 people. Darlene Petrie, program manager for McMan Youth, Family and Community Service Association, said it's only getting worse as youth shelters turn more people away every year. 'In the past three months, it's been close to 100,' she said, noting that's a 50 per cent increase over last year.

Some of the increase in youth homelessness has been attributed to the growth of the city, with a rising number of youth fleeing homes facing tough economic times. In addition, youth who are homeless have higher needs than adults. The homeless foundation's paper suggested 43 per cent of homeless youth have been diagnosed with childhood mental illness, 57 per cent have thought about suicide, 33 per cent have a physical disability and 37 per cent have a learning disability. Once they are on the street, 94 per cent of youth use alcohol or drugs, and 45 per cent of girls have been asked to engage in prostitution. Richter said the plan will try to address some of those complex needs. 'We know it's a major problem,' he said. 'One of the major challenges we have is that we don't fully understand the scale. Part of our work is going to be making sure we get a better handle on it.'

Source: Colette Derworiz. *Calgary Herald*. Calgary, AB: April 5, 2010. p. A.1.

Key Terms

homeless youth	street-involved youth
life-cycle model	throwaways
runaways	youth-centric programming model
squeegee kids	

Review Questions

1. Identify structural factors that may contribute to the involvement of youth in street life in Canada.

2. Identify and describe key factors that contribute to young people becoming involved in the street.

3. Why are typologies useful in providing a framework for working with street-involved youth in Canada?

4. What kinds of risks are street-involved youth exposed to? Why?

Critical Thinking Questions

1. How would you propose getting an accurate count of the number of street-involved youth currently living in a major Canadian city?

2. What factors do you think would be important in developing a public awareness program for street-involved youth?

3. How would you counter the debate that shelters and outreach services make it too easy for children to remain living on the street and that there is no incentive for them to get off the street?

4. Identify a group of street-involved youth (e.g., youth involved in survival or obligatory sex, or injection drug use). If you were designing a new program, what program components would be a priority for meeting their immediate and long-term needs? How would you know if the program was successful?

Suggested Readings

Gaetz, S. (2004). Safe streets for whom? Homeless youth, social exclusion, and criminal victimization. *Canadian Journal of Criminology and Criminal Justice, 46*(4): 423–55.

Karabanow, J. (2004). Changing faces: The story of two Canadian street youth shelters. *International Journal of Social Welfare, 13*(4): 304–14.

Kufeldt, K., and Burrows, B.A. (1994). *Issues affecting public policies and services for homeless youth.* Calgary, AB: University of Calgary.

Public Health Agency of Canada. (2006b). *Street youth in Canada: Findings from enhanced surveillance of Canadian street youth, 1999–2003* (No. HP5-15/2006). Ottawa: Minister of Health.

Roy, E., Lemire, N., Haley, N., Boivin, J.F., Frappier, J.Y., and Claessens, C. (1998). Injection drug use among street youth: A dynamic process. *Canadian Journal of Public Health, 89*(4): 239–40.

Thompson, S.J., McManus, H., Lantry, J., Windsor, L., and Flynn, P. (2006). Insights from the street: Perceptions of services and providers by homeless young adults. *Evaluation and Program Planning, 29*, 34–43.

Worthington, C., MacLaurin, B., Huffey, N., Dittmann, D., Kitt, O., Patten, S., et al. (2008). *Calgary, youth, health and the street—Final report.* Calgary, AB: University of Calgary.

Suggested Weblinks

Boys and Girls Clubs of Canada

www.bgccan.com

- The Boys and Girls Clubs have been in operation for more than 100 years in communities across Canada and serve young people in the community as they grow to adulthood. Many of these clubs offer services for street-involved youth.

Calgary Youth, Health and the Street: Final Report

www.aidscalgary.org/files/publications/Calgary%20Youth%20Health%20and%20the%20Street.pdf

- This is the location for the final report for the Calgary, Youth, Health and the Street study conducted in Calgary, Alberta, and prepared by the chapter authors.

Canada—Missing Children

http://missingkids.ca/app/en

- This website is for MissingKids.ca, the missing children resource centre for Canada. This organization offers families support in finding their missing child and provides educational materials to help prevent children from going missing.

Covenant House

www.covenanthouse.org

- Covenant House was founded almost 40 years ago and offers food, shelter, immediate crisis care, and essential services to homeless, throwaway, and runaway youth in multiple sites in Canada, the United States, Mexico, and Central America.

The Homeless Hub

www.homelesshub.ca

- The Homeless Hub was created to address the need for a single place to find information on homelessness in Canada. Launched in 2007, the Homeless Hub is a web-based research library and information centre using technology to enhance knowledge mobilization and networking.

John Howard Society of Canada

www.johnhoward.ca

- John Howard Society of Canada is designed to advocate to the government of Canada for correctional and criminal justice policy as well as to deliver practice services reflective of these principles. It is shown to be economically responsible and accountable to communities.

Kids Help Phone

http://org.kidshelpphone.ca/en

- The Kids Help Phone is a free, anonymous, and confidential phone and online professional counselling service for youth. It is designed to address all concerns experienced by youth and is offered 24 hours a day, 365 days a year.

Missing Children Society of Canada

http://mcsc.ca

- The Missing Children Society of Canada was established in 1986 and offers comprehensive search programs to assist police and searching families in the active and ongoing search for missing children.

National Network for Youth (nn4y)

www.nn4youth.org

- The National Network for Youth uses a network of member organizations to champion the needs of runaway, homeless, and other disconnected youth through advocacy, innovation, and services.

National Runaway Switchboard

www.nrscrisisline.org

- The National Runaway Switchboard (NRS) is designed to ensure that runaway, homeless, and at-risk youth in the United States are safe and off the streets. This service offers education and solution-focused interventions and support in a confidential manner for at-risk youth and their families, 24 hours a day.

Youth in Care Canada

www.youthincare.ca

- Youth in Care Canada is an organization organized by youth and alumni who are from care with the purpose of ensuring that the voices of these youth are heard and valued. This organization conducts research on topics related to youth in care, presents findings to a range of audiences, provides support to youth in and from state care, and guides the development of local and provincial Youth in Care Networks.

PHAC Street Youth in Canada

www.phac-aspc.gc.ca/std-mts/reports_06/youth-eng.php

- Enhanced Surveillance of Canadian Street Youth (E-SYS) was initiated in 1998 and is the result of strong collaboration between local, provincial, and federal public health stakeholders in addition to universities. Information collected from E-SYS is intended to assist with enhancing social and public health programs aimed at improving the emotional, physical, and psychological well-being of Canadian street youth.

Safe Place

www.nationalsafeplace.org

- Safe Place is a national youth outreach program in the United States that educates thousands of young people every year about the dangers of running away or of trying to resolve difficult, threatening situations on their own. This easily replicated community initiative involves the whole community to provide safe havens and resources for youth in crisis.

Street Connect

www.streetconnect.org

- StreetConnect was developed as a multi-purpose resource site focusing on homeless and street-involved youth that was developed through a partnership between youth service providers, youth, and researchers in the United States.

Youthline

www.youthline.ca

- The Lesbian Gay Bi Trans Youth Line is a toll-free, Ontario-wide peer support phone line provided by youth for youth. It is designed to offer support, information, and referrals specific for youth who identify as lesbian, gay, bisexual, transgender, transsexual, two-spirit, or queer.

References

Abate, G. (2001, February 20). Squeegee ban violates charter, lawyer argues. *The Globe and Mail*, p. A23.

Adlaf, E.M. and Zdanowicz, Y.M. (1999). A cluster analytic study of substance abuse problems and mental health among street youths. *American Journal of Drug and Alcohol Abuse, 25*(4): 639–59.

Anonymous. (2010a, October 20). Guest comment: Why youth homelessness is an important social issue. *Victoria News*, p. 1.

Anonymous. (2010b, October 29). Scope of youth homelessness largely unknown. *The Prince George Citizen*, p. 27.

Appathurai, C. (1987). *Runaway behaviour: A background paper.* Toronto: Ministry of Community and Social Services.

Auerswald, C.L. and Eyre, S.L. (2002). Youth homelessness in San Francisco: A life cycle approach. *Social Science and Medicine, 54*: 1497–1512.

Ayerst, S.I. (1999). Depression and stress in street youth. *Adolescence, 34*(135): 567–85.

Baer, J.S., Peterson, P.L., and Wells, E.A. (2004). Rationale and design of a brief substance use intervention for homeless adolescents. *Addiction Research and Theory, 12*(4): 317–34.

Baron, S.W. (2003). Self-control, social consequences, and criminal behavior: Street youth and the general theory of crime. *Journal of Research in Crime and Delinquency, 40*(4): 403–25.

Baron, S.W. (2004). General strain, street youth and crime: A test of Agnew's revised theory. *Criminology, 42*(2): 457–83.

Baron, S.W. and Hartnagel, T.F. (1997). Attributions, affect, and crime: Street youths' reactions to unemployment. *Criminology, 35*(3): 409–34.

Baron, S.W. and Hartnagel, T.F. (1998). Street youth and criminal violence. *Journal of Research in Crime and Delinquency, 35*(2): 166–89.

Baron, S.W. and Hartnagel, T.F. (2006). Street youth, strain theory, and crime. *Journal of Criminal Justice, 34*(2): 209–23.

Barry, P.J., Ensign, J., and Lippek, S.H. (2002). Embracing street culture: Fitting health care into the lives of street youth. *Journal of Transcultural Nursing, 13*(2): 145–52.

Barth, R.P. (1990). On their own: The experiences of youth after foster care. *Child and Adolescent Social Work,* 7: 419–40.

Barwick, M.A. and Siegal, L.S. (1996). Learning difficulties in adolescent clients of a shelter for runaway and homeless street youths. *Journal of Research on Adolescence, 6*(4): 649–70.

Bassuk, E.L., Rubin, L., and Lauriat, A. (1984). Is homelessness a mental health problem. *American Journal of Psychiatry, 141*(12): 1546–50.

Biehal, N. and Wade, J. (2000). Going missing from residential and foster care: Linking biographies and contexts. *British Journal of Social Work, 30*: 211–25.

Boivin, J.F., Roy, E., Haley, N., and Galbaud du Fort, G. (2005). The health of street youth: A Canadian perspective. *Canadian Journal of Public Health, 96*(6): 432–37.

Booth, R.E. and Zhang, Y. (1997). Conduct disorder and HIV risk behaviors among runaway and homeless adolescents. *Drug and Alcohol Dependence, 48*: 69–76.

Brands, B., Leslie, K., Catz-Biro, L., and Li, S. (2005). Heroin use and barriers to treatment in street-involved youth. *Addiction Research and Theory, 13*(5): 477–87.

Bronfenbrenner, U. (1974). Towards an experimental ecology of human development. *American Psychologist, 52*: 513–31.

Brooks, R.A., Milburn, N.G., Rotheram-Borus, M.J., and Witkin, A. (2004). The system-of-care for homeless youth: Perceptions of service providers. *Evaluation and Program Planning, 27*(4): 443–51.

Burt, M. (2001). *What will it take to end homelessness?* Washington: Urban Institute.

California Department of Social Services. (CDSS). (2002). *Report on the survey of the housing needs of emancipated foster/probation youth.* Independent Living Program Policy Unit. Child and Youth Permanency Branch. Sacramento: Author.

Carlson, J.L., Sugano, E., Millstein, S.G., and Auerswald, C.L. (2006). Service utilization and the life cycle of youth homelessness. *Journal of Adolescent Health, 38*: 624–27.

Carmichael, A. (1997, October 28). On the streets. *The Toronto Star*, p. C1.

Cauce, A.M., Tyler, K.A., and Whitbeck, L.B. (2004). Maltreatment and victimization in homeless adolescents: Out of the frying pan and into the fire. *The Prevention Researcher, 11*: 12–14.

Chase, S. and Ketcham, B. (1997, June 3). Province to toughen prostitution penalties. *The Calgary Herald*, p. B1.

Chen, X., Tyler, K.A., Whitbeck, L.B., and Hoyt, D.R. (2004). Early sexual abuse, street adversity, and drug use among female homeless and runaway adolescents in the Midwest. *Journal of Drug Issues, 34*(1): 1–21.

City of Calgary. (1996). *The 1996 count of homeless persons.* Calgary, AB: City of Calgary, Community Strategies.

City of Calgary. (2006). *Results of the 2006 count of homeless persons in Calgary: Enumerated in emergency and transitional facilities, by service agencies, and on the streets.* Calgary, AB: City of Calgary, Policy and Planning Division, Community & Neighbourhood Services.

Clarke, M. and Cooper, M. (2000). *Homeless youth: Falling between the cracks.* Calgary, AB: Youth Alternative Housing Committee.

Clatts, M., Goldsamt, L., Yi, H., and Gwadz, V. (2005). Homelessness and drug abuse among young men who have sex with men in New York City: A preliminary epidemiological trajectory. *Journal of Adolescence, 28*: 201–14.

Clatts, M., Rees-Davis, W., Sotheran, J.L., and Atillasoy, A. (1998). Correlates and distribution of HIV risk behaviours among homeless youth in New York City: Implications for prevention and policy. *Child Welfare, 77*(2): 195–207.

Community Action on Homelessness. (2009). *Halifax report card on homelessness 2009.* Halifax, NS: Community Action on Homelessness.

Community Action on Homelessness. (2010). *Halifax report card on homelessness 2010.* Halifax, NS: Community Action on Homelessness.

Cook, R.J. (1994). Are we helping foster care youth prepare for their future? *Children and Youth Services Review, 16*(3/4): 213–29.

Courtney, M.E. (2001). Foster youth transitions to adulthood: A longitudinal view of youth leaving care. *Child Welfare, 80*(6): 685–717.

Courtney, M.E. and Dworsky, A. (2006). Early outcomes for young adults transitioning from out-of-home care in the USA. *Child and Family Social Work, 11*: 209–19.

Dachner, N. and Tarasuk, V. (2002). Homeless 'squeegee kids': Food insecurity and daily survival. *Social Science and Medicine, 54*, 1039–49.

De Rosa, C.J., Montgomery, S.B., Hyde, J., Iverson, E., and Kipke, M. (2001). HIV risk behavior and HIV testing: A comparison of rates and associated factors among homeless and runaway adolescents in two cities. AIDS *Education and Prevention, 13*(2): 131–48.

DeMatteo, D., Major, C., Block, B., Coates, R., Fearon, M., Goldberg, E., et al. (1999). Toronto street youth and HIV/AIDS: Prevalence, demographics and risks. *Journal of Adolescent Health, 25*: 356–66.

deOliviera, W. (1992, July). *Street children and safe sex: Opportunities and barriers for changing behaviors.* Paper presented at the International Conference on AIDS VIII. Amsterdam, The Netherlands.

Derworiz, C. (2010, April 5). Youths get help to leave streets; 'Plan within a plan' to end homelessness. *The Calgary Herald*, p. A1.

Diaz, T., Conover, S., Edwards, V., Monterroso, E., and Susser, E. (1998, July). *Drug using behaviors of young and recent initiate injection drug users in New York City: A unique opportunity for prevention of HIV.* Paper presented at the International Conference on AIDS XII, Geneva, Switzerland.

Dittmann, D., MacLaurin, B., Worthington, C., and Kitt, O. (2009). *Criminal activities among Calgary's street-involved youth: Calgary youth, health and the street* (Fact Sheet #11). Calgary, AB: University of Calgary.

Doherty, M.C., Gafein, R.S., Monterroso, E., Brown, D., Huang, H., Park, M., et al. (1996, July). *Younger age of initiating injection drug use is associated with risky behaviors and HIV infection in short-term injectors.* Paper presented at the International Conference on AIDS XI, Vancouver, BC. Duval, D.M., and Vincent, N. (2009). Affect regulation of homeless youth once in the child welfare system. *Child and Adolescent Social Work Journal, 26*: 155–73.

Elise, R., Frappier, J.Y., Nadeau, D., Girard, M., Morin, D.A., and Morin, D.H. (1993, June). *Adolescent injection drug users: No sweet sixteen.* Paper presented at the International Conference on AIDS IX, Berlin, Germany.

Farrow, J.A., Deisher, R.W., Brown, R., Kulig, J.W., and Kipke, M.D. (1992). Health and health needs of homeless and runaway youth. *Journal of Adolescent Health, 13*: 717–26.

Fisher, J. (1989). *Missing children research project, volume 1: Findings of the study—A focus on runaways* (No. 1989-07). Ottawa: Solicitor General of Canada.

Fitzgerald, M.D. (1995). Homeless youths and the child welfare system: Implications for policy and service. *Child Welfare, 74*(3): 717–31.

Freundlich, M. and Avery, R.J. (2006). Transitioning from congregate care: Preparation and outcomes. *Journal of Child and Family Studies, 15*: 507–18.

Gaetz, S. (2004). Safe streets for whom? Homeless youth, social exclusion, and criminal victimization. *Canadian Journal of Criminology and Criminal Justice, 46*(4): 423–55.

Gaetz, S., O'Grady, B., and Vaillancourt, B. (1999). *Making money: The Shout Clinic report on homeless youth and employment.* Toronto: Central Toronto Community Health Centres.

Garbarino, J. (1982). *Children and families in the social environment.* New York: Aldine DeGruyter.

Ginzler, A.J., Cochran, B.N., Domenech-Rodriguez, M., Cauce, A.M., and Whitbeck, L.B. (2003). Sequential progression of substance use among homeless youth: An empirical investigation of the gateway theory. *Substance Use and Misuse, 38*(3-6): 725–59.

Gleghorn, A.A., Marx, R., Vittinghoff, E., and Katz, M.H. (1998). Association between drug use patterns and HIV risks among homeless, runaway, and street youth in northern California. *Drug and Alcohol Dependence, 51*(3): 219–27.

Goar, C. (2009, November 23). Street kids' toughness only skin deep. *The Toronto Star*, p. A13.

Goering, P., Tolomiczenko, G., Sheldon, T., boydell, K., and Wasylenki, D. (2002). Characteristics of persons who are homeless for the first time. *Psychiatric Services, 53*(11): 1472–4.

Greene, J.M., Ennett, S.T., and Ringwalt, C.L. (1997). Substance use among runaway and homeless youth in three national samples. *American Journal of Public Health, 87*(2): 229–36.

Greene, J.M. and Ringwalt, C.L. (1996). Youth and familial substance use's association with suicide attempts among runaway and homeless youth. *Substance Use and Misuse, 31*(8): 1041–58.

Greene, J.M. and Ringwalt, C.L. (1998). Pregnancy among three national samples of runaway and homeless youth. *Journal of Adolescent Health, 23*(6): 370–7.

Grover, S. (2002). On meeting Canada's Charter obligation to street youth. *International Journal of Children's Rights*, 10: 313–44

Hagan, J. and McCarthy, B. (1997). *Mean streets: Youth crime and homelessness.* Cambridge: University Press.

Hahn, J., Shafer, K., and Moss, A.R. (1998, July). *High rate of HIV infection in homeless young injectors: Sex poses greatest risk.* Paper presented at the International Conference on AIDS XII, Geneva, Switzerland.

Haley, N., Roy, E., Leclerc, P., Boudreau, J-F., and Boivin, J-F. (2004a). Characteristics of adolescent street youth with a history of pregnancy. *Journal of Pediatric and Adolescent Gynecology, 17*(5): 313–20.

Haley, N., Roy, E., Leclerc, P., Boudreau, J-F., and Boivin, J-F. (2004b). HIV risk profile of male street youth involved in survival sex. *Sexually Transmitted Infections, 80*(6): 526–30.

Halifax Region Municipality. (2005). *Homelessness in HRM: Portrait of streets and shelters, Volume II.* Halifax, NS: Halifax Regional Municipality, Planning and Development Services.

Hammer, H., Finkelhor, D., and Sedlak, A.J. (2002). *Runaway/thrownaway children: National estimates and characteristics.* Washington: Office of Juvenile Justice and Delinquency Prevention.

Hathazi, D., Lankenau, S., Sanders, B., and Bloom, J. (2009). Pregnancy and sexual health among homeless young injection drug users. *Journal of Adolescence, 32*(2): 339–55.

Health Canada. (2002a). *HIV/AIDS Epi update: Prevalent HIV infections in Canada: Up to one-third may not be diagnosed.* Ottawa: Centre for Infectious Disease Prevention and Control.

Health Canada. (2002b). *HIV/AIDS Epi update: HIV and AIDS among youth in Canada.* Ottawa: Centre for Infectious Disease Prevention and Control.

Hyde, J. (2005). From home to street: Understanding young people's transitions into homelessness. *Journal of Adolescence, 28*: 171–83.

Janus, M.D., Archambault, F.X., Brown, S.W., and Welsh, L.A. (1995). Physical abuse in Canadian runaway adolescents. *Child Abuse and Neglect, 19*(4): 433–47.

Johnson, K.D., Whitbeck, L.B., and Hoyt, D.R. (2005). Predictors of social network composition among homeless and runaway adolescents. *Journal of Adolescence, 28*: 231–48.

Karabanow, J. (2004). Changing faces: The story of two Canadian street youth shelters. *International Journal of Social Welfare, 13*(4): 304–14.

Kidd, S.A. (2003). Street youth: Coping and interventions. *Child and Adolescent Social Work Journal, 20*(4): 235–61.

Kidd, S.A. (2006). Factors precipitating suicidality among homeless youth: A quantitative follow-up. *Youth and Society, 37*(4): 393–422.

Kipke, M., Montgomery, S., Simon, T., and Iverson, E. (1996, July). *Homeless youth: Variations in HIV risk according to peer group affiliation.* Paper presented at the International Journal on AIDS XI, Vancouver, BC.

Kipke, M., Unger, J.B., Palmer, R., and Edgington, R. (1996). Drug use, needle sharing, and HIV risk among injection drug-using street youth. *Substance Use and Misuse, 31*(9): 1167–87.

Kral, A.H., Lorvick, J., and Edlin, B.R. (1999, August). *Differences between young and old injection drug users in San Francisco* (Abstract 533). Paper presented at the National HIV Prevention Conference, Atlanta, GA.

Kraus, D., Eberle, M., and Serge, L. (2001). *Environmental scan on youth homelessness.* Ottawa: Canada Mortgage and Housing Corporation.

Kufeldt, K. and Burrows, B.A. (1994). *Issues affecting public policies and services for homeless youth.* Calgary, AB: University of Calgary.

Kufeldt, K. and Nimmo, M. (1987a). Kids on the street, they have something to say: Survey of runaway and homeless youth. *Journal of Child Care, 3*(2): 53–61.

Kufeldt, K. and Nimmo, M. (1987b). Youth on the street: Abuse and neglect in the Eighties. *Child Abuse and Neglect, 11*: 531–43.

Kufeldt, K. and Perry, P. (1989). Running around with runaways. *Community Alternatives: International Journal of Family Care, 1*(1): 85–97.

Larke, B. (2001). *HIV/AIDS surveillance.* Edmonton, AB: Alberta Health, Disease Control and Prevention.

Leach, M.P., Wolitski, R.J., Goldbaum, G.M., Fishbein, M., and The AIDS Community Demonstration Projects (1997). HIV risk and sources of information among urban street youth. *Psychology, Health and Medicine, 2*(2): 119–34.

Lenz-Rashid, S. (2006). Employment experiences of homeless young adults: Are they different for youth with a history of foster care? *Children and Youth Services Review, 28*: 236–59.

Leslie, B. and Hare, F. (2000). *Improving the outcomes for youth in transition from care.* Toronto: Working Group of the Children's Aid Society of Toronto, Covenant House and Ryerson University Research Project.

McCarter, B. (2010, November 18). Growing up on streets trumps dysfunctional home life; Family dynamics—not drugs or alcohol—is the main reason why thousands of teens choose to run away from home. *The Vancouver Sun,* p. A17.

McCormack, A., Janus, M.D., and Burgess, A.W. (1986). Runaway youths and sexual victimization: Gender differences in an adolescent runaway population. *Child Abuse and Neglect, 10*: 387–95.

MacDonald, M. (1997, September 19). Pair fight child sex business. *The Toronto Sun,* p. 22.

McIntyre, S. (1999). The youngest profession—the oldest profession: A study of sex work. In C. Bagley and K. Mallick (Eds.), *Child sexual abuse and adult offenders: New theory and research* (pp. 159—92). Aldershot: Ashgate Publishers.

MacLaurin, B. (1991). *A program evaluation of exit outreach services.* Calgary: University of Calgary.

MacLaurin, B. and Bala, N. (2004). Children in care. In N. Bala, M.K. Zapf, R.J. Williams, R. Vogl, and J.P. Hornick (Eds.), *Canadian child welfare law* (pp. 111–38). Toronto: Thompson Educational Publishing Inc.

MacLaurin, B., Trocmé, N., Fallon, B., McCormack, M., Pitman, L., Forest, N., et al. (2006). *Alberta incidence study of reported child abuse and neglect—2003 (AIS-2003): Major findings report.* Calgary, AB: University of Calgary, Faculty of Social Work.

MacLaurin, B., Worthington, C., Dittmann, D., and Kitt, O. (2009a). *Education among Calgary's street-involved youth: Calgary youth, health and the street* (Fact Sheet #14). Calgary, AB: University of Calgary.

MacLaurin, B., Worthington, C., Dittmann, D., and Kitt, O. (2009b). *Maltreatment among Calgary's street-involved youth: Calgary youth, health and the street* (Fact Sheet #1). Calgary, AB: University of Calgary.

MacLaurin, B., Worthington, C., Dittmann, D., and Kitt, O. (2009c). *Substance use among Calgary's street-involved youth: Calgary youth, health and the street* (Fact Sheet #2). Calgary, AB: University of Calgary.

McLean, L. (2005). *Seeking sanctuary: An exploration of the realities of youth homelessness in Calgary—2005.* Calgary, AB: Broadview Applied Research Group.

Marshall, B.D.L., Kerr, T., Qi, J., Montaner, J.S.G., and Wood, E. (2010). Public injecting and HIV risk behaviour among street-involved youth. *Drug and Alcohol Dependence, 110*: 254–58.

Milburn, N.G., Rotheram-Borus, M.J., Batterham, P., Brumback, B., Rosenthal, D., and Mallett, S. (2005). Predictors of close family relationships over one year among homeless young people. *Journal of Adolescence, 28*: 263—79.

Miller, D., Miller, D., Hoffman, F., and Duggan, R. (1980). *Runaways—Illegal aliens in their own land: Implications for service.* Westport: Praeger Publishing.

Min Park, J., Metraux, S., and Culhane, D.P. (2005). Childhood out-of-home placement and dynamics of public shelter utilization among young homeless adults. *Children and Youth Services Review, 27*(5): 533–46.

Molnar, B.E., Shade, S.B., Kral, A.H., Booth, R.E., and Watters, J.K. (1998). Suicidal behaviour and sexual/physical abuse among street youth. *Child Abuse and Neglect, 22*(3): 213–22.

O'Grady, B. and Bright, R. (2002). Squeezed to the point of exclusion: The case of Toronto squeegee cleaners. In J. Hermer and J. Mosher (Eds.), *Disorderly people: Law and politics of exclusion in Ontario* (pp. 79–90). Halifax: Fernwood Publishing.

O'Grady, B., Bright, R., and Cohen, E. (1998). Sub-employment and street youths: An analysis of the impact of squeegee cleaning on homeless youths. *Security Journal*, 11: 315–23.

O'Grady, B. and Greene, C. (2003). A social and economic impact study of the Ontario safe streets act on Toronto squeegee workers. *Online Journal of Justice Studies 1*(1). Retrieved 21 January, 2011, from http://web.archive.org/web/20060113223626/ojjs.icaap.org/issues/1.1/ogrady-greene.html

Pennbridge, J., MacKenzie, R.G., and Swofford, A. (1991). Risk profile of homeless pregnant adolescents and youth. *Journal of Adolescent Health, 12*: 534–38.

Peressini, T., McDonald, L., and Hulchanski, D. (1995). *Estimating homelessness: Towards a methodology for counting the homeless in Canada—Background report.* Toronto: Centre for Applied Social Research

Public Health Agency of Canada. (2006a). *Sexually transmitted infections in Canadian street youth: Findings from enhanced surveillance of Canadian street youth, 1999–2003* (No. HP5-14/2006). Ottawa: Minister of Health.

Public Health Agency of Canada. (2006b). *Street youth in Canada: Findings from enhanced surveillance of Canadian street youth, 1999–2003* (No. HP5-15/2006). Ottawa: Minister of Health.

Radford, J.L., King, A.J.C., and Warren, W.K. (1991). *Street youth and AIDS.* Kingston, ON: Queens University, Social Program Evaluation Group.

Ray, J. (1993). Survival methods of young street mothers. *Child and Adolescent Social Work Journal, 10*(3): 189–205.

Rees, G. (1993). *Hidden truths: Young people's experiences of running away.* London: The Children's Society.

Reilly, T. (2003). Transition from care: Status and outcomes of youth who age out of foster care. *Child Welfare, 82*(6): 727–46.

Rew, L. and Horner, S.D. (2003). Personal strengths of homeless adolescents living in a high-risk environment. *Advances in Nursing Science, 26*(2): 90–101.

Robert, M., Pauze, R., and Fournier, L. (2005). Factors associated with homelessness of adolescents under supervision of the youth protection system. *Journal of Adolescence, 28*: 215–30.

Rotheram-Borus, M.J., Mahler, K.A., Koopman, C., and Langabeer, K. (1996). Sexual abuse history and associated multiple risk behaviour in adolescent runaways. *American Journal of Orthopsychiatry, 66*(3): 390–400.

Rotheram-Borus, M.J., Meyer-Bahlburg, H., Koopman, C., Rosario, M., Exner, T.M., Henderson, R., et al.
(1992). Lifetime sexual behaviours among runaway males and females. *The Journal of Sex Research, 29*(1):
15–29.

Roy, E., Haley, N., Leclerc, P., Cedras, L., Bedard, L., and Allard, R. (2002). Seroprevalence and risk factors for
hepatitis A among Montreal street youth. *Canadian Journal of Public Health, 93*(1): 52–53.

Roy, E., Haley, N., Leclerc, P., Cedras, L., and Boivin, J. F. (2002). Drug injection among street youth: The first
time. *Addiction, 97*(8): 1003–10.

Roy, E., Haley, N., Leclerc, P., Roivin, J. F., Cedras, L., and Vincelette, J. (2001). Risk factors for hepatitis C virus
infection among street youths. *Canadian Medical Association Journal, 165*(5): 557–60.

Roy, E., Haley, N., Lemire, N., Boivin, J.F., Leclerc, P., and Vincelette, J. (1999). Hepatitis B virus infection
among street youth in Montreal. *Canadian Medical Association Journal, 161*(6): 689–93.

Roy, E., Lemire, N., Haley, N., Boivin, J.F., Frappier, J.Y., and Claessens, C. (1998). Injection drug use among
street youth: A dynamic process. *Canadian Journal of Public Health, 89*(4): 239–40.

St. Lawrence, J.S., Crosby, R.A., and O'Brannon III, R. (1999). Adolescent risk for HIV infection: Comparison
of four high risk samples. *Journal of HIV/AIDS Prevention and Education for Adolescents and Children, 3*(3):
63–86.

Schneiderman, D. (2002). The constitutional disorder of the safe streets act: A federalism analysis. In J. Hermer
and J. Mosher (Eds.), *Disorderly people: Law and politics of exclusion in Ontario* (pp. 79–90). Halifax: Fernwood Publishing.

Slonim-Nevo, V., Ozawa, M.N., and Auslander, W.F. (1991). Knowledge, attitudes and behaviors related to AIDS
among youth in residential centers: Results from an exploratory study. *Journal of Adolescence, 14*(1): 17–33.

Stiffman, A.R. (1989). Suicide attempts in runaway youths. *Suicide and Life-Threatening Behaviour, 19*(2):
147–59.

Sullivan, T.R. (1996). The challenges of HIV prevention among high-risk adolescents. *Health and Social Work,
21*(1): 58–65.

Swart-Kruger, J. and Richer, L.M. (1997). AIDS-related knowledge, attitudes and behaviour among South African street youth: Reflections on power, sexuality and the autonomous self. *Social Science and Medicine,
45*(6): 957–67.

Thompson, S., Bender, K., Lewis, C., and Watkins. (2008). Runaway and pregnant: Risk factors associated
with pregnancy in a national sample of runaway/homeless female adolescents. *Journal of Adolescent Health,
43*(2): 125–32.

Thompson, S.J., McManus, H., Lantry, J., Windsor, L., and Flynn, P. (2006). Insights from the street: Perceptions of services and providers by homeless young adults. *Evaluation and Program Planning, 29*: 34–43.

Thompson, S.J., Zittel-Palamara, K.M., and Maccio, E.M. (2004). Runaway youth utilizing crisis shelter services: Predictors of presenting problems. *Child and Youth Care Forum, 33*(6): 387–404.

Thrane, L.E., Hoyt, D.R., Whitbeck, L.B., and Yoder, K.A. (2006). Impact of family abuse on running away,
deviance, and street victimization among homeless rural and urban youth. *Child Abuse and Neglect, 30*:
1117–28.

Tutty, L., Bradshaw, C., Waegemakers-Schiff, J., Worthington, C., MacLaurin, B., Hewson, J., Dooley, D., Kean,
S., McLeod, H. (2010). *Risks and assets for homelessness prevention: A literature review for the Calgary homeless
foundation*. Calgary: University of Calgary.

Tyler, K.A. and Cauce, A.M. (2002). Perpetrators of early physical and sexual abuse among homeless and
runaway adolescents. *Child Abuse and Neglect, 26*: 1261–74.

Tyler, K.A. Cauce, A.M., and Whitbeck, L.B. (2004). Family risk factors and prevalence of dissociative symptoms among homeless and runaway youth. *Child Abuse and Neglect, 28*: 355–66.

Tyler, K.A. and Johnson, K.A. (2006). Pathways in and out of substance use among homeless-emerging adults.
Journal of Adolescent Research, 21(2): 133–57.

Unger, J.B., Simon, T.R., Newman, T.L., Montgomery, S.B., Kipke, M.D., and Albornoz, M. (1998). Early adolescent street youth: An overlooked population with unique problems and service needs. *Journal of Early
Adolescence, 18*(4): 325–48.

van der Ploeg, J. and Scholte, E. (1997). *Homeless youth*. London: Sage Publications.

Verma, S. (1999, July 22). Police target squeegee kids. *The Toronto Star*, pp. B1, B4.

Viner, R. and Taylor, B. (2005). Adult health and social outcomes of children who have been in public care:
Population-based study. *Pediatrics, 115*(4): 894–99.

Weber, A.E., Boivin, J.F., Blais, L., Haley, N., and Roy, E. (2002). HIV risk profile and prostitution among female street youths. *Journal of Urban Health, 79*(4): 525–35.

Whitbeck, L.B., Chen, X., Hoyt, D.R., Tyler, K.A., and Johnson, K.D. (2004). Mental disorder, subsistence strategies, and victimization among gay, lesbian, and bisexual homeless and runaway adolescents. *Journal of Sex Research, 41*(4): 329–42.

Whitmore, E. and McKee, C. (2001). Six street youth who could . . . In P. Reasor and H. Bradbury (Eds.), *Handbook of action research: Participative inquiry and practice* (pp. 396–402). London: Sage Publications.

Worthington, C., MacLaurin, B., Dittmann, D., and Kitt, O. (2009a). *Mental health among Calgary's street-involved youth: Calgary youth, health and the street* (Fact Sheet #5). Calgary, AB: University of Calgary.

Worthington, C., MacLaurin, B., Dittmann, D., and Kitt, O. (2009b). *Physical health among Calgary's street-involved youth: Calgary youth, health and the street* (Fact Sheet #6). Calgary, AB: University of Calgary.

Worthington, C., MacLaurin, B., Dittmann, D., and Kitt, O. (2009c). *Resilience among Calgary's street-involved youth: Calgary youth, health and the street* (Fact Sheet #15). Calgary, AB: University of Calgary.

Worthington, C., MacLaurin, B., Dittmann, D., and Kitt, O. (2009d). *The sex trade among Calgary's street-involved youth: Calgary youth, health and the street* (Fact Sheet #16). Calgary, AB: University of Calgary.

Worthington, C., MacLaurin, B., Dittmann, D., and Kitt, O. (2009e). *Sexual health among Calgary's street-involved youth: Calgary youth, health and the street* (Fact Sheet #4). Calgary, AB: University of Calgary.

Worthington, C., MacLaurin, B., Huffey, N., Dittmann, D., Kitt, O., Patten, S., et al. (2008). *Calgary, Youth, Health and the Street—Final report.* Calgary, AB: University of Calgary.

Wright, J.D. (1991). Health and the homeless teenager: Evidence from the National Health Care for the Homeless Program. *Journal of Health and Social Policy, 2*(4): 15–35.

Yoder, K.A., Hoyt, D.R., and Whitbeck, L.B. (1998). Suicidal behaviour among homeless and runaway adolescents. *Journal of Youth and Adolescence, 27*(6): 753–71.

Yoder, K.A., Whitbeck, L.B., and Hoyt, D.R. (2003). Gang involvement and membership among homeless and runaway youth. *Youth and Society, 34*(4): 441–67.

Zilde, M.R. and Cherry, A.L. (1992). A typology of runaway youths: An empirically based definition. *Child and Adolescent Social Work Journal, 9*(2): 155–68.

13 Under the Radar: The Sexual Exploitation of Young Men in Western Canada

Susan McIntyre

Overview

This chapter offers an overview of the research on the issue of sexually exploited young persons with a specific attention directed toward young men in Western Canada. It focuses on the background of these young men prior to their involvement in the sexual exploitation trade. The demographics of the 157 young men interviewed were considered in the areas of Aboriginal heritage, age, running away, education, and background of sexual or physical abuse. The chapter explores how an individual enters the trade, at what age, and for how long, and also discusses family relations. In addition, the chapter reviews the dangers of the sexual exploitation trade, such as gay bashing, violence, lack of safety, and drug use. In closing, the chapter explores how a person is able to work, what services they need, and their attempts at exiting.

Key Objectives

After reading this chapter, you should be able to:

- Identify that there are both young women and young men in the sexual exploitation trade.
- Understand how and why young men enter the sexual exploitation trade.
- Understand the experience young men will have with the sexual exploitation trade.
- Understand the challenges of exiting the sexual exploitation trade.
- Understand the stigma the sexual exploitation trade brings to young men.
- Identify the difference between personal sexual identity and a 'work' sexual identity.

Introduction

Most readers of this chapter are likely somewhat familiar with the issue of sexually exploited females. Comparatively speaking, this issue has been both well researched and resourced (Farley 2003). However, the body of literature and research on sexually exploited young males is very limited. In fact, most of the existing literature in this latter area has been almost exclusively in Canada. Therefore, given the unique nature of this aspect of the topic, this chapter will focus on the **sexual exploitation** of young males. For some general background information of the sexual exploitation of females, see the suggested readings at the end of this chapter.

First, we will provide the background that led to the study 'Under the Radar: The Sexual Exploitation of Young Men in Western Canada'. Second, we will discuss key demographics and findings from this study. Third, we will discuss the actual work life of sexually exploited young men. Fourth, we will examine the process of attempting to exit the sexual exploitation trade. In closing, we will provide an overview of the recommendations that emerged from this study.

sexual exploitation
The abuse of children and youth by exchanging sexual activity for money, drugs, and/or basic needs.

Factors Leading to 'Under the Radar: The Sexual Exploitation of Young Men'

Young men are invisible and ignored in the issue of sexual exploitation. In the 2006 ECPAT Global Monitoring Report on Canada, young men were virtually ignored. The report spoke about children, yet it spoke predominantly if not exclusively about young women, as illustrated in this quote: 'The increase in prostitution of children is causing growing concerns. Young girls are seduced by pimps and subsequently conned into prostitution or forced to work in strip clubs. They are recruited in public places, such as shopping malls, metro stations and bus stops, even on the street' (ECPAT Global Monitoring Report 2006, p. 11).

In 1994, Dr Susan McIntyre released 'The Youngest Profession, the Oldest Oppression', which was a study conducted in Calgary, Alberta. A total of 50 young people participated in the study. Forty-one young women and nine young men were interviewed. At the time these young people were typically viewed as criminals, often charged with prostitution-related offences, most likely under Section 213 of the Criminal Code of Canada (see Box 13.1), which speaks to the issue of communicating for the purpose of prostitution. This charge can be brought against a consumer or a sex-trade worker. The 'Youngest Profession' (McIntyre 1994) revealed that this population began working in the prostitution trade at the age of 14 and that over 80 per cent had a background of sexual abuse prior to their involvement with the sex trade. Based on these findings, we identified that these were not adults choosing a lifestyle. These were children and young adolescents who, by and large, were either forced or coerced into the sex trade by an adult. In most cases, these young people did not identify their involvement with the sex trade as a 'choice', and most viewed it as a means of survival. Following the release of the study, the identification of this population began to shift from viewing them as prostitutes to considering them as being sexually exploited. Various legislation ensued, such as the Alberta Protection of Sexually Exploited Children Act (see Box 13.2), to deal with the issue of child sexual exploitation.

In 2002, McIntyre returned to interview some of the original participants from the 1992 study. The report 'Strolling Away' was released in 2002, which included interview findings from a total 41 (82 per cent) of the original 50 participants. A reoccurring observation from the study was that until this point, the issue of sexual exploitation had focused primarily on the female perspective. It was

customer
An individual who is a consumer and pursues the opportunity to purchase activity from a sex-trade worker.

Box 13.1 Youth Justice in Action

Communicating Law: Criminal Code, R.S.C. 1985, c. C-46, ss. 213.

Every person who in a public place or in any place open to public view (a) stops or attempts to stop any motor vehicle, (b) impedes the free flow of pedestrians or vehicular traffic or ingress to or egress from premises adjacent to that place, or (c) stops or attempts to stop any person or in any manner communicate or attempts to communicate with any person for the purpose of engaging in prostitution or of obtaining the services of a prostitute is guilty of an offence punishable on summary conviction.

A 'public place' includes any place to which the public have right of access as of right or by invitation, express or implied, and any motor vehicle located in a public place or in any place open to public view.
Note: Even though we have the Communicating Law, males are virtually never charged with this offence. In order to bring about such a charge, a male undercover officer would have to pose as a **customer** seeking out a male sex-trade worker. As this very rarely happens, however, young men are virtually ignored from the enforcement position of Communicating Law.

Box 13.2 Youth Justice in Action

Protection of Sexually Exploited Children Act

Help is available to children sexually exploited through prostitution through the Protection of Sexually Exploited Children Act. The act recognizes that children involved in prostitution are victims of sexual abuse and allows police and caseworkers to remove sexually exploited children from dangerous situations to ensure their safety and well-being.

Under the legislation, sexually exploited children and youth involved in prostitution can access a variety of voluntary community services, including medical assistance, drug and alcohol counselling, psychological services, educational programming, placement resources, and life-skills support.

A child who does not want to end his or her involvement in prostitution can be apprehended by police or a child protection worker. The police or child protection worker would then take the child to a safe, secured facility, where the child can be confined for up to five days. At this safe, secured facility, the child receives emergency care, treatment, and an assessment. The development of a long-term plan to assist the child to exit prostitution begins.

Under the act, those who exploit children can be charged with child sexual abuse and fined up to $25 000, jailed for up to two years, or both.

—Government of Alberta

Source: www.child.alberta.ca/home/533.cfm

for this reason that the study 'Under the Radar, The Sexual Exploitation of Young Men in Western Canada' was launched in the provinces of Alberta, British Columbia, Saskatchewan, and Manitoba. A total of 157 young men in the four Western provinces of Canada were interviewed. This study involved 48 nonprofit organizations, 6 research coordinators, and 20 research assistants. Eight of the research assistants self-identified as **experiential**: they had been involved with, and had exited, the sexual exploitation trade. They brought with them invaluable insights of the realities faced by sexually exploited children and youth.

experiential
Refers to an individual who has worked and lived the lifestyle of a sex-trade worker.

Consultations with Youth in Care Networks

During the development of earlier studies (years 2002 and 2004), the principal investigator had consulted with young people (18 to 24 years of age) in and from child-welfare care to ensure that the views and experiences of youth at risk influenced the design and style of the questionnaires, as well as the interview format. As this approach had proven to be effective, youth from care were once again consulted in the development of the 'Under the Radar' study questionnaire. Primarily, these consultations were with youth members of the Alberta Youth in Care and Custody Network.

Provincial and local Youth in Care Networks can be found across Canada (see Box 13.3). These organizations are the outcome of a national movement started in 1985 by a small group of young people between the ages of 14 and 24 who were in, and from, child welfare/government care. Their vision was to develop a network that would connect their peers from all provinces and territories so they would know they were not alone. This movement has taken many of the principles of social networking theory and brought them into practice.

National Youth in Care Network
An organization run by youth and former youth from government care who advocate for youth in care.

Box 13.3 Youth Justice in Action

What Is Youth in Care Canada?

Youth in Care Canada (also known as the **National Youth in Care Network**) is an organization driven by youth and alumni from care. We are committed to making connections and making change.

Youth in Care Canada exists to voice the opinions and concerns of youth in and from care and promote the improvement of services for them.

We are the only national constituency-driven consumer-focused organization in the child welfare sector. We are the longest-running national child welfare organization in Canada, and the oldest national youth-directed organization in Canada.

Source: www.youthincare.ca

The relevance of youth in care to the 'Under the Radar' study is important as the findings revealed that 55 per cent of respondents reported some degree of child welfare intervention during childhood or adolescence. While not all young men, or women, involved with the sexual exploitation trade have a child-welfare background, we have learned that the vast majority of respondents had a history of physical and/or sexual abuse, or had witnessed familial aggression during their childhood or adolescence. This would indicate that these young men should have received child protective services. In either case, it is clear that at some point these young men were failed by the very people who were supposed to care for them.

Key Demographics from Study

The following sections provide key demographic findings from the study 'Under the Radar, The Sexual Exploitation of Young Men in Western Canada'. In addition to offering a descriptive review, the data speak to a number of the key risk factors for young male sexual exploitation victims: 'Risk factors can be defined as life events or experiences that are associated with an increase in problem behaviors, such as drug use or gang activities. For example, being the child of a single-parent who is often absent from the home and lacks adequate support, can be considered a risk factor. The negative influence of a friend or sibling can be another, (Howell 2005, pp. 334–6).

Aboriginal Heritage

According to the Office of Correctional Investigator (2010) in Canada, only about 2.7 per cent of the population has Aboriginal ancestry. However, 18.5 per cent of offenders now serving federal sentences are Aboriginal. In Western Canada, this population escalates to 60 per cent. Research has shown that Aboriginal young people are sent to jail at a younger age and for longer periods of time (www.afn.ca/cmslib/general/NAOs.pdf). 'Under the Radar' (McIntyre 2009: 15) found that 61 per cent of the 157 interviewed identified themselves as Aboriginal. Aboriginal young men are at an alarmingly high risk of entering the sexual exploitation trade and the criminal justice system.

Of the respondents who participated in the 'Under the Radar' project who self-identified, 56 per cent indicated that they felt they were connected to their traditional Aboriginal culture, while 44 per cent indicated they had no connection to their Aboriginal culture. In each of the provinces, the percentage of Aboriginal respondents varied: British Columbia revealed the lowest percentage (40 per cent), 85 per cent of Saskatchewan respondents identified themselves as Aboriginal, 65 per cent of Manitoba respondents and 54 per cent of Alberta respondents indicated Aboriginal heritage (McIntyre 2009).

Involvement with Child Protective Services

It is estimated that over 200 000 children and youth will be involved with child protection authorities annually in Canada (Trocmé et al. 2005). Mulcahy and Trocmé (2010) found that on any day within Canada there are 65 000 children and youth residing in or out of home care.

Dating back to the work of J.J. Kelso at the end of the 1800s (also see Chapter 1), the services speak to the plight of young persons and the long-standing position of the state in acting as a protectorate of youth at risk (Hennick and Stuart 2005). However, these services have not been without their critics—hence, the Alberta Child Intervention Review Panel put forth 14 recommendations in June 2010.

In relation to the main study being reviewed here, just over half of those interviewed had experienced some degree of intervention through government-legislated child welfare authorities. The additional 45 per cent were at risk given backgrounds of abuse and running away, but they were not directly connected to the child welfare system. Interestingly, the majority of these young men identified that they had not received adequate information on sexual development or health while growing up. This lack of information and knowledge places these young men in a vulnerable situation as they have gaps and misinformation in reference to their sexual development. Boys are not encouraged to talk about the changes that are happening to their bodies. They receive less guidance about their reproductive role, despite being provided with information and support around the experiences of puberty (Powelson 2004, p. 5). While most authorities assume that young men have received the knowledge about sexual biology and socialization that they require, this is not always the case.

Education

It was important to ascertain the level of education this population had completed, at the same time gaining understanding of the educational disruptions they had experienced. Thirty-five per cent of all the respondents indicated that they had, at minimum, completed high school, with 10 per cent of that population having completed either college- or university-level programs. As well, 15 per cent of the total number of respondents indicated they had only completed grade school while 85 per cent indicated they had completed some level of high school, varying from grades 9 to 12.

Three significant factors play against this population of sexually exploited young men. First of all, in looking at Labour Statistics Canada for 3 November, 2010, young men were more likely to drop out of high school than young women. Young men represent 10.3 per cent of school dropouts where young women represent only 6.6 per cent. Second, 22.6 per cent of dropouts are Aboriginal young men. A third challenge for this group of young men is that 55 per cent of them grew up in government care. The Alberta Child and Youth Advocate reported the following in reference to youth growing up in care while being educated:

> Considerable evidence from across North America and Europe indicates children and youth in care do not experience the same success in school as their peers. Children and youth in care are more likely to perform below grade level and to fall behind their peers as they get older. They are over-represented in special education and vocational classes and are more likely to be identified as having behavioral disorders, severe learning disabilities or mild intellectual disabilities. They are more likely to be suspended or expelled from school and are less likely to complete high school. While we were unable to find data specific to the school experience of Alberta children and youth in care, it is safe to suggest their experiences mirror those reported for children and youth in other jurisdictions. (Child and Youth Advocate 2008, p. 5)

Running Away

While most young people threaten to run away from home at some point in time during their formative years, actually doing so is, fortunately, a relative rare occurrence. Therefore, when young people do run away, it generally reflects considerable distress or conflict in the family (MacLaurin 2005). There is value in ascertaining how a young person ends up having to survive on the streets. Over 83 per cent of the youth interviewed for this study had the experience described by MacLaurin (2005) of being runaways, throwaways, or both. According to MacLaurin (2005), a runaway describes a youth who exits his or her place of residence without permission and is absent at least one night. MacLaurin (2005) describes a throwaway as a youth who is asked to leave and has no alternative accommodations provided for him or her.

Eighty-three per cent of the study's total respondents indicated that at some point they had run away or were exited from home during childhood or adolescence. Sixty-one per cent of the total respondents indicated that when they ran they were offered food and shelter. What becomes important about this finding is that 45 per cent of those who were offered food and shelter had conditions attached, most of which were sexual in nature. A similar finding occurred with the Public Health Agency of Canada study on street youth (2006), where 25.7 per cent of young male street youth took part in obligatory sex for food, shelter, money gifts, and/or drugs: 'For young people who are homeless, the implications are clear. Their lives are played out in spaces that bring them into contact with hostile strangers, potential offenders, other homeless people with serious substance abuse issues or mental health problems' (Gaetz 2009, p. 3).

Many of those interviewed indicated that their first introduction to hustling/working in the sexual exploitation trade occurred while they were 'on the run' and trying to survive. One young man said that when he was approached, it was 'sex for food and shelter'. When offered accommodation, another young man said it was clear he was to 'put out or get out'.

As evidenced by these quotations, the risks associated with being a runaway and being lured into the sexual exploitation trade for survival are high. Obligatory sex is clearly a form of survival for the runaway and homeless male populations (Public Health Agency of Canada Street Youth 2006; McIntyre 2009).

Getting Thrown Out[1]

McIntyre (1994, 2002, and 2009) clearly identified the population interviewed for the study as being at risk of running away. At the same time, this population was also at risk of being thrown out of their place of residence:

> The loss of family and community supports encourages street youth to identify more strongly with other street people. Acquaintance-based networks and relationships support the transitions to a life on the streets. When such networks are absent, youth are at increased risk. They lack the required knowledge about how, when and where to get the resources related to their basic needs, such as health care, food and shelter. (MacLaurin 2005, pp. 192–3)

Fifty-one per cent of respondents indicated that they had been thrown out of the family home (i.e., told to leave). One young man said he was thrown out of the house because of his sexuality and 'because I wanted to dress like a girl'. As a result, these 51 per cent of respondents sought temporary accommodation or sleeping outdoors. Respondents indicated various reasons for being thrown out of the family home. These rationales ranged from not fitting in socially, spiritually, sexually, or culturally.

Sexual and Physical Violation

The topic of sexual and physical violation of young people in Canada received virtually no attention until the mid-1980s. David Finkelhor (1979) attributes the women's movement with raising awareness of sexual abuse in North America. The consequence of this awareness was the Canadian landmark study by the Badgley Commission (1985), which looked at the issue of sexual abuse and prostitution in Canada. From this report, discussion began on the actual definitions of *abuse*. The following are the definitions that were agreed upon in 2009 by the Department of Justice Canada:

> *Physical abuse* may consist of just one incident or it may happen repeatedly. It involves deliberately using force against a child in such a way that the child is either injured or is at risk of being injured. Physical abuse includes beating, hitting, shaking, pushing, choking, biting, burning, kicking or assaulting a child with a weapon. It also includes holding a child under water, or any other dangerous or harmful use of force or restraint. Female genital mutilation is another form of physical abuse.

> *Sexual abuse and exploitation* involves using a child for sexual purposes. Examples of child sexual abuse include fondling, inviting a child to touch or be touched sexually, intercourse, rape, incest, sodomy, exhibitionism, or involving a child in prostitution or pornography. (Family Violence Initiative 2009)

Referring to the 'Under the Radar' project, 75 per cent of respondents in all four Western provinces identified themselves as being sexually violated. In other words, many had a history of sexual abuse prior to their involvement with the sex trade. The 75 per cent of respondents described being sexually violated many times and at very early ages as children. Eighty-five per cent reported a history of physical violation, or physical abuse. They spoke of fighting and name calling, being struck with a cast-iron pot to the head, and choking. This population experienced varying degrees of sexual and physical violation. We must caution, however, that not all who experience this degree of violation turn to sexual exploitation. Nevertheless, coupled with runaway or throwaway experience, sexual and physical violation can increase the probability of possible recruitment into the sexual exploitation way of survival.

In summary, this is a population with a substantial history of both sexual and physical violation prior to their involvement with the sexual exploitation trade. Furthermore, this population experienced extensive victimization within their homes and communities and within the sexual exploitation trade.

Witnessing Aggression While Growing

In 1999, Statistics Canada Juristat Canadian Centre for Justice Statistics produced findings of 'Children Witnessing Family Violence'. According to the survey, 37 per cent of children heard or saw one parent assaulting the other. This report by Dauvergne and Johnson (2001) determined that witnessing family violence also links to negative behaviours in children. These children are more likely to exhibit aggression, have emotional disorders and hyperactivity, and act in a delinquent manner toward property. Blanchette et al. (1998), found that of those who had grown up witnessing violence 56 per cent replicated this violence in their adult lives.

Indeed, the population interviewed for 'Under the Radar' reported that 86 per cent of them had personally witnessed violence. This is at least twice as high as the national average reported by Dauvergne and Johnson (2001). This population of sexually exploited young men spoke about seeing their mothers being beaten and the explosive nature of family gatherings that involved alcohol.

Involvement with Police

In our study, 79 per cent of respondents reported having a background involvement with the police. This involvement resulted from either their family of origin, their involvement in the general community, or more recently in their involvement with the street. The data would reflect that such criminal activities were primarily summary convictions and were in the context of social and community disorder. Of the 157 individuals interviewed, none of them had served any substantial incarcerated time.

What is important is that they had, however, experienced being 'labelled'. This labelling is further ingrained and illustrated as they become a population of runaways and throwaways. People vary in their vulnerability or sensitivity to the reaction of others; if the original self-image is not strong enough, the labelled person may come to accept the image offered by others and change the self-image accordingly. And the more often a person is labelled the more likely it is that this change will take place (Williams and McShane 1994, p. 138).

In summary, this population is characterized by several risk factors, such as a background of abuse, criminal activity, community disorder, and running away and/or being thrown away. Evidently, young males who are sexually exploited are at a significant level of risk of being victimized: 'The evidence is clear. Those in prostitution have experienced extremely high rates of childhood trauma, violent victimization while in prostitution, substance abuse, and psychiatric disorders' (Ross, Farley, and Schwartz 2003, p. 202).

We will now shift to examine how young men enter into the sexual exploitation trade.

The Work Life/Hustling of Sexually Exploited Young Men

Entering the Sexual Exploitation Trade

Throughout the research, many factors present themselves as possible reasons for an individual to enter the sexual exploitation trade. What we know for certain is that this is not attributable to any one factor but is often the outcome of multiple contributing factors, including physical, mental, and emotional health; necessity and survival (e.g., food, clothing, and shelter); drug and alcohol dependency; as well as family history. In other words, the reasons for entering into sexual exploitation result from complex, myriad personal and interpersonal factors:

> Rotheram-Borus et al. (1996) estimate that street youth are five times as likely as domiciled youth to report having been victims of sexual abuse as children. These young people are likely to experience low self-esteem, an impaired ability to form affective and trusting relationships with adults, higher rates of depression and suicide attempts, running away or being kicked out of home. (Gaetz 2009, p. 2)

None of the respondents identified having had 'a goal' to enter into, or to remain involved with, the sexual exploitation trade. In fact, over 69 per cent of the total respondents saw this activity as a short-term method to make money in order to survive. These respondents also shared that this was a means of escape from something and/or someone. Other responses indicated that individuals had a desire to feel wanted and to belong to a culture or peer group. Those who reported that they were 'on the run' at the time they were first introduced to the sex exploitation trade recalled feeling isolated, feeling a sense of 'anomie' from their families and communities. Both Durkheim and Merton agree that the source of deviance is anomie, the sense of normlessness and frustration that is a product of the way society is organized. Organization or disorganization of society causes anomie, which leaves people confused about what norms should regulate their behaviour (Cao 2004, p. 71).

Many spoke about how they felt compromised, strange, or immoral in what they were doing. Through their involvement with the 'trade', however, they found a camaraderie and level of acceptance they had not previously known or that had been missing from their lives. They found a place to attach to. The challenge is that it is not a healthy environment to be aligned with. Social control theory speaks to deviance as a way of attaching and belonging, and as a means of commitment and involvement (see Williams and McShane 1994, p. 191).

As noted earlier, 81 per cent of those who had run away were offered food and/or shelter. As one respondent noted, 'it was survival, food, shelter then drugs'. Of this group, 45 per cent reported that there were conditions attached to this type of offer. These conditions were sexual in nature and, as such, these respondents identified this as their introduction to the sexual exploitation trade.

It is important to gain some background information on exactly how someone discovers and enters the sexual exploitation trade. Remember that 83 per cent had a running away or throw-away background. A total of 51 per cent learned about the sex trade through a 'friend'. Most of the responses indicate that while on the street a friend introduced these young men to the sexual exploitation trade as a means of survival.

Thirty-four per cent of the total respondents explained that they learned the 'protocol' of sex work by observing others and mimicking their actions. Fifteen per cent reported that they had met a customer, or 'trick', who had offered to teach them how the sex trade works. Young men from the study spoke about how they just fell into the surroundings of the sexual exploitation trade. They saw it and this became their entrance into the trade. Some learned about the trade from friends or from those who had violated them but then provided them with cash.

Age at Beginning Hustling/Working

Based on the studies completed by the author of this chapter, 73 per cent of youth entered the sexual exploitation trade under the age of 18 (see Table 13.1). The youngest person entered the sexual exploitation trade at 8 years of age and the oldest was 25. This reflects a vast differential in ages and personal development.

Twenty-seven per cent entered this life when they were adults (over 18 years of age). Lack of employment skills and work experience often lead to a need for survival for this older population. The sexual exploitation trade was about economic survival for the population both over and under the age of 18. This finding shows that the male sexual exploitation trade is not one that only targets children and adolescents. However, that those under the age of 18 are at greater risk:

> When they do find work, it is often in short-term, dead-end jobs or in unregulated work on the margins of the economy. As a result they engage in risky money making strategies, some of them illegal or quasi-legal, including the sex trade, panhandling (begging), squeegeeing (cleaning car windshields), and criminal acts such as theft and drug dealing. (Gaetz 2009, pp. 5–6)

As reported earlier, the majority of this population had a background of sexual and/or physical abuse. This finding confirms that physical or sexual violation/abuse as a child (and particularly when untreated) can affect an individual later in adulthood. As the study indicates, this might also trigger, or prompt, an individual's introduction into the sexual exploitation trade.

Time Spent Hustling/Working

It is important to understand the length of time respondents had been hustling/working because it will affect the intervention plan and the needs a person will require when considering exiting. The majority (83 per cent) had been in the sex trade longer than two years. Only 9 per cent of the total population of respondents had been in the sex trade for less than one year. These young men remain out of sight, however. They are not quickly identified as they 'work' in a rather underground manner; neither are these young men quick to self-identify themselves as 'sex-trade workers' or as individuals who are being exploited. As such, preventative support services and other forms of outreach services are not as readily available or as accessible. As respondents suggested, such circumstances often limit the ability of social support services to connect with these individuals, at least until these young men are fully entrenched in the sexual exploitation trade.

As was discovered in *Strolling Away* (McIntyre 2002), males enter the trade earlier and stay a

Table 13.1 Under the Radar, The Sexual Exploitation of Young Men in Western Canada, 2009

Age Started	Per cent
8–9 years	3
10–11 years	4
12–13 years	15
14–15 years	22
16–17 years	29
18–19 years	16
20–21 years	6
22–23 years	2
24 years plus	3

Source: McIntyre, S. (2009). *Under the Radar: The Sexual Exploitation of Young Men—Western Canada.* Calgary, AB: The Hindsight Group.

minimum twice as long as their female counterparts. Young men stay longer as they have fewer options. By contrast, young women often leave the sexual exploitation trade to birth a child.

Once again, this comparative finding would suggest a gross lack of both preventative and intervention-based supports and services that are specific to young men. This finding also points to a general lack of understanding in terms of what is required to ease the transition from 'working' to exiting the sexual exploitation trade for young men. As noted, many young women exit to birth children, which brings with it family and state support. Again, this is not an option for young men. Based on the author's research findings, there are very few supports for young men exiting in Canada.

Work Locations

The study identified a variety of work locations. Most worked in cars, hotels, and apartments, while some worked at truck stops and parks. Young men working are often undetectable as they wear everyday clothing. They tend to walk and keep moving. Young men work in various locations where potential customers are found, such as chat lines, house parties, bars, lobbies, washrooms, and street.

Shelter Stays

Because members of this population are often runaways and throwaways, they will, out of necessity, seek out shelter. This often results in temporary homeless accommodations. Sixty-four per cent of total respondents reported staying in shelters. The others had never stayed in a shelter (36 per cent). For many, shelters were the only option available to them. As with many adult men, their ability to gain government support given their age and personal circumstances was minimal. Entrance into and continuation of the sexual exploitation trade often results in a distinct lack of options.

Homelessness is a reality for many of these young men. MacLaurin (2005) speaks extensively about the risks and outcomes of being homeless. The sex trade can present a means to avoid homelessness. A small number of respondents reported negative or unsafe experiences within homeless shelters, which had discouraged them from accessing this service. For instance, respondents reported that due to the high-barrier structure of certain shelter services they had been turned away from accessing shelter beds once they had disclosed their involvement with the sexual exploitation trade: 'As an outcome of their homelessness, street youth are typically pushed into places and circumstances that impair their ability to ensure their safety and security and, consequently, increase their risk of criminal victimization' (Gaetz 2009, p. 5).

In summary, respondents reported that the sex trade is a means of making a living in the world, and a way to obtain food, shelter, and other material goods. Initially, the sex trade is most often seen as a short-term, viable option for both young women and young men (McIntyre 1994). The reality for most of these young men, however, is that they eventually become entrenched in a long-term cycle of victimization and trauma.

Dissociation

The majority of these young men reported that they did not enjoy 'working' in the sexual exploitation trade. They felt victimized or traumatized in this lifestyle. Their responses reinforced that their involvement in the activity is based on their need to survive rather than for enjoyment or lifestyle choice. Unresolved abuse issues were a clear theme in the quotes of young men discussing their thoughts and feelings while working and after working:

> According to the trauma model of dissociation . . . pathological dissociation is a core element of the response to chronic, severe childhood trauma which includes sexual, emotional, and verbal abuse, neglect, loss of primary caretakers through death, divorce, addiction, mental illness or imprisonment, family chaos and violence, violence outside the home, medical and surgical trauma, and severely disturbed family dynamics (Ross, Farley, and Schwartz 2003, p. 200).

Indeed, one of the young men from this study clearly articulated how he would dissociate by saying 'I mentally would send myself somewhere else, I was there in body and they were doing that to me but I wasn't there in mind.'

This is not an activity that people engage in proudly, or with a strong sense of safety or security. As such, disassociating from one's reality is common for both young men and young women in the sexual exploitation trade. Young men spoke about how they felt 'awful, full of shame', as well as sick, dirty, drained, and burned out. One young man stated that he felt 'crappy because I know I won't have any more drugs until I do it again, or steal something'.

Family Relations

As noted earlier, family relations are often strained and challenged and this is evident by the high rates of abuse, aggression, and child-welfare experiences. Referring to family knowledge of a person's involvement in the sexual exploitation trade, the following was discovered: 69 per cent of the population interviewed said at least one family member was aware of their involvement with the sexual exploitation trade. Respondents reported that initially they are able to keep their involvement a secret but that eventually family members become aware of what is occurring. Thirty-two per cent of those interviewed believed that their family was unaware of their involvement in the trade.

Fifty-four per cent of this population had difficult or nonexistent relationships with their families. Once a family becomes aware of the sexual exploitation trade in the child's life, anger, fear, and confusion result. People find it difficult to understand or accept. This experience is common among all youth regardless of gender. However, when family members discovered that the customers of sexually exploited young men are predominantly male, respondents reported that this put further strain on the family relationship. These young men spoke about the reaction of family members. As one young man stated, 'it is no good my grandfather hates me and I told them all I was bi-sexual and they look down upon me'.

Advice to Other Youth

All respondents were in agreement that the sexual exploitation trade is not something one should become involved with. They spoke about the downsides and negative results, and the loss of respect that comes from this continuous victimization with no clear escape route. One young man said, 'think carefully, it destroys your life'. Respondents strongly recommended that people explore alternative options for survival and income.

Those immersed in the life clearly warn and challenge people to re-think their decision prior to entering the sexual exploitation trade. They speak about the harm and shame they experience, yet this population often ended up staying.

We will now shift to looking at those that stay in the sexual exploitation trade for a period of time.

Experiences of Youth Who Stay in Sexual Exploitation Trade

As noted earlier, the majority of respondents in the study had remained in the sexual exploitation trade for extensive periods of time. Eighty-three per cent, in fact, had been in the trade for more than two years. These youth are subject to a variety of experiences and traumas.

Gay Bashing

Violence is an issue that both genders are subject to while in the sexual exploitation trade. Humiliation and violence from customers and the general community was cited as a daily occurrence. In previous studies, women had reported more violence from customers while males were at a higher risk of homophobia and **gay bashing** (McIntyre 2009) (see Box 13.4).

   The fear of gay bashing is prevalent at all times for young men involved in the sexual exploitation trade. Forty-four per cent of the respondents experienced gay bashing and indicated that their safety was at risk each time they had worked. This potential fear is always top of mind for sexual exploitation workers. This risk of violence for male sex trade workers is heightened through the bar scene within the inner city: 'Queer bashing by drunken revelers turned out from the bars after closing is another danger' (West and de Villers 1993, p. 84). This bashing is often cited as a fear of homosexuality and a product of homophobia: 'Hatred of homosexuality may induce some heterosexual "queer bashing" to select a rent boy for victimization' (West and de Villers 1993, p. 103).

gay bashing
The humiliation and violence workers are at risk of from customers and the community.

Common Fears

During the interviews, we asked individuals what they feared most while they were hustling/working. Twenty-nine per cent of the total population indicated that their greatest fear was a 'bad date', meaning

Box 13.4 Youth Justice in Action

Port Moody Man Arrested in Vancouver Gay-Bashing Case

By Simone Blais

A Port Moody man has been charged in an alleged gay-bashing incident near Tinseltown in early October. Vancouver police announced Wednesday that Port Moody's Michael Anton Hostland, 22, has been arrested.

   Shortly after 3 a.m. on Oct. 8, police were called to an assault in progress near International Village at Abbott and West Pender streets. Two men were initially taken into custody at the scene, but were released while the case was being investigated.

Const. Lindsey Houghton said in a release that an extensive investigation was conducted, which led to charges against Hostland and another suspect, 20-year-old Dustin James Sciog from Fort St. John.

   Sciog has been charged with three counts of assault, while Hostland will face one count of assault. Houghton said neither Hostland nor Sciog were previously known to police.

   They are scheduled to appear in the downtown community court on Nov. 22.

Source: Simone Blais, *Coquitlam NOW,* November 19, 2010

Note: Cases of gay bashing occur in the communities where male sex trade workers ply their trade to survive. Gay bashing is a direct homophobic reaction to male sex-trade workers, which often occurs after the bars shut down as was evidenced by the case outlined in this box. The men charged in this case had no history of previous criminal behaviour yet reacted in a homophobic rage in an inner-city, gay-friendly neighbourhood.

a customer who would harm them and potentially kill them. The fear is always present. Eighty per cent had experienced a 'bad date'. The threat of being beaten, raped, or attacked with a weapon is the most prominent worst experience reported by respondents in all four Western provinces.

Almost unanimously, the participants also spoke of not being allowed to leave, of enduring threats of death, of being given drugs, of being kidnapped and taken out of town, and of the fear of a drive-by shooting taking place:

> Street youth are more likely to be in contact with others who may be deviant or dangerous and they may place themselves in a more vulnerable position relative to more powerful criminals (pimps, drug suppliers). Because their money making activities are highly visible (prostitution, panhandling, squeegeeing) and produce cash-in-hand on a daily basis, street youth present attractive targets, despite their seeming poverty. (Gaetz 2009, p. 6)

A total of 85 per cent of those interviewed saw hustling/working in the sexual exploitation trade as always dangerous. They witnessed and personally experienced the dangers of the sexual exploitation trade in varying degrees. They also spoke of the violence that friends had experienced, including murder. One young man stated that 'I have seen people overdose, suicide, murdered and be bashed. I fear being raped and dumped outside the City on winter days'. Youth are in constant fear of what could occur; they are always at risk and need to be prepared:

> Street youth are vulnerable to exploitation whether by petty criminals, sexual predators, unscrupulous landlords or employers, or a whole range of other individuals who can wield power over them, because potential perpetrators recognize that young people who are homeless have few resources to defend themselves and little recourse to challenge them. (Gaetz 2009, p. 13)

Common Preoccupations

Respondents shared that while hustling/working their thoughts often turned to concerns for their own safety, as well as how and when they would/might exit the trade. One individual feared that he would never get out of the trade. He also wondered if he would ever be able to find himself again. None of the respondents reported having positive thoughts about the activity of hustling/working, nor did they glorify this activity in any way. However, they did acknowledge the income the sexual exploitation trade provided, whether for daily survival, for substance use, or for maintaining a lifestyle free of the dangers of absolute homelessness.

McIntyre (2009) found that 58 per cent reported that while not working, their thoughts often centred on ways to change and improve their lives, as well as the lives of their families. Respondents also shared that they had hopes and dreams for a safer and more rewarding lifestyle that they could take pride in. A resounding theme identified from all four provinces involved in this study was the desire to successfully exit the trade.

Working Safely

There are specific techniques young men rely on to maintain their safety while hustling/working. While these techniques are far from foolproof, respondents reported that they provided them with a sense of control and safety:

> The high rate of criminal victimization experienced by street youth means that they are forced to live from day to day with the very real fear of theft and robbery, of being attacked

or sexually assaulted. For some, this becomes just another hazard associated with life on the streets; for others, the trauma associated with the victimization has a devastating effect and can present yet another barrier to moving successfully off the streets. (Gaetz 2009, p. 13)

Thirty per cent of the total population indicated that they do not hustle/work alone. Usually they will do so with friends close by and will usually stay in areas that are 'safe' and 'well-lit'. Respondents from all four provinces also indicated the need to rely heavily on their own personal instincts or 'intuition' in order to maintain their personal safety.

Young men in the trade often seek out a 'sugar daddy' for security. Respondents shared that this type of 'relationship' protects them and has the potential to limit the amount of time and risk they would experience on the street. A sugar daddy can provide a regular source of income as well as other material goods. One young man described having a sugar daddy as an 'opportunity to have my expenses taken care of for a number of months'. While respondents did not suggest in any way that a sugar daddy relationship is one a young man should seek out, they perceived such a relationship to be safer than the alternative methods of hustling/working on the street.

Respondents also revealed that a sugar daddy would typically profile the young man he chooses, seeking him out in public places or at events. Most often the sugar daddy is seeking a public relationship with the chosen young man. Such a relationship often involves exclusivity and a live-in role. Findings revealed that in this type of relationship the sexual orientation of both individuals is homosexual (see West and de Villers 1993).

A **gay for pay** young man would not seek out such a public display; these individuals self-identify as heterosexual but work as a gay young person to earn an income. Their sexual orientation is gay only when they are involved in the sexual exploitation trade. This population would be more inclined to seek a regular customer in private and have an impersonal distant relationship with that client.

gay for pay
A person who is heterosexual but who, in order to survive, will work in the sexual trade as a homosexual.

Hustling/Working and Drugs

There is a strong relationship between drug use and the sexual exploitation trade. For some respondents, substance abuse (i.e., drugs and alcohol) was first introduced to them once they began working in the trade. The Badgley Report (Canada, Committee on Sexual Offences Against Children and Youths, 1984) found that one in four of the young persons interviewed were frequent or heavy users of alcohol. The committee also found that one in three were considered to be heavy consumers of drugs.

Close to 100 per cent of respondents reported that drugs eventually became a 'way of life' once they had become entrenched in the trade. Initially, drugs were viewed as a reward, providing an escape from the continual exploitation and humiliation experienced from hustling/working. Respondents suggested that the longer they remained in the trade, the more interdependent the relationship became between hustling/working and substance abuse.

The initial introduction to hustling/working is often driven by the need to obtain basic survival: food, shelter, and clothing. These are the first stage of Maslow's hierarchy of needs (Maslow 1943)—physiological needs. However, these needs often become replaced by, or adjoined to, a need to feed drug addiction. While close to half of those interviewed avoid the use of drugs while they are hustling/working on the street, nearly all of them spoke of some drug use in their private time. For these individuals, we learned that drug use in their private life often fuels their need to work and enables them to remain in the trade.

Part III At-Risk and Criminalized Youth in Canada

Sexual Orientation

Both young women and young men in the sexual exploitation trade often were divided by who they were when they worked and who they were in their own time. For young women, this was demonstrated by having a 'working name' they only used during working hours. What became clear to the principal investigator over time is the distinct difference between how individuals define their sexual identity while working/hustling versus when they are in their personal 'non-work' time. 'Confused' is how one person identified his sexual identity, particularly while hustling or working. Definitions of these sexual orientations are explained in Box 13.5. The following three descriptors are particularly important in understanding how this population is able to survive in the sexual exploitation trade:

- As mentioned, *gay for pay* refers to a young man who is heterosexual in his non-hustling/working life. During the time period in which he is hustling/working he is 'gay for pay', meaning he will become involved in sexual activities with male customers. Respondents who identified as 'gay for pay' reported that customers found the potential opportunity to alter a young man's heterosexual orientation very attractive.
- **Straight for pay** refers to a gay male who will take on the persona of a heterosexual male while hustling/working. Respondents reported that some male customers found it attractive to engage with these young men as this presents the challenge and potential to alter their sexual identity.
- A person will work as a heterosexual male 'straight' but have a private identity of **transgender**. Often this reflects a need for safety—i.e., it is safer to appear as a male, whether straight or gay for pay.

Respondents of the study self-identified their *working* sexual orientation as shown in Table 13.2. As we have learned, some respondents described their sexual identity as different from their actual sexual identity or orientation.

Helping Young Men Exit the Sexual Exploitation Trade

Why Do They Stay?

Many might wonder why someone would remain in the sexual exploitation life. The following quote speaks to the challenges in preparing to leave: 'Regaining self-respect and recreating an emotional life is far more difficult. It is as hard as reconstructing a hundred crown bill from ashes' (Hoigaard and Finstad 1992, p. 115). If we are to be effective in assisting individuals to successfully exit the

Table 13.2 Sexual Orientation of Respondents of 'Under the Radar: The Sexual Exploitation of Young Men in Western Canada'

Working Sexual Orientation	Non-Working Sexual Orientation
Gay (38%)	Gay (42%)
Gay for pay (14%)	
Straight for pay (3%)	Straight (19%)
Tranny (19%)	Tranny (16%)
Bisexual (18%)	Bisexual (14%)
Confused (7%)	Confused (8%)
Don't know (1%)	Don't know (1%)

straight for pay
A person who is homosexual but who, in order to survive, will work in the sexual exploitation trade as a heterosexual.

transgender
A person who crosses gender roles in one way or another, including transsexuals, drag queens, and transvestites.

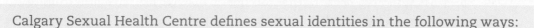

Box 13.5 Youth Justice in Action

Calgary Sexual Health Centre defines sexual identities in the following ways:

Sexual Orientation

The physical and emotional attraction people have for someone of the same gender or another gender than themselves. Not everyone acts on their attractions and you can know your sexual orientation without ever having sex.

Heterosexual 'Straight'

Someone who is physically and emotionally attracted to people of the opposite gender—in other words, women who like men and men who like women.

Homosexual

Someone who is physically and emotionally attracted to people of the same gender. The term 'homosexual' has historically been used in hurtful ways, which is why many people now use other terms like lesbian, gay and bisexual.

Lesbian

A woman who is physically and emotionally attracted to other women. This word is derived from 'Lesbos', a Greek island home to Sappho, a poet and teacher who loved other women.

Bisexual

Someone who is attracted physically and emotionally to people of the same or different genders. Bisexual people are not necessarily attracted equally to men and women and not always attracted to both men and women at the same time. Bisexuality is often thought of as a 'phase' on the way to coming out as gay or lesbian, but for many people, being bisexual is a life-long sexual identity.

Transgendered

A self-identifying term for someone whose gender identity or expression differs significantly from the gender they were assigned at birth. Transgendered is also a political umbrella term used to refer to everyone who crosses gender roles in one way or another including transsexuals, drag queens and transvestites. Some people ('transgenderists') live in a gender other than the one they were assigned at birth but without wanting to change their genitalia.

Transsexual

Someone whose gender identify is different from the biological sex that they were assigned at birth. A transsexual person might change their physical sex by having surgery (known as Sex Reassignment Surgery or SRS), take hormones (testosterone or estrogens), do electrolysis and/or wear gender specific clothing. This process of change is known as transitioning. Transsexuals may be referred to as female-to-male (FTM: a trans man) or male-to-female (MTF: a trans woman). A trans woman should absolutely be referred to as 'she' and a trans man as 'he'. Transsexual or transgendered people may identify as gay, lesbian, straight or bisexual or otherwise.

Two-Spirited

A First Nations term used in various ways by people who are lesbian, gay, bisexual, transgendered or transsexual, or who literally embody both a male and female identity and perspective. This term particularly refers to gender. Two-Spirited people had positive and elevated status among some Aboriginal nations prior to the arrival of Europeans.

Note: These definitions provide a guide for understanding sexual orientation for this population in their private and their sex-trade lives. The use of definitions assists in understanding how a person can create a construct in order to be able survive as a male sex-trade worker. People can see themselves as heterosexual in their personal life but as gay for pay while working the sex trade in order to survive.

sexual exploitation trade, we must understand what motivates them to continue hustling/working. Almost an equal number of individuals indicated that they either have no choice or options (48 per cent), or that their addictions are what keep them hustling (47 per cent). Responses across the four Western provinces varied significantly; in Alberta, a much higher number of respondents indicated the need to stay hustling because of addictions (65 per cent).

It comes as perhaps no surprise to the reader that everyone we interviewed wanted to leave the sexual exploitation trade. This is consistent with both young women and young men (McIntyre,

two-spirited

A First Nations term that refers to persons who are lesbian, gay, bisexual, transgendered, or transsexual, or to persons who embody both a male and female identity.

2002, 2005). No one person identified positive benefits or a desire to remain. All respondents identified at least one reason to exit the sex trade. All respondents reported that they had at some point attempted to leave the trade or had taken a break from it. However, most eventually returned, citing factors such as necessity, survival, or addiction to drugs and/or alcohol as the main reasons.

What is important to understand about these youth is that they are a diverse, complex population surviving in whatever way they can survive in their personal and work lives. It is clear that this population needs supports and protective program strategies and services.

Services That Would Help

Throughout the interviews, we were curious about the type of services these young men felt should exist. A major theme was that existing services were predominantly female-oriented. Compared to studies on females working in the sexual exploitation trade, there is little known about the unique needs, challenges, and 'working style' of males. It is not surprising, then, that the delivery of appropriate and accessible services were viewed as limited or nonexistent.

Respondents shared that by participating in this study, they hoped to provide the clarity required to ensure relevant services and supports are established for these young men. Ignoring sexually exploited young men has occurred in numerous settings across the world as is clearly illustrated in a recent study that came out of London, England in 2005:

> A total of 507 separate cases of young people were identified in London where sexual exploitation was known or indicated. In approximately one third of cases (n=175), sexual exploitation was 'known' rather than 'indicated'. Cases were identified in every borough in London. The vast majority of cases involved young women (n=490).
>
> Young men at risk of sexual exploitation were rarely identified by interviewees. Practitioners acknowledged that they do not focus their concerns on young men. (Harper and Scott 2005, p. 6)

One of the strongest recommendations put forward in 'Under the Radar' came from 61 per cent of respondents regarding the need for residential support services for this population. Many of these respondents indicated that this would or could eliminate the need to trade sexual favours for basic survival, such as a place to sleep. They indicated that this type of service would also help them to find their independence and, ultimately, exit the sexual exploitation trade.

Attempts at Exiting

The group that indicated residential support services would help was committed to wanting to pursue traditional and conventional lives. There was a clear sense of Hirschi's (1969) social control theory:

> Commitment represents the investment one has already built up in conventional society. This investment may take such forms as the amount of education, a good reputation, or the establishment of a business. Those with these forms of commitment to conventional society have more to lose if they are caught engaging in deviant behavior. (Williams and McShane 1994, p. 189)

Respondents did not perceive the sex trade as a long-term lifestyle. However, knowing how to leave this life is a process we must understand if we are to design supports accordingly. As noted by Gaetz (2009), homeless youth and sexually exploited youth have been socially isolated from home, family, education, employment, health and community support, and understanding. We need to be patient with this population and understand that exiting the sex trade is similar to quitting smoking—it often takes a number of attempts. Indeed, the Capital Health (2002) reported that on average it took five attempts at quitting smoking to be successful.

Understandably, it is difficult to imagine anyone (regardless of age) wanting to be a victim of such violation. Reflecting on the primary study of focus of this chapter, some 24 per cent of the respondents said that limited resources and a change in the life circumstances they had grown used to were the most challenging aspects of leaving the trade. In addition, 20 per cent indicated that missing their friends, roommates, and others they had bonded with was a significantly difficult adjustment. These respondents said that by leaving the sex trade, they had lost their community and were therefore isolated:

> Street youth can not easily obtain support from authority figures (parents, teachers, and the police) to protect them or their property or to assist them when they are victims of crime. Street youth depend heavily on other street youth (whose capital is likewise weak, and who may also be potential offenders) and the staff at street youth agencies to provide these resources.
>
> Unfortunately, alienation and difficulty in forming attachments and trusting relations with adults—and with other street youth, for that matter—may be one consequence of victimization, which, in turn may increase risk. (Gaetz 2009, p. 6)

Returning to the Sexual Exploitation Trade

Almost half (48 per cent) of the respondents reported that they had returned to hustling/working because they were stranded, unemployed, and/or feared becoming homeless. Within this group, respondents shared their belief that hustling/working was the only thing they knew how to do to avoid becoming homeless or going hungry. This push and pull that occurs in the sexual exploitation trade can be explained by Reckless's containment theory:

> Emphasizing inner containment, Reckless said that a self concept exists in people and is formed when they are quite young. This self-concept provides either a 'good' or 'bad' image of the self and acts as a buffer to outside influences. He also stressed that there are a variety of 'pushes' and 'pulls' toward deviant behavior that all individuals experience. (Williams and McShane 1994, p. 186)

We must remember that all of these young men had lived either as runaways, throwaways, or were homeless and had experienced the shelter system. Although they may decide to stop working/hustling, the majority choose to continue associating with friends and living with roommates who work in the sex trade (McIntyre 2002, 2009). Unfortunately, living on the periphery of this lifestyle can present challenges to successfully and permanently exiting. We have learned from respondents that maintaining such close ties to the trade can result in returning to it.

Reactions after Exiting

Drawing on the data used in preparing this chapter, 63 per cent of all respondents experienced symptoms of stress once they stopped hustling/working. In most cases, this stress was a direct result of worrying about how they would provide for themselves and, in some cases, their families.

Most of the individuals had limited experience with other forms of employment. Their experiences in the trade did not prepare them for the demands of mainstream or 'legitimate' employment:

> The problematic backgrounds and difficult home lives of street youth can inhibit their ability to fully participate in society as teenagers and later as adults. Once they are on the streets, their exclusionary trajectory intensifies as their inadequate access to housing, limited educational and employment opportunities, and restricted access to public spaces increase their vulnerability to crime. (Gaetz 2009, p. 11)

During periods of time when young men exited the trade, over 56 per cent experienced difficulty sleeping. Street life entails long, late hours. However, it was not just the adjustment to change in waking/sleeping hours. Often difficulty sleeping had to do with other changes, including drug withdrawal, sleep disturbances, and nightmares.

Moreover, 58 per cent of the total respondents experienced flashbacks once they left the street. Flashbacks are a very real disturbance for many individuals. Often these youth recall some of the difficult times that occurred while in the sexual exploitation trade or experience unresolved issues they suppressed while in the trade. These reactions are common for persons who have experienced trauma in their lives. Both young women and young men from the sexual exploitation trade have had such experiences while attempting to exit and successfully exiting the sexual exploitation trade (McIntyre 1994, 2002, 2009).

Messages for Service Providers

'Under the Radar' had a clear purpose: to understand sexually exploited young men and their need for services. It is important to hear what these young men wanted to tell service providers. An overwhelming number wanted to let service providers know that it is not easy to leave the trade. As was found in *Strolling Away* (McIntyre 2002), nearly everyone left at least once. We must understand that the process of leaving is a challenge as these youth often do not have the resources or the skills to exit successfully. Add to that their level of substance abuse addiction, lack of employment, and limited resources, and we can see why a 'successful' exit often resulted in homelessness and/or shelter stays.

The young men in this study reported that they did not feel understood by service providers, and they did not believe that appropriate services were available to them. Sadly, little if anything has changed in the past 20-plus years, as was discussed by Livy Visano in 1987 in 'This Idle Trade', where he interviewed 33 young men in Toronto: 'Recently established reception and therapeutic facilities were perceived by all prostitutes as ineffective and coercive. Very few opportunities exist for prostitutes to engage in positive programs directed toward skill development' (Visano 1987, p. 329). For example, Hustle Men On the Move, a Vancouver PEERS program, is virtually the only program designed specifically for young male sex-trade workers. And this outreach support program, designed by experiential young men, has only been going for three years.

Sixty-six per cent of the respondents explained the difficulty in leaving the trade, and all the issues that surround leaving the trade for young men. They indicated that there was a need for the service providers, health-care providers, and the legal system to understand the differences between being a male hustler and a female hustler and to realize the lack of support for young men. The issue of drug rehabilitation programs was critical. Young men engage in sexual exploitation at a very young age and remain in the trade longer than women. Consequently, they have longer and more severe experiences of drug addiction.

Through this study, however, these youth felt that their voices about needing services to meet their needs were finally being heard. While condoms and coffee programs assist, there is a desire for more in-depth services.

Summary

This chapter set out to shed some light and awareness on the under-the-radar topic of sexually exploited young men. Sexual exploitation occurs regardless of gender. All of our street trade youth—both young woman and young men—have comparable backgrounds of sexual and physical abuse prior to the sexual exploitation trade. These youth, who run away or are thrown away, are placed in vulnerable circumstances that can put them at risk within our communities. The risk is comparable for young women and young men to enter the sexual exploitation trade in order to survive, and this lifestyle is often heavily associated with drugs.

It is perhaps ironic that in an age where the rights of women and children who are being sexually exploited, trafficked, and/or smuggled across borders or across jurisdictions are being championed at all levels of government, comparatively nothing is being done for young males. Society has enabled young men in the sexual exploitation trade as there remains a level of discomfort and confusion regarding male sexual exploitation—a form of reverse discrimination. We have supported and facilitated young men in flying under the radar. As evidenced in this chapter, the longer a young male stays street involved the more distant and strained he becomes from his family and community.

Young men stay in the sexual exploitation trade twice as long as young women. Young women often leave the sexual exploitation trade to birth children. With this exit comes state and family support. This is not an option available to young men. We have looked at the issue of sexual exploitation through a female lens. Young men have specific service needs, and we need to recognize this and protect them and assist them in exiting the sexual exploitation trade.

Researching justice issues is also about research policy. In the end, data and information gathered about any issue should have some fundamental return on investment to the community. In addition to recognizing and acknowledging the plight of young male sexual workers, the most effective strategies to address the problem should focus on all three levels of prevention/intervention—primary, secondary, and tertiary—in the following areas:

- Addiction treatment
- Counselling and clinical support
- Crisis services
- Education
- Employment
- Housing

Key Terms

customer
experiential
gay bashing
gay for pay
National Youth in Care

sexual exploitation
straight for pay
transgender
two-spirited

Review Questions

1. What role does running away play for young men in the sexual exploitation trade?

2. What do you believe are the risk factors that lead young men into the sexual exploitation trade?

3. Which of the theoretical explanations do you think best describe how and why young men become involved in the sexual exploitation trade?

4. How might the risk factors differ from young females in the sex trade?

Critical Thinking Questions

1. Why do you think the issue of sexual exploitation of young men has been ignored?

2. Why do you think that Aboriginal young men are overrepresented in the population of sexually exploited young men in Canada?

3. What differences do you see between young women and young men in the sexual exploitation trade?

4. What are the possible challenges to actualizing the proposed prevention/intervention strategies?

Suggested Readings

Farley, M. (2003). *Prostitution trafficking, traumatic stress disorder.* Binghamton, New Jersey: The Haworth Maltreatment and Trauma Press.

Sheff, N. (2007). *TWEAK: Growing up on methamphetamines.* New York: Atheneum Books for Young Readers.

Sterry, H.D. (2002). *Chicken: Self portrait of a young man for rent.* New York: Harper Collins Publisher Inc.

Weisberg, D.K. (1985). *Children of the night: A study of adolescent prostitution.* Lexington: D.C. Heath.

Suggested Weblinks

ECPAT International
www.ecpat.net
- An organization dedicated to ending child prostitution, child pornography, and trafficking of children for sexual purposes.

News Reports: Sexual Exploitation
See www.hindsightgroup.com, or www.child.alberta.ca/home/590.cfm
- The home webpage for the Alberta Children and Youth Services.

PEERS Vancouver
www.peersvancouver.com/#!vstc1=about-us
- An organization that assists sex workers to leave the sex trade.

Endnote

1. In recent years there has been considerable attention give to the fact that a notable number of sexually exploited young females are being trafficked either domestically or internationally. However, to the author's best knowledge this problem appears far less prevalent among young men. Based on research conducted by the author, young men are more likely to be exploited for labour than in the sex trade. This is in part due to the fact that they tend not to have pimps, they move to where the work is, and they are much more collegial than their female counterparts.

References

Alberta Child Intervention Review Panel. (2010, June 30). *Closing the gap between vision and reality: Strengthening accountability, adaptability and continuous improvement in Alberta's child intervention system.* Edmonton, AB: Child Intervention Review Panel.

Bagley, C. (1985). Child sexual abuse and juvenile prostitution: A commentary on the Badgley report on sexual offences against children and youth. *Canadian Journal of Public Health, 76* (January/ February): 65–66.

Blanchette, K., Robinson, D., Alksnis, C., and Serin, R. (1998). Assessing treatment change among family violent offenders: Reliability and validity of a family violence treatment assessment battery. Ottawa: Research Branch, Correctional Service Canada.

Canada, Committee on Sexual Offences Against Children and Youths. (1984). *Sexual offences against children* (2 vols; Chairman: R. Badgley). Ottawa: Minister of Justice and the Attorney General of Canada and the Minister of National Health and Welfare.

Canada, Office of the Correctional Investigator. (2010). Backgrounder: Aboriginal Inmates. http://www.oci-bec.gc.ca/rpt/annrpt/annrpt20052006info-eng.aspx

Capital Health. (2002). *Population health survey 2002.* Edmonton, AB: Capital Health.

Cao, L. (2004). *Major criminological theories: Concepts and measurement.* Belmont, CA: Wadsworth/Thomson Learning.

Child and Youth Advocate. *Annual report 2006–2007.* (2008). Edmonton, AB: Government of Alberta. Retrieved 8 June, 2011, from http://advocate.gov.ab.ca/home/documents/AR2006to2007.pdf

Cottle, C.C., Lee, R.J. and Heilbrun, K. (2001). The prediction of criminal recidivism in juveniles: A meta-analysis. *Criminal Justice and Behavior*, 28, 367-394.

Crenshaw, S.J.N. (2005). The role of systemic public education in the retention and attrition of students placed at risk: Closing or creating the achievement gap. (Doctoral dissertation: Auburn University, 2005). *Dissertation Abstracts International*, 66/04: 1220.

Dauvergne, M. and Johnson, H. (2001). Children witnessing family violence. *Juristat, 21*(6). Canadian Centre for Justice Statistics, Statistics Canada.

Deane, L., Bracken, D.C., and Morrissette, L. (2007). Desistance within an urban Aboriginal gang. *Probation Journal. 54*(2): 125–41.

Deschamps, G. (1998). *2 Spirited people of the First Nations.* Toronto: Author.

Donnellan, M.B., Trzesniewski, K.H., Robins, R.W., Moffitt, T.E., and Caspi, A. (2005). Low self-esteem is related to aggression, antisocial behavior, and delinquency. *Psychological Science, 16* (4): 328–35.

Duke, D.L. (1977). What can students tell educator about classroom dynamics? *Theory into Practice, 16*(4): 262–71.

ECPAT. (2006). Global monitoring report on the status of action against commercial sexual exploitation of children: Canada. Bangkok: ECPAT International. http://www.ecpat.net/A4A_2005/PDF/Americas/Global_Monitoring_Report-CANADA.pdf

Family Violence Initiative. (2009). Ottawa: Department of Justice. Retrieved 8 Jun 2011, from http://www.justice.gc.ca/eng/pi/fv-vf/about-aprop/

Farley, M. (Ed.) (2003). *Prostitution, trafficking and traumatic stress.* San Francisco: Haworth Press.

Farrington, D.P. (2007). Advancing knowledge about desistance. *Journal of Contemporary Criminal Justice. 23*(1): 125–34.

Finkelhor, D. (1979). *Sexually victimized children.* New York: Free Press.

Gaetz, S. (2009) Whose safety counts? Street youth, social exclusion and criminal victimization. In: J.D. Hulchanski, P. Campsie, S. Chau, S. Hwang, and E. Paradis (Eds.), *Finding home: Policy options for addressing homelessness in Canada* (pp. 1–23). Toronto: Cities Centre, University of Toronto.

Harper, Z. and Scott, S. (2005). Meeting the needs of sexually exploited young persons in London. Barking-side, Essex: Barnardo's.

Haynie, D.L. (2001). Delinquent peers revisited: Does network structure matter? *American Journal of Sociology, 106*(4): 1013–57.

Hennick, J. and Stuart, P. (2005). *Encyclopaedia of social welfare history in North America*. Thousand Oaks, CA: Sage.

Hirschi, T. (1969). *Causes of delinquency*. Berkeley, CA: University of California Press.

Hoigaard, C. and Finstad, L. (1992). *Back streets: Prostitution, Money and Love*. Cambridge: Polity Press.

Howell, J.C. (2005). Moving risk factors into developmental theories of gang membership. *Youth Violence and Juvenile Justice 3*(4): 334–54.

Kegan, R. and Lahey, L.L. (2001). *How the way we talk can change the way we work*. San Francisco, CA: Jossey-Bass.

Kelly, K. and Caputo, T. (2007). Health and street/homeless youth. *Journal of Health Psychology. 12*: 726–36.

Kingsley, C. and Mark, M. (2000). *Sacred lives: Canadian aboriginal children & youth speak out about sexual exploitation: Save the Children Canada*. http://publications.gc.ca/collections/Collection/RH34-12-2000E.pdf

Kirby, L.D. and Fraser, M.W. (1997). Risk and resilience in childhood. In M.W. Fraser (Ed.), *Risk and resilience in childhood: An ecological perspective*. Washington: NASW Press.

Kuo, F.E. and Sullivan, W.C. (2001). Aggression and violence in the inner city: Effects of environment via mental fatigue. *Environment and Behavior, 33*: 543–71.

Law Commission of Canada. (2003). *What is a crime? Challenges and alternatives*. Law Commission of Canada. Online resource www.lcc.gc.ca accessed May 24, 2010.

McCreary Centre Society (2002). *Accenting the positive: A developmental framework for reducing risk and promoting positive outcomes among BC youth*. Burnaby, BC: The McCreary Centre Society.

McIntyre, S. (1994). *The youngest profession: The oldest oppression*. Unpublished doctoral dissertation. Great Britain: University of Sheffield.

McIntyre, S. (1999). The youngest profession—The oldest oppression: A study of sex work. In C. Bagley and K. Mallick (Eds.), *Child sexual abuse and adult offenders: New theory and research* (pp. 159–92). Calgary, AB.

McIntyre, S. (2002), *Strolling away*. Ottawa: Department of Justice Canada Research and Statistics Division.

McIntyre, S. (2009). *Under the radar: The sexual exploitation of young men—Western Canada*. Calgary, AB: The Hindsight Group.

MacLaurin, B. (2005), Street youth in Canada. In J. Winterdyk, and K. Okita (Eds.), *Issues and perspectives on young offenders in Canada* (3rd ed.) (pp. 177–202). Toronto: Harcourt.

Maslow, A.H. (1943). A theory of human motivation. *Psychological Review, 50*(4): 370–96.

Matsueda, R.L. and Anderson, K. (1998). The dynamics of delinquent peers and delinquent behavior. *Criminology, 36*(2): 269–308.

Mazzotta, M.A. (2004). Perceptions about schooling and substance abuse treatment success from court mandated adolescent males. (Doctoral dissertation, Oregon State University, 2004). *Dissertation Abstracts International, 65/02,* 412. Retrieved February 20, 2009 from www.proquest.umi.com.

Mercredi, O. (2000). *Aboriginal gangs: A report to the Correctional Service of Canada on Aboriginal youth gang members in the Federal Corrections system*. Ottawa, ON: Government of Canada. Electronic resource accessed May 18, 2006 from www.csc-scc.gc.ca

Mulcahy, M. and Trocmé, N. (2010). Children and youth in out-of-home care in Canada. CECW 2010 # 78E.

Ooi, Y.P., Ang, R.P., Fung, D.S.S., Wong, G., and Cai, Y. (2006). The impact of parent-child attachment on aggression, social stress and self-esteem. *School Psychology International, 27*: 552–66.

Parker, K.G. and Reckdenwald, A. (2008). Concentrated disadvantage, traditional male role models, and African-American juvenile violence. *Criminology, 46*(3): 711–35.

Powelson, K. (2004). *A moment for boyz*. Vancouver: McCreary Youth Foundation.

Public Health Agency of Canada. (2006, March). *Street youth in Canada: Findings from enhanced surveillance of Canadian street youth, 1999–2003.*

Reyes, J.C., Robles, R.R., Colón, H.M., Negrón, J., Matos, T.D., Calderón, J., & Pérez, O.M. (2008). Neighborhood disorganization, substance use, and violence among adolescents in Puerto Rico. *Journal of Interpersonal Violence, 23*(11): 1499–512.

Raveaud, M. (2005). Hares, tortoises and the social construction of the pupil: Differentiated learning in French and English primary schools. *British Educational Research Journal, 31*(4): 459–79.

Ross, C.A., Farley, M., and Schwatrz, H.L. (2003). Dissociation among women in prostitution. In M. Farley (Ed.), *Prostitution, trafficking and traumatic stress* (pp. 199–212). Bingham, NY: The Haworthne Press, Inc.

Rotheram-Boris, M.J., Mahler, K.A., Koopman, C., and Langabeer, K. (1996). Sexual abuse history and associated multiple risk behaviour in adolescent runaways. *American Journal of Orthopsychiatry, 66*(3): 390–400.

Schonert-Reichl, K. (2000). *Children and youth at risk: Some conceptual considerations.* Paper prepared for the Pan-Canadian Educational Research Agenda Symposium "Children and Youth at Risk", April 6–7, Ottawa, Canada. Sponsored by the Canadian Statistics Council and HRDC.

Statistics Canada. (2006). Aboriginal people as victims and offenders. *The Daily,* June 6, 2006. Government of Canada. Electronic resource accessed October 6, 2009 from www.statcan.gc.ca.

Trocmé, N., Fallon, B., MacLaurin, B., Daciuk, J., Felstiner, C., Black, T., et al. (2005). *Canadian incidence study of reported child abuse and neglect—2003.* Ottawa: Minister of Public Works and Government Services Canada.

Visano, L. (1987). *This idle trade: The occupational patterns of male prostitution.* Concord, ON: VitaSana Books.

Volpe, R. (2000). *What have we learned documenting and evaluating school-linked services for children and youth at risk?* Electronic resource accessed April 30, 2010 from http://www.cesc-csce.ca/pceradocs/2000/00Volpe_e.pdf.

Walsh, A. and Beaver, K.M. (2009). *Biosocial Criminology.* New York: Routledge.

Wente, M. (2000). *Urban Aboriginal homelessness in Canada.* Faculty of Social Work. University of Toronto. Electronic resource accessed November 16, 2010 from http://action.web.ca/home/housing/resources.shtml?x=67148&AA_EX_Session=463ec326fd1796cc64313e93908dff7f.

West, D.J. and Villers de Buz (1993). *Male prostitution.* Binghamton: Haworth Press Inc.

Weyers, S., Dragano, N., Mobus, S., Beck, E., Stang, A., Möhlenkamp, S., Jockel, K.H., Erbel, R., and Siegrist, J. (2008). Low socio-economic position in association with poor social networks and social support: Results from the Heinz Nixdorf Recall Study. *International Journal for Equity in Health, 7*(13): 1–13.

White, R. (2008). Disputed definitions and fluid identities: The limitations of social profiling in relation to ethnic youth gangs. *Youth Justice, 8*: 149–61.

Williams, F.P. and McShane D.M. (1994). *Criminological theory* (2nd ed.). Englewood Cliffs, NJ: Prentice Hall.

Wolfgang, M.E., Thornberry, T.P., and Figlio, R.M. (1987). *From boy to man, from delinquency to crime.* Chicago, IL: The University of Chicago Press.

Wotherspoon, T. & Schissel, B. (2001). The business of placing Canadian children and youth at-risk. *Canadian Journal of Education, 26*(3): 321–39.

Wright, J.P., Tibbetts, S.G., and Daigle, L.E. (2008). *Criminals in the making: Criminality across the life course.* Thousand Oaks, CA: Sage.

Ybrandt, H. (2008). The relation between self-concept and social functioning in adolescence. *Journal of Adolescence, 31*: 1–16.

Part IV
Keeping Kids Out of the System:
Restorative Justice and Other Progressive Approaches to Youth Crime and Justice

To this point in the book we have studied the history of youth justice in Canada and the impact and evolution of youth justice legislation, provided an examination of youth crime, and discussed a number of key types of youth crime and problems. In this concluding section, we include three chapters that explore some unique, if not promising, approaches to dealing with youth crime and youth problems.

In Chapter Fourteen, Louis-Georges Cournoyer, Jacques Dionne, Michèle Goyette, and Pierre Hamel provide a comprehensive overview of the unique Québec approach to keep young offenders out of the justice system. While many textbooks have given passing attention to the Québec experience, this chapter represents one of the first (if not the first) detailed accountings of how and why Québec has adopted a social welfare, psycho-educational approach toward dealing with youth at risk. While still operating within the parameters of the YCJA, Québec has managed to forge a model of juvenile justice that shows promise and that is, in fact, gaining wider acceptance. As descriptive and informative as the chapter is, it should serve as an example of what might be possible for Canada as a whole. The reader will hopefully be inspired to debate and explore the potential of the Québec model. And, as the authors note in the concluding remarks, the Québec approach is 'more in keeping with what is found in western European countries . . .'. This in turn will also hopefully motivate you to explore and examine youth justice systems outside of Canada because, in the end, there is always room for improvements.

Chapter Fifteen, authored by Brenda Morrison and Colleen Pawlychka, focuses on juvenile justice and the development of restorative justice in Canada. Although the authors draw on Canadian and some international material to ground their discussion, they rely on the situation in British Columbia to ground their overview and development of restorative justice. Restorative justice (RJ) is widely seen to represent a strong and viable alternative to conventional youth justice practices, not only in Canada but internationally. And now that the Youth Criminal Justice Act has legal provisions for the application of RJ, it is appropriate, after almost 10 years of the act being enacted, to examine its relative merits. Morrison and Pawlychka begin by providing a broad overview of the youth justice system in Canada and argue that in spite of legislative reforms, young offenders are still largely subject to 'a system of social control'. The authors then provide a clear overview of how several different models of RJ can apply, and have been applied, in different strategic justice contexts. These strategic initiatives are also examined with a critical lens and serve to help identify theoretical and practical issues that should be addressed if RJ is to become more mainstream. For example, Morrison and Pawlychka examine whether RJ programs should be state operated or supported through community-based NGO groups. The chapter concludes with a thought-provoking query: referring to the commentary of other noted RJ champions, the authors point out that while RJ has a rich history in Canada, we do not appear to have capitalized on its potential for youth justice. Indeed, with the recent introduction of the omnibus bill (Bill C-10) in 2011 (and likely to pass in 2012), RJ is likely to continue to struggle for acceptance within the youth justice system.

The final chapter in this section was written by Susan Reid and Sarah Gilliss. While the previous two chapters discuss opportunities for keeping youth at risk out of the system, Chapter Sixteen addresses the issue of the value and need to maintain a separate system of youth justice. Referring to national legislation and the UN Convention on the Rights of the Child, the authors present a robust discussion of why we need to avoid the adulteration of youth crime. However, Reid and Gilliss point out that with the 2011 introduction of Bill C-10 (the Safe Streets and Communities Act), the future for young offenders may be a return to a more punitive model of justice. The authors then go on to examine some of the challenges faced by youth. They frame their examination of youth challenges and needs within the socio-legal framework that recognizes the complex needs (e.g., emotional, personal, physical, social, etc.) of young offenders. The discourse is further enriched by placing the needs within a 'risk' framework. As is well established in the literature, in order to understand youth offending, we must look at the range of risk and protective factors. And as has been reiterated throughout this textbook, Reid and Gilliss conclude by pointing out that there are no easy or simple solutions to approach youth at risk. They call for a dynamic approach that calls for a separate youth justice system and that also provides youth with a voice.

We do not, however, consider Part Four or Chapter Sixteen as the final word. Instead, we hope that the material presented, not only in the last three chapters but throughout this book, will further stimulate your thinking as well as your desire to become involved in the quest to better understand and address youth crime, youth justice, and/or its related problems through one or more of the intervention, prevention, or control strategies discussed.

14 Québec's Experience in Keeping Youth Out of Jail

Louis-Georges Cournoyer, Jacques Dionne, Michèle Goyette, and Pierre Hamel

Overview

This chapter presents an overview of some key moments in the history of the efforts to rehabilitate young offenders in Québec—key moments that have served to lay the foundation for how young offenders are dealt with in Québec today. The chapter describes the evolution of Québec's legislative youth justice framework as well as the evolution of the province's various intervention strategies, and focuses particularly on the views of rehabilitation in the province that led to the actual structure of services offered to youth offenders. Together, these elements are intended to help explain why a majority of the Québec population is opposed to some of the fundamental principles of the Youth Criminal Justice Act. The chapter attempts to provide the reader with insight into how and why Québec's focus has moved away from the gravity of the offence to try instead to address the needs and capacity of young persons who are recognized as at-risk youth.

Introduction

The Province of Québec has a unique socio-political context in Canada. It is the only province to have French as the only official language. Under the provincial political system, Québec also has a unique organization of public services (e.g., finance, justice, health, education, etc.). In addition, Québec maintained the Napoleonic civil code that it inherited from France, although in terms of criminal justice, the Canadian Criminal Code applies. This distinction goes back to the founding of Canada as the union of Upper and Lower Canada and has in some ways influenced the conceptualization and application of law to youth offenders, as will be discussed herein.

The Québec Intervention Model for Young Offenders: The Right Measure at the Right Time

Before 1950, in Québec, as in the rest of Canada and some occidental countries, young offenders found themselves in adult prisons (Parizeau 1976; Foucault 1984). It was several decades before the incarceration of minors disappeared in Québec. This chapter describes the evolution of this process from various perspectives over the past 100 years. The changes made to the judicial system during that time were accompanied by new concepts of intervention and more extensive criminological, psychological, and psycho-educational research. The dynamic relationship between research and intervention has also played a major role in defining a **differential intervention** approach that has become more explicit and is now recognized as the basis of the intervention model used in Québec. We will describe the past and current organization of services for youth offenders in Québec and the difficulties associated with the implementation of the Youth Criminal Justice Act (YCJA) in the province.

differential
intervention
Based on the
identification of the type
of delinquency associated
with the behaviours of
young offenders. The
interventions must then
be tailored to meet young
offenders' treatment
needs and the level of risk
they pose to society
(risk of recidivism).

Evolution of Québec's Legislative Framework

In 1857, Canada adopted the Act for the More Speedy Trial and Punishment of Juvenile Offenders in an effort to avoid long imprisonments before trial proceedings. It was at that time that the government decided to play a role in the protection of minors who had committed an offence (see Chapter 1 in this textbook for further discussion). Between 1868 and 1925, more than 80 000 poor children were sent from England to Canada without family, and some with delinquency issues. They were initially placed in asylums before being integrated into Canadian families as farm labourers or domestic servants (see Carrington 1999 for further discussion). To protect these abandoned children from delinquency, in 1869 Québec adopted two laws that established institutions to take charge of these children: the Industrial Schools Act, which ensured housing and education for children under 14 years old who had been abandoned or were not being properly taken care of, and the Reform School Act, which aimed to rehabilitate offenders under 16 years old. Prisons were, at that time, overflowing with minors. This system remained in place until 1892, when a change in law obliged municipalities to pay for half of the cost for youth offenders placed in industrial and reform schools. Municipalities avoided paying these new costs, and, once again, youth offenders were sent to adult courts and prisons (Joyal 2000).

In 1908, the adoption of The Juvenile Delinquents Act (JDA) marked a societal shift inspired by the American experience. As described in Chapter 1, this law was based on a paternalistic philosophy whereby minors were no longer seen as criminals but as poorly raised; therefore, they could not be held responsible for their actions (see Platt 1977). Similar to abused and neglected children, delinquent children were seen as victims of their environment and deemed to need care, encouragement, and supervision. Intervention centred on helping these young people instead of reprimanding them for their delinquent behaviour. This 1908 law conferred a special legal status on youth who had committed offences and constituted major social progress. Distinct tribunals and legal procedures for young offenders allowed them to receive help and remain with their family instead of being systematically incarcerated and/or treated like adults. Judges were now expected to act with reasonable and due care when it came to judicial proceedings involving young offenders.

By the beginning of the twentieth century in Québec, religious institutions cared for abandoned children free of charge. The intention was to morally and physically 'save' these children. Children were placed in big halls and dormitories, their basic needs were provided for, and they received minimal instruction. In 1951, Québec passed the School Act of Youth Protection, a law that abolished reform and industrial schools. This new act instituted youth protection schools and the court of social welfare; judges were expected to hear the youth's situation. The spirit of this law favoured the substitution of the state for parents when the child was in need of protection. The tribunal responsible for applying this law was the same one responsible for the federal 1908 Juvenile Delinquents Act. With the School Act of Youth Protection, however, the rules of law were minimal since the legislation did not acknowledge the notion of rights for young people. The procedures in the court of social welfare were very basic; the judge was expected to act with reasonable and due care. The principles of the act were aligned with those of the federal law in effect at the time—the 1908 JDA. The procedures applied by the judge could be seen as a concrete implementation of the state as the *parens patriae*.

In 1977, Québec adopted the Youth Protection Act (YPA), which came into effect in January 1979. Adopting this act was a major step that influenced the course of intervening with young offenders. In addition to dealing with children in need of protection, this law also deals with young persons charged with an offence under the Criminal Code or under provincial or municipal laws.[1] Provisions are included that define voluntary measures that can be offered to young offenders as an alternative to judicial proceedings and are deemed to be in their best interest. These provisions allow the youth protection director to either propose a voluntary measure, refer the matter to court, or close the case. This process was invalidated with the Supreme Court of Canada declaring in 1981 that criminal law, including procedures, is a federal jurisdiction (Procureur général du Québec c. Lechasseur et autre [1981] 2 R.C.S. 253). However, the impact of this incursion of provincial legislation on federal jurisdiction has been to introduce a recourse for young offenders outside of judicial procedures. This legislation affirms the notion of the 'precedence of social intervention over court intervention',[2] which constitutes an important milestone for differential intervention.[3]

It was at this time that the Québec National Assembly held the Charbonneau Special Parliamentary Commission addressing youth protection. Taking into account the Supreme Court's decision and the enactment of the YOA in 1982, the Charbonneau Commission proposed the adoption of an alternative measures program that balanced social and judicial obligations. In this program, the first step consists of an examination of the evidence by the solicitor followed by a decision from the youth protection director as to which regime is applicable, by either proposing alternative measures to the youth or by making a recommendation to the solicitor to press charges against the offending youth. The Charbonneau Commission also recommended that the youth protection director be made provincial director under the YOA, thereby giving the youth protection network responsibility over the rehabilitation services provided to young offenders. Hence, the notion of precedence of social intervention was reaffirmed with the adoption of the YOA. As soon as the act came into effect in 1984, Québec adopted its alternative measures program (Commission Charbonneau, part II). As detailed in Chapter 3, the YOA considered that youth were able to assume, up to a certain point, responsibility for their actions while also insisting on protecting society. At the same time, the YOA emphasized the principle of considering adolescents' special needs in treating delinquency (see sec. 3(1)(c)).

The nature and gravity of the offence are not the only elements considered when imposing judicial decisions; a juvenile's needs and circumstances must be taken into account when explaining his or her behaviour. Inspired by Québec's experience using extrajudicial measures, the YOA instituted the Alternative Measures Program (AMP), which allowed Québec and other jurisdictions of Canada to elaborate on and implement these measures. Québec rapidly adopted a decree to institutionalize this option. Under the AMP, the prosecutor was expected to evaluate the evidence and determine if an offence had been committed. If such was the case, for the majority of offences each jurisdiction was obliged to transfer the young offender to the director of Youth Protection Services for assessment and to determine how best to apply the program options. For some offences or specific situations, the prosecutor had discretion to either refer the offender to the director of Youth Protection Services or directly proceed with legal proceeding.

The methods of intervention used with young offenders and the place the nonjudicial measures occupy are the result of the experience and thinking of the 1960s and 1970s (to be discussed subsequently). In 1984, Québec became one of the first provinces to take advantage of these provisions by adopting the decree 'the Alternative Measures Program' as a program outside of the court was part of the YOA. Since 1984, the directors of Youth Protection Services have been designated provincial directors according to the YOA and, consequently, have responsibility to oversee the Alternative Measures Program. And since 2003, the provincial directors have the same responsibilities under the new YCJA. In the same manner, the rehabilitation centres responsible for youth protection were designated detention centres for young offenders with custodial sentences.[4]

Since 1984, the number of juveniles who have benefited from alternative measures has continued to grow. In 2009, 5604 teens were given extrajudicial sanctions[5] compared to 3723 juveniles who received sentences and who were under the responsibility of the provincial director. Indeed, since 2000, approximately 8000 young offenders a year have been supervised by **alternative justice agencies** in alternative measures programs.

In **extrajudicial programs**, the assessment carried out by the provincial director must examine certain key factors: the offence committed as well as who is responsible for the offence; the character of the offender and of his/her family; and the social environment. This allows the director to identify not only the nature of the action but its meaning and significance for the young person, as well as the risk to society. This program is still in effect and has been extended under the YCJA as the Extrajudicial Sanctions Program.

When implementing the YCJA, the provincial directors confirmed their support for a differential approach to the intervention option. A differential intervention is based on identifying the type of delinquency associated with the young offender's behaviours. The distinction here is between a common young offender and a distinctive young offender, a distinction that is fundamental to intervening with young offenders (Le Blanc 1983). To do so, one must take into consideration the young offender's conduct and personality, and undertake a psycho-social evaluation. Such an assessment aims to identify the right measure at the right time for the right person.[6]

alternative justice agencies
Québec-based agencies responsible for the application of the extrajudicial programs for youth that are either referred by the police or by the provincial director under the YCJA. Measures can include information and awareness programs on shoplifting, drugs, and law reinforcement as well as mediation or damage repair for the victim, or, if that is not possible, repairing the damage in terms of the community.

extrajudicial programs
Measures that are designed to hold youths responsible for their actions without creating a criminal record. They are generally applied to youths who are not engaged in a serious delinquent trajectory.

The right measure at the right time is based on the offence for which the adolescent must assume responsibility according to his capacity to do so. The measure must be determined within the limits of the gravity of the offence. Within these limits, the aim is to protect and reaffirm reprobation for the offence while favouring education and rehabilitation measures; it also targets the needs and rights of victims. This measure takes into consideration the adolescent's entire situation to be influenced through tailor made decisions and measures that take into account specific needs.

. . . This measure is the result of an equilibrium that is difficult to reach among the following concerns: taking proper, fair, moderated and personalized decisions and measures; the need to take into consideration the gravity of the offence and the reprobation of society; and the importance of intervening at the right moment. The choice and application of such measures are clearly challenging.[7]

In accordance with the YCJA, prosecution in youth court and the imposition of specific sentences should be limited to adolescents in situations (1) where the criminal conduct is an indication of a 'distinctive delinquency' (Le Blanc and Fréchette 1989), (2) where there are risks for public security, or (3) where the offences are serious. Serious interventions ordered by the court are designed for juveniles with important developmental deficiencies. These measures take into account both the young person's actions and the meaning these actions have for the young offender. This approach depends on the differential evaluation of each situation, taking into account the specific needs of young offenders, especially in terms of rehabilitation and social reintegration. The intervention model in Québec for young offenders is based on a differential evaluation before any intervention measures are taken. This approach was the result of extensive dialogue among judges, prosecutors, lawyers, and psycho-social professionals, following the YOA's implementation. This was evident in Judge Jasmin's 1995 report and has been supported since the 1970s by experts from both the judicial and social systems who have agreed to value prevention and rehabilitation.

As a consequence of this judicial evolution, there have been profound and dynamic transformations in the way interventions are designed, whether the youth offenders are in open custody, in secure custody, or in the community, or whether alternative measures are being used.

The Evolution of Interventions

Transformation of Open-Custody Interventions

Beginning in the 1950s, during the creation of the court for 'social welfare', uprisings against youth imprisonment and large repressive institutions intensified. At the same time, groups of professionals began setting up pilot experiments in rehabilitation, like that of **Boscoville** (Rumilly 1978), which will be discussed subsequently (see Box 14.1). Educators and other professionals took young offenders out of prisons and integrated them into newly designed rehabilitation programs, considered as alternatives to adult prisons and reform schools.

Boscoville became the new rehabilitative project for young delinquents in Montreal and had an important influence on the evolution of rehabilitation throughout the rest of Québec. At the time, in the larger institutions there were 200 to 300 young people along with only a few staff members, who were members of the church without any specific training (Ménard 2003). On the other hand, at Boscoville, there were only about 50 teens. They were divided into small groups of 12 to 15, and lived in cottages similar to family homes. There were no guardians, only educators who lived with the youth and led this innovative program, which included academics, sports, art, and social activities. The intention of the program was to contribute to the youths' re-education. This approach was

Boscoville

A unique program introduced in the 1950s in Québec that was based on a social welfare and psycho-educative model and that introduced elements in its program designed to teach delinquent youth the necessary skills, values, and attitudes that would allow them to develop a sense of social responsibility.

inspired by innovations from European (see Capul and Lemay 1996) specialized educators after the Second World War and by the Americans Redl and Wineman (1951). Boscoville was structured as systematic action research, which led to a theoretical concept of rehabilitation (Guindon 1970) as well as to a method of intervention (Gendreau 1978).

The program at Boscoville contributed to psycho-education with one of its areas of specialty being the rehabilitation of troubled youth. The **psycho-education model** was unique to Québec. This profession was created on the basis of several assumptions. The first assumption was that 'love' was not sufficient for working with youth. Contrary to beliefs in some religious environments, this model proposed that the worker must have certain relative, competent skills. Therefore, educators working with young offenders in the program had to develop specific competencies to intervene efficiently (e.g., everyday life skills, the capacity to plan and direct rehabilitative activities, knowledge of normal and abnormal adolescent development, the capacity to perform educational clinical evaluations and to conduct educational monitoring interviews). The second assumption was that re-education of young offenders must be integrated into every activity throughout the day and shared with the psycho-educator so that these youths would have a chance to change and take responsibility for their development. Intense interactions between the young offenders and the educator were seen as crucial for effective rehabilitation. At the time this concept was new and there was resistance from both those who defended a more conservative concept, by limiting worker competencies and incorporating a dose of religious idealism and physical force, and those who were passionate about new therapeutic approaches. For the latter, it was important to offer competent workers who were capable of using psychotherapy with young people. Unfortunately, psychotherapy failed with these young persons (Trieshman, Brendtro, and Whittaker 1969).

Training for special educators working with young offenders and other troubled youth began to take shape with a program first developed at the University of Montreal. Today, five Québec universities offer a bachelor's and master's degree in this area, and two of them dispense a doctorate in psycho-education (Université de Montréal and Université du Québec à Trois-Rivières).

Box 14.1 Youth Justice in Action

Elements of the Boscoville Program

- Rehabilitation centre for delinquent teens ages 14 to 18 years
- Initiated as a summer camp toward the end of the 1940s
- Six groups of 15 adolescents in duplex-style apartments
- Staffed by trained educators who specialized in psycho-education (undergraduate- or masters-level education)
- Known as the birthplace of the psycho-educational treatment model and of psycho-education as a profession
- Program composed of activities addressing adolescent development, including academics, arts and crafts (theatre, ceramics, etc.), sports, group meetings; democratic means of engaging youths in collective arrangements, decisions, and individualized treatment; all activities aimed at achieving rehabilitation

Results of an evaluation conducted by Le Blanc (1983) showed that compared to similar programs Boscoville resulted in lower recidivism rates than most other programs reviewed. For example, one year after attending the program, the adolescents who participated in the program had a rate of non-recidivism of 65 per cent and showed significant improvement in their social functioning.

Since 2000, psycho-education has been recognized and structured by a professional organization. The model used for the **psycho-educative** intervention has been the subject of both qualitative and quantitative research (see Szabo and Le Blanc 1994 and Le Blanc 1983). This research was conducted over a 10-year period and evaluated the effects of programs used in open custody. Le Blanc showed that the Boscoville process, in using the psycho-educative intervention model, was able to create a positive social atmosphere. In other words, the social situation is a countervailing force on the negative effects of the delinquent subculture, which is often created in environments where young offenders are housed. The results of the study also show that 68 per cent of the youth who participated in the program were not involved in any recidivist activity for up to one year. These results are among the most significant reported in the literature on intervention programs for young offenders. The research also shows how effective rehabilitation programs can be in comparison to the absence of specific interventions and to strict detention. In fact, only 10 per cent of young offenders appearing before a youth court and placed in detention centres without rehabilitation programs did not recidivate a year after the end of their sentence compared to the 68 per cent from the Boscoville program who did not.

Another important contributor to the differential perspective for treating youth is the Philippe-Pinel Institute (see Box 14.2), which is a psychiatric penitentiary hospital with a special unit for teens with mental-health problems associated with their delinquency; the institute also provides a specialized assessment service. In the 1960s, some judges and political authorities made it possible to integrate young offenders who had committed homicide into the rehabilitation program. This practice made it clear that it was possible to re-educate even these young offenders in open custody with intervention programs adapted to their needs and societal expectations. Approximately 10 young offenders participated in this experiment throughout the 1960s. Most youth convicted of murder took part in Boscoville's internal program for three to five years, followed by two to three years of support in the community while they were being reintegrated into society. Both social adaptation and non-recidivism proved to be a success (Boisvert, Bisaillon, and Adam 1988; Ducharme 1999).

Research at the Philippe-Pinel Institute showed how important the differential intervention concept is when trying to rehabilitate young offenders. Clearly, the intervention model used at Boscoville had many positive effects for some teen delinquents. According to Le Blanc (1983), the program was more effective with youth offenders presenting neurotic disorders (e.g., anxiety) than with highly criminalized teens presenting psychopathic disorders. However, it was not effective

psycho-educative model

Developed in Québec, this model followed the Boscoville experience and is now recognized as a profession specializing in the intervention of troubled youths.

Box 14.2 Youth Justice in Action

The Philippe-Pinel Institute

Created in 1970, the Philippe-Pinel Institute is:

1. A forensic psychiatric hospital.
2. A leading-edge evaluation and treatment facility for forensic psychiatry. Multi-disciplinary teams treat patients suffering from severe mental-health disorders who pose threats to society. These teams apply treatment programs designed to address specific mental-health disorders among adults. It also houses a special unit for adolescents that is dedicated to offering forensic evaluation and rehabilitation beyond the capacity of youth centres.

3. A research centre studying mental-health disorders with a purpose of enhancing evaluation and treatment methods. For instance, since the 1970s, the Philippe-Pinel Institute's team and its associated researchers have produced numerous studies and reports on prisoners and mental-health problems, as well as on the characteristics and treatment of sexual abusers, of murderers, and of other types of aggressors and on their personalities.

enough for certain types of offenders. This convinced researchers of the need to create a new generation of intervention programming, whereby the type of program would match the type of young offender. This differential perspective has prevailed in many innovative attempts since the early 1990s (see Le Blanc, Dionne, Grégoire, Proulx, and Trudeau-Le Blanc 1998; Cournoyer and Dionne 2007). The results of the various studies showed that evaluating the psycho-educative model applied at Boscoville convinced many authorities that rehabilitation with rigorous and well-implemented programs is necessary. Like Boscoville, institutions were interested in applying the best practices developed elsewhere. For example, inspired by Boscoville, many tried using for the first time the Interpersonal Maturity Levels Theory for young offenders as a model of differential intervention. This typology, developed in the United States (Sullivan, Grant, and Grant 1957) was used to assess different levels of maturity, which are associated with modes of reaction and for which a specific intervention can be put in place. This was the groundwork for the first attempts at differential intervention (Warren 1966). Early in the 1970s, researchers became involved with intervention centres and contributed to their development and implementation in Québec. Other factors and events, including the evolution of secure custody interventions, were also partly responsible for improving the service delivery system for young offenders in Québec.

The Transformation of Secure-Custody Intervention

By the mid 1970s, Montreal had a detention centre with a structure similar to that of a prison, called le Centre Berthelet. In 1975, a violent riot broke out there, and many young offenders were injured and the premises were ransacked and set on fire. The riot attracted considerable media attention and prompted an important reorganization of the centre. This reorganization had an enormous influence on how other secure custody centres in the province operated. Although change and reform were gradual, the process leading up to the changes provided new knowledge about the conditions necessary to support rehabilitative efforts within a secure custody centre.

Even though Martinson (1974) and some of his supporters believed that 'nothing works' with offenders, Boscoville and other programs contradicted that view and confirmed that rehabilitation was possible in open custody. For high-recidivism-risk teens requiring secure custody, however, rehabilitation was still thought to be impossible. Besides initiatives such as that by Agee (1979) in the United States, few attempts at rehabilitation have been recorded in such environments. After the Berthelet riot, a new team of directors took over le Centre Berthelet. They changed the name of the centre to Cité des Prairies and concentrated restructuring efforts on putting in place a rehabilitation program able to satisfy the needs of youth offenders as well as the need for public protection. The main guidelines were as follows:

1. *To take the necessary means to find competent and well-trained employees.* The hiring process for the management, educators, and security staff was rigorous. The selection was completed by a continual training mechanism for all the staff. This exhaustive process of changing the organizational culture favoured rehabilitation over physical control and confinement.

2. *To implement programs with activities intent on socializing the clientele and inspired by intervention methods proven to be effective.* This second principle led to the implementation of a program with academic, sport, and art activities that emphasized rehabilitation. The program included an individual clinical support process for each young offender, which consisted of a thorough psycho-social assessment, an individualized intervention plan, regular educative sessions, as well as meetings with the family/guardians. In addition, there were a series of activities and measures to support a harmonious social reinsertion for each youth.

3. *To establish an adequate equilibrium between dynamic and static security.* Secure-custody institutions are preoccupied with static security, that is, the physical control of the incarcerated person, comprised of different dimensions such as the height of the walls, locks on doors, the use of surveillance cameras, and the presence of security guards. **Dynamic security** is ensured by the relational dimension within the institution. In a secure-custody rehabilitation centre, dynamic security is achieved by the constant presence of educators and the bonds built between the youth and the educators. As a result, the quality of the social climate is improved among peers, which in turn contributes to the security of the institution. While reorganizing the new centre, there were enormous tensions for months between the security staff, who were ensuring static security, and the educators, who were securing their relationships with the youth to ensure the dynamic security. This tension demanded efforts and dialogue to resolve conflicts between the two parties and to find a new equilibrium between rehabilitation practices and the necessity of a certain level of physical control (Le Blanc 1991).

dynamic security
Security that is ensured by the relational dimension. It is achieved by the constant presence of educators and the bonds built between the youth and them. As a result, the quality of the social climate is improved among peers, who in turn contribute to the security of the institution.

After a few years of difficult teamwork, the concept materialized and transformed the centre, which had a major influence on new centres that were being implemented or on existing ones that were being reorganized in the province. The transformation of Cité des Prairies, which was a secure-custody centre for young offenders, was the first demonstration of the feasibility of modifying the marginalized and delinquent subculture that was known to prevail in prisons and detention centres, and transforming it into a pro-social subculture that valued rehabilitation and that was able to counter the iatrogenic effects felt in secure-custody establishments. Unfortunately, it was not possible to evaluate the results on a large scale as was done at Boscoville (Borgo 1987). However, researchers have observed positive effects of this reorganization on the organizational culture as well as a change in behaviour among the clientele (Le Blanc et al. 1998).

The Evolution of Community Intervention

Since the early 1960s in Québec, there has been enormous progress in community follow-up methods, whether the offender is on probation or under an extrajudicial measure. In the past, the Justice Department took care of the intervention while the youth offenders were on probation, and there was no difference between services for adults or young offenders. Probation officers were responsible for a great number of cases (about 100 per case worker), which did not encourage meaningful intervention. Interventions were more-or-less intermittent in their effectiveness. The transfer of juvenile probation services to the Ministry of Health and Social Services (ministère de la Santé et des Services sociaux du Québec) in 1976 marked a turning point in the philosophy and means of intervention. From then on, juveniles on probation received intensive services based on supervision, monitoring, and guidance as well as help and counselling. The YOA brought an important expansion to developing clinical interventions during probation, and there was an awareness, as mentioned earlier in the chapter, of the 'right measures at the right time'. Youth centres invested in training for their staff, notably on evaluation tools (e.g., the Jesness Inventory, which is a short, 55-question survey that measures a number of different asocial tendencies); or on intervention models, such as reality therapy (Glasser 1990) or the rational-emotive approach (Ellis and Dryden 1997); or on the implementation of the interpersonal maturity theory (Sullivan, Grant, and Grant 1957; Warren 1969;1966).

The 1990s began with different intensive probation experiments in Québec. Results from research projects carried out in the US (Armstrong and Altshuler 1991) and Great Britain made this possible. The first documented experiment, for which there was a formal evaluation, was done by Québec's Youth Centre (Piché and Fréchette 1995). Others in Montérégie, Estrie, and Montreal followed.

Research conducted in Ontario and elsewhere in Canada on the risk-need-responsivity model for offender assessment and rehabilitation (Andrews and Bonta 1998), as well as some experiments on intensive supervision in probation and parole (Armstrong and Altshuler 1991; Gendreau, Coggin, and Fulton 2000), inspired studies of intensive probation follow-ups with treatment for offenders presenting moderate to high risks of recidivism (Cournoyer and Dionne 2007). The research showed that the program significantly lowered the risks of criminal recidivism of the youths. In fact, 76 per cent of those who participated in the program did not recidivate one year after they completed the program. This study led to the implementation in 2009 of a new pilot program of intensive differential follow-up (SID or 'suivi intensif différencié') in Montréal, which was to undergo evaluation in 2011 (see www.publicsafety.gc.ca/prg/cp/ythgng/cpa03-gdr-eng.aspx, accessed 18 September, 2011).

In addition to the efforts made to improve rehabilitation methods in institutions and to the rigorous community follow-up for moderate to high-risk offenders, there was also an opportunity for creating community interventions with lower risk offenders. These represented the first steps in creating alternative justice agencies.

The alternative justice measures were significantly influenced by one of the first projects called Projet Intervention Jeunesse de Montréal (Montreal's Youth Intervention Project), which was carried out from 1977 to 1979. The project's aim was to help young offenders avoid the judiciary process by offering alternative solutions: community work, direct reconciliation with the victim, paying for damages, or participation in measures that would improve social aptitudes. These were options proposed as alternative measures to prosecution, particularly as a consequence of the implementation of Chapter 40 of the Act of Youth Protection from 1979 to 1984 in Québec. In some ways, as described earlier in the chapter, it is possible to say that the exchange measures program, elaborated in 1984 within the framework of the YOA, gets its roots from these projects.

The Evolution of Criminological Research

Another important factor in keeping young offenders out of Québec prisons was the dynamics of the research in criminology, psychology, psycho-education, social work, and at times in psychiatry (see Szabo and Le Blanc 2004). These studies shed light on youth characteristics, their evolution, and the characteristics of institutions for minors and the effects of their intervention programs (Le Blanc 1998).

As mentioned earlier, open-custody research, conducted by Le Blanc (1983), and the study of the trajectories of 400 criminalized delinquents done by Le Blanc and Fréchette (1989) helped distinguish between 'common' delinquency and 'distinctive' delinquency. These notions are the basis for the differential intervention model used in many Québec youth centres. According to these authors, common delinquency is committed by a large number of teens and represents an epiphenomenon that is part of the developmental process in teens. The results of the studies show that most youth commit an infraction in the process of exploring their social environment without their actions being due to important personal, family, or social deficits. Even though common delinquency is not usually a serious or repetitive commission of delinquent gestures, some acts are serious or repetitive. Intervention involving education, awareness, and the repairing of damages can provoke feelings of responsibility if we are dealing with 'conventional' teens who have the necessary acquired knowledge and experience for adequate social development. Taking into account the potential the majority of teens have for social adaptation, even without intervention, this type of delinquency usually disappears by itself (Le Blanc and Fréchette 1989). Using the youth court with this type of delinquency appears unnecessary and even abusive.

The second category of delinquency deals with crimes that are more repetitive and that become a lifestyle that continues to more advanced stages. This includes about 5 per cent of youth. Making the distinction between the transition of young offenders exhibiting a typical personality development process and real criminal activities that appear at the same age is essential for intervention. Therefore, adolescent young offenders demand a particular approach that is focused on their needs during their personal and social development phase. This type of delinquency, described in studies done by Fréchette and Le Blanc (1987), is qualified as 'distinctive' delinquency. It is distinctive because of the important personality deficits identified in these young offenders and is characterized by a behavioural state where the offensive gestures appear early, persist, are abundant, and are serious. Even though this type of offending is present in only a limited number of teens, it still represents an important part of offences committed by young persons. The behaviour associated with this type of delinquency is diverse and includes serious crimes.

Differential intervention is based on identifying the type of young offender by the behavioural, social, and psychological course that the young person takes. The distinction between common or distinctive delinquency is fundamental for intervention measures with young offenders. This is done by taking into account the delinquent conduct and the teen's personality, and by confirming this based on a psycho-social assessment. As previously mentioned, this evaluation aims to fulfill *the right intervention, at the right moment, with the right person.*

Today's Services for Young Offenders

Over the past 40 years in Québec, services for young offenders have been under the responsibility of Health and Social Services. Youth rehabilitation centres, social service centres, and youth protection centres joined forces in 1993. At the same time, 16 youth centres were created throughout the province of Québec. These centres, under the Youth Protection Act, the Youth Criminal Justice Act, the Act on the Health and Social Services (Loi sur le système de santé et les services sociaux), and the Civil Code of Québec, offer juveniles and their parents psycho-social services and rehabilitation. In each of the youth centres, a director of youth protection (DYP), named according to the Youth Protection Act Québec, is responsible for receiving reports concerning a child who may have his or her security or development compromised as a result of physical or sexual abuse, neglect, psychological cruelty, abandonment, or serious behavioural problems. The DYP is also responsible for evaluating the reports and proposing either voluntary measures or court measures in order to address and ameliorate the situation, as indicated previously in this chapter. When the Young Offenders Act came into effect in Québec in 1984, the duties accorded to the provincial director under the act were devolved to the DYPs of the province. This disposition was maintained under the Youth Criminal Justice Act (YCJA). Therefore, the provincial director (PD) is responsible for applying many aspects of the YCJA. To do so, she or he delegates authority to a number of people. These delegated members work, for the most part, in one of the 16 youth centres in the province.

In addition to the youth centres, Québec provides a network of community centres. These centres are under the authority of the Ministry of Health and Social Services of Québec and are mainly concerned with how teens reconcile with their victims or the community for their wrongdoings. Known as alternative justice agencies, they are united in a provincial organization and are first to collaborate with the youth centres in applying the YCJA. Centres can be found throughout Québec and they all offer the same types of services. Services offered for extrajudicial sanctions are determined by an agreement between the alternative justice agencies and the youth centres, which standardizes the underlying philosophy for intervention and how the roles are assigned.

Québec is a vast province composed of different regions, each with their own characteristics. No matter where the adolescent lives, however, he or she will receive roughly the same service with the same rehabilitation perspective. The provincial director (PD), under the Québec's Youth Centres Association, and after enforcement of the YCJA, reaffirmed a number of statements of principles that guide staff working with youth throughout the province. The following section will briefly describe the steps for applying the act by specifying each clinical position supported by the PDs and the Québec's YCJA working group. This group produced a reference manual guiding the application of the YCJA in youth centres (Hamel and Paradis 2004) that is based on the scientific literature and on the values derived from the evolving services.

Extrajudicial Measures

Police Measures

The YCJA introduced a preliminary step that was referred to as 'exchange measures'. The legislation considered that a certain number of youth committing offences could benefit from measures applied directly by the police. Besides the possibility of laying charges, the police could decide to not apply any measure, to give a warning, or to direct the adolescent to a community centre where measures would be taken. The inter-ministerial committee of the YCJA in Québec prepared a framework for these measures before implementing the law. The framework anticipates the type of offence and the measures that are necessary according to the severity of the offence, to traces of the offences left in the youth's police file (Centre Renseignement Policier Québec), and to the role each partner plays in applying measures (i.e., police officers, prosecutors, alternative justice agencies, provincial director). The framework also includes allowances for regional committees under the authority of the provincial director who follows its progress. The alternative justice agencies take care of some of the measures for teens referred by the police. Most of these measures are information and awareness programs on shoplifting, drugs, law reinforcement, etc. Though nonparticipation has no consequences, since 2003 young offenders in Québec have participated in significant numbers.

Extrajudicial Sanctions

As mentioned in the previous section, extrajudicial measures define some offences where the young offender can be held liable for criminal and penal prosecution. All other offences are referred to the PD for evaluation and implementation of the possible extrajudicial sanctions. Every youth centre has staff dedicated to this task. Staff members meet the adolescent and the parents for a brief evaluation of the circumstances surrounding the offence, the adolescent's situation, and his or her personal and social functioning. If possible, the provincial director's delegate proposes a measure to the youth. The outline of the agreement in alternative justice agencies—youth centres anticipates that before the delegate carries out the evaluation the alternative justice agency contacts the victim. That way, when meeting with the adolescent the delegate has the victim's point of view regarding the damages and can consider measures suitable for the youth to address the damage. The agreement in question also provides for a hierarchy of measures: the first measure allows some damage repair for the victim; if that is not possible, repairing the damage in terms of the community would be considered. While the responsibility for evaluation and orientation resides with the professionals at the youth centres, the alternative justice agency sets the conditions so the adolescent can carry out the measure.

During the evaluation process, the youth delegate must determine if the youth is considered normal in terms of social and psychological development (i.e., determine if the youth is manifesting 'common' delinquency) (Fréchette and Le Blanc 1987), and if applying an extrajudicial measure appears sufficient to assist the young person. If the evaluation of the situation surrounding the minor (i.e., including prior offences, behaviour, and social and psychological difficulties) leads the delegate to believe that she or he is getting into 'distinctive' delinquency (Fréchette and Le Blanc 1987), the delegate can choose to return the case to the prosecutor and legal action may then be taken with measures geared toward establishing a structure and path that will discourage delinquency.

This program has been in place since 1984 and recent annual statistics collected by the PD between 2003 and 2010 indicate that 90 per cent of young offenders with extrajudicial sanctions have successfully carried out the measures imposed. Although these results are encouraging, studies on young offenders returning to the justice system are needed to get a better sense of what these numbers mean. However, since the YCJA came into effect, the program has been used much less. The number of evaluations/orientations done by the PD went from 10 383 in 2002 to 7525 in 2007 (Ministry of Health and Social Services 2008). This drop might be a result of the fact that many prospective cases had measures dictated by the police. This introduces at least two problems: first, the decisions taken by police are not based on psycho-social assessments nor on the risk of recidivism; second, the decisions generally do not consider the victim's opinion or measures aimed at repairing damages.

The Role of Social Proceedings in Provisional Detention: The Liaison Services in Place and Supervision before Sentencing

Youth Centres in many parts of Québec have implemented liaison mechanisms with the judicial services. In most regions, a youth delegate must liaise with the prosecutor and with youth-centre services. This same delegate handles the evaluations requested by the prosecutor, the reports demanded by the court, and rulings involving the PD. These services allow the exchanges to run more efficiently and effectively. In so doing, the judicial system is ensured that requests sent to the PD arrive quickly and that rulings are applied the day they come into effect.

As well as the liaison service, most youth centres, under Health and Social Services, implement voluntary services for adolescents and their parents before going to court. For example, when a young person is released, support and concrete help are offered to both the parents and the adolescent. In particular, in cases with family violence, where the family is in crisis and requires immediate help, youth centres provide educative support or temporarily lodge the adolescent in another environment. Whether the program is referred to as 'rapid intervention for delinquency' (*intervention rapide en délinquance*) or 'follow-up programs before sentencing' (*programme de suivi avant peine*), it allows for rapid intervention and often prevents further deterioration of a potentially explosive family situation (Duret 2004).

The Pre-sentence Reports

The Youth Tribunal can request a pre-sentence report if more clarification of the case is required before making a ruling. If necessary, the court asks the PD to file the pre-sentence report. As well as answering the judge's questions to assist in the ruling, the report will trace the young person's differential profile and suggest measures according to his or her needs and the perceived risk of recidivism. To further the goals of the differential intervention perspective, youth centres train their staff to use clinical tools that allow them to establish the youth's profile and situation so they can suggest the best measures likely to impact recidivism and rehabilitation. The pre-sentence report will deal with the elements related to the present and past history of the adolescent's delinquency, including early manifestations of delinquent episodes, aggravation, polymorphism, and persistence. The report will also determine if the offence(s) are premeditated and organized, if the youth is alone or involved in some type of organized group, etc. In addition to the behavioural variables mentioned, the report will also provide information about the youth's social history, including family history, school records, working experiences, participation in leisure activities, friends, and present and past social life, to assess the youth's social capacities as a basis for intervention. Finally, the psychological profile will be informed by observations during interviews, through information given by the parents, or through psychometric testing. The tools most often used in Québec are the Jesness Personality Inventory (Jesness 1971), a research version of the Youth Level of Service-Case Management Inventory (Hoge and Andrews 1994), or the Crimino-Metric Grid (Piché and Fréchette 1995). These tools allow for a better assessment of the youth's risk level and criminal capacity, as well as help to identify potential protective factors (i.e., his or her social capacity).

In Québec a pre-sentence report is always accompanied by a series of recommendations made by the youth delegate. The recommendations typically include measures thought to have a real impact on recidivism and on the youth's ability to reintegrate back into society.

Sentence Follow-ups

Whether the pre-sentence measures involve follow-up in the community or in custody, clinical intervention undertaken by the PD is systematic. Before examining specific aspects of each measure, the general characteristics of clinical intervention of the young offender in youth centres will be examined.

A Planned Intervention

The Québec legislation on Health and Social Services mandates participation in developing an intervention plan for anyone who receives services from any Health and Social Services organization. No client subject to the YCJA is exempt from this intervention plan. The plan must be signed by the young person and his or her parent(s) or guardian and is subject to review every six months.

Community intervention necessarily requires various conditions that the young offender must respect. There is a need for clinical and legal conditions. The youth must participate in the clinical structure, which includes pro-social activities as well as activities that help him or her learn new skills. The youth offender's family is also integrated into the intervention. The aim is to support parents and guardians to take control over the family structure and to help them learn to resolve conflict. Intervention plans are also prepared if the young offender is in custody. In such cases, the intervention plan clarifies the work that the youth must undertake while in custody as well as the responsibilities of the youth delegate in contact with the parent(s) or guardian(s). Intervention of this kind is re-adaptive, not repressive, and continues to protect society.

An Individualized Intervention: The Differential Approach

A well-judged intervention is based on an extensive assessment that measures the criminal risks as well as the adolescent's personal and social strengths and weaknesses. Such an intervention will be modulated to fit the adolescent's specific characteristics, and the intensity of the support, supervision, and control will vary depending on the type of offender.

A Specialized Intervention

Whether follow-up is in the community or in custody, intervention with young offenders is completed by a psycho-social or rehabilitation professional. Criminologists, social workers, psycho-educators, and special educators may work with the young offender in youth centres. Throughout their career, qualified staff members receive training on evaluation tools and intervention approaches or models. The intervention is, therefore, very specialized and structured by rigorous practice standards.

Follow-up in the Community

There are a number of provisions in the YCJA (Chapters 102 to 109) that allow for follow-up in the community through a court order. The most commonly used provision is probation. According to the Québec guide on juvenile probation (Piché 2006), probation is defined as 'a judicial measure of re-socialization which at the same time guarantees public protection and endeavours to establish personal social functionality of the youth offender . . . while ensuring structure and assistance . . . so he can learn to adjust to the requirements of life in society'. Probation, therefore, unites control and support with the aim of facilitating the development of the necessary tools in the youth for enhancing social capacity while controlling the temptation of engaging in criminal activities.

Probation follow-up normally consists of interventions that impose conditions in order to control the adolescent, and of clinical measures such as addressing social obligations: going to school, working, and participating in structured leisure activities or clinical group activities. Intervention will also offer support and assistance since it is aiming to help the teen's efforts toward social integration. Probation can consist of regular group and individual meetings at a local probation office. The nature of the follow-up depends on the young offender's identified needs and criminal risk. For example, in Montreal a tool exists to help make decisions about the intensity of the services needed, which can go from one meeting every two weeks for regular probation to at least three direct interventions a week for those following an intensive differential program (SID; Laporte 2005).

In addition to providing support for the youth, the delegate also offers support to the parents or guardians. This 'wrap-around' service is designed to defuse conflicts between the parents and child.

When appropriate, the surrounding community will also be involved in the intervention. Whether it is at school, at work, or during leisure activities, the delegate will mobilize surrounding resources to collaborate in restructuring and supporting the adolescent. Indeed, some measures embedded in the YJCA (e.g., Chapter 42) imply follow-up in the community. Some examples are the obligation to participate in an intensive program offering support and supervision; deferred custody and supervision; and post-custody supervision. The intervention method and the objectives of these measures are the same as in probation but are intensified because those adolescents subjected to these measures generally have a higher criminal risk.

Only a few regions in Québec (e.g., Québec City and Montérégie) have developed support and supervision programs approved by the PD. Although there is a lack of approval for these programs in other regions, all centres are able to offer intense follow-up in the community. The organization and resources of these services, however, varies from one region to another. In Montreal, for example, intervention cells consisting of several members who work together allow them to do a more intensive intervention in a community follow-up program.

Placements under Custody

Every youth centre has a number of units reserved for youth held in provisional detention or in secure custody. Adolescents placed in open custody are placed in open resources that are, in many regions, dedicated to teens presenting serious behavioural problems, such as those under the Youth Protection Act.

The young offenders placed in secure custody are confined to a physical space where they cannot leave without permission. Any youth placed in secure custody is subject to participating in a rehabilitation program that aims to increase awareness and to make changes to modes of thinking and behaving. Often based on a psycho-educative model, the program consists of a variety of elements that create equilibrium between different mediums and, therefore, allows the adolescent to develop skills in many different areas. Schooling is mandatory whether it is an academic program or in preparation for integration into the labour force. Participation in activities in order to complete social and personal development is also mandatory: sports, artistic expression, and activities to develop social competencies. Every moment of the day is employed to facilitate rehabilitation.

In addition, there are also group clinical activities aimed at learning social skills, anger management, problem solving, moral reasoning, and empathy development. The program also touches on the issue of drug consumption through group activities or individual activities.

Québec's Guidelines for Youth Offenders' Rehabilitation

In Québec, the PDs recommend differential intervention at each level of intervention. The introduction of Bill C-7 in penal law for adolescents provoked an uproar in the province. Québec was for the most part opposed to the idea that the federal government wanted to modify the foundations of the Young Offenders Act. An important coalition of professionals from the justice department, social and community services, universities, and professional associations, such as the Québec Bar, manifested their opposition to the bill. Particularly, representatives from both the justice department and the social networks who work daily with young offenders were concerned about the impact this new bill could have. Principles like 'sentencing' were introduced and inspired by rules applied to adults and, thus, facilitated subjecting teens to adult sentencing. Specifically, introducing the principle of proportionality of the sentence with the gravity of the offence as a guiding principle in determining the sentence was in total opposition to the approach used in Québec (Trépanier 2004). As was indicated earlier, Québec's approach encouraged an assessment of the situation the adolescent was living in, including the offence, its gravity, and the circumstances of its perpetration, but also the psychosocial and developmental aspects of the adolescent.

In Québec, it was agreed that the Young Offenders Act was excellent and the foundations of its principles should be maintained. If there were problems, they were most likely related to its enforcement. A few amendments would have been sufficient to correct it. In reaction to Bill C-7, the Québec government requested that the Québec Court of Appeal pronounce on the legality of certain aspects of the bill. Thus, on September 5, 2001, the Québec government adopted Decree 1021-2001 concerning an amendment to the Court of Appeal relating to Bill C-7 and its penal justice for adolescents. This decree asked the court to examine questions related to the conformity to the United Nations agreement on children's rights, to the international pact of civil and political rights, and to rights guaranteed by clause 7 and paragraph 15(1) of the Canadian Charter of Rights and Freedoms.

On March 31, 2003, the Court of Appeal of Québec pronounced its verdict. To answer the questions of the decree, the court ruled that the clauses on sentencing proposed with articles 38 to 82 did indeed infringe on the rights guaranteed by clause 7 and paragraph 15(1) of the Canadian Charter of Rights and Freedoms. This was based on the rules of presumption, which would send juveniles to the penal justice system as adults at the age of 14. This was also true for the presumption of exceptions to confidential information when an adolescent is subjected to adult sentencing or to presumption related to this type of sentencing. The Supreme Court also declared that presuming an adult sentence in the ruling of *R. v. D.B.*, 2008 CSC 25 was unconstitutional.

Even though these rulings declared certain dispositions on subjecting adolescents to adult sentencing unconstitutional in Québec, those involved in intervention remained concerned. The dispositions targeted a minority of the youth involved with the penal justice system, but for the majority the dispositions of the YCJA applied completely. For example, the YCJA's priority to the principle of sentence proportionality and the criteria limiting the recourse for custody goes against the principle of the right measure at the right moment at the right time, which, in turn, imposes a series of measures based only on the nature of the offence and its gravity, and accords little importance to the adolescent's needs or criminal risk. The effect of this approach delays the ability to apply the right measure at the right time. The right measures applied too late in the lives of teens are less likely to result in positive change.

As mentioned previously, when the YCJA came into effect, the values and the principles at the base of the Québec intervention model were confirmed and guided interventions with young offenders during the application of legal proceedings.[8] The PDs recommended a clinical approach based on differential assessment of each adolescent. The implementation of the YCJA in Québec is based on two premises:

- Preserving the established Québec young offender intervention model
- Taking advantage of all possibilities offered by the YCJA to preserve the psycho-social and rehabilitation interventions

The PDs recommend that interventions with young offenders rely on the values and the clinical vision of the following principles:

- The young person is a developing individual who has not reached full maturity, and thus has different needs from adults. The intervention must correspond to this state of development;
- The particular characteristics of each young person's situation have to be taken into account to provide the right service at the right time. For this, it is important that professionals working with the youth have the required skills. Young offenders need interventions with diversified approaches, methods, and resources. This principle highlights the need to adapt intervention to the nature and amplitude of the problem without a predetermined schedule;
- Rapid intervention is necessary since the notion of time for an adolescent is significantly different, particularly because changes happen rapidly during this phase of development. In the case of distinctive delinquency, pinpointing it early can be a turning point. It is necessary to intervene before the delinquent behaviour becomes entrenched;
- Parental involvement in intervention is essential. It must be sought out, valued, and supported throughout the intervention;
- The victims must be considered and the impact of the offence on them must be kept in mind. The young offender must be made aware of his actions and the damage caused. If appropriate, a process to repair damages must be proposed.
- Success of social intervention requires partners with existing resources around the adolescent.

PDs consider the young offender's differential assessment to determine services and to promote a differential approach during all phases of the intervention process. The assessment relies on the adolescent's delinquent trajectory and on his or her evolution in different areas of life. The assessment situates the risk of recidivism and identifies factors responsible for delinquency and its persistence. The differential assessment also helps determine the intensity and objective of the needed intervention in order to both protect the public and resolve the adolescent's problems related to recidivism risk factors. Throughout the intervention, assessment must be continuous in order to adjust the intervention to the adolescent's evolution. This individualized approach allows the adolescent's needs to be prioritized during the intervention. To help reach targeted objectives, a choice of resources is established. As described earlier, Québec has a network of community organizations with specialized staff who can offer young offenders a variety of quality services.

Differential assessment of young offenders is the foundation of all phases of intervention in delinquency: extrajudicial sanction programs, pre-sentence reports, community follow-up, custody and supervision in the community, reviews, etc. As well, PDs support the use of a variety of clinical tools, which contribute to systemizing data collection according to validated instruments and evaluating certain personality dimensions less accessible during interviews. Objectives of differential assessment include the following:

- to determine the adolescent's level of involvement in delinquency;
- to identify the factors contributing to delinquency;
- to determine the risk of recidivism;
- to assess the adolescent's resources and his/her capacity to benefit from available resources and services, as well as that of his/her family;

- to identify the most appropriate services to prevent recidivism using supervision, monitoring, guidance, help, and counselling; and
- to establish intervention objectives.

Efforts to elaborate on principles that guide intervention for young offenders and to implement the necessary resources were spread out over the past 20 years and provided Québec with a justice system and a system of intervention and rehabilitation that is recognized for its flexibility and efficiency.

The intervention model for young offenders and their families that is applied in Québec youth centres can be summarized as follows:

- It is a differentiated intervention;
- It is based on a differential assessment of the young offender's situation;
- It is supported by known theories and validated clinical tools;
- It favours alternatives to judicial measures and prioritizes mediation with victims for adolescents presenting 'common' delinquency;
- It uses the most appropriate measures within the judicial system of the YJCA to satisfy specific needs of adolescents with 'distinctive' delinquency;
- It involves parents as well as the collaboration of community resources;
- It takes into account the victims' interests.

Summary

Québec has had the lowest custody rate of young offenders in Canada for a number of years (Bala, Carrington, and Roberts 2009). As a result, there have been a number of inquiries as to why and as to what the implications have been. Without comparing the evolution of the youth-offender systems in other provinces to that of Québec's, it appears that many answers to these questions can be found in Québec's unique cultural, social, and political history related to the evolution of approaches to young offenders. Most of what is presented in this chapter is intended to help provide insight into the opposition in Québec to the YCJA when it was submitted as well as to the amendment proposed in Bill C-4. There was also opposition to the YCJA elsewhere in Canada, especially from the Canadian Criminal Justice Association (1998).

From a historical standpoint, one of the first elements presented in this chapter was the implementation of modalities to take charge of youth offenders that were distinct from those for adults, recognizing their different needs. In terms of Québec, the Juvenile Delinquents Act of 1908 is another important moment regarding the history of the youth offender system (Dubois and Trépanier 1999). In the 1950s, a series of initiatives in Québec demonstrated that it is possible to implement effective rehabilitation programs for youth offenders being held in open custody (Le Blanc 1983). The opening of the Philippe-Pinel Institute enabled the creation of specialized assessment and treatment programs for young offenders who presented with severe mental disorders. Throughout the 1970s, four events had a major impact on improving rehabilitation services for youth offenders in Québec: (1) initiatives that tested alternative measures for young offenders; (2) the major reorganization of all social services; (3) the creation of social-service centres; and (4) the Youth Protection Act of Québec. Within the act, youth protection directors were appointed, and later, in the 1980s, they were mandated under the Young Offenders Act. All of these events were significant in the development of today's services and today's philosophy behind the care of young offenders in Québec.

Following the experiment in Boscoville, it became clear that one unique method of rehabilitation was not sufficient for all youth offenders. Research demonstrated the need to develop a differential perspective. As noted in the Jasmin II Report (1995), a consensus of all actors of the judicial and social-service systems stated that it is possible to implement effective interventions that respect youth rights and offer the right measure at the right time. Assessments were recognized as fundamental in determining the best measures for young offenders. In addition to providing assistance to less serious types of young offenders, it became evident that there was a need to develop specialized programs for high-risk offenders. Programs involving intensive probation with treatment were then tested for youth offenders (offenders that would have normally been placed in custody) who were receptive to the intervention, and who had families to support them and participate in the rehabilitation process.

Because of the YCJA's emphasis on the gravity of the offence and because the act does not take into account the youth's needs, recourse to such a differential approach became almost impossible. For example, for professionals, it appeared it was no longer possible to direct young offenders who had committed serious offences to intensive follow-up programs in the community. The overall rigidity of the YCJA is one of the main reasons for Québec's opposition to the act. Specifically, it has been recognized for some time now that the offence for which a young person gets arrested is rarely a realistic reflection of his or her criminal capacity, or of his or her prior offences (Le Blanc 1986).

The development of psycho-education and criminology as professions also contributed to the improvement of practices and influenced the move toward the rehabilitation of young offenders in Québec. The training given to the personnel working with youth offenders during the 1960s and the 1970s was particularly important; indeed, most youth workers today have a university education in their field.

The principles associated with the rehabilitation of young offenders in Québec have been supported by a meta-analysis (see Lipsey meta-analyses, especially that of 2009). The 'Québec model' has also been supported by the research work of Canadian experts in the field. For example, Andrews and Bonta (2004) have documented the necessity of choosing the best measure when considering offenders' risk of recidivism, their criminogenic needs, and the most effective approach for treatment given their characteristics. Supported by research and reinforced by the historical evolution of measures for youth offenders in the province of Québec, provincial directors, clinicians, researchers, politicians, and a large part of the Québec population have opposed, and still firmly oppose, the YCJA, which for them, gives too much importance to the gravity of the offence to the detriment of the adolescents' needs and capacity.

But is the position of Québec really different from the rest of Canada? As cited by Trépanier (2004) a Federal-Provincial-Territorial Task Force on Youth Justice (1996) already exposed that important differences do exist between Québec and the rest of Canada:

> Quebec's approach to youth justice appears to be more in keeping with what is found in western European countries: the over-arching goal is the rehabilitation of young offenders within a framework that respects the rights of young persons . . . Quebec's approach to youth justice cannot be simply transplanted to the rest of the country. Quebec's approach serves as an important reminder, however, that the apparent 'need' to reform the *Act* is as much or more a function of values, attitudes and perceptions as it is of real (or objectifiable) needs.[9]

Is this still true? . . . History will speak for itself.

Key Terms

alternative justice agencies

Boscoville

differential intervention

dynamic security

extrajudicial programs

psycho-educative model

Review Questions

1. Explain why the expression 'the right measure at the right time for the right person' is particular to Québec.

2. Identify five measures applied in Québec under the YCJA that exemplify the principle 'the right measure at the right time for the right person'.

3. How do you understand Québec's opposition to the YCJA?

4. How does psycho-education apply to young offenders' rehabilitation?

5. Name seven characteristics of the intervention model used by Québec's youth centres.

Critical Thinking Questions

1. After comparing this chapter to others in the book, do you have any information that demonstrates that Québec's rehabilitation model is really different than that of other provinces?

2. How do you explain the difference in custody rate between Québec and the rest of Canada?

3. After reading this chapter, do you consider that the precedence of social intervention over court intervention is justified?

4. Explain how the meta-analyses of the past decades on offenders' rehabilitation can justify Québec's position toward the rehabilitation of youth offenders.

Suggested Readings

Bala, N., Carrington, P.J., and Roberts, J.V. (2009). Evaluating the Youth Criminal Justice Act after five years: A qualified success. *Canadian Journal of Criminology and Criminal Justice, 51* (2): 131–68.

Barber, J, and Doob, A.N. (2004). An analysis of public support for severity and proportionality in the sentencing of youthful offenders. *Canadian Journal of Criminology and Criminal Justice, 46*(3): 327–42.

Hogeveen, B. (2005). If we are tough on crime, if we punish crime, then people get the message: Constructing and governing the punishable young offender in Canada during the late 1990s. *Punishment and Society, 7*(1): 73–89.

Joyal, R. (2000). *L'évolution de la protection de l'enfance au Québec: Des origines à nos jours.* Sainte-Foy, QC: Presses de l'Université du Québec.

Lipsey, M.W. (2009). The primary factors that characterize effective interventions with juvenile offenders: A meta-analytic overview. *Victims & Offenders, 4*(2): 124–47.

Trépanier, J. (2004). What did Quebec not want? Opposition to the adoption of the Youth Criminal Justice Act in Quebec. *Canadian Journal of Criminology and Criminal Justice, 46*(3): 276–300.

Suggested Weblinks

Québec Justice Department: The Youth Criminal Justice Act: The Legal Procedure

www.justice.gouv.qc.ca/english/publications/generale/projud-a.htm

● This website presents an explanation of the YCJA. Other relevant links are also given.

Jeune pour Jeunes: Your Rights and Obligations

www.jeunepourjeunes.com/en

● A Québec site on laws. Some sections explain the judicial procedures for youth. Other sections aim to inform Québecers of their rights and obligations by providing legal information in everyday language.

Endnotes

1. Article 40: If a person has reasonable cause to believe that a child has committed an offence against any act or regulation in force in Québec, the youth protection director shall be informed of the case before the institution of any judicial proceeding.

2. In Québec, the director of youth protection and others authorized by the director (professionals in humane sciences, including social workers, psychologists, and criminologists) are competent to choose the measures. These professionals are the people in the best position to evaluate each youth's particular situation and choose the best orientation for him or her.

3. 'Precedence of social intervention over court intervention' is defined as the optimal match between the troubled juvenile's needs and intervention. See: Le Blanc, M., Dionne, J., Proulx, J., Grégoire, J. C. and Trudeau-Le Blanc, P. (1998). Intervenir autrement: un modèle différentiel pour les adolescents en difficulté. Montréal, Québec: Presses de l'Université de Montréal.

4. All custody measures in Québec consist of a rehabilitation program allowing a series of systematic and intensive interventions, using the most appropriate techniques that aim to redirect the juvenile delinquent. In every rehabilitation centre, only trained professionals intervene, not the keepers or guardians.

5. Bilan des Directeurs de la protection de la jeunesse /Directeurs provinciaux 2009, Association des centres jeunesse du Québec (Results from Directors of Youth Protection/Provincial Directors 2009, Association of Youth Protectors of Québec). Retrieved from www.acjq.qc.ca/public/a14178bc-45b5-4a12-b27e-38017be2da39/mes_documents/bilans/bilan_dpj_2009.pdf.

6. Ministère de la Justice et ministère de la Santé et des Services sociaux du Québec (1995). Les jeunes contrevenants : Au nom . . . et au-delà de la loi, rapport du groupe de travail chargé d'étudier l'application de la Loi sur les jeunes contrevenant au Québec (Rapport Jasmin ll), 36–37.

7. Unofficial translation from excerpts of Ministère de la Justice et ministère de la Santé et des Services sociaux du Québec (1995). Les jeunes contrevenants: Au nom . . . et au-delà de la loi, rapport du groupe de travail chargé d'étudier l'application de la Loi sur les jeunes contrevenant au Québec (Rapport Jasmin II), 36–37.

8. In order to correctly reflect the positions of the provincial directors, from this point up to the summary section, the text is composed of some excerpts taken from the 'Reference manual guiding the application of the Youth Criminal Justice Act in youth centers' (2004) of Hamel, P. and Paradis, R. for the Ministry of Health and Social Services in Québec, 11–55. The translation of the text hereby presented is not official.

9. Fuller accounts can be found in McGuire (1997).

References

Agee, V.L. (1979). *Treatment of the violent incorrigible adolescent.* Lexington, MA: Lexington Books.

Andrews, D.A. and Bonta, J. (1998). *The psychology of criminal conduct* (2nd ed.). Cincinnati, OH: Anderson Publishing Co.

Andrews, D.A. and Bonta, J. (2003). *The psychology of criminal conduct* (3rd ed.). Cincinnati, OH: Anderson Publishing Co.

Armstrong, T.L. and Altshuler, P.M. (1991). *Intensive interventions with high risks youths: Promising approaches in juvenile probation and parole.* Monsey, NY: Criminal Justice Press.

Association des centres jeunesse du Québec. (2009). *Bilan des directeurs de la protection de la jeunesse/directeurs provinciaux* (Results from directors of youth protection/provincial directors, Association of Youth Protectors of Québec). Retrieved from http://www.acjq.qc.ca/public/a14178bc-45b5-4a12-b27e-38017be2da39/mes_documents/bilans/bilan_dpj_2009.pdf

Bala, N., Carrington, P.J., and Roberts, J.V. (2009). Evaluating the Youth Criminal Justice Act after five years: A qualified success. *Canadian Journal of Criminology and Criminal Justice, 51* (2), 131–68.

Boisvert, Y, Bisaillon, C., and Adam, J. (1988) *Les jeunes auteurs d'homicide: Rétrospective et prospective: L'expérience de Boscoville.* Montréal: Les Cahiers de Boscoville.

Borgo, J. (1987). Treating the violent offender. In J.M. MacLatchie (Ed.), *Insights into Violence in contemporary Canadian society* (pp. 298–304). Ottawa: The John Howard Society of Canada.

Canadian Criminal Justice Association. (1998). *Comments of the Canadian criminal justice association on strategy for the renewal of youth justice.* Ottawa: Canadian Criminal Justice Association.

Capul, M. and Lemay, M. (1996). *De l'éducation spécialisée.* Paris: Érès.

Cournoyer, L.G. and Dionne, J. (2007). Efficacité du programme de probation intensive du centre jeunesse de Montréal-Institut Universitaire: La récidive officielle. *Criminologie, 40*(1) : 155–83.

Dubois, P. and Trépanier, J. (1999). L'adoption de la loi sur les jeunes délinquants de 1908. Étude comparée des quotidiens Montréalais et Torontois. *Revue d'histoire de l'Amérique française, 52*(3): 345–81.

Ducharme, J. (1996). Boscoville de 1941 à 1996: Un centre en constante réadaptation. *Revue canadienne de psycho-éducation 25*(2): 107–19.

Ducharme, J. (1999). *Saute d'abord! Un parcours de trente-cinq ans en psychoéducation.* Montréal: Sciences et Culture.

Duret, A. (2004). LSJPA: La mobilisation du jeune et de ses parents dans le continuum de services aux jeunes contrevenants: Deuxième partie: Le projet intervention rapide en délinquance (Mobilisation of the youth and the parents in the continuum of services to youth offenders: The rapid intervention project for delinquency). *Défi jeunesse, 10*(2): 8–13.

Ellis, A. and Dryden, W. (1997). *The practice of rational emotive behavior therapy.* New York: Springer.

Foucault, P. (1984). *Aider . . . malgré tout: Essai sur l'historique des centres de réadaptation au Québec.* Montréal: Les Éditions des centres d'accueil du Québec.

Fréchette, M. and Le Blanc, M. (1987). *Délinquances et délinquants.* Chicoutimi, QC: Gaëtan Morin.

Gendreau, G. (1978). *L'intervention psychoéducative: Solution ou défi?* Paris: Éditions Fleurus.

Gendreau, P., Coggin, C., and Fulton, B. (2000). Intensive supervision in probation and parole. In C.R. Hollin (Ed.), *Handbook of offender assessment and treatment* (pp. 195–204). Chichester, Great Britain: John Wiley.

Glasser, W. (1990). *Reality therapy: A new approach to psychiatry.* New York: Harper Row.

Guindon, J. (1970). *Les étapes de la rééducation des jeunes délinquants et des autres . . .* Paris: Fleurus.

Hamel, P. and Paradis, R. (2004). *L'application de la loi sur le système de justice pénale pour les adolescents dans les centres jeunesse: Manuel de référence* (Reference manual guiding the application of the Youth Criminal Justice Act in youth centres). Ministère de la santé et des services sociaux du Québec. Québec: Gouvernement du Québec.

Hoge, R.D. and Andrews, D.A. (1994). *The youth level of service/Case management inventory and manual.* Ontario: Department of Psychology, Carleton University.

Jesness, C.F. (1971). *Manual for the Jesness personality inventory.* Palo Alto, CA: Consulting Psychologist Press.

Joyal, R. (2000). *L'évolution de la protection de l'enfance au Québec: Des origines à nos jours.* Sainte-Foy, QC: Presses de l'Université du Québec.

Laporte, C. (2005). *Suivi intensif différencié dans la communauté* (Differentiated intensive follow-up in the community) (Unpublished manuscript). Montréal: Centre d'expertise sur la délinquance des jeunes et les difficultés du comportement, Centre jeunesse de Montréal-Institut universitaire.

Le Blanc, M. (1983). *Boscoville: La rééducation évaluée.* Montréal: HMH.

Le Blanc, M. (1986). Pour une approche intégrative de la conduite délinquante des adolescents. *Criminologie, 19*(2): 73–96.

Le Blanc, M. (1994). Les mesures pour jeune délinquant. In D. Szabo et M. Le Blanc (Eds.), *Traité de criminologie empirique* (2e éd.). Montréal: Presses de l'Université de Montréal.

Le Blanc, M., Dionne, J., Grégoire, J., Proulx, J., and Trudeau-Le Blanc, P. (1998). *Intervenir autrement: Un modèle différentiel pour les adolescents en difficulté.* Montréal: Les Presses de l'Université de Montréal.

Le Blanc, M. and Fréchette, M. (1989). *Male criminal activity from childhood through youth: Multilevel and developmental perspectives.* New York: Springer-Verlag.

Lipsey, M.W. (2009). The primary factors that characterize effective interventions with juvenile offenders: A meta-analytic overview. *Victims & Offenders, 4*(2): 124–47.

McGuire, M. (1997). C-19—An act to amend the Young Offenders Act and the Criminal Code: 'Getting tougher?' *Canadian Journal of Criminology, 39*: 185–214.

Martinson, R. (1974). What works? Questions and answers about prison reform. *The Public Interest, 35*: 22–54.

Ménard, S. (2003) Des enfants sous surveillance: La rééducation des jeunes délinquants au Québec (1840–1950). Montréal: VLB Éditeur.

Ministry of Health and Social Services. (2008). Statistical annual report of youth centers (AS-480 forms) (Unpublished manuscript). Québec: Ministère de la Santé et des Services sociaux.

Ministère de la Justice et Ministère de la Santé et des Services Sociaux du Québec. (1995). Les jeunes contrevenants: *Au nom . . . et au-delà de la loi* (In the name of the law and beyond it*): Rapport du groupe chargé d'étudier l'application de la loi sur les jeunes contrevenants au Québec (Rapport Jasmin II).* Québec: Gouvernement du Québec.

Parizeau, A. (1976). Le droit des mineurs et l'emprisonnement des jeunes au Québec. *Criminologie, 9*(1-2) : 118–47.

Piché, J.-P. (2006). *L'encadrement des jeunes contrevenants dans la communauté: Guide d'intervention en matière de probation juvénile,* Ministère de la Santé et des Services Sociaux (The follow-up of youth offenders in the community: Intervention guide in juvenile probation). Québec: Gouvernement du Québec.

Piché, J-P. and Fréchette, M. (1995). Mesure probatoire intensive pour adolescents contrevenants: Application et efficacité. Québec: Les Centres jeunesse de Québec.

Platt, A.M. (1997). *The child savers: The invention of delinquency.* Chicago: University of Chicago Press.

Redl, F. and Wineman, D. (1951). *Children who hate.* New York: Free Press.

Renou, M. (1991). La psychoéducation: Une critique rétrospective de la conception traditionnelle. *Revue Canadienne de Psycho-Éducation 20*(2): 151–67.

Rumilly, R. (1978). *Boscoville.* Montréal: Éditions Fides.

Sullivan, C., Grant, M.Q., & Grant, J.D. (1957). The development of interpersonal maturity: Applications to delinquency. *Psychiatry, 20*(4): 373–95.

Szabo, D. and Le Blanc, M. (1994). *Traité de criminologie empirique.* Montréal: Les Presses de l'Université de Montréal.

Szabo, D. and Le Blanc, M. (2004). *Traité de criminologie empirique* (2e éd.). Montréal: Les Presses de l'Université de Montréal.

Trépanier, J. (2004). What did Quebec not want? Opposition to the adoption of the Youth Criminal Justice Act in Quebec. *Canadian Journal of Criminology and Criminal Justice, 46*(3): 276–300.

Trieschman, A.E., Brendtro, L.K., and Whittaker, J.K. (1969). *The other 23 hours: Child-care work with emotionally disturbed children in a therapeutic milieu.* Piscataway, NJ: Transaction Publishers.

Warren, M.Q. (1966). Interpersonal maturity level classification: Juvenile diagnosis and treatment for low, middle and high maturity delinquents. Sacramento, CA: Youth Authority.

Warren, M.Q. (1969). The case for differential treatment of delinquents. *The Annals of the American Academy of Political and Social Science, 381*: 47–59.

15 Juvenile Justice and Restorative Justice: Reflecting on Developments in British Columbia

Brenda Morrison and Colleen Pawlychka

Overview

This chapter focuses on the development of restorative justice in British Columbia within a wider theoretical and institutional analysis of justice reforms in British Columbia and Canada. The chapter begins with broad reflections on juvenile justice practice and outcomes, suggesting that despite various legislative reforms the juvenile justice system remains focused on the juvenile as the bad apple, within a system of social control. The theory and practice of restorative justice widens the humanistic lens of justice, moving from a mechanism of social control to one of social engagement. The chapter also reflects on legislative and diversionary restorative practices that have influenced developments in British Columbia, in particular, victim offender reconciliation programs, circle sentencing, and conferencing, as well as the development of community accountability programs. The chapter then reflects on these current practices, based on propositions put forward in the Green Paper recently released in the UK, and on an innovative youth-at-risk program, ROCA, based in Chelsea, Massachusetts. The findings suggest that holistic reform within the Canadian juvenile justice system has yet to come, because the justice system has yet to embrace the theoretical and practical research and development that has emerged internationally regarding potentially effective restorative justice programs.

Introduction

Over 20 years have passed since *Taking Responsibility*, a report authored by a House of Commons Justice Committee (the Daubney Committee), recommended the use and evaluation of restorative justice in Canada. The report stated that the '. . . Committee found the evidence it heard across the country about the principles of restorative justice [RJ] compelling', and recommended that governments at all levels support the expansion and evaluation of RJ programs at all stages of the criminal justice process (Daubney 2010). In particular, Recommendation 19 of the report recommended that the federal government, preferably in conjunction with provincial/territorial governments, support the expansion and evaluation throughout Canada of **victim–offender reconciliation programs (VORP)** at all stages of the criminal justice process that (a) provide substantial support to victims through effective victim services, and (b) encourage a high degree of community participation.

In 1996 Canada became the first country in the world to include restorative justice, through the provision of reparations to victims and communities, as a legitimate option within the Criminal Code (see Section 718.2 (e)). While Canadians have much to be proud of for their contributions to the development and expansion of **restorative justice (RJ)** programs and practices internationally, restorative justice remains at the margins of the justice system in Canada compared to developments in other countries. This chapter explores the history of the development of restorative justice as it relates to juvenile justice, using developments in British Columbia as a case study.

Juvenile Justice Legislation: Social Control to 'Off Ramps'

Canada has come a long way since the Juvenile Delinquents Act of 1908. Under this act, youth were convicted of juvenile delinquency rather than criminal behaviour, and were considered to be misguided products of improper upbringing by their family (Green and Healy 2003; Tustin and Lutes 2010; see also Chapter 1 in this textbook). Because youth were not considered responsible for their actions, the focus of conviction was on rehabilitation, re-education, and guidance, with the state taking over the parental role and decision making of the youth.

In 1984, the Juvenile Delinquents Act was replaced by the Young Offenders Act (YOA), reflecting then dominant societal views of young offenders and crime—specifically, that youth were responsible for their behaviour and should be held accountable for their crimes. While this act protected youth by guaranteeing due process, it extended much the same treatment to youth as was extended to adults. Youth were referred to as offenders rather than as delinquents, were represented by counsel in court proceedings, and, similar to courts of adults, courts dealing with young offenders were open to the public (Green and Healy 2003). Young offenders, like adult offenders, became viewed as

victim–offender reconciliation programs (VORP)
A process through which a trained mediator, often a volunteer, brings offenders and victims in a criminal event together to achieve a resolution that is satisfactory to both parties (Community Justice Initiatives Association 2011).

restorative justice (RJ)
While conceptualized in many different ways—*encounter*, *reparative*, and *transformative*—RJ is a theory of justice that emphasizes repairing the harm caused or revealed by unjust behaviour. Restoration is best accomplished through inclusive and cooperative processes (Johnstone and Van Ness 2011).

the 'bad apples' of society, requiring punishment, mainly in the form of custody, as an institutional mechanism to challenge and change their behaviours.

While the YOA increased the use of custody for young offenders, various societal factors contributed to wide criticism that the justice system was not tough enough on them, overprotecting repeat offenders while allowing increasing victimization of innocent, law-abiding citizens. Inaccurate or incomplete media reports of individual cases combined with misconceptions, even within the justice sector, eroded public confidence in the YOA, fuelling a growing 'us v. them' mentality as well as public demand for a more punitive response to youth crime (Tustin and Lutes 2010). By the 1990s, even though youth crime was decreasing, the public believed that levels were significantly higher, and there was 'clearly . . . a gap between fact and public perception of youth crime levels' (Green and Healy 2003, p. 32). The response was increased use of custody as an answer to youth crime, until 1999, when Anne McLellan, Canada's Justice Minister at the time, declared that we 'incarcerate youth at a rate of four times that of adults and twice that of many US states' (in Green and Healy 2003, p. 32). In fact, Canada's youth incarceration rate was the highest in the Western world (Tustin and Lutes 2010, p. 2).

Although earlier chapters of this textbook (see in particular Chapter 3) have outlined specific provisions of the Youth Criminal Justice Act (YCJA), we will highlight here particular parts of the act that are relevant to promoting the use of restorative justice measures and programs. In April 2003, the YCJA replaced the YOA, providing legislative direction to reduce the use of custody in all but the most serious and violent offences. The YCJA also provides legislative direction that recognizes that an effective response to youth crime must consider the limited developmental capacity of youth and must integrate the various factors affecting their lives, such as education, mental health, family, and community. Specific restorative justice values that may be seen to underlie the legislation include:

- Societal responsibility to address developmental challenges and needs of young persons in order to guide them into adulthood;
- Communities and families should work in partnership through multidisciplinary approaches to address crime prevention by addressing its underlying causes, providing guidance and support to young persons, particularly those at risk;
- Information regarding youth justice, crime and measures taken to address youth crime should be publicly available;
- Young persons have rights and freedoms, including those set out in the United Nations Convention on the Rights of the Child, in the Canadian Charter of Rights and Freedoms and the Canadian Bill of Rights;
- The youth criminal justice system should command respect, and take into account the interests of victims;
- The youth justice system should foster responsibility and ensure accountability through meaningful consequences and effective rehabilitation and reintegration; and
- The youth justice system should reserve its most serious interventions for the most serious crimes and reduce over-reliance on incarceration. (Department of Justice 2002)

While these are general principles outlined in the Preamble of the act, overall they reflect the acceptance of an approach that is consistent with restorative justice. For instance, the YCJA aims to prevent crime by addressing underlying circumstances of offending behaviours and by emphasizing rehabilitation and reintegration of young persons into society, with specific consideration for the reduced level of maturity and greater level of dependency of young persons on adults. Consequences resulting from crime are to be meaningful to the young person, and must promote accountability while being fair and proportionate to the crime. The YCJA also makes specific provisions for young persons to be heard and involved in the processes that lead to decision making. Finally, Sec. 3(1) of the act emphasizes that measures taken against young persons should:

(c) (i)   Reinforce respect for societal values;

   (ii)   Encourage the repair of harm done to victims and the community;

  (iii)   Be meaningful for the individual young person given his or her needs and level of development and, where appropriate, involve the parents, the extended family, the community and social or other agencies in the young person's rehabilitation and reintegration, and

  (iv)   Respect gender, ethnic, cultural and linguistic differences and respond to the needs of aboriginal young persons and of young persons with special requirements. (Department of Justice 2002)

Thus, although the YCJA makes no direct reference to restorative justice, there is general agreement that the act 'does seem to open the door to the development of initiatives generally associated with restorative justice' (Charbonneau 2005, p. 75). For example, numerous extrajudicial measures form an essential first response to youth crime rather than a possible alternative to court as was the case under the YOA. That is, the act requires that police and Crown attorneys consider extrajudicial measures, including informal warnings, police or Crown cautions, police referrals to community programs or agencies, referrals to pre-charge screening programs or youth justice committees, or conferences (Tustin and Lutes 2010; see also Chapters 3 and 4 in this textbook).

Two of the primary methods of allowing for restorative justice initiatives are the inclusion of victims in the process, and the authorization of restorative justice conferences at various stages of the process. Under Section 5, the YCJA directs (in part) that extrajudicial measures must:

- encourage acknowledgement and reparation of harm to the victim and community;
- encourage families, including extended families, of young persons, and the community to become involved in the design and implementation of those measures; and
- provide an opportunity for victims to participate in decisions related to the measures selected and to receive reparation.

While conferences were not included in the YOA, the YCJA authorizes their use by a youth justice court judge, the provincial director, a police officer, a justice of the peace, a prosecutor or youth worker, or a youth justice committee. Defined in the YCJA, Sec. 2(1), as 'a group of persons who are convened to give advice in accordance with section 19', conferences refer to various types of processes in which affected or interested parties come together to formulate plans to 'address the circumstances and needs involved' (Department of Justice Canada 2002, p. 6) and may take the form of **family group conferencing**, youth justice committees, community accountability panels, **sentencing circles** and inter-agency case conferences' (Department of Justice Canada 2002, p. 6). The inclusion of conferences in the YCJA and the broad nature of their mandate allow for some restorative justice initiatives through the inclusion of victims in the process of reparation of harm, and through the healing of young persons and communities.

With the new requirement that extrajudicial measures, including restorative justice initiatives, be considered, there has been a decline in young persons charged by police, 'with a 30 per cent rate of youths cleared otherwise' since implementation of the YCJA (Tustin and Lutes 2010, p. 27). This indicates some measure of success in the YCJA (see also Chapter 4 in this textbook for additional data in support of this argument). However, use of these extrajudicial measures is not mandatory; rather, police and Crown attorneys need only consider such measures in order to satisfy legislative

family group conferencing

'. . . a process of collaborative planning in situations where decisions need to be made for children or youth. It is a formal meeting where members of a child or youth's immediate family come together with extended kin and members.' (*Source:* BC Ministry of Children and Family Development 2005, p. 2)

sentencing circles

'Sentencing circles . . . invite . . . members of the community to join the judge, prosecutor, defence counsel, police, social service providers, community elders, along with the offender, the victim and their families and supporters, [to] meet in a circle to discuss the offence, factors that may have contributed to it, sentencing options, and ways of reintegrating the offender into the community.' (*Source:* Department of Justice Canada 2002) requirements. Therefore, it is important to examine not only the reduction in charges but also the primary factors that play a role in the police and Crown attorney decision making regarding whether to divert these youth, and where these youth should be diverted to. That is, as Tustin and Lutes (2010, p. 30) point out, given that the police and prosecutors play a key role in ensuring that youth are diverted out of the formal system, there must be adequate 'off ramps' toward which we can divert youth. These 'off ramps', referring to diversionary measures or extrajudicial measures, might include existing community programs, school mediation programs, or programs operated by local agencies. It is equally important that police and Crown attorneys not only are aware of these initiatives but that they support them or consider them to be the best possible avenue to hold the youth accountable. To this end, the reality is that although there are numerous initiatives available within communities, programs tend to be widely used and recognized only if they are endorsed by the Attorney General to whom Crown attorneys are accountable (Tustin and Lutes 2010, p. 30).

Despite these legislative changes in Canada, which have certainly influenced restorative justice initiatives for youth, particularly initiatives within BC, current evidence suggests that these legislative changes alone are not enough. Focusing on youth as 'bad apples' while not providing and supporting initiatives that embrace a truly holistic approach to reform leaves our youth, and our youth justice system, unengaged and vulnerable to criminal or antisocial behaviours.

The Development of Restorative Justice in BC: The Intersection of Three Practices

Victim–Offender Reconciliation Programs

The restorative justice movement in Canada traces its modern inception to a landmark juvenile justice case in Elmira, Ontario, in 1974, which launched the Kitchener Experiment (see Peachy 1989), where two young men destroyed the property of 22 victims. In a courageous and insightful move, the decisions and actions of Mark Yantzi, a Mennonite probation officer, and Judge Gordon McConnell set a precedent for a new response to juvenile delinquency in Canada. Officer Yantzi, with the encouragement and support of Dave Worth of Mennonite Central Committee, attached an addendum to the back of the pre-sentence report, recommending that the offending juveniles be ordered to knock on the doors of their victims, apologize for their crimes, listen to what the victims had to say to them, determine the amount of restitution, and ask for forgiveness. Judge McConnell saw no legal precedence to order these actions by the juveniles. Officer Yantzi, weighing the benefits offered by the court with those of a face-to-face meeting with the victims, spoke with the juveniles, convincing them that volunteering to perform these acts of restoration would allow the judge to include them as part of a probation order. Russ Kelly (2010) was one of those two young offenders:

> On that day, my life changed forever as I managed to overcome the challenges of a punitive society and turn my life around. Meeting my victims taught me a valuable lesson in humanity and I never damaged anyone's property after that, but I still had a problem. It took another 20 years to kick my addiction to drugs and alcohol. I was tired of waking up sick and tired. And, I was tired of going to funerals. I was on the road to nowhere. So, I had to make a choice. I moved, changed jobs, stopped going to hotels, and stopped hanging out with the people that could feed my established habit. Still, I was taking 2 steps forward and 1 step back. The journey ahead was a rough one as I tried to escape my self-destructive life. That is when I met Irene and we fell in love. She gave me purpose and reason. My life

improved as I strive to be a better person. . . . My circumstance led me down a dead-end road . . . my courage allowed me to find another path. (Kelly 2010).

This landmark case marked the beginning of Kitchener's victim–offender reconciliation program (VORP) and became a foundation program for community justice initiatives in Kitchener-Waterloo, Ontario. As interest grew within Mennonite communities, this influence spread across Canada to Langley, in the Fraser Valley of British Columbia.

David Gustafson received British Columbia's first victim–offender reconciliation program (VORP) referral in May 1982, with funding support coming from the Langley Mennonite Fellowship. In 1985, after being awarded an alternative measures contract with British Columbia's Ministry of the Attorney General, the Fraser Valley Community Justice Initiatives (FVCJI) was formed to operate VORP and other related programming for both juveniles and adults (Gustafson 2004). Over time VORP expanded into the adjacent cities of Surrey, White Rock, and Delta. In 2002, provincial funding was cut for adult cases, limiting the program to juveniles. Despite these cutbacks, as reported in FVCJI's annual reports (cited in Table 15.1), the evidence of VORP's effectiveness of youth accountability to the community is remarkable.

FVCJI's funding for juveniles, from the Ministry of Children and Family Development, ended July 31, 2004, and with this came the end of VORP in British Columbia. Despite this loss of funding and recognition, FVCJI remained committed to serving young people in its community. Through building on local partnerships, FVCJI developed a new funding structure, and developed Restorative Youth Services to replace VORP.

Research and development of VORP has been more fully realized in the United States. Following the Kitchener experiment, VORP was initiated in Elkhart, Indiana, in 1978, under the direction of Howard Zehr, also a Mennonite, and then spread across the country (Claasen and Zehr 1989; Gehm and Umbreit 1985). For example, Central Valley, California, began using VORP in 1982, and since 2002 VORP has been administered by the Center for Peacemaking and Conflict Studies at Fresno Pacific University. The Center's data shows that between 1983 and 2009, 10 474 cases have been managed by the Central Valley Program. In 2000, VORP programs across six counties in California (Los Angeles, Mendocino, Orange, Santa Barbara, Santa Clara, and Sonoma) were evaluated (Evje and Cushman 2000). This matched comparison study found 'that generally, as compared with juveniles not participating in the program, juveniles in VORPs paid more restitution and were less likely to re-offend, and that VORP participants (both victims and offenders) were satisfied with the program'

Table 15.1 Fraser Valley Community Justice Initiatives (FVCJI) Data on VORPs

2002/2003

City	Cases	Agreements Fulfilled
Langley	31	88%
Surrey	58	100%

2003/2004 (not a full year, hence the lower numbers below)

City	Cases	Agreements Fulfilled
Langley	5	100%
Surrey	38	100%

(Evje and Cushman 2000, p. 1). In 1998, a survey administered by the Center for Restorative Justice and Peacemaking at the University of Minnesota estimated that about 300 programs exist in the United States (Umbreit and Greenwood 1998). No such national survey has been conducted in Canada. Other than the meta-analysis carried out by the Department of Justice (Latimer, Dowden, and Muise 2001), there has been little effort to collect systemic data across the country, from mapping the existing programs, to process- and outcome-based evaluations.

VORP is widely considered to be the foundational program within the rise of the restorative justice movement, particularly in North America (see Zehr 1990). The influence of VORP has also spread beyond North America, particularly to Europe and the United Kingdom. Given this influence, the rise and fall of VORP in British Columbia, a community-based program with solid evaluation data, begs answers to deeper questions of policy and praxis.

Sentencing/Peacemaking Circles

In Canada, the harsh realities of the justice system for Aboriginal people began to be more fully recognized in the late 1980s and early 1990s, with disproportional representation and high recidivism and crime rates being widely recognized (see Dickson-Gilmore and La Prairie 2005). This was particularly true in Canada's northern territories and Prairie provinces. Recognizing that a shift in judicial practice needed to take place, Judge Barry Stuart of the Yukon Territorial Court adjourned the case of *R. v. Moses* (1992)—who pled guilty to carrying a baseball bat with the intention of assaulting a police officer—and convened the first sentencing circle, drawing on traditional Aboriginal practice in the Yukon Territory (see Stuart 1996).

Since that decision, sentencing circles have been used in many Aboriginal communities throughout Canada. These sentencing circles are attempting to incorporate what are identified as Aboriginal traditions and values. The sentencing circle itself is not a traditional practice of Aboriginal peoples in Canada that is now being re-instituted. Rather, it is very much a creation of the existing system, introduced within Aboriginal communities for the most part by the judiciary serving these communities (Crnkovich 1995, p. 2).

Traditional practice is based on three guiding premises: (1) a criminal offence represents a breach of relationship between the offender and the victim/community; (2) the well-being of the community is dependent on healing these breaches; and (3) the community is the best resource to address these breaches. A sentencing circle, as it was originally conceived, is a community-directed process that partners with the criminal justice system in an effort to build consensus on a sentencing plan (Griffiths and Hamilton 1996; Pranis 2005). Sentencing circles include a wide range of community members in the process: victims, victim supporters, offenders, offender supporters, judge, prosecutor, defence counsel, police, and court workers. In the early days, judges were the primary facilitators of circle hearings and this evolved to community members co-facilitating the circles (Crnkovich 1995).

The use of sentencing circles was supported by the Supreme Court of Canada in 1999 in the case of *R. v. Gladue* '. . . as an approach to remedying crime in which it is understood that all things are interrelated and that crime disrupts the harmony which existed prior to its occurrence, or at least which it is felt should exist . . . appropriateness of a particular sanction is largely determined by the needs of the victim, and the community, as well as the offender'. The Gladue case encouraged the use of alternatives to incarceration and, in endeavouring to remedy the dramatic overrepresentation of Aboriginal Canadians in our prisons and penitentiaries, recognized that restorative approaches resonated with traditional Aboriginal ways of dealing with conflict. Subsequently, the Gladue decision was legislated in the Criminal Code amendment (Section 718.2) in the sentencing principle that 'all available sanctions other than imprisonment that are reasonable in the circumstances should be considered for all offenders, with particular attention to the circumstances of aboriginal offenders'.

The use of sentencing circles facilitated or co-facilitated by judges never took hold in British Columbia. However, the use of **peacemaking circles**, facilitated by elders and community members, rests on the three same guiding principles and has been widely adopted in British Columbia as an important aspect of the Aboriginal Justice Strategy (AJS). This program is cost-shared at a federal level, with approximately 31 programs being supported. The program supports the use of traditional justice in Aboriginal communities, which may (or may not) include the use of peacekeeping circles. For example, the Vancouver Aboriginal Transformative Justice Services Program provides prevention, diversion, and alternative measures to Aboriginal people in the city of Vancouver. The program's main objectives are to offer a community-based process that focuses on repairing relationships among those affected by crime—i.e., the victim, the offender, their families, and the community—and to empower individuals to formulate appropriate responses and strategies to deal with the crime and participate directly in processes that affect the community's overall well-being. To accomplish these objectives, the Society utilizes a community council forum made up of volunteers, an elder, the victim and offender, and their support people to discuss the offence, its effects, and the causes of the behaviour that led to the offence. At the forum's conclusion, a healing plan is developed with the goal of making amends and positively reintegrating the offender into the community.

Again, there is no systematic data on the extent of use of sentencing or peacekeeping circles, and the outcomes achieved, in British Columbia. Instead, the most rigorous evaluations of sentencing circles to date have been conducted in New South Wales (NSW), Australia, where a pilot program in Nowra began in February 2002. In the first 12 months of the program's operation, 13 offender participants (11 male and 2 female) and 8 cases were examined. Surveys were completed by defence solicitors, police, prosecutors, the magistrate, defendants, and victims. The evaluation supported the effectiveness of sentencing circles, noting that this alternative justice process was effective in reducing barriers between the courts and Aboriginal people; raising the level of support for Aboriginal people; incorporating victim support; empowering the Aboriginal community; offering relevant sentencing options with community support; and reducing recidivism. The only deficit noted was the significant time commitment required to process an offender through a sentencing circle. The report recommended that sentencing circles be expanded to other regions of the state, where Aboriginal people reside. Based on this recommendation, other programs began operating throughout NSW.

A rigorous evaluation of sentencing circles was commissioned in 2006 (see New South Wales Attorney General's Department 2008), examining three aspects of recidivism (within a 15-month period): (1) reduction in frequency; (2) time to reoffend; and (3) reduction in seriousness of offending. Compared to the court processes, this study suggested that circle sentencing has no effect on any of these recidivism outcomes. As such this more rigorous study does not replicate the finding of the pilot study, which did report a reduction in recidivism. However, as this second study concludes, this finding should not be generalized to conclude that circle sentencing has no value simply because, at this time, it appears that the process has no short-term impact on reoffending. This study did not examine the impact of any of the other objectives of sentencing circles. For example, if the process strengthens the informal social controls in the communities served by the sentencing circle, the process may have a crime prevention value that cannot be quantified in studies of reoffending. It also may be the case that other objectives, such as increasing the confidence of Aboriginal communities in the sentencing process, must be first realized before the reoffending objective is realized. Beyond the justice system, other systemic influences (e.g., family, peer groups, alcohol and drug programs) may also need to be addressed through integrated community support mechanisms. The review of sentencing circles commissioned by the New South Wales Attorney General's Department concludes this:

peacemaking circles

Peacemaking circles draw directly from the tradition of the talking circle, common among indigenous people of North America. The physical format of the circle symbolizes shared leadership, equality, connection, and inclusion. Using very intentional structural elements—ceremony, a talking piece, a facilitator or keeper, guidelines, and consensus decision-making—circles aim to create a safe space for authentic dialogue.

> One of the most important unintended benefits of Circle Sentencing is the positive impact that participation has had for many of the Elders involved. Many of the Elders included in the research had a strong sense of achievement as a result of their participation, with discussions about the impact on their levels of pride, confidence and community status. (New South Wales Attorney General's Department 2008, p. 7)

Other unintended benefits include perceptions that community members take more responsibility for the actions of other members through their involvement in circle sentencing. It was also suggested in one location that circle sentencing has reduced the impact of factional issues. Several stakeholders highlighted the benefits of circle sentencing as a community-based approach for addressing domestic violence within Aboriginal communities, although more research and development is needed on this issue.

Family Group Conferencing

Family group conferencing (FGC) is likely the most internationally recognized model of restorative justice. Developed in New Zealand, this model was legislated through the Children, Young Persons and Their Families Act in 1989 as a youth justice mechanism that includes police warnings, police youth diversion, and family group conferences. Rather than being diverted from court to restorative justice (as is the case in British Columbia), young offenders in New Zealand are directed from restorative justice to court when an FGC, alone, is not deemed appropriate. In New Zealand, youth court is typically reserved for very serious offences. Like VORP, an FGC involves a facilitator; however, the range of participants is much broader and brings together the family and friends of the offender and victim. The mandate of an FGC is to (a) build understanding of the consequence of the crime, allowing young offenders to hear the full impact of the crime; and (b) develop a reparative plan. In New Zealand, an important step in this process is private family time between these two stages. This process is widely held to be derived from traditional Maori practice. For example, the *Handbook of Restorative Justice Programs* (United Nations 2006, p. 20), describes an FGC as

> based on the centuries old sanctioning and dispute resolution traditions of the Maori, the New Zealand aboriginal group. The model is now also widely used in modified form as a police-initiated diversion approach in South Australia, South Africa, Ireland, Lesotho, as well as cities in Minnesota, Pennsylvania and Montana.

It is interesting that neither Canada nor British Columbia is mentioned here, even though the *Handbook* was written by two Canadian researchers from British Columbia. Nevertheless, what appears most important is the Maori influence in the change of legislation, as Shannon Pakura (2005, p. 2) states:

> Regarding the origins of this development, let me emphasize that the law changed primarily because Maori were dissatisfied with the way professionals made decisions about them. Maori were distressed about the impact on them of these decisions and were no longer prepared to tolerate legal or professional systems that gave little weight to Maori customs, values and beliefs.

While there are historical connections with the Maori people in New Zealand, the connection between the indigenous peoples of New Zealand and family group conferencing has been deeply criticized (Cunneen 1997; Tauri 1999; Snyder 2001; Hakiaha 2004). In particular, the inclusion of family group decision making within a Western system of common law falls out of step with the larger cultural context of traditional Maori life and, as such, has not served to create more just responses for the indigenous people of New Zealand. Indeed it has been argued that extracting only certain elements of Maori traditional justice out of a broader system of Maori justice leads to 'selective and ahistorical claims . . . about indigenous social control conforming with the principles of restorative justice, while conveniently ignoring others' (Cunneen 2007, p. 43). Despite these criticisms, FGC is widely used internationally.

From New Zealand, FGC jumped the Tasman Sea to Australia in the early 1990s. In some states the private family group time remained part of the FGC process while in others it was dropped. For example, the well-known scripted Wagga Wagga (or Real Justice) model of an FGC does not include private family time; instead, all participants (victims, offenders, and their respective communities of care) remain together throughout the process as the emphasis is on the *encounter* between the parties affected by the harm (see McDonald, Thorsborne, Moore, Hyndman, and O'Connell 1995). This model was brought to British Columbia in the late 1990s and was adopted by the Royal Canadian Mounted Police (RCMP) as a diversion process from court (see Chatterjee and Elliott 2003). While sometimes known as an FGC, this scripted model has also been called a **community justice forum** and a community conference. For example, in 1998 Corporal James Cooley of the Royal Canadian Mounted Police 'E' Division was trained and began facilitating *community justice forums* and mentoring other individuals interested in restorative justice. In 2003 he became RCMP 'E' Division's restorative justice program director. This program is under the direction of the RCMP's Aboriginal Policing Branch yet serves a diverse range of communities, including schools. Again, no systematic data is readily available.

The British Columbia Ministry of Child and Family Development (MCFD) started to use FCG shortly after the implementation of the YCJA (2003). MCFD (2010) has the provincial government mandate for youth justice, and the YCJA emphasized extrajudicial measures. MCFD has 10 conference specialists who work on both youth-justice and child-protection cases. Probation officers can also facilitate FGC. Referrals for restorative conferencing are based on a judge's order and can be requested by a probation officer, by Crown counsel, or by defence counsel. Referrals are based on the voluntary participation of the victims and the young person, and on the consent of both defence and Crown counsel, who can consider all categories of offences for youth (although there are some limitations on sexual offences). There is no readily available data on the extent of use, and the outcomes achieved, by this program at the provincial level.

The most rigorous testing of FGC (the scripted version, with no private family time) has been in Australia and England through the ongoing reintegrative shaming experiments (RISE), using randomized control trials. On repeat offending, Sherman and Strang (2007, p. 8) conclude as follows:

> In general, RJ seems to reduce crime more effectively with more, rather than less, serious crimes. . . . works better with crimes involving personal victims . . . works with violent crimes more consistently than with property crimes . . . These findings run counter to conventional wisdom, and could become the basis for substantial inroads in demarcating when it is 'in the public interest' to seek RJ rather than CJ [criminal justice].
>
> Victims also benefit through increased satisfaction in the outcome and feelings of safety, and decreased likelihood of revenge. They are more likely to receive an apology and reduce their post-traumatic stress symptoms.

This level of research and development has not been carried out in Canada.

community justice forum (RCMP)

A safe, controlled environment in which the offender, the victim, and their families or supporters are brought together under the guidance of a trained facilitator. Together, using a scripted dialogue process, they discuss the offence and how they have all been affected, and jointly develop a plan to correct what has occurred.

British Columbia's Justice Reforms

An understanding of how different models of restorative justice have worked in British Columbia must be framed within the context of strategic justice reforms that have been initiated in BC. A news release on November 13, 1996, from the Attorney General's office expressed the initial intention of the ministry to adopt a restorative justice approach to criminal justice. This was followed by the release of a number of documents, including *Strategic Reforms of British Columbia's Justice System* (April 1997), *Restorative Justice Framework* (January 1998), and *Community Accountability Programs Information Package* (1998, 2004).

The overall policy shift reflected in these reforms and framework was stated by the Attorney General at that time, Ujjal Dosanjh, as a belief 'in a restorative justice system that gives communities a primary role in developing policies and programs'. At that time the restorative justice portfolio was located within the Community Programs Division of the Attorney General's office. In 2001/02, the Ministry of the Attorney General was split into the Ministry of Public Safety and Solicitor General (Community Safety and Crime Prevention) and the Ministry of the Attorney General. The restorative justice portfolio moved to the office of the Ministry of Public Safety and Solicitor General, and the 2004 version of Community Accountability Programs Information Package was produced. This information package specifies the scope of community accountability programs (CAP): they must be volunteer based; adhere to the ministry's Framework for Restorative Justice; demonstrate community and criminal justice support, including victims organizations; and accept referrals for category 3 and 4 offences only (i.e., for less serious offending, e.g., mischief and property crime).

The Directory of Restorative Justice Programs (2010) lists 49 community-based restorative justice groups, many of which are in the greater Vancouver area and Vancouver Island, as well as in the Central Interior, east to the Rockies (e.g., Invermere), and as far north as Fort Nelson. Most of these programs take police diversion cases for first-time offenders; a few take referrals from Crown counsel; and others take referrals from schools and the community at large. These community-based groups could use any one of the models of restorative justice described above, as well as other models (e.g., other forms of circles and community panels/boards).

While there is little written on these community-based programs in British Columbia, Dhami and Joy (2007) offer a rare overview of the challenges in establishing volunteer-run, community-based restorative justice programs. A community-based program in Victoria is used as a case study, and the paper concludes this:

> As RJ programs are associated with the criminal justice system and its programs and processes, there is danger that rather than altering the state's way of doing business, these programs will themselves be co-opted and diluted by the pull of retributive and punitive practices. One of the greatest challenges will be to ensure that volunteer-run, community-based RJ programs, with their personal and humanizing appeal for participants at all levels, do not become so routine and formal that they lose their flexibility, their vitality, and eventually their effectiveness. (Dhami and Joy 2007)

It is difficult to know whether or not this concern has efficacy, as there is little time for reflective practice and development within these small community-based programs. Indeed, only a handful of CAP programs have been evaluated, including Abbotsford (Squires 2009), Communities Embracing Restorative Action in Coquitlam (Roberts and Couch 2009), and North Shore Restorative Justice (Roberts 2010).

Looking back over this past decade of reforms and development in British Columbia, there has been a notable amount of growth. But what marks the substance of that growth? For example, one of the most promising community-based programs—VORP—has been lost. This program enjoyed a much more substantial and sustainable community-based juvenile justice role in the province compared to the current community accountability programs, particularly in relation to funding and referrals. Yet despite the challenges, a few of these community programs have been creative in carrying out evaluations through partnering with their local universities. In contrast, the provincial government programs are much better funded but have yet to be evaluated. Thus, in terms of fulfilling at least one recommendation (19) of the House of Commons Standing Committee on Justice, British Columbia has failed in that VORP is no longer supported in the province and there is a very poor evidence base across existing programs that have replaced VORP. In other words, BC lacks the research and development that was recommended over 20 years ago. Thus, both in practice and evaluation, restorative justice remains a marginal practice on the fringes of the justice system in British Columbia. The larger question that criminologists need to address is whether the marginal experience of restorative justice programs in British Columbia is being replicated in other jurisdictions across Canada and elsewhere.

Chris Cunneen and Carolyn Hoyle point out that even in Australia, where they do have some level of evaluation, restorative justice, as a theory of justice, lacks praxis:

> Despite all the words that have been written on restorative justice over the last 25 years, one cannot escape the feeling that restorative justice is essentially a peripheral add-on to the main workings of the criminal justice system. In New South Wales, Australia, . . . there are clearly articulated legislative and administrative procedures for the use of conferences. The system has been in place since the later 1990s, developed after various trials of restorative justice for young people which date back to the early 1990s. . . . So after nearly 20 years, what has been the net outcome? Depending on the year, between 2 and 4 per cent of police interventions involving young people result in referral to a youth justice conference. . . . At the other end of the legal process—the courts—restorative justice has not faired any better. For every one young person who appears in a restorative justice conference, about 15 appear in court, . . . And this is in a jurisdiction viewed as one of the pioneers in the 1990s in developing restorative justice practices for young people. (2010, pp. 184–185)

Cunneen and Hoyle (2010) conclude that restorative justice does not actively engage in research development of current restorative justice practices within the context of the broader justice system. To move beyond the margins of the justice system, there needs to be a constantly reflexive, dialectical relationship between theory and practice. In other words, restorative justice 'lacks an analysis of its own significant shortcomings; it lacks an analysis of political power and social power; it lacks a transformative politics' (p. 186). In particular, much like Canada, reduced to a marginal normative theory, Cunneen and Hoyle argue that restorative justice has failed indigenous youth in Australia.

Based on the evidence to date, these claims ring true for British Columbia and for Canada as well. There has been no consistent support to engage in praxis, particularly in praxis that engages community- and state-based policy, programs, and practice. There is no good reason, other than political will, that the practice of restorative justice should remain relegated to a marginal normative theory when restorative justice's theoretical roots span both normative and explanatory theory (see Braithwaite 2002a, 2002b for an overview) and when there are community groups willing to engage in research and development; that is, engage in praxis.

ROCA—The Praxis of Engagement

While the development of peacekeeping circles in British Columbia has lacked praxis, this is certainly not the case in Chelsea, MA, where the use of peacekeeping circles as an organizational strategy has made a significant impact on a community-based organization called Roca. This out-come-driven organization has a clearly defined mission: to help disengaged and disenfranchised young people, ages 14 to 24, move out of violence and poverty. Their vision is clear:

> Young people will leave the streets and gangs to take responsibility for their actions and have jobs. Young immigrant mothers will raise their children in safety and will be rec-ognized for their contributions to society. Our communities will have the ability to keep young people out of harm's way and in turn, thrive through their participation and leader-ship. (Roca 2010)

Roca describes its peacemaking circle strategy as a method that

> teaches young people and families an alternative communication method that allows them to deal with extremely painful and difficult issues, how to manage their own heal-ing process, and how to make agreements that promote safety so they can live in a healthy way. Circles are effective for identifying real issues and seeking appropriate solutions when there are conflict situations, when there is a need for healing or understanding, or a desire to reach consensus. (Roca 2010)

Mentored by the Tagish Tlingit people in the Yukon, along with Barry Stuart and Kay Pranis, Roca finds that 'circles bring people together in a way that creates trust, respect, intimacy, good will, belonging, generosity, mutuality and reciprocity. The process is never about changing others but, rather, is an invitation to change oneself and one's relationship with the community' (2010). Roca uses the circle process in a variety of ways with and without young people, internally and externally, often partnering with other agencies, groups, and community members.

Building on its peacemaking circle strategy is Roca's **engaged institutions (EI) strategy**. This strat-egy recognizes that a range of institutions are important and influential to the economic, social, and emotional well-being of a young person's life, including schools, local government, agencies, and organizations. As such, Roca creates a strong community base of partnerships with these institutions and organizations. Wheeler (2006) articulates the purpose and outcomes of the engaged institutions strategy as being to 'ensure that the systems and institutions contribute to young people's self-suf-ficiency and help them to be out of harm's way' (p. 44). As a community-based organization, Roca seeks to (1) increase institutions' ability to understand and be more responsive to youth needs; (2) be accountable for services they provide; and (3) understand the impact they have on young people's lives. The processes of engaging institutions mirrors that of those used to engage young people:

> The strategy is marked by an investment in building trusting relationships no matter how long it takes, frequent, consistent, honest communication between Roca staff and staff within the institutions or organizations, and the use of *peacemaking circles* to hear and understand each other and the young people.
>   The long term aim is to enact alternative restorative policies in communities that will, in turn, result in a systemic change of how communities address the needs of this high-risk youth population. (Pierce 2009, p. 44)

The evidence to date is very promising: in the 2009 financial year (FY), Roca actively served 664 youth and young adults through its high-risk youth intervention model. While most programs strug-gle with serving and retaining this population, Roca does not lose these young people: 91 per cent of the target population participants who were initially engaged in FY 2008 were retained through

engaged institutions (EI) strategy (Innovation Centre for Community and Youth Development 2006)

The engaged institutions (EI) strategy recognizes that positive collaboration between institutions, through the use of peacemaking circles, can originate from core organizational values regardless of any financial or practical incentives. For example, Roca realized that its core values of belonging, generosity, competence, and independence needed to be lived not only among staff members and participants of the organization, but in its relationships with other public and private agencies in its locality.

Roca's high-risk youth intervention model through FY 2009 and are still engaged in relationships and programming to support their change processes. Of young people in transformational relationships (Phase 1 and Phase 2), 84 per cent participated in stage-based life skills, education, and/or employment programming; 72 per cent of participants in Phase 2 made positive progress through the stages of change related to specific behaviour changes indicated on their service plans; 76 per cent who were engaged in educational programming made academic gains; 88 per cent who were engaged in prevocational training achieved skill gains; 91 per cent being worked with toward employment obtained employment; 81 per cent who successfully completed transitional employment were placed in jobs; and 74 per cent of these retained their employment. Roca is now involved in further implementation, outcome, and impact evaluations, including a replication, with possible random assignment, in Springfield, MA. Through its commitment to youth, Roca is building the foundation of a rich evidence base of innovation and change at the individual, community, and institutional level.

When Roca was founded in 1988, many thought that, like other nonprofits that serve vulnerable communities, the program was destined to fail. Yet, more than two decades later, more than 15 000 teens and young adults have been served by Roca's high-risk youth intervention model. Roca has grown into a solid community-based organization where others have failed, and now is being replicated in the community of Springfield, MA. As part of this next step in sustainable development, Roca is partnering with Lesley University, and is grounded in an integrated set of core academic, professional, and personal values. This strategic model is based on a philosophy of social engagement of young people at risk. This is a significant shift in praxis, moving from a paradigm of social control to one of social engagement (Morrison 2010). This engagement strategy aligns with Roca's mission to 'help disengaged and disenfranchised young people move out of violence and poverty—and we do it through relentless outreach, education, and partnering with engaged institutions' (Baldwin 2011). As an evidence-based organization, Roca's track record in achieving this mission is strong: 'In recent years, more than 90 per cent of kids engaged in the program remain with it. Of graduates over the last two years, a staggering 98 per cent ended criminal or delinquent behavior; 84 per cent were connected to furthering their education or employment' (Lesley University 2011). The city of Chelsea's city manager adds that 'the real story is larger than that. Roca's work, their success with individuals, their bringing together community partners to work together for common goals all make Chelsea a much stronger community (Lesley University 2011). As Molly Baldwin, the founder of Roca concludes:

> We know of no other community-based, non-mandated authority driving to outcomes and tracking efforts at this level. . . . In turn, we hope this will aid in others learning from what we have learned in the field. . . . Our penal system—the primary provider of 'services' to the young people we work most with—isn't effective and it's dangerous and expensive. We've gone a long way to showing there are better ways—and we want to bring it further. (Lesley University 2011)

Roca is a prime example of a thriving and sustainable community based 'off ramp' from the justice system. At the level of the state, the mantra of justice is 'order and control'; at the level of community, the mantra can be, as exemplified by Roca, engagement and transformation. This resonates with Van Ness's (1990) suggestion that the government can bring order, but only the community can bring peace.

Off-Ramps: The Importance of NGOs

Over a decade ago at a conference in Nova Scotia, John Braithwaite (1996, p. 9) put forward a strong argument for the importance of NGOs to deliberative problem solving, restorative justice, community, and democracy:

> The lived experience of modern democracy is alienation. The feeling is that elites run things, that we do not have a say in any meaningful sense. . . . Once citizens learn to be actively responsible as opposed to learning to rely totally on protection by a state that enforces passive responsibility, they will become active in social movement politics. NGOs offer the second great avenue for revitalizing meaningful forms of citizen participation in a democracy. . . . NGO influence can feed back into restorative justice conferences as advocacy of making the personal political, by invoking the possibility of agitating for structural change. The most important way this happens is when the justice of the people puts pressure on the justice of the law to change. (Braithwaite 1996, p. 9)

The importance of NGOs to driving active responsibility through participatory deliberation has continued to be an emergent factor of Braithwaite's (2006, 2010, for example) current work on comparative peace building in the South Pacific. This resonates with Christie's (1977) seminal paper on 'Conflict as Property', in which he argues the need to address a range of problems inherent in state-based justice:

> This loss is first and foremost a loss in *opportunities for norm-clarification*. It is a loss of pedagogical possibilities. It is a loss of opportunities for a continuous discussion of what represents the law of the land. How wrong was the thief, how right was the victim? Lawyers are, as we say, trained into agreement on what is relevant in a case. But that means a trained incapacity in letting the parties decide what *the*y think is relevant. (Christie 1977, p. 8)

Interestingly, what British Columbia gained in terms of the emergence of restorative justice in the early 1990s through community justice initiatives and VORP has been lost again to the state. Community-based NGOs have much more capacity to evoke the experience of civil society and meaningful deliberation, when the core of restorative justice for juveniles is community-based rather than state-based. Based on the experience of NGOs in BC, Christie's point is even more salient in that the state has now stolen the conflict, and the deliberative process, back from the community. In seeking state-based social control of restorative justice, the state has failed to deliver justice to communities and an evidence base to support its practice. Roca, as a community-based NGO, has delivered on this front by being true to its mission statement of delivering hope for a sustainable future to young people, and for those young people to live out of harm's way. Roca has indeed captured the essence of Braithwaite's (2002b) work in coupling restorative justice with responsive regulation through its two levers of change that work hand in hand: programmatic and organizational. The fundamental premise is that individual change is best leveraged through responsive regulation at a community level.

The practice of restorative justice, coupled with responsive regulation, enables communities to tap into the rich ecologies of an individual's life by creating safe spaces to dialogue through storytelling and listening in places close to home. Communities cut across institutional domains of social control and order and can respond in ways that broaden the scope for achieving safe and productive communities (see Morrison 2010).

Developing community-based civic capacity is good for the state too, as communities have a capacity for problem solving that is often thwarted by leaders at a state level, resulting in process paralysis (Briggs 2008). The role of mediating institutions, at the level of community, has long been argued in public policy. For example, Berger and Neuhaus (1977) argue that community-based institutions serve as alternate mechanisms to provide for social welfare, allowing the public to continue to respond to major social problems, yet without creating the sense of alienation characteristic of the state. Fundamental questions arise then in implementing restorative justice for juveniles, such as: What is the proper role of government in restorative justice? How can the government empower community based NGOs and maintain its need for order? These are bold questions that require bold governance and policy direction. England is now engaging with these very questions.

The Green Paper: The UK's Response to Engaging Communities in Criminal Justice

Twenty years following Canada's development of *Taking Responsibility* in response to concerns raised in the House of Commons, England's Justice Committee (2009/10) was asked to respond to similar concerns and produced *Cutting Crime: Case for Justice Reinvestment*. As with Canada, a number of recommendations were put forward including

- community-based services to prevent potential offenders from entering the criminal justice system and to divert them from the offending behaviour, which can lead to custody; and
- the creation of a well-resourced, credible, nationally available but locally responsive system of community sentences that our evidence shows would be more effective than custody in reducing re-offending.

However, unlike Canada, England quickly turned the recommendations put forward by the Justice Committee into a Green Paper for wider public consultation and feedback. Youth justice is covered in Chapter 5 of the Green Paper *Breaking the Cycle* and puts forward the policy recommendation:

> To increase the use of Restorative Justice we will build on the role currently performed by volunteer youth offender panel members and ensure that referral orders have a strengthened restorative approach. We will support panel members to increase their skills and confidence in using Restorative Justice in referral orders. (Ministry of Justice 2010)

In addition, Chapter 6 of the Green Paper recognizes the importance of community engagement through neighbourhoods. Public feedback has been enormous, with the Restorative Justice Council of the UK (2011) making the following conclusion:

> Overall, the focus from the national level should be on putting in place measures to engage communities in a meaningful way which has real impact, while expanding the use of restorative justice, which has proven positive effects, and carrying out a broader examination of the potential benefits of justice reinvestment. This follows considerable recent interest in the latter issue, including from the House of Commons Justice Committee, the All Party Parliamentary Local Government Group and the Commission on English Prisons Today. (Ministry of Justice 2010)

This speaks to the questions raised about the role of the relationship between the state and the community. Many other individuals, communities, NGOs, and government committees continue to respond. Only history can now reveal how these bold recommendations will unfold. What is clear, at this point in history, is that England, through engagement with a range of stakeholders, has turned the page that Canada failed to turn 20 years ago.

Summary

This chapter calls for a shift from social control to social engagement as a practical approach to dealing with problems surrounding youth crime. The evidence that has emerged from this analysis suggests that Barry Stuart's (Balanced and Restorative Justice Conference 2007) reflections on his experience of restorative justice in Canada still ring true: 'Canada's role in the development of restorative justice is as an exporter. We invent it, and others develop it in a fuller capacity'. One of the common adages in the field of restorative justice is to create opportunities to learn from our mistakes. Canada has the opportunity, and the capacity, to learn from this international experiment in restorative justice to which it has so proudly contributed. Moreover, Canada has the capacity to renew the promise of restorative justice as a domestic import. The lesson learned is that we must engage in praxis locally, provincially, nationally, and internationally. We must import as much as we export, and develop the sustainable capacity of 'off ramps' to community. For government and community, this will take the same courage and compassion of those early pioneers: from Judge Gordon McConnell, to probation officer Mark Yantzi, to members of communities and NGOs like Dave Worth, and indeed to the young people themselves, such as Russ Kelley. It is in these people's hands that the promise of restorative justice resides. As stated by Eleanor Roosevelt many years ago,

> Where, after all, do universal human rights begin? In small places, close to home—so close and so small that they cannot be seen on any map of the world. Yet they *are* the world of the individual person: The neighborhood he lives in; the school or college he attends; the factory, farm or office where he works. Such are the places where every man, woman, and child seeks equal justice, equal opportunity, equal dignity without discrimination. Unless these rights have meaning there, they have little meaning anywhere. Without concerted citizen action to uphold them close to home, we shall look in vain for progress in the larger world. (Eleanor Roosevelt, 'In Your Hands' 1958)

Key Terms

community justice forum   restorative justice (RJ)
engaged institutions strategy   sentencing circles
family group conferencing   victim–offender reconciliation programs
peacemaking circles

Review Questions

1. What is a diversionary process, and what are possible avenues (or points or referral) for entry of youth into diversion? What other 'off ramps' do youth need?

2. Discuss Christie's (1977) argument that state-based justice results in a 'trained incapacity' (p. 8) for decision making and norm clarification.

3. What is VORP, and how has it contributed to the history of restorative justice in Canada and British Columbia?

4. What is Roca? What is Roca's primary vision and how are peacekeeping circles important to Roca in achieving its vision?

Critical Thinking Questions

1. Consider the impact of data collection on development and implementation of restorative justice programs for youth.

2. Discuss the potential to meet the provisions of the YCJA that require addressing youth's developmental challenges and needs as they grow into adulthood, through restorative justice processes as opposed to traditional criminal justice processes.

3. Do you think it is more effective for justice officials (police, Crown prosecutors, etc.) to make decisions as to diversion on a case-by-case basis, or do you think a system-wide directive such as that in New Zealand where *all* youth experience restorative justice as a first approach is more effective? Why or why not?

4. What is *Taking Responsibility*? When was it developed, and what, in particular, did Recommendation 19 contribute to youth justice in Canada?

Suggested Readings

Boyes-Watson, C. (2008). *Peacemaking circles and urban youth: Bringing justice home.* St. Paul, MN: Living Justice Press.

Christie, N. (1977). Conflict as property. *British Journal of Criminology, 17*(1), 1–14.

Elliott, E. M. (2011). *Security with care: Restorative justice & healthy societies.* Winnipeg, MB: Fernwood Publishing.

Suggested Weblinks

Correctional Service Canada
www.csc-scc.gc.ca/text/rj/index-eng.shtml
• An explanation of restorative justice.

Roca
www.rocainc.org
• See this homepage of Roca.

Restorative Justice in British Columbia
www.rjbc.ca
• 'This website is intended for restorative justice (RJ) practitioners, community partners, and others with an interest in RJ.'

The Centre for Restorative Justice
www.sfu.ca/cfrj
• Part of the Simon Fraser University School of Criminology.

References

Berger, P. and Neuhaus, R. (1977). *To empower people: The role of mediating structures in public policy.* Washington, DC: American Enterprise Institute.

Braithwaite, J. (1996). Restorative justice and a better future. *The Dalhousie Review, 76*(1): 9-32. Reprinted in E. McLaughlin, R. Fergusson, G. Hughes, and L. Westmorland (Eds.), (2003). *Restorative justice: Critical issues.* London: Sage.

Braithwaite, J. (2002a). Restorative justice and responsive regulation. New York: Oxford University Press.

Braithwaite, J. (2002b). Setting standards for restorative justice. *British Journal of Criminology, 42*(3): 563–77.

Braithwaite, J. (2006). Accountability and responsibility through restorative justice. In M.D. Dowdle (Ed.), *Public accountability, designs, dilemmas and experiences* (pp. 33–51). Cambridge, UK: Cambridge University Press.

Briggs, X.S. (2008). Democracy as problem solving: Civic capacity in communities across the globe. Cambridge, MA: MIT Press.

British Columbia Ministry of Children and Family Development. (2005, August). *Family group conference reference guide.* BC: Child and Family Development Division. Retrieved from www.mcf.gov.bc.ca/child_protection/pdf/fgc_guide_internet.pdf

Charbonneau, S. (2005). The Canadian Youth Criminal Justice Act 2003: A step forward for advocates of restorative justice. In E. Elliot and R.M. Gordon (Eds.), *New directions in restorative justice:Issues, practice, evaluation* (pp. 75–86). Cullompton, UK: Willan Publishing.

Chatterjee, J. and Elliott, L. (2003). Restorative policing in Canada: The Royal Canadian Mounted Police, community justice forums, and the youth criminal justice act. *Police Practice and Research*, 4(4): 1.

Christie, N. (1977). Conflict as property. *British Journal of Criminology, 17*(1): 1–14.

Claasen, R. and Zehr, H. (1989). *VORP: Organizing a foundation in the church* (Mennonite Central Committee US). Elkhart, IN: Office of Criminal Justice.

Community Justice Initiatives Association. (2011). Victim offender reconciliation. Retrieved from www.cjibc.org/victim_reconciliation

Crnkovich, M. (1995). Report on sentencing circles in Nunavik. In Pauutuutit Women's Association, *Inuit women and justice: Progress report no. 1.*

Cunneen, C. (1997). Community conferencing and the fiction of Indigenous control. *Australian and New Zealand Journal of Criminology, 30*(3): 292–311.

Cunneen, C. (2007). Reviving restorative justice traditions. In J. Johnstone and D. Van Ness (Eds.), *The handbook of restorative justice.* Cullommpton, UK: Willan Publishing.

Cunneen, C. and Hoyle, C. (2010). *Debating restorative justice.* Oxford: Hart Publishing.

Daubney, D. (2010, November). The role the 1987–88 justice committee of the House of Commons played in encouraging the use of restorative justice in Canada. Paper presented at Restorative Justice Week 2010, Canada.

Department of Justice Canada. (2002). The Youth Criminal Justice Act: Summary and background. Retrieved from http//www.justice.gc.ca/en/ps/yj/ycja/explan.html

Dhami, M.K. and Joy, P. (2007). Challenges to establishing volunteer run community-based restorative justice programs. *Contemporary Justice Review, 10*, 9–22.

Dickson-Gilmore, J. and La Prairie, C. (2005). *Will the circle be unbroken: Aboriginal communities, restorative justice and the challenges of conflict and change.* Toronto: University of Toronto Press.

Evje, A. and Cushman, R. (2000). *A summary of the evaluations of six California victim offender rehabilitation programs.* San Francisco, CA: Judicial Council of California, Administrative Office of the Courts.

Gehm, J. and Umbreit, M. (1985). *National VORP directory.* Valparaiso, IN: National VORP Resource Center.

Green, R. and Healy, K.F. (2003). *Tough on kids: Rethinking approaches to youth justice.* Saskatoon, SK: Purich Publishing.

Griffiths, C.T. and Hamilton, R. (1996). Sanctioning and healing: Restorative justice in Canadian Aboriginal communities. In B. Galaway and J. Hudson (Eds.), *Restorative justice: International perspectives* (pp. 175–92). Monsey, NY: Criminal Justice Press.

Gustafson, D. (2004). Is restorative justice taking too few, or too many risks? In H. Zehr and B. Toews (Eds.), *Critical issues in restorative justice* (pp. 299–309). Monsey, NY, and Cullompton, UK: Criminal Justice Press & Willan Publishing.

Hakiaha, M. (2004). What is the state's role in indigenous justice processes? In H. Zehr and B. Toews (Eds.), *Critical issues in restorative justice* (pp. 351–59). Monsey, NY, and Cullompton, UK: Criminal Justice Press and Willan Publishing.

House of Commons. (1998). Taking responsibility: Report of standing committee on justice and Solicitor General on its review of sentencing, conditional release and related aspects of corrections. Canada: Standing Committee on Justice and Solicitor General.

House of Commons Justice Committee. (2010). *Cutting crime: The case for justice reinvestment.* (HC 94-1). London: The Stationary Office Limited.

Howard, Z. (2002). Critical issues in restorative justice: An inadequate and overlapping outline. *VOMA Connections, 12*(Autumn). Retrieved from http://www.voma.org/docs/connect12.pdf

Johnstone, J., and Van Ness, D. (Eds.) (2007). *The handbook of restorative justice.* Cullommpton, UK: Willan Publishing.

Kelly, R. (2010, November). *The Elmira case . . . and beyond!* Paper presented at Restorative Justice Week 2010, Canada. Retrieved from www.csc-scc.gc.ca/text/rj/rj2010/kit/3-eng.shtml.

Latimer, J., Dowden, C., and Muise, D. (2001). *The effectiveness of restorative justice practices: A meta-analysis.* Ottawa: Department of Justice, Research and Statistics Division.

Lesley University. (2011). *Roca, driving positive outcomes for the most at-risk youth.* Retrieved 15 April, 2011, from http://news.lesley.edu/2011/01/roca-driving-positive-outcomes-for-the-most-at-risk-youth.shtml

Lode, W. (2008). Restorative justice: An alternative for responding to crime? In S. Shoham, S., Giora, O. Beck, and M. Kett (Eds.), *International handbook of penology and criminal justice* (pp. 613–89). Florida: Taylor & Francis Group.

McDonald, J., Thorsborne, M., Moore, D., Hyndman, M., and O'Connell, T. (1995). *Real justice training manual: Coordinating family group conferences.* Pipersville, PA: Piper's Press.

Ministry of Children and Family Development. (2004). Best practice approaches: Child protection and violence against women. Victoria, BC: Author.

Ministry of Justice. (2010). Breaking the cycle: Effective punishment, rehabilitation and sentencing of offenders. (Cm 7972). UK: The Stationary Office Limited.

Ministry of Public Safety and Solicitor General. (1998). *Community accountability programs.* (Information package). British Columbia.

Ministry of Public Safety and Solicitor General. (2004). *Community accountability programs.* (Information package). British Columbia.

New South Wales Attorney General's Department. (2008). *Evaluation of circle sentencing program report.* Leichhardt, NSW: Cultural and Indigenous Research Centre Australia.

Pakura, S. (2005, March). The family group conference 14-year journey: Celebrating the successes, learning the lessons, embracing the challenges. Symposium conducted at the American Humane Association's Family Group Decision Making Conference and Skills-Building Institute, Pennsylvania.

Peachey, D.E. (1989). The Kitchener experiment. In M. Wright and B. Galaway (Eds.), *Mediation and criminal justice: Victims, offenders and community* (pp. 14–26). London: Sage Publications.

Penny, J. and Mandeep, D.K. (2006). Challenges to establishing volunteer-run, community-based restorative justice programs. *Contemporary Justice Review, 10*(1): 9–22.

Pierce, B.A. (2009, December). Roca's high risk youth intervention model: Initial implementation evaluation report. Boston, MA: Crime and Justice Institute.

Restorative Justice Council. (2011). A new way of doing justice—Restorative Justice Council response to Breaking the Cycle Green Paper. Retrieved 15 April, 2011, from http://www.restorativejustice.org.uk/resource/a_new_way_of_doing_justice__restorative_justice_council_response_to_breaking_the_cycle_green_paper_5hybc/

Roberts, M.L. (2010). Evaluating evaluation: An investigation into the purpose and practice of evaluation in restorative justice based programs. Paper presented as thesis defence at Simon Fraser University, School of Criminology.

Roberts, M. and Couch, L. (2009). CERA program evaluation report. Coquitlam, BC: CERA.

Roca. (2010). *In the streets and in their lives.* (Annual report). Chelsea: MA.

Sharpe, S. (1998). *Restorative justice: A vision for healing and change.* Edmonton, AB: Mediation and Restorative Justice Centre.

Sherman, L.W. and Strang, H. (2007). *Restorative justice: The evidence.* London: The Smith Institute.

Snyder, T.R. (2001). *The Protestant ethic and the spirit of punishment.* Grand Rapids, MI: William B. Eerdmans Publishing Company.

Stuart, B. (1996). Circle sentencing in Yukon Territory, Canada: A partnership of the community and the criminal justice system. *International Journal of Comparative and Applied Criminal Justice, 20*(1 & 2): 291–309.

Tauri, J.M. (1999). Family group conferencing: The myth of Indigenous empowerment in New Zealand [Special issue]. *Native Law Centre 4*(1).

Tustin, L. and Lutes, R.E. (2010). *A guide to the Youth Criminal Justice Act.* Toronto, ON: Butterworths.

Umbreit, M.S. and Greendwood, J. (1998). *National survey of victim offender mediation programs in the United States.* US: Department of Justice.

United Nations. (2006). *Handbook on restorative justice programs: Criminal justice handbook series.* United Nations Office on Drugs and Crime.

Van Ness, D. W., and Strong, K. H. (2006). *Restoring justice: An introduction to restorative justice* (3rd ed.). Cincinnati, OH: Matthew Bender & Company, Inc., Anderson Publishing Co.

Victim Services and Crime Prevention. (2010). *Directory of restorative justice programs, agencies, and contacts.* Abbotsford: BC.

Wachtel, T. (1997). *Real justice: How we can revolutionize our response to wrongdoing.* Pipersville, PA: The Piper's Press.

Weitekamp, E.G.M. (1999). The history of restorative justice. In B. Bazemore and L. Walgrave (Eds.), *Restorative juvenile justice: Repairing the harm of youth crime.* Monsey, NY: Criminal Justice Press.

Wheeler, W. (2006, February 7). *Encircling institutions: Surrounding youth in crisis with mutual engagement and trust.* Takoma Park, MD: Innovation Center for Community and Youth Development.

Zehr, H. (1990). *Changing lenses: A new focus for crime and justice.* Scottsdale, PA: Herald Press.

Statutes Cited

Criminal Code, R.S., c. C-46 (1985). Retrieved from http://laws.justice.gc.ca/en/C-46/index.html

Juvenile Delinquents Act, S.C. c. 40. (1908). Retrieved from http://www.justice.gc.ca/eng/pi/icg-gci/jj2-jm2/sec02.html.

R. v. Gladue, 1 S.C.R. 688 (1999). Retrieved from http://www.indigenousbar.ca/cases/gladue.htm

R. v. Moses, 71 C.C.C 347 (1992). Retrieved from http://www.usask.ca/nativelaw/factums/view.php?id=124

Young Offenders Act, S.C. c. Y-1 (1985). Retrieved from http://laws-lois.justice.gc.ca/P DF/Y-1.pdf.

Youth Criminal Justice Act, S.C. c. 1 (2002). Retrieved from http://www.justice.gc.ca/en g/pi/yj-jj/ycja-lsjpa/ycja-lsjpa.html.

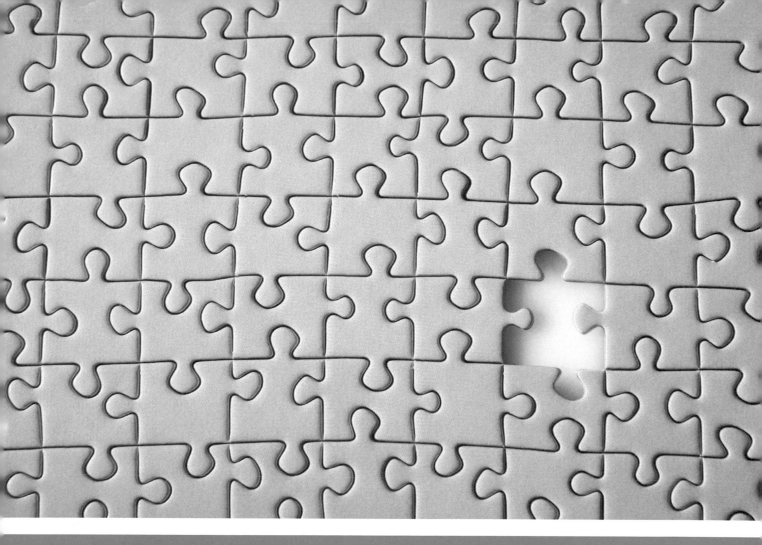

16 Key Challenges in Hearing the Voice of Youth in the Youth Justice System

Susan A. Reid and Sarah Gilliss

Overview

This chapter analyzes the continuing issue regarding the maintenance of a separate system of youth justice versus trends promoting the 'adulteration' of youth who commit crimes. A focus on the articles within the UN Convention on the Rights of the Child draws attention to the importance of a youth voice in decisions that affect youth. This chapter discusses the literature on what works with youth at risk and youth with highly complex needs in light of recent Canadian cases and crime prevention programs.

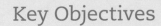

Key Objectives

After reading this chapter, you should be able to:

- Understand the difference between what works and what does not work for youth-at-risk programming.
- Understand the principles behind a separate system of justice for youth.
- Understand the challenges faced by youth with complex needs in the youth criminal justice system.
- Understand the importance of recognizing the articles of the UN Convention on the Rights of the Child in hearing the voice of youth in all matters.

Introduction

The chapters that have made up this volume have drawn attention to the myriad issues that are involved in the implementation of youth justice in Canada. This chapter is intended to draw attention to the positive developments in the juvenile justice policy field as well as to some of the challenges that are still ahead as we continue to draw on our research and evidence of the most appropriate means of intervening in the lives of troubled youth.

The Legal Regulation of Childhood and Adolescence

The law that regulates criminal conduct for children and youth is based on a binary system, where the state focuses on the protection of children until such time as they cross the threshold, known as the *age of majority,* to adulthood. Prior to the age of majority, children and youth receive the protection from the state in the form of restrictions on their freedom and investment in their development with the intent that such policies will pay dividends in terms of the promotion of competent adults as productive members of society. While there is variation in the upper age jurisdiction of the youth court throughout the world, the age of majority assumes that the individual in question has reached a period in their development wherein they can be seen as fully autonomous individuals who are responsible for their choices and actions and no longer require the state's protection. The problem with this binary system, which focuses only on *immature children* and *competent adults*, is that there is no opportunity to include the evolving capacities of children as they mature during their adolescent years.

Where there have been changes to the age of consent, these policies have been put in place to allow for changing capacities of young people based on the notion that social welfare and the welfare of the young person can both benefit through such a reclassification. One example is related to the age of consent for a minor to receive medical treatment. By lowering the age of consent, there is a benefit to the young person and to the larger community in the form of reduced health costs associated with pregnancy, sexually transmitted disease, and other social welfare costs. In the case of **youth justice**, however, the rationale for lowering the age is not focused on the promotion of the welfare of youth. Rather, treating a youth like an adult for the purposes of criminal responsibility is more of a reflection of societal values reflected in the adage 'adult crime equals adult time'. There are also a number of juvenile justice statutes that undermine the principle of confidentiality in youth justice proceedings by increasing the number of opportunities to share information about the youth defendant with criminal justice, education, social service agencies, and the media. This punitive stance toward young people has been underscored by such repressive policies as zero tolerance, curfews, naming and shaming rituals, and the targeting of pre-criminal disorder and incivility through anti-social behaviour orders that were prevalent in the United Kingdom in recent years.

youth justice

A separate and distinct criminal justice system that explicitly meets the unique needs of young people.

The **best interests of the child** doctrine, which is a key principle of the United Nations Declaration on the Rights of the Child, appears to be in direct opposition to an increasing trend toward the **adulteration** of youth crime throughout the world. There are now provisions in juvenile criminal statutes throughout the world that provide for the transfer of youth who commit criminal offences to the adult system, either for adjudication or for punishment. The research evidence is clear, however, that increased criminal justice processing of youth runs counter to the reduction of youth crime. Further, imposing adult penalties and including young people in adult prisons has led to serious problems for young people as evidenced in New Brunswick with the case of Ashley Smith (see Box 16.1 later in the chapter).

The Codification of a Separate System of Youth Justice in Canada

In 1985, the UN Standard Minimum Rules for the Administration of Youth Justice, known as the Beijing Rules, recognized the special needs of young people and the promotion of diversion from court proceedings. Further, these standards underscored the principle that custody should be used as a last resort for children and that all proceedings against young people should be anonymous in order to protect children from lifelong stigma and **labelling**. The United Nations Convention on the Rights of the Child (UNCRC) expanded on these rules and was proclaimed in 1989. The UNCRC has been ratified in more than 190 countries, and reiterates that children have a right to be protected from degrading and cruel punishment and to receive special treatment in the justice system. Further, it states that children below a minimum age shall be presumed to lack the capacity to infringe the penal law.

The United Nations Convention on the Rights of the Child (UNCRC) states in Article 3 that 'In all actions concerning children and the courts of law, the best interests of the child shall be a primary consideration'. Article 40 requires that children who have violated the penal law be treated in a manner consistent with the child's age and the desirability of promoting the child's **reintegration** and his or her taking up a constructive role in society. The UN Convention underscores diversion from criminal proceedings and extrajudicial solutions, and socio-educational interventions. It recommends deprivation of liberty only as a last resort when dealing with young people who offend.

Canada's international obligations to all children who have committed offences support a presumption that juvenile offenders are not to be treated like adults. However, Canada has continually violated the spirit of the UN Convention on the Rights of the Child by insisting on a reservation under Article 34 with respect to the rule about housing adults and youth in separate facilities.

The UNCRC has laudable objectives in its principles and articles, and it is the most ratified of all human rights instruments, but it is also perhaps the most violated of the human rights treaties. Breaching the provisions of the UNCRC does not lead to any formal sanction. In a lot of cases, the UNCRC has not been incorporated into domestic law in countries that have ratified it. In other cases, countries have put in reservations around specific issues regarding juvenile justice to allow for alterations to the provisions in the case of housing youth offenders with adult offenders and other key issues that may promote the best interests of the young person. Even such fundamental principles as children not being exposed to inhumane or degrading treatment or punishment can be liberally construed in light of the controversy over the age of criminal responsibility and the ability of state parties to bend these rules to provide for more invasive and punitive sanctions for youth under the age of 18 years.

While there has been in Canada a formal system of youth justice that is separate and apart from the adult justice system since the proclamation of the Juvenile Delinquents Act (JDA) in 1908, it was not until the Youth Criminal Justice Act (YCJA) expressly stated in s.3(1)(b) 'the criminal justice system for young persons must be separate from that of adults', in 2002, that Canada was explicit in its law

best interests of the child
When the interests of a young person are paramount in decision-making regarding his or her experience in the criminal justice system.

adulteration
The dismantling of a distinct system of criminal justice for youth and the remerging with systems of justice for adults.

labelling
The stigmatization of a young person as deviant.

reintegration
The introduction of the young person back into the community as a productive member of society.

that there were two distinct systems of justice. Prior to this time, Canada did not expressly adhere to the UN Convention on the Rights of the Child, even though Canada had ratified it in 1991.

Diverting Children from a Life of Crime: Sustaining the Original Purpose of a Separate System of Youth Justice

If we consider the origins of the juvenile justice system in North America, at the turn of the century the 'child savers', as they were known, attempted to divert young people from the harshness of the adult system. The years that followed the enactment of the Juvenile Delinquents Act of 1908 have been replete with arguments for policy changes that centre on the culpability of children as criminals. The concept of a separate system of youth justice has been debated many times over the past century, but to date the juvenile court has remained separate and distinct from the adult system (also see Chapters 1 and 3).

The JDA was marked by a singular approach focusing on social welfare concerns with a strong emphasis on the 'best interests' doctrine of child welfare and protection hearings. As more and more attention was drawn to the inequities of justice that were being meted out in the youth court to young people without legal representation, there was a cry for more procedural safeguards to the confidential juvenile justice proceedings. Equally, adults began to question whether or not the 'discipline' of the youth court was sufficient to provide the community with protection from the sometimes heinous acts of young people. This 'care' versus 'control' argument has been the mainstay of the controversy surrounding the most suitable way to handle youth in conflict with the law since the mid 1960s and the release of a pivotal discussion document, Juvenile Delinquency in Canada (1965).

While the successor of the JDA heralded a change in youth justice with the elimination of social welfare concerns under the Young Offenders Act, there were still a number of provisions within the legislation that recommended that alternatives to the court system, albeit a mitigated accountability court system, were to be preferred for first-time, minor offenders. However, the implementation of the YOA, with its contrary goals of **rehabilitation** and the protection of society, led to an increased use of the youth court and to an even greater use of **custodial sanctions** than had been experienced under the former legislation. As Tustin and Lutes (2008, p. 2) point out, 'Instead of promoting the use of diversionary programs to keep young people out of custody, the introduction of the Young Offenders Act increased the use of custody to the point where Canada had the highest rate of youth incarceration in the western world'.

Over a decade ago, a federal/provincial/territorial task force was established by the then ministers responsible for justice to complete a review of the former legislation, the Young Offenders Act, to assist and complement the work of the then Standing Committee on Justice and Legal Affairs in their efforts to improve the youth justice system. The group determined at that time that there were six broad priority areas to be addressed, with *diversion* being seen as an important part:

> Matters related to diversion, pre-trial detention, community-based sanctions, and custodial processes, including the potential to *deal more efficiently and effectively with young persons by making greater use of diversion from formal court proceedings and community-based alternatives to custody* [emphasis added]. (Canada 1996)

In 1998, the Department of Justice released its *Strategy for the Renewal of Youth Justice*, which underscored the need for 'crime prevention' and 'meaningful consequences' for youth who came in conflict with the law. Between 1998 and 2002, the Youth Criminal Justice Act was introduced and re-introduced as Bills C-68, C-3, and C-7. Bill C-7 incorporated 160 amendments in response to reactions to the earlier versions. The YCJA was finally enacted in 2002 and came into force in April 2003.

rehabilitation

A fundamental concept of the Youth Criminal Justice Act that holds that a young person can be reformed or changed as a result of appropriate treatment programs.

custodial sanctions

Under the Youth Criminal Justice Act, the sentencing of a young person to custody.

Across Canada, the YCJA has had the effect of reducing the number of young people who have been sentenced to custody. The focus on alternatives to the formal system are reiterated as has been the case through history, but the YCJA also stresses the importance of reserving the youth court for the small number of serious and persistent young offenders. Tustin and Lutes (2008) suggest that the YCJA legislates the intent of the act as well as building on the 'best practices' learned throughout the implementation of the YOA. The purpose of the legislation, as they state, is as follows: 'Where possible, youths are to be dealt with outside of the more formal justice system, reserving the courts only for serious violent and repeat offenders' (Tustin and Lutes 2008, p. 3).

Whyte (2005, p. 19) argues that research supports the use of diversion as 'spontaneous desistance' can be achieved by many young people without intervention. Early prevention and intervention through school networks, through communities, and through the assistance of families helps to avoid stigma and labelling and may be the most suitable alternative for the majority of young people who offend. There will always be, however, a small number of young people who are persistent offenders and who require a range of multidisciplinary assistance set within a clear path over a fairly substantial period of time. Where we make our biggest mistake is when we provide intensive treatments to our low-risk offenders and set them off on a trajectory of net widening and further entrenchment within the system.

Diversion programs were developed to respond to the research evidence that suggests that keeping youth in their family and communities and supported by a package of services aimed at their individual needs has been shown to have a positive effect and has been successful in reducing recidivism (Foster, Qaseem, and Connor 2004; Lipsey, Wilson, and Cothern 2000; Latimer 2001; Whitaker, Severy, and Morton 1984). Keeping youth in their community allows for a 'holistic intervention approach' focused on identifying individual, family, and community risks and strengths and treating them comprehensively (Sullivan, Veysey, Hamilton, and Grillo 2007).

The Youth Criminal Justice Act is based on research that shows that incarcerating young people can do more harm than good, and that our most successful interventions should be doing less criminal justice processing for the majority of offenders who present as low-risk, low-need offenders. For these reasons, and as mentioned in earlier chapters, the YCJA places increased emphasis on extrajudicial measures to appropriately respond to youth while keeping them out of the formal justice system, and on noncustodial sentences for those youth who are formally charged and found guilty. Custodial sentences are seen as a measure of last resort for the highest-risk offenders. The continued success of the YCJA, however, is extremely vulnerable from a number of perspectives:

- The use of extrajudicial measures is based on police and Crown prosecutors exercising discretion and considering those measures as the first course of action.
- The existence of a number of extrajudicial measures and noncustodial sentences depends on the approval and funding of programs by provincial directors and governments.
- The success of many programs depends on the active co-operation of different sectors and individuals.

Last year, the government introduced amendments to the Youth Criminal Justice Act through Bill C-4. According to Rob Nicholson, Minister of Justice, in his comments to the Standing Committee on Justice and Human Rights,

> Our government has introduced an important piece of legislation, known as Sébastien's Law, to make the protection of society a primary goal of our youth criminal justice system. It would also give Canadians greater confidence that violent and repeat young offenders will be held accountable. It would simplify the rules to keep these offenders off the streets,

---

and would require the courts to consider publishing the name of a violent young offender in individual circumstances when necessary to protect society. (House of Commons 2010a)

There were a number of proposed changes to the legislation that were contrary to the research evidence, which may prove to further erode the distinctive nature of the youth court from the adult system. In testimony before the same committee, Mr Bernard Richard, Child and Youth Advocate for the province of New Brunswick, admonished the government for its proposed changes:

> In my view, none of these things—publishing the name, adding denunciation and deterrence, providing for more pre-sentence detention of youth, and most of the amendments that are proposed—will do anything to address or to change the impulsive, irrational, often reckless behaviour of teenagers. I'm not convinced, at all, that it will bring us to where we want to be as a country, with a lower crime rate. I think we can do much better. It takes more of a long-term view, I agree, and often that's not easy. We're much better if we invest the same kinds of resources in addressing those youth who are suffering from mental illness, severe behaviour disorders, or addictions, and I would wager that accounts for a very large proportion of youth crime. (House of Commons 2010b)

Bill C-4 died on the order paper during the spring session and a new election led to a majority government for the Conservative party. In the fall of 2011, the changes proposed in Bill C-4 became part of the Conservative's omnibus crime bill (Bill C-10), entitled the Safe Streets and Communities Act. By putting together nine separate bills related to crime that were debated but not passed during the last Parliament, the Tory government, now in a majority position, will be able to push through these measures. C-10 purports to be 'comprehensive legislation that will target crime and terrorism and provide support and protection to victims of crime', according to the Minister of Justice. Critics of the bill say that the provisions go overboard with respect to increased sentencing for minor crimes and, as such, will put thousands more into prisons. The bill also toughens penalties for youth, which will make it significantly more likely that there will be more young people in custody. Estimates of the cost to the provinces of this omnibus legislation are between $2 billion and $13 billion over the next five years.

Now retired Justice Merlin Nunn was quoted recently in the *Chronicle Herald* as being deeply disappointed with the provisions, which do not respond to the need for help and assistance for troubled youth. While the Conservatives have noted repeatedly that the report of the Nunn Commission helped to frame the amendments to the Youth Criminal Justice Act, it is deeply disappointing that the author of this report is troubled by the interpretation of his recommendations.

Challenges Faced by Youth with Highly Complex Needs

As mentioned in Chapter Five, in the fall of 2004, a high-speed police chase involving a young offender in a stolen vehicle led to the tragic death of Theresa McEvoy when the car she driving was struck by the vehicle driven by the fleeing youth. As the youth in question had a long history of youth-related offences and had been released from custody two days prior to the fatal incident, the Nova Scotia government called for a public inquiry and appointed a retired justice of the Nova Scotia Supreme Court, Hon. D. Merlin Nunn, as the commissioner. The Nunn Commission resulted in a 381-page report that provided a series of 34 recommendations with respect to youth justice administration and accountability, youth crime legislation, and the prevention of youth crime.

The first recommendation that came out of this commission was that there should be additional training and adequate funding for assessment and early intervention in the education system for children and youth with learning disabilities and other mental and psychological disabilities that may increase the likelihood of their coming into conflict with the law (Nunn 2005). This recommendation was made in light of the information that was presented to the commission showing that approximately 80 per cent of repeat young offenders are living with disabilities, including mental-health disabilities (Nunn 2005, p. 269).

Indeed, there is a growing and diverse body of research that has concluded that youth who are involved in the youth justice system have significantly more mental-health and substance-abuse problems compared to other youth (Elliot, Huizinga, and Menard 1989; Loeber et al. 1998; Dembo and Schmeidler 2003; OJJDP 1998; Rosenblatt, Rosenblatt, and Biggs 2000; Wasserman et al. 2002). Some estimates are that up to 90 per cent of young people before the juvenile courts exhibit the general symptoms of conduct disorder or oppositional defiance disorder. Cocozza and Skowyra (2000, p. 6) indicate that one-third of youth before the youth courts suffer from either attention deficit disorder (ADD) or attention deficit hyperactivity disorder (ADHD). Their analysis of the research literature has led them to conclude that at least 20 per cent of young offenders suffer from *severe* mental-health disorders.

Despite the fact that these studies have found a correlation between mental health disorders and youth crime, this does not imply a causal relationship. There are many other factors related to the individual, family, school, and community that present a social context that may contribute to risk or provide protection from the effects of any single risk factor. Understanding the correlation between mental-health disorders (i.e., lack of impulse control or aggression) and youth crime, as suggested by Cueller McReynolds, and Wasserman (2006), and then targeting the disorder through treatment may reduce the likelihood of recidivism. In fact, empirical evidence has shown that mental-health treatment reduces subsequent detention rates among foster-care children (Cuellar, Markowitz, and Libby 2004).

While there have been a number of programs that have been designed to divert less serious youth offenders from the juvenile court in order to avoid stigmatizing the offending youth (Moyer 1980), it has only been in recent years that programs applying the theory of *therapeutic jurisprudence* have been developed (Winick 2003). Mental-health courts and mental-health diversion programs are designed to be treatment-oriented and are based on the assumption that for certain types of individuals, problem-solving responses are more appropriate than punishment (Wexler 2000). The intent of such specialized services is to improve coordination across justice and social-service agencies, improve efficiency, increase predictability of the court proceedings, and ultimately improve the quality of justice (Gilbert, Grimm, and Parnham 2001). The provision of diversion for youth with mental-health needs not only provides more effective and appropriate treatment but also facilitates the further development of community-based mental-health services. Further, reviews of the research on such programs has pointed to the improvement in working relationships of cross-systems groups, an expedited court processing of youth into appropriate services, and a greater likelihood of encouraging family participation in treatment plans (Cocozza and Skowyra 2000; Skowyra and Powell 2006).

Skowyra and Powell (2006) argue that many youth with significant mental-health issues are in the juvenile justice system for relatively minor offences and are placed in jail by default. A study by the National Alliance for the Mentally Ill (2001) found that 36 per cent of the survey respondents had to place their children in the juvenile justice system in order to access mental-health services. Similarly, a report issued by the US House of Representatives (2004) documented the inappropriate use of juvenile detention in 33 states where youth were being held with no charges against them, but simply due to the fact that there was no place for them to go. Similar problems were experienced and divulged in the New Brunswick Ombudsman and Child and Youth Advocate report, *Connecting the Dots* (Child and Youth Advocate 2008a).

In an effort to gather national data on the utilization of mental-health diversion programs for juveniles, the National Centre for Mental Health and Juvenile Justice conducted a study to identify those programs that target youth with mental-health needs. In order to ensure that the programs were indeed diversion programs, there was an initial screening of 779 programs that operated formal programs that were aimed at reducing justice involvement and maintained linkages to community-based services. From this a second survey was sent out asking for more in-depth information about the programs. A 30 per cent response rate yielded 230 programs responding. The programs self-rated on the variable of whether or not their program was simply a general diversion program (n=111) or a mental-health diversion program (n=105). Both the general diversion programs and the mental-health diversion programs reported limiting eligibility of participants in terms of the seriousness of the current offence and the number of prior arrests or convictions. However, Skowyra and Powell (2006) found that the mental-health programs were more likely to admit youth with more serious charges and with a prior history of involvement with the justice system.

In this study, the majority of programs accepted youth from multiple points of entry, but the most common point of diversion was at probation intake. The study found that mental-health programs were more likely to admit youth at later stages of their adjudication process than the more general diversion programs. This suggests that early identification of mental-health needs was not being uncovered at the young person's earliest point of contact with the system; most youth were not diagnosed until they were put into some form of juvenile detention. The lack of diagnosis at an earlier stage may be explained by the data that showed that just a little over one-half of all programs conducted some form of screening and assessment. Even in the mental-health diversion programs, however, there was no consistent response to the use of a standardized screening instrument, with many programs relying on questions developed by the program itself.

Skowyra and Cocozza (2007), in their *Blueprint for Change*, outline a Comprehensive Model for the Identification and Treatment of Youth with Mental Health Needs who come in contact with the youth justice system. They have set out the following underlying principles:

Guiding Principles:

1. Youth should not have to enter the juvenile justice system solely in order to access mental health services or because of their mental illness.
2. Whenever possible and when matters of public safety allow, youth with mental health needs should be diverted from the juvenile justice system into evidence-based treatment in a community setting.
3. If diversion out of the juvenile justice system is not possible, youth should be placed in the least restrictive setting possible, with access to evidence-based treatment.
4. Information collected as part of a pre-adjudicatory mental health screen should not be used in any way that might jeopardize the legal interests of youth as defendants.
5. All mental health services provided to youth in contact with the juvenile justice system should respond to issues of gender, ethnicity, race, age, sexual orientation, socio-economic status and faith.
6. Mental health services should meet the developmental realities of youth. Children and adolescents are not simply little adults.
7. Whenever possible, families and/or caregivers should be partners in the development of treatment decisions and plans made for their children.
8. Multiple systems bear responsibility for these youth. While at different times, a single agency may have primary responsibility, these youth are the community's responsibility, and all responses developed for these youth should be collaborative in nature, reflecting the input and involvement of the mental health, juvenile justice and other systems.

9. Services and strategies aimed at improving the identification and treatment of youth with mental health needs in the juvenile justice system should be routinely evaluated to determine their effectiveness in meeting desired goals and outcomes. (p. 11)

secure custody

A form of custody under the Youth Criminal Justice Act whereby youth are removed from a community and confined to an institution.

Based on these principles, consider the New Brunswick case of Ashley Smith and ask yourself what might have been put in place at the early stages of her involvement in the youth justice system to alter the course of events that led to her accidental death in an adult penitentiary at the age of 19 (see Box 16.1).

Box 16.1 Youth Justice in Action

Ashley Smith

Ashley Smith, a 19-year-old woman from Moncton, New Brunswick, died on October 19, 2007, while in federal custody at Ontario's Grand Valley Institution. Ashley had spent three years in and out of the New Brunswick Youth Centre, which is the only **secure custody** young offender institution in the province of New Brunswick. During those three years, Ashley spent two-thirds of her time in segregation—that is, in solitary confinement in an eight-by-ten cell for more or less 23 hours a day, with lights on 24 hours a day. She faced 501 institutional charges during those three years and 70 criminal charges during her lifetime, more than half for incidents inside the institution. She had 168 self-harm incidents, and she was tasered twice, as a youth, before she reached the age of 19 in an adult prison while waiting for transfer to the federal institution where she eventually died. The coroner's report revealed that Ashley died accidentally as a result of asphyxiation. She did place a ligature around her neck, but she did not intend to die.

After Smith's death, Bernard Richard, the New Brunswick Provincial Ombudsman and Child and Youth Advocate, launched an investigation into her death at the urging of Smith's mother. Richard released *The Ashley Smith Report* in 2008, which put forth 25 recommendations to 'revamp' the youth criminal justice system in order to take full advantage of the provisions of the Youth Criminal Justice Act. Richard argued that 'youth who commit *punishable acts* but who are not, themselves, forcibly *punishable*' (Child and Youth Advocate 2008b, p. 8) should not be held in closed custody facilities. Ashley, he concluded, fell under this category.

Smith's story was also featured on CBC's *the fifth estate*, first with 'Out of Control', which introduced viewers to the life and death of Ashley Smith in January 2010, and then again with 'Behind the Wall' in November 2010, which delved further into the Ashley Smith case and shocked viewers by broadcasting institutional footage of her death.

While a tremendous amount of attention has been given to the Ashley Smith case after her death, it is important that attention also stay focused on Canadian youth, like Ashley, who are involved in the criminal justice system but should not be criminalized. Most recently, in January 2011, the *National Post* reported the story of a 13-year-old girl with severe, diagnosed mental illnesses who had to be court-ordered to a treatment facility in Utah because there were no treatment facilities available to her in her home province of Ontario. However, the girl had to be discharged from the facility as a result of violent behaviour, and now her parents wonder where she will end up. There are no adequate facilities for her in Ontario, and because her mental illnesses can cause violent outbursts her mother fears she will end up in a closed custody facility. This case has been compared to the Ashley Smith case by the former president of the Schizophrenia Society of Kingston, Pat Forsdyke. Speaking of both cases, Forsdyke urges that 'jail must be avoided at all costs when attempting to treat the mentally ill—a remedy that Canada has so far failed to address'.

What do we do with our mentally ill young people?

Critical Thinking Questions

1. What was meant by Bernard Richard's comment 'not forcibly punishable'?
2. Article 40 of the UN Convention on the Rights of the Child requires that children who have violated the penal law be treated in a manner consistent with the child's age and with the desirability of promoting the child's reintegration and his or her taking up a constructive role in society. Was this article followed in the case of Ashley Smith?

What Does Not Work?

It has become almost common knowledge that in order to understand youth offending, one must look at a range of factors, broadly grouped as individual factors, family factors, school factors, and community factors. Research to date suggests that individual characteristics include such things as impulsivity, anti-social attitudes, continued contact with anti-social peers, and alcohol and other drug abuse. Family factors include such items as parenting styles, inconsistent and harsh discipline, parental criminality, and poor parental supervision. Truancy, poor academic performance, a lack of school engagement, and aggressive behaviour at school have been shown to relate to youth offending. Finally, disorganized communities, the availability of drugs and alcohol, a lack of amenities such as access to sports, leisure, and other activities are factors that contribute to a lack of belonging and an increased risk for youth crime. It is not uncommon that youth will have multiple **risk factors**, and the cumulative risk factors sometimes make it difficult to untangle the effects of individual risk factors (Loeber and Farrington 1998). The more problems that a youth has, the more difficult it becomes to address his or her needs. To do so, it is important to first identify potential sources of problem behaviour and then address these problems with a package of services aimed at the individual needs of youth.

Individual characteristics such as impulsivity, low empathy, poor internalized norms, and attitudes supporting offending may indeed be factors that foster anti-social behaviour, but they are often long-term problems and not easily changed. However, some factors are situational and short term and may be amenable to intervention. Such items as boredom, frustration, alcohol or drug misuse, status with peers, and perceived costs and benefits of offending (Farrington 1996). Andrews refers to such intermediate factors as **criminogenic** needs, which, if targeted appropriately, can result in effective outcomes (Andrews and Bonta 1997). Such needs tied to effective outcomes include the following:

- Changing anti-social attitudes and feelings through cognitive-behavioural programming
- Reducing the number and opportunities for anti-social peer associations
- Fostering and promoting family affection, communication, monitoring, and supervision
- Increasing self-control, self-management, and problem-solving skills
- Finding and maintaining positive social role models
- Ensuring that the offender is able to recognize 'risky' situations and has concrete and well-rehearsed plans for dealing with those types of situations and circumstances
- Confronting and working toward changing the personal and circumstantial barriers that are in the way of effective outcomes

However, it is essential when considering the effectiveness of any program that we look at the unpredictability of even evidenced-based programs as a 'one-size fits all' solution. The same structured program may work in different ways in different circumstances, and sometimes it will not work at all.

Criminal behaviour in young people cannot simply be tackled as an episode of individual criminality disassociated from the social context or from the available child-welfare, education and health, social, and recreational provisions (Whyte 2005, p. 9). The social context is as important as the individual personal and skill development outcomes are because 'social circumstances and relationships with others are both the object of the intervention and the medium through which change can be achieved' (Farrall 2002, p. 21). We know from the **resiliency** literature, for example, that not all children and young people exposed to multiple risk factors become offenders, nor do all children and young people who offend grow up in low socio-economic classes (Graham 1998; Ungar 2004; Steinberg, Blatt-Eisengart, and Cauffman 2006).

risk factors
Factors that may cause a young person to be more likely to offend. These factors can be individual, environmental, etc.

criminogenic
Producing or tending to produce crime or criminals.

resiliency
The ability of children and youth to develop positive self-esteem and self-efficacy despite facing crisis, challenges, or adversity.

What Does Work?

Effective programs appear to have the following characteristics:

- They are designed to target crime-related characteristics that can be changed (dynamic factors) and that are predictive of future criminal activities.
- Individuals must spend sufficient time considering the changes desired.
- They are implemented in such a way that it is appropriate for the participant's age and stage of development, using methods based on social learning or cognitive behavioural theories of change that emphasize positive reinforcement and provide contingencies for social behaviour.
- They are delivered by well-trained staff who are knowledgeable and skilled.
- The most intensive programs are delivered to those at the highest risk of re-offending and are individualized as much as possible.

Perhaps the last point is the most important to underscore when discussing alternative measures, diversion, and the youth justice system.

While we must base our interventions on the best available research evidence, perhaps we need to be mindful of the ever-present issue relating to the determination of what works for who under what circumstances (Hoge, Guerra, and Boxer 2008). We have sufficient evidence to date to tell us that reserving our most serious interventions for our most serious offenders is essential. That should be enough in itself to move away from trying to implement 'treatment' programs for the majority of young people who come into the system. Again, for most youth, doing nothing may be the most effective outcome.

Guerra, Kim, and Boxer (2008, p. 98) offer a set of principles to guide effective treatment for juvenile offenders:

- Closer to home principle
- Rehabilitation principle
- Evidence-based principle
- Risk-focused, strength-based principle

In looking at the literature with respect to juvenile diversion, the *closer to home principle* has been outlined many times over. Guerra, Kim, and Boxer (2008) argue that

> Whenever possible, youth should receive treatment in the communities where they live, with incarceration in state institutions used as a last resort for purposes of community safety. When youth cannot live with their families of origin, they should be assigned to residential, community-based facilities that provide treatment in small cottages or homes with foster families or teaching family support. Incarcerated youth should still retain ties with their home communities in order to develop a positive support system. (p. 99)

The *rehabilitation principle* is underscored in a system where there is institutional and political support and when that support becomes 'part of the culture of practice' and becomes a set of organizing beliefs to guide programs and services. Treatment that follows *evidence-based principles* should be structured and address dynamic risk factors that are most likely to change and most likely to be able to generalize (Guerra, Kim, and Boxer 2008, p. 99). Finally, the *risk-focused, strength-based principle* needs to recognize the multiple types of risk that young people face and must capitalize on the tools that are available to match the level of service to specific profiles of risk while reserving the most serious interventions for the highest risk offenders. Emphasis should be placed on building strengths to promote desistance from an offending lifestyle, and treatment should identify and leverage youth strengths in order to reduce risk (Guerra, Kim, and Boxer 2008, p. 99).

The implementation of a strong program based on the principles of effective correctional treatment—with standardized assessment and screening tools and myriad services within the community to be able to address individual needs as a wraparound program—seems to show the most promise to date. Packaged interventions provide little room for active participation in determining the social context in which the program is being delivered. Hoge, Guerra, and Boxer (2008, p. 119) suggest that through greater collaboration and partnerships between researchers and juvenile justice practitioners, research may be able to keep pace by determining which program elements of these packages are essential and which components can be implemented with greater flexibility (see Box 16.2).

Box 16.2 Youth Justice in Action

Quantum Opportunities Program: Connecting Youth at Risk of School Failure to their Communities

In 1998, the Quantum Opportunities Program (QOP) was listed as a model program through Blueprints for Violence Prevention. Even though the program is fairly expensive to implement, Elliott (1998) suggests that it is more cost effective in the long run than the criminal justice system. The Quantum Opportunities Program has been rated as a promising program by the US Surgeon General's Report (2001), and an exemplary program by Mihalic and Aultman-Bettridge (2004). Taggart (1995) reported a 70 per cent reduction in arrests for the youth in QOP compared to their control group counterparts by the time of expected high school graduation.

QOP is a long-term, multi-component intervention program that aims to reduce dropout rates, pregnancy, and delinquency among disadvantaged high school students. QOP does this by directly addressing low academic achievement, problematic life choices such as drug or alcohol abuse, and anti-social, aggressive, or violent behaviour. The program targets students entering grade 9 who come from low-income families and supports them for the full four years that they are in high school. The research literature has shown consistently that both academic failure and school dropout are risk factors highly correlated with criminal activity.

According to Elliott et al. (2002) the QOP provides education, development, and service activities coupled with a 'sustained relationship with a peer group and a caring adult' throughout the four years of high school. The interventions of the program fall into three general components: (1) educational activities, (2) developmental activities, and (3) service activities.

The program requires that the students complete 250 hours of activity per year in each of these components, for a total annual participation of 750 hours and a total of 3000 hours of participation over the project's four-year duration.

1. Educational Activities

These activities are intended to improve academic achievement and increase the likelihood of graduation from high school and attending post-secondary education. As the youth who are referred to the program have already been identified as being at risk of not completing high school, they each have an individual learning plan that has been developed by the referral school and that will form the basis of the educational activities for each individual youth. Activities normally consist of tutoring, homework help, computer skills training, learning skills and strategies (organizational skills, time management, effective study habits), and coaching to help overcome challenges posed by learning disabilities or low literacy skills.

2. Developmental Activities

These activities are intended to reduce risky behaviours, problematic life choices, and anti-social, aggressive, or violent behaviour. This component provides life skills training for personal development. Activities include training and coaching related to effective decision-making skills, employment skills, healthy lifestyles, relationship skills, social skills, and knowledge of how to access community resources.

3. Service Activities

These activities are intended to help youth develop a sense of pride and responsibility for themselves as well as for others in their neighbourhood; feel a sense of belonging and ownership in their community; learn teamwork and other critical skills related to planning, judgment, and social skills; develop interests leading to future education and employment choices; connect to resources that will be helpful in creating opportunities; and break down their social exclusion and marginalization through engagement in positive community activities and events.

Activities can include volunteering, participating in community events, fundraising, participating in campaigns, neighbourhood clean-ups and environmental improvements, sport teams, public speaking, team building, and other similar activities.

Motivation and Retention

An important element of the Quantum Opportunities Program is the reinforcement of desired behaviour through a system of motivational incentives that allow the project to recognize effort, progress, and achievement on the part of the youth involved.

The project develops a system of tangible recognition for the participants, which acknowledges the work required to fulfill the program's educational, developmental, and service components. As young persons achieve certain weekly, monthly, quarterly, or annual milestones (e.g., completing 250 hours of annual activity in a particular component of their contract), they will be offered incentive opportunities, such as field trips to cultural or social events in the community, attendance at sports events, enrolment in recreational and sports activities, etc.

One of the essential ingredients of this program is the continued involvement of the QOP counsellors in the lives of the young people, regardless of whether or not these youth have been removed from the formal school system through expulsion. In addition to expulsion from school, students who are ill, who become incarcerated, or who move to a different neighbourhood will continue to be supported in the program.

Current Canadian Program Implementation of the Quantum Opportunities Program

The QOP is being funded through the National Crime Prevention Centre in two provinces for the next four years. The non-government agency responsible for the administration and implementation of this program is the John Howard Society of New Brunswick and Ontario.

Since 1929 the John Howard Society has been committed to providing effective programs and services that assist in reducing crime and its causes. The John Howard Society of Canada's mission is 'Effective, just and humane responses to the causes and consequences of crime'. As such, both the John Howard Society of New Brunswick and Ontario have argued consistently 'that longer prison sentences are not an effective method of rehabilitation, nor an effective way of reducing crime', which echoes the research literature discussed earlier. The John Howard Society of New Brunswick applies specific operational principles and criteria to all its programs: all programs must be **evidence-based**; there must be sufficient resources and facilities for effective program development and implementation; only trained and qualified volunteers/employees are recruited to plan and deliver programs.

The John Howard Society supports prevention-focused social programs and the provision of adequate social supports to reduce rates of crime and victimization in all of our communities. For a list of all John Howard Societies in Canada, refer to the weblink at the end of this chapter.

Critical Thinking Questions

1. What potential risk and protective factors are addressed in this program? How does this prevention program assist in reducing the likelihood of youth becoming entrenched in the youth criminal justice system?

2. Consider the list of principles and criteria that are used for the programs and services delivered by the John Howard Society of New Brunswick. In what way(s) do these principles reflect the research evidence on 'What Doesn't Work'?

Principles for Developing Youth Policy and a Youth Voice

In her discussion of a move toward more effective youth policy, Bessant (2005, p. 5) argues that the problem with current discussions about youth policy is that adult policy-makers try to 'imagine

evidence-based principles
Principles based on a foundation of reliable research.

what young people want or what they believe they ought to want or need'. This, she argues, has produced a history of youth policy-making where 'policy makers create knowledge about young people' and act as spokespersons for them and as a 'substitute for young people' (Bessant 2005, p. 5).

Brank and Lane (2008) suggest that even though young people have a unique perspective, they are rarely asked for their opinions. In their study they questioned juvenile attitudes toward parental responsibility for crimes for which they were now incarcerated. Previous beliefs held that there was a link between absentee parenting and higher chances of a youth committing crime; the 150 incarcerated youth studied, however, did not believe this to be the case! Seventy-seven per cent of the youth indicated that their parents were more than a little involved (22.4 per cent) or completely involved (54.4 per cent) in their lives the year before they were committed to the young offender facility. Further, in terms of parental monitoring, 15 per cent of the youth reported that their parents *always* knew where they were, 23 per cent indicated their parents usually knew where they were, and 23 per cent said their parents knew of their whereabouts 'more than half the time'. More than 75 per cent of the young people incarcerated said that their parents were not at all responsible for their criminal behaviour, with only 9 young incarcerates stating that their parents were completely responsible.

Hoge, Guerra, and Boxer (2008) point out that young offenders are a 'heterogeneous group with multiple potential pathways to delinquency', which means that a 'one-size fits all' treatment approach does not meet the needs of youth at risk. These youth need to be invited to the conversation as they are an important source of information. Indeed, the UN Convention on the Rights of the Child outlines, in articles 12, 13, and 14, the right of children under 18 years of age to fully participate in decisions that affect them, to be able to express their ideas and concerns in any way that is appropriate for them, and to have access to full information about situations that affect them.

In order to make appropriate recommendations with respect to youth policy, then, we must ask the young people who will be the direct recipients of such policy. To actively engage young people, adults need to work as partners with them in a supportive manner. Rather than working in isolation of the individuals and communities whose perceptions and actions they seek to transform, young people can be engaged with 'adult allies' who support and advocate with them every day (Fletcher and Vavrus 2006). We need **youth engagement** in policy formation.

Investing in Youth and Social Management of Risk is a project of the Policy Research Initiative of Human Resources and Skills Development Canada. In January 2010, a research paper by Sandra Franke (2010) was released that outlines an analytical framework for youth-related policy development and research in Canada. In the review of the academic literature, two conclusions were drawn, which form the basis of the model framework proposed:

1. The importance of decompartmentalizing how researchers and policy-makers think about youth by favouring a holistic approach that factors in all aspects of young people's lives: personal, psychological, educational, family, social, and community
2. The importance of adopting a positive view of youth by building on their strengths and their contribution to society's well-being

The positive youth development framework and the holistic approach to youth engagement and intervention are the trademarks of the proposed expansion to the Centre of Excellence on Youth Engagement. Franke goes on to suggest that it may not be necessary for the government of Canada to create a pan-Canadian youth policy if it takes a 'leadership role in establishing a shared vision and in coordinating youth-focused policy'.

Strong youth–adult partnerships serve a variety of different purposes: they protect youth rights for participation, particularly in terms of decision-making; they facilitate positive youth development; and they work to steer youth toward improving their communities and civil society (Zeldin,

youth engagement
'The meaningful participation and sustained involvement of a young person in an activity, which has a focus outside of him or herself' (Centres of Excellence for Children's Well-Being, www.tgmag. ca/centresnew/files/ Whatis_WEB_e.pdf). Full engagement consists of a behavioural component, an affective component, and a cognitive component.

Camino, and Mook 2005). With adults' civic attitudes and participation rooted in their adolescent experiences of civic participation (Stolle and Hooghe 2004), it is important to examine pathways, such as youth–adult partnerships, toward the development of meaningful youth engagement.

In an effort to understand what young people had to say about improving the youth justice system, two focus groups were held in the spring of 2009. One of the assemblies included youth who were currently attending either a high school or an alternative education program while the other focus group was held at the New Brunswick Youth Centre (see Box 16.3).

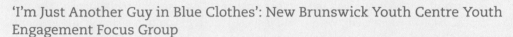

Box 16.3 Youth Justice in Action

'I'm Just Another Guy in Blue Clothes': New Brunswick Youth Centre Youth Engagement Focus Group

A group of youth incarcerated at the New Brunswick Youth Centre (NBYC) were invited to participate in a focus group where they would be given the opportunity to share their experiences of being a young person involved with the criminal justice system. The fact that 15 young people (out of a total count of 35 young offenders) agreed to participate in the two-hour focus group was an overwhelming response. They described lives filled with risk factors and very few protective factors. We were encouraged by their honesty as they shared very disturbing details of their home life and the pains of imprisonment. We were met with a group of polite and respectful young people who very much wanted to share their opinions (Reid 2009).

We asked the youth to tell us some things about what worked well for them and what might work well for others who have not been sentenced to custody. We asked them the following questions:

1. Why do youth commit crimes?
2. What would be ideal programming?
3. What would have stopped you from committing crimes?
4. What are your concerns about reintegration?

In terms of the reasons given by the youth at the NBYC as to the causes of crime, many of them felt that drugs had a large role to play in the commission of their offence. Others stated that they 'Need money for drugs, need a way to get drugs' and that their past experience led them to commit crimes; some people act out what they experience and some argued that it was out of necessity. When asked whether they committed crime because they were bored, a couple of them said that there was no way, 'that's a stupid reason. You don't come here because you are bored'.

Another youth stated that 'I was never bored, I grew up on reserve I didn't have to pay for anything'.

Some youth shared that their family was dysfunctional and that their reasons were different. One young person commented that 'We're all unique' and this was underscored by a later comment about how they have to wear uniforms and they have no individuality left, 'just another guy in blue clothes'. One youth stated 'If I had a family it would have saved me from this; foster care that's what messed me up'. He really felt that the only reason the foster family took him in was for the money: 'I'll take in this troublesome kid so I can get a couple hundred dollars for keeping him'. The youth understood what it felt like to be moved around from one placement to another: 'When I get comfortable in a foster home they move me'.

Other youth identified a number of key issues with the lack of 'matching' when it came to child welfare placements. One youth remarked that he was 'a different race than my foster family'. Another youth spoke of the problems in the home and of not being believed: 'My foster brother beat me up all the time'.

Family factors were important for the youth and one youth pointed out that there is not much attention paid to the fact that a number of young people who are at the NBYC are not only young offenders but also parents. He said that it would be different this time when he was released because he had the responsibilities of fatherhood and that would help him to stay away from drugs and crime. Another young person also discussed the importance of family, commenting that he was upset that since he had been incarcerated his younger brother no longer knew who he was. He also felt that he wasn't providing a good role model for his younger brother and he didn't want him to grow up and 'follow in his footsteps'.

When the youth were asked about their concerns about reintegration, it was clear that some of these young people were afraid of breaching their conditions of release. Youth said that there were too many conditions to release, conditions that made it impossible for them to be successful and they wanted to have some opportunity to work toward reducing the controls as they proved that they were successful: 'While we are in here we work on levels, and if you achieve points you get more privileges. When you are released you start back at nothing with a six o'clock curfew, requirements to attend programs, attend school, attend counseling and no opportunity to improve'. Another youth said, 'We're not robots, we can't go from being in here for six months or a year talking to our friends, to having no friends to talk to. We can't change overnight'. There was acknowledgement that the probation officers had a job to do in terms of reporting to the court, but their complaints stemmed from the inability of officials to have the time to 'see the positive things' and be able to 'cut some slack'.

The young people did offer some suggestions for ways that they would be able to be with their 'peers' even if there was a non-association order. They made the point that there is no problem with them 'associating' with young offenders when they are in custody, and there is no problem when they are released to associate with young offenders at anger management and other 'programs'. They questioned why a program couldn't be set up so that they could go to the gym or play a game of basketball with these same peers.

The youth liked the idea of having peer helpers and felt that they would be good peer helpers to other youth who were following the path into crime. A number of young people offered to be a 'peer mentor' as an alternative measures program offering. While these comments only scratch the surface of the myriad issues related to youth in custody, it is essential that there are provisions for 'alternatives' for those young people who are completing their term of custody and reintegrating back into their communities. Without choice, services, and resources, there is a strong likelihood that these young people will breach their many conditions and return to custody to once again become 'just another guy in blue clothes'.

Critical Thinking Question

1. What value is there in engaging youth in the formulation of legislation that pertains to them?

Summary

There is no one, ideal way to approach youth at risk. Youth justice legislation and youth-at-risk programming cannot be developed as a one-size-fits-all model because in doing so, the needs of so many youth are not met. This chapter presented many of the unique challenges of developing effective policies for youth.

The binary function of the youth justice system, as it is designed today, does not allow for the best interests of youth to be addressed. The chapter also made the point that, increasingly, youth have been pushed into the adult system through a variety of loopholes prior to reaching the age of majority. This phenomenon is known as adulteration.

Throughout the evolution of youth criminal justice in Canada, the fundamental belief was that all avenues should be exhausted to prevent youth from embarking on a life of crime. As the research demonstrates, this is best achieved by reserving custodial sentences for the most severe of cases and, instead, imposing meaningful consequences that will promote rehabilitation and reintegration. Extrajudicial measures, diversion, and noncustodial sentences limit the occurrences of stigmatization and labelling and are more in line with serving the best interests of the child. This need to focus on noncustodial sentences is most apparent with youth with highly complex needs. High numbers of incarcerated youth have been shown to have mental illness or conduct disorders, and their needs cannot be met in a correctional facility. Mental-health diversion programs are the only answer to help these youth. The case of Ashley Smith was held up as a key example of how the system has failed.

Within diversion programs, individualized programs must be developed for youth to overcome their dynamic risk factors. Evidence-based principles must be used in order to capitalize on each youth's strengths in order to promote resiliency. One such program is the Quantum Opportunities Program, which helps youth work within their strengths, and pushes them to develop new ones in order to allow for positive outcomes.

Finally, in order to truly understand the needs of youth, youth themselves must be consulted. The UN Convention on the Rights of the Child demands this and as a signatory to this human rights treaty, Canada must respond. Allowing youth to have a voice in their own experience empowers and lends a sense of responsibility to take ownership of their own path. Further, although adults may have the best of intentions they may not interpret the needs of youth in a way that is beneficial. Simply put, youth and adults must come together with the common goal of meeting the 'best interests' of the child.

Key Terms

adulteration

best interests of the child

criminogenic

custodial sanctions

evidence-based principles

labelling

rehabilitation

reintegration

resiliency

risk factors

secure custody

youth engagement

youth justice

Review Questions

1. What is meant by the 'best interests of the child'? How does this concept relate to the current legal regulations of young persons?

2. What is meant by 'adulteration'?

3. Describe the type of youth justice model that best describes the JDA and YOA. How do these models differ from the youth justice model that characterizes the YCJA?

4. What is the significance of the Nunn Commission and its recommendations?

5. Describe three to four of the key characteristics for effective youth-at-risk programs. How do they compare to the effective treatment principles for young offenders?

Critical Thinking Questions

1. How important do you think it is to maintain a separate system for young offenders in Canada?

2. To what extent do you feel the UN Convention on the Rights of the Child is, or is not, important for empowering and protecting young persons?

3. What are the critical factors that differentiate programs that work vs. those that don't work? Briefly discuss the implications of these (if any) differences.

4. How might we best address the challenges that youth at risk face today?

Suggested Readings

Barron, C. (2000). *Giving youth a voice: Rethinking adolescent violence.* Halifax: Fernwood.

Brendtro, L. K., Brokenleg, M., and Van Bockern, S. (2002). *Reclaiming youth at risk: Our hope for the future* (rev. ed.). Bloomington, IN: Solution Tree Press.

Schissel, B. (2000). *Still blaming children: Youth conduct and the politics of hate.* Halifax: Fernwood.

Scott, E.S. and Steinberg, L. (2008). *Rethinking juvenile justice.* Cambridge, MA: Harvard University Press.

Suggested Weblinks

The Students Commission/Centre of Excellence for Youth Engagement

www.tgmag.ca

- This site provides links to the research on youth engagement as well as materials and resources related to youth voice and youth engagement. A series of publications on youth engagement, young decision makers models, UN Convention on the Rights of the Child, and Project PEACE (an anti-gang crime prevention program) are outlined and discussed.

The John Howard Society of Canada

www.johnhoward.ca

- This site provides links to John Howard Societies across Canada as well as to a number of resources related to research and program evaluation, advocacy, and position papers on various aspects of the youth and adult criminal justice system. A series of short fact sheets on issues related to crime and criminal justice as well as position papers and research documents are housed with the Ontario society through its Research and Policy Centre.

The Office of the Child and Youth Advocate: New Brunswick

www.gnb.ca/0073/Child-YouthAdvocate/publications-e.asp

- A number of reports referred to in this chapter are available for downloading from this site, including the Ashley Smith report, *Connecting the Dots.* To obtain information about other provincial child and youth advocates, refer to the list of members of the Canadian Council of Provincial Child and Youth Advocates available at http://provincialadvocate.on.ca/main/en/ccpcya/.

The Library of Parliament

www2.parl.gc.ca/Sites/LOP/VirtualLibrary/ResearchPublications-e.asp

- There are a substantial number of research publications prepared to assist parliamentarians, and Senate and House of Commons committees and parliamentary associations.

Canadian Coalition for the Rights of Children

http://rightsofchildren.ca

- Its purpose is to exchange information, provide public education materials about the UN Convention on the Rights of the Child, monitor implementation of the Convention in Canada, and engage in dialogue with government officials on child rights issues.

The Campbell Collaboration Group

www.campbellcollaboration.org/library.php

- This is an international research network that produces systematic reviews and meta-analysis of the effects of social interventions. The searchable data base provides an array of articles and reviews on key aspects of youth justice, delinquency, and crime prevention.

Center for the Study and Prevention of Violence

www.colorado.edu/cspv/blueprints

- Blueprints programs provide research and resources on model and promising crime prevention programs.

References

Andrews, D. and Bonta, J. (1997). *The psychology of criminal conduct* (2nd ed.). Cincinnati: Anderson.

Bessant, J. (2005). Principles for developing youth policy. *Policy Studies, 26*(1): 103–16.

Brank, E. and Lane, J. (2008). An experimental juvenile probation program; Effects on parent and peer relationships. *Crime Delinquency, 54*(2): 193–224.

Caloz, M. (Producer/director). (2010). *The fifth estate: Behind the wall.* [Television Series]. Canada: CBC.

Caloz, M. (Producer/director). (2010). *The fifth estate: Out of control.* [Television Series]. Canada: CBC.

Canada. (1965). Juvenile delinquency in Canada. The report of the department of justice committee on juvenile delinquency. Committee on Juvenile Delinquency: Queen's Printer.

Canada. (1996). A review of the Young Offenders Act and the youth justice system in Canada: Report of the federal provincial territorial task force on youth justice. Department of Justice Canada.

Centre of Excellence on Youth Engagement. (2008). *What is youth engagement?* Retrieved from http://www.tgmag.ca/centresnew/files/Whatis_WEB_e.pdf

Child and Youth Advocate: Ombudsman. (2008a). Connecting the dots: A report on the condition of youth-at-risk and youth with very complex needs in New Brunswick. Fredericton, NB: New Brunswick Ombudsman and Child and Youth Advocate.

Child and Youth Advocate: Ombudsman. (2008b). *The Ashley Smith report.* Fredericton, NB; New Brunswick Ombudsman and Child and Youth Advocate.

Cocozza, J. and Skowyra, K. (2000). Youth with mental health disorders: Issues and emerging responses. *Office of Juvenile Justice and Delinquency Prevention Journal, 7*(1): 3–13.

Cuellar, A.E., Markowitz, S., and Libby, A. (2004). Mental health and substance abuse treatment and juvenile crime. *Journal of Mental Health Policy and Economics, 7*(2), 59–68.

Dembo, R. and Schmeidler, J. (2003). Classification of high risk youths. *Crime and Delinquency, 49*(2), 201–30.

Department of Justice. (1908). *Juvenile delinquents act.* Ottawa: Government of Canada.

Department of Justice. (1985). *Young offenders act.* Ottawa: Government of Canada.

Department of Justice. (2002). *Youth Criminal Justice Act.* Ottawa: Government of Canada.

Elliott, D.S. (1998). *Prevention programs that work for youth: Violence prevention.* Boulder, CO: Centre for the Study and Prevention of Violence.

Elliott, D.S., Grady, J.M., Heys, L., Bell, H., Woodward, B., and Williams, S. (2002) *Safe communities- safe schools: A guide to effective program selection.* Boulder, CO: Centre for the Study and Prevention of Violence.

Elliot, D., Huizinga, D., and Menard, S. (1989). *Multiple problem youth: Delinquency, substance use and mental health problems.* New York: Springer.

Farrall, S. (2002). *Rethinking what works with offenders: Probation, social context and distance from crime.* London: Willan.

Farrington, D. (1996). *Understanding and preventing youth crime.* New York: Joseph Rowntree Foundation.

Feld, B.C. (1998). Juvenile and criminal justice systems responses to youth violence. In M. Tonry and M.H. Moore (Eds.), *Youth violence: Crime and justice, a review of research*, Vol. 24 (pp. 236–37). Chicago, IL: University of Chicago Press.

Fletcher, A. and Vavrus, J. (2006). *The guide to social change led by and with young people.* Olympia, WA: CommonAction.

Foster, E., Qaseem, A., and Connor, T. (2004). Can better mental health services reduce the risk of juvenile justice system involvement? *American Journal of Public Health, 94*(5): 859–65.

Franke, S. (2010). Current realities and emerging issues facing youth in Canada: An analytical framework for public policy research. Ottawa: Government of Canada, Policy Research Institute.

Gilbert, J., Grimm, R., and Parnham, J. (2001). Applying therapeutic principles to a family-focused juvenile justice model. *Alabama Law Review, 52*: 1196–97.

Gotfredson, D.C., Wilson, D.B., and Najaka, S.S. (2002). School based crime prevention. In L.W. Sherman, D.P. Farrington, B.C. Welsh, and D.L. Mackenzie (Eds.), *Evidence-based crime prevention* (pp. 56–164). New York: Routledge.

Government of New Brunswick (2009). Reducing the risk, addressing the need; Being responsive to at-risk and highly complex children and youth. Government Report, Public Safety.

Graham, J. (1998). *Schools, disruptive behavior and delinquency.* London: Home Office.

Guerra, N.G., Kim, T., and Boxer, P. (2008). *Principles of best practice.* In R. Hoge, N.G. Guerra, and P. Boxer (Eds.), Treating the juvenile offender (pp. 79–102). New York: Guilford Press.

Hahn, A., Leavitt, T., and Aaron, P. (1994). *Evaluation of the quantum opportunities program (QOP): Did the program work?* A report on the post-secondary outcomes and cost effectiveness of the QOP program. Unpublished manuscript, Brandeis University, Waltham, MA. As cited in Gotfredson et al., (2002). Ibid.

Hoge, R.D., Guerra, N.G., and Boxer, P. (2008). *Treating the juvenile offender.* New York: Guilford.

House of Commons (2010a, Tuesday, May 11). Standing Committee on Justice and Human Rights, Evidence. 3rd session, 40th Parliament, Number 016.

House of Commons (2010b, Thursday, June 10). Standing Committee on Justice and Human Rights, Evidence. 3rd session, 40th Parliament, Number 023.

Kong, R. (2009). Youth custody and community services Canada, 2007/2008. *Juristat, 29*(2).

Latimer, J. (2001). A meta-analytical examination of youth delinquency, family treatment, and recidivism. *Canadian Journal of Criminology, 43*(2): 237–53.

Lipsey, M.W., Wilson, D.B., and Cothern, L. (2000). *Effective intervention for serious juvenile offenders.* Washington, DC: OJJDP.

Loeber, R. and Farrington, D. (1998). Serious and violent juvenile offenders: Risk factors and successful interventions. Thousand Oaks, CA: Sage.

Loeber, R., Farrington, D., Stouthamer-Loeber, M., Kammen, W., and Van, W.B. (1998). Multiple risk factors in multi-problem boys. In R. Jessor (Ed.), *New perspectives in adolescent risk behaviour.* New York: Cambridge University Press.

McKee, M. (2009). Together into the future: A transformed mental health system for New Brunswick. NB: New Brunswick Department of Health.

Mair, G. (2004). *What matters in probation?* London: Willan.

Mears, D.P. and Butts, J.A. (2008). Using monitoring to improve the accountability, operations, and effectiveness of juvenile justice. *Criminal Justice Policy Review, 19*(3): 264–84.

Mendell, R. (2000). Less hype, more help. Reducing youth crime: What works and what doesn't? Washington, DC: American Youth Policy Forum.

Mihalic, D. and Aultman-Bettridge, S. (2004). A guide to effective school based prevention programs. In W.L. Turk (Ed.) *School crime and policing.* Englewood Cliffs, NJ: Prentice Hall.

Moyer, S. (1980). Diversion from the juvenile justice system and its impact on children: A review of the literature. Ottawa: Queen's Printer.

National Alliance for the Mentally Ill. (2001). Families on the brink: The impact of ignoring children with serious mental illness. Arlington, VA: NAMI.

National Crime Prevention Centre. (2008). *Promising and model crime prevention programs.* Ottawa: Public Safety Canada.

Nunn, D.M. (2005). Spiraling out of control: Lessons learned from a boy in trouble. NS: Nova Scotia Government.

Office of Juvenile Justice and Delinquency Prevention (OJJDP). (1998). *Mental health disorders and substance abuse problems among juveniles.* Washington, DC: OJJDP.

Pitts, J. (2008). Korrectional karaoke: New labour and the zombification of youth justice. *Youth Justice, 1*(2), 1–16.

Raynor, P. (2008). Community penalties and home office research: On the way back to 'nothing works'? *Criminology and Criminal Justice, 8*(1), 73–87.

Regoli, R., Wildermann, E., and Pogrebin, M. (1985). Using an alternative evaluation measure for assessing juvenile diversion programs. *Child and Youth Services Review, 7*: 21–38.

Reid, S.A. (2009) 125 warnings: A review of extrajudicial measures and sanctions in the province of New Brunswick. (Unpublished report for NB Department of Public Safety).

Rosenblatt, J., Rosenblatt, A., and Biggs, E.E. (2000). Criminal behavior and emotional disorder: Comparing youth served by the mental health and juvenile justice systems. *Journal of Behavioral Health Services and Research, 27*: 227–37.

Schirm, A., Rodriguez-Planas, N., Maxfield, M., and Tuttle, C. (2003) *The quantum opportunity program demonstration: Short term impact.* Washington, DC: U.S. Department of Labor, Employment and Training. Mathematic Policy Research Inc.

Shelden, R.G. (1999). *Detention diversion advocacy: An evaluation.* Washington, DC: OJJDP.

Skowyra, K.R. and Cocozza, J.J. (2007). Blueprint for change: A comprehensive model for the identification and treatment of youth with mental health needs in contact with the juvenile justice system. Delmar, NY: National Center for Mental Health and Juvenile Justice.

Skowyra, K. and Powell, S.D. (2006). *Juvenile diversion: Programs for justice-involved youth with mental health disorders.* National Centre for Mental Health and Juvenile Justice.

Steinberg, L., Blatt-Eisengart, I., and Cauffman, E. (2006). Patterns of competence and adjustment among adolescents from authoritative, authoritarian, indulgent and neglectful homes: Replication in a sample of serious juvenile offenders. *Journal of Research on Adolescence, 16*: 47–58.

Stolle, D. and Hooghe, M. (2004). The roots of social capital: Attitudinal and network mechanisms in the relation between youth and adult indicators of social capital. *Acta Politica, 39*: 422–41.

Sullivan, C.J., Veysey, B.M., Hamilton, Z.K., and Grillo, M. (2007). Reducing out-of-community placement and recidivism: Diversion of delinquent youth with mental health and substance use problems from the justice system. *International Journal of Offender Therapy and Comparative Criminology, 51*: 555–77.

Taggart, R. (1995). *Quantum opportunity program.* Philadelphia, PA: Opportunities Industrialization Centres of America. As cited in Gotfredson et al., (2002).

Tustin, L.A. and Lutes, R. (2008). *A guide to the Youth Criminal Justice Act.* Toronto: Lexis Nexis.

Ungar, M. (2004). Resilience among children in child welfare, corrections, mental health and educational settings: Recommendations for service. *Child and Youth Care Forum, 34*(6), 445–64.

UN General Assembly. (1989). *Convention on the rights of the child.* United Nations, Treaty Series, Vol. 1577.

United States House of Representatives. (2004). Incarceration of youth who are waiting for community mental health services in the United States. Washington, DC: Committee on Government Reform.

US Surgeon General. (2001). Youth violence: A report of the Surgeon General.

Wallace, K. Teen caught in limbo in mental health system. (2011, January 24). *National Post.*

Wasserman, G.A., McReynolds, L.S., Lucas, C.P., Fisher, P., and Santos, L. (2002). The voice DISC-IV with incarcerated male youths: Prevalence of disorder. *Journal of the American Academy of Child and Adolescent Psychiatry, 41*(3), 314–21.

Wexler, D. (2000). Just some juvenile thinking about delinquent behavior: A therapeutic jurisprudence approach to relapse prevention planning and youth advisory juries. *University of Missouri at Kansas City Law Review, 69*, 93–114.

Whitaker, J., Severy, L., and Morton, D. (1984). A comprehensive community based youth diversion program. *Child Welfare, 63*(2), 175–81.

Whyte, B. (2005). Effectiveness, research and youth justice. *Youth Justice, 4*(1), 1–21.

Winick, B. (2003). Therapeutic jurisprudence and problem solving courts. *Fordham Urban Law Journal, 30,* 1055–76.

Zeldin, S., Camino, L. and Mook, C. (2005). The adoption of innovation in youth organizations: Creating the conditions for youth-adult partnerships. *Journal of Community Psychology, 33*(1), 121–35.

Glossary

Aboriginal: Includes individuals who identify as First Nations, Métis, or Inuit.

adjudication: The making of the decision by a court as to the guilt of the accused person. A person may also be adjudicated not guilty or not criminally responsible due to a mental disorder.

administrative offences: Offences against the administration of justice, that is, violations of court-ordered behavioural requirements, such as complying with a curfew, attending mandated programs, and following through on all manner of bail conditions and probation orders. Under sec. 4 of the YCJA there are provisions under the extrajudicial measures that allow for charges to be laid if the young person fails to comply with his or her disposition or fails to appear before the court. The charge can be initiated by either the police or the Crown.

adolescence: A term popularized by the child-development expert G. Stanley Hall to refer to the stage of life during which a person progresses, both biologically and emotionally, from being a child to being an adult.

adulteration: The dismantling of a distinct system of criminal justice for youth and the remerging with systems of justice for adults.

alternative justice agencies: Québec-based agencies responsible for the application of the extrajudicial programs for youth, which are either referred by the police or by the provincial director under the YCJA. Measures can include information and awareness programs on shoplifting, drugs, and law reinforcement as well as mediation or damage repair for the victim, or, if that is not possible, repairing the damage in terms of the community.

apprehended person: A person who has been identified by police as an offender and against whom a charge could be laid; also known as a *chargeable person.*

best interests of the child: When the interests of a young person are paramount in decision-making regarding his or her experience in the criminal justice system.

bifurcated youth justice system: Literally, a two-pronged justice system, meaning that it provides avenues for the diversion of first-time and less serious young offenders out of the system, while at the same time making possible more punitive forms of punishment for more serious offenders.

binge drinking: Heavy alcohol consumption over a short period of time for the purpose of becoming intoxicated. Generally, the concept is operationalized as the consumption of five or more drinks on one occasion (four or more for females).

biopsychosocial model: An approach that addresses biological, psychological, and social risk factors related to criminality that has been applied to the study of youth female criminality and youth gang involvement.

Boscoville: A unique program introduced in the 1950s in Québec that was based on a social welfare and psycho-educative model and that introduced elements in its program designed to teach delinquent youth the necessary skills, values, and attitudes that would allow them to develop a sense of social responsibility.

breach of probation: Violation of one or more of the conditions of a probation order.

charge ratio: The proportion of chargeable persons who were charged.

chargeable person: A person who has been identified by police as an offender and against whom a charge could be laid; also known as an *apprehended person.*

coercion: A personal or impersonal force that compels or frightens individuals to behave in a certain way.

colonization: Refers to historical and ongoing processes that began with the arrival of Europeans to the country and that include attempts to dominate and assimilate indigenous peoples.

community-based sentence: A sentence that is served in the community (and, therefore, not in a custodial facility); also known as a *noncustodial sentence.*

community justice forum: A safe, controlled environment in which the offender, the victim, and their families or supporters are brought together under the guidance of a trained facilitator. Together, using a scripted dialogue process, they discuss the offence and how they have all been affected, and jointly develop a plan to correct what has occurred.

co-morbidity: Two or more independent and coexisting medical conditions.

compensatory intervention: An intervention designed to make up for something that is absent, especially in the learning and social environment of young people.

conferencing: A collaborative and nonconventional approach to decision making in youth court.

context analysis: Analyzing media content for themes such as sensationalism or distortion.

control balance: The degree of control individuals perceive that they have over their environment relative to the degree of control they perceive their environment has over them.

convergence: When a current issue is framed in terms of its relation to a previous one.

Crime Severity Index (CSI): Developed and introduced by Statistics Canada, the CSI uses a weighting system to measure (youth) offences according to their seriousness. Although introduced in 2009, CSI data are available back to 1998.

criminalization: The process whereby individuals are assigned the label of 'criminal'.

criminogenic: Producing or tending to produce crime or criminals.

critical criminology: Scholarship on crime and justice that seeks to examine and alter inequalities, marginalization, and social exclusion.

critical discourse analysis: An approach in socio-linguistics that links discourse with political structure.

cultivation hypothesis: The hypothesis that the media inundates the public with ideas about crime.

cumulative continuity: A developmental model that outlines how crime in adolescence has negative consequences for future life chances, including education, relationships, and employment, and increases the likelihood that criminal behaviour will continue into adulthood. These in turn undermine further life chances, escalating the probabilities of continued, persistent criminal behaviour.

custodial sanctions: Under the Youth Criminal Justice Act, the sentencing of a young person to custody.

custodial sentence: A sentence that is served in a custodial facility; under the YCJA this may be an open or a closed facility.

custody and supervision order: A period of youth imprisonment followed by a period of community supervision.

customer: An individual who is a consumer and pursues the opportunity to purchase activity from a sex-trade worker.

dark figure of crime: Refers to incidents of crime or delinquency that go undetected or unreported by the police.

deconstruction: Involves opening up words to their hidden or closed-off possibilities in an attempt to reveal what is going on behind language.

deferred custody and supervision order (DCSO): In the YCJA, a community-based alternative to a custodial sentence, under which the young person will serve his or her sentence in the community under a set of strict conditions. If these conditions are not followed, the young person may be sent to custody to serve the balance of that sentence.

dependence: When an individual feels that use of a substance is necessary for normal daily functioning or when substance use leads to tolerance. Abruptly stopping use may lead to symptoms of withdrawal.

deterrence: A penological theory that criminal sanctions will discourage people from committing crime; a penological practice based on that theory.

differential intervention: Based on the identification of the type of delinquency associated with the behaviours of young offenders. The interventions must then be tailored to meet young offenders' treatment needs and the level of risk they pose to society (risk of recidivism). Takes into account that people do not come in one-size-fits-all packages and therefore refrains from applying the same approach to each person involved in a class, program, or other form of group-based change process.

differential treatment: An approach to treatment that takes individual differences fully into account. Treatment is individually designed and flexible enough to allow for variation as this need emerges and is based on the identification of the type of delinquency associated with the behaviours of young offenders. The interventions must then be tailored to meet young offenders' treatment needs and the level of risk they pose to society (risk of recidivism).

diminished criminal responsibility: The general view that individuals who are not adults should not be held fully responsible for their criminal behaviour.

disposition: For young offenders, this is the equivalent of sentencing for adults. Under the YCJA, a disposition should in theory be more rehabilitative and/or restorative than retributive.

disrupted social control: Events or life circumstances that weaken or destroy the relationships, attachments, and activities that provide barriers to engaging in criminal activities.

diversion: A justice-system practice, procedure, or program that substitutes an informal response to offending for a formal response, thus diverting people out of the formal justice system.

doli incapax: A legal doctrine that literally translated means 'incapable of doing harm' and refers to the English common-law presumption that children between 7 and 14 years of age could not be prosecuted for committing criminal offences, unless this presumption was contested by the Crown.

drug recognition expert (DRE) evaluation: A standardized procedure performed by a trained drug recognition expert—involving visual cues, vital signs, questioning, and the provision of bodily fluids by the potentially impaired driver—that is used for determining impairment by drugs or a drug in combination with alcohol.

dynamic security: Security that is ensured by the relational dimension. It is achieved by the constant presence of educators and the bonds built between the youth and them. As a result, the quality of the social climate is improved among peers, who in turn contribute to the security of the institution.

engaged institutions (EI) strategy (Innovation Centre for Community and Youth Development 2006): The engaged institutions (EI) strategy recognizes that positive collaboration between institutions, through the use of peacemaking circles, can originate from core organizational values regardless of any financial or practical incentives. For example, Roca realized that its core values of belonging, generosity, competence, and independence needed to be lived not only among staff members and participants of the organization, but in its relationships with other public and private agencies in its locality.

ethnography: A form of participatory research that involves immersion in the field of study. Because it allows for rich and descriptive findings on areas that are often hidden from view, ethnographic research is fundamental to cultural criminology.

evidence-based principles: Principles based on a foundation of reliable research.

experiential: Refers to an individual who has worked and lived the lifestyle of a sex-trade worker.

extrajudicial measures: Under the YCJA, measures other than judicial proceedings (i.e., youth court) that are used to deal with a young person alleged to have committed an offence (including extrajudicial sanctions).

extrajudicial programs: Measures that are designed to hold youths responsible for their actions without creating a criminal record. They are generally applied to youths who are not engaged in a serious delinquent trajectory.

extrajudicial sanctions: Under the YCJA, relatively formal diversion programs that have been authorized by the provincial authorities.

family group conferencing: '. . . a process of collaborative planning in situations where decisions need to be made for children or youth. It is a formal meeting where members of a child or youth's immediate family come together with extended kin and members'. (Source: BC Ministry of Children and Family Development, August 2005, p. 2)

fear-based communication: Messages used to frighten youth away from experimentation with substances by emphasizing the potential negative effects of use.

fetal alcohol spectrum disorder (FASD): The umbrella term used to describe the entire continuum of disabilities, from most severe to least severe, of prenatal exposure to alcohol. It includes the related conditions of fetal alcohol syndrome (FAS), fetal alcohol effects (FAE), alcohol-related birth effects (ARBE), and alcohol-related neurodevelopmental disorder (ARND).

folk devils: Any group that is unjustifiably perceived to pose a threat to the traditional values and institutions of society.

frame analysis: Analyzing media content to see how crime and criminals are depicted.

gay bashing: The humiliation and violence workers are at risk of from customers and the community.

gay for pay: A person who is heterosexual but who, in order to survive, will work in the sexual trade as a homosexual.

gender gap: Acknowledges the difference in the rates at which males and females do things. In the field of criminology, there exists a persistent and well-documented difference in the arrest rates for males and females, with males consistently committing significantly more crime than females.

gender role theories: Those explanations of delinquent and criminal behaviour that focus on the role that gender plays in the lives and behaviours of both females and males.

harm-reduction strategies: Any policies or programs that are designed to reduce the level of harm associated with substance use and abuse without requiring the cessation of use.

homeless youth: Youth who have either left or have been urged to leave home with the full knowledge or approval of legal guardians. They have no alternative home in which to live.

hospitality: An unrestrained welcome to a stranger. It calls for open spaces that welcome the other as they arrive.

ideological flexibility: Where the portrayal of persons is ambiguous—e.g., a youth offender is portrayed as both villain and victim.

incarceration rate: The rate (usually per 100 000) of persons in custodial facilities on an 'average' day of the year; it is the sum of the sentenced custody and the remand custody rates.

indeterminate sentences: Sentences of incarceration that have no fixed expiration date, which means that a person can be held in custody until he or she is deemed by correctional officials to either to be rehabilitated or to no longer pose a threat to society.

informal social control: The control over people's behaviour that develops as a result of relationships and attachments to significant others and investments in conventional activities that could be damaged by engaging in illegal activities.

intersectionality: Refers to a movement away from thinking categorically and toward thinking about the connections and crossroads between social facets. Intersectional thinking and theorizing recognizes the multiple, changing, and often overlapping dimensions, demographics, roles, and identities of criminals, victims, other individuals, and collectives.

intervention: Approaches that address the needs of youth once they are involved in gangs.

justice (Derrida): For Derrida, justice is a messianic promise of a more just future 'to come'.

juvenile courts: Specialized courts first created in the late nineteenth century to apply juvenile justice laws in the care of dependent and delinquent children.

juvenile delinquency: The legal term, which came into popular use in the nineteenth century to describe violations of the law by persons who had not reached the legal age of adulthood.

Juvenile Delinquents Act (JDA): Canada's first juvenile delinquency legislation enacted in 1908 and in force until 1984.

labelling: The stigmatization of a young person as deviant.

life-course turning points: Events such as marriage/divorce or employment/unemployment that serve to direct an individual's developmental criminal career path toward either desistance or onset.

life-cycle model: This model proposes a series of stages that youth encounter on the street and includes an initial engagement in street life, a stage where youth become more comfortable with street life, and, finally, periods of crisis during which some youth may transition off the street. A cyclical pattern is noted, however, in that many youth who exit the street may become re-involved.

low self-control: A trait made up of impulsivity, short-sightedness, risk-taking, physicality, insensitivity, and low frustration tolerance, which leaves individuals less able to refrain from activities that provide short-term pleasure or gain.

marginalization: The partial exclusion of certain groups from mainstream society who routinely suffer as the result of gross inequalities.

method of administration: The path by which a drug or other substance is brought into contact with the body. Common methods include smoking, ingestion, injection, and intranasal inhalation.

moral panic: Exaggerated fears about social problems, including youth deviance, partly generated by the media.

National Youth in Care Network: An organization run by youth and former youth from government care who advocate for youth in care.

noncustodial sentence: A sentence that is served in the community (and therefore, not in a custodial facility); also known as a *community-based sentence.*

official data: The Canadian Centre for Justice Statistics, a branch of Statistics Canada, collects offender and offence data from the police, courts, and corrections for administrative purposes. The Centre produces regular reports that are readily available to the public.

parens patriae: The legal doctrine that the state has a duty to assume the role of a substitute parent in the case of delinquent or dependent children who do not have parents who are able to adequately control or care for them.

parent: Includes any person who is under a legal duty to provide for a young person or any person who has the custody or control of a young person.

peacemaking circles: Peacemaking circles draw directly from the tradition of the talking circle, common among indigenous people of North America. The physical format of the circle symbolizes shared leadership, equality, connection, and inclusion. Using very intentional structural elements—ceremony, a talking piece, a facilitator or keeper, guidelines, and consensus decision-making—circles aim to create a safe space for authentic dialogue.

post-adjudication: Occurring after adjudication.

power (Foucault): Rather than as a quantity held or possessed by the state, Foucault understood power to be relational, positive, and exercised.

power-control theory: Refers to John Hagan and colleagues' 1989 integrated (conflict and social control theories), feminist-informed explanation of the role of gender socialization on crime distributions.

pre-adjudication: Occurring before adjudication.

presumption: A rule of law that permits a court to assume something is true until such time as there is evidence that disproves (rebuts) the presumption.

presumptive offence: Under the YCJA, an offence for which, if a young person is found guilty, there is a presumption of an adult sentence.

pre-trial detention: The practice of holding a person in a custodial facility before or during his or her court appearance(s); also known as *remand custody.*

prevention: Approaches that prevent young people from joining gangs.

proactive police work: Enforcement activities that are police initiated, rather than in response to a call for service.

psycho-educative model: Developed in Québec, this model followed the Boscoville experience and is now recognized as a profession specializing in the intervention of troubled youths.

psychosis: A symptom of mental illness involving a substantial alteration to an individual's personality and a loss of contact with objective reality.

punishable young offender: A term coined by Bryan Hogeveen (2005) to describe the discursive construction of some young offenders as 'troublesome' and therefore requiring punishment in order to make them accountable for their criminal acts.

punitive turn thesis: The argument that in recent decades the criminal justice systems of many Western countries have become more punishment oriented, with longer prison sentences and higher rates of incarceration.

rate per 100 000: The number of persons who experience some event during some period of time, divided by the number of persons in the population who are at risk of experiencing the event.

rebuttable presumption: A presumption that can be disproved by evidence to the contrary.

recidivism: Repetition of criminal and/or delinquent behaviour. Recidivism can be measured through official sources or through self-report surveys.

recorded youth crime rate: The annual rate (usually per 100 000) of young persons identified by police as offenders and against whom a charge could be laid.

reformable young offender: A term coined by Bryan Hogeveen (2005) to describe the discursive construction of some young offenders as 'troubled' and therefore needing intervention in the hope they can be rehabilitated.

rehabilitation: A fundamental concept of the Youth Criminal Justice Act that holds that a young person can be reformed or changed as a result of appropriate treatment programs. Also, a penological theory that an offender can be returned by appropriate programs to a state of nonoffending; also, practices and programs based on that theory.

reintegration: The introduction of the young person back into the community as a productive member of society.

remand custody: The practice of holding a person in a custodial facility before or during his or her court appearance(s); also known as *pre-trial detention.*

resiliency: The ability of children and youth to develop positive self-esteem and self-efficacy despite facing crisis, challenges, or adversity.

restorative justice (RJ): While conceptualized in many different ways—*encounter, reparative,* and *transformative*—RJ is a theory of justice that emphasizes repairing the harm caused or revealed by unjust behaviour. Restoration is best accomplished through inclusive and cooperative processes (Johnstone and Van Ness 2007).

risk: The calculated probability of an event or circumstance. Risks are calculated and managed through class, gender, age, and race categories.

risk factors: Factors that may cause a young person to be more likely to offend. These factors can be individual, environmental, etc.

risk society: This refers to a break with modernity into an emerging societal form characterized by the production of risks and tools for their management. In contrast to the view that social problems are to be solved, issues in the risk society (i.e., crime) are risks to be managed.

runaways: Youth who run away from their family or child-welfare placement, at least overnight, without parental or caretaker permission. They often leave as a result of family conflict or maltreatment.

secure custody: A form of custody under the Youth Criminal Justice Act whereby youth are removed from a community and confined to an institution.

self-report (SR) survey: A social-science questionnaire survey designed to ask respondents to report on their involvement in criminal or delinquent activities.

sentenced custody: Being held in a custodial facility as a result of a court sentence (as opposed to *remand custody*).

sentencing circles: 'Sentencing circles . . . invite . . . members of the community to join the judge, prosecutor, defence counsel, police, social service providers, community elders, along with the offender, the victim and their families and supporters, [to] meet in a circle to discuss the offence, factors that may have contributed to it, sentencing options, and ways of reintegrating the offender into the community.' (Source: Department of Justice Canada 2002).

sexual exploitation: The abuse of children and youth by exchanging sexual activity for money, drugs, and/or basic needs.

sitters: Individuals who are paid to tend to and protect the plants in a marijuana growing operation. Sitters may also appear to legitimately occupy a residence to avoid drawing suspicion.

situated choice: The choices individuals make to become involved in certain relationships, be they work or personal, that are situated under certain structural and historical conditions and that can influence future behaviour.

social bonds: The degree to which individuals, through socialization, have connections to people and institutions in a society and believe in the rules of the society. These connections serve as restraints against criminal opportunities and behaviour.

social constructionism: An approach that sees social problems as constructed in the media; see *moral panic*.

social desirability effects: Biases in research caused by respondents' desire to provide what they feel is the socially acceptable response or 'what the researcher wants to hear'.

squeegee kids: A group of street-involved youth who are resourceful in attempting to develop and maintain a livelihood and means of survival by offering to clean windshields at major intersections.

status offences: Behaviours that are considered delinquent or criminal only because the person who engages in the behaviour is not yet an adult. Examples include truancy (skipping school), underage drinking, and promiscuous sexual behaviour.

stigma: A behaviour or attribute that causes an individual to be discredited, rejected socially, or negatively stereotyped.

straight for pay: A person who is homosexual but who, in order to survive, will work in the sexual exploitation trade as a heterosexual.

strain: Experiences or situations that individuals perceive as being negative, creating a negative emotional reaction that provides the possible incentive for using crime as a coping mechanism.

street-involved youth: Youth 25 years of age or younger who do not have a safe home or are underhoused; who have been forced to leave their families of origin; who have run away from their homes without the consent of their parent or guardian or who left foster or group-care placements; or who are not living on the street but who experiment and engage in street-involved activities and identify with street culture and street peer groupings.

substance abuse: Excessive, unhealthy use of a substance such as alcohol, tobacco, or illicit drugs.

suppression: Policing approach to dealing with gangs.

surveillance: The direct or indirect observation of conduct, which is intended to produce a desired outcome (i.e., conformity).

throwaways: Youth who are asked, or encouraged, to leave home by their parents/guardians, with the purpose of ending parental responsibility for the well-being of the youth.

trace: The silent elements that provide words with their essential meaning (Spivak 1976) and that underlie all language.

trajectories: Paths or avenues of development throughout the lifespan. These are long-term patterns of behaviour that often consist of marriage, parenthood, employment, and involvement in criminal activities.

transgender: A person who crosses gender roles in one way or another, including transsexuals, drag queens, and transvestites.

trauma: Experience that is psychologically painful, distressful, or shocking (such as suffering sexual abuse or witnessing serious violence) and that often results in long-term mental or physical effects (such as depression, anxiety, or insomnia). Also, the community-level and individual-level damage, pain, and suffering of indigenous peoples—physically, spiritually, emotionally, and psychically—as a result of the historical and current processes of colonization.

triangulation: A research methods technique that involves using more than one source of criminological data to access the validity of what is being observed. For example, this technique can include combining official crime data with self-report data to obtain a clearer picture of crime or delinquency facts.

two-spirited: A First Nations term that refers to persons who are lesbian, gay, bisexual, transgendered, or transsexual, or to persons who embody both a male and female identity.

unofficial data: Refers to data that is collected and usually published by private or independent researchers or research facilities. The primary data collection techniques are self-report surveys and victimization surveys. Unofficial data is often used to enrich official data.

values: A collective conception of what is considered proper, desirable, and good—or improper, undesirable, and bad—in a culture.

victimization: The experience of being a victim, which can be linked to future criminalization.

victimization survey: A social-science questionnaire survey designed to measure the experiences of respondents as victims of crime(s).

victim–offender reconciliation programs (VORP): A process through which a trained mediator, often a volunteer, brings offenders and victims in a criminal event together to achieve a resolution that is satisfactory to both parties (Community Justice Association).

Young Offenders Act (YOA): The federal legislation that replaced the Juvenile Delinquents Act from 1984 to 2003.

young person: A youth aged 12 to 17 years charged under the YCJA with having committed an offence.

youth at risk: Refers to young people who are 'at risk' of offending or being victimized because of various social, family, and/or personal factors.

youth court: The court in which young people charged with an offence under the Criminal Code or the Controlled Drugs and Substances Act appear, in order to enter a plea and then to have their trial or to be sentenced.

Youth Criminal Justice Act (YCJA): The federal legislation enacted in 2002 to replace the Young Offenders Act, and which came into effect on 1 April, 2003.

youth criminal justice systems: A term often used today as a substitute for *juvenile courts*. Critical criminologists argue that it signifies a shift toward treating young offenders more like adults offenders.

youth engagement: 'The meaningful participation and sustained involvement of a young person in an activity, which has a focus outside of him or herself' (Centres of Excellence for Children's Well-Being, www.tgmag.ca/centresnew/files/Whatis_WEB_e.pdf). Full engagement consists of a behavioural component, an affective component, and a cognitive component.

youth justice: A separate and distinct criminal justice system that explicitly meets the unique needs of young people.

youth-centric programming model: Youth play a significant role in developing and evaluating programs, and agencies continue to be flexible in adapting to the changing needs of street-involved youth.

Index